Will Moreton
with Diane Naughton, Alison Bewsher and John Peebles

INTERMEDIATE

Total English

Teacher's Resource Book

Longman

Contents

UNIT	LESSON 1	LESSON 2	LESSON 3	VOCABULARY	COMMUNICATION
1 **Friends** page 5 Lead-in vocabulary: relationship	**1.1 What's normal?** **Grammar:** auxiliary verbs **Vocabulary:** verbs/adjectives + prepositions **Can do:** make generalisations **Skills:** **speaking and listening:** talk about your spare time activities; listen to people describing their activities **reading:** read about the differences in men and women's lifestyles **pronunciation:** saying numbers **speaking:** make generalisations about specific topics	**1.2 Any friend of yours …** **Grammar:** Present Simple and Present Continuous **Vocabulary:** using a computer **Can do:** write an informal email **Skills:** **speaking and listening:** talk about friendship; listen to people describing how they met their friends **reading:** read about how two friends met through a website **writing:** emails (**Writing bank** page 162); write an email introducing yourself to a new friend	**1.3 Brotherly love?** **Grammar:** Present Perfect Simple and Past Simple **Vocabulary:** for and since **Can do:** retell a simple narrative in your own words **Skills:** **speaking and listening:** listen to people talking about someone they fell out with; discuss falling out with someone you know/knew **reading:** read about the story of the Dassler brothers' fall out and how they founded their companies, Adidas and Puma **pronunciation:** have	**Vocabulary:** Phrasal verbs **Lifelong learning:** revising new vocabulary	**Can Do:** describe personal relationships
	Film Bank: Best friends (Students' Book page 151 and Teacher's Resource Book page 178) **Photocopiable materials:** Vocabulary, Grammar and Communication (Teacher's Resource Book page 104)				
2 **Media** page 19 Lead-in vocabulary: news collocations	**2.1 Media First** **Grammar:** the passive **Vocabulary:** talking about the media **Can do:** give opinions and agree/disagree **Skills:** **speaking and reading:** talk about the media world and its popularity; read about some of the 'firsts' and 'bests' of the media world **pronunciation:** sentence stress **listening:** listen to an interview with a journalist **Lifelong learning:** interact with English outside the classroom	**2.2 When it all goes wrong** **Grammar:** defining relative clauses **Vocabulary:** TV programmes **Can do:** deal with problems **Skills:** **listening:** listen to four people talking about what can go wrong on a live TV show **speaking:** act out mini problem-solving dialogues **reading:** read about two TV quiz show contestants who were caught cheating	**2.3 Seen the news?** **Grammar:** Past Simple and Past Continuous **Vocabulary:** common collocations **Can do:** describe an important event from your life **Skills:** **speaking and reading:** talk about the credibility of newspapers; read some unusual newspaper stories **pronunciation:** /t/, /d/ and /ɪd/ **speaking and writing:** talk about important events in your life; write a short text describing your event	**Vocabulary:** In the news **Skills:** **writing:** write a newspaper report	**Can Do:** compare and contrast alternatives, discussing what to do
	Film Bank: Breaking News (Students' Book page 152 and Teacher's Resource Book page 179) **Photocopiable materials:** Vocabulary, Grammar and Communication (Teacher's Resource Book page 110)				
3 **Lifestyle** page 33 Lead-in vocabulary: homes and lifestyle	**3.1 Your Place or mine** **Grammar:** talking about the future **Vocabulary:** describing homes **Can do:** write a letter of complaint **Skills:** **speaking and reading:** talk and read about house swapping holidays **listening:** listen to two families talk about their home exchange plans, then listen to the families describing their holiday experiences **writing:** letters of complaint (**Writing bank** page 161); write a letter of complaint from one of the home exchange families	**3.2 Top cities** **Grammar:** comparatives and superlatives **Vocabulary:** adjectives describing places **Can do:** compare cities **Skills:** **listening and speaking:** listen to a song about someone missing home; discuss what makes a city good or bad **reading:** read about the World's top ten cities and discuss the findings **listening:** listen to two people discussing the survey **speaking:** discuss the top five for a category of your choice	**3.3 Homes that think** **Grammar:** future probability **Vocabulary:** compound nouns **Can do:** make a formal phone call **Skills:** **reading:** read a text about new technology and its impact on our lives **speaking and listening:** discuss the difficulty in making phone calls in English; practise making formal phone calls	**Vocabulary:** Prefixes and suffixes **Lifelong learning:** one word in six words!	**Can Do:** understand straightforward factual information about common topics, identifying both general messages and specific information
	Film Bank: City or country? (Students' Book page 153 and Teacher's Resource Book page 180) **Photocopiable materials:** Vocabulary, Grammar and Communication (Teacher's Resource Book page 116)				
4 **Wealth** page 47 Lead-in vocabulary: time and money	**4.1 Can you catch me?** **Grammar:** question tags **Vocabulary:** phrasal verbs **Can do:** make small talk at a party **Skills:** **reading and listening:** read about the true story of a fake; listen to a summary of the same story and correct the mistakes **speaking:** Retell the story	**4.2 Getting rich quick** **Grammar:** modal verbs of obligation and prohibition **Vocabulary:** personal qualities **Can do:** make and respond to invitations **Skills:** **speaking:** discuss ways to become rich **listening:** listen to the first part of a seminar and complete the notes **pronunciation:** sentence stress and the elision of /t/ **speaking:** discuss how to be a good public speaker/student/employer/employee **writing:** evaluate the use of letters and emails	**4.3 Spend more!** **Grammar:** First Conditional with if/when/unless/as soon as **Vocabulary:** opposites **Can do:** write a short classified advertisement **Skills:** **reading and speaking:** read advertising strategies and convey the information; discuss the use of advertising and its related successes **pronunciation:** word stress **Lifelong learning:** mark the stress! **writing:** design an advertisement	**Vocabulary:** Confusing words **Lifelong learning:** usage; keeping notes on how to use new vocabulary	**Can do:** express belief, opinion, agreement and disagreement politely
	Film Bank: From rags to riches (Students' Book page 154 and Teacher's Resource Book page 181) **Photocopiable materials:** Vocabulary, Grammar and Communication (Teacher's Resource Book page 122)				

Syllabus outline

UNIT	LESSON 1	LESSON 2	LESSON 3	VOCABULARY	COMMUNICATION
5 **Spare time** page 61 Lead-in vocabulary: leisure activities	**5.1 Are you creative?** **Grammar:** Present Perfect Simple vs. Present Perfect Continuous **Vocabulary:** creative activities **Can do:** suggest and respond to ideas **Skills:** **listening:** listen to three people discussing their creativity **pronunciation:** contracted forms of *have* **reading:** read about three ways to be more creative **speaking:** suggest and respond to ideas	**5.2 The book or the film?** **Grammar:** verb patterns with *-ing* or infinitive **Vocabulary:** describing books and films **Can do:** describe a film or book **Skills:** **speaking:** describe a book or film **pronunciation:** /æ/, /e/ and /ɑ:/ **listening:** listen to an interview with a film maker describing how she spends her free time	**5.3 Memorable meals** **Grammar:** countable and uncountable nouns **Vocabulary:** food **Can do:** recommend a restaurant **Skills:** **reading:** read about a strange restaurant experience **listening and speaking:** listen to someone describing a restaurant; recommend a restaurant **writing:** write a summary of a film description (**Writing bank** page 164)	**Vocabulary:** Explaining what you mean **Lifelong learning:** explain yourself by using other words to communicate your meaning	**Can do:** give a clear, detailed description on a topic of interest with relevant supporting detail
	Film Bank: Favourite films (Students' Book page 155 and Teacher's Resource Book page 182) **Photocopiable materials:** Vocabulary, Grammar and Communication (Teachers' Resource Book page 128)				
6 **Holidays** page 75 Lead-in vocabulary: travel	**6.1 Across Africa** **Grammar:** Past Perfect Simple **Vocabulary:** descriptive language **Can do:** describe a memorable photo **Skills:** **reading:** read an extract from *Travels Across Africa* **pronunciation:** *had* in the Past Perfect **listening and speaking:** listen to three people describing photos; talk about photos	**6.2 Out and about in Dublin** **Grammar:** uses of *like* **Vocabulary:** places to visit in a city **Can do:** get around a new place **Skills:** **listening:** listen to two people's conversations as they travel around Ireland **pronunciation:** intonation **speaking:** asking for and relaying travel information **reading and speaking:** read a city guide; decide which places you'd like to visit **writing:** write a city guide	**6.3 Travellers' tales** **Grammar:** articles **Vocabulary:** describing nature **Can do:** show interest and surprise **Skills:** **reading and speaking:** read about strange events that have happened when travelling; discuss the events **pronunciation:** expressing surprise or interest **speaking:** practise showing surprise or interest in short dialogues	**Vocabulary:** Expressions with *get* **Lifelong learning:** using mind maps	**Can do:** plan a day trip
	Film Bank: Dream holidays (Students' Book page 156 and Teacher's Resource Book page 183) **Photocopiable materials:** Vocabulary, Grammar and Communication (Teacher's Resource Book page 134)				
7 **Education** page 89 Lead-in vocabulary: learning	**7.1 Learning from experience** **Grammar:** subject and object questions **Vocabulary:** education **Can do:** describe a learning experience **Skills:** **listening:** listen to people describing a learning experience **reading:** read about inventions that were developed by mistake **Lifelong learning:** learn from your mistakes!	**7.2 Great teachers** **Grammar:** *used to/would* **Vocabulary:** teachers **Can do:** describe a teacher from your past **Skills:** **reading and speaking:** read an extract from *Matilda*; discuss what you remember about your first day at school **listening:** listen to people discussing their teachers **pronunciation:** *used to* and *didn't use to* **speaking:** describe a teacher from your past **writing:** descriptions (**Writing bank** page 163); write an entry for a website	**7.3 It's never too late** **Grammar:** modals of ability, past and present **Vocabulary:** old age **Can do:** talk about abilities in the past and present **Skills:** **listening:** listen to three people discussing the issues of old age **reading:** read about three remarkable people **pronunciation:** modals of ability, past and present **speaking:** talk about abilities, past and present	**Vocabulary:** Idioms about learning	**Can do:** narrate a true story
	Film Bank: Cambridge (Students' Book page 157 and Teacher's Resource Book page 184) **Photocopiable materials:** Vocabulary, Grammar and Communication (Teacher's Resource Book page 140)				
8 **Change** page 103 Lead-in vocabulary: expressions with *change*	**8.1 Changing the rules** **Grammar:** Second Conditional **Vocabulary:** talking about cities **Can do:** talk about cause and result **Skills:** **speaking:** discuss what you know about New York City **reading:** read about recent changes in New York City **pronunciation:** First and Second Conditionals **speaking and listening:** discuss making changes to your town/city; listen to four people talking about the changes they would make to their cities **writing:** newspaper articles (**Writing bank** page 164); write a newspaper article about an issue you'd like to change	**8.2 Change the world** **Grammar:** adverbs **Vocabulary:** global issues **Can do:** talk about change/ lack of change **Skills:** **Lifelong learning:** record new words in pairs **listening and speaking:** listen to two people discussing how the world has changed since they were children; discuss five things that have made the world better/worse in the last twenty-five years **reading:** read about the Live 8/Live Aid concerts	**8.3 The right decisions** **Grammar:** Third Conditional **Vocabulary:** life changes **Can do:** describe the effect of important decisions **Skills:** **speaking:** discuss making decisions and the results **listening:** listen to three people talking about important decisions they have taken **pronunciation:** Third Conditional **speaking:** talk about how much your life has changed in the past ten years **writing:** write about a life-changing event	**Vocabulary:** Word building	**Can do:** discuss potential changes in your life
	Film Bank: From cradle to grave (Students' Book page 158 and Teacher's Resource Book page 185) **Photocopiable materials:** Vocabulary, Grammar and Communication (Teacher's Resource Book page 146)				

UNIT		LESSON 1	LESSON 2	LESSON 3	VOCABULARY	COMMUNICATION
9	**Jobs** page 117 Lead-in vocabulary: the working environment	**9.1 Democracy at work** **Grammar:** *make, let, allow* **Vocabulary:** work **Can do:** present ideas to a group **Skills:** **speaking:** discuss whether you agree with a series of quotes about work **reading:** read a text about the innovative way Semco is run **listening and speaking:** listen to a speaker giving a talk about a new business; discuss setting up a company and design its profile **Lifelong learning:** prepare before giving a presentation	**9.2 Good Boss, bad boss.** **Grammar:** reported speech **Vocabulary:** *-ing /-ed* adjectives **Can do:** report information **Skills:** **listening and speaking:** listen to people talking about their managers; discuss what makes a good/bad boss **reading:** read a story about *The Engineer and the Manager* **listening:** listen to a job interview	**9.3 New on the job** **Grammar:** past obligation/ permission **Vocabulary:** job requirements **Can do:** state job routine requirements **Skills:** **reading and speaking:** read about how two amateurs became famous; discuss being famous and whether you would like to be famous **listening:** listen to people talking about their jobs **speaking:** describe your current/ideal job	**Vocabulary:** UK and US English	**Can do:** prepare and carry out a job interview
		Film Bank: The ideal workplace (Students' Book page 159 and Teacher's Resource Book page 186) **Photocopiable materials:** Vocabulary, Grammar and Communication (Teachers' Resource Book page 152)				
10	**Memories** page 131 Lead-in vocabulary: memories	**10.1 Losing your money** **Grammar:** *I wish/if only* **Vocabulary:** memory **Can do:** talk about wishes **Skills:** **reading and writing:** read three stories about memory; write a title and an ending for each story **listening:** listen to two people talking about the things they remember/ forget **speaking:** talking about skills you wish you had **reading:** read a poem about a memory **pronunciation:** stress patterns and rhythm **Lifelong learning:** make it rhyme to learn new words	**10.2 Famous women** **Grammar:** review of past tenses **Vocabulary:** biographies **Can do:** say different types of numbers **Skills:** **listening and speaking:** listen to descriptions of famous women; talk about heroes of the 20th century **reading:** read about the story of another famous woman in history **listening:** listen and correct the summary of Coco Chanel's life **pronunciation:** numbers **speaking:** talk about important five numbers	**10.3 Saying goodbye** **Grammar:** phrasal verbs **Vocabulary:** common phrasal verbs **Can do:** write a thank you letter **Skills:** **listening:** listen to a variety of ways to say goodbye **reading and speaking:** two texts about ways to say goodbye; relay the information and discuss whether they are good ways of saying goodbye **listening:** listen to the song, *Leaving on a jet plane* **writing:** thank you letters (**Writing bank** page 162); write a thank you letter	**Vocabulary:** The senses **Skills:** **writing:** write a poem	**Can do:** talk about memories in detail
		Film Bank: Icons (Students' Book page 160 and Teacher's Resource Book page 187) **Photocopiable materials:** Vocabulary, Grammar and Communication (Teacher's Resource Book page 158)				

Test A: Units 1 – 5 (Teacher's Resource Book page 196)
Test B: Units 1 – 5 (Teacher's Resource Book page 202)
Test A: Units 6 – 10 (Teacher's Resource Book page 208)
Test B: Units 6 – 10 (Teacher's Resource Book page 214)

Introduction

Teaching and learning are unpredictable experiences. Learners can be dynamic and engaged one lesson and then demotivated, tired or even absent the next. The aim of *Total English* is two-fold: firstly to set new standards in terms of interest level, teachability and range of support materials; and secondly to address the reality of most people's unpredicatable teaching experience as it is, not as we hope it will be.

Research for *Total English* suggested three classroom 'realities' that need to be addressed in a coursebook: 1) learners often lack direction and purpose – they are often not sure about the relevance of what they are learning and where they are going with English; 2) learners need to be genuinely engaged in coursebook content just as they are in the newspapers, TV programmes and films that they see around them; 3) learners often miss lessons and this creates extra work for the teacher to make sure that no-one falls behind.

Finding direction and purpose

Learners need a clear sense of where they are going and how they are going to get there. They need to know what they are learning, why they are learning it and how it can be applied outside the classroom. Clear goals and objectives are crucial. *Total English* contains a clear grammar syllabus and plenty of practice. Each input lesson is organised on a double-page spread and has a grammar and *Can Do* learning objective clearly stated at the start. The *Can Do* objectives give a purpose and reason for learning and mean that students know why they are studying that lesson and how they can use the new language.

The learning objectives in Total English are derived from the *Can Do* statements in the Common European Framework which means teachers can feel confident that *Total English* covers the language areas their students need. The levels of *Total English* correlate to the Common European Framework in the following way:

Elementary	Covers A1 and goes towards A2
Pre-intermediate	Covers A2 and goes towards B1
Intermediate	Covers B1 and goes towards B2
Upper Intermediate	Covers B2
Advanced	Covers C1

Engaging learners' interest

Motivation through engagement is equally important for successful language learning. *Total English* lessons give a new twist to familiar topics – topics that reflect learners' needs and interests. This ensures that learners will always have something to say about the content of the lesson. There are frequent opportunities for learners to exchange ideas and opinions and engage with the material on a personal level. Activities have been designed to be as realistic as possible so that learners can see how the language they're learning can be applied outside the classroom.

In addition to the wide range of topics, texts and activities, each level of the *Total English* Students' Books has a DVD which adds an extra dimension to the course. Containing a range of authentic material from film and TV, the DVDs expose learners to a variety of different English media and give them a feel for how the language is used in real life. Each unit of the Students' Books has a corresponding DVD extract and the Film banks at the back of the Students' Books offer material to use in class or at home while watching the DVD.

Helping learners catch up

One of the most common problems that teachers face is irregular attendance. Learners often have busy lives with work, study or family commitments and attending English classes on a regular basis is not always possible. *Total English* recognises this problem and has been designed to help learners catch up easily if they miss lessons. In addition to the practice exercises in each lesson, there is a Reference page and a Review and practice page at the end of each unit. These provide an accessible summary of the main grammar and vocabulary covered.

The *Total English* Workbooks also have freestanding CD-ROMs that include interactive self-study 'catch-up' material to present and practise language from any lessons learners have missed. With this extensive range of animated presentations, interactive practice exercises and games, *Total English* ensures your students don't get left behind if they miss lessons.

The course package

Total English has five levels and takes learners from Elementary to Advanced. Each level consists of the following:

- **Students' Book**
The *Total English* Students' Books are divided into 10-12 units and contain approximately 80-120 hours of teaching material. Each unit contains a balanced mix of grammar, vocabulary, pronunciation and skills work including writing.

- **DVD**
The 'with DVD' version of the Students' Books has a freestanding DVD which provides additional listening practice linked to the topic areas in the Students' Books.

- **Video**
The DVD material is also available on video (PAL and NTSC).

- **Class Cassettes/CDs**
Total English Class Cassettes/CDs contain all the recorded material from the Students' Books.

- **Workbook**
The *Total English* Workbooks contain further practice of language areas covered in the corresponding units of the Students' Books.

- **Workbook 'Catch-up' CD-ROM**
The *Total English* Workbook CD-ROMs provide extra support for students who miss lessons. In addition to the recorded material from the Workbooks, the Workbook CD-ROMs feature 'catch-up' material related to the key grammar areas covered in the Students' Books.

- **Teacher's Resource Book**
The *Total English* Teacher's Resource Books provide all the support teachers need to get the most out of the course. The Teacher's Resource Books contain teaching notes, photocopiable worksheets, DVD worksheets and tests.

- **Website**
Total English has its own dedicated website. In addition to background information about the course and authors, the website features teaching tips, downloadable worksheets, links to other useful websites as well as special offers and competitions. Join us online at www.longman.com/totalenglish.

The Students' Book

Each unit of the *Total English* Students' Books follows the same structure making the material very easy to use:

- **Lead-in page**
  - acts as a springboard into the topic of the unit and engages students' interest.
  - introduces essential vocabulary related to the topic so that students start with the same basic grounding.

- **Input lessons**
  - three triple-page input lessons, thematically linked, offer interesting angles on the unit topic.
  - each input lesson leads towards a *Can Do* learning objective in line with the Council of Europe's *Can Do* statements.
  - each 90-minute lesson focuses on a specific grammar area and includes vocabulary, pronunciation and skills work.
  - each unit contains at least two reading texts and a substantial listening element.
  - How to ... boxes develop students' competence in using language, in line with the Common European Framework.
  - Lifelong learning boxes offer tips and strategies for developing students' study skills.

- **Vocabulary page**
  - extends students' knowledge on lexical areas such as phrasal verbs, prefixes and suffixes, etc.
  - provides further practice of topic-related language.

- **Communication page**
  - revises language taught in the previous three lessons in a freer, more communicative context.
  - each communication task practises a range of skills and has a measurable goal or outcome.

- **Reference page**
  - summarises the main grammar points covered in each unit and provides a list of key vocabulary.
  - helps learners to catch up if they miss lessons and is an essential revision tool.

- **Review and practice page**
  - provides a range of exercises to consolidate key grammar and vocabulary covered in the unit.
  - can be used to check progress, enabling teachers to identify areas that need further practice.

- **Film bank pages**
  - support the DVD which is attached to the back of the 'with DVD' version of the Students' Books.
  - feature a range of exercises designed to stimulate interest in each DVD extract and make the authentic material contained on the DVD accessible to students.

The Total English Students' Books also feature the following:

- **Do you know?**
  - an optional page to be covered before learners start the course which teaches basic language areas such as the alphabet, numbers and classroom language.

- **Writing bank**
  - provides models and tips on how to write emails, letters and postcards as well as guidance on different writing skills such as punctuation, spelling and paragraph construction.

- **Pronunciation bank**
  - provides a list of English phonemes, guidance on sound-spelling correspondences and weak forms.

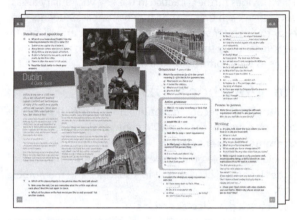

The Workbook

The *Total English* Workbooks contain 10-12 units which correspond to the Students' Book material. Each Workbook contains:

- **Additional practice material**
  Extra grammar, vocabulary, skills and pronunciation exercises practise language covered in the corresponding units of the Students' Books.
- **Review and consolidation sections**
  These occur after each unit and contain additional practice of the grammar and vocabulary covered in the unit.
- **Vocabulary bank**
  This provides further practice in the key vocabulary areas covered in each unit of the Students' Books. Students can refer to this after studying a particular topic and record the new vocabulary they have learned. They can also add new items as they come across them.

The Workbook CD-ROM

In addition to the recorded material from the Workbook, the 'catch-up' section of the CD-ROM contains the following:

- **Grammar presentations**
  Simple, accessible grammar explanations summarise the target language of each unit in a succinct and memorable way.
- **Self-check practice exercises**
  A range of practice exercises (two for each grammar point) enable students to practise the target language.
- **'Can do' game**
  This provides communicative practice of the target language.

The Teacher's Resource Book

The Teacher's Resource Books are divided into the following sections:

- **Introduction**
  This explains the aims and rationale of the course and provides a complete description of the course package.
- **Teaching notes**
  These provide step by step instructions on how to exploit each unit as well as background notes and suggestions for warm-up, lead-in and extension activities.
- **Photocopiable resource banks**
  The photocopiable resource banks contain 60 photocopiable worksheets (6 worksheets for each unit of the Students' Books). The worksheets are designed to practise the grammar and vocabulary covered in the Students' Book units in a freer, less structured and enjoyable context. Detailed instructions on how to use each worksheet are also provided in the Teacher's Resource Book.
- **DVD worksheets**
  In addition to the Film bank pages in the Students' Books, the Teacher's Resource Books also have 10 DVD worksheets. Containing Before viewing, While viewing and Post viewing activities, the DVD worksheets provide more detailed exploitation of the DVD material. Instructions on how to use each worksheet including warm-up and extension activities are also provided.
- **Tests**
  Four photocopiable progress tests are included in the Teacher's Resource Books. Each test covers grammar, vocabulary, reading, listening and writing skills.

The Test Master CD-ROM

The Teacher's Resource Book includes a Test Master CD-ROM which provides an invaluable testing resource to accompany the course.

Easy to use

- The tests are based strictly on the content of Total English Intermediate, providing a fair measure of students' progress.
- An interactive menu makes it easy to find the tests you are looking for.
- Keys and audio scripts are provided to make marking the tests as straightforward as possible.
- Most tests come in A and B versions. This makes it easier for you to invigilate the test by making it harder for students to copy from each other.
- The audio files for the listening tests are conveniently located on the same CD.

Types of test
The Test Master CD contains five types of test.

- Placement Test/s
- Module Tests
- Progress Tests
- Mid Course Test
- End of Course Test

Flexible
You can print the tests out and use them as they are – or you can adapt them. You can use Microsoft® Word to edit them as you wish to suit your teaching situation, your students or your syllabus. Here are some of the things you may wish to do.

- Delete or add exercises to make the test shorter or longer.
- Delete exercises or items which relate to points which you decided to skip.
- Add in exercises to cover extra content you introduced into the course.
- Edit exercises to make them harder or easier, or to introduce key vocabulary.
- Edit the format of exercises so that they are consistent with other exams that you use.
- Personalise the content of exercises to bring them to life. For example, incorporate the names of students in the class, other teachers in the school, famous people and places from your country …
- Use the audio scripts to create extra listening exercises – for example by removing words to create gap fills, adding options to create multiple choice exercises or introducing deliberate mistakes for the students to correct.
- Add in the name and/or logo of your school at the head of the test, and finally, save your version on your hard drive.

Using this CD
The ideal way to use this CD-ROM is to treat it as a master. Copy the tests to the hard drive of your computer and burn the audio files to CD or copy them on to cassette.

- Test files – The installation wizard will copy the files to your hard drive.
- Audio files – If you don't have a CD burner or if you prefer to teach with cassettes, you can simply put the Test Master CD into the CD drive of an ordinary hi-fi and copy the audio files onto a blank cassette.

Levels
Test Master CDs are available from Starter to Advanced levels of Total English.

Teaching approaches

Grammar

Total English covers all the main language areas you would expect at each level and gives learners a thorough foundation in grammar based on the following principles:

- **Clear presentation/analysis**
  Each triple-page lesson has a clear grammar aim which is stated at the top of the page. New language items are presented in context via reading and/or listening texts and grammar rules are then analysed and explained via the Active grammar boxes which are a key feature of each lesson.

> ### Active grammar
>
> *I'm starting the course next month ...*
> *Geoff is working in the US again in March ...*
>
> 1 Which tense are the sentences?
> 2 Has Joanna decided to do the course?
> 3 Has Geoff organised his stay in the States?
> 4 Are the sentences describing an action in the present or in the future?

Total English takes a 'guided discovery' approach to grammar and learners are actively invited to think about grammar and work out the rules for themselves.

- **Varied, regular practice**
  Once learners have grasped the important rules, all new language is then practised in a variety of different ways so that learners are able to use the grammar with confidence. Practice activities include form-based exercises designed to help learners manipulate the new structures as well as more meaningful, personalised practice. Additional grammar practice exercises can be found in the Review and practice sections at the end of each unit as well as in the Workbooks and on the Workbook CD-ROMs. The Teacher's Resource Books also contain an extensive bank of photocopiable grammar activities which are designed to practise the language in freer, more communicative contexts.
- **Accessible reference material**
  In addition to the explanations contained in the Active Grammar boxes, there is a Reference section at the end of each unit which summarises the rules in greater detail and provides extra information and examples.

Vocabulary

Total English recognises the central role that vocabulary plays in successful communication. The emphasis is on providing learners with high-frequency, useful vocabulary which is regularly practised and revised. New vocabulary is presented and practised in a variety of different ways – via the Lead-in pages which provide a springboard into the topic of each unit enabling teachers to elicit vocabulary that learners already know as well as pre-teach essential vocabulary for the rest of the unit; via the reading and listening texts and related exercises; via special vocabulary sections in the main lessons; via the detailed vocabulary page at the end of the unit. Additional vocabulary practice is provided in the Review and practice sections of the Students' Book, in the practice exercises in the Workbook and special vocabulary worksheets in the Teacher's Resource Book.

Speaking

The key aim for most learners is spoken fluency but low level learners cannot express themselves easily without support. *Total English* develops spoken fluency in a number of ways – by giving learners discussion topics they want to talk about; by setting up situations where they are motivated to communicate in order to complete a specific task; by providing clear models and examples of how to structure discourse and by encouraging them, wherever possible, to express their own ideas and opinions. All lessons feature some speaking practice and there are regular How to … boxes throughout the course which focus on the words and expressions learners need to carry out specific functions.

> **HOW TO …** **order in a fast food restaurant**
>
> | Ask questions | _____ you have salads? |
> | Say what you want | I'd _____ a cheese sandwich, please. |
> | Ask about prices | How _____ is that? |

Communication pages at the end of each unit engage learners in a variety of problem-solving tasks and involve learners in a number of different skills – including speaking. The photocopiable activities in the Teacher's Resource Book are also specifically designed to promote speaking practice.

Listening

Listening is one of the most difficult skills to master and *Total English* pays particular emphasis to developing learners' confidence in this area. Listening texts include short dialogues as well as longer texts (conversations, interviews, stories and songs). There are lots of simple 'Listen and check your answer' exercises as well as more challenging activities where learners have to listen to longer extracts in order to find specific information. The recorded material features a variety of accents including British, American, Australian and some non-native speakers. There is additional listening practice in the Workbooks and the DVDs further enhance learners' confidence in understanding the spoken word.

Pronunciation

Total English pays particular attention to pronunciation which is integrated into all the lessons which present new language. The pronunciation syllabus includes word and sentence stress, weak forms, intonation and difficult sounds. The Pronunciation banks at the back of the Students' Books include a list of English phonemes, guidance on sound-spelling correspondences and weak forms. There is additional pronunciation practice in the Workbooks and on the Workbook CD-ROMs.

Reading

There is a wide variety of reading texts in *Total English* ranging from simple forms and advertisements to short texts from newspapers and magazines. Texts have been chosen for their intrinsic interest as well as for their usefulness in providing a vehicle for the particular grammar and vocabulary points in focus. Many all of the texts have been adapted from authentic, real-life sources (magazines, websites etc.) and related tasks have been carefully selected to develop learners' confidence in dealing with written texts. Activities include comprehension and vocabulary work as well as practice in dealing with different reading sub-skills such as reading for gist. There are a number of jigsaw readings where learners work together and share information. The length and complexity of the texts get more challenging as the course progresses.

Writing

With the growth of email, writing is becoming an increasingly important skill. *Total English* acknowledges this by including regular writing tasks in the Students' Books. These are carefully structured with exercises and examples designed to ensure that learners are actually able to carry out the tasks. Models of different types of writing – emails, postcards, formal and informal letters are provided in the Writing Bank at the back of the Students' Books as well as additional advice and guidance on different writing sub-skills such as punctuation, spelling and paragraph construction.

Revision and testing

There are plenty of opportunities for revision in *Total English* and language is constantly recycled throughout the course. At the end of every unit, there are special Review and practice pages which take the form of mini progress checks enabling learners to identify areas where they might need further practice.

In addition to the Review and practice pages, there are ten Review and consolidation sections in the accompanying Workbook, and a whole range of additional practice material on the 'Catch-up' CD-ROMs. The Teacher's Resource Books include four photocopiable progress tests which cover grammar, vocabulary, reading, listening and writing skills.

Learner training

Total English places a strong emphasis on learner training and good study habits are encouraged and developed via the Lifelong learning boxes which are a featured in many lessons. The Lifelong learning boxes provide useful tips and suggestions on how to continue learning outside the classroom. .

Lifelong learning

Personalise it!
When you want to learn new words, it is useful to write them in a personal sentence.
fridge – *My fridge is very old – it's useless!*
cupboard – *I have a big cupboard in my bedroom.*

Total English and exams

The table below shows how the different levels of Total English relate to the Common European Framework levels and the University of Cambridge ESOL main suite examinations in terms of the language taught and the topics covered;

Elementary	Covers A1 and goes towards A2	Useful for KET
Pre-Intermediate	Covers A2 and goes towards B1	Useful for PET
Intermediate	Covers B1 and goes towards B2	Useful for FCE
Upper Intermediate	Covers B2	
Advanced	Covers C1	Useful for CAE

While *Total English* is not an examination preparation course, a student who has, for example, completed the Upper Intermediate level would have sufficient language to attempt the Cambridge ESOL FCE (First Certificate in English) examination. Many of the exercises in the *Total English* Students' Books, Workbooks and photocopiable tests are similar in format to those found in the Cambridge ESOL main suite examinations but specific training is required for all EFL examinations and we would strongly recommend this.

For further information on the University of Cambridge ESOL examinations, contact:

Cambridge ESOL
1 Hills Road
Cambridge
CB1 2EU

Tel. +44 (0) 1223 553355
Fax. +44 (0) 1223 460278
Email: ESOL@ucles.org.uk
www.CambridgeESOL.org

Total English authors

Total English Elementary

Mark Foley has worked in English language teaching for over 23 years and has extensive experience in teaching (mostly in the UK and Spain), teacher training, examining and materials writing. He is the co-author of a number of publications, including the Longman ELT advanced titles, Distinction and Advanced Learner's Grammar. He is co-author, with Diane Hall, of *Total English* Elementary Students' Book and Workbook.

Diane Hall has worked in English language teaching for over 25 years and has extensive experience in teaching (mostly in the UK and Germany), publishing and materials writing. She is co-author of a number of publications, including the Longman ELT advanced titles, Distinction and Advanced Learners' Grammar. She is co-author, with Mark Foley, of *Total English* Elementary Students' Book and Workbook.

Total English Pre-intermediate and Upper Intermediate

Richard Acklam lives in North London and has been involved in English Language teaching since 1982. He has taught and trained teachers in Egypt, France and the UK and has an M.A. (TEFL) from the University of Reading. His publications include components of the 'Gold 'series and he is co-author, with Araminta Crace, of *Total English* Pre-intermediate and Upper Intermediate Students' Books.

Araminta Crace lives in North London with her two young daughters, Petra and Lola. She has been involved in English Language teaching since 1984 and has taught and trained teachers in Brazil, Egypt, Portugal, Spain and the UK. Her ELT publications include Language to Go and Going for Gold. She is co-author, with Richard Acklam, of *Total English* Pre-intermediate and Upper Intermediate Students' Books.

Total English Intermediate and Advanced

Antonia Clare graduated from University College London in Psychology, and has enjoyed teaching (both adults and younger learners), and teacher training in Europe Asia and South Africa. She is now a full-time writer and freelance teacher trainer based in the UK. Her publications include Language to Go Upper Intermediate and she is co-author, with JJ Wilson, of *Total English* Upper Intermediate and Advanced Students' Books and Workbooks.

JJ Wilson trained at International House London and has taught in Egypt, Lesotho (where he ran a student theatre), Colombia, the UK, Italy and the U.S. His main interests in the field include vocabulary acquisition and the development of innovative methods and materials for the classroom. His short fiction is published by Penguin and Pulp Faction. He is co-author, with Antonia Clare, of *Total English* Upper Intermediate and Advanced Students' Books and Workbooks.

1 Friends

Overview

Lead-in	**Vocabulary:** relationships
1.1	**Grammar:** auxiliary verbs
	Vocabulary: verbs/adjectives + prepositions
	Can do: make generalisations
1.2	**Grammar:** Present Simple and Present Continuous
	Vocabulary: using a computer
	Can do: write an informal email
1.3	**Grammar:** Present Perfect Simple and Past Simple
	Vocabulary: time expressions
	Can do: retell a simple narrative in your own words
Vocabulary	Phrasal verbs
Com. Focus	The tree of friends
Reference	
Practice	

Summary

Lesson 1: Ss listen to five people talking about their lives. They then read two texts about 'normal' men and women and exchange information about their texts.

Lesson 2: Ss listen to people talking about how they met their friends. They then read a text about *friendsters.com*, which helps people form friendships on the Internet.

Lesson 3: Ss listen to three people talking about someone they fell out with. They go on to read a text about the Dassler brothers, the founders of the companies Adidas and Puma.

Vocabulary: Ss look at meaning of different phrasal verbs connected with relationships and ask each other questions using these phrasal verbs.

Communication: Ss make notes about some of their friends and share this information with their partners. They discuss possible friendships between each other's friends.

Film bank: Best friends (3'34")

One extract is from famous British comedy duo Laurel and Hardy and a second is from a classic British sitcom.

The first extract from a Laurel and Hardy film shows two friends discussing their departure from Paris, one of whom doesn't want to leave Paris and explains why. The second extract from the British sitcom shows two friends' attempt to rescue a children's ball from the top of a very old building which goes wrong.

Possible places to use this short film are:
➤ Before the Lead-in to introduce the topic of friends
➤ At the end of the unit to round up the topic and language

For ways to use this short film in class, see Student's Book page 151 and Teacher's Book page 178.

Lead-in

OPTIONAL WARMER

Ss write their name in the centre of a piece of paper. They then write the names of family and friends around their name. The people who they are closest to should be written closest to their name, the ones they are not so close to should be put further away. In pairs Ss explain who the people around their names are.

1➤ In pairs Ss tell each other if they have ever been in situations like the ones shown. Ss discuss what type of relationships the photos show. Get feedback from the class.

Answers: Main photo: old/best/close friends
Top photo: old friends/close friends
Middle photo: classmates   Bottom photo: colleagues

2➤ In pairs Ss put these words into the four groups. If there are any words the Ss don't know, encourage them to explain them to each other. Check the answers with the class. Practise saying any words the Ss have pronunciation problems with.

Possible combinations:
a work/school: boss, classmate, colleague, team mate
b family: husband, stepmother, father-in-law
c friends: close/best/old friends   d other: acquaintance, stranger, ex-girlfriend, friend of a friend

➤ In pairs Ss add any more words they know to each group. Go round and monitor to check correct spelling. Get feedback from the class and write Ss' words on the board.

3➤ Tell Ss to cover column B of the table. In pairs Ss read column A of the table. With their partner Ss discuss what these phrases in bold mean. Get feedback from various Ss. Ss uncover column B of the table. Ss match the phrases in bold in A with a definition in B. Check answers with the class. Ask for volunteers to explain the meanings with example sentences.

Answers: 1 h 2 d 3 e 4 a 5 c 6 b 7 g 8 f

4➤ Ss choose four people from Ex. 2. Before describing their relationship with them to their partners Ss think of adjectives to describe the people. Monitor and assist where necessary. Ss can use these adjectives: *I get on really well with my boss. He's really funny and outgoing …* Get feedback from the class.

EXTEND THE LEAD-IN

On the board write: *Someone who …*
… you try to keep in touch with/… you have a lot in common with/… you have lost touch with/… you have got to know recently/… whose company you enjoy/… who you have fallen out with/… you get on well with/… has the same sense of humour as you
Tell Ss to write the name of people they know who fit these characteristics. Ss swap information with their partner. Get feedback from the class.

1.1 What's normal?

There have been many studies to investigate if men and women behave differently. Findings have shown that there are significant differences between the way men and women spend their free time, the topics they talk about and how much time they spend doing housework.

In this lesson Ss look at verbs/adjectives and their dependent prepositions and then listen to people talking about their lives. Ss then do a grammar analysis of auxiliary verbs. Ss also read texts about men and women and share information about these texts.

OPTIONAL WARMER

In a monolingual class Ss decide what a typical person from their part of their country is like. To help them, write the following areas on the board: *job, car, clothes, hobbies, pets, relationships*. Ss build up a lifestyle of the typical person then share their descriptions with their partners. Ss can then tell you about how people can be different in each part of their country.

In a multilingual class Ss think of different regions in their countries and how people differ from region to region. Ss then share this information with a student from a different country. Get feedback from the class.

Speaking and vocabulary

1➤ In groups of three or four, Ss discuss the questions 1–3. Get feedback from class, asking Ss to explain their answers.

2a➤ Focus Ss on the gapped sentences 1–10. In pairs Ss complete the spaces in the sentences 1–10 with the correct prepositions from the box. Ss compare their answers with another pair. Check answers with the whole class.

Answers: 1 about 2 for 3 at 4 on 5 about
6 on 7 about 8 in 9 to 10 in

---

b➤ Divide the class into groups of three or four. In their groups Ss choose five of the questions in Ex. 2a to ask other Ss in the class. Pair Ss so they are working with a partner from a different group. Ss ask each other the questions and write down the information.

➤ Ss then swap partners so they are working with a new student. Ss ask the questions again. Repeat the activity until Ss have asked the questions to five other Ss. Get feedback from the class by asking Ss to report on their findings.

Listening

3a➤ Focus Ss on the table. Play recording 1.1. Ss listen and write the question numbers from Ex. 1a next to the dialogue number in the first column. Ss compare their answers in pairs.

Answers: Dialogue 1 – question 3
Dialogue 2 – question 9   Dialogue 3 – question 6
Dialogue 4 – question 8   Dialogue 5 – question 10

---

b➤ In pairs Ss write one key word in the middle column of the table. Check the key words the Ss have written.

c➤ Play recording 1.2. Ss add any other information they hear in the right-hand column. Ss compare their answers with their partners. Check the answers with the class.

Answers:

Question?	Answer?	More information
3	singing	in a band, plays at parties
9	chess	daughter plays every day
6	running	in the park three or four times a week
8	Mexican	likes the culture, went to Mexico on holiday
9	one	English. Studied French and Spanish. Learned some Italian.

Grammar

OPTIONAL GRAMMAR LEAD-IN

Tell Ss a hobby or sport that you do. Write *1 No, I don't* on the board and the number of times you do the hobby/sport a week e.g. *2 Two or three times a week*. In pairs Ss think of questions they can ask you to give these two answers. Elicit the Ss' questions and write correct questions above each answer. Elicit/teach the difference between the two questions. (1 is a *Yes/No* question and 2 is a *Wh-* question.) Focus Ss on answer 1 and explain it is a short answer and uses the auxiliary verb from the question. Explain that it is a negative answer and elicit/teach the negative auxiliaries used in first and third person for the present, past and Present Perfect.

4➤ Ask two students to read the dialogue. Then in pairs Ss read the Active grammar box and match the sentences from the dialogues to the examples (a–d). Check the answers with the class and write the sentences on the board.

Active grammar

a) *Yes/No* questions: sentence 2 (Do you do it regularly?)   b) *Wh-* questions: sentence 4 (Where do you run?)   c) Short answers: sentence 3 (Yes, I do.)   d) Negatives: sentence 5 (I don't run very fast.)

➤ Refer Ss to Reference page 17 and give them a few minutes to read the notes. Ask: **Q: What auxiliary verbs do we use to make questions, short answers and negatives and to form tenses?** *Do, be* and *have.* **Q: What auxiliary verb do we normally use with 'simple' tenses?** *Do.* **Q: What verb do we use with the continuous form?** *Be.* **Q: What verb do we use to make perfect forms?** *Have.*

5➤ Write the example sentence on the board: *Where are you come from?* Ask Ss what is wrong with the sentence. If they can't see the error lies with the auxiliary verb, underline *are* and ask them to replace it with another auxiliary. Elicit *do* and write it in the sentence instead of *are*.

➤ In pairs Ss find the mistakes in sentences 1–10. Check the answers with the class.

Answers: 1 **Do you use** the Internet a lot?
2 She **doesn't** like Maths. 3 **I'm not** keen on
football. 4 He doesn't **live** here any more.
5 **Do** they like playing tennis? 6 **What do you**
talk about with your friends? 7 Are you from
Switzerland? No, **I'm not.** 8 Have you seen the film
yet? Yes, I **have.** 9 Did they stay long? No, they
didn't. 10 Do you play the violin? No, I **don't.**

6a➤ On the board write one piece of information about
yourself similar to that in answers 1–8 in Ex. 6a. Ask Ss to call
out a question for this answer and write it on the board. Ss
then write questions for the answers in Ex. 6a.

b➤ Ss compare their questions with a partner. Get feedback
from various pairs by asking them to read out their questions.

Suggested answers: 1 What's your favourite
sport? 2 Who do you live with? 3 Do you like Elton
John? 4 What's your favourite food? 5 Have you
ever eaten paella? 6 Do you like cabbage? 7 What
time are they arriving? 8 Which team do you like?

Person to person

7➤ Focus Ss on the diagram. Ss write four things that they
think most of the class don't know about them in the spaces
in the diagram. Then, in pairs Ss compare diagrams. Ss think of
questions to ask about the answers in the diagram. Encourage
Ss to ask follow-up questions. Monitor conversations and take
note of errors. Write the errors on the board and encourage Ss
to self-correct. Praise Ss for use of correct language.

Reading

OPTIONAL LEAD-IN

Ss in groups of three or four. Write the following
activities on the board: *watching TV, working in
the kitchen, doing the housework, going to the gym,
doing yoga, going for a walk, driving, talking about
relationships, talking about sport, dieting.* In their
groups Ss decide if a man or a woman is more likely to
do each activity. Ss change groups to compare their
answers and to discuss why they think a man or a
woman is more likely to do each activity. Go round the
class monitoring Ss' work and making any corrections.

8a➤ Ss in pairs, A and B. Each pair decide if the sentences
1–6 are true or false and why. Get feedback from the class.

b➤ Student A reads text A and finds the answers to
sentences 1–3. Student B reads text B on page 8 and finds the
answers to sentences 4–6. In pairs Ss correct Ex 8a.

Answers: 1 F 2 F 3 T 4 F 5 T 6 F

9a➤ In pairs Ss decide what the numbers in the box refer
to, looking back at the texts if necessary. Ss write sentences
about what the numbers refer to. Encourage Ss not to copy
sentences directly from the texts but to write the sentences in
their own words.

Suggested answers: 80.2: the average women in
the developed world lives until this age €790: men
earn this amount per week €170: men spend this
on leisure 90%: women who don't like their body
35%: men do no physical exercise 2 hours 18
minutes: women do this much housework a day
7,000: number of words women use each day

b➤ Ss discuss questions 1 and 2 in pairs. Monitor the
conversations and take note of any errors. Get feedback from
the class. Finally, write the errors on the board and encourage
Ss to self-correct.

Pronunciation

10a➤ Play recording 1.3. Ss listen and repeat the numbers
in the box in Ex. 9a.

b➤ Check that Ss know how to say decimal points (point)
and when to use *and* (before numbers under 100). Focus Ss
on the stress on the numbers between 100 and 999. (e.g. we
stress *six* in the number **six** *hundred and sixty.*

c➤ Play recording 1.4. Ss write down the numbers they hear.
Check answers with the class and write them on the board.

d➤ In pairs Ss say the numbers aloud.

Answers: a 238 b €3,475 c 65.7 d 22%
e $423 f 98.2% g 10,937 h €474 i 32.9%
j 6,292

OPTIONAL EXTENSION

Dictate a series of numbers to Ss. Include percentages,
decimals, hours/minutes and numbers over a
thousand. Ss write down the numbers then compare
with their partners. Ask Ss to call the numbers out to
you and write them on the board. Ss in pairs, A and B.
Ss write a list of their own numbers. Student A dictates
the numbers to student B who writes them down. B
checks the numbers with A. Repeat the activity with
student B dictating numbers and student A writing
them down.

Speaking

11a➤ Focus Ss on the How to … box. Ss scan the texts
quickly and tick the expressions which are included. Check
answers with the class.

Answers: *The average man/woman … On average,
… In general, … generally, … Women tend to talk a lot
Men don't tend to get married until they are 27.*

b➤ Ss read the list of topics. In pairs Ss make as many
generalisations as possible about these topics in five minutes.

➤ Go round and monitor for errors and correct language.
When Ss have finished, write the errors on the board and
discuss them with the class. Write up examples of correct
language Ss have used and praise Ss for using it.

1.2 Any friend of yours …

The use of the Internet has changed the way people relate to each other. One specific example of this is how it is used by people to meet each other. There are now many web pages which are devoted to helping people meet new friends.

In this lesson Ss listen to people talking about how they met their friends. Ss then read a text about Internet services which help people find new friends. Through this text Ss look at the grammar of Present Simple and Present Continuous.

> **OPTIONAL WARMER**
>
> Give Ss one minute to write down as many words as they can think of connected to a friend of theirs. Ss then talk to their partner and explain how these words are related to their friend.

Speaking and listening

1a➤ Focus Ss on the quotes. Ask Ss if there are any words they don't understand and encourage Ss to explain difficult words to each other before doing it yourself. Ss then tick the quotes they agree with, then compare their ideas in pairs.

b➤ Ss complete the sentence in the way they think best.

c➤ Ss read their sentences to the class. Discuss with the class which sentence is the best definition of a real friend.

2a➤ Focus Ss on the questions 1–5. Play recording 1.5. Ss match the speakers with the numbers 1–5. Ss compare their answers. Check answers with various Ss.

> **Answers:** 1 Speaker 4   2 Speaker 3   3 Speaker 2
> 4 Speaker 5   5 Speaker 1

b➤ Ss read the gapped sentences. Play recording 1.5 again. Ss complete what each speaker says. Check the answers.

> **Answers:** Speaker 1: lost touch   Speaker 2: sense,
> humour   Speaker 3: her company   Speaker 4: in
> common   Speaker 5: kept, touch

3➤ In pairs Ss discuss the questions. When Ss have finished, re-pair them so they are working with a different partner. Ss tell their new partner what they have learned about their previous partner. Monitor for errors. When Ss have finished, read out some of their errors then elicit the correct form from the Ss. Write the corrections on the board and get feedback.

Vocabulary

> **OPTIONAL LEAD-IN**
>
> Write: *1 Do you like using a computer? Why/Why not?*
> *2 When did you last use a computer? 3 What did you use it for? 4 How often do you use the Internet? 5 Could you survive without a computer?* on the board.
>
> In pairs Ss discuss the questions. Get feedback from the class. Monitor and take note of errors by writing them on the board. Encourage Ss to self-correct.

4a➤ Focus Ss on the the box. In pairs Ss decide which of the things in the box a computer can do.

b➤ Ss make a list of other things a computer can do, then compare their list with their partner's list. Get feedback and write Ss' ideas on the board.

5a➤ Write *work/print/shop/research* on the board. In pairs Ss think of any nouns which go with these words. Get feedback and write correct collocations on the board. Write *online* on the board and ask Ss which verb it does not collocate with. (*print*)

➤ Ss choose the verb in numbers 1–5 which does not collocate with the noun. Check answers with the class.

> **Answers:** 1 catch   2 switch on   3 shut
> 4 stop   5 surf

b➤ In pairs Ss write other verbs which collocate with the nouns in Ex. 5a. Get feedback and write Ss' ideas on the board.

> **OPTIONAL VARIATION**
>
> Organise Ss into five groups. Each group takes one of the groups of verbs 1–5. In their groups Ss make a list of words that collocate with each of the verbs. Go round and check the collocations Ss are writing. Re-organise Ss so there is one student from each of the previous groups together. Ss share the collocations they have made with the other Ss in the group.

c➤ In pairs Ss discuss which of the things in Ex. 5a they have done in the last week and which they do most days. Get feedback from the class.

Reading

6➤ Ss read quickly through the text and answer the questions. Tell them not to worry about any words they don't understand at this stage. Ss compare their answers with a partner. Check answers with the whole class.

> **Answers:** 1 They're friends who met on the Internet.
> 2 It's a way to meet friends from different countries.

7➤ Ss read the text again carefully and answer the questions in pairs. Check the answers with the class.

> **Answers:** 1 Every day.   2 Louise lives in London and Juanita lives in Vancouver, Canada.   3 The 'new social trend' is making friends on the Internet.
> 4 People join these websites by being invited by their real-life friends.   5 You can meet your friends' friends without going out to parties to meet them.   6 They are both doing photography courses.   7 She uses the site to make new friends because she thinks it is not easy to do so in today's society.   8 The main idea is that everyone in the world is connected by no more than six 'degrees' of separation.

➤ Ask Ss if there are any words or phrases in the text that they don't understand. Encourage Ss to answer each others' questions before explaining the words or phrases yourself.

8➤ Ss in groups of three or four. Focus Ss on questions 1–3 in Ex. 8. Ss discuss the questions in their groups. Go round and monitor for errors. Get feedback from the class. Finally, write the errors on the board and encourage Ss to self-correct.

Grammar

> **OPTIONAL GRAMMAR LEAD-IN**
>
> Write the following sentences on the board: *1 I am a teacher. 2 I'm wearing _____* (complete this sentence with something you are wearing that day). In pairs Ss discuss the difference between the two sentences. Elicit/explain that the first sentence describes a general state and that the second sentence is something which is true at that moment. Ask Ss what the names of these two grammatical structures are (Present Simple and Present Continuous). Ss write two similar sentences about themselves, one using Present Simple and one using Present Continuous. Ss read their sentences to their partner. Check the sentences as a class.

9a➤ Ss read the sentences (1–5) in the Active grammar box and match them with the rules (a–e).

> **Active grammar**
>
> a) habits/routines: sentence 3   b) things that are always true/permanent: sentence 4   c) describing a state: sentence 5   d) things that are happening now at this precise moment: sentence 2   e) temporary situations that are happening around now: sentence 1

➤ Explain that some verbs such as *hate, want* and *need* are not normally used in the continuous form and that these verbs are known as state verbs.

b➤ In pairs Ss discuss the difference between the two sentences. Check the answer with the class.

> **Answers:**   1 Present Simple – asking for general opinion   2 Present continuous – specific, at this moment – What are you thinking about <u>now</u>?

➤ Refer Ss to Reference page 17. Ask: **Q: What structure do we use for habits/routines, things that are true/ permanent or describing a state?** Present Simple. **Q: Do we use the Present Continuous for describing things that are happening now?** Yes. **Q: Do we use the Present Simple for temporary situations that are happening around now?** No, we use the Present Continuous.

➤ Focus Ss on the time expressions used with the Present Simple and Present Continuous. Refer Ss to the list of state verbs not usually used in the continuous form.

10➤ In pairs Ss complete the sentences 1-10 using the verbs in the correct form of the Present Simple or Present Continuous.

> **Answers:**   1 Are you reading   2 doesn't work   3 need   4 Do you want   5 don't have   6 are you living   7 Do you understand   8 are you thinking   9 don't want, hate   10 'm staying

11➤ Write the prompt from number 1 on the board: *What/you/do*, and ask Ss students to make a question about a job. (*What do you do?*) Write the full question on the board.

➤ In pairs Ss make questions from the other prompts 2–10. Ss compare their answers with another pair. Check answers with the whole class.

> **Answers:**   1 What do you do?   2 What are you doing at work/school at the moment?   3 How often do you go out with friends?   4 What do you like doing?   5 What films do you like watching?   6 What do you usually do at the weekends?   7 Are you reading a good book at the moment?   8 Are you playing (or watching) any sports these days?   9 Why are you studying English this year?   10 Are you doing any other courses at the moment?

Person to person

12➤ Ss ask their partners the questions in Ex. 11 and note the answers. Get feedback from the class.

> **OPTIONAL EXTENSION**
>
> Ss in pairs, A and B. Ss choose three time expressions used with the Present Simple and three used with the Present Continuous from Reference page 17. Ss write six sentences about themselves. Ss A read their sentences to Ss B. Ss B ask at least one follow-up question to Ss A to find out more information. Repeat the activity with Ss B reading their sentences and Ss A asking questions. Monitor for errors and interesting language Ss use and write them on the board for Ss to discuss at the end of the activity.

Writing

13➤ Write *Who? What? Why? How Long?* on the board. Using the question words as prompts Ss tell their partner about the last email they wrote. Get feedback from the class.

➤ In pairs Ss read the email and find ten mistakes. Check answers with the whole class.

> **Answers:**   My name is Stefano and I'm **an** Italian student. I **come** from Rome, which I **think** is the most beautiful city in the world. At the moment **I'm** studying Engineering at university in Pisa, so I **live** in a flat with three other students. We have a lot in common and **share** the same sense of humour. Most nights we listen **to** music, and on Saturdays we usualy go to a disco and dance all night. All except Marco, who is studying Chemistry. He is very boring and never **goes** out. This year I**'m studying** English twice a week because I would really like to work for an American company when I **finish** my degree.
>
> Look forward to hearing from you soon.
>
> All the best,
>
> Stefano
>
> PS I have attached some photos of me and the Leaning Tower.

1.3 Brotherly love?

Adidas and Puma are two of the leading brands of sports equipment and in particular sports shoes. The companies were founded by two brothers, Adolph and Rudolph Dassler, who fell out with each other and became rivals. Adidas has generally been the more successful company, reflected in their deal with Real Madrid and English football star David Beckham to wear their sports clothes. This deal was reputedly worth $150,000,000 to Beckham.

In this lesson Ss listen to people talking about someone they fell out with. They then read about the Dassler brothers and through this text look at the grammar of the Present Perfect Simple and the Past Simple.

Listening and speaking

> **OPTIONAL WARMER**
>
> Write these words on the board: *fight, argue, discuss, fall out with*. In pairs Ss talk about the meaning of these words and decide which word is the odd one out. (Answer: *Discuss* is the odd one out as it does not necessarily imply a disagreement.)

1a➤ Focus Ss on the pictures. With their partner Ss decide what the relationship between the people in each photo is. Get feedback from the class.

➤ Play recording 1.6. Ss match the speaker to the photos. In pairs Ss compare their answers before checking with the class.

> **Answers:** Speaker 1: b Speaker 2: a Speaker 3: c

b➤ Play recording 1.6 again. Ss complete the notes in the table. Pause between each speaker so that Ss have time to write in their answers.

c➤ Ss check answers with their partners.

> **Answers:**
>
> | Speaker: | 1 | 2 | 3 |
> |---|---|---|---|
> | **Who do they talk about?** | Father | *Romina – best friend* | Sarah, a colleague |
> | **How long have they known/ did they know each other?** | All his life | Twelve years | *1 year* |
> | **Why/When did they fall out?** | Aged 15, he came home at five in the morning and didn't call to say he'd be late. | They had an argument over money while they were on holiday. | Sarah was unfriendly and said bad things about her. She said she was lazy and a bad worker. |
> | **How is their relationship now?** | Fine. He's has always been very kind to him | They haven't seen each other since that day. | There is no relationship. She says, 'I don't know what she's doing now.' |

2➤ Ss discuss the questions 1–3 in pairs or small groups. Monitor and take note of errors. Write the errors on the board and encourage Ss to self-correct.

Reading

3a➤ Focus Ss on the pictures. In pairs Ss predict what they think the story is about. Re-pair Ss so they are working with a different partner. Ss swap their stories with their new partner. Get feedback from various Ss.

b➤ Ss read quickly through the text on page 13 and put the pictures in order. Tell them not to worry about any words they don't understand at this stage. In pairs Ss compare their order of the pictures. Check the order of the story with the class.

> **Answers:** Pictures B, A, D, C, E

4➤ Ss read the text again slowly and mark the sentences 1-6 (*T*) if true and (*F*) if false. Check the answers with the class.

> **Answers:** 1 F He was a shoemaker.   2 T   3 F They probably argued about money or women.   4 T
> 5 F Adidas sells more shoes than Puma.   6 F Some of the Adidas and Puma employees still don't talk to each other.

5➤ Focus Ss on the words in the box. In pairs Ss discuss the significance of the words in the story. If Ss need to they can refer back to the text. Check answers with the class.

> **Answers:** a wild cat: Puma was named after a wild cat.   a river: The two companies are on different sides of the River Aurach.   a shoemaker: The Dasslers' father was a shoemaker.   a nickname: Adolph Dassler's nickname was Adi, which later became part of his company's name.   the 1932 Olympic Games: The Dassler brothers' first company provided the shoes for Germany's athletes at the 1932 Olympic Games.   an argument: The Dassler brothers argued which led them to found separate companies, Adidas and Puma.

6➤ Focus Ss on the definitions 1–4. In pairs Ss find the verbs in the text.

> **Answers:** 1 supplied   2 founded   3 relocated   4 rival

7➤ In pairs Ss take it in turns to retell the story to each other. Tell Ss to use the words, phrases, verbs and pictures from exercises 5 and 6 to help them.

Grammar

> **OPTIONAL GRAMMAR LEAD-IN**
>
> Write the following sentences on the board *1 I lived here since 2001. 2 I have seen him yesterday*. Tell Ss that the sentences are not correct. In pairs Ss correct the sentences. Get feedback and write the corrections on the board, underlining the verbs: *1 I have lived here since 2001. 2. I saw him yesterday*.
>
> Elicit/Teach the name of these structures: *1 Present Perfect Simple. 2 Past Simple*. In pairs Ss discuss why we use these structures. Get feedback from the class.

8a➤ Focus Ss on the three sentences. In pairs Ss decide what tense the underlined verbs are. Get feedback.

> **Answers:** sentences 1 and 2: Present Perfect Simple, sentence 3 Past Simple

b➤ Focus Ss on the Active grammar box. Ss choose the correct alternative. Ss compare their answers with a partner. Check answers with the class.

> **Active grammar**
> 1 Present Perfect Simple   2 Present Perfect Simple
> 3 Past Simple

➤ Focus Ss on the form of the Present Perfect Simple. Ask: **Q: What auxiliary verb do we use with the Present Perfect Simple?** *Have/*Has. **Q: What form of the verb follows the verb *have*?** The past participle. Write *have/has + past participle* on the board.

c➤ In pairs Ss find two more examples of the Present Perfect Simple in the text on page 13. Check answers with the class.

> **Answers:** have supplied have suggested
> has survived has always been has been split

➤ Refer Ss to Reference page 17. Ask: **Q: What structure do we use to describe an action that started in the past and continues in the present?** Present Perfect Simple. **Q: What structure do we use for an action that happened in the past but has a result in the present?** Present Perfect Simple. **Q: What structure do we use for something that happened at a specific time in the past?** Past Simple.

9➤ Ss correct the mistakes in the sentences 1–6. Ss compare their answers in pairs. Get feedback from the whole class.

> **Answers:** 1 **Have** you bought those expensive shoes yet?   2 These are my favourite trainers. I **bought** them last year.   3 **I've known** him for six years. We're still friends now.   4 Oh! **You've had** a haircut. It's … nice.   5 I **haven't seen** him for several weeks.   6 While I was in Italy I **ate** lots of pizza.

10a➤ Focus Ss on the verbs in the box. Ss complete the dialogues with the verbs. Ss compare answers with their partners. Check the answers with the whole class.

> **Answers:** 1 did you decide   2 haven't had   3 had   4 Have you seen   5 saw   6 've found   7 've lost   8 put

b➤ Play recording 1.7. Ss listen and check their answers.

Pronunciation

11a➤ Focus Ss on the sentences in Ex. 10a again. Play recording 1.7 again and Ss notice that *have* often gets contracted in positive sentences if it follows a pronoun. The contracted form is pronounced as /və/. *Have* in full positive sentences also uses the schwa /həv/. This contrasts with the pronunciation of *have* in short answers e.g. *Yes, I have* which is /hæv/ and in negative sentences /hævənt/.

b➤ Ss practise reading the dialogues with their partners. Ss close the books and repeat the dialogues without looking at the book. Go around the class correcting errors and ask some more confident pairs to perform the dialogues for the class.

> **OPTIONAL EXTENSION**
> On the board write five things about yourself which started in the past and continue till now, e.g. *I have lived in London for five years*. One of the sentences that you write on the board should not be true. To find out which of the sentences is not true Ss ask you questions about each one, using the Past Simple. When they think that they have found the sentence which is not true they can tell you using the Present Perfect Simple: '*You haven't …*' Ss then write five similar sentences about themselves using the Present Perfect Simple, one of which is not true. Ss show their partners the sentences who must ask questions with the Past Simple to find out which one is not true.

Grammar

12a➤ Write the two sentences about Adidas and Puma on the board. Underline *for* and *since*. In pairs Ss discuss the difference between *for* and *since*. Get feedback from the class.

➤ Ss read the active grammar box and choose the correct alternative in rules 1 and 2. Check answers with the class.

> **Active grammar**
> 1   We use *for* + **period of** time.
> 2   We use *since* + **point in** time.

b➤ Focus Ss on the time expressions in the box. Give an example by writing *yesterday* and *a few weeks* on the board and asking which one goes with *for* and which one with *since*. Then, working in pairs, Ss decide which expressions in the box go with *for* and which ones go with *since*. Ss compare their answers with another pair. If they need more help, refer them to the Reference section on page 17.

> **Answers:**
> *for*: a couple of months, fifteen years, a while
> *since*: last night, this morning, the moment when …, last weekend, the day before yesterday

c➤ In pairs Ss complete the sentences with *for* and *since*. Check answers with the class.

> **Answers:** 1 since   2 for   3 since   4 for   5 since   6 for

Person to person

13a➤ Ss change the sentences in Ex. 12c so that they are true for them. Ss add more information after each sentence, using either the Present Perfect Simple or the Past Simple.

b➤ Ss compare their sentences with other Ss. Encourage Ss to ask follow-up questions. Get feedback from various Ss who tell you about other students in the class.

Vocabulary: Phrasal verbs

In this lesson Ss look at phrasal verbs connected to the theme of families and relationships. Ss then use these phrasal verbs to talk about their childhood and family.

> **OPTIONAL WARMER**
>
> Write the following phrasal verbs on the board: *look after*, *get on with*, *carry on*, *grow*. Ask Ss which is the odd one out and why. Answer: *grow* because it is not a phrasal verb. Explain that phrasal verbs are formed with a verb and a preposition, a verb and two prepositions, or a verb and an adverb.

1► Ss discuss the questions about phrasal verbs with a partner. Get feedback from Ss. Ss then check their answers on page 17.

2► In pairs Ss choose the correct alternative to complete the sentences.

> **Answers:** 1 up 2 up 3 off 4 after 5 after
> 6 on 7 up 8 on

3► Ss discuss the meaning of the phrasal verbs in Ex. 2 and write a definition for each one. Get feedback.

► Ss match the phrasal verbs in column A with the definitions in column B, referring to the sentences in Ex. 2 to help. Check answers with the class.

> **Answers:** 2 h 3 e 4 g 5 d 6 f 7 a 8 b

4► Ss complete the text using the correct form of the phrasal verbs in Ex. 3. Check answers with the class.

> **Answers:** 1 grew up 2 looked after 3 told us off 4 carried on 5 got on 6 looked up to
> 7 took after

5► Ss in groups of three or four. Ss read the questions 1–7. Ss answer the questions in their groups. Get feedback from the groups by getting various Ss in each group to tell the class one interesting thing about another member of their group.

Lifelong learning

► Think of an example of something you have learned recently and tell the class how you learned it including whether you used any techniques for remembering things while you were learning.

► Ask Ss how they record and try to remember new vocabulary. Brainstorm ideas on the board.

► Ask Ss how many times they think they need to see vocabulary before they remember it. Get feedback from various Ss, then tell Ss to read the Lifelong learning box.

► Ss tell their partners about the different ways they revise vocabulary. Get feedback from the class.

Communication: The tree of friends

In this lesson Ss think about six of their friends and exchange information with their partners about these friends. Then Ss decide if their friends would get on with their partner's friends before writing a paragraph about their relationship with a close friend.

> **OPTIONAL WARMER**
>
> Ss in two teams, A and B. Ask a student from each team to come to the front of the class and sit with their backs to the board. Write one of these words/phrases from Ex. 1 on the board: *friend, impression, in common, character, keep in touch, job, hobbies*.
>
> Without saying the word or phrase, the other Ss define the word so that the student from their team can guess the word/phrase. The student who guesses the word first wins a point for their team.
>
> Repeat the activity with different Ss until all the words and phrases have been guessed. The team with the most points at the end is the winner.

1► Ss choose six of their friends. If Ss want to, they can draw their friends' faces in the boxes around in the tree. If they do not want to draw, they can write their friends' names in the boxes around the tree.

► Focus Ss on the questions 1–8. Ss write notes about each of their friends using the questions as prompts. Tell Ss they do not have to write full sentences.

2a► Ss draw a line between the friends that know each other. If the friends know each other well then the line can be drawn thicker or in a different colour.

b► Ss work in pairs. Ss swap books with their partners and describe the friends on the trees and talk about which of the friends know each other and how.

c► Ss then discuss which of their friends would get on with their partner's friends and why. Ss find five things these friends have in common with their partner's friends. Get feedback from the whole class.

> **OPTIONAL EXTENSION**
>
> Tell Ss that they have to plan a social event (e.g. a dinner party) for the friends that would get on well from Ex. 2c. Ask the Ss to consider what kind of event would appeal to the group of friends and to think about the following: *Who would you invite? What would they be doing? Where would it be?* Ask them to compare their ideas with their partner. Get feedback by asking which member of the pair had planned the best event for their friends and ask them to explain their choice.

3► Ss write a paragraph about their relationship with a close friend, using the questions from Ex. 1 and their notes to help. Ss should think about how they met their friends and how their relationship has developed.

► Ask various Ss to read out their paragraphs to the class. Encourage the Ss listening to ask follow-up questions about the friends.

Review and practice

1➤

> **Answers:** 1 Has 2 are 3 Have 4 don't
> 5 Are 6 has 7 Doesn't 8 Haven't

2➤

> **Answers:** 1 *Do*/are 2 Do/don't 3 Are/don't
> 4 Do/don't/have 5 Do/are 6 Have/haven't
> 7 are/ 'm 8 Have/have

3➤

> **Answers:** 1 it doesn't snow 2 He's learning
> 3 are you doing 4 makes 5 Do you know
> 6 I'm living

4➤

> **Answers:** 1 isn't raining 2 has 3 's staying
> 4 want 5 don't believe 6 's working

5➤

> **Answers:** 1 have played 2 didn't have, was
> 3 invented 4 became 5 have played 6 has won

6➤

> **Answers:** 1 didn't call 2 Have you ever eaten
> 3 has influenced 4 stopped 5 haven't seen
> 6 has been 7 have never heard 8 woke up

7➤

> **Answers:** 1 stranger 2 have a lot in 3 fluent in
> 4 forward 5 deleted 6 couple 7 while
> 8 carried on

Notes for using the Common European Framework (CEF)

CEF References

1.1 Can do: make generalisations

CEF B1 descriptor: can identify the main conclusions in clearly signalled argumentative texts. Can recognise the line of argument in the treatment of the issue presented, though not necessarily in detail. (CEF page 70)

1.2 Can do: write an informal email

CEF B1 descriptor: can write personal letters describing experiences, feelings and events in some detail. (CEF page 83)

1.3 Can do: retell a simple narrative in your own words

CEF B1 descriptor: can paraphrase short written passages in a simple fashion, using the original text wording and ordering. (CEF page 96)

CEF quick brief

The Common European Framework is a reference document for teachers. It is about 260 pages long. You can download it for free from www.coe.int. The CEF recommends that Ss use a *Portfolio*. This is a document that aims to help Ss reflect on, record and demonstrate their language learning. There is a free downloadable *Total English* Portfolio.

Portfolio task

Download the Total English Portfolio free from www.longman.com/totalenglish.

Objective: help Ss to understand the purpose and value of the Portfolio.

This task can be done in Ss' own language.

➤ Make sure that each student in your class has a copy of the Total English Portfolio.

1➤ Ask Ss to complete their personal details on the Portfolio and explain its purpose: to help Ss learn more effectively and demonstrate their language abilities and experiences to others.

2➤ Explain that you will ask them to update their Portfolio at regular intervals but you will not 'mark' their Portfolio – it is an aid to learning, not a focus for learning itself.

Overview

Lead-in	**Vocabulary:** news collocations
2.1	**Grammar:** the passive
	Vocabulary: talking about the media
	Can do: give opinions and agree/disagree
2.2	**Grammar:** defining relative clauses
	Vocabulary: TV programmes
	Can do: deal with problems
2.3	**Grammar:** Past Simple and Past Continuous
	Vocabulary: common collocations
	Can do: describe an important event from your life
Vocabulary	In the news
Com. Focus	The front page
Reference	
Practice	

Summary

Lesson 1: Ss read a text about some of the 'firsts' and 'bests' of the media world. They then listen to an interview with a journalist talking about what she thinks about her profession.

Lesson 2: Ss listen to four people talking about what can go wrong on a live TV show. Then they read texts about two contestants who were caught cheating on quiz shows and exchange information about them.

Lesson 3: Ss read some newspaper stories and study related collocations. They describe a significant event in their lives.

Vocabulary: Ss study and practise different news collocations.

Communication: Ss role play a situation in which editors of a newspaper decide which stories go on the front page of a newspaper.

Film bank: Breaking news (3'59")

Three news reports covering the fall of the Berlin Wall, the election of Nelson Mandela and a solar eclipse.

In the first report we see the journalist interviewing some revellers at and on the Berlin Wall. In the second report we see queues of thousands of people in South Africa waiting to cast their first vote in a democratic election and the resulting celebrations. The third report finds the journalist describing the total eclipse of the sun in the south-west of England as it happens.

Possible places to use this short film are:
➤ After Lesson 3 to extend the topic of describing an important event from your life
➤ At the end of the unit to round up the topic and language

For ways to use this short film in class, see Student's Book page 152 and Teacher's Book page 179.

Lead-in

OPTIONAL WARMER

Write *media* on the board. Explain that there are different forms of media, for example the TV, radio and Internet. In pairs Ss brainstorm words related to the media. Get feedback from the whole class and write the words on the board.

1➤ Ss read the text. Tell them not to worry about any words they don't understand at the moment. Using the text, Ss discuss in pairs if newspapers in their country are similar to newspapers in the UK. Get feedback from the whole class.

2a➤ Ss identify the words in bold in the photos. Check the answers by holding up the book and pointing to the correct part of the photos so that Ss can see. Explain any words that Ss don't understand or encourage Ss to explain words and expressions to each other.

Answers: The main photo: front page, headlines, main stories, Sunday papers, sports section, articles, review section, financial section   Top photo: celebrities   Middle photo: online news   Bottom photo: journalists

---

b➤ Ask Ss what they can see in the main photo. Write *newspaper* on the board in the following three ways: *newspaper, newspaper, newspaper.* Ask Ss which is the correct pronunciation. Ss practise saying the word with their partners.

➤ Ss copy the table into their notebooks and write the words in bold in the correct spaces in the table. When they have completed the table, ask Ss to underline the stressed syllables.

c➤ Play recording 2.1. Ss listen and check their answers. In pairs Ss practise saying the words.

Answers: People: journalists, celebrities, editor
Things you find in a newspaper: main stories, the front page, headlines, sections; financial section, sports section, review section, reports, articles, interviews, advertisements   Other: the Sunday papers, the daily papers, online news.

3➤ Focus the Ss on the questions 1–3. Ss discuss the questions in pairs. Get feedback from the whole class. In a monolingual class ask Ss to explain to you what newspapers are like in their country. In a multilingual class students of different nationalities can explain the system of newspapers in their countries to each other.

EXTEND THE LEAD-IN

Write the following words on the board: *TV, the Internet, radio, newspapers.* In pairs Ss discuss the different media and decide which is the best way to receive news and why. Monitor conversations and note errors. Write the errors on the board and encourage Ss to self-correct. Congratulate Ss on their use of any interesting or correct language.

2.1 Media first

A 'first' is an expression used in English to refer to the first time something happens or is invented. In the media there have been many notable firsts, such as the first TV 'ad' and the first video recorder.

In this lesson Ss read a text about some of the most popular forms of media as well as about some 'firsts' in the media world. Ss then analyse the grammar of the passive and then go on to practise this structure. Ss also listen to a modern-day interview with a journalist and through this context, categorise and use expressions for giving opinions, agreeing and disagreeing.

> **OPTIONAL WARMER**
>
> On the board write: _reality TV show_, _search engine_, _film_, _quiz show_, _newspaper_. Check that the Ss understand the words. Ss ask a partner what their favourite reality TV show, search engine, film, quiz show and newspaper are and why. Get feedback by asking Ss to explain their partner's choices to the rest of the class.

Speaking and reading

1➤ Ss look at the words in the box and decide in pairs in what order the things were invented. Get feedback from various Ss. Ss check page 145 for the answers. Ss then decide which have been the most important for the world, for them personally and their country. Get feedback from the group.

> **Answers:** newspapers, radio, TV, video, the Internet

2a➤ In pairs Ss write the answers to the quiz. Get feedback and discuss Ss' answers.

b➤ Ss read the text quickly to find the answers. Tell them not to worry about any words they don't understand at this stage. Ss check their answers with a partner then check with the whole class.

> **Answers:** 1 _Big Brother_   2 India   3 Google
> 4 _Citizen Kane_   5 _Who wants to be a millionaire?_
> 6 The US   7 _Yomiuri Shimbun_

3a➤ Ss read the text more carefully and mark the sentences (_T_) if true, (_F_) if false or (_NI_) for no information if the answer is not in the text. Tell Ss to underline any words or phrases that they don't understand. Check answers with the group.

> **Answers:** 1 F 2 NI 3 T 4 F 5 F 6 T
> 7 T 8 NI

➤ Ask Ss if there are any words or phrases in the text that they don't understand. Encourage Ss to work out the meaning of the words and expressions from the context.

b➤ Ss tick any information in the text they already knew before reading it and mark with an exclamation mark any information they found surprising. Ss compare with a partner. Get feedback from the whole class.

Grammar

> **OPTIONAL GRAMMAR LEAD-IN**
>
> Write the following words on the board:
> _Orson Welles_   make   _Citizen Kane_
> In pairs Ss make a correct sentence using the words in this order. Tell Ss to change the form of the verb if necessary. (Orson Welles **made** Citizen Kane.) Now write the words on the board in the following order:
> _Citizen Kane_   make   _Orson Welles_
> In pairs Ss make a correct sentence using the words in this order. Tell Ss to change the form of the verb and add extra words if necessary. (Citizen Kane **was made by** Orson Welles.) Ask Ss what the name of this grammatical structure is. (the passive)
> In pairs Ss write more sentences using the passive about famous films, books and songs. Go round and check the sentences Ss write.

4➤ Ss look back at the text and complete the spaces in the Active grammar box. Copy the sentences on the board and elicit the answers to fill the gaps. Ss then read the rules a–c and match them with the sentences 1–3.

> **Active grammar**
> Many films **are made** in India. The TV **was invented** by John Logie Baird. _Big Brother_ **has been broadcast** in over twenty countries. Lots of information **can be found** by searching Google.
> Rules: a) 2   b) 3   c) 1

➤ Check the answers with the class. Ask Ss to identify verb forms used in the passive (_to be_ + past participle) and write this on the board. Refer Ss to Reference page 31 and give them time to read the notes. Ask: **Q: What happens to the object of an active sentence when this is changed into a passive sentence?** It becomes the subject. **Q: What is the main focus of a passive sentence?** The person (or thing) affected by the action. **Q: What preposition do we use if we want to include the person who did the action in a passive sentence?** _by_.

5➤ Ss complete the sentences in pairs. Check answers with the class.

> **Answers:** 1 is removed   2 is given   3 stop   4 is told   5 is found   6 wins   7 open   8 are played

6a➤ Write sentence 1 on the board and ask Ss to give you one extra word to make the sentence correct. In pairs Ss add one word to sentences 2–8.

b➤ Play recording 2.2. Ss listen and check their answers.

> **Answers:** 1 The story has been told many times.
> 2 Last week's article was written by our leading journalist.   3 The magazine is sold in twenty countries now.   4 The newspaper will be printed at 3.00a.m.   5 'This news report has been brought to you by Fox Cable News, USA.'   6 The World Wide Web was invented by Tim Berners-Lee.   7 These days, over 10,000 books are published every week.   8 The growth of television can't be stopped.

Pronunciation

7a➤ Focus Ss on the sentences in Ex. 6a. Replay recording 2.2. Ss should mark the stress on the main verb not the auxiliary verb. Allow Ss to compare their answers in pairs before getting feedback from various Ss. Write the sentences on the board with the stress marked on the main verbs.

b➤ Ss practise saying the sentences in pairs. Then, chain around the class, with different Ss saying the sentences.

Person to person

8a➤ Write the first sentence on the board as an example and complete it so it is true for you. Tell the Ss another piece of information about the present you were given. Encourage Ss to ask you follow-up questions about the present. Ss complete the sentences 1–4 so they are true for them.

b➤ Ss tell other Ss their sentences, adding extra information for each one. Encourage Ss to ask follow-up questions to find out more details. Get feedback from the whole class and discuss who has had similar experiences.

Listening

> **OPTIONAL WARMER**
>
> Ask Ss in pairs to brainstorm the positive and negative aspects of being a journalist. Get feedback from various Ss. Alternatively, ask Ss in pairs to make a list of all the things they think a journalist does in their job. Get feedback from the whole class.

9a➤ Focus Ss on the question. Play recording 2.3. Ss listen to the first part of the interview and decide what the journalist is talking about. Get feedback from the group.

> **Answer:** b types of story

b➤ Give Ss time to read the topics that the journalist talks about in the rest of the interview. In pairs Ss predict what they think the journalist might say about each of the topics.

➤ Play recording 2.4. Ss number the topics in the order the journalist talks about them. Check the answers with the class.

> **Answers:** 1 d 2 a 3 c 4 b

c➤ Tell Ss they are going to listen again and that this time they should take notes about the four topics.

➤ Play recording 2.4 again and Ss take notes. Ss compare answers with a partner. Get feedback from the whole class.

> **Answers:** Good stories: There are two types of story: ordinary people in strange or funny situations, and stories about celebrities who do something wrong. Celebrities: they make mistakes and people like reading about them. Ethics: It is not ethical to follow celebrities on their private holidays, but if they are acting in the public interest, we need to check what they are doing. Types of papers: There are two types: serious news, and gossip papers. Photographers: They need celebrities like celebrities need photographers.

➤ In pairs Ss decide if they agree or disagree with what the journalist says. Get feedback from the class. If Ss use any correct expressions for giving opinions, agreeing or disagreeing, write them on the board.

10➤ Focus Ss on the headings. In pairs Ss put the headings in the correct place in the How to ... box. Elicit the answers.

> **Answers:** a Giving an opinion b Asking for an opinion c Agreeing d Disagreeing e Saying it may change (according to what happens)

11a➤ Tell Ss they are going to listen to some statements which they will agree or disagree with. Ss write numbers 1–5. Play recording 2.5. Ss listen and tick if they agree with the statement and write a cross if they disagree. Refer to the tapescript on page 169 if necessary.

b➤ Play recording 2.5 again, pausing after each statement. Give Ss time to write a response from the How to ... box.

c➤ Ss discuss their answers with a partner. Encourage Ss to use expressions from the How to ... box while discussing their answers. Check answers with the class.

> **OPTIONAL EXTENSION**
>
> Ss in pairs, A and B. Tell Ss to write down the names of five famous people who are often in the public eye. Ss share the names they have written with their partner. Ss A have one minute to talk about this famous person, using expressions from the Active grammar box. Ss B listen and can either agree or disagree with Ss A. While doing so, they should also use expressions from the Active grammar box. After one minute, Ss change roles. To make sure Ss try and use the expressions, tell them to tick the expressions each time they use them. Continue until the Ss have discussed all the famous people. Monitor and give feedback at the end.

Lifelong learning

➤ Individually Ss think of the last time they used English outside class and tell their partners.

➤ Focus Ss on the Lifelong learning box. Ss write a list of the different ways they interact with English outside class. Ss compare their lists with a partner. Get feedback from various pairs and explain how important it is for Ss to have contact with English outside class.

➤ For homework Ss find short English language articles from the Internet, magazines or newspapers and bring them to class the following day. Ss read each other's articles.

> **OPTIONAL VARIATION**
>
> Ask Ss to find a website in English which they find interesting for homework. Tell Ss they will give a short presentation to the rest of the class the following day. Encourage Ss to use as much of the language covered in unit 2.1 as possible. Ss explain the website to the rest of the class and talk about what they found interesting. Ss can then look at the sites they heard about and want to investigate either in class or for their next homework. Ask Ss to give feedback on their new websites.

2.2 When it all goes wrong

The quiz show *Who wants to be a millionaire?* was first shown in the UK in 1998, and has since been broadcast all over the world. In 2001 a contestant, Charles Ingram, was caught cheating on the programme. *Twenty-One* was one of the most popular quiz shows in the USA In the 1950s. One of the contestants, Charles Van Doren, admitted to cheating on the show. His story was made into a film called *Quiz Show*.

In this lesson Ss listen to people talking about what can go wrong on a live TV show. Half the Ss then read about Charles Ingram and half read about Charles Van Doren. Ss then swap information. Using the texts Ss consider the grammar of relative clauses.

> **OPTIONAL WARMER**
> Give Ss a few minutes to write down what they think are the three most popular TV programmes in their countries are. Ss compare their lists in small groups.

Vocabulary

1➤ In pairs Ss discuss what type of TV programmes they can see in the photos and whether they enjoy them. They then talk about the other types of programmes they like to watch.

> **Answers:** A Chat show   B Quiz show

2a➤ In pairs Ss match the words in the box to their descriptions 1–6. Get feedback from the whole class, paying attention to pronunciation. Ask Ss to mark the stress on the words. Ss practise saying the words with their partners.

> **Answers:** 1 **cam**eraman, pro**du**cer, **news**reader, pre**sen**ter, **ac**tress   2 **quiz** show, docu**men**tary, **chat** show, **soap**   3 **mic**rophone, **TV** camera 4 con**test**ant   5 **live** performance   6 **au**dience

b➤ In pairs Ss use the words Ex 2a to describe the photos.

3➤ Ss discuss the statement with a partner and decide what could go wrong on a live TV show. Monitor conversations and note errors. Get feedback from the class and write Ss' ideas on the board, giving/eliciting corrections if necessary.

> **OPTIONAL EXTENSION**
> Tell Ss that they are going to plan a Saturday evening's viewing on TV in their country. They can choose any programme from any channel for their viewing. If there are pairs of Ss of the same nationality they can plan their viewing together. If not they can write the programmes individually then explain it to other Ss.

Listening

4a➤ Give Ss time to read the problems and check that Ss understand them. Ss tell a partner if they have ever seen any of these problems while watching a live TV show or an outtake programme which shows a collection of clips of things going wrong. Ss describe to each other what happened.

> Play recording 2.6. Ss listen and write the number of the speaker next to the problems. Ss compare their answers with a partner. Check the answers with the class.

> **Answers:** 2 Speaker 2   3 Speaker 1   4 Speaker 4 5 Speaker 3   6 Speaker 3   7 Speaker 2   8 Speaker 4

b➤ Play recording 2.6 again and Ss take notes about what was said about each thing. Ss compare their answers with a partner. Get feedback from the group.

> **Answers:** 1 These are the worst things.   2 It can be difficult.   3 One man forgot to take it off when he'd finished so everyone could hear his rude comments about the producer.   4 She closed a door and the window fell off!   5 When you start laughing sometimes it is difficult to stop.   6 This means they don't say anything.   7 Some of these are difficult to pronounce.   8 It's very embarrassing when everything else is fine and you forget your words.

5➤ Ss put the words and expressions in the correct place in the How to … box. Check answers with the class.

> **Answers:** 1 What's the matter   2 out of order 3 is broken   4 deal with

6a➤ In pairs Ss decide what problems the people in the pictures are having. Get feedback from various Ss.

> Ss complete the dialogues 1–3. If necessary refer Ss back to the How to … box. Ss then match the dialogues to the pictures and compare their answers with a partner.

> **Answers:** 1 C   2 A   3 B

b➤ Play recording 2.7. Ss listen and check their answers.

> **Answers:** 1 matter   2 broken   3 call   4 keeps 5 Try   6 working   7 deal with

c➤ Give Ss a few minutes to read the dialogues. Ss practise the dialogues with a partner. Ss can then close their books and repeat the dialogues without looking at them. Alternatively, they adapt the dialogues to talk about a different problem.

Speaking

7a➤ Ss in two groups, Ss A and Ss B. Give Ss time to read the situation and to think about what they are going to say. Pair Ss A and Ss B. Ss A tell Ss B about their problem and Ss B offer help. Encourage Ss to use the expressions from the How to … box. Go round the class monitoring the conversations.

b➤ Ss change roles and repeat the conversations. Monitor the conversations again. Ask one or two of the more confident pairs to act out their conversation for the rest of the class.

Reading

8a➤ Ss discuss the question in pairs. Get feedback.

b➤ Divide the class into two groups, A and B. Ss A look at the text on page 24 and Ss B look at the text on page 147.

➤ Ss read their texts and answer the questions. Tell them to help each other with any difficult vocabulary or to ask you.

	Student A	Student B
What was the TV programme?	Who wants to be a Millionaire?	Twenty-One
What did the contestants win?	£1 million	money ($100,000)
Why was there a scandal?	The contestant, Charles Ingram, cheated	The contestant Charles Van Doren was given the answers before the show
Who was involved in the scandal?	Charles Ingram, his wife, and their friend, Tecwen Whittcock.	The producer and the contestant
What happened in the end?	They were found guilty and had to pay fines, but they didn't go to prison	Another contestant revealed the truth.

c➤ Form pairs, A and B. Ss A tell Ss B about their text. Encourage Ss to do so in their own words rather than reading from the text. Then Ss swap roles. Alternatively the pair take turns to ask each other the questions 1–5.

9➤ Ss discuss the questions in pairs. Get feedback.

Grammar

OPTIONAL GRAMMAR LEAD-IN

Tell Ss you are going to check their knowledge of the media. Ask them to write down the following:

a) The name of the person who invented the TV. (*John Logie Baird*)   b) The country whose film industry is nicknamed Bollywood. (*India*)   c) The country where the programme *Who wants to be a millionaire?* started. (*the UK*)   d) The year when the first 'ad' was made. (*1941*)   e) The search engine which is used by most people. (*Google*)   f) The reality TV show that has been broadcast in over twenty countries. (*Big Brother*)

Check the answers with the class and copy them onto the board. Ask the Ss who John Logie Baird was. If the Ss can't give you '*He was the person who invented the TV*', write it on the board. Ss write similar clauses for b–f. Write these clauses on the board. Underline the defining relative clauses. Elicit/Tell Ss the name of the structure, then ask them to read the notes on page 31.

10a➤ Focus Ss on sentences 1–6. Ss use the words in the box to complete the gaps. Check the answers with the class.

Answers: 1 who   2 which   3 where   4 whose
5 that   6 When

b➤ Ss complete the gaps in the Active grammar box using the words from Ex. 10a. Check the answers with the class.

Active grammar

Use *who* or *that* for people. Use *which* or *that* for things or animals. Use *where* for places. Use *whose* for possessions. Use *when* for time.

➤ Explain to Ss that these clauses give extra information that is necessary to understand the noun. Draw three houses on the board. Write underneath the picture: *The house was sold*. **Q: Do we know which house was sold?** No. Draw a tree in front of one of the houses. Change the sentence so it reads: *The house which has the tree in front of it was sold*. **Q: Do we know which house was sold?** Yes. Ask Ss to identify the relative pronoun in the sentence (*which*).Tell Ss that there is a full explanation on page 31 and give them time to read it.

11a➤ In pairs Ss add a pronoun to the sentences. Check the answers with the whole class.

Answers: 1 That's the studio *where* the last Bond film was made.   2 He's the man *that/who* helps the director.   3 I've seen the new film *which/that* won an award at Cannes.   4 The quiz show host is the same woman *who/that* reads the news.   5 Did she like the camera *which/that* you bought her?   6 Here's the house *where* I grew up.

b➤ Ss decide which sentence in Ex.11a doesn't need a relative pronoun, then check with a partner. (Sentence 5 doesn't need a relative pronoun. Explain that *who*, *which* or *that* can be omitted if they are the object of the clause.)

12➤ Read through the example sentences with the class. In pairs Ss make similar sentences with the pairs of sentences 1–10. Explain there may be more than one possible answer for each pair of sentences. Check answers with the whole class.

Answers: 1 Last year I met a boy whose father is a pilot.   2 She loves the city where she was born.
3 This is her new novel which has already sold 500,000 copies.   4 We work for a small company (which/that) you haven't heard of.   5 I like the start of spring when flowers begin to grow.   6 He's an actor (who/that) I have never seen perform.   7 We met the artist whose exhibition was in town.   8 The children like to stay on the beach where they can play.   9 I had a great time when my cousins from New Zealand stayed with us.
10 That's the man who won the big prize.

Speaking

13a➤ Divide the class into two groups, A and B. As look at page 145 and Bs look at page 148. Ss work with a partner from their group and complete the quiz questions with the correct relative pronoun. Monitor carefully, correcting any errors.

Answers:
Student A: *Sport:* 1 who 2 who 3 whose
The Arts: 1 which 2 who 3 where
Geography: 1 which 2 which 3 which
Student B: *Cinema:* 1 whose 2 which 3 who
Nature: 1 which 2 where 3 whose
Science and technology: 1 who 2 which 3 whose

b➤ Reorganise the class so that Ss A are working with Ss B. Ss ask each other the questions from the quiz. Ss note their partner's score.

➤ When the Ss have finished asking and answering the questions, check who the class quiz champion(s) is (are).

2.3 Strange news?

Some newspapers in the UK, known as tabloids, have a reputation for not always being accurate in their reporting. They also often include strange stories which are hard to believe.

In this lesson Ss read some strange newspaper stories and through this context analyse the grammar of the Past Simple and Past Continuous. They then talk about events in their lives using the Past Simple and Past Continuous.

OPTIONAL WARMER

Write *newspaper* on the board. In one minute Ss in pairs write as many words as they can think of related to newspapers. Ask Ss how many words they have written. The pair with the most words read out their words. Write them on the board. If the other Ss have any different words, write them on the board. In pairs Ss put the words on the board into groups using any categories they want to. Get feedback from the class.

Speaking

1➤ Focus Ss on the questions and tell them to discuss their answers in pairs. Get feedback from the class.

2a➤ Check Ss understand all the words in the box and then they work in pairs to complete the sentences. Check the answers with the whole class.

> **Answers:** 1 deliver 2 takes 3 escapes 4 saves 5 survives 6 inherits

b➤ In pairs Ss match the headlines to the pictures and describe what they think is happening in each one.

> **Answers:** A 6 B 4 C 2 D 1 E 3 F 5

Reading

3a➤ Ss read quickly through the text and choose a headline for each story. Tell them not to worry about any words they don't understand at this stage. Ss check their answers with a partner. Check answers with the whole class.

> **Answers:** A 2 B 4 C 6 D 3 E 5 F 1

b➤ Explain that some of the stories cover similar topics. For example both stories B and D mention restaurants. In pairs Ss try to find other similarities between the stories. Get feedback from the class.

➤ Ss look at the list of topics 1–7 and write the number of the stories beside the topics.

c➤ Ss compare their answers with a partner.

> **Answers:** 1 B, D 2 A, E 3 B, C, D 4 A, E
> 5 B, C, (D), E 6 C, F 7 E, F

4➤ Ss read the text again slowly and answer the questions in pairs. Check the answers with the class.

> **Answers:** 1a She wanted to go to the supermarket in Calais. 1b Because she was too embarrassed. 2 He ate seagulls and a turtle. 3 Because the cat inherited a house and money from its owner. 4 She dropped a vase, threw paper towels around and flooded a restaurant. 5a Because he thought the lobster was a fine creature and had had been alive longer than he had. 5b He put the lobster back in the sea. 6a He can give first aid to motorists and help mothers as they give birth. 6b Because his passenger was having a baby.

➤ Check if there are any words or expressions that Ss don't understand in the text.

5a➤ In pairs Ss complete the gaps in the collocations 1–7 with the verbs then match them with the definitions a–g. Get feedback from the whole class.

> **Answers:** 1 take; f 2 get; e 3 move; b
> 4 cause; g 5 return; c 6 give; d 7 take; a

OPTIONAL VARIATION

Before doing Ex. 5a focus the Ss on the verbs in the box. Give Ss in pairs one minute to think of expressions which use these verbs. Ss pair off with another partner and compare expressions. Get feedback and write the expressions on the board.

---

b➤ Ss cover the text. In pairs Ss take it in turns to retell the stories, using the phrases to help. Monitor closely and note errors. Write the errors on the board and encourage Ss to self-correct.

c➤ Ss discuss the questions in pairs. Get feedback.

OPTIONAL EXTENSION

Ss write their own strange newspaper story and read it to the class. It could be a strange story they have heard, or one which they have made up.

6a➤ Focus the Ss on question 1. In pairs Ss write the past form of the verbs in Ex. 2a.

➤ In question 2 ask Ss which verb is irregular.

➤ In pairs Ss look at the different groups of verbs in question 3 and discuss why they think the verbs are in these groups. Get feedback and explain why the verbs are organised in these groups. Write the past forms on the board.

> **Answers:**
> 1 delivered, took, escaped, saved, survived, inherited
> 2 took
> 3 The past form endings all have a similar pattern/pronunciation.
> Group 1: know, fly, grow, draw, blow
> Group 2: get, lose, shoot, forget
> Group 3: bring, teach, fight, buy, think, catch
> Group 4: hit, put, cost, cut, let, hurt, shut
> Group 5: wake, speak, choose, break, write

➤ Ask Ss individually to read the different groups of verbs. In pairs Ss add the verbs in the box to the correct groups 1–5.

b➤ Form pairs, A and B. Ss A close their books. Ss B read out a verb from the Groups 1–5 in Ex. 6a number 3. Ss A say the past tense of the verb. Continue until Ss B have read out ten verbs. Following the same procedure Ss A read out ten verbs. Go around the class listening to pronunciation, correcting errors if necessary.

Pronunciation

7a➤ Ss look at the table with the verbs in the three columns. Play recording 2.8 while Ss read the verbs. Play recording 2.8 again, pausing for Ss to repeat the verbs. Discuss the pronunciation rules for -ed endings with Ss: If the last sound in the verb is unvoiced, we pronounce -ed as /t/. If the last sound in the verb is voiced we pronounce -ed as /d/.

➤ In pairs Ss take turns practising saying the verbs. Monitor carefully to check Ss are using the correct pronunciation.

b➤ Ss choose the correct answer.

> **Answer:** a We pronounce the past ending /ɪd/ for verbs ending in *t* or *d*.

➤ Ss add more verbs to each list. Get feedback and write the verbs on the board.

c➤ Play recording 2.9 and Ss write the sentences. Ss compare with a partner. Play the recording again. Students practise saying the sentences in pairs.

> **Answers:** 1 The bank robbers escaped. 2 She saved the young boy. 3 They waited for her for an hour. 4 Who delivered this parcel? 5 She spent all the money she inherited. 6 We all helped them to do it.

Grammar

> **OPTIONAL GRAMMAR LEAD-IN**
> Ss tell a partner what they can remember about the story about Mrs Bright (page 26). Ask Ss the question below and tell Ss to write a full sentence as an answer. **Q: When did Mrs Bright lose her way?** Mrs Bright lost her way as she was driving round Calais. Tell Ss to underline the verbs in the sentence and ask: **Q: What grammatical structures are in this sentence?** Elicit/ Teach Past Simple and Past Continuous.

8a➤ Ask Ss to look at the Active grammar box and tell them to answer questions 1 in pairs. Elicit the answer.

> **Active grammar**
> 1 The underlined verbs describe something temporary and in progress.

b➤ Ss read rules a and b then find more examples of the Past Continuous in the text and underline them. Ask various Ss to read them aloud. Tell Ss that the Past Continuous is used in the following cases: to describe something temporary and in progress, to say that something happened in the middle of a longer action and to set the scene at the beginning of a story.

➤ In pairs Ss then discuss question 2. Elicit the answer.

> **Active grammar**
> 2 Verbs not normally used in the continuous form are state verbs such as *like, love, hate, want, need, prefer, know, understand, believe, remember.*

➤ Tell Ss to look at Reference page 31 and give them a few minutes to read through the notes. Ask: **Q: Which tense do we use for complete, finished actions in the past?** Past Simple. **Q: Which tense is used for the action which interrupts the Past Continuous?** Past Simple. **Q. Do we use the Past Simple for temporary actions and situations?** No. **Q: Do we use Past Continuous for longer or permanent situations?** No.

➤ Focus on the pronunciation of the weak forms of *was* /wəz/ and *were* /wə/. Ss practise saying the sentences in the reference section on page 31.

9➤ Ss complete the sentences then compare them with a partner's. Check the answers with the whole class.

> **Answers:** 1 was working/met 2 was/liked 3 arrived/was cooking 4 knew/met 5 didn't break /was playing/fell 6 checked/were sleeping 7 was listening/didn't hear 8 saw/Were you wearing

10➤ In pairs Ss discuss what is happening in the picture. Get feedback from various Ss. With their partners Ss write the first four sentences of the story. Get feedback and check the correct use of the Past Continuous.

11➤ Ss put the verb phrases into the story in the correct places. Check the answers with the class.

> **Answers:** I remember when my little sister was born. I was ten years old, and I *was staying* in London with my parents. I knew my mother *was expecting* a baby, but I *didn't know* how soon it would arrive. I was really *hoping* for a girl. It happened when I *was* at a friend's house. It was her birthday and so she *was having* a party. My grandmother came to collect me, but when she told me the news I was so excited that I ran down the stairs, and I *fell* and broke my arm. I *visited* my mother and sister in hospital, and I had to spend the night there with my arm in plaster too.

Speaking and writing

12a➤ Ss choose one of the events in the box and make notes using the questions as a guide. Explain that they do not have to write full sentences.

b➤ Form pairs, A and B. Ss A ask Ss B questions about their events. Ss B answer using the Past Continuous where relevant. Following the same procedure Ss A tell Ss B about their events. Ss then re-pair with other Ss and repeat their stories.

13➤ Ss write a short text about their events, using the notes they took in Ex. 12a as a guide. Go round the class monitoring and helping Ss to self-correct where possible.

➤ Ss swap their text with a partner they have not talked to previously about the event. Ss read their partner's text. Get feedback from various Ss about their partner's event.

Vocabulary: In the news

In this lesson Ss look at different verb + noun collocations and their use in the context of newspaper articles. Ss then write their own newspaper report using these collocations.

OPTIONAL WARMER

Write *take a* _____ on the board. In pairs Ss think of different ways of completing the phrase. Get feedback from the class, and write the Ss' ideas on the board if they are correct phrases. Explain that some verbs are often followed by certain nouns, and that this is called collocation.

1➤ In pairs Ss look at sentences 1–9 and decide in each one which noun does not collocate with the verb. Check the answers with the whole class.

Answers: Odd ones out: 1 b 2 c 3 a 4 b
5 a 6 b 7 a 8 c 9 a

2➤ Focus the Ss on the different newspaper pages in the box. In pairs Ss discuss which of these sections of a newspaper they would normally read and why/why not.

➤ In pairs Ss discuss on which pages they would find the collocations from Ex. 1.

Answers: 1 science/business news 2 current affairs, arts/business news 3 sports news 4 home/international news 5 science 6 current affairs 7 arts news 8 home/international news 9 sports news, current affairs

3➤ Ss complete the sentences 1–7 with the collocations in Ex. 1. Explain that they may have to change the tense of the verb to fit the context of the sentence. Check answers with the whole class.

Answers: 1 performed the song 2 came into
3 made a discovery 4 develops a product
5 have plastic surgery 6 commit a crime
7 caused an accident

4a➤ Ss write the name of a famous person for each of the prompts. Go around helping Ss with names if necessary.

b➤ Ss compare their list with a partner. Get feedback.

OPTIONAL VARIATION

Ss write the list of famous people in a different order from that in Ex 4. Ss show their lists to a partner who guesses who each person is, using a collocation from Ex. 1: 'I think Elton John *performs songs* on TV.' etc.

5a➤ Ss work in small groups to continue the report. Encourage Ss to use the expressions from Ex. 1 in the report. Monitor the Ss' work and encourage them to self-correct where possible.

➤ In their groups Ss write a headline for their reports.

b➤ Each group reads the other groups' reports and decides which one is the best. Get feedback from all the groups.

Communication: The front page

In this lesson Ss perform a role play in which editors of a newspaper decide which stories are to go on the front page of the newspaper.

OPTIONAL WARMER

Write the headline: *Talking mouse created by scientists* on the board. Ask Ss what words they think are missing from the headline that would turn it into a complete sentence. Add the correct words to the sentence on the board: A *talking mouse* was *created by scientists*. Elicit what type of words the added words are and explain that newspaper headlines often don't use articles (*the, a* or *an*), or the verb *to be* in passives. Then ask Ss to work out which of the other headlines in Ex. 2 miss out these words. Elicit the answers from the class.

1➤ Divide the class into groups, A, B and C. Ss A look at the information on page 145, Ss B look at page 146, Ss C look at page 148. Give Ss time to read through the information with a partner from the same group. Check that Ss understand the role and if there are any words they don't understand. Encourage Ss to explain words to each other and help Ss if necessary.

2a➤ Focus the Ss on the headlines 1–10. In their groups the Ss choose six of the stories to go on their front page.

b➤ Focus the Ss on the How to … box on page 22. Give Ss time to read through the box again.

3➤ Re-group the Ss so there is a student A, student B and student C in each group. Give them a limited time (e.g. ten minutes) to discuss which stories should go on the front page. Encourage Ss to use the expressions from the How to … box while doing so. Monitor discussions and note errors and examples of correct use of language. Write the errors on the board and encourage Ss to self-correct. Write the correct language Ss have used on the board and praise them for using it.

➤ In their groups Ss write the headlines for their front page and map out the layout using the main photo on page 19 for guidance. Go round and help where necessary.

4➤ Ss return to their original groups of Ss A, Ss B and Ss C. Ss compare their front pages and discuss how similar or different they are.

OPTIONAL EXTENSION

For homework ask Ss to write a story for one of the headlines of their front page. In the following class Ss swap their stories with a partner and read each other's stories. Alternatively Ss stick their stories on a large piece of paper and create their own newspaper front pages which can be displayed on the classroom walls.

Review and practice

1▶

> **Answers:** 1 is made   2 has recorded   3 have been given   4 will be sent   5 called   6 are employed   7 sold   8 aren't shown   9 was invented 10 are spoken

2a▶

> **Answers:** 1 when   2 which   3 where   4 who   5 whose   6 who   7 when   8 which   9 where   10 where   11 who

2b▶

> **Answers:** The pronoun can be omitted in the following sentences:
>
> The quiz show <u>which</u> asks contestants about the place where they were born.
> Follow the progress of two restaurants <u>which</u> famous chefs have visited.
> *that* can be used in sentences 2, 4, 6, 8, and 11.

3▶

> **Answers:** 1 was/started   2 were watching/heard   3 were you doing/was reading   4 saw/was looking   5 crashed/was going   6 Were they winning/were losing   7 was studying/found   8 Did you see/was wearing/Didn't you notice

4▶

> **Answers:** 1 the front page   2 documentary   3 plastic surgery   4 sections   5 profit   6 contestant 7 accidents   8 performance   9 record   10 article

Notes for using the Common European Framework (CEF)

CEF References

2.1 Can do: give opinions and agree/disagree

CEF B1 descriptor: can generally follow the main points in an informal discussion with friends provided speech is clearly articulated in standard dialect. Can give or seek personal views and opinions in discussing topics of interest. (CEF page 77)

2.2 Can do: deal with problems

CEF B1 descriptor: can explain why something is a problem, discuss what to do next, compare and contrast alternatives. (CEF page 79)

2.3 Can do: describe an important event from your life

CEF B1 descriptor: can write accounts of experiences, describing feelings and reactions in simple connected text. Can write a description of an event, a recent trip – real or imagined. (CEF page 62)

CEF quick brief

The Common European Framework is produced by the Council of Europe. The Council of Europe is concerned with issues like human rights, European identity, education and more. This identity is based on diversity and the Common European Framework gives equal importance to all languages of Council of Europe member nations.

Portfolio task

Download the Total English Portfolio free from www.longman.com/totalenglish.

Objective: help Ss to use the Portfolio to assess their skills.

This task can be done in Ss' own language.

➤ Portfolios are divided into three main sections. The first section is called the 'Passport'. The Passport is designed to summarise relevant language learning experiences and qualifications. This can be shown to others, for example new teachers, employers, etc. Firstly, however, it is helpful for learners to give their own assessment of their abilities in the different skills areas.

1▶ Help Ss to understand the self-assessment grids (there are many translations available as this is a standard document) for levels A1 to B1.

2▶ Ask Ss to assess their own abilities in the different skills areas (listening, reading, spoken interaction, spoken production, and writing). Ss complete the language skills profile by shading in the relevant boxes.

3▶ Explain that Ss can update this profile as they progress and they can fill in profiles for other languages.

Overview

Lead-in	**Vocabulary:** homes and lifestyle
3.1	**Grammar:** talking about the future
	Vocabulary: describing homes
	Can do: write a letter of complaint
3.2	**Grammar:** comparatives and superlatives
	Vocabulary: adjectives describing places
	Can do: compare cities
3.3	**Grammar:** future possibility
	Vocabulary: compound nouns
	Can do: make a formal phone call
Vocabulary	Prefixes and suffixes
Com. Focus	Your dream house
Reference	
Practice	

Summary

Lesson 1: Ss read about a website where families can exchange houses with other families for a holiday. They then go on to read about two families talking about their experiences of this type of holiday.

Lesson 2: Ss listen to a Simon and Garfunkel song, *Homeward Bound*, before going on to read a text about a survey conducted on cities around the world. Ss then listen to two people discussing the survey.

Lesson 3: Ss read a text about how mobile phones will be able to help control houses in the future. Ss also listen to different telephone conversations then role play the same scenarios.

Vocabulary: Ss look at and practise prefixes and suffixes.

Communication: Ss read about a competition to win a house for a year then listen to two people trying to win the competition. Ss then do a role play where they take on the roles of competition entrants and judges of the competition.

Film bank: City or country? (3'09")

Four speakers; Ajay, Emlyn, Jennifer and Sarah describe their experience of life in the city or the country.

Ajays starts by describing what it is like being a student in Leeds and why he likes living there. Emlyn follows on to describe why he really enjoys living in the country having escaped from busy city life. In contrast, Jennifer is a city dweller who enjoys the hectic lifestyle and has no immediate plans to move. Lastly, Sarah is a definite country lover who can find no fault with living in the country.

Possible places to use this short film are:
➤ After Lesson 2 to build on vocabulary group of adjectives describing places

➤ After Lesson 3 to review and consolidate grammar

➤ At the end of the unit to round up the topic and language

For ways to use this short film in class, see Students' Book page 153 and Teacher's Book page 180.

Lead-in

OPTIONAL WARMER
Tell Ss that you are going to tell them about your home. Give Ss five minutes to work in pairs and think of questions they can ask you. Go round and check the questions the Ss write, correcting where necessary. Ss take turns to ask you the questions. Answer giving as much information as you like. Encourage Ss to ask follow-up questions if they want to find out more.

1a➤ Focus Ss on the question. Give Ss a few minutes to think about their home. Ss write notes about the prompts.

b➤ Ss compare their ideas with other Ss in the group. Get feedback from the whole class.

2➤ Ss in groups of three or four. Ss look at the table and check they understand the words and expressions. If there is any vocabulary Ss don't understand, encourage them to answer each others' questions. They can also consult their dictionaries or ask you.

b➤ Draw the table with the headings of the columns on the board and the existing words. Ask Ss to give you words and expressions that they think can be added to each column. Get feedback and write correct words or expressions on the board in the columns as the Ss tell you the words.

➤ Check the meaning of the words and expressions as a class and clarify any vocabulary Ss do not understand. Elicit example sentences to check Ss can use the vocabulary in context and are using the correct pronunciation from the whole class. Encourage Ss to correct each other before doing so yourself.

b➤ In pairs Ss add other words to each section. Check these words with the class and write them on the board in the relevant column.

3a➤ Ss in pairs take it in turns to describe the houses in the pictures. Encourage Ss to use words and expressions from Ex. 2 while doing so.

b➤ Ss describe the place where they live and their lifestyle to their partners. Encourage Ss to ask follow-up questions to find out more. Monitor and assist where necessary.

➤ Ss then swap partners so they are working with a new student. Ss repeat their descriptions.

➤ Get feedback from the class by asking Ss to tell you something about their first and second partner's house or flat and their lifestyle. Encourage Ss to compare the lifestyles and ask whether anyone found two people who sounded similar.

EXTEND THE LEAD-IN
Focus Ss on the pictures of the places to live. In pairs Ss discuss the pictures and rank the houses in order from 1–4; 1 being the place they would like to live the most, 4 the place they would least like to live. Ss tell the rest of the class their order, explaining why they have decided on that order.

3.1 Your place or mine?

There are now organisations which offer house swapping holidays where families exchange their homes with other families in another country for the holidays. The advantage for the families is a saving on the cost of accommodation.

In this lesson Ss read about two homes in Seville and London which are advertised on a website which arranges house swapping holidays. Ss then listen to two families talking about their plans for a house exchange. Through the listening, Ss look at different ways of talking about the future.

> **OPTIONAL WARMER**
>
> Write the following questions on the board: *Where did you stay? What was the area like?* In pairs Ss talk about their last holiday, answering the questions. Get feedback from the class.

Reading and speaking

1➤ Ss talk about the questions in pairs. Get feedback.

2➤ Write *Yourhome-Myhome.com* on the board. In pairs Ss discuss what they think the purpose of this website is.

➤ Ss read quickly through the texts and match them to the photos. Tell them not to worry about any words they don't understand at this stage. Ss check their answers with a partner. Get feedback from the class.

> **OPTIONAL VARIATION**
>
> Ss in pairs, A and B. Ss A read about property 1, Ss B read about property 2. Ss then exchange property information and match the texts to the photos.

3a➤ Ss read the text more carefully and answer the questions 1–6. Check the answers with the class. Ask Ss to tell you the part of the text which gave them each answer.

> **Answers:** 2 property 2   3 property 1   4 property 2
> 5 property 1   6 property 2

➤ Ask Ss if there are any words or phrases in the text that they don't understand. Encourage Ss to answer each others' questions before asking you.

b➤ Ss discuss which of the two properties they would prefer to live in for a month and why. Get feedback from the class.

Listening

4a➤ Give Ss time to read the activities 1–6 and check that they understand them.

➤ Play recording 3.1. Ss listen and write 1 for the Dos Santos family and 2 for the Armitage family beside the activities 1–6. Check answers with the whole class.

> **Answers:** visit museums 1   see cathedrals 2
> enjoy the local cuisine 2   go shopping 1
> visit friends 1   sit outside and enjoy the sun 2

b➤ Focus Ss on the extracts from the dialogues and give them time to read them. With their partners Ss predict which verb forms are used in the conversations.

➤ Play recording 3.1 again and Ss choose the correct verb forms. Check answers with the whole class.

> **Answers:** 1 're spending 2 'll love 3 'm going to
> 4 'll give 5 're going to 6 will 7 are going to 8 'll be

Grammar

> **OPTIONAL GRAMMAR LEAD-IN**
>
> Write the following sentence halves on the board:
> 1 *I'm going to*   have the soup.
> 2 *For the starter I think I'll*   visit America one day.
> 3 *I'm meeting*   John at six on Saturday.
> Ask Ss to match the sentence halves. (*1 visit America one day, 2 have the soup, 3 John at six on Saturday*) Ss then make their own sentences using the underlined forms. Ss compare their sentences with their partners.

5➤ Give Ss a few minutes to read the Active grammar box. In pairs Ss find examples of each structure for talking about the future in Ex. 4b. Check answers with the class.

> **Answers:** a 3, 5, 7   b 4   c 1   d 2, 6

➤ Refer Ss to the Reference on page 45. Give Ss time to read through the notes. Ask: **Q: What structure do we use if we want to talk about intentions or plans in the future?** *going to.* **Q: What structure do we use for fixed arrangements for the future?** Present Continuous. **Q: What structure do we use for decisions made at the time of speaking?** *will.* **Q: What structures do we use for making general predictions about the future?** *going to* or *will.* Focus Ss on the contracted forms of *will* and *will not* (*'ll* and *won't*).

6➤ In pairs Ss complete the text with the words from the box. Check answers with class.

> **Answers:**
> Sarah and Jeremy: I**'m starting,** we**'ll** need, we**'re going** to, we**'ll** have
> Miriam and Carlos: mother**'s moving** in, She **is going** to sell, I hope **won't** be, She **is going** to share, it**'ll**

7➤ Copy the sentences onto the board and ask Ss to correct the mistakes. Do the first one with them as an example, if necessary. Ss correct the mistakes in sentences 2–9. Elicit the answers and write the corrections on the board. In some cases, there is more than one possible answer.

> **Suggested answers:** 1 I'm sorry, I have to leave early. I'm playing squash this evening. 2 Tomorrow I'm going on a trip to Cambridge. 3 A: That's the telephone. B: OK. I'll get it. 4 Hurry up, or we're going to be late again! 5 A: Would you like a drink? B: Yes, I'll have a glass of water, please. 6 Are you going to stay here for long? 7 When I grow up, I'm going to be a firefighter. 8 We are getting married in August. 9 A: How do I get to the airport from here? B: Don't worry, I'll show you.

Person to person

8a➤ In pairs Ss write three or four questions to ask other students about their plans for the topics in the box. Go round the class monitoring Ss' work, helping where necessary.

b➤ Regroup the Ss so they are working in groups of four. Ss take turns to ask questions to each other. Encourage Ss to ask follow-up questions. Monitor and take note of errors which can be looked at with the class at the end of the activity.

Listening

9a➤ Focus Ss on the pictures of Jeremy and Miriam during their home exchange. In pairs Ss predict what the problems were. Get feedback from various Ss and write their predictions on the board.

b➤ Play recording 3.2 and Ss check their ideas using the predictions on the board.

c➤ Play recording 3.2 again. Ss take notes about what happened next to each picture. Get feedback from the class.

➤ In pairs Ss take it in turns to describe what happened, using the pictures as prompts.

> **Suggested answers:** Picture 1: The house – old and dark. Picture 2: Nothing worked properly – no shower. Picture 3: The flat – small. Had big arguments. Picture 4: Bar downstairs – played loud music until 4.00a.m.

> **OPTIONAL EXTENSION**
> Give Ss a short time to think of a problem that they had (or someone they knew had) while on holiday. Ss in groups of three or four take turns to tell each other the problem. Encourage Ss listening to ask follow-up questions about the problem. When all the Ss have talked about their problems, Ss decide which was the worst problem. Get feedback from the groups.

Reading and speaking

10➤ Ss read Miriam's letter of complaint and underline the different problems she writes about. Ss compare thir answers with a partner. Check the problems Miriam had as a class.

> **Answers:** Problem 1: (the information said) the house was near the city centre... it took over two hours to get there. Problem 2: the directions for finding the house were difficult to follow and sometimes incorrect. Problem 3: the house was in a terrible mess. There were dirty dishes and cups everywhere, the bathroom was filthy, and there were no clean sheets or towels as promised. Problem 4: the central heating wasn't working, so the house was freezing, and there was no hot water! Problem 5: the man who answered (the phone at the office) was very rude and unhelpful.

11➤ Organise Ss into two groups, A and B. Group A reads the information on page 145. Group B reads the information on page 147. In their groups Ss prepare what they are going to say. Go round and help Ss as necessary.

➤ Pair Ss so that Ss A are working with Ss B. Ss hold the meeting. Monitor carefully and take note of errors and correct language used by the Ss. When Ss have finished the conversation, get feedback and check if the 'Miriams' in the class feel their problem was dealt with satisfactorily. Write the errors on the board and ask Ss to correct them. Finally, write the examples of correct language used by the Ss on the board and congratulate them for using it.

Writing

> **OPTIONAL ACTIVITY**
> Ask Ss to read the letter from Miriam Dos Santos to *Yourhome-Myhome.com* again. In pairs Ss write down any features of formal letters that they can see in the letter. Get feedback from the class and write the features on the board.
> Features include: greeting: Dear Sir/Madam, Formal language, no contractions, signing off: Yours faithfully, signing and printing name.
> To help students record the vocabulary in a logical way, suggest using the following table.
>
> | Introduction | I am writing to complain about … |
> | Explaining the facts | According to the website/ the information I received … In fact,/However,/Actually,/ Unfortunately, … In addition to this …/Also … I am/was very disappointed … |
> | Action to be taken | I expect to receive a full refund … I would also like … |
> | Conclusion | I look forward to receiving a satisfactory reply. |

12a➤ Refer Ss to the Writing bank on page 161. Ss complete Ex. 1 with a partner. Tell Ss there is more than one possible answer to each question. Check answers with the whole class.

> **Answers:** 1 B 2 A 3 A (or C) 4 D (or B)

➤ In the Writing skills section, Ss match the meanings to the paragraphs in the letter. Ss compare their answers with their partners. Check answers with the whole class.

> **Answers:** a 2, 3 b 1 c 7 d 4, 5, 6

b➤ Ss write a letter of complaint from Jeremy to *Yourhome-Myhome.com* using the pictures in Ex. 9a as prompts.

➤ When Ss have finished writing, they give the letter to their partner to read. If there is time, ask Ss to write a reply to their partner's letter. Direct Ss back to the Writing bank on page 161 for a quick review of the format for a formal letter.

➤ Ss read their partner's reply and decide if it is a good response. Get feedback from the class.

3.2 Top cities

Paul Simon and Art Garfunkel were one of the most popular singing duos of the 1960s and 70s. Their hits included the song *Bridge Over Troubled Water* and the soundtrack to the film *The Graduate*. They later both pursued solo careers, Paul Simon enjoying considerably more success as a solo artist than Art Garfunkel.

In this lesson Ss listen to a Simon and Garfunkel song, *Homeward Bound*. Ss then look at some adjectives for describing places. They then read a text about a survey done to discover the world's top cities and listen to some people discussing the survey. Through this context Ss look at the grammar of comparatives and superlatives. Finally, Ss write their own top five list for something they are interested in.

OPTIONAL WARMER

Ss think of their favourite city. This can be either in their own country or in a foreign country they have visited. Ss make notes about this city for a few minutes. Monitor and help Ss with vocabulary as necessary. Ss then describe this city to their partners and tell each other why this is their favourite city. Encourage Ss to ask each other follow-up questions. Get feedback from the class and write the names of cities that Ss have chosen on the board. As a class Ss can then choose the top five cities from the ones on the board.

Listening and speaking

1a➤ Ask Ss if they know anything about Simon and Garfunkel. Get feedback and tell the Ss about them if they have not heard of them before.

➤ Draw Ss' attention to the photo of the man in the station. In pairs Ss discuss where they think he might be going and why he is carrying a guitar.

➤ Play recording 3.3. Ss listen to the song and answer the question. Get feedback.

Answer: '*Homeward Bound*' signifies going home

b➤ Ss discuss the three questions in groups of three. Get feedback from various groups.

Answers: 1 sad 2 A musician who is missing his partner. 3 He goes to different cities to play his music.

2➤ Ss read the three different summaries of the song. Check any vocabulary the Ss don't understand. Play recording 3.3 again. Students listen and decide which is the best summary of the song.

Answer: Summary 3

3a➤ Ss discuss the questions 1 and 2 with their partners. Ss then share their ideas with another pair. Get feedback from the whole class.

➤ With their partners Ss write a list of all the good and bad points of living in a city.

➤ Ss compare their lists with other Ss. Get feedback from the whole group and write Ss' ideas on the board in two columns.

b➤ Ss write down a list with the names of cities which they think are good or bad to live in. Have a class discussion about the cities they think are good or bad to live in and why.

OPTIONAL EXTENSION

Ss in pairs, A and B. Tell Ss A that they are in favour of living in the city and that Ss B are against living in the city. Give Ss a few minutes to prepare what they are going to say. Ss can use the ideas they talked about when discussing Ex. 3. Pair Ss off so that Ss A are working with Ss B. Students try to convince their partner that they are right. Monitor and take note of errors. When Ss finish the conversations write errors on the board and have Ss correct them.

Vocabulary

4a➤ Focus Ss on the adjectives used to describe cities in the box. With their partners Ss find pairs of words that mean the opposite. If Ss have any problems with the vocabulary encourage them to use a dictionary before asking you.

Answers: modern – historical   ugly – picturesque   tiny – enormous   clean – polluted   noisy – peaceful   dull – lively

b➤ In pairs Ss think of a town or a city which could be described by each adjective. Ss compare their answers with another pair. Get feedback from the whole group.

Reading

5➤ Focus Ss on the pictures of the cities. With their partners Ss discuss which cities can be seen in the photos. Ss share their ideas with other Ss. Ss then decide if these cities look like good cities to live in or not. Get feedback from the group.

➤ Ss read the text quickly and check if it mentions any of the cities they thought of in Ex. 3 and Ex. 4b. Tell them not to worry about any words they don't understand at this stage. Get feedback from the class.

6a➤ Ss read the text more carefully and answer questions 1–8. Tell Ss to underline any words or phrases they don't understand while reading. In pairs Ss compare their answers.

Answers: 1 It is one of the world's largest Human Resources consultancies. 2 He compared the cities by giving marks for various criteria including political, economic and social environment, healthcare, educational provision, recreation and transport infrastructure. 3 Zurich came in joint first place (with Vancouver, Berne and Vienna). 4 Switzerland 5 US cities have high crime rates. 6 Climate and traffic 7 Brazzaville, in the Congo, came last because of its lengthy ongoing civil war. 8 It compares big cities with smaller cities; smaller ones are easier to run.

➤ Check any vocabulary in the text that Ss didn't understand and write it on the board. Encourage Ss to answer each others' questions or explain the words yourself.

b➤ Ss discuss the three questions in groups of three or four. Get feedback from the class and if anyone in the class has been to any of the cities mentioned ask them to tell the class how much the survey corresponds to the experience they had while visiting it.

Listening

7➤ Tell Ss they are going to hear two people discussing the survey. Play recording 3.4. Ss write the names of the cities mentioned in the conversation. Ss compare their answers with their partners. Check answers with the whole class.

> **Answers:** Paris, San Francisco, Tokyo, London

8➤ Give Ss time to read sentences 1–4. Play recording 3.4 again and Ss mark the sentences (*T*) if true, and (*F*) if false. Ss compare their answers with their partners. Check the answers with the whole class.

> **Answers:** 1 T 2 F 3 F 4 T

Grammar

> **OPTIONAL GRAMMAR LEAD-IN**
>
> Write the following gapped sentences on the board:
> 1 _____ is tal*ler* than _____ .
> 2 _____ is the tall*est* in the class.
> Invite a student to complete the spaces on the board with names of Ss in the class. Ss then discuss the endings of the adjectives and when to use them.

9a➤ Refer Ss to the tapescript on page 170. In pairs Ss find examples of superlatives and comparatives in the text and discuss what these structures are and why they are used. Get feedback from the class.

> **Answers:**
>
> COMPARATIVES: much bigger, much easier, bigger, more beautiful, not as expensive as
> SUPERLATIVES: the best (x2), the biggest, the most interesting, the most important

b➤ Focus Ss on the Active grammar box. Ss match the rules a–e to the sentences 1–6 then compare their answers with their partners. Check answers with the class.

> **Active grammar**
>
> 1 *Rule a) superlative*   2 Rule d) comparative
> 3 Rule c) comparative   4 Rule e) comparative
> 5 Rule b) comparative   6 Rule b) superlative

➤ Refer Ss to Reference page 45 and give them time to read through it and ask you questions if they have any.

10➤ Write the first sentence on the board as an example. Ask Ss what is wrong with the sentence and ask them to correct it. Write the correct form on the board. In pairs Ss correct the mistakes in sentences 2–8. Ss compare their answers with another pair. Check answers with the class.

> **Answers:** 1 Lagos is **larger** than Milan.   2 Cape Town is **smaller** than Mexico City.   3 Auckland is windier **than** Sydney.   4 Cairo is **the** most important city in Egypt.   5 Rio de Janeiro is **more** picturesque than Brasilia.   6 Katowice isn't as historical **as** Krakow.   7 Prague is **prettier** than Kolin.   8 The food in Madrid is **better** than the food in Edinburgh.

11➤ Focus Ss on the Web log: Day 24. In pairs Ss complete the spaces using the word in brackets to make comparative or superlative sentences. Check answers with the class and write the answers on the board.

> **Answers:** 1 the biggest 2 the most interesting 3 more comfortable 4 better than 5 friendlier than 6 as cold 7 the most delicious 8 the oldest

12➤ Ss in groups of three or four. Tell Ss to think about the cities they have been to, either in their own country or in other countries. Ss write sentences about the cities using the words in the box as prompts and the comparatives and superlatives language from the Active grammar box. Ss compare their answers with the other Ss in their groups. Encourage Ss to ask follow-up questions about the cities.

➤ Get feedback from all the groups and discuss which is the nicest city Ss have been to and why.

> **OPTIONAL EXTENSION**
>
> Organise Ss into pairs. Tell Ss to think of two cities in their country and write five or six sentences comparing the two. Ss A read their sentences to their partners but only read the name of one of the cities. For example, 'Madrid is much older than _____.' After listening to all of the sentences, their partners must guess the city their partner has not mentioned. Repeat the activity with Ss A reading their sentences and Ss B guessing the cities. In a monolingual class get feedback and ask Ss to tell you more about the cities in their country. In a multilingual class have Ss tell each other more about the cities in their countries.

Speaking

13a➤ Write your own Top Five films on the board. Encourage Ss to ask you follow-up questions about your favourite films and why you chose these particular ones.

➤ Ss choose one category they are interested in. Give Ss a few minutes to think of their own Top Five for that area.

b➤ Organise Ss into groups of four. Ss tell the other Ss in their groups why they chose this category and explain how they chose their number 1. Encourage Ss to use language of comparatives and superlatives from the Active grammar box while doing so. Have the Ss listening ask follow-up questions.

➤ Get feedback from the class and check if any of the Ss chose the same things in their Top Fives.

3.3 Homes that think

Mobile phones have evolved rapidly over the last few years. The latest developments from Japan include phones which can help you stay in contact with your home and the electrical appliances in it.

In this lesson Ss look at some compound nouns connected with household appliances. Ss then read a text about how mobile phones will help control electrical appliances in homes in the future. Through this text Ss analyse ways of talking about future possibility. Ss then go on to look at telephone language. Finally, Ss practise a telephone conversation.

> **OPTIONAL WARMER**
>
> Ss write down the names of all the electrical appliances that they have in their houses. Ss compare their lists with their partners. Ask a student to tell you their list and write it on the board. If other Ss have any different words write them on the board too. Practise any words Ss have pronunciation difficulties with.

Vocabulary

1a➤ Tell Ss to cover column B of the table. In pairs Ss think of words to connect to the words in column A to finish each compound noun. Ss compare their compound nouns with another pair. Get feedback and write correct compound nouns on the board.

➤ Ss uncover column B and match the nouns from column A with the nouns from column B to make compound nouns.

➤ Check answers with the class and make sure Ss understand what each compound noun is.

> **Answers:** 2 h washing machine
> 3 a air conditioner   4 f central heating
> 5 g mobile phone   6 d burglar alarm
> 7 e DVD player   8 b alarm clock

b➤ Focus Ss on the functions in the box. In pairs Ss match the items in Ex. 1a to the functions. Check answers with the whole class.

> **Answers:** clean clothes: washing machine, stay warm: central heating, speak to people: mobile phone, stay cool: air conditioner, leave messages: answer phone, watch films: video recorder, wake up on time: alarm clock, keep the home safe: burglar alarm

Pronunciation

2a➤ Write *answer phone* on the board and ask Ss where the stress is. Mark the stress above the first word. Ss practise saying this compound noun with their partners, concentrating on the stress. Explain that most compound nouns are stressed on the first word and that if the first word is an *-ing* word it is always stressed, e.g. <u>wash</u>ing machine.

➤ Play recording 3.5. Ss listen and mark the stress on the compound nouns in the correct place. Ss compare their answers with their partners.

> **Answers:** 1 <u>answer</u> phone   2 <u>washing</u> machine
> 3 <u>air</u> conditioner   4 central <u>heating</u>
> 5 mobile <u>phone</u>   6 <u>burglar</u> alarm   7 <u>DVD</u> player
> 8 <u>alarm</u> clock

b➤ Play recording 3.5 again, pausing to give Ss time to repeat the words.

Speaking

3➤ Organise Ss into groups of three. Ss discuss the three questions with their group. Monitor for errors and take notes. Get feedback from the class and discuss each group's ideas. Write any errors on the board and encourage Ss to self-correct. Finally, write up examples of correct language you have heard Ss use and praise them for using it.

Reading

4a➤ In pairs Ss make a list of all the things that a mobile phone can be used for apart from calling and texting. Get feedback from one pair and write their ideas on the board.

➤ Ask the rest of the class if they have any other ideas and add them to the list on the board.

b➤ Ss read quickly through the text and choose the best title. Tell them not to worry if there are any words they don't understand at this stage. Ss check their answers with a partner. Get feedback from the class.

> **Answer:** 1 New reasons to phone home

5a➤ Ss read the text more carefully and answer the questions 1–4. Ss compare their answers with a partner. Check the answers with the group.

> **Answers:** 1 Mobile phones changed our lives because they allowed us to make phone calls while travelling.   2 'Echonet' is already on sale.
> 3 'Echonet' allows you to communicate with your fridge, air conditioner, washing machine, oven and burglar alarm.   4 Mitsubishi's new technology is for forgetful shoppers.

b➤ Ss read the text again and mark the sentences 1–5 (*T*) if they are true and (*F*) if they are false. Check answers with the whole class.

> **Answers:** 1 T   2 F   3 F   4 T   5 T

c➤ Ask students to correct the false sentences and to compare their answers in pairs.

➤ Ask Ss if there are any words or phrases in the text that they don't understand. Encourage Ss to answer each others' questions or to use a dictionary before asking you.

> **Answers:** 2 The phone won't close the door but it will send you a warning message.   3 The phone won't call the police but it will tell you there are burglars in the house.

6a Tell Ss to reread the text and underline all the changes in mobile phones they can find. In pairs Ss write numbers 1–5 beside these changes, depending on how useful they think each change will be; 1 being not useful - 5 being very useful.

b Ss discuss their opinions with another pair of Ss. Get feedback from the whole group.

Grammar

> **OPTIONAL GRAMMAR LEAD-IN**
>
> Write the following sentence prompts on the board:
> *1 Astronauts/travel to Mars. 2 Scientists/find a cure for AIDS. 3 My country/win the World Cup. 4 Spanish /become the most important language in the world. 5 I/speak English perfectly.*

➤ Ss talk to their partner and decide how likely it is that these things will occur in the next ten years. Go around the class, taking note of how Ss express future possibility. Get feedback and write some of the Ss' ideas on the board.

7 Ss complete the Active grammar box using the underlined words from the text.

> **Active grammar**
>
> Certain + *New Technology will certainly change our lives.*
> Probable + *It will probably arrive in Japan first.* – *It probably won't be cheap.*
> Possible + *Customers may/might/could find it difficult to use.*

➤ Refer Ss to Reference page 45 and give them time to read through it. Focus Ss on the use of *will* before the adverb in affirmative sentences and the use of *won't* after the adverb in negative sentences. Also draw Ss' attention to the use of the infinitive without *to* after *may/might/could*.

8 Ss choose the correct alternatives in sentences 1–6 then compare their answers in pairs. Check answers with the class.

> **Answers:** 1 might   2 I'll probably   3 may not
> 4 probably win   5 probably won't   6 may come

9 Write *Computers _____ get faster in the next twenty years.* on the board. Ask Ss to complete the sentence using an expression of future possibility. Elicit answers from various Ss.

➤ Ss complete the sentences 1–6 with a partner. Tell Ss there is more than one possible answer for each sentence. Get feedback and encourage Ss to explain their choices.

> **Possible answers:**   1 may 2 will probably 3 might
> 4 will probably 5 will certainly/definitely 6 may

Person to person

10a Tell Ss they are going to make predictions about other Ss in the class. Ss think about other Ss in the class and write seven predictions without writing the Ss' names. While writing the predictions, encourage Ss to use the ways of expressing future possibility seen in Ex. 7. Monitor what Ss are writing and help them with vocabulary as necessary.

b Ss tell other Ss in the class their predictions. The Ss guess who they think each of the predictions is about.

➤ Get feedback from the class and ask Ss if they think the predictions made about them will come true.

Speaking and listening

11a In pairs Ss discuss the questions. Get feedback from the whole class.

b Ss work in pairs to complete the How to … box with the words. Check answers with the group.

> **Answers:**   Hello I'd <u>like</u> to speak to …   (May I ask) who's <u>calling</u>, please?   <u>This</u> is John Fox.   I'll put you <u>through</u>.   Can I <u>take</u> a message?   Could he call me <u>back</u>?   Can I leave a <u>message</u>?

12a Focus Ss on the table. Play recording 3.6 and Ss complete the table. Give Ss time to compare their answers.

b Play recording 3.6 again and Ss check their answers.

> **Answers:**
>
> | | Call 1 | Call 2 | Call 3 |
> |---|---|---|---|
> | *Caller's name* | Mr Sharp | Gabriella Jones | Andrea Jackson |
> | *Message* | Ask Mrs Davies to call back about Friday's meeting | Call back | Ricardo Villas must fax an invoice |
> | *Caller's number OR fax number* | 202 943 8226 | Line 6 | 682 3149 |

c Ss look at the tapescipts of the conversations on page 170 and practise the conversations with their partners.

➤ Ss then close their books and repeat the conversations without looking at the tapescripts.

13a Write *John please there Is?* on the board and ask Ss to put this sentence in the correct order. Write the words in the correct order on the board.

➤ In pairs Ss order the words in sentences a–h. Check answers with the class.

> **Answers:**   a Yes, I'll do that.   b Johnson and Johnson. How may I help you?   c I'm afraid she's not in the office at the moment.   d Hello. This is Mr Brown. I'd like to speak to Maria Cardusio please.
> e Yes, of course.   f Can you ask her to call me back?
> g Oh. Can I leave a message?   h Thank you. Goodbye.

b Ss put the sentences in order to make a complete telephone conversation. Ss compare their answers in pairs, then check the answers with the class.

> **Answers:**   1 b 2 d 3 c 4 g 5 e 6 f 7 a 8 h

➤ Ss practise the conversation in pairs.

14 Ss in pairs, A and B. Student A looks at the role cards on page 42, student B looks at the role cards on page 148. Give Ss time to read their roles and to prepare their dialogue. If possible, to make the role play more realistic, organise the chairs so that Ss are sitting back to back with their partners. Ss have the telephone conversations. Monitor the conversations for errors. Write errors on the board and ask Ss to correct.

Vocabulary: Prefixes and suffixes

In this lesson Ss look at different prefixes and suffixes and how they are used to modify words.

1a➤ Ss look at the words in the box and discuss which part of the words are prefixes, which are suffixes, and what they mean. Elicit prefixes go at the start of the word they are modifying and suffixes go at the end.

> **Answers:** prefixes: *un-* suffixes: *-ful, -less, -y*
> *un-* gives a negative or opposite meaning to a word.
> *-ful* and *-y* mean that the person or thing contains the quality of the adjective, *-less* means that the person or thing does not have the quality of the adjective.

b➤ In pairs Ss read the table and add more examples to the right-hand column. If Ss need help, encourage them to use dictionaries or tell them to ask you.

2a➤ In pairs Ss add prefixes from the table in Ex. 1b to the words in the box. Check answers with the class.

> **Answers:** misunderstanding, ex-wife, unusual, revisit, disagree

b➤ Ss complete the sentences 1–5 using the new words they made in Ex. 2a. Check answers with the class.

> **Answers:** 1 revisit 2 disagreed 3 unusual
> 4 misunderstanding 5 ex-wife

Lifelong learning

➤ Ss read the Lifelong learning box then discuss how they could organise their notebooks to note the different forms a word has. Get feedback from the class and discuss the different ways Ss could organise their notebooks.

3a➤ Focus Ss on the table. Discuss how adding suffixes to a word can change the word type. Ask Ss to identify which adjectives were formed from nouns and which from verbs.

> **Answers:** Adjectives formed from nouns: dirt, friend, help, use, care; Adjectives formed from verbs: create, attract, care, use, enjoy, comprehend

b➤ Ss add their own examples to the right-hand column. Check examples with the class.

4➤ In pairs Ss change the base words in bold to complete the gaps in the ads. Check answers with the class.

> **Answers:** Advert 1: airy / peaceful / friendly / weekly
> Advert 2: attractive / homeless / responsible / sunny
> Advert 3: careful / expensive / breakable / messy

Writing

5➤ In pairs Ss write a short advert. Encourage Ss to include at least three words with prefixes or suffixes.

➤ Stick the ads on the classroom wall. Ss go round and read the ads. Tell Ss they must respond to one of the ads and write an answer in an email which could be written for homework.

Communication: Your dream house

In this lesson Ss read and discuss an advertisement for a competition. Ss then listen to two people trying to win the competition and do a role play where they explain why they should win the competition.

> **OPTIONAL WARMER**
> In groups of three or four Ss discuss if they have ever entered or won a competition. Get feedback and ask what type of competitions Ss have entered and what prizes they have won if any.

1➤ Focus Ss on the pictures of the houses. In pairs Ss describe the houses and discuss which one they prefer.

➤ Ss read the advertisement for the competition and answer the questions in pairs. Check answers with the class.

> **Answers:** The prize is a house for a year and entrants must answer three questions: why they want to stay there, what they will do during the year, which house they prefer and why.

2a➤ Focus Ss on the table and give them time to read it carefully. Check Ss understand the vocabulary in the table.

➤ Play recording 3.7. Ss complete the notes in the first two columns of the table. Allow Ss to compare their answers.

b➤ Play recording 3.7 again and Ss check their answers. Check answers with the class.

> **Answers:** 1 city 2 house in the country 3 nature
> 4 honey 5 work 6 boring and quiet 7 city
> 8 cultures 9 gym 10 another language 11 stay

c➤ Ss in small groups four discuss whether Speaker 1 or Speaker 2 should win the competition and why. Get feedback.

3a➤ Tell Ss they are going to enter the competition. Give them time to prepare what they are going to say and to make notes in the right-hand column in the table. Monitor and help Ss as necessary.

b➤ Organise Ss into groups of six. In each group there should be three speaker and three judges. Give the speakers a limited time (three or four minutes) to make a speech explaining why they should win the house/apartment for a year. The judges listen and ask questions to find out more information. Monitor and take note of errors. When all the speakers have spoken, the judges decide who should win the competition.

➤ Change roles so the speakers become judges and the judges become speakers. Repeat the activity.

c➤ Ask Ss to tell you who won the competition in each group and why.

➤ Read out any errors you heard while Ss were talking. Discuss the errors with the class and write the correct forms on the board.

Review and practice

1➤

Answers: 1 am thinking   2 Are you going   3 is working   4 I'll go   5 are you going to   6 am playing   7 I'll do   8 are you doing

2➤

Answers: 1 I'll probably stay at home and watch TV.   2 Mark probably won't be able to come to lunch.   3 Australia might win the next Rugby World Cup.   4 I'm working late tomorrow so I might not see you.   5 We'll probably buy a flat next year.   6 My father may not come home for another two months.

3➤

Answers: 1 He's taller than me.   2 Everest is the highest mountain in the world.   3 Her first book was more interesting than her second.   4 Hospitals are not as efficient as they were in the past.   5 She earns much more than me.

4➤

Answers: 1 quieter   2 more crowded than
3 further   4 more old-fashioned than
5 colder / than   6 more picturesque
7 more polluted than   8 easier / than

5➤

Answers: 1 polluted / dirty   2 touristy
3 cramped   4 tiny   5 untidy   6 noisy
7 dull   8 unhelpful

Notes for using the Common European Framework (CEF)

CEF References

3.1 Can do: write a letter of complaint

CEF B1 descriptor: can convey information and ideas on abstract as well as concrete topics, check information and ask about or explain problems with reasonable precision. (CEF page 83)

3.2 Can do: compare cities

CEF B1 descriptor: can work out how to communicate the main point(s) he/she wants to get across, exploiting any resources available and limiting the message to what he/she can recall or find the means to express. (CEF page 64)

3.3 Can do: make a formal phone call

CEF B1 descriptor: can find out and pass on straightforward factual information. Can obtain more detailed information. (CEF page 81)

CEF quick brief

The Common European Framework describes itself as 'a common basis for the elaboration of language syllabuses, curriculum guidelines, examinations, textbooks, etc'. It is not intended to be a definitive description of what to teach but it is designed to offer a 'framework' which the user can build on. In addition it believes that language learning can be measured not by how much grammar or vocabulary a learner knows, but by what a learner can achieve with the language that they know. Grammar and vocabulary are only important in terms of what they empower a learner to do. This is an 'action-oriented' approach to language.

Portfolio task

Download the Total English Portfolio free from www.longman.com/totalenglish.

Objective: help Ss to complete the record of their 'language qualifications' as well as their 'language and cultural experiences' sections of their Passport.

This task can be done in Ss' own language.

1➤ Remind Ss that their Passport enables them to demonstrate their relevant experiences and qualifications.

2➤ Explain that recording language qualifications and considering language and cultural experiences are important in this. The Total English Portfolio has two separate sections for Ss to give information about these.

3➤ Give some examples of your own relevant qualifications and experiences (exams, certificates, exchange trips, holidays, courses, friends with that first language, etc).

4➤ Ask Ss to write a list of their own relevant experiences and show a partner.

5➤ Ask Ss to complete these sections of their Passport.

6➤ Remind Ss that they can update this at any time.

4 Wealth

Overview

Summary

Lesson 1: Ss read a text about Frank Abagnale, a famous American trickster. They then listen to a summary of Frank's story and look at phrasal verbs in the text.

Lesson 2: Ss listen to a seminar about how to be an entrepreneur. Ss then go on to look at different letters and emails and write a letter of invitation to a famous person to give a talk at their school.

Lesson 3: Ss discuss different advertisements and advertising before reading a text about how advertising convinces people to buy things. Ss then write an advertisement for an object they want to sell.

Vocabulary: Ss look at some confusing words in English and write sentences about their classmates using these words.

Communication: Ss read a text about some of the most expensive things in the world. Ss then discuss whether they feel these things are a waste of money or not.

Film bank: From rags to riches (3'14")

An extract from a classic British film. *The Lavender Hill Mob* was made in 1951 and stars Alec Guinness as Holland, a bank clerk who dreams of being extremely rich. He befriends some criminals and the group plot to steal some gold bullion from the bank. This extract shows Holland comfortably settled in South America enjoying the good life.

Possible places to use this short film are:

➤ Before the Lead-in to introduce the topic of wealth

➤ At the end of the unit to round up the topic and language

For ways to use this short film in class, see Students' Book page 154 and Teacher's Book page 181.

Lead-in

OPTIONAL WARMER

Focus Ss on the photos. In pairs Ss decide what sort of lifestyle each photo shows. They then decide which of the lifestyles they would prefer to lead and why. Ss then discuss the disadvantages of each lifestyle.

1a➤ In pairs Ss read the quotations and decide if any of the quotations are reflected in the photos. Monitor conversations for errors. Get feedback from the class. Write any errors on the board and discuss them.

Answers: 'Money never made a man happy': bottom left photo 'Happiness comes from spiritual wealth, not material wealth': main photo 'Time is money': bottom left photo

---

b➤ Ss decide with their partners if they agree or disagree with the quotations. Get feedback and ask Ss if there are any quotations related to money in their own languages.

2a➤ Focus Ss on the verbs and phrases in the box. Ss write them in the correct column in the table. If there are any expressions the Ss are not sure of, encourage them to answer each others' questions.

Answers:

MONEY:	MONEY AND TIME:
lend, It's not worth the, good value for, earn, inherit, steal	*spend*, run out of, make, use your … wisely, save, have got … to spare, waste, not have enough, invest … in

---

b➤ Ss add other words and phrases they know to the table. Check the words and phrases Ss have written and write correct expressions on the board.

3a➤ Check that Ss understand the vocabulary in the prompts 1–6. Ss write down answers for each of the prompts.

b➤ Ss share their ideas with other Ss. Encourage Ss to ask follow-up questions. Get feedback and as a class talk about what the Ss have written.

OPTIONAL VARIATION

Ss write their answers in a different order to the prompts, then swap their notebooks with their partners. Ss guess what each thing their partner has written is: 'Do you think clothes are a waste of money?' 'No, clothes are something I spend a lot of money on.' Encouage Ss to expand each topic by explaining their answers: 'No, clothes are something I spend a lot of money on because I want to look good.'

4.1 Catch me if you can

Frank Abagnale was a famous American trickster who was played by Leonardo Di Caprio in the 2002 film *Catch me if you can* directed by Steven Spielberg. In the 1960s Abagnale ran away to Manhattan when his parents separated. He supported himself by posing as an airline pilot, a doctor and a lawyer and by the age of twenty-one had earned $2.5 million dollars by his cheating. Abagnale cashed false cheques in over twenty-six countries before he was eventually caught in France by FBI man Joseph Shea, played in the film by Tom Hanks.

In this lesson Ss read a text about Frank Abagnale. They then listen to a summary of Frank's story. Through this context Ss look at various phrasal verbs. They then go on to analyse and practise the grammar of question tags.

> **OPTIONAL WARMER**
>
> Ss in pairs. With their partners Ss discuss if they know of or have seen any films which are based on a true story. Get feedback from the class. Ask different pairs to tell the class about the films they have seen.

Reading and listening

1a➤ Focus Ss on the photos. In pairs Ss describe what they can see in the photos. Ss discuss if they know why the character played by Leonardo Di Caprio became famous and if they have seen the film. Get feedback from the class. If any of the Ss have seen the film they can tell the rest of the class what the film is about.

b➤ In pairs Ss look at the words in the box and predict what they think the text might be about. If there are any words Ss don't understand, encourage Ss to explain them to each other.

Get feedback from the class and decide as a group whose prediction sounds the most likely.

c➤ Ss read the text quickly and match the headings to the correct paragraph. Tell them not to worry about any words they don't understand at the moment. Ss compare their answers with a partner. Check answers with the whole class.

> **Answers:** paragraph a: heading 5
> paragraph b: heading 3   paragraph c: heading 1
> paragraph d: heading 4   paragraph e: heading 2

2a➤ Ss read the text more carefully and answer the questions 1–7. Ss compare their answers with their partners. Check answers with the class.

> **Answers:** 1 He was sixteen.   2 He was good-looking with greying hair (and dressed well).
> 3 He used magnetic ink to change bank code numbers and stole bank customers' money.
> 4 He got the uniform by saying his was lost at the dry cleaners and that he had an urgent flight.
> 5 He was the FBI man who arrested Frank and later became his friend. He was probably very determined but is fair.   6 Frank is a successful security consultant.
> 7 He thinks he was egotistical and self-centred.

➤ Ask Ss if there are any words or phrases in the text that they don't understand. Encourage Ss to answer each others' questions before asking you.

> **OPTIONAL VARIATION**
>
> Ss in groups of three or four. Ss read the first paragraph of the text. Ask Ss the following questions: What did Frank Abagnale pretend to be? A pilot, a doctor and a lawyer. How much money did Frank Abagnale earn from his cheating? $2.5 million.
>
> Each student now reads one of the paragraphs b–e. Ss take notes of any important information and decide which of the headings 1–4 go with their paragraphs. Without looking at the text again, each student tells the other students in the group about their paragraph and say which heading they think goes with the paragraph. Ss then read the other three paragraphs to check the information and which heading goes with each paragraph. Check the correct headings with the class. Ss then answer the questions 1–7. Ss compare their answers with their partners. Check answers with the class then ask Ss if there are any words they don't understand in the text.

b➤ Tell Ss to close their books and that they are going to hear a summary of Frank's story. Play recording 4.1. Ss find seven differences between the text and the summary.

➤ Check the differences with the class. Play recording 4.1 again if necessary.

> **Answers:** 1 Frank Abagnale wasn't English. He was American.   2 He tricked and cheated his way to $2.5 million, not $250 million.   3 He was wanted in 26 countries, not cities.   4 His mother was French, not German.   5 He said his uniform was lost, not stolen.   6 He didn't pretend to be a footballer. He pretended to be a doctor.   7 He went to prison in France.   8 He advises companies on security, not on how to cheat their customers.

3➤ In groups of three or four Ss discuss the questions. Monitor and take note of errors. Get feedback from the class then write the errors on the board. Encourage Ss to correct.

Vocabulary

4➤ Write *phrasal verb* on the board and ask Ss what a phrasal verb is (verb + particle(s)). In pairs Ss make a list of phrasal verbs they know. Get feedback from Ss and write correct phrasal verbs on the board and discuss their meaning.

➤ Focus Ss on the text again and tell them to underline any phrasal verbs they can see.

➤ Ss put the phrasal verbs in the correct place in the diagrams. Go round and check Ss' diagrams. Check answers with the whole group.

> **Answers:**
> Up: a pick up   b make up   c end up
>   d catch up with   e break up   f grow up
> Out: a work out   b run out   c drop out

5➤ Write the example sentence on the board with the three possible endings. In pairs Ss decide which of the endings is not possible. Cross out *his exams* and elicit/explain the meaning of the verb *drop out*.

➤ Ss cross out the wrong endings in sentences 1–7. Ss compare their answers with their partners. Check answers with the class and explain the meanings of any verbs Ss do not know.

> **Answers:** 1 b my relationship   2 c acting
> 3 c wrong   4 c a new haircut   5 a enough milk
> 6 b myself   7 b work as a doctor

6➤ In pairs Ss retell the story of Frank Abagnale using the phrases to help them. Go round the class and monitor. Take notes of any errors. Finally, write the errors on the board and discuss them with the whole class. Give feedback.

> **OPTIONAL EXTENSION**
> Ss look back at the diagram and choose four phrasal verbs. Ss write a sentence for each phrasal verb, but leave a space where the phrasal verb goes in the sentence. Go round and check the sentences Ss have written. Ss swap their sentences with a partner. Their partner tries to fill in the gaps in the sentences with the correct phrasal verb. To check their answers, Ss show the phrasal verbs they have included in the sentences to their partners. Get feedback from the whole class.

Grammar

> **OPTIONAL GRAMMAR LEAD-IN**
> Write the following sentences on the board:
> *1 I think you work in fashion.*
> *2 You work in fashion, _____ _____?*
> In pairs Ss decide how they could complete the gaps in sentence 2 so that it has the same meaning as sentence 1. Get answers from the class and write the correct words in the gaps (*don't you*). Elicit/explain that sentence tags are used to confirm information in a sentence.
> Organise Ss into pairs, A and B. Ss A close their books and try to remember facts about Frank Abagnale. They confirm these facts with Ss B who are looking at the text: 'Frank Ran away from home when he was sixteen, didn't he?' Monitor carefully and take note of where Ss have difficulties so you can explain them fully after looking at the Active grammar box.

7a➤ In pairs Ss read through the dialogues and complete the gaps. Ss compare their answers with other pairs. Check answers with the whole class and write the correct question tags on the board.

> **Answers:** 1 don't, do.   2 haven't, have
> 3 isn't, is   4 aren't   5 weren't, would

b➤ Play recording 4.2 and Ss check their answers. Ss practise saying the dialogue with their partners.

➤ Ss close their books and try to repeat the dialogues without reading them. Ask pairs of Ss to repeat the dialogues for the rest of the class.

8➤ Focus Ss on the Active grammar box and give them a few minutes to read through it. Individually Ss choose the correct alternatives to complete the rules 1–4. Ss compare their answers with their partners. Check the answers with the whole group.

> **Active grammar**
> 1 To make question tags, we repeat <u>the auxiliary verb</u>.
> 2 If the question is in the positive, the question tag is <u>negative</u>.
> 3 If the question is in the negative, the question tag is <u>positive</u>.
> 4 If there is no auxiliary verb, the question tag <u>uses *do, does or did*</u>.

➤ Refer Ss to Reference page 59 and give them time to read through the notes. Ask: **Q: What answer do you expect if you use a negative tag?** Yes. **Q: what answer do you expect if you use a positive tag?** No. **Q: What verb do we use in a question tag if there is no auxiliary verb?** *do, does, did* and their negatives. **Q: If you want to give a short answer, do you need to use the main verb?** No, only the auxiliary verb.

9➤ Focus Ss on the questions with the missing tags 1–10. With their partners Ss add the correct tags to the questions. Check answers with the class and write the question tags on the board.

> **Answers:** 1 can't you?   2 don't you?
> 3 isn't it?   4 haven't you?   5 did we?
> 6 do you?   7 aren't you?   8 won't you?
> 9 wouldn't they?   10 is it?

10➤ Give Ss time to think what their answers would be to the questions in Ex. 9. Now tell Ss they are to imagine they are at a party. If possible, get students to stand up and mingle and ask other students the questions in Ex. 9 using question tags.

➤ Go round and monitor and take note of errors and correct use of question tags. When Ss have finished, write the errors on the board.

➤ In pairs Ss discuss the errors and decide how to correct each one. Get feedback and write the corrections on the board. Finally, congratulate the group on correct use of question tags.

> **OPTIONAL EXTENSION**
> Tell Ss to think about any information that they know about the other Ss in the class. Individually Ss write five or six questions using question tags that they can ask the other Ss to confirm this information. Go round and check the sentences Ss write. Ss stand up and mingle and ask the other Ss the questions using the question tags. Get feedback and ask Ss if they have learned anything new about their classmates.

4.2 Getting rich quick

There are several well-known multimillionaire businesspeople that are often in the news. Recently businessman Donald Trump has appeared on his own TV programme, *The Apprentice*, which spawned a British version with Alan Sugar. The Russian businessman Roman Abramovich is also often in the news because of the vast amounts of money he has spent on Chelsea football club.

In this lesson Ss look at vocabulary connected with being an entrepreneur and listen to a seminar about how to be one. They then analyse the grammar of modals of obligation and prohibition and write a letter inviting a famous person to give a talk at their school.

> **OPTIONAL WARMER**
>
> On the board write the following ways of making money: *gambling, the stock market, investing in property, starting a business, getting a job*. In pairs Ss rank these ways of making money from 1–5; 1 being the best way of making money, 5 being the worst. Get feedback from the whole group.

Speaking

1➤ In groups of three or four, Ss discuss the questions 1–3. Get feedback from the class. In a monolingual class Ss tell you about any famous rich people from their country. In a multilingual class Ss tell each other about famous rich people from their countries.

> **Suggested answers:** 1 win the lottery, rob a bank, write a bestseller, invent something, etc. 2 Oprah Winfrey; popular US chat show host who owns a production company, Stella McCartney; successful fashion designer with a famous dad, Richard Branson; built the Virgin Empire (includes Virgin Airlines, Trains and Records), Paul Newman; used to be a film star and used some of his earnings to start a successful salad cream company 3 JK Rowling, Bill Gates, Madonna

Vocabulary

2a➤ Focus Ss on the expressions in the box. In pairs Ss check the meanings of the expressions. Ask for volunteers to explain each expression by providing example sentences.

b➤ In pairs Ss discuss the questions. Elicit feedback.

Listening

3a➤ Play recording 4.3. Ss listen and answer the questions. Check answers with the class.

> **Answers:** 1 The seminar is for young entrepreneurs. 2 The topic is how to get rich.

b➤ Focus Ss on the expressions in Ex. 2a again. Play recording 4.4. Ss listen and tick the expressions mentioned by the speaker. Check answers with the whole class.

> **Answers:** Be mean, don't be too generous, don't be too extravagant, be confident, work long hours, be ambitious.

c➤ Give Ss time to read the notes. Play recording 4.4 again and Ss complete the notes. Check answers with the class.

> **Answers:** 1 Be mean. You **shouldn't** <u>be too</u> <u>generous</u> 2 You **should** start <u>early</u> 3 You **mustn't** <u>waste</u> your money Bill Gates doesn't care about looking good because he **doesn't have to** <u>look good</u> 4 Be confident. You **must** <u>believe</u> in yourself 5 You **have to** work <u>hard</u>

4a➤ Focus Ss on the words in the box. In pairs Ss discuss how the words are connected to the seminar. Elicit answers.

> **Answers:** Payphone: John Paul Getty put *payphones* in the bedrooms of his house so his friends couldn't make free phone calls. Mice: Matthew Freud sold *mice* to his friends when he was at school. Suit: Bill Gates doesn't wear *suits* becuase he knows he doesn't have to look good. 5 o'clock: Rupert Murdoch goes to *five o'clock* meetings (in the mornings).

b➤ Ss think about whether they would be a good entrepreneur or not and why/why not. Ss discuss in pairs. Get feedback by asking Ss to tell you about their partners.

Grammar

> **OPTIONAL GRAMMAR LEAD-IN**
>
> Write the following advice on the board:
>
> 1 You <u>have to</u> do your homework.
> 2 You <u>should</u> write new vocabulary in your notebook.
> 3 You <u>must</u> study before the exam.
> 4 You <u>shouldn't</u> try to use English outside class.
>
> Tell Ss that one of the sentences is not true. In pairs Ss decide which sentence is false and how they could change it so that it is true. (Sentence 4 should read: *You <u>should</u> try to use English outside class.*)

5➤ Refer Ss back to Ex. 3c. Ss put the words in bold into the correct column in the Active grammar box then answer the questions.

> **Active grammar**
>
> It is an obligation *must*/*have to* It is a good idea *should* It is prohibited *mustn't* It isn't a good idea *shouldn't* It is not necessary. You can do it if you want to *don't*/*doesn't have to*
>
> 2 a Sentence 2 2b Sentence 1

➤ Refer Ss to Reference page 59. Give Ss time to read through the notes. Ask: **Q: What modal is often used for rules and regulations?** *have to.* **Q: What modal do we use when the obligation comes from the speaker?** *must.* **Is it correct to say *must to* or *should to*?** No. *must* and *should* are never followed by *to*. **Q: What is the negative form of should?** *shouldn't.*

6➤ Write the example sentence on the board: *It's a good idea to take an aspirin if you have a headache.* Underneath write: *You* _____ *an aspirin if you have a headache.*

➤ Ask Ss how to complete the sentence using a modal verb. Write *should take* in the space.

➤ Ss complete the sentences 1–7 using the words in brackets. Tell Ss they must use between two and five words when doing so and that they must not change the form of the word in brackets. Ss compare their answers with their partners. Check answers with the whole class.

> **Answers:** 1 don't have to 2 should buy
> 3 has to switch off 4 have to get a passport
> 5 mustn't smoke 6 shouldn't wash your hair

Pronunciation

7a➤ In pairs Ss discuss where they think the stress lies in sentences 1–5. Get feedback from various Ss.

➤ Play recording 4.5. Ss listen and mark the stress.

> **Answers:** 1 You **have** to buy a ticket. 2 You **don't** have to pay. 3 You **should** send a card. 4 I **must** remember. 5 You **mustn't** smoke.

b➤ Ask Ss how *to* is pronounced in (*don't*) *have to*. Check the answer with the class and practise saying the weak form of *to* /tə/ in *have to* and *don't have to*.

c➤ Ask Ss if the *'t*'s are pronounced in *don't/must/mustn't* in sentences 2, 4 and 5 in Ex. 7a. (*'t'* in 2, 4 and the first one in 5 isn't pronounced. The sentences *sound like* the following: 2 You *don* have to pay. 4 I *mus* remember. 5 You *musn't* smoke.) Practise saying the sentences slowly and quickly to compare.

d➤ Play recording 4.5 again. Pause to give Ss time to repeat the sentences.

8a➤ Ss change the modal verbs in sentences 1–6 to make true sentences.

b➤ Ss compare their answers with other Ss. Check answers with the whole group.

> **Answers:** 1 You *don't have to* pay by credit card when you go shopping in the supermarket.
> 2 You *must* bring some identification when you open a bank account. 3 You *have to* pay for English lessons. 4 You *shouldn't* carry a lot of money with you late at night in dangerous areas. 5 You *don't have to* pay to go to the library. 6 You *have to* buy a ticket to see a film at the cinema.

Speaking

9a➤ In pairs Ss discuss how to be a good public speaker, student or teacher and employer or employee.

b➤ Ss write down their ideas. Encourage Ss to use modals of obligation and prohibition.

➤ Ss compare their answers with another pair. Get feedback from the class and discuss the ideas and which the most difficult thing to be good at is.

> **OPTIONAL EXTENSION**
> Tell students you are going to give them information about a place and they have to guess the place. Read the following sentences: *You must be quiet. You should bring your card if you want to borrow books. You don't have to borrow a book every time you go.* Ss guess the place (library). Ss then write down a list of six public places and decide what people are expected to do in these places and write sentences using modals to describe what is expected. Ss read their sentences to their group who guess the places.

Writing

10➤ Ss read the letters and emails. Ask Ss if there are any words they don't know the meaning of. Encourage Ss to answer each others' questions.

➤ Ss discuss the three questions with their partners. Get feedback from the class.

> **Answers:** 1 The left email/letter are invitations. The right email/letter are acceptances. 2 Maria Pesaro could be the events co-ordinator at Intra Solutions. Paul Sharp is probably a well-known businessman. 3 The letters are formal, the emails are informal. Characteristics of formal letters include: Dear, Yours sincerely, full names and addresses, no contractions. Characteristics of informal writing include: Hi, XXX, first names only, contractions used.

11➤ Focus Ss on the How to … box. Ss put the missing words in the correct place in the box.

> **Answers:**
> | | |
> |---|---|
> | **Inviting** | Informal; *I'm having a party on Saturday 21st June. Would you like to come?* Formal: *I am writing to invite you to…* |
> | **More information** | I have enclosed/attached a map/programme. *Can you give me confirmation of…* |
> | **Accepting** | Informal: *I'd love to come.* Formal: *I will be pleased to attend.* |
> | **Refusing:** | Informal: *Sorry, I can't make it because…* Formal: *I am afraid I am unable to attend due to…* |

12a➤ In groups of three or four Ss discuss questions 1–3. Ss share their ideas with the rest of the class.

b➤ In their groups the Ss write the letter to the famous person. Go round and monitor the Ss' work, encouraging Ss to use expressions from the How to … box.

c➤ When Ss have finished writing they swap letters with another group. Ss look at the other group's letter and discuss ways the letter could be improved. Ss write comments on the other group's letter. Encourage Ss to write positive as well as negative comments. Monitor carefully so that Ss don't correct anything that is correct in the letters.

➤ Ss return their letters to the other groups. Ss read the comments from the other group and decide how many of the comments they would like to incorporate into their letter.

d➤ Each group writes a final version of the letter. Collect the letters and correct them for the following class.

4.3 Spend more!

Nowadays advertising agencies charge companies huge amounts of money for designing advertisements. These agencies use a number of techniques to try to convince people to buy things.

In this lesson Ss discuss advertising, supermarkets and salespeople. Ss then go on to read a text about one of these areas and exchange information about the texts. Ss look at vocabulary from the texts and their opposites and then go on to look at the grammar of the first conditional with *if/when/unless/as soon as*. Ss practise the conditional by making sentences about themselves using this structure.

OPTIONAL WARMER

Collect some popular adverts from magazines and/or newspapers and remove/cover up the slogans. Write *slogan* on the board and elicit/explain what it means. Ask Ss to guess what the slogans are. Then ask Ss in pairs to make a list of all the advertising slogans they can think of. These slogans can be in English or in their own language provided they try and translate the slogan into English. Get feedback from the class and check if any pairs have written the same slogans. Ss decide which is the best slogan and why it is effective.

Reading and speaking

1➤ Focus Ss on the five advertisements. Ss answer questions 1–3 in pairs. Go around the class monitoring the conversations and making note of any errors. Get feedback about the questions, and then go through the errors with the whole class, encouraging Ss to self-correct before explaining yourself.

2➤ In pairs Ss look at the sentences about supermarkets, advertising and salespeople and decide what information completes the sentences. Tell them to look carefully each sentence, particularly at the words immediately before and after each gap if they need help.

➤ Check answers with the class and write Ss' ideas on the board.

3➤ Organise the Ss into three groups, A, B and C. Refer group A to the text on page 54, group B to the text on page 146, and group C to the text on page 149.

➤ Give Ss time to read the texts in their groups. If there are any words or expressions they don't understand, encourage them to answer each other's questions, or to ask you.

Answers: 1 75% 2 play music 3 shopping baskets 4 celebrities 5 funny 6 mouth waters 7 anything, to anybody, any time 8 hobbies, family, lifestyle 9 body language

---

4a➤ Regroup Ss into groups of three so there are students from group A, B and C together. Ss swap information in their groups to check their answers to Ex. 2.

b➤ Ss discuss if any of the information in the texts surprised them. Get feedback from the class and discuss why this information was surprising.

5➤ In their groups of three Ss discuss questions 1–3. Monitor and take note of errors. Ask each group to report what they have talked about to the rest of the class. Finally, write the errors on the board and discuss them with the class before giving feedback.

OPTIONAL EXTENSION

In pairs Ss write their own slogan for an English school. Ss then share their slogans with the rest of the class. Decide as a class which slogan is the best one for advertising a language school.

Vocabulary

6a➤ Write *succeed* on the board and elicit the opposite adjective. Write *fail* on the board.

➤ In pairs Ss write opposites for the words 1–9 using the words in the box. Check answers with the class and write the opposites on the board.

Answers: 1 reward 2 sell 3 produce 4 respond 5 success 6 punishment 7 buyer 8 consumer 9 response

---

b➤ Ss complete the sentences with a suitable word from the box in Ex. 6a. Ss compare their answers with a partner. Check the answers with the class and write them on the board.

Answers: 1 response 2 advertisement 3 reward 4 punish 5 failure 6 success 7 advertise 8 produce

---

Pronunciation

7a➤ Write *succeed* on the board and ask Ss where the stress is on this word. Mark the stress over the word and practise saying it with the class.

➤ Play recording 4.6 and Ss mark the main stress on the words from Ex. 6a. Allow them to compare with a partner before checking with the whole group. Write the words on the board and mark the stress above the words.

Answers: suc**ceed**, **fail**, re**ward**, **pu**nish, **buy**, **sell**, pro**duce**, con**su**me, **ad**vertise, res**pond**, suc**cess**, **fail**ure, re**ward**, **pu**nishment, **bu**yer, **se**ller, pro**du**cer, con**su**mer, ad**ver**tisement, res**ponse**

---

b➤ Play recording 4.6 again. Pause to give Ss time to repeat the words.

Lifelong learning

➤ Tell Ss about the importance of noting stress on new words they write in their notebooks. Ss look back at words they have recorded in their notebooks recently and mark the stress on ten of them.

➤ Ss practise saying these words with a partner. Ask various Ss to write on the board the words they have marked stress on. Practise saying these words with the group.

c➤ Play recording 4.7. Ss listen and answer the questions. Ss compare their answers with their partners

> **Answers:** 1 fail 2 reward 3 a seller 4 success 5 punishment 6 buy 7 a producer 8 advertisement

8➤ Focus Ss on the questions 1–6. Ss ask their partners the questions. Encourage Ss to ask follow-up questions to find out more information. Monitor for errors.

➤ Get feedback from the class by asking Ss about their partners. Finally, write errors on the board and go through them with the group.

> **OPTIONAL EXTENSION**
>
> Ss write questions for other Ss in the class which contain words from Ex. 6a. Monitor and give help where necessary. Ss stand up and mingle and ask other Ss the questions. Get feedback by asking Ss to report information about other Ss they have discovered.

Grammar

> **OPTIONAL GRAMMAR LEAD-IN**
>
> Write the following sentence on the board: *If you read English outside class, you'll improve more quickly.* Ask Ss if they know the name of this structure in English. (First Conditional.) Focus Ss on the structure of the First Conditional: *if* + Present Simple + *will* + infinitive without *to*. With their partners Ss write more sentences about studying English which include the First Conditional. Ss read out their sentences to the class.

9a➤ Give Ss time to read through the sentences 1–5. Ss choose the correct underlined alternatives in the Active grammar box. Ss compare their answers with their partners. Check answers with the whole class.

> **Active grammar**
>
> a) Use *if* + Present Simple + *will* to talk about <u>real possibilities</u> in the future.
> b) Use <u>*when*</u> for events in the future that are certain.
> c) Use <u>*if*</u> for events in the future that are not certain.
> d) Use <u>*as soon as*</u> to emphasise that an event happens immediately.
> e) *Unless* + positive verb means the same as <u>*if not*</u>.

b➤ Tell Ss to underline six more examples of the first conditionals in the three texts in Ex. 3. In pairs, Ss compare the sentences they underline. Check the sentences with the class.

> **Suggested answers:** Text A: Unless your mouth waters, a chocolate advert is probably a failure. If a product costs a lot of money, it won't necessarily be good quality. Text B: If I buy lots now, I won't need to come back later. If the experience is relaxing, you will stay in the shop longer. Text C: If you really believe in a product, this will help you sell it. If customers think of the salesperson as a friend, they will probably keep coming back to the same man or woman.

➤ Focus Ss on Reference page 59. Give Ss time to read the notes about the First Conditional then ask: **Q: What words do we use to form the First Conditional?** *if* + Present Simple + *will*. **Q: Is it possible to use other verbs instead of *will*?** *Yes*, modals like *can*, *should* and *may* can be used. **Q: Can First Conditionals also be used to describe events that are always true?** Yes. Focus Ss on the use of contractions for *will* ('*ll*) and *will not* (*won't*).

10➤ Ss cover column B of the table. With their partner Ss think of ways of completing the beginnings of the sentences in column A. Tell Ss to use the First Conditional while doing so. Get feedback from the whole group and write correct sentences on the board.

➤ Ss uncover column B and with their partners match the beginnings of the sentences in column A with the endings of the sentences in column B. Check answers with the class.

> **Answers:** 1 c 2 f 3 a 4 d 5 e 6 b

11➤ Ss complete the sentences with the correct verb forms. Ss compare their answers with their partners. Check answers with the class.

> **Answers:** 1 offer, 'll take 2 see, 'll tell 3 don't pay, 'll get 4 won't phone, is 5 finds, 'll have to 6 'll buy, can

Person to person

12a➤ Focus Ss on the sentence prompts 1–6. Ss complete the prompts so they are true for them. Go round and check the sentences Ss are writing and check them for correct use of the First Conditional.

b➤ Ss discuss their sentences with their partners. Encourage Ss to ask follow-up questions. Ss change pairs and tell a new partner about their sentences.

Writing

13➤ Refer Ss to the advertisements on pages 54 and 55 and give them time to decide what they want to advertise. Ss write their advertisements. If you wish, Ss can exchange their writing and let other Ss read it to decide which is the best one.

> **OPTIONAL EXTENSION**
>
> Divide Ss into two groups, A and B. Tell Ss in group A that they are receptionists in a language school. Tell group B that they are Ss looking for a school. Group A should think of reasons why their school is a good school to learn English in. While doing so they should try and think of sentences using the First Conditional: *If you do a course with us, you'll have full access to our resource centre.* If there is time, they should write an advertisement for the school. Group B should think of questions they can ask the receptionists using the First Conditional: *If I study with you for two years, will I be able to pass the First Certificate exam?* Re-pair Ss so that each receptionist is talking to a different student. Monitor and take note of errors. When Ss have finished, write errors on the board and discuss them with the class.

Vocabulary: Confusing words

In this lesson Ss look at and practise using words which are easily confused such as *rob* and *steal*. The exercises will help Ss analyse the differences between these words.

> **OPTIONAL WARMER**
>
> Write *borrow* and *lend* on the board. Give Ss two minutes to discuss the difference between the words and to write one sentence for each word. Get feedback. Tell Ss that they are going to be looking at easily-confused words such as these ones.

1➤ In pairs Ss choose the correct word in each of the sentences in 1–8. Alllow Ss to compare their answers with another pair before checking the answers with the class.

> **Answers:** 1 miss, lost 2 trip, travel 3 fun, funny 4 told, said 5 job, work 6 lend, borrow 7 remind, remember 8 robbed, stolen

➤ In small groups Ss discuss the difference between each pair of words. Get feedback from the class.

2➤ Focus Ss on the notes. Give Ss time to read the notes. In pairs Ss write similar notes for the other underlined words in Ex. 1. Check the answers with the whole class.

> **Example notes:**
> ***work vs job:*** *Work* is what you do to earn money. A *job* is the particular type of work that you do.
> ***lend vs borrow:*** If you *lend* something to someone, you give it to them so that they can use it for a short time. If you *borrow* something from someone, you take something that belongs to them, use it, and return it.
> ***remind vs remember:*** If you *remember* something, it comes back into your mind. To *remind* someone to do something, you let them know they need to do it.
> ***lose vs miss:*** If you *lose* something, you cannot find it. If you are late for something, e.g. a bus, say you *miss* it.

Lifelong learning

Discuss with the class the importance of recording how to use new vocabulary. Explain how a good dictionary can be helpful in this respect.

3➤ Tell Ss to cover the words in Ex. 1. Ss then complete the sentences 1–8 with an appropriate word. Tell Ss to change tenses to fit the context of the sentences. Check answers with the whole class.

> **Answers:** 1 told 2 lend 3 remember 4 stolen 5 trip 6 job 7 funny 8 missed

4a➤ Write a true sentence on the board about one of the Ss in the class which includes a word from Ex. 1. Ss then write similar sentences about their classmates using the sentence prompts 1–8. Go around and check the sentences Ss write.

b➤ Ask various Ss to read out some of their sentences to the class to check if what they have written is correct. The other Ss listen and say if the information is correct or not.

Communication: What a waste!

In this lesson Ss look at some of the most expensive things in the world. Ss then consider whether these things were a waste of money or not.

> **OPTIONAL WARMER**
>
> In pairs Ss discuss how much they would be willing to pay for a meal in a restaurant. Get feedback and discuss whether Ss think that spending a lot of money in a restaurant is a waste of money or not.

1a➤ Focus Ss on the pictures. In pairs Ss decide what is happening in the photos and how much money was spent on each thing. Ss match the figures to the pictures. Get feedback from the class.

b➤ Ss read the text quickly to check their answers. Tell Ss not to worry about any words they don't understand at this stage as you will be dealing with them later.

> **Answers:** 1 C 2 A 3 D 4 B

➤ Give Ss time to read the text more carefully. Ask Ss if there are any words they don't understand. Tell Ss to try to explain words to each other before asking you.

2a➤ Divide the Ss into two groups, A and B. Group A chooses three facts from the text and decides why they think these are a terrible waste of money. Group B chooses three facts also from the text and decides why it is/was a good idea to spend this money.

b➤ Pair Ss off so they are working with a student from the other group. With this partner Ss discuss their facts and why they think they were a waste of money or worth spending money on.

➤ Monitor the conversations and take note of errors. Write the errors on the board and encourage Ss to work together to correct the errors.

c➤ Ss discuss the question in groups of three or four. Get feedback from the class.

3a➤ Tell Ss they are going to do a survey about the spending and saving habits of the class. In groups of three or four, Ss prepare five or six questions about saving and spending money they can ask the other Ss.

➤ Go round and help Ss with the questions where necessary.

b➤ Ss work with a student from another group and ask each other the questions.

➤ Get feedback from the class and decide which Ss are money-wasters and which are money-savers.

> **OPTIONAL EXTENSION**
>
> Organise Ss into groups of three or four. Tell Ss that they have $1,000,000 to spend on anything they like, but that they must spend it on at least five different things. Give Ss five minutes in their groups to decide what they would spend the money on and why. Get feedback from the class and discuss which groups of Ss came up with the best way of spending the money.

Review and practice

1➤

> **Answers:** 1 can I? 2 don't I? 3 won't they?
> 4 didn't she? 5 isn't it? 6 aren't I? 7 aren't
> we? 8 have they? 9 should I? 10 didn't you?

2➤

> **Answers:** 1 c 2 g 3 i 4 j 5 e
> 6 f 7 b 8 a 9 d 10 h

3➤

> **Answers:** 1 never 2 ✔ 3 to 4 ✔
> 5 not 6 ✔ 7 to 8 be 9 have

4➤

> **Answers:** 1 mustn't 2 don't have to 3 mustn't
> 4 doesn't have to 5 mustn't 6 doesn't have to

5➤

> **Answers:** 1 when 2 Unless 3 If 4 if
> 5 unless 6 when 7 unless 8 when

6➤

> **Answers:** 1 If I see you tomorrow, I will give you
> the book. 2 She won't act in the film unless she
> receives her normal salary. 3 We'll go as soon as the
> taxi arrives. 4 If I drink another cup of coffee, I won't
> be able to sleep tonight. 5 I can't hear you unless
> you shout. 6 When I next go shopping, I'll buy some
> milk. 7 If you drive carefully, you won't crash.
> 8 As soon as you see him, call me.

7➤

> **Answers:** 1 run 2 value 3 up 4 picked
> 5 figures 6 success 7 advert 8 trip

Notes for using the Common European Framework (CEF)

CEF References

4.1 Can do: make small talk at a party

CEF B1 descriptor: can follow clearly articulated speech directed at him/her in everyday conversation, though will sometimes have to ask for repetition of particular words and phrases. Can enter unprepared into conversations on familiar topics. (CEF page 76)

4.2 Can do: make and respond to invitations

CEF B1 descriptor: can write personal letters and notes asking for or conveying simple information of immediate relevance, getting across the point he/she feels to be important. (CEF page 83)

4.3 Can do: write a short classified advertisement

CEF A1 descriptor: can exploit a wide range of simple language flexibly to express much of what he/she wants (CEF page 124)

CEF quick brief

Chapters four and five of the Common European Framework set out 'reference levels' as a way to describe someone's ability in language. There are six basic reference levels: A1, A2, B1, B2, C1, C2 which are designed to describe ability in any language, not just English, and are mostly written in the form of 'Can do' statements. Teachers, syllabus designers, writers, etc. can write and add their own statements according to the needs of their users.

Portfolio task

Download the Total English Portfolio free from www.longman.com/totalenglish.

Objective: to introduce students to the Biography section of Portfolio.

This task can be done in Ss' L1.

The second section of the Portfolio is the 'Biography'. The Biography is for the students to keep a more detailed and personal record of their language learning history, objectives and progress so that they can reflect on successful as well as unsuccessful language learning experiences and hence further develop their language learning skills.

1➤ Explain the purpose of the Biography section of the Portfolio and its benefits.

2➤ Ask Ss to think about their language learning objectives and to make a list of these. Give examples of your own objectives in a different language to add clarity.

2➤ Ask Ss to write details of their English language learning history (12 years at school, etc.) and encourage Ss to reflect critically on what has been successful and what hasn't been successful for them.

4➤ Ask Ss compare their notes with a partner before completing the relevant sections of their Biography.

5 Spare time

Overview

Lead-in	**Vocabulary:** leisure activities
5.1	**Grammar:** Present Perfect Simple vs Present Perfect Continuous
	Vocabulary: creative activities
	Can do: suggest and respond to ideas
5.2	**Grammar:** verb patterns with -ing or infinitive
	Vocabulary: describing books and films
	Can do: describe a film/book
5.3	**Grammar:** countable and uncountable nouns
	Vocabulary: food
	Can do: recommend a restaurant
Vocabulary	Explaining what you mean
Com. Focus	What are you good at?
Reference	
Practice	

Summary

Lesson 1: Ss listen to people talking about creativity. They then go on to read a text about ways of becoming more creative before solving problems in groups.

Lesson 2: Ss describe a favourite film or a book, then listen to a film-maker talking about what she did with her time in a month.

Lesson 3: Ss read a text about a restaurant in Iran. Ss then listen to someone describing a restaurant and talk about a restaurant they would recommend.

Vocabulary: Ss look at different common expressions for clarifying what you are talking or writing about and for giving further explanation. Ss review the use of adjectives to describe shape, weight, size and texture.

Communication: Ss listen to someone talking about Capoeira, a Brazilian martial art, then go on to talk about a skill they have.

Film bank: Favourite films (9'06")

An extract from *Casablanca,* a classic Hollywood film

Set against the backdrop of World War II, *Casablanca* tells the story of two men vying for the same woman's love. Humphrey Bogart and Ingrid Bergman play the starring roles. Famous lines from this 1942 film are '*Here's looking at you kid*' and '*Play it again Sam*'.

This extract shows Ilsa (Ingrid Bergman) coming back into Bogart's life and the drama that surrounds this.

Possible places to use this short film are:

➤ After Lesson 2 to extend the topic of describing books and films

➤ At the end of the unit to round up the topic and language

For ways to use this short film in class, see Student's Book page 155 and Teacher's Book page 182.

Lead-in

OPTIONAL WARMER

Focus Ss on the pictures. In pairs Ss rank the activities in the photos in order of preference from 1–4. Ss compare their order with another pair's order. Get feedback from the class and discuss the differences.

1➤ Focus Ss on the pictures. In groups of three or four Ss discuss if they do any of the activities and what type of person likes doing each one.

➤ Get feedback from the Ss. If Ss use any adjectives to describe the type of people who do these activities, write them on the board.

2a➤ In groups of three or four Ss put the words in the box into the correct column in the table.

➤ Draw the table on the board. Check answers with the whole class and write the words into the table on the board.

Answers:
PLAY: **cards**, **squash**, **chess**, compu**ter games**, **vo**lleyball, a **mu**sical **in**strument, **foot**ball

GO: **fish**ing, **skii**ng, **jog**ging, **swim**ming, **dan**cing, **sail**ing, **sur**fing, **cy**cling

DO: ae**ro**bics, **ex**ercise, **gar**dening, ath**le**tics, ka**ra**te, pho**to**graphy

NO VERB: **rea**ding, **pain**ting, **coo**king, **draw**ing

---

b➤ Play recording 5.1 and Ss check their answers.

➤ In pairs Ss mark the stress on the words. Play recording 5.1 again and pause for Ss to check their answers. Chain around the class, with different Ss pronouncing the words.

3➤ Ss work in pairs to choose three activities from the table which they enjoy. Ss decide what is needed for each of the activities and write the words under the headings of *Equipment, People, Place*.

➤ Get feedback from the class and write Ss' ideas on the board. Practise saying any words Ss have pronunciation problems with.

4a➤ In pairs Ss discuss the four questions.

b➤ Get feedback by asking Ss to tell the class some information they have found out about their partners.

EXTEND THE LEAD-IN

Ss in pairs, A and B. Ss A choose one of the activities from the box. To find out which activity A has chosen, Ss B must ask *Yes/No* questions. While asking the questions, encourage Ss to use any vocabulary they have thought of in Ex. 3. When Ss B have guessed Ss A's activities, Ss change roles so that Ss B choose an activity and Ss A ask *Yes/No* questions.

5.1 Are you creative?

There are many different ways of becoming more creative. Techniques include taking unrelated ideas and finding links between them, imagining that normal limitations don't exist and looking at the situation from a different point of view.

In this lesson Ss discuss their own creativity before listening to three people talking about their creativity. Through this context Ss look at the grammar of Present Perfect Simple and Present Perfect Continuous. Ss then read about ways of becoming more creative and use these ideas to solve some interesting dilemmas.

OPTIONAL WARMER

Ss look back at the activities in Ex. 2a on page 61. With their partner Ss discuss which of the activities are creative ones, and why/why not. Get feedback from the whole class and discuss what makes an activity creative.

Speaking

1➤ In pairs Ss discuss the questions 1–5. Monitor and take note of any important errors. Get feedback from the class. Finally write the errors on the board and ask Ss to self-correct.

2a➤ Give Ss time to read through the activities 1–10. If Ss don't understand the meaning of all the activities, encourage them to answer each others' questions or to ask you. Ss tick the activities that they have done in their lives.

b➤ Ss stand up and mingle to find Ss who have done each of the activities. Encourage Ss to ask follow-up questions.

c➤ Get feedback from the group by asking Ss to report what they have learned about other Ss in the class.

OPTIONAL EXTENSION

Ss in two teams decide which of the activities in Ex. 2a you have done in your life. Get feedback and award points for each correct guess. Encourage Ss to ask you follow-up questions about the activities you've done. The team with the most points at the end is the winner.

Listening

3a➤ Tell Ss they are going to hear three people talking about their own creativity. Play recording 5.2 and students mark the activities from Ex. 2 which the speakers mention. Ss compare their answers. Check answers with the class.

Answers: Speaker 1 made something with her hands. Speaker 2 invented new recipes. Speaker 3 entertained children for hours.

b➤ Give Ss time to read through the phrases. Play recording 5.2 again. Ss listen and write 1, 2 or 3 beside each phrase, depending on which speaker said each one.

Answers: 1 Speaker 1   2 Speaker 3   3 Speaker 2
4 Speaker 3   5 Speaker 1   6 Speaker 2

Grammar

OPTIONAL GRAMMAR LEAD-IN

On the board write the following gapped sentence: *I've been studying English for ___ years.* Tell Ss to complete the sentence so that it is true for them. Elicit Ss' answers and ask how long they have been studying English. Then elicit the name of the underlined structure.

4a➤ Focus Ss on the sentences in Ex. 3b. In pairs Ss mark (*S*) for the sentences which are Present Perfect Simple and with a (*C*) for the sentences which are Present Perfect Continuous. Check answers with the whole class.

Answers: 1 S   2 C   3 S   4 S   5 C   6 C

b➤ Ss read the Active grammar box and circle the correct alternatives. Ss compare their answers with a partner. Check answers with the class.

Active grammar
1 isn't   2 finished

c➤ Ss look at sentences 2 and 6 in Ex. 3b. In pairs Ss decide which of the rules in the Active grammar box fit these sentences. Check answers with the class.

Active grammar
Sentence 2 fits rule 2, sentence 6 fits rule 1.

➤ Focus Ss on Reference page 73 and give them a few minutes to read through the notes. Point out how the Present Perfect Continuous emphasises the continuation of an activity (recently finished or unfinished) rather than the result.

5➤ Focus Ss on sentences 1–8. Ss complete the sentences using the verbs in brackets. Check answers with the class.

Answers: 1 've broken   2 haven't washed
3 has been writing   4 have you been waiting
5 haven't seen   6 Have you been running
7 have been eating   8 have you had

6➤ In pairs Ss read through the sentences 1-6 and discuss why the underlined tenses are wrong. Check answers with the whole class.

Answers: 1 I**'ve been reading** ... (Use the Present Perfect Continuous as the action is unlikely to have finished)   2 I**'ve been swimming**. (Use the Present Perfect Continuous as we can see the results of a recently finished action – wet hair)   3 She**'s known** him all her life. (Use the Present Perfect Simple as *know* is a state verb not normally used in the continuous form)   4 How many exams **have** you **taken**? (Use the Present Perfect Simple because it emphasises the activity rather than the result)
5 I**'ve given up** smoking! (Use the Present Perfect Simple as it emphasises the result)   6 How long **have** you **been learning** Chinese? (Use the Present Perfect Continuous as it focuses on the length of the activity)

Pronunciation

7➤ On the board write *I have been reading Underworld this morning*. Ask Ss if it is possible to contract any of the verbs in the sentence. Elicit *I've been reading* and write it underneath the first sentence. Practise saying the contracted form using different pronouns with the class.

➤ Play recording 5.3 and ask Ss to listen for the contracted form of *have*. Ask Ss to identify which sentences use the contracted form.

➤ Play recording 5.3 again and pause to let Ss repeat the sentences.

Person to person

8a➤ Focus Ss on the sentence prompts and ask them to complete them so that they are true for them. Go round and monitor what Ss are writing.

b➤ Ss work in pairs. Ss take turns to ask each other questions using the prompts in Ex. 8a. Encourage Ss to ask follow-up questions. Monitor conversations and take note of errors. When Ss have finished, write the errors on the board and discuss them with the class.

> **OPTIONAL EXTENSION**
>
> Give Ss a few minutes to prepare a short talk about a hobby or activity which they do in their spare time. Encourage Ss to include both the Present Perfect Simple and Present Perfect Continuous in the talk. Ss present their talk to the rest of the class. Encourage the other Ss to ask follow-up questions about the hobby or activity.

Reading

> **OPTIONAL WARMER**
>
> Before looking at the questions in Ex. 9, write the following words on the board: *imagine, inspire, create*. In pairs Ss write as many different forms of these words as possible, by adding or changing suffixes and prefixes. Check the words the Ss have written and write correct words on the board.

9➤ Focus Ss on the questions 1–4. Ask Ss if there are any words they don't understand and encourage Ss to explain difficult words to each other before doing it yourself. Ss then discuss the questions in groups of three or four. Get feedback.

10a➤ Ss read the first paragraph of the text and decide which of the questions in Ex. 9 it discusses. Tell Ss not to worry about any vocabulary they don't understand at this stage. Check answers with the class. Ss tell their partners if they think they are imaginative or not and why/why not.

> **Answer:** 1 and 3

b➤ Ss read the rest of the text quickly and put the paragraph headings in the correct place. Ss compare their answers with their partners. Check answers with the class.

> **Answers:** Paragraph 1: Making connections
> Paragraph 2: No limits! Paragraph 3: Be someone else!

11➤ Ss read the text more slowly and answer the questions 1–5. Check answers with the class.

> **Answers:** 1 c 2 a 3 b 4 b 5 c

➤ Ask Ss if there are any words or phrases in the text that they don't understand. Write the words and phrases on the board and encourage Ss to explain them to each other. If there are still words or phrases that Ss don't understand, explain them to the group yourself.

Speaking

12➤ Focus Ss on the How to … box. With their partners Ss complete the sentences using the words above the box. Ss compare their answers with another pair. Check answers with the whole class.

> **Answers:**
>
> | Presenting an idea | *Why **don't** we do this? Shall we try this?* |
> |---|---|
> | Accepting | *That's a good **idea**. OK, let's go **with** that.* |
> | Rejecting | *The problem with that is … I'm not **sure** about that.* |
> | Presenting an alternative | ***Wouldn't** it be better to do this? Or we could do this.* |

13a➤ Organise the class into groups of four. Refer Ss to page 145. In their groups Ss work together to try and solve the problems. Encourage Ss to use the creativity techniques they discovered in the reading while doing so.

b➤ Pair off Ss so that they are working with Ss from other groups. Ask Ss to tell each other what they had discussed, the creativity techniques they used when solving the problem, and what solutions they found. Monitor the conversations to take note of errors and examples of correct language.

➤ Get feedback from the class. Ask the class to decide which group found the best solutions to the problems.

➤ Write the errors on the board and encourage Ss to self-correct. Write up examples of correct language Ss used and praise them for using it correctly.

c➤ Refer Ss to page 149 so they can check the solutions to the problems. Check which groups of Ss (if any) found the correct solutions.

> **OPTIONAL EXTENSION**
>
> Divide the Ss into groups A, B, C & D. Give the groups a few minutes to think of and write down another problem using the ones in Ex 13a as an example and their imagination. Then, ask Ss to exchange their problems with another group. In their groups Ss work together to find a solution to the problem. Ask the groups to present their problems and solutions to the class. Get feedback from the class by asking if the orginial group agrees with the solution.

5.2 The book or the film?

The Godfather was written by Mario Puzo and later turned into a film by Francis Ford Coppola, starring Marlon Brando. There were three Godfather films in all. The Shakespeare play *Romeo and Juliet* was filmed by Baz Luhrmann and released in 1996 in the US. This version was set in modern-day Los Angeles and featured a rock soundtrack. *The Lord of the Rings* was written by JRR Tolkien in 1954. A film trilogy of the Lord of the Rings shot in New Zealand became some of most successful films of all time.

In this lesson Ss look at vocabulary connected with books and films and speak about their favourite film or book. Ss then listen to a film-maker talking about how she spends her time and look at the grammar of gerunds and infinitives.

OPTIONAL WARMER

Form pairs, A and B. Ss A think of a famous film or book. Ss B ask Ss A questions to find out what film or book they are thinking of using *Yes/No* questions. When Ss B have discovered Ss As' films or books, repeat the activity with the As now asking the Bs the questions.

Vocabulary

1➤ Focus Ss on the pictures of the films. In pairs Ss discuss the questions 1–4. Get feedback from the whole group.

2a➤ Write the example sentence about *The Lord of the Rings* on the board and ask Ss if the sentence is about a film, a book or both. Elicit the meaning of *plot* from the Ss.

➤ Ss read sentences 1–9 and decide if the statements are about a book, a film or both, and what book or film the statement is about. Get feedback from the whole class.

Answers: 1 book: *The Lord of the Rings* 2 film: *Romeo and Juliet* 3 book and film: *The Godfather* 4 book: *The Lord of the Rings* 5 book: *The Lord of the Rings* 6 book and film: *Romeo and Juliet* 7 film: *The Godfather* 8 film: *The Lord of the Rings* 9 film: *The Godfather*

➤ In pairs Ss decide what the words or phrases in bold mean. Get feedback from the class.

Answers: chapter: one of the parts into which a book can be divided **soundtrack:** the recorded music from the film **main character:** the central person in a book, film or play, etc **was written by:** refers to the author **descriptions:** a piece of writing that gives details about what someone or something is like **is set in:** a place where a story takes place **is about:** describes the plot **was directed by:** refers to the person who instructs the actors, camermen, etc working on a film or play **sequel:** a book, film or play, etc that continues the story of an earlier one, usually written or made by the same person **was dubbed:** the original spoken language of the film was changed into another language **stars:** whoever stars in a film or play is one of the main characters **performance:** refers to how well the actors/cast/star did their job

b➤ In pairs Ss put the words in bold in the sentences in Ex. 2a into the correct column in the table. Beside the words Ss write (*n*) if it is a noun, (*v*) if it is a verb and (*adj*.) if it is an adjective.

➤ Copy the table onto the board. Check answers with the class and write the words into the correct place in the table on the board, marking the case of the words as you write them.

Answers:

Film OR Book	Film	Book
plot (n)	*soundtrack (n)*	*chapter (n)*
(main) characters (n)		
It was written by (v)		
is set in (v)		
sequel (n)		
was directed by (v)		
was dubbed (v)		
stars (n) (v)		
performance (n)		
descriptions (n)		

Speaking

3➤ Ss think of one of their favourite films or books. Ss complete the sentences in the How to … box about the film or book. Give Ss a few minutes to prepare their descriptions.

➤ Organise Ss into groups of four. Ss describe their books or films to the other Ss in the group. Encourage the other Ss to ask follow-up questions about the film or book. Get feedback from each of the groups.

Pronunciation

4a➤ Write the following sounds on the board: /æ/ /e/ /ɑː/. Ss practise saying the sounds with their partners.

➤ Focus Ss on the picture of the film by asking what kind if film is being shown. (A cowboy film.) With their partners Ss find as many objects as they can which contain the sounds. Ss write the words in the correct column in the table.

Answers:

man /æ/	ten /e/	car /ɑː/
fat man	pen	bar
hat	dead men	star
camera	leg	cards
bag	head	guitar
cat		
can		

b➤ Ss compare the words they have written in the columns with another pair.

➤ Ss add other words they know which contain the sounds into the spaces in the table.

5a➤ Play recording 5.4. Tell Ss to listen and write a tick beside the sentences they hear. Check answers with the class.

Answers: 1 a 2 a 3 b 4 a 5 b 6 b 7 b 8 a

b➤ Play recording 5.4 again, pausing to give Ss time to repeat the sentences.

c➤ In pairs Ss say the nonsense sentences as fast as possible. Get various Ss to read out one sentence each to the class.

> **OPTIONAL EXTENSION**
>
> Ss in groups of three or four. Each group chooses one of the sounds from Ex. 4a. Ss write a list of as many words as they can think of which contain that sound. Then, give Ss five minutes to write a short story which includes all the words they have written in the list. Ss read out their story to the rest of the class.

Listening

6a➤ Ss discuss with their partners how much of their free time they spend doing these activities. Get feedback.

b➤ Ss decide which of the activities they would like to do more of and which they would like to do less of and why. Get some general feedback from the whole class.

7a➤ Ss read about Hannah Cheung and look at the diagram. Check that Ss understand the amount of time she dedicates to each activity by asking Ss what percentage of time she spends doing each one. To help students understand the meanings of these percentages, ask how many days twenty percent of one month would be. (Based on a month of thirty days twenty percent is six days.)

b➤ Play recording 5.5. Ss listen and complete the information in the diagram. Check answers with the class.

> **Answers:**
> 7% **Cooking and eating**
> 15% Watching TV
> 10% Reading
> 8% **Shopping**

8a➤ Play recording 5.5 again. Ss listen and complete the notes about what Hannah says.

b➤ Refer Ss to the tapescript on page 171. Ss check their answers.

Grammar

> **OPTIONAL GRAMMAR LEAD-IN**
>
> Write the following sentence prompts on the board:
> *I can't stand …*
> *I enjoy …*
> *When I was younger I decided …*
> Ss copy the prompts into their notebooks and complete the sentences so they are true for them. Go round and check the sentences Ss have written, correcting the verb forms if necessary. Ss tell their partners about what they have written. Get feedback from the class and focus Ss on the form of the verb which follows *can't stand, enjoy* and *decided*. Tell Ss that there are some verbs which are followed by a gerund (*-ing* form) and some which are followed by an infinitive (*to + verb*).

9a➤ Focus Ss on the Active grammar box. Ss write the words in bold from Ex. 8a in the correct column in the table. Ss compare their answers with their partners.

➤ Copy the table onto the board. Check answers with the whole class and write the verbs in the correct column on the board.

> **Active grammar**
>
> | Verb + *ing*: | Verb + infinitive: | Verb + object + infinitive: |
> |---|---|---|
> | can't stand, don't mind, enjoy, look forward to, love | expect, 'd prefer, try, manage, seem, 'd like | invite |

b➤ Ss add the verbs in the box to the correct columns of the table in the Active grammar box. Check answers with the class and write the verbs in the table on the board.

> **Active grammar**
>
> | Verb + *ing*: | Verb + infinitive: | Verb + object + infinitive: |
> |---|---|---|
> | hate, finish, adore | forget, agree, refuse | remind, advise |

➤ Focus Ss on Reference page 73. Give Ss time to read through the notes. Check that Ss realise that there is no rule to verb patterns and that they must try and remember the patterns. Ask: **Q: If I stop eating, do I eat first, then stop?** Yes. **Q: If I stop to eat, do I stop what I am doing to eat?** Yes.

10➤ In pairs Ss choose the correct verb form in sentences 1–6. Check answers with the whole class.

> **Answers:** 1 to do 2 to do 3 doing 4 to do 5 to do 6 doing

11➤ Focus Ss on the advertisement for the book club. In pairs put the underlined words into the correct form. Remind Ss to use the Present Simple when doing so.

➤ Ss compare their answers with another pair. Check answers with the class.

> **Answers:** 1 invite you to join 2 you enjoy reading 3 expect to receive 4 you want to choose 5 advise you to join 6 finish reading 7 forget to include

Person to person

12a➤ Ss in groups of three or four. Focus Ss on the questions in Ex. 10. Ss ask each other the questions in their groups and remember as much information as possible about the other Ss. Monitor the conversations taking note of errors.

b➤ Pair Ss so they are working with a student from another group. Ss tell their new partners what they found out about the Ss in their groups. Finally, write errors on the board. Ask Ss to come up and correct the errors on the board.

> **OPTIONAL EXTENSION**
>
> Ss draw their own diagrams similar to Hannah Cheung's diagram in Ex. 7b to show how they spend their free time. Ss swap diagrams with their partners and ask questions about each others' diagrams. When asking and answering the questions, remind Ss to use correct verb patterns.

5.3 Memorable meals

Iran is a country with a rich cuisine. Iranian cuisine is famous for soups made from rice, herbs and meat. Main courses include rice and meat or chicken dishes as well as more exotic meals like Maghz (fried brains with herbs). Its desserts include many delicious dishes often made from yoghurt and almonds.

In this lesson Ss read about a strange restaurant experience. Ss then look at the grammar of countable and uncountable nouns, before listening to someone describing a restaurant. Ss then talk about a restaurant they would recommend and go on to write a synopsis of the film *Babette's Feast*.

OPTIONAL WARMER

Ss think about the typical food of their country and write notes about it. In a monolingual class, Ss compare their notes in small groups then tell you about the cuisine of their country. In a multilingual class, allow Ss to share their information with a partner. Get feedback.

Vocabulary

1➤ Focus Ss on the questions. Ss discuss the questions with their partners. Get feedback from the class.

2a➤ In pairs Ss decide what the difference is between the pairs of words. Encourage Ss to use their dictionaries for help.

b➤ Tell Ss to check their answers on page 146. Then ask Ss to provide example sentences to check understanding. Elicit the sentences from various Ss and correct if necessary.

Reading

3a➤ Focus Ss on the photos. In pairs Ss decide what country this might be and what type of food they eat in this place. Get feedback from the class.

➤ Tell Ss to cover the right-hand column of the table. With their partners Ss make expressions by adding words to the words in the left-hand column. Check the expressions with the class and write correct expressions on the board.

➤ Ss uncover the right-hand column and match the two sides of the table. Check answers with the class.

Answers: 1 c 2 f 3 a 4 d 5 b 6 e

b➤ In pairs, Ss work to predict what happens in the story. Ss use the expressions in Ex. 3a and the photo to help them.

➤ Ss swap partners and tell their new partners what they think happens in the story. Get feedback from the class and write their predictions on the board.

4➤ Ss read the story quickly to check their ideas. Tell Ss not to worry about any words they don't understand at the moment. Check if any Ss had made any correct predictions.

➤ With their partners Ss discuss why they think the man never found the café again. Get feedback from the class.

5➤ Ss read the text more carefully. Ask Ss if there are any words or phrases in the text that they don't understand. Encourage Ss to answer each others' questions.

➤ Ss read the summary and find eight mistakes. Ss compare the mistakes they have found with their partners. Ss correct the mistakes with their partners. Check answers with the class.

Answers: They were not driving through *a busy area* in Iran, they were driving through an **isolated place**. They didn't stop in a *small city*, they stopped in **a village**. The owner didn't speak *a little* English, he spoke **perfect** English. The meal was *not expensive*, it was **astonishingly cheap**. His friends didn't think it possible to find a *good* restaurant in such a remote area, not a **poor** restaurant. The engineer didn't return with his *wife*, he returned with his **colleague**. They couldn't find the **café**, not the *train station*. The local man had been there for **forty** years, not *thirty* years.

Grammar

OPTIONAL GRAMMAR LEAD-IN

Write the following sentences on the board:
1 *There are much restaurants in the centre of London.*
2 *Have you got many furniture in your house?*
In pairs Ss correct the sentences. Get feedback from the Ss and swap *much* and *many* in the sentences on the board. Ss write six more sentences and questions, three with *much* and three with *many*.

6➤ Give Ss a few minutes to read through the Active grammar box. In pairs Ss complete the tables in the box with the headings. Allow Ss to compare their answers with another pair before checking answers with the whole class.

Active grammar

a) Countable nouns b) Uncountable nouns
c) None d) A small amount e) A large amount

7➤ Refer Ss to reference page 73. Give Ss time to read through the notes. Then write: *Would you like chocolate? They're delicious.* on the board and ask a student to come up to the board and add one word to make the question correct. (*Would you like a chocolate.*)

➤ Focus Ss on the sentences 1–10. In pairs Ss add *a*, *an*, or nothing to the sentences to make them correct. Give Ss time to compare their answers with another pair. Then, check the answers with the whole group.

Answers: 1 nothing 2 That was **a** terrible meal! 3 nothing 4 Mummy, can I have **an** ice cream? 5 nothing 6 Let's go to **a** café for breakfast. 7 nothing 8 nothing 9 I live in **a** village in Santa Catarina. 10 nothing.

8➤ In pairs Ss choose the correct quantifier in sentences 1–8. Check answers with the whole class.

Answers: 1 a lot of 2 many 3 much 4 much 5 much 6 a lot of 7 a lot, no quantifier 8 a lot of

Person to person

9➤ Ss in pairs. Ss ask their partner the questions in Ex. 8 and take note of their partner's answers, listening out for correct use of quantifiers.

➤ If some Ss finish early, they can swap partners and relay their previous partner's answers.

Listening and speaking

> **OPTIONAL LEAD-IN**
>
> Write the following countries on the board: *Mexico, Japan, China, Argentina, France, Italy*. In pairs Ss discuss what they know about the cuisine from these countries. Get feedback from the class and write any information the Ss have told you beside the countries. Ask Ss if they have tried all of these types of cuisine. Discuss with the class which country has the best cuisine and why.

10➤ Tell Ss they are going to hear someone describing a restaurant. Give Ss time to read the four summaries.

➤ Play recording 5.6 and Ss write a tick next to the correct summary. Check the answer with the class.

> **Answer:** The best summary is d.

11➤ Focus Ss on the How to … box and give Ss time to read through the notes. Check that Ss understand the vocabulary and expressions. If they don't understand any vocabulary, encourage them to answer each others' questions before giving the explanations yourself.

➤ Play recording 5.6 again and Ss tick any expressions in the How to … box that the speaker uses. Allow Ss to compare their answers with their partners. Check answers with the whole class.

> **Answers:**
>
> | | |
> |---|---|
> | Location | *It's on a small street…* ✔ |
> | Atmosphere | *very lively* ✔ |
> | Menu | *The menu is (very) traditional* ✔ |
> | | *The (meat) is fresh and good quality* ✔ |
> | Service | *the waiters are (really) friendly* ✔ |
> | Prices | *the prices are (very) reasonable* ✔ |
> | Recommendation | *If you're in …, you must go* ✔ |

12a➤ Tell Ss to think about a restaurant they know which they could recommend. Focus Ss on the How to … box and tell them to use these expressions in their recommendation. Give Ss a few minutes to prepare what they are going to say. Go around the class helping with any vocabulary if necessary.

b➤ Organise Ss into groups of four. Ss tell their groups about their restaurants. Encourage the Ss listening to ask follow-up questions about the restaurant.

➤ Monitor the conversations and take note of errors. Write the errors on the board and discuss them with the class and write the correct form on the board.

➤ Get feedback by asking Ss in their groups to decide which of the restaurants recommended sounds the best and why.

Writing

13a➤ Write the following words on the board: *after, in the end, when*. Ask Ss what these words/expressions have in common. Elicit/Explain that the words/expressions are linking expressions, which tell us about the sequence in which events happen.

➤ With their partners Ss brainstorm any other linking expressions they know. If some of the Ss finish early, they can also pick out the non-defining relative clauses.

➤ Focus Ss on the summary in Ex. 5 on page 68. Ss underline the linking expressions in the summary. Ss compare the expressions they have underlined with their partner. Check answers with the class.

> **Answers:**
>
> *Linking words to specify time and sequence are* <u>underlined</u>. *Non defining relative clauses are in* **bold**.
>
> <u>While</u> two engineers, **who were hungry**, were driving through a busy area in Iran, they stopped in a small city. They found a little café. The owner of the café, **who spoke a little English**, offered to serve the men a meal. The meal, **which was delicious**, was surprisingly expensive. <u>After</u> they had finished eating, the restaurant owner asked the engineers to recommend his restaurant to their friends. They did this, but the engineer's friends didn't believe it was possible to find such a poor restaurant in such a remote area. <u>In the end,</u> the engineer returned to the village with his wife. However, <u>when</u> they arrived, they couldn't find the train station. <u>Eventually,</u> they asked a local man about the restaurant. He said he had never heard of such a place, and he had been there for thirty years.

b➤ Refer Ss to the Writing Bank on page 164. Ss read the description of Babette's Feast and mark the statements in number 1 (*T*) if true and (*F*) if false.

> **Answers:** 1 F They are from Jutland, Denmark. 2 F They are both single. 3 T 4 F She worked for free. 5 F Babette cooks the fantastic meal. 6 T

➤ Direct Ss to the second exercise of the Writing bank on page 164 and ask Ss to discuss Ex. 2a and Ex. 2b with their partner. Get feedback from the class.

c➤ In pairs Ss write a synopsis of the film *Babette's Feast*. Encourage Ss to use the sentences and phrases in the Useful phrases box on page 164 in their synopsis. Go round and help Ss as necessary.

➤ Ask various Ss to read out their synopses to the class.

> **OPTIONAL EXTENSION**
>
> Ss describe how to prepare a dish which is typical to their country. When preparing their descriptions, encourage Ss to use the linking words which specify time and sequence. Go round and help Ss with any vocabulary they need. In a monolingual class different pairs describe to you how the dish they have chosen is made. In a multilingual class each student prepares a description of how to make a typical dish from their country. Ss then mingle and tell other Ss in the class how the dish is made. Get feedback from the class.

Vocabulary: Explaining what you mean

In this lesson Ss look at different common expressions for clarifying what you are talking or writing about and for giving further explanation. These expressions have similar meanings but collocate with either countable or uncountable nouns. Ss also review the use and correct order of adjectives to describe shape, weight, size and texture.

> **OPTIONAL WARMER**
>
> In pairs Ss look back through their books and write a list of ten words they have seen in the course up till now. Re-pair Ss so they are working with a different student. Ss take turns to explain the words in their list to their partners who guess what word is being defined.

1a➤ In pairs Ss think of different situations in which they need to explain something, using the prompts 1–4 to help.

b➤ Ss compare the situations they have written with another pair. Get feedback from the class.

2a➤ In pairs Ss decide what is being described in sentences 1–5. Get feedback from the class. Tell Ss to turn the book upside down to check the answers at the bottom of the page.

b➤ Ask Ss to look at the questions and work out the uses of the expressions in bold and whether they are used with countable or uncountable nouns.

> **Suggested answers:** 1 The expressions are common ways of explaining something when we don't know the exact word. 2 *thing* is used for countable nouns and *stuff* is used for uncountable nouns

➤ Tell Ss that *type, kind,* (and *sort*) can be used for countable and uncountable nouns and have same meanings in these situations. What *type of* car do you have? What *kind of* music do you like? What *sort of* food do you want to eat tonight? If you are saying that something is partly true or are not being exact, use *sort of* or *kind of* rather than *type of*. E.g. It was *kind of* funny but I didn't laugh much. It was a *sort of* square shape.

3➤ In pairs Ss put the words in sentences 1–6 into the correct order to make sentences. Ss compare their answers with another pair. Check answers with the class.

➤ Ss then match the sentences with the pictures.

> **Answers:** 1 It's something you find in front of windows. 2 It's a type of cheese which you put on pasta. 3 It's something you use for opening wine bottles. 4 It's a kind of rice dish from Spain. 5 It's the stuff you use for washing your hair. 6 It's a large figure made of stone.
> Picture order: 1 F 2 A 3 B 4 E 5 D 6 C

4a➤ In groups of four Ss complete the notes. Tell Ss to use a dictionary if there are any words they don't understand or to ask you. Get feedback from the class.

b➤ Play recording 5.7. Ss listen and check if their ideas are mentioned on the recording.

c➤ Play recording 5.8, pausing so Ss can repeat the words in Ex. 4a.

5➤ Write *crossword* on the board and ask Ss to explain to you what a crossword is. Explain what it is if they don't know and tell Ss that horizontal words in a crossword are known as the 'across' words and that vertical words are known as 'down' words.

➤ Ss in two groups, A and B. Group A turn to page 146, group B to page 148. Each group prepares definitions for the words they have in their crosswords.

➤ Ss pair of with someone from the other group and explains their words to each other so their partner can fill in the crossword.

Lifelong learning

➤ Focus Ss on the Lifelong learning box. Read through the suggestion with the whole class and discuss the usefulness of this advice with the Ss. Stress the importance of being able to explain what you mean by using alternative words and synonyms by giving the Ss an example of when you have had to use these strategies. Then elicit examples from the class.

Communication: What are you good at?

In this lesson Ss listen to someone talking about Capoeira, a martial art which originated in Brazil. Ss then prepare a talk about a skill they enjoy or are good at and tell the class.

1a➤ Focus Ss on the photo on page 72. In pairs Ss discuss what they think the people in the photo are doing. Get feedback from the class and discuss Ss' ideas.

b➤ Tell Ss that the people in the photo are doing Capoeira. Give Ss time to read the expressions in the chart. If there are any words or expressions that Ss don't know, encourage them to answer each others' questions or to ask you.

➤ Play recording 5.9. Ss listen and write a tick next to the expressions in the chart as Pedro uses them.

2➤ Tell Ss to think of a skill which they are good at or enjoy doing. Give Ss a few minutes to prepare what they can say about this skill. Encourage Ss to use the expressions in bold in the chart while preparing.

➤ Go round and monitor as the Ss prepare and help where necessary.

3➤ Ss tell the rest of the class about their skills. Tell Ss that while they listen they should write two questions they can ask the student speaking about his/her skill. Take note of errors while the Ss are talking.

➤ When the Ss finish talking about their skills the other Ss ask them the questions they have written.

➤ When all the Ss have finished talking, write the errors on the board and discuss them with the class.

> **OPTIONAL EXTENSION**
>
> As the Ss talk about their skills, write them on the board. When all the Ss have spoken, in pairs Ss choose the three most interesting skills from the ones on the board. Get feedback from the class.

Review and practice

1▶

> **Answers:** 1 been working 2 known 3 been dancing 4 met 5 finished 6 been learning 7 played 8 been coming, seen 9 been watching 10 cleaned / cleaned

2▶

> **Answers:** 1 A: You look exhausted. What <u>have</u> you <u>been</u> doing? B: I've <u>been playing</u> squash. 2 A: You're late! I've <u>been waiting</u> for nearly an hour. B: I'm sorry. I've <u>been working</u> late in the office. 3 A: I'm really hungry. I <u>haven't eaten</u> all day. B: Sit down. I've just <u>finished</u> making dinner. 4 A: I haven't seen you for hours. What <u>have you been doing</u>? B: I've <u>been playing</u> with the dog. 5 A: <u>Have</u> you <u>spoken</u> to Alexander yet? B: No, I haven't. I've <u>been trying</u> to phone him all week. 6 A: <u>Have</u> you <u>left</u> any messages for him? B: Yes, I've <u>left</u> four messages. 7 A: There's paint on your clothes! <u>Have</u> you <u>been decorating</u>? B: Yes, I've <u>been painting</u> the living room. It's nearly finished. 8 A: How many countries <u>have</u> you <u>visited</u> this year? B: This year? I've <u>visited</u> four countries.

3▶

> **Answers:** 1 seeing 2 to give 3 to stay 4 listening 5 to go 6 to entertain 7 going out 8 to bring 9 to ask 10 to leave 11 to bring

4▶

> **Suggested answers:** 1 In the evening I love listening **to music**. 2 We went out to **a** lovely restaurant. 3 Hurry up! We don't have **much** time. 4 I don't think I can come to the theatre, because I **don't have much** money. 5 Would you like **milk** in your coffee? Yes, **a** little. 6 The show was cancelled. That's **very** bad news. 7 I'm going to the market to buy some **bread**. 8 I don't like **salt** on my food.

5▶

> **Answers:** 1 going 2 to go 3 doing 4 playing 5 soundtrack 6 sequel 7 service 8 tip

Notes for using the Common European Framework (CEF)

CEF References

5.1 Can do: suggest and respond to ideas

CEF B1 descriptor: can make his/her opinions and reactions understood as regards solutions to problems or practical questions of where to go, what to do, how to organise an event (e.g. an outing). (CEF page 77)

5.2 Can do: describe a film/book

CEF B1 descriptor: can relate the plot of a book or film and describe his/her reactions. (CEF page 59)

5.3 Can do: recommend a restaurant

CEF B1 descriptor: can reasonably fluently relate a straightforward narrative or description as a linear sequence of points. (CEF page 59)

CEF quick brief

Though the reference levels in the Common European Framework suggest that students progress 'vertically', from B1 to B2, etc., the Framework itself says that 'learning a language is a matter of horizontal as well as vertical progression'. This means that some learners might like to move from B1 level in a business context to B2 level in a tourist context. The CEF identifies four basic 'domains' that help to understand this horizontal language development: the public domain, the personal domain, the educational domain and the occupational domain.

Portfolio task

Download the Total English Portfolio free from www.longman.com/totalenglish.

Objective: to help Ss complete the 'important language and cultural experiences' section of their Portfolio Biography.

This task can be done in Ss' own language.

➤ Ss can further improve their language learning skills by reflecting on significant experiences that have helped them to learn another language or about another culture.

1▶ Refer Ss back to the section of their Passport where they listed their language and cultural experiences.

2▶ Ask Ss to choose the most important experiences that have helped them learn a language or learn about a culture. It can help to give examples of your own.

3▶ Ask Ss to compare with each other and explain why they were important.

Holidays

Overview

Lead-in	**Vocabulary:** travel
6.1	**Grammar:** Past Perfect Simple
	Vocabulary: descriptive language
	Can do: describe a memorable photo
6.2	**Grammar:** uses of *like*
	Vocabulary: places to visit in a city
	Can do: get around a new place
6.3	**Grammar:** articles
	Vocabulary: describing nature
	Can do: show interest and surprise
Vocabulary	Expressions with *get*
Com. Focus	London in a day
Reference	
Practice	

Summary

Lesson 1: Ss read a text about travelling in Africa and then go on to listen to three people describing photos. Finally Ss speak about their own memorable photos.

Lesson 2: Ss listen to a conversation between people who are travelling round Ireland. Ss then read a guide to Dublin Ss and write a guide to a city they know well.

Lesson 3: Ss read a text about strange things that can happen while travelling. Ss then go on to look at ways of expressing interest and surprise.

Vocabulary: Ss look at different expressions with *get* and write a story using some of these expressions.

Communication: Ss read information about entertainment in London. Ss then plan a day trip to London and tell the class about the trip.

Film bank: Dream holidays (3'00")

A documentary style film describing three dream holiday destinations

The narrator takes us to three great destinations to discover what type of holidays we can enjoy there. The journey starts in the tropical Maldives where you can learn to dive, then it's on to New Zealand for a hiking (known as 'tramping') holiday before finally heading to Egypt to see the mighty pyramids and to travel down The River Nile by the small boats called *falukas*.

Possible places to use this short film are:
➤ After Lesson 1 to extend the theme of descriptive language

➤ After Lesson 2 to extend the topic of getting around a new place

➤ After Lesson 3 to develop the vocabulary theme of describing nature

For ways to use this short film in class, see Student's Book page 156 and Teacher's Book page 183.

Lead-in

OPTIONAL WARMER

Focus Ss on the photos of the different types of holidays. With their partners Ss choose the holiday they would most like to go on and tell their partner why they would like to go on that holiday. Get feedback from the class and with the group rank the holidays in order of preference. (1 being the best and 4 being the least.)

1a➤ Focus Ss on the types of holiday in the box. Ss match the holidays with the photos. If Ss don't understand the vocabulary, tell them to use their dictionaries or to consult you. Check answers with the whole class.

Answers: Main photo: safari/adventure holiday, top photo: beach holiday, middle photo: river cruise, bottom photo: sightseeing holiday

OPTIONAL EXTENSION

In pairs Ss mark the stress on the types of holiday. Check answers with the class and write the words on the board with the stress marked. Practise saying any words Ss have difficulties with.

b➤ Ss decide which category they would put the types of holiday in and why. Ss compare their answers with a partner. Get feedback from the class.

2a➤ Write *traveller* and *tourist* on the board. Ask Ss what they think the difference between these two words is. Ss discuss the difference with their partners.

➤ Elicit the answer from one of the pairs. Write any characteristics Ss suggest underneath the words. Then encourage the rest of the class to add any other words they associate with the two words and write them on the board.

➤ Ss read the texts and find out if they are travellers or tourists. If Ss have any problems with the vocabulary in the texts, encourage them to answer each other's questions or to use a dictionary.

b➤ Focus Ss on the sentence prompts 1–4. Ss choose one of the options in each sentence and complete it so that it is true for them. In pairs Ss compare their answers. Get feedback from the whole class.

EXTEND THE LEAD-IN

Ss in groups of three or four. Focus Ss on the types of holiday in the box in Ex. 1a. In their groups Ss decide what five items they would take on each type of holiday and why. Ss pair off with a student from another group and explain their choices. Get feedback from the class and talk about the type of things Ss normally take on holiday with them.

6.1 Across Africa

Travelling in Africa has become much easier and organised safari tours are nowadays very common. However, there are still many people who prefer to travel in Africa on their own.

In this lesson Ss read an extract from a book called *Travels Across Africa* then look at descriptive language in the text. Ss then go on to analyse the grammar of the Past Perfect Simple. Finally Ss listen to people describing travel photos and then describe one of their own photos they can remember.

> **OPTIONAL WARMER**
>
> Write *Africa* on the board. Give Ss one minute to write down as many words as they can which are related to Africa. Get feedback and write the words on the board. Ask Ss if anyone has travelled to Africa and if not, whether they would like to go there and why/why not.

Reading

1a➤ Write *keep a _____, take _____, buy _____, send postcards/letter _____* on the board. In pairs Ss think of ways they can complete these phrases. Get feedback from the class and write correct phrases on the board.

➤ Focus Ss on the words in the box. Ss use these words to complete the phrases. Check answers with the group.

> **Answers:** 1 keep a <u>diary</u> 2 take <u>photos</u> 3 buy <u>souvenirs</u> 4 send postcards/letter/<u>emails</u>

➤ Ss discuss in pairs if they normally do any of these things when travelling. Get feedback from various pairs.

2➤ Focus Ss on the photo. In pairs Ss discuss the questions. Get feedback from the class.

3➤ Ss read the text quickly and answer the questions 1–3. Tell Ss not to worry about any words or phrases they don't understand at this stage.

➤ Ss compare their answers with their partners. Check answers with the whole class.

> **Answers:** 1 They are in the Karoo desert in South Africa. 2 Ss' own answers 3 Daniel likes to use a camera, Sophie (the narrator) likes to write down her experiences in notebooks.

4➤ Ss read the text again more carefully and write (*T*) for true, (*F*) for false and (*DK*) for don't know next to the sentences 1–8. Tell Ss to underline any words or expressions they don't understand as they read.

➤ Ss compare their answers with their partners. Check answers with the class.

> **Answers:** 1 F They 'shot through' the desert. 2 T 3 DK 4 T 5 F He was asleep. 6 DK 7 F 'almost close enough to touch' 8 F Sophie woke Daniel up an hour later.

➤ Ask Ss if there are any words in the text they don't understand. Ss can use their dictionaries, help each other or ask you.

Vocabulary

5➤ Write *shoot/shot/shot* on the board and ask Ss what this verb normally means. Elicit/explain that it is normally used for the action of firing of a gun.

➤ Focus Ss on line 1 of the text and ask them what they think *shot* means in this context. Elicit that it means *moved very fast*.

➤ Focus Ss on the descriptive language taken from the text. Ss choose the correct meaning for this language and answer the questions. Ss compare their answers with their partners. Check answers with the class.

> **Answers:** 1 incredible 2 makes a loud noise 3 it became very quiet 4 noticed something and looked at it 5 very well

Grammar

> **OPTIONAL GRAMMAR LEAD-IN**
>
> Write the following sentences on the board:
> *1. I ate breakfast. 2. I left the house.*
> Ask Ss which action was first, which was second.
> Underneath the two sentences write:
> *After _____ the house.*
> In pairs Ss complete the gaps in the sentence so that it has the same meaning as the first two sentences. Check the sentences Ss have written and write the answer on the board with the tenses underlined: *After I <u>had eaten</u> breakfast I <u>left</u> the house.* In pairs Ss discuss what the underlined tenses are and why they are used. Elicit/explain that the first underlined structure is the Past Perfect Simple and the second is the Past Simple.

6a➤ In pairs Ss read the Active grammar box and choose the correct alternatives. Check answers with the whole group.

> **Active grammar**
> a) We saw things.
> Use the <u>Past Perfect</u> to show that one event happened before another one in the past.
> We make the Past Perfect using *had/hadn't* + <u>past perfect</u>.

➤ Copy the timeline onto the board and write 1 under the first action and 2 under the second action.

b➤ Ss find other examples of the Past Perfect in the text. Ss check their examples with their partners.

> **Answers:** I **had** already **finished** three notebooks and was into the fourth … The road was empty – we **hadn't seen** another car for hours. I didn't know how long they **had been** there next to us. When Daniel woke up an hour later I told him what **had happened.**

7➤ Focus Ss on sentences 1–8. In pairs Ss put the verbs in brackets into the correct tense, Past Simple or Past Perfect Simple. Check answers with the class.

Answers: 1 had eaten 2 hadn't lived 3 met
4 had died 5 had already left 6 hadn't
drunk 7 did you go 8 got

8➤ Tell Ss to cover the right-hand column of the table. Ss complete the sentences in column A in any way they like. Encourage them to use the Past Perfect Simple while doing so. Ss compare their answers with their partners. Get feedback from the class.

➤ Ss uncover the right-hand column of the table. In pairs Ss connect the beginnings of the sentences in column A with the endings in column B. Make sure that Ss know they have to change a verb in column B to the Past Perfect.

➤ Check answers with the class.

Answers: 1 c I got lost in the city because I hadn't been there before. 2 e The evening went well because I'd planned it carefully. 3 b I went to the film because I'd heard it was good. 4 f I was qualified for the job because I'd studied the subject at university. 5 a I found the exam easy because I'd spent a lot of time studying before it. 6 d It was a big day but I was tired because I hadn't been able to sleep the night before.

Pronunciation

9a➤ Play recording 6.1. Focus Ss on how *had* and *hadn't* are pronounced in the Past Perfect Simple.

Answers: In the Past Perfect positive, *had* is contracted to *'d*. In the negative, we use the full form *hadn't*.

b➤ Play recording 6.1 again, pausing to give Ss time to repeat the sentences, paying attention to the pronunciation of *had* and *hadn't*.

Person to person

10➤ Focus Ss in the situations in Ex. 8. In pairs Ss discuss if they have ever been in situations like these ones and if so, what happened in each situation. Encourage Ss to use the Past Perfect Simple while talking about the situations. Monitor for errors.

➤ Get feedback by asking Ss to report what they have found out about their partner to the class.

➤ Write the errors on the board and discuss them with the class. Finally, write up examples of correct language Ss have used and congratulate them on its use.

Listening and speaking

11➤ Focus Ss on the photos. In pairs Ss describe the photos and answer the questions 1–4. Go round and help Ss with vocabulary where necessary, or encourage Ss to use their dictionaries.

➤ Get feedback from the class and ask Ss if any of them have ever been on holidays similar to the ones shown in the photos.

OPTIONAL VARIATION

Ss in pairs A and B. Student A looks at the photos on page 78 and describes them to student B. Student B draws the pictures into his/her notebook. When student A has finished describing all the photos, student B opens the book and compares the drawings with the photos. Ss then discuss the questions 1–4.

12a➤ Tell Ss they are going to hear three people describing the photos. In pairs Ss write a list of words they think the people might say about each photo. Ss compare their list of words with a partner then check the lists of words with the class and write the words on the board.

➤ Play recording 6.2 and Ss decide which photos the speakers are talking about.

Answers: Speaker 1 E Speaker 2 A Speaker 3 B

b➤ Play recording 6.2 again and Ss complete the notes in the table. Give Ss time to compare their answers, before eliciting the answers from the class.

Answers:

	1 Which place?	2 When did they take the photo?	3 What had they heard about the place?
Speaker 1	Great Wall of China	A week into his holiday	You can see it from the moon
Speaker 2	Grand Canyon	After a few hours of walking	How amazing it was
Speaker 3	Machu Picchu	Just after they arrived at the place	Some people cry when they see it

c➤ Give Ss time to read through the *How to…* box. If they have any problems with the vocabulary encourage them to help each other or to ask you. Play recording 6.2 again and Ss tick the phrases in the How to … box that the speakers use.

Answers: This photo shows ✔ It was ✔ In the background ✔ On the left ✔ We had heard ✔ We felt very happy ✔ We were very excited ✔ We'd always wanted to see ✔

13➤ Give Ss a few minutes to think of a photo they want to describe and which expressions from the How to … box they can use while describing the photo. If they don't have a photo with them, they can use one of the photos on page 149.

➤ Ss describe their photos to their partners for about a minute. Their partners should listen and think of follow-up questions they can ask about the photo. Monitor the conversations and write any errors on the board.

➤ Discuss the errors on the board and ask Ss to correct the errors with their partners. Elicit the corrections from the Ss and write them on the board.

OPTIONAL EXTENSION

In small groups Ss rank the types of holidays shown in the pictures in Ex. 11 in order of danger; 1 being the most dangerous, 5 the least dangerous. Ss pair off with Ss from other groups and compare their rankings. Get feedback from the whole class and discuss if Ss like the idea of doing dangerous/adventurous things on holiday.

6.2 Out and about in Dublin

In the last ten to fifteen years the boom in the Irish economy (known as the Celtic Tiger) has transformed the city of Dublin and its people. It is now one of the most thriving cities in Europe, as well as being one of the most expensive. However, it has not lost its rich literary and cultural heritage and is also famous for its nightlife.

In this lesson Ss look at vocabulary related to places to visit in a city. Ss then listen to two people travelling around Ireland and go on to read a guide to Dublin. Ss also look at the different uses of *like* and write their own quick guide to a city they know well.

OPTIONAL WARMER

Write the words from Ex. 1a on the board with the letters in a jumbled order. In pairs Ss write the letters into the correct order to make words. Ss spell the words to you. Write the correct words on the board and ask Ss where the stress is in each word. Practise saying the words with the class.

Vocabulary

1a➤ Focus Ss on the pairs of words. In pairs Ss discuss the differences between the pairs of words. Ss write down a sentence for each pair of words to explain the difference between them.

Check the differences between the words with the class.

Suggested answers: 2 Museums can contain many things (e.g. antiques, art), art galleries contain only art. 3 Pubs always sell alcohol but sometimes don't sell food and are open in the evenings. Cafés don't often serve alcohol and usually close in the evenings. 4 A park is usually large, and usually open to the public, often for games. A garden can be large or small, private or public. You can't usually play games in public gardens. 5 A lake is a large area of water surrounded by land. A fountain is man-made, usually using stone, often with statues. The water comes out in a jet. 6 A bookshop is where you buy books. A library is where you borrow books. 7 A shop is usually inside, with fixed prices and permanent buildings. A market is often outside. The sellers come at special times. You can sometimes negotiate prices.

---

b➤ Ss decide what are their top three choices from the list of things to visit when they travel to a new city.

➤ Ss share their list of top three places with their partners and explain to each other why they like to visit those places in a new city. Get feedback from the class and ask Ss if there are any places in Ex. 1a that they would not be interested in visiting and why they wouldn't be interested in visiting them.

OPTIONAL VARIATION

Ss work in pairs, A and B. Ss A tells B their choices of the top three things to visit when travelling to a new city. Ss B must disagree with Ss A and try to convince them that their three places to visit are more interesting ones.

Listening

2➤ Tell Ss they are going to hear a conversation between two people who are travelling around Ireland. In pairs Ss brainstorm anything they know about Ireland. Get feedback and write anything Ss know on the board.

➤ Ss in five groups. Each group looks at one of the series of words 1–5. In their groups Ss think of words they know which they associate with the three places in their series. Get feedback from the groups and write their words on the board.

➤ Play recording 6.3. Ss listen to the five conversations between Stefan and Karina and choose the correct answers. Elicit the answers from the class and encourage Ss to tell you which words helped them choose the correct answer.

Answers: 1 a 2 c 3 b 4 b 5 c

3➤ Play recording 6.3 again and Ss note down the problems in each dialogue. Give Ss time to compare their answers, before eliciting the answers from the whole class.

Answers: Conversation 2 – The museum is closed
Conversation 3 – The post office closed at 6
Conversation 4 – The bus only goes hourly
Conversation 5 – The student had to pay full price because she/he forgot his/her student card.

OPTIONAL EXTENSION

Ss in groups of three or four. Ss tell the others in their groups any problems which they have had while travelling and how these problems were solved. Get feedback from the whole class.

Pronunciation

4a➤ Focus Ss on the How to … box and give them time to read through it. In pairs Ss predict how the sentences in the box could be completed. Get feedback from the class.

➤ Play recording 6.4 and Ss complete the sentences. Check answers with the whole class.

Answers: What time does the museum <u>open</u>? Is there a <u>bank</u> near here? Can you recommend a <u>good</u> restaurant? How much is a <u>return</u> to the city centre? <u>Does</u> this bus go to the airport? Could you tell me what time the train <u>leaves</u>? Do you know <u>where</u> platform 1 is? Can you tell me the way <u>to the station, please</u>? Just go straight on. It's on <u>your left</u>.

---

b➤ Tell Ss that when asking questions in English we often use high intonation at the start of the question because it helps to sound polite. Play recording 6.5 and ask Ss to notice the intonation in the questions.

c➤ Play recording 6.5 again, pausing so that Ss can repeat the questions. Ask various Ss to repeat the questions, concentrating on the intonation.

5➤ Ss work in pairs, A and B. Student A looks at the role card on page 79. Student B turns to the one on page 147. Give Ss time to read through their information and make sure that they understand the situation.

➤ Student B asks student A questions to find out the information about the trains to Cambridge. Then Student A asks student B questions to find out about the exhibitions at the Tate Gallery. Monitor carefully, encouraging Ss to use high intonation at the beginning of their questions to sound polite.

> **OPTIONAL EXTENSION**
> Ss think of five questions they can ask about the city or town where they are studying at the moment. Ss write the questions using expressions from the How to … box. Ss stand up and mingle to ask the other Ss the questions. The winner is the student who can all the answers to his/her questions first.

Reading and speaking

6a➤ In pairs Ss mark the statements 1–5 (*T*) for True and (*F*) for false. Get feedback from various pairs.

b➤ Ss read the Quick Guide to Dublin quickly to check their answers. Tell Ss not to worry about words and expressions they don't understand at this stage. Get feedback.

> **Answers:** 1 T   2 T   3 F Molly Malone was a fishmonger.   4 T   5 T

7a➤ Focus Ss on the photos. In pairs Ss decide which of the places in the photos the text talks about. (The text talks about all of the photos.)

b➤ Ask Ss to cover the text so they can only see the photos. In pairs tell each other what they can remember about each place in the photos.

➤ Ss uncover the text and read it again carefully to check.

➤ Ask Ss if there are any words or expressions that they don't understand. Encourage Ss to answer each others' questions or to use a dictionary before explaining them yourself.

c➤ Ss think about the different places in the text and decide which of the places they would like to visit. Ss then tell their partners about the places they would like to visit and why. Monitor their conversations and take note of any errors.

➤ When they have finished, write the mistakes on the board. Ask Ss to try to correct them.

Grammar

> **OPTIONAL GRAMMAR LEAD-IN**
> Write *like* on the board. In pairs Ss think of as many different ways of using this word as they can. Get feedback and write on the board any Ss' ideas which coincide with the ones in the Active grammar box.

8➤ Ss match the sentences a–e to the correct meaning 1–5 in the Active grammar box. Check the answers with the class.

> **Active grammar**
> 1 e *What do you like doing on holiday?*   2 a *What would you like to do?*   3 c *What does it look like?*   4 d *What's it like?*   5 b *It tastes like chicken.*

➤ Focus Ss on Reference page 87 and give Ss time to read through the notes.

9➤ Ss complete the dialogues 1–9 using expressions with *like*. Ss compare their answers with their partners. Check answers with the whole class.

> **Answers:** 1 What is it like?   2 What would you like to do?   3 Yes, it looks like an airport terminal!   4 What did you like most about Krakow?   5 Really? What was it like?   6 What does he look like?   7 It was like rubber.   8 A: I don't really like modern art. B: The paintings often look like the work of children.   9 Yes, I thought it looked like an enormous cake!

Person to person

10➤ Ss think of three questions using the different expressions with *like* that they can ask their partners. Go round and check the questions that Ss write.

➤ Ss ask their partners the questions and take note of the answers. Ss then tell another student in the class what they have learned about their partner.

➤ Get feedback from the whole class.

Writing

11a➤ Ss read the questions about the town or city they were born or a place they know well. Ss write down notes. Tell Ss they do not have to write full answers to the questions.

➤ In pairs Ss ask each other the questions. Encourage Ss to ask follow-up questions. Monitor the conversations and take note of any important errors.

➤ Get feedback from the pairs.

➤ Write the errors on the board. Ask different Ss to come to the board and correct the errors.

b➤ Focus Ss on the Quick Guide to Dublin again. In pairs Ss underline expressions which the guide uses to advise people what to do in Dublin.

➤ Ss write a Quick Guide to a city that they know well, recommending things a visitor should do. Encourage Ss to use the expressions they underlined in the Quick Guide to Dublin and the expressions on page 81.

➤ If Ss need any vocabulary for their Quick Guides, encourage them to answer each others' questions, before giving them the words or expressions yourself.

c➤ Ss swap their Quick Guides with other Ss. Ss read the other Ss' guides. Encourage Ss to ask each other follow-up questions about each others' places.

➤ Ss decide which of the cities they would like to visit and why. Get feedback from the class.

> **OPTIONAL VARIATION**
> Form groups of three or four. Ask Ss to present their Quick Guides to the rest of the group and encourage the listeners to ask follow-up questions. At the end of the presentations ask Ss to choose their favourite place.

6.3 Travellers' tales

Many strange things can happen to people (and animals) when travelling. Stories include people who find rings they lost when visiting a place ten years previously or pets that travel 4,800 kilometres to get home.

In this lesson Ss read a text about strange things that have happened to people while travelling. Through this context Ss look at the grammar of articles then go on to look at ways of showing interest and surprise. Finally, Ss practise using these ways of showing interest and surprise.

OPTIONAL WARMER

Write the word *coincidence* on the board and elicit/explain what it means. Ss think of any strange coincidences that have happened to them or that they have heard of. Ss tell their partners about the coincidences. Get feedback from the class and discuss which coincidence is the most incredible.

Vocabulary

1a➤ Focus Ss on the photos of the different places. Ss describe the photos in pairs.

➤ Ss match the adjectives from box A with a noun from box B then label the photos with this vocabulary.

➤ Get feedback from the group and practise saying any words the Ss have pronunciation problems with.

Answers: A tropical rainforest B mountain range C sandy beach D green valley E rocky coastline F desert island

b➤ In pairs Ss make a list of other natural places. Go around the class helping Ss with vocabulary where necessary. Also encourage them to ask their partner or to use their dictionaries.

➤ Get feedback from the group and write the places the Ss have written on the board.

c➤ Ss discuss the questions in groups of three or four, using the prompts on the board. Get feedback from the class.

Reading and speaking

2a➤ Focus Ss on the three pictures. In pairs Ss decide what strange events or coincidences connected with travelling the pictures show.

➤ Get feedback from various pairs and discuss their ideas with the class.

b➤ Ss read the text quickly to check the predictions they made about the pictures. Tell Ss not to worry if there are any words they don't understand at this stage.

➤ Get feedback from the class and check if any of the Ss' predictions were correct.

3➤ Ss read the text more slowly and answer the questions. Ss compare and discuss their answers with a partner. Get feedback from the whole class.

➤ Ask Ss if there are any words or phrases in the text that they don't understand. Encourage Ss to answer each others' questions if they can before explaining them yourself.

4➤ Ss work in pairs. Using the key words in prompts 1–4 Ss take it in turns to re-tell the stories from the text. Go round the class, making note of any important errors.

➤ Ask various Ss to repeat the stories for the rest of the class. Finally, write the errors on the board and encourage Ss to self-correct and then congratulate Ss on any interesting or correct language they have used while retelling the stories.

Grammar

OPTIONAL GRAMMAR LEAD-IN

Write the first lines of this children's song on the board with the articles underlined:
I knew an old woman who swallowed a fly, I don't know why she swallowed the fly, perhaps she'll die.
In pairs Ss discuss the use of articles in the song.

5➤ Focus Ss on the Active grammar box. With their partners Ss match the rules 1–6 with the example sentences a–f. Check answers with the whole class.

Active grammar
1 e   2 a   3 f   4 c   5 d   6 b

➤ Refer Ss to reference page 87. Give Ss time to read through the notes about articles. Ask: **Q: What do we use when it's the first time we mention the subject?** *a/an.* **Q: What do we use with jobs?** *a/an.* **Q: Do we use *a* when we are talking about something we have mentioned previously?** No. **Q: What do we use if the subject is unique?** *the.* **Q: What do we use with superlatives?** *the.* **Q: When do we not need to use an article?** When we make generalisations with plurals and uncountable nouns.

➤ Check Ss understand the use of articles in place names and ask them to write two more places for each of the examples 1–4. Check the places that Ss write and write them on the board.

6➤ Focus Ss on the sentences 1–8. Explain that all of the sentences contain at least one mistake with articles. Ss find the mistakes and correct them. Ss then compare their answers with their partners. Check the answers with the whole class.

Answers: 1 Travellers should always respect other people's culture.   2 Europe is not the most beautiful continent.   3 A good way to see a country is to go by train.   4 It'd be really relaxing to go on a trip along a river, like the River Nile, for example.   5 Delayed flights are one of the greatest problems travellers face these days.   6 Before going abroad, you should learn a few words of the local language.   7 Travel is a bit boring for me.   8 I hate travelling in aeroplanes.

4➤ In pairs Ss read the stories and write *a/an/the* or – (nothing) in the spaces. Ss compare their answers with another pair. Check answers with the whole class.

Answers: 1 a   2 The   3 the   4 the   5 a   6 – 7 a   8 the   9 the   10 –   11 the   12 the

OPTIONAL VARIATION

When you have checked the answers to Ex. 7 ask Ss to close their books. Write the words which follow the articles in each story in Ex. 7 on the board in two columns. At the top of the column with the words from the story about the guitar, write *guitar*. At the top of the column with the words from the story about the hotel in Warsaw, write *Warsaw*. Ss retell the stories in pairs, using the words on the board from the stories as prompts. Monitor for correct use of articles and take note of any errors. When Ss have finished telling the stories, write the errors on the board and discuss them with the class.

OPTIONAL EXTENSION

In groups of three or four Ss plan a trip round the world. Tell Ss they can visit any places they like; countries, rivers, deserts, oceans, cities. They must also make a list of things they would like to take with them, and who will be responsible for buying these items. Before starting to make plans refer Ss back to the Active grammar box and the rules about using articles. While Ss are discussing their trip monitor closely for correct use of articles. Get feedback by asking different groups to present their plans for the trip to the rest of the class.

Person to person

8➤ Ss in groups of three or four. Ss read the sentences in Ex. 6 again and write (*Y*) if they agree with the sentences completely, (*N*) if they disagree and (*DK*) if they don't know.

➤ Ss discuss their answers with the other Ss in their group. Tell Ss they should come to a consensus about each statement.

➤ Re-pair Ss so that they are working with a student from another group. Ss tell each other what their groups decide and why.

Pronunciation

OPTIONAL LEAD-IN

Tell the class an interesting or surprising incident that has happened to you recently. Make the incident as interesting as possible. If Ss do not react in any way while you tell them about the incident, stop and ask them if they can think of any ways of showing interest and surprise when somebody is speaking. Ss brainstorm ideas in pairs. Write Ss ideas on the board. If Ss do react and show interest or surprise, write the expressions they use on the board and discuss them. In pairs Ss then think of any more expressions they can to express interest and surprise.

9a➤ Focus Ss on the dialogues. Give Ss time to read through the dialogues. Play recording 6.6 and Ss complete the sentences.

➤ Ss compare their answers with a partner. Check answers with the whole class.

> **Answers:** 1 Did/Really 2 How/amazing
> 3 Does/interesting 4 she/That's

b➤ Write *Really?! That's amazing! Oh no!* and *How awful!* on the board. Tell Ss that to emphasise words we sometimes make the vowel sounds very long. In pairs discuss which vowel sounds in the words and phrases you have written on the board are long ones.

➤ Ss discuss their answers with another pair. Get feedback from the whole class.

c➤ Play recording 6.7 and Ss check their answers.

> **Answers:** 1 R**ea**lly! 2 That's am**a**zing! 3 Oh n**o**!
> 4 How **aw**ful!

d➤ Play recording 6.6 again, pausing to give Ss time to repeat the dialogues and copy the intonation.

e➤ In pairs Ss practise the dialogues. Tell Ss to concentrate on their intonation. Monitor and help Ss with the intonation as necessary.

➤ Ss close their books and try to repeat the dialogues from memory. Ask various pairs of Ss to act out the dialogues for the rest of the class.

10a➤ In pairs Ss discuss how the listeners in Ex. 9a showed they are interested in what the speakers were saying. Get feedback from various pairs of Ss.

➤ Ss read the How to … box to check their ideas.

b➤ Ss work in pairs, A and B. Student A reads one of the sentences to student B who shows interest and surprise. Student B then reads a sentence and student A reacts with interest and surprise. Ss continue till they have read all the sentences. Monitor the conversations and correct intonation where necessary.

Speaking

11➤ Ss in pairs, A and B. Tell Ss A to turn to page 146. Ss B turn to page 148. Ss read their sentences to each other and react with interest and surprise. Tell Ss to ask follow-up questions where possible. Encourage them to be imaginative. Go around the class checking they are using the expressions and intonation patterns correctly.

OPTIONAL EXTENSION

Ss think of something interesting or surprising that has happened to them recently. Give Ss a few minutes to write notes about the incident. Encourage Ss to use their imaginations or even lie to make the story sound more interesting. Ss work in pairs, A and B. Ss A tell their story to Ss B. Ss B react showing interest and surprise where relevant. Ss then change roles so Ss B tell their story and Ss A react with surprise. Monitor the conversations and take note of any errors. At the end of the activity write the errors on the board and encourage Ss to self-correct.

Vocabulary: Expressions with *get*

In this lesson Ss look at different expressions formed with *get* by filling in a word map. Ss then go on to write a story using these phrases.

OPTIONAL WARMER

In pairs Ss make a list of all the expressions they know with *get*. Get feedback and write the Ss' expressions on the board if correct. Make sure Ss know the meaning of all the expressions on the board.

1➤ Focus Ss on the word map. In pairs Ss read through the map and tick any expressions with *get* that they know.

➤ Ss check the expressions they have ticked with another pair. Ss explain expressions to each other where possible.

➤ Get feedback from the class and have various Ss explain the expressions. If there are any expressions Ss have not seen before, explain them to the class.

2➤ Focus Ss on sentences 1–10. With their partners Ss complete the sentences with the words and phrases in the box. Ss compare their answers with their partners.

4➤ Check answers with the whole group and write the expressions with *get* on the board.

Answers: 1 some stamps 2 getting 3 get 4 hungry 5 tickets 6 is getting 7 lost 8 train 9 got on 10 back

---

3a➤ Ss in groups of three or four. Focus Ss on the expressions with *get* in the box. In pairs Ss check that they know the meaning of all the expressions. If there are any expressions Ss don't know, encourage them to answer each others' questions before asking you.

➤ In their groups Ss prepare a story using the phrases with *get* from the box and any other expressions with *get* they want to include. If Ss need help with vocabulary, encourage them to use their dictionaries or to ask you.

b➤ In their groups Ss write their stories for other Ss to read. Tell Ss to leave spaces where there is an expression with *get* in the story.

➤ Ss swap their stories with another group. Each group reads the other group's story and decides what expression with *get* goes in each space.

➤ Ss check their answers with the group who wrote the story.

Lifelong learning

➤ Ask Ss if they have ever used maps like the *get* map before. If Ss have, ask them to describe their maps, telling the class what kind of language it recorded and how useful it was.

➤ Discuss how this can be an effective way of recording and remembering vocabulary and encourage Ss to use maps to record vocabulary in the future.

Communication: London in a day

In this lesson Ss read information about what's on in London. Ss then plan a day trip to London and tell the rest of the class about their plans.

OPTIONAL WARMER

Write *London* on the board. In groups of three or four Ss brainstorm everything they know about London. Get feedback and write Ss ideas on the board. Ask Ss if anyone in the class has been to London. If someone has visited London previously, ask them to tell the rest of the class about the city.

1➤ Ss talk about the question in groups of three or four. Get feedback and discuss what Ss enjoy/don't enjoy doing when they visit another city.

2➤ Ss read quickly through the information about London and find the different things mentioned in the text. Tell Ss not to worry about words they don't understand at the moment. Check answers with the class.

Answers: 1 a Big Red Bus tour 2 Camden market 3 30 minutes 4 *Les Miserables* 5 The Royal Festival Hall 6 Madame Tussaud's and The British Museum 7 Harrods

---

➤ Ss read through the information again and underline any words or expressions they don't know. Encourage Ss to explain vocabulary to each other or to ask you.

3➤ Tell Ss they are going to hear three people planning a day trip. Play recording 6.8 and Ss write down three things they decide to do.

Answers: tour London on a bus, go to The British Museum, go to Camden

---

4a➤ In groups of four Ss plan their day using the information in the text. Tell Ss they can spend up to £100 each and they must plan activities for the morning, afternoon and evening. Ss should try and include activities that everyone in the group will enjoy. Go round and help where necessary.

b➤ Get feedback by asking each group to tell the rest of the class about their plans for the day out.

OPTIONAL EXTENSION

Ss plan a day out in their own city. In a monolingual class abroad Ss work in pairs to plan the day out and tell the rest of the class what they have planned to do. In a multilingual class Ss plan a day out in a city they know well in their own country and tell their partner about the day out.

Review and practice

1➤

> **Answers:** 1 had lived   2 got, had cooked   3 went
> 4 had never seen   5 had all gone   6 kissed   7 had
> grown / had   8 hadn't seen

2➤

> **Answers:**   1 What is it like? I haven't been there
> before.   2 I like watching films at home but I prefer
> going to the cinema.   3 Don't you think Maria looks
> like her sister?   4 I can't wait to see what the house
> will look like when it is finished.   5 Tim doesn't like
> getting up early.   6 Would you like to come in and
> have a drink?   7 What is your new job like?   8 Do
> you like my new hairstyle?   9 I like walking around
> when I am in a new city.   10 I'd like two tickets for the
> exhibition, please.

3➤

> **Answers:**   1 the Canary Islands   2 Africa   3 the
> Czech Republic   4 the Andes mountains   5 the
> River Nile   6 Canada   7 the United Arab
> Emirates   8 northern Europe   9 the Atlantic
> Ocean   10 Mount Kilimanjaro   11 the Sahara
> Desert   12 the Mediterranean Sea

4➤

> **Answers:**   1 The food   2 aeroplanes   3 the
> man   4 Cats   5 A   6 the most

5➤

> **Answers:**   1 go   2 see   3 getting   4 sandy
> 5 tropical   6 about   7 getting   8 get
> 9 there   10 Get

Notes for using the Common European Framework (CEF)

CEF References

6.1 Can do: describe a memorable photo

CEF B2 descriptor: can give clear, systematically developed descriptions with appropriate highlighting of significant points, and relevant supporting detail. (CEF page 58)

6.2 Can do: get around a new place

CEF B1 descriptor: can exploit a wide range of simple language to deal with most situations likely to arise whilst travelling. (CEF page 74)

6.3 Can do: show interest and surprise

CEF B1 descriptor: can express and respond to feelings such as surprise, happiness, sadness, interest and indifference. (CEF page 76)

CEF quick brief

The reference levels in the Common European Framework (A1–C2) allow a correlation with common international exams as well as exams within a country or institution. This means that employers can have a more accurate idea of what a student with a particular qualification can actually do. For more information see the introduction at the start of this Teacher's Book.

Portfolio task

Download the Total English Portfolio free from www.longman.com/totalenglish.

Objective: to help Ss start using the Portfolio to assess their progress and priorities in English.

This task can be done in Ss' own language.

➤ The Biography section of the Portfolio contains the Can do statements from each lesson in the book. Ss can use this section to review and keep track of their progress. It is helpful to remind students to complete the tick boxes in this section at a regular intervals, perhaps at the end of every unit or at the end of semester.

1➤ Ask Ss to look at the Can do statements in the Biography section of their Portfolio. Show how the statements relate to the work they have completed in their coursebooks.

2➤ Ask Ss to look through the statements at B1 level and complete the tick boxes.

3➤ Explain that as they progress through the course, they will be able to achieve more Can do goals at B1 and will also start to complete goals at B2 level.

Overview

Lead-in	**Vocabulary:** learning
7.1	**Grammar:** subject and object questions **Vocabulary:** education **Can do:** describe a learning experience
7.2	**Grammar:** *used to / would* **Vocabulary:** teachers **Can do:** describe a teacher from your past
7.3	**Grammar:** modals of ability, past and present **Vocabulary:** old age **Can do:** talk about abilities in the past and present
Vocabulary	Idioms about learning
Com. Focus	School days
Reference	
Practice	

Summary

Lesson 1: Ss listen to people talking about how they learned how to do things. They then read a text about how people have learned from mistakes they have made.

Lesson 2: Ss read an extract from *Matilda* by Roald Dahl. Ss then listen to two people discussing their teachers and go on to write an entry to a website about a favourite teacher.

Lesson 3: Ss read different texts about some remarkable old people and share the information they have read. Ss then go on to speak about abilities they have or once had.

Vocabulary: Ss look at different idioms connected with learning.

Communication: Ss listen to a childhood story then tell other Ss in the class stories about their school days.

Film bank: Cambridge (5'00")

The narrator interviews students and townspeople to find out about life in Cambridge

This documentary on Cambridge and its world famous university looks at the history of some of the colleges. A variety of students are interviewed to find out why they chose Cambridge and whether they like being a student at the university. A local woman also gives her thoughts on the university's influence on the town.

Possible places to use this short film are:
➤ after Lesson 1 to build on the vocabulary topic, education

➤ before the Lead-in to introduce the topic of education

➤ at the end of the unit to round up the topic and language

For ways to use this short film in class, see Student's Book page 157 and Teacher's Book page 184

Lead-in

OPTIONAL WARMER

Write *education* on the board. Ss write down five words connected with education. Organise Ss into pairs, A and B. Student A describes his/her words to student B without saying the word. Student B guesses the words. Ask Ss to change roles so that Student B is describing the words and Student A is guessing the words.

1➤ Focus Ss on the photos of the different learning situations. Ss discuss the questions with their partners. Get feedback and discuss Ss' answers as a class. Decide as a group which learning situations are the most effective.

2➤ Focus the Ss on the box and the table. Ss write the nouns in the table to make as many verb/noun collocations as possible.

➤ Go round the class and help Ss with the meanings of any words or expressions they don't know.

➤ Copy the table onto the board. Ask various Ss to come up to the board and write up the correct collocations in the columns.

Answers:
GET: a degree, good marks, to lectures, to class
TAKE: an exam, a course, notes, a subject
DO: a degree, an exam, a course, some research, a subject
PASS: an exam, a subject
FAIL: an exam, a course, a subject
REVISE: notes, a subject
GO: to lectures, to class
MAKE: *a mistake*, progress
GRADUATE: from university

➤ In pairs Ss add more nouns to each verb in the table. Check the words the Ss have added and write them in the correct column in the table on the board.

3a➤ Focus Ss on the sentences 1–5. Ss complete the sentences with the correct form of the verbs. Remind Ss they will have to change the form of the verb to fit each sentence. Ss compare their answers with their partners. Check answers with the whole class.

Answers: 1 revise 2 making 3 taken 4 go 5 make

b➤ In pairs Ss ask and answer the questions. Monitor and take note of errors. When Ss have finished, tell them you are going to read out some errors. Read out the errors and elicit the correct form from Ss.

OPTIONAL EXTENSION

If you feel Ss need extra practice, tell them to write five questions of their own using some of the collocations in the table. Then working in pairs Ss take turns to ask each other their questions. Encourage Ss to self-correct. Go around the class and correct any errors if necessary.

7.1 Learning from experience

Inventors must be persistent if they are to succeed. The ability to learn from previous mistakes is also important for inventors. Sometimes an invention unintentionally comes about. Things like the post-it note, bread and crisps were all unexpected inventions.

In this lesson Ss listen to people talking about how they learned to do something. Ss then look at vocabulary connected with education. Ss go on to read a text about different inventions and how they came about. Through this context Ss look at the grammar of subject/object questions and finish with a quiz.

> **OPTIONAL WARMER**
> Organise Ss into pairs, A and B. Ss A look at the pictures in Ex. 1. Ss B have the book closed. Student A describes the pictures to student B. Student B listens and decides what the pictures have in common. Get feedback from the class and check what Ss B think the pictures have in common. Ss B open the book and check the pictures.

Listening

1a➤ In pairs Ss discuss what they think the people in the pictures are doing. Get feedback and discuss the Ss' ideas.

b➤ Play recording 7.1 and Ss write the number of the speaker next to the picture. Ss compare their answers. Check answers with the whole class and check if any of the Ss' predictions were correct.

> **Answers:** A Speaker 2   B Speaker 4   C Speaker 1
> D Speaker 3   E Speaker 5

2a➤ Focus Ss on the phrases and sentences a–j taken from the listening. Give them time to read through them. In pairs Ss match the phrases and sentences to the pictures. Get feedback and ask Ss to give you reasons for their answers.

b➤ Play recording 7.1 again and Ss check their answers. Check answers with the whole group.

> **Answers:**   a B   b D   c E   d E   e C   f D
> g A   h B   i C   j A

Vocabulary

3➤ Write the words from the box on the board. In pairs Ss use these words to make phrases or expressions they know. Check Ss' answers and write correct phrases and expressions on the board.

> Focus Ss on the words in the box. With their partners Ss complete the phrases and expressions 1–9 with the words from the box. Ss compare their answers with another pair. Check answers with the class.

> **Answers:**   1 fast   2 strict   3 perfect   4 steep
> 5 heart   6 by doing   7 up   8 deep   9 bring

4➤ Ss discuss the questions 1–3 with their partners. Get feedback from the whole class.

5a➤ Ask Ss to think about a good or bad learning experience they have had. With their partners Ss make questions about the learning experience. Check the full questions with the class and write them on the board. Practise saying the questions with the class as necessary.

> **Answers:**   1 What were you learning? Why?
> 2 Why was the experience good or bad?
> 3 How did you learn?   4 Did you learn in a
> group or on your own?   5 Was it easy or difficult
> to learn?   6 How did you make progress?
> 7 Did you learn useful techniques?

b➤ Ss answer the questions individually and make notes about the learning experience. Go round and help Ss with vocabulary where necessary.

c➤ Tell Ss they are going to describe their learning experience. Focus Ss on the How to … box and give them time to read through it.

> Ss look back at the vocabulary in Ex. 3 and decide how they could use it when telling their partner about the learning experience.

> In pairs Ss tell each other about their learning experience. Encourage Ss to use the language from the How to … box and the vocabulary from Ex. 3. The Ss listening should think of follow-up questions they can ask. Go round and monitor the conversations for errors.

> Get feedback by asking Ss to tell you about their partner's experience and why it was a good or bad one.

> When Ss have finished put some of the important errors on the board and ask various Ss to come up to the board and correct the errors. Praise Ss for correct use of target language.

> **OPTIONAL VARIATION**
> When you have got feedback about all of the learning experiences, ask Ss to choose the top five most difficult learning experiences the Ss have mentioned. In groups Ss discuss which Ss had the most difficult learning experiences and why. Get feedback from the groups.

Reading

6➤ Write the following words on the board: *light bulbs, crisps, bread, post-it notes*. In pairs Ss think what the connection between these items is. Get feedback from the whole class.

> Ss read the text quickly to find out what the connection between the items is. Tell Ss not to worry if there are words they don't understand at the moment. Get feedback from the class. (The items were invented after failures or mistakes.)

7a➤ Ss cover the text. Ss complete the sentences 1–7 then compare their answers with a partner.

b➤ Ss read the text more carefully and check their answers and correct any which they have not completed in the right way. Check answers with the whole class.

> **Answers:**   1 make   2 light bulb / mistakes
> 3 inventions   4 sleep   5 a customer / thin
> 6 cost / not / experience   7 learn

➤ Ask Ss if there are any words or expressions in the text which they don't understand. Encourage Ss to answer each others' questions or to use a dictionary, before giving the explanations yourself.

8➤ Ss discuss the questions in groups of three or four. Get feedback from the class.

Lifelong learning

➤ Ask Ss to decide with their partners if there is a connection between the text and learning English. Get feedback from the class and refer Ss to the Lifelong learning box.

➤ Discuss the importance of being adventurous when speaking and writing English. Tell Ss that making a mistake is a natural part of the learning process and one which they shouldn't feel negatively about.

➤ Explain that it is a good idea for Ss to keep notes of common errors they make in their notebooks so they can try and correct themselves.

Grammar

OPTIONAL GRAMMAR LEAD-IN

Write the following questions on the board:

1 What time did the class begin?

2 Who arrived last in the class today?

In pairs Ss answer the questions. Check answers with Ss and write the full answers on the board under the questions. Ask Ss if they can see a difference between the two questions. Elicit that the first question contains an auxiliary verb, the second one doesn't.

In pairs Ss discuss why there is an auxiliary in the first question but not in the second. Get feedback from various pairs and elicit/explain that the first question is an object question, the second a subject question. Go on to look at the Active grammar box.

9➤ Focus Ss on the Active grammar box and give Ss time to read through the notes and complete the rules. Give Ss time to compare their answers with their partners. Check answers with the whole class.

Active grammar

The light bulb is the <u>object</u> of the question.
Thomas Edison is the <u>subject</u> of the question.

➤ Refer Ss to Reference page 101. Give Ss time to read through the notes. Ask: **Q: When a *Wh-* question word is the object of the question, what word order do we use?** The normal question word order: Question word + auxiliary + subject + verb. **Q: When a *Wh-* question word is the subject of the question, what word order do we use?** The same order as an affirmative sentence: Question word + verb + object. **Q: Do we need an auxiliary verb in a subject question?** No. **Q: What are the most common type of questions, subject or object questions?** Object questions.

10a➤ Divide the class into two groups, A and B. Each group looks at their corresponding statements 1–10. Together Ss write questions for the statements. Remind Ss to use the correct type of question form when writing the questions.

➤ Go round the class and monitor, helping where necessary. When Ss have finished writing the questions, check them with each group.

Answers:

Quiz A

1 Who painted *Guerrica* in 1937?
2 When did Mozart start composing music?
3 Who discovered penicillin in 1928?
4 Which of the world's greatest scientist lived from 1879–1955?
5 Which famous city is nicknamed The Big Apple?
6 What invention is Guglielmo Marconi responsible for?
7 Which is the largest desert in the world?
8 Who earned $34 million per day during the 1990s?
9 Which country is the oldest surviving republic in the world?
10 When did Boris Becker become the youngest ever man to win the men's singles at Wimbledon?

Quiz B

1 Which islands did Christopher Columbus discover in 1492, before he discovered America?
2 Who painted the Sistine Chapel?
3 What book made Umberto Eco famous?
4 Which European country has the smallest area?
5 Which team did David Beckham join in 1993?
6 Who wrote the song *Imagine* in 1971?
7 What did John Logie Baird invent?
8 Which is the world's longest river?
9 Which famous writer lived from 1564–1616?
10 When did Hong Kong become part of China again?

b➤ Pair Ss so there is a student from group A working with a student from group B. Refer Ss A to the answers to Quiz A on page 146 and Ss B to the answers to Quiz B on page 149. Give Ss time to check the answers.

➤ Ss ask each other their quiz questions. Ss give their partners a point for each question answered correctly.

➤ When they have finished asking and answering the questions, Ss count the points and check who won the quiz.

➤ Get feedback from the class and discuss which questions Ss found most difficult.

11➤ In pairs Ss write their own quiz questions and answers. Encourage Ss to include both subject and object questions in their quiz. Go round and check the questions Ss are writing. Ss read out the questions for other pairs and see if they can answer them.

OPTIONAL EXTENSION

Ss in pairs. Ss think of five things they think they know about their partners. Ss write down the five things. Ss then think of questions for these five things. The questions must include subject and object questions. If the original five questions don't include both subject and object questions, tell Ss to change some of them to include both types of questions. Ss now ask their partner the questions and compare their partners' answers to the answers they originally wrote.

7.2 Great teachers

Roald Dahl wrote many very successful books for children such as *James and the Giant Peach* which was turned into an animated film and *Charlie and the Chocolate Factory*, which was also made into a film, starring Gene Wilder. A new version of the film was released in 2005, starring Johnny Depp. *Matilda* was also turned into a film, starring Danny De Vito. Roald Dahl also wrote for adults. His short stories are famous for having an unexpected twist at the end of them. Some of his stories were televised in Britain as *Tales of the Unexpected*.

In this lesson Ss read an extract from *Matilda* by Roald Dahl about Matilda's school. Ss go on to look at vocabulary related to teachers and listen to two people talking about their teachers. Ss then look at the grammar of *used to* and *would* and end the lesson by writing a website entry about a favourite teacher from their past.

Reading and speaking

OPTIONAL WARMER

Dictate the following words taken from the extract from *Matilda*: *exercise book, pencils, headmistress, strict discipline, argue, liquidise* (liquidize AmE), *laugh, eager* Check that Ss understand these words and phrases. In pairs Ss decide how these words and phrases could be related to a first day at school. Get feedback from the whole class and discuss Ss' ideas.

1➤ Focus Ss on the questions. Ss discuss their answers to these questions with a partner. Get feedback from the pairs.

2a➤ In pairs Ss look at the cartoon and discuss what they think the teacher in the cartoon is like. Ss exchange their ideas with another pair.

➤ In pairs Ss predict what they think the writer might say about the teacher. Get feedback by asking various pairs their predictions.

b➤ Ss read the extract quickly to check their predictions about the teacher. Tell Ss not to worry about any words or expressions they don't understand at this stage.

➤ Get feedback and check if any of the Ss' predictions were correct.

3➤ Focus Ss on sentences 1–8. Ss read the text more carefully and write (*T*) if the sentences are true, (*F*) if the sentences are false. Ask Ss to underline the parts of the text which give them the answers.

➤ Ss compare their answers with their partners. Check answers with the whole class.

Answers: 1 T 2 F 'You have all brought your own pencils, I hope,' she said. 3 T 4 F It is the beginning of eleven years of schooling, six of which are spent at the school, Crunchem Hall. 5 F Miss Trunchbull is the headmistress. 6 T 7 F She advises them not to argue with Mrs Trunchbull. 8 T

4➤ Ss look at the words and phrases taken from the text and underline the correct definition. Ss compare their answers with their partners. Check the answers with the group.

Answers: 1 making people *obey rules* 2 *do what I suggest* 3 *act like a good child* 4 *disagree with someone by talking or shouting* 5 *reply rudely* 6 *punishes* 7 behaves in the *incorrect* way

➤ Check if there are any other words or expressions in the text that Ss don't understand.

5a➤ Ss complete the sentences 1–5 using some of the words and phrases from Ex. 4. Check the answers with the Ss.

Answers: 1 behave 2 strict discipline 3 take, advice 4 argue 5 deals severely

b➤ Ss change the sentences so that they are true for them. Ss then share the new sentences with their partners.

Vocabulary

OPTIONAL LEAD-IN

Write the following subjects on the board: *Maths, Art, English, Geography*. In groups of three or four Ss discuss what they think the typical teacher of these subjects is like. They can refer to their own experience of teachers.

6➤ Focus Ss on the table. In pairs Ss check they understand the meaning of the phrases in the table. Ss then put the phrases into two groups, qualities of a good teacher and qualities of a bad teacher. Ss compare their answers.

➤ Draw two columns on the board and write *Positive* at the top of the left-hand column and *Negative* at the top of the right-hand column. Check answers with the class and write the words into the correct column. There are no definite answers here as it depends on Ss' opinion.

➤ Practise saying any of the phrases that Ss have problems saying correctly.

OPTIONAL VARIATION

Ss in two groups, A and B. Group A looks at the things a teacher does in the left-hand column of the table. Group B looks at the things a teacher is in the right-hand column of the table. Check Ss understand the phrases. Ss then decide if the qualities are of a good or a bad teacher. Monitor carefully and help Ss where necessary. Re-organise Ss into pairs, A and B. Ss take turns to explain the phrases in their columns to each other.

7➤ Focus Ss on the sentences 1–8. In pairs Ss choose the correct alternative in each sentence. Ss compare their answers with another pair. Check answers with the whole class.

Answers: 1 boring 2 loses her temper 3 patient 4 knowledgeable 5 shouts at 6 understanding 7 shout 8 inspiring

Listening

8➤ Play recording 7.2. Ss listen to two people discussing their teachers and complete the information in the table. Ss compare their answers with their partners.

Answers:

	Subject	Good /Bad qualities	Other information:
Mr Halsworth	History	Boring, shouted a lot,	Short, terrible glasses
Miss Matthews	Music	Inspiring, patient	Beautiful, played Mozart, relaxing, enjoyable lessons
Madame Bouchier	French	Frightening, punished students	Asked difficult questions
Mr Ford	Religious Studies	Open-minded, knowledgeable, never lost temper	Taught about different religions and astronomy

9► Play recording 7.2 again and check their answers. Ss also write down any expressions from the previous exercises which the speakers use to describe each teacher. Ss compare their answers with their partners. Check answers with the class.

Answers: he was really boring he used to shout she was inspiring so patient she was frightening she would punish you he was so open-minded he was very knowledgeable he never lost his temper

Listening

OPTIONAL GRAMMAR LEAD-IN

Write the following sentence prompts on the board:
1 When I was five I _used to_ like _____ at school.
2 When I was five I _would_ often _____ at school.
Ss complete the sentences so they are true for them. Ss discuss their answers with a partner. Ask Ss why we use the underlined words.

10a► Ss complete the sentences a–d by looking at the tapescript on page 173. Ss then choose the correct options to complete the rules 1–3. Elicit the answers from the class.

Active grammar

1   Use _used to_ + verb and _would_ + verb to talk about repeated actions in the past which don't happen now.
a) We _would_ throw paper at him. (Action)
b) She _used to_ play us Mozart. (Action)
2   Only use _used to_ + verb to talk about states in the past.
c) We _didn't use to_ like her lessons at all.
3   _would_ is usually contracted to 'd in spoken English.
d) We _'d_ learn about the stars.

► Refer Ss to Reference page 101. Give Ss time to read through the notes. Draw Ss attention to the spelling of _used to_ in negatives and questions (without '_d_').

b► Focus Ss on the tapescript on page 173. Ss underline other examples of _used to_ and _would_. Check Ss' answers.

Answers: We _would throw_ paper … He _used to shout_ so much he _would go_ red in the face. She _used to play_ us Mozart and teach … I _didn't use to like_ her lessons … she _used to tell_ me … she _would punish_ you. He _used to teach_ us … we_'d learn_ about the stars too. Not even when we _used to_ …

11► Ss read the text and circle the correct forms. Check answers with the class.

Answers: 1 use to   2 would   3 used to   4 used to be   5 would 6 used to be

12a► In pairs Ss complete the sentences 1–8 using _use(d) to_ and a suitable verb from the box. Ss compare their answers with another pair. Check answers with the group.

Answers: 1 use to be   2 used to like   3 didn't use to watch   4 used to live   5 didn't use to go   6 use to eat   7 used to do   8 didn't use to behave

b► Ss change the sentences so they are true for them and answer the questions.

c► Ss compare their answers with their partners. Encourage Ss to ask follow-up questions. Get feedback from various pairs.

Pronunciation

13► Play recording 7.3. Ss notice how _used to_ /juːstə/ (/juːs tuː/) and _didn't use to_ / /dɪdən(t)juːstə/ are pronounced. Ss decide which letters are silent. ('_d_' in _used to_, '_t_' in _didn't use to_ are silent.)

Speaking

14a► Ss think about a good or bad teacher from their past that they do not have now. Using the questions Ss write notes about the teacher. Tell Ss it is not necessary to write full sentences. Go round and help Ss as necessary.

b► Ss work in groups of three or four. Ss tell each other about their teachers. Encourage Ss to use _used to/would_ as appropriate while doing so. Encourage the Ss listening to ask follow-up questions.

► Monitor the conversations for errors. When Ss have finished, write the errors on the board and encourage Ss to correct them. Finally, congratulate Ss on correct use of _used to_ and _would_.

Writing

15► Refer Ss to the writing bank on page 163. Ss complete the exercises.

Answers:
2 Physical: short, slightly chubby, very good-looking, have (her) hair tied back, a friendly face Clothing: dressed conservatively Character: knowledgeable, calm and understanding, enthusiastic, encouraging, kind and polite, organised, respectful and interesting
3 Ss own suggestions
4 1 a great imagination 2 dresses conservatively 3 calm, understanding 4 enthusiastic 5 kind, polite
5 Ss own answers

16► Ss write an entry to the website about a favourite teacher from their past. Go round and help Ss where necessary. When Ss have finished writing, ask various Ss to read out their entries to the class.

7.3 It's never too late

In many countries in the western world, life expectancy is rising, as are retirement ages. Nowadays some old people are doing sports and hobbies even after they have turned 100.

In this lesson Ss look at vocabulary related to old age and listen to three people talking about old age. They then read different texts about remarkable old people and share information about what they have read with their partners. Through the context of the texts Ss analyse the grammar of modals of ability and ask each other about different abilities they had in the past and have now.

OPTIONAL WARMER

Write the following questions on the board: *Do you know any remarkable old people? Why are they so special?* Ss think about these questions and share information with their partners. Encourage Ss to ask each other follow-up questions to find out more information about the old people. Get feedback by asking Ss to share their stories with the rest of the class.

Vocabulary

1➤ Focus Ss on the words in bold in sentences 1–4. With their partners Ss discuss the meaning of these words. Ss then match these words to the definitions a–f. Ss compare their answers with their partners. Check answers with the class.

Answers: 1 retire: e   2 senior citizens: b, pension: d   3 elderly: c, nursing homes: a   4 respect: f

---

OPTIONAL VARIATION

Organise the class into pairs, A and B. Ss A look at the sentences 1–4 and cover the definitions a–f. Ss B look at the definitions a–f and cover the sentences 1–4. Ss A read out the words in bold to Ss B who find the definition for the words. When student A has read out all the words, the pair uncover the definitions or sentences and check their answers together. Elicit the answers from the whole class.

2➤ Tell Ss they are going to hear three people discussing three of the questions in Ex. 1a. Play recording 7.4. Pause after each part of the conversation so Ss can decide with their partners which questions the people talk about. Check the answers with the whole class.

Answers: Part 1 4   Part 2 3   Part 3 1

3➤ In pairs Ss read the sentences 1–5 and decide which they think is the correct option in each sentence.

➤ Play recording 7.4 again and Ss circle the correct phrase.

➤ Give Ss time to compare their answers with their partners. Check answers with the class.

Answers: 1 are involved in family decisions   2 can do some things for free   3 live with extended family   4 can be very good   5 don't retire

---

4➤ In groups of three or four Ss discuss the questions in Ex. 1. Monitor the conversations for errors. Get feedback from various groups.

➤ Write any important errors on the board. In pairs Ss correct the errors. Get feedback and write the correct version underneath the errors.

Reading

5a➤ Organise Ss into two groups, A and B. Tell Ss A to read the three texts on page 96–97. Tell Ss B to read the three texts on page 150. While reading, Ss take notes for each of the three people using the areas in the box. Tell Ss not to copy directly from the text, but to write the information in their own words.

➤ If there are any words or phrases that Ss don't understand encourage them to answer each others' questions or to use a dictionary before asking you.

Answers:

Student A's answers:

Name	Ella Scotchmer	Elizabeth Collins	Max Jones
Age	104	94	71
Activity/ achievement	Travel, dance, tai chi	art	Running
Personal philosophy/ attitude to being old	'Wait and see what happens.'	She thinks about dying, but 'it's not the right time'	Doesn't consider himself old

Student B's answers:

Name	Louisa May	Mary Wesley	Kyra Vane
Age	88	86	82
Activity/ achievement	composer	writer	singer
Personal philosophy/ attitude to being old	Knows she might die soon. Her music means more to her than her life	Age doesn't make any difference to her. She has friends who are younger than her	Need to keep brain alert, interested in things and people. Her friends are much younger than her

---

b➤ Re-pair the Ss so they are working with someone from the other group. Ss tell their partners about the three people they have read about.

➤ In pairs Ss decide which of the old people is the most remarkable and why. Ss compare their answers with another pair. Discuss the questions with the whole group.

6➤ Ss discuss the questions 1–4 in groups of four. Ss share information with a student from another group. Get feedback from the class.

7➤ Focus Ss on the sentences 1–6. In pairs Ss complete the sentences using the phrases from the box. Ss compare their answers with another pair. Check answers with the class.

Answers: 1 b   2 e   3 c   4 f   5 a   6 d

Grammar

OPTIONAL GRAMMAR LEAD-IN

Write five sentences on the board about yourself and your present and past abilities. Use the following modals of ability: *can, could, was able to* and *managed to* in your sentences. Ss can ask you follow-up questions to find out more about your abilities. Discuss the use of the modal verbs of ability in the sentences with the class

---

8▶ Refer Ss back to the sentences in Ex. 7. Ss complete the Active grammar box with the words and phrases in the box. Ss compare their answers with their partners. Check the answers with the whole class.

> **Active grammar**
>
> To describe general ability in the present, we say:
> + I **can** swim.
> – She **can't** play the violin.
> To describe general ability in the past, we say:
> When I was/we were young …
> + We **could** climb trees.
> + I **was able to** dance for hours.
> – I **couldn't** drive.
> – We **weren't able to** speak French.
> To describe something that happened at a particular moment in the past, we say:
> Yesterday …
> + They **were able to** finish their work.
> + I **managed to** book the holiday.
> – She **wasn't able to** go to the meeting.
> – They **weren't able to** find a hotel.
> – He **didn't manage to** visit his friends.

➤ Focus Ss on Reference page 101. Give Ss a few minutes to read through the notes. Ask: **Q: What modal verb do we use when we are talking about general ability in the present?** can. **Q: What verb do we use when we are talking about general ability in the past?** could. **Q: When do we use *was able to*?** When we talk about general ability in the past or a particular situation in the past. **Q: What modal verb do we use if we want to emphasise that the action is difficult?** *Manage to*. **What modal verbs can we use in the negative when we are talking about one particular moment?** Couldn't, wasn't able to, didn't.

9▶ Focus Ss on the sentences 1–5. Ss rewrite the sentences using the word in brackets using two to four words for each sentence. Give Ss time to compare their answers in pairs before checking answers with the whole class.

> **Answers:** 1 John Parr finally <u>managed</u> to climb Mount Everest in 1994. 2 Orgosky <u>was able to</u> write music when he was a child. 3 We <u>weren't able to</u> go out because of the bad weather. 4 He <u>couldn't meet</u> his friends. 5 <u>didn't manage to</u> buy the cards because the shop was closed.

10▶ Focus Ss on the gapped sentences 1–8. In pairs Ss correct the modals of ability in the sentences.

➤ Ss compare their answers with another pair. Check answers with the whole group.

> **Answers:** 1 I didn't manage **to** finish my homework. 2 We **couldn't eat** out because we had no money. 3 Were you able to **sleep** last night? 4 Did you **manage** to speak to Shen Yung last night? 5 When he was younger he could **speak** four languages. 6 I was **able** to call for help on my mobile phone. 7 How **did** you manage to work with all that noise yesterday? 8 Was she **able to pay** her bills last month?

Pronunciation

11▶ Focus Ss on the pairs of sentences 1–6. Play recording 7.5 and Ss tick the sentence they hear in each pair. Ss compare their answers with a partner. Check the answers with the class.

> **Answers:** 1 a 2 b 3 b 4 a 5 b 6 a

➤ Ss practise saying the sentences with their partners. Go around the class listening to the pronunciation, correcting errors if necessary.

Person to person

12▶ Ss discuss the three questions in groups of three or four. Encourage Ss to use modals of ability when doing so. Also encourage Ss to ask each other follow-up questions to find out more information.

➤ Get feedback from the class by asking Ss to report what they have learned about other Ss in their groups to the rest of the class.

Speaking

13▶ Ss in pairs. Focus Ss on the table. Give Ss time to look at the areas in the left-hand column of the table and to make questions about these areas. Check that Ss understand all of the words and phrases in the column. Encourage Ss to explain words and phrases to each other before asking you.

➤ Go round and check the questions Ss are writing. Ss stand up and mingle, asking other Ss questions and writing their names in the box in the appropriate spaces. Encourage Ss to ask follow-up questions to help them fill in the last column of the table. Monitor the conversations and take note of any important errors.

➤ Get feedback by asking Ss to tell the rest of the class information they have learned about other Ss.

➤ Finally, read out some of their errors to the class and ask Ss to correct them. Finally praise Ss for any correct use of modals of ability and comment on any interesting language they have used while doing the task.

> **OPTIONAL EXTENSION**
>
> Tell Ss that their homework task is to interview an old person they know. In class Ss can prepare the questions they want to ask that old person in groups of three or four. Tell Ss to include the grammar they have seen in this unit in the questions they prepare.
>
> Grammar to include: subject/object questions, *used to/ would* and modals of ability: *can, could, was able to* and *managed to*.
>
> The interview itself can be done in their own language if necessary. Ss write up the information they have gained from the interview. In the following class Ss tell the rest of the class about the old person.

Vocabulary: Idioms about learning

In this lesson Ss look at the meaning of different idioms about learning and practise using them.

1a➤ In pairs Ss decide which subjects they associate with the sentences 1–9. Ss compare their answers with another pair. Check answers with the group.

> **Answers:** 2 Mathematics (Maths) 3 Languages (Polish) 4 Science (Biology) 5 History 6 Music 7 Philosophy 8 Art 9 Geography

b➤ Ss match these words and expressions in bold to the definitions a–i. Check answers with the group.

> **Answers:** a 9 b 5 c 2 d 7 e 8 f 6 g 1 h 4 i 3

2➤ Ss look at the pictures and decide with their partners which idioms the pictures illustrate.

> **Answers:** A 1 B 9 C 8 D 3

3➤ Ss choose the best alternative to complete the sentences 1–4. Ss compare their answers with their partners. Check the answers with the group.

> **Answers:** 1 hasn't got a clue 2 learned it by heart 3 picked up 4 bookworm

4➤ Tell Ss that in each of the sentences 1-9 there is a mistake. With their partners Ss correct the mistakes. Get feedback from the whole group.

> **Answers:** 1 This is too difficult for me. Can you give **me** a hand? 2 I have to brush **up on** my German before I go to Austria. 3 We learned all the Maths formulas **by** heart. 4 She asked him a difficult question so he **made** a wild guess. 5 I picked **up some** Chinese when I was in Beijing last year. 6 She knows the poems of Sylvia Plath **inside out**. 7 I understand the question but I haven't got **a** clue how to answer it. 8 He always brings presents for the teacher. He's the **teacher's pet**. 9 You read all the time! I've never met such a **bookworm**.

5➤ Focus Ss on the gapped sentences 1–9. Tell Ss to complete five of the sentences so that they are true for them.

6➤ Ss compare their sentences in pairs. Ss must ask at least one follow-up question for every sentence their partner tells them. Go round and monitor and take note of important errors. Write these errors on the board and have Ss correct them. Praise Ss for correct use of the idioms about learning.

Communication: School days

In this lesson Ss listen to a childhood story and then tell their own childhood stories.

1a➤ In pairs Ss describe the photos and decide when and where the photos were taken. Ss discuss if their own school days when they were young were similar to any of the photos.

➤ Play recording 7.6 and Ss decide which photo illustrates the story being told. Check the answer with the class.

> **Answer:** Photo C

b➤ Ss read the questions 1–9. Ss answer as many questions as they can. Ss compare their answers with their partners.

c➤ Play recording 7.6 again. Ss compare their answers with their partners. Check answers with the whole class.

> **Answers:** 1 Eight or nine 2 The speaker was at a large school in the city centre. Her class didn't know anything about the countryside so their teacher decided to take the class on a trip out of London. 3 in the countryside 4 the girl, her class and her teacher 5 A beautiful sunny day 6 They went horse riding in the afternoon. The girl's horse ran off and it took her a while to stop it. 7 frightened and embarrassed 8 Afterwards she was so frightened she was shaking for about an hour. 9 She learned that she didn't get on well with horses so she has never been on a horse since then.

d➤ Refer Ss to the tapescript on page 174. With their partners Ss find the words and expressions which match definitions 1–5. Check answers with the class.

> **Answers:** 1 one day 2 Anyway, 3 all of a sudden 4 Eventually, 5 I'll never forget it.

2➤ Focus Ss on instructions 1–5. Ss think of two stories from their school days or when they were young. Ss use the questions in Ex. 1b to help them. Then, in the same way Ss invent another story about their school days which is not true.

➤ Give Ss time to prepare what they are going to say about each of the stories. Ss work in pairs, A and B. Ss A tell Ss B their stories. Encourage Ss B to ask follow-up questions. Ss B should try and guess which story is not true. Then Ss change roles so that Ss B are telling their stories and Ss A are listening, asking follow-up questions and guessing which story is not true.

Review and practice

1➤

> **Answers:** 1 Who phoned you last night? 2 When does he get the train? 3 Who taught Maria to play the piano? 4 Why did he fail the exam? 5 What fell on the floor? 6 Who lives in that house? 7 Which office did she run into? 8 How did they meet?

2➤

> **Answers:** 1 used to get 2 used to stay 3 use to have 4 used to love 5 use to study 6 used to spend 7 use to go out 8 used to stay 9 used to read 10 used to dream

3➤

> **Answers:** 1 Sam **used** to smoke but now he has given up. 2 Correct 3 Tomas **would go** to the market every day with his father. 4 Emil used **to** love riding horses on the beach. 5 Correct 6 Tom didn't use **to** have a girlfriend but now he has lots. 7 Myra used to **be** a dancer when she was younger. 8 She would dance for **me when** I came to visit.

4➤

> **Answers:** 1 could 2 managed to 3 wasn't able to 4 could 5 managed to 6 aren't able to 7 can't 8 couldn't

5➤

> **Answers:** 1 *inside out* 2 brush 3 bookworm 4 up 5 clue 6 wild 7 learn 8 give

Notes for using the Common European Framework (CEF)

CEF References

7.1 Can do: describe a learning experience

CEF B1 descriptor: can give detailed accounts of experiences, describing feelings and reactions. (CEF page 59)

7.2 Can do: describe a teacher from your past

CEF B2 descriptor: can write clear, detailed descriptions of real events and experiences, marking the relationship between ideas in clear connected text, and following established conventions of the genre concerned. (CEF page 62)

7.3 Can do: talk about abilities in the past and present

CEF B1 descriptor: can enter unprepared into conversation on familiar topics, express personal opinions and exchange information on topics that are familiar, of personal interest or pertinent to everyday life (e.g. family, hobbies, work, travel and current events). (CEF page 74)

CEF quick brief

One of the key ideas within the Common European Framework is that learning a language is a lifelong task; it requires 'lifelong learning' skills. Like all skills, we can improve how we learn and one of the teacher's responsibilities is to show Ss how to do this. The Lifelong learning boxes in Total English offer help in this task and showing Ss how to use their Portfolio is another way that teachers can help.

Portfolio task

Download the Total English Portfolio free from www.longman.com/totalenglish.

Objective: to introduce Ss to the Dossier section of their Portfolio.

This task can be done in Ss' own language.

➤ The Dossier section of the Portfolio allows Ss to record and store examples of good work in English to show other people. It can include anything from stories to recorded interviews to videos.

1➤ Explain the purpose of the Dossier section of the Portfolio to Ss.

2➤ Ask Ss to look back at their work over the last few months and choose one or two pieces of work which they feel proud of.

3➤ Ask Ss to compare the work in groups and explain why they feel proud.

4➤ Ask Ss to record details of the work relevant section of their Dossier and store the work separately in a Dossier folder. If necessary, learners might like to redo the work, correcting mistakes from the original version.

8 Change

Overview

Lead-in	**Vocabulary:** expressions with *change*
8.1	**Grammar:** Second Conditional **Vocabulary:** talking about cities **Can do:** talk about cause and result
8.2	**Grammar:** adverbs **Vocabulary:** global issues **Can do:** talk about change/lack of change
8.3	**Grammar:** Third Conditional **Vocabulary:** life changes **Can do:** describe the effects of important decisions
Vocabulary	Word building
Com. Focus	Time for a change
Reference	
Practice	

Summary

Lesson 1: Ss read a text which deals with changes which have taken place in New York. Ss then go on to listen to four people talking about what they would like to change about their cities.

Lesson 2: Ss listen to two people discussing how the world has changed since they were children. Ss then go on to read about the Live Aid concerts of 1985.

Lesson 3: Ss listen to three people talking about important decisions they have taken. They then go on to write a paragraph about an important turning point in their lives.

Vocabulary: Ss look at different prefixes and suffixes and how they can build different words with them.

Communication: Ss talk about different things they would change in their lives if they could. Ss go on to listen to five speakers talking about change.

Film bank: From cradle to grave (3'44")

A documentary style film giving facts and figures on life from birth until death

The film starts with a small baby called Charlotte and shows her growing up. During this process the narrator gives us biological and social facts and figures on various things that happen during her lifetime, for example, how much chocolate she'll eat, how long she'll talk for, etc., up until the age she is likely to die.

Possible places to use this short film are:
➤ before the Lead-in to introduce the topic of change

➤ after Lesson 2 to consolidate can do statements

➤ at the end of the unit to round up the topic and language

For ways to use this short film in class, see Student's Book page 158 and Teacher's Book page 185.

Lead-in

OPTIONAL WARMER
Give Ss a few minutes to think about how they could change the way they study English to become more effective Ss. Ss make a list of ideas. Ss then share their list with their partners. Get feedback by asking various Ss how they could study more effectively. Tell Ss that the topic of the unit they are going to study is 'Change'.

1➤ Focus Ss on the photos. In pairs Ss discuss if they or anyone they know have experienced any of these changes recently.

➤ Ss discuss the questions in groups of three or four. Get feedback from the class. As a group Ss decide which are the most and least dramatic changes and why.

2➤ Write *change* on the board. With their partners Ss think of any expressions they know which are made with this word. Get feedback from the class and write any correct expressions on the board.

➤ Focus Ss on the words and phrases in the box. In pairs Ss decide which of these words go with the word *change*. Elicit answers from the class.

> **Answers:** All of the words in the box go with *change* except the following: *time, your head, your happiness, talking*

3a➤ Focus Ss on the expressions with *change* in bold in the dialogues 1–3. Ss read the dialogues and discuss in pairs what they think the expressions mean. Get feedback from the class.

➤ Ss practise saying the dialogues in pairs. Ss close their books and try to repeat the dialogues without looking at them.

b➤ Focus Ss on the beginnings of the sentences. Ss complete the sentences so that they are true for them. Go around the class, correcting errors.

c➤ Ss in groups of four. Ss read their sentences to the other Ss in the group. Encourage Ss listening to ask follow-up questions.

➤ Get feedback from each group by asking them to tell the class about the most interesting changes.

EXTEND THE LEAD-IN
Tell Ss they have to write a story using as many expressions with *change* as possible. Give Ss a few minutes to think and make brief notes about what they want to write. Have them work with a partner to write the story and give them a limited time to do it, e.g. five minutes. Go round and help where necessary. Ask various pairs to read out their stories to the class.

8.1 Changing the rules

New York, nicknamed the Big Apple, has always had a reputation for being a bustling, noisy, dangerous city where anything goes. Recently, however, that reputation has changed, largely because of a city-wide ban on smoking in public places. The smoking ban and other new laws have infuriated some of the citizens of New York, while they have been applauded by others.

In this lesson Ss read a text about the changes in the laws in New York. Through this context Ss analyse the grammar of the Second Conditional. They then go on to speak about laws that they would introduce if they were the mayor of their town or city. Ss then listen to people talking about changes they would make to their cities and finish by writing a newspaper article about issues they would like to change.

> **OPTIONAL WARMER**
>
> Ask Ss to draw two columns in their notebooks. At the top of the first column Ss write *New York*, at the top of the second column Ss write the name of their town or city. Ss compare the two places by writing words in each column connected to each place e.g. *subway* in the first column and *bus* in the second column. Get feedback from the class and discuss how they think New York is different from their own towns or cities.

Speaking

1➤ Ss discuss the questions 1–4 with their partners. Get feedback from various pairs.

Reading

2➤ Focus Ss on the title of the text. In pairs Ss predict what they think the text will be about. Get feedback from the class.

➤ Ss read the text quickly and check which of the ideas they discussed in Ex. 1, question 2 are mentioned in the text. Tell Ss not to worry about any words or expressions they don't understand at this stage. Get feedback from the class.

3➤ Ss read the text again more slowly and write (*T*) next to the statements 1–9 which are true, and (*F*) next to the statements which are false. Ss underline the parts of the text which give them the answers. Ss compare their answers with their partners. Check answers with the class and ask Ss to read out the parts of the text which gave them the answers.

> **Answers:** 1 T 2 F It is illegal to smoke or drink in public. 3 F It is illegal to feed your sandwich to the birds in the park. 4 F the police think that the new laws are stupid. 5 F It is illegal to uses two seats on the subway. 6 T 7 T 8 T 9 T

➤ Ask Ss if there are any words or expressions in the text which they don't understand. Encourage Ss to explain them to each other, before doing so yourself.

4➤ Ss in groups of three or four. Ss discuss the questions 1–5 in their groups. Monitor the conversations for errors.

➤ Get feedback from the groups. Finally, write any important errors on the board and encourage Ss to self-correct.

> **OPTIONAL EXTENSION**
>
> Divide Ss into two groups, A and B. Group A take the role of the tourist who fell asleep on the subway, Group B take the role of the police officers who woke him up to fine him. Group A must think of reasons why they should not pay any fine, Group B why the tourist must pay the fine.
>
> In their groups Ss prepare what they are going to say. Ss then pair off with someone from the other group and perform the role play. Monitor the role plays for errors. When Ss have finished, read out the errors and ask Ss to correct them.

Grammar

> **OPTIONAL GRAMMAR LEAD-IN**
>
> Write the following sentence prompt on the board: *If I spoke English perfectly* …. Ss complete the sentence then compare it with their partners. Get feedback from various Ss and write their sentences on the board if correct. Ask Ss what type of sentence this is. Elicit/Explain that it is a Second Conditional sentence. In pairs Ss discuss why this type of conditional is used in English.

5➤ Focus Ss on the Active grammar box. Give Ss time to read through it. With their partners Ss choose the correct alternatives. Check answers with the class.

> **Active grammar**
>
> 1 Use the Second Conditional to describe <u>an imaginary situation</u> in the present or future and its result.
> 2 In the *if* clause, use <u>the Past Simple</u>.
> 3 In the result clause, *would* (or *'d*) is used because the situation is <u>imaginary (hypothetical)</u>
> 4 It is possible to use a modal verb such as *could* or *might* instead of *could*, if you are <u>not sure</u> of the result
>
> **First and Second Conditional:**
>
> In a real situation use the <u>First Conditional</u>.
> In a hypothetical situation use the <u>Second Conditional</u>.
> The <u>First Conditional</u> uses the Present Simple + *will*.
> The <u>Second Conditional</u> uses the Past Simple + *would*.

➤ Refer Ss to Reference page 115. Ss read through the notes. Ask: **Q: What conditional do we use with an unreal, imaginary or hypothetical situation?** Second Conditional. **Q: What is the form of the Second Conditional?** *if* + Past Simple + *would ('d)/wouldn't*. **Does the 'if clause? always have to come first in a Second Conditional sentence?** No, it can be the first or second phrase. **If the 'if clause' is the second phrase, do we need a comma?** No. **Is it possible to say *If I were*?** Yes. **What conditional do we use to talk about possible or real situations?** First Conditional.

6➤ In pairs Ss complete the gaps in sentences 1–8 to make Second Conditional sentences, using the verbs in brackets. Check answers with the class.

Answers: 1 were / would you arrest 2 wouldn't like / lived 3 would you go / wanted 4 didn't make / wouldn't exist 5 wouldn't be / had to 6 didn't have / would find 7 existed / would they 8 would be / had

7➤ Ss read the situations in the box. Check that Ss understand all the words and expressions.

➤ Ss write (R)/(P) next to the situations that Ss think are real or possible situations in their life. In pairs Ss then decide what they *will / would* do in each situation in the box. Get feedback from the class.

OPTIONAL VARIATION

Organise Ss into pairs, A and B. First, Ss think about what they *will/would* do themselves in each of the situations in the box. Then Ss think about what their partner *will/would* do in each of the situations. Ss A tell Ss B what they think B *will/would* do in each situation. Ss B tell Ss A if their guesses are correct or not. Ss B then tell Ss A what they think Ss A *will/would* do in each situation and Ss A confirms if they are correct or not.

Pronunciation

6➤ Give Ss time to read through the dialogues 1–4. Play recording 8.1. Ss underline the words that they hear in the dialogues. Check answers with the class. Focus Ss on the weak contracted forms of *will* and *would*.

Answers: 1 would 2 didn't 3 I'd 4 won't

b➤ Ss practise saying the dialogues with a partner, then repeat the dialogues with their books closed. Ask various pairs to repeat the dialogues for the class.

Speaking and listening

9a➤ Ss in groups of three or four. Ss imagine they are representing the mayor of their towns or cities. Give Ss a few minutes to think of five new laws that they would introduce before they start discussing them as a group. Ask Ss to make note of their group's laws. Encourage Ss to use the Second Conditional while doing so.

b➤ Each group takes turns to tell the rest of the class about their laws/proposals. Encourage the Ss listening to ask follow-up questions.

➤ As a class Ss choose the five best laws/proposals.

10a➤ Write the following names of cities on the board: *Mexico City, São Paulo, Manchester, Naples*. In pairs Ss discuss what they know about these cities. Get feedback from the class and write Ss' ideas on the board.

➤ Tell Ss that they are going to hear four people talking about their cities. Check that Ss understand the words and phrases in the box. Play recording 8.2. Ss match the speakers to the subjects in the box.

Answers: 1 c pollution 2 d disabled facilities 3 a noise 4 b buildings

b➤ Play recording 8.2 again and Ss complete the extracts with the correct words.

c➤ Ss check their answers with the tapescript on page 174.

Answers: 1 so 2 because of /so 3 caused by / So 4 Because of / which means

11a➤ Refer Ss to the How to … box. In pairs Ss put the formal expressions in the correct place in the table. Check answers with the class.

Answers:
Describe cause	*It's caused by* (+ noun or gerund) … *because (of)*… *As a result of* (+ noun) …
Describe result	*so* … *which means* … *Therefore,* … *This leads to* (+ noun or gerund) … *As a result,* …

b➤ Ss decide which of the words/expressions can start a sentence in written English and which can join two clauses. Give Ss time to compare their answers with a partner. Check answers with the whole class.

Answers: The words and expressions that can start a sentence are: *It's caused by* (+ noun or gerund) …, *As a result of* (+ noun) …, *Therefore, This leads to, As a result* The words and expressions that can join two clauses: *because (of), so …, which means …*

c➤ Focus Ss on the sentences 1–8. Ss complete the sentences in any way they like. Ss compare their sentences with a partner. Check the sentences with the whole class.

OPTIONAL VARIATION

Ss write similar sentences to the ones in Ex. 11c about their own cities or towns. Encourage Ss to use the expressions from the How to … box. In a monolingual class Ss tell you about their cities or towns. In a multilingual class form groups of three or four. Ss tell the other Ss in their group about their cities or towns.

Writing

12a➤ Refer Ss to the article in the Writing Bank on page 164. Ss do the exercises with their partners.

Answers:
1 1 F Diseases such as lung cancer and heart disease can be caused by second-hand smoke. 2 T 3 F In New Mexico every year between 230 and 390 deaths are caused by second-hand smoking. 4 T
2 A 4 B 3 C 2 D 1

b➤ Ss choose one of the laws they proposed in Ex. 9. Ss write an article for a newspaper about the issue they would like to change. Encourage Ss to use the useful phrases on page 164 in the articles. This could be done for homework.

8.2 Change the world

In July 1985 Bob Geldof, the organiser of Band Aid, arranged a day of concerts in London and Philadelphia. The concerts raised £140 million for the starving of Africa. Since then global problems such as third world debt are ever present in the news. Twenty years after the original concerts, another series of concerts known as Live 8 was organised by Bob Geldof. The purpose of these concerts was to put pressure on the leaders of the world's richest countries to release developing countries from their debts.

In this lesson Ss look at vocabulary related to global issues and listen to two people discussing how the world has changed since they were children. Ss then read a text about the original Live Aid concerts and through this context Ss analyse the grammar of adverbs.

Vocabulary

OPTIONAL WARMER

In pairs Ss make a list of the five most important problems facing the world today. Go round and help Ss if they need any vocabulary or expressions. Ss compare their lists with their partners. Get feedback and try to come to a consensus as a class of the five most important global problems.

1▶ Focus Ss on the photo. In pairs Ss discuss the questions 1–3 and make a list of ways to initiate change. Get feedback from the whole class.

2▶ Tell Ss to organise the words in the box into pairs. The pairs may be opposites or words with similar meanings. Ss compare their answers with a partner. Check answers with the whole class.

> **Answers:** developed countries – developing countries lifestyle – standard of living famine – starvation security – crime war – peace disease – cure the environment – pollution

3a▶ Ss use the words from Ex. 2 to fill the gaps in the sentences 1–5. Ss compare their answers with their partners. Check answers with the class.

> **Answers:** 1 pollution, the environment 2 famine, starvation 3 cure, diseases 4 Developed countries, developing countries 5 war, peace (solutions)

b▶ Ss discuss the questions in Ex. 3a in pairs. Ss share their ideas with another pair. Get feedback and discuss the questions as a group.

Lifelong learning

➤ Focus Ss on the Lifelong learning box and give them time to read through it. Ask if any of the Ss have tried this method and encourage them to say how successful it was.

➤ Discuss with the class the benefits of recording new vocabulary in pairs.

OPTIONAL EXTENSION

Organise Ss into pairs, A and B. Ss A define a word or phrase in the box for Ss B. Ss B must guess the word. Ss then take turns defining the words in the box until all the words and phrases have been defined.

Listening and speaking

4▶ Focus Ss on the issues in the box in Ex. 2 again. Tell Ss they will hear two people discussing how the world has changed since they were children.

➤ Play recording 8.3. Ss listen and decide which of the issues from the box in Ex. 2 the speakers mention. Ss compare their answers with a partner. Get feedback from the whole class.

> **Answers:** cures and diseases, developing countries, lifestyle

5▶ Give Ss time to read the expressions in the How to … box. Play recording 8.3 again and Ss tick the phrases in the box they hear..

> **Answers:**
>
> | Talk about change | It has got better/worse ✓ |
> | | The situation (in …) has deteriorated/improved ✓ |
> | | (Laws) have become … more/less … ✓ |
> | Talk about lack of change | … is/are still … ✓ |
> | | … is/are the same … |
> | | The situation … hasn't changed. ✓ |
> | Express your attitude towards the change | Luckily, … ✓ |
> | | Unfortunately, … ✓ |
> | | (Not) surprisingly, … ✓ |
> | | Interestingly, … |

6a▶ Organise Ss into two groups, A and B. Tell Ss that group A is the optimists' group and that the group B is the pessimists' group.

➤ Ask group A to think of five things which have made the world better in the last twenty-five years. Group B thinks of five things that have made the world worse in the last twenty-five years. Go around the groups helping Ss with vocabulary as necessary and encourage Ss to use the phrases from the How to … box where relevant.

b▶ Re-pair Ss so there is a student from group A working with a student from group B. Ss read their sentences to their partner who must respond with the different point of view. Monitor conversations for errors. When Ss have finished, write the errors on the board and discuss them with the class. Praise Ss for correct use of phrases from the How to … box.

OPTIONAL VARIATION

In a monolingual class Ss discuss with their partner how their country has changed over the last twenty-five years, using the phrases from the How to … box. Get feedback from the group. In a multilingual class Ss think about how their own countries have changed. Ss then tell other Ss in the class about these changes.

Reading

OPTIONAL LEAD-IN

Write the following ways of raising money for charity on the board: *1 hold a concert   2 ask for money in the street   3 hold a dinner and sell tickets for it   4 organise a sports event   5 broadcast a special television show.* In pairs Ss discuss these ways of raising money for charity and rank them in order of preference; 1 being the best way of raising money, 5 being the worst way. Get feedback from various pairs and discuss the Ss' ideas as a class

7a➤ In pairs Ss discuss what they think is the connection between the photos. Get feedback from various pairs of Ss.

➤ Ss in groups of three or four. In their groups Ss write down three things they know or think they know about the Live 8/ Live Aid concerts in 2005/1985 (respectively) and three things they would like to know about the concerts.

b➤ Ss read the read the text quickly to find out or check their information. Tell Ss not to worry about any words or phrases they don't understand at the moment. Allow Ss to compare their information. Get feedback from the whole class.

8➤ Tell Ss to read the text more carefully and look for the significance in the text of the words, phrases and numbers in the box. Ss share their answers with their partners. Check answers with the whole group.

Answers: One and a half billion people watched the Live Aid concerts. There was a terrible **famine** in sub-Saharan Africa. The concert raised **£140 million**. Live Aid was a **miracle**; because the concert achieved things that previously people didn't think were possible. In 1985 there were no **mobile phones** and **computers** were outside the experience of most ordinary people. **Ten** cities around the world held the Live 8 concerts. Bob Geldof says the **lingua franca** is rock music, not English. English is often described as a 'lingua franca', because people all over the world use it to communicate. Live Aid started **new ways of thinking** and behaving in broadcasting, in putting political pressure on governments and in raising money. Previously, people hadn't thought about using a huge concert to raise money, or to change politics. They hadn't considered how simultaneous broadcasting could be used to unite people around the world. The message that Live Aid delivered was **the need for change**. The concert raised awareness of the terrible situation in Africa, and how the developed countries were partly responsible. People realised that this situation should change. There were **simultaneous concerts** on two different continents. The concerts were broadcast all over the world at the same time. Concorde was **put on stand-by** for the concerts so it could be used if necessary.

9➤ Ss answer the questions 1–4 with a partner. Get feedback by asking various pairs their answers and discussing them with the whole class.

➤ Ask Ss if there are any words or expressions in the text that they don't understand. Encourage Ss to help each other with the vocabulary or to use a dictionary before asking you.

Grammar

OPTIONAL GRAMMAR LEAD-IN

Write the following sentence on the board: *Bob Geldof thought that Africa* urgently *needed help.* Ask Ss what type of word *urgently* is. Elicit/explain that it is an adverb. Focus Ss on the *-ly* ending and explain that this is a typical ending for adverbs. Ask Ss if there are any typical endings for adverbs in their own languages. Tell Ss to read back through the text in Ex. 7 and underline any examples of adverbs they can find. Get feedback from the class and write the adverbs on the board

10a➤ Give Ss time to read through the Active grammar box. Ss match the example sentences 1–4 with the rules a–d in the box. Ss compare their answers with a partner. Check answers with the whole class.

b➤ With their partners Ss choose the correct underlined alternatives to complete the rules in the Active grammar box. Elicit the answers from various Ss.

Active grammar

a 3 These adverbs usually come <u>after</u> the main verb.
b 1 These usually come <u>before</u> the main verb.
c 4 These usually come <u>before</u> the main verb.
d 2 These often come at the <u>beginning</u> of the sentence.

➤ Refer Ss to Reference page 115. Tell Ss to read through the notes carefully and answer any questions they have.

11a➤ Focus Ss on the adverbs in the box. Check that Ss know the meaning of all the adverbs. With their partners Ss mark the stress on the adverbs. Check the stress with the class and write the adverbs on the board. Tell Ss to come up and underline the stressed syllables on the board. Ss practise saying the adverbs with their partners.

➤ In pairs Ss match the adverbs in the box to their uses 1–8. Elicit the answers and write the adverbs on the board.

Answers: 1 fortunately   2 surprisingly
3 hopefully 4 personally   5 actually
6 basically   7 definitely   8 obviously

b➤ Ss read the sentences 1–8 and delete the adverb which cannot be used in the sentences. Check answers with the whole class.

Answers: 1 surprisingly   2 Definitely
3 Personally   4 hopefully   5 hopefully
6 fortunately   7 Hopefully   8 personally

Person to person

12a➤ Organise Ss into groups of three or four. In their groups Ss discuss the questions 1–4. Get feedback from the class and write the different groups' answers on the board.

b➤ Refer Ss to the answers on page 150. With their partners Ss discuss if they found any of the facts surprising, interesting or shocking. Encourage Ss to use adverbs while doing so.

8.3 Making the right decisions

In this lesson Ss read about a woman who is not happy with her life and discuss possible solutions. Ss then listen to people talking about important decisions they have taken. Through this context Ss look at the grammar of the Third Conditional before talking about how much their lives have changed in the past ten years. Finally, Ss write a paragraph describing an important turning point in their lives and the effect this had.

> **OPTIONAL WARMER**
>
> Tell Ss about a moment in your life when you had to make a decision about something important. In pairs Ss decide what decision you took at that moment, and what happened to you because of the decision you took. Get feedback from the class and check if any Ss correctly guess your decision and the consequences it had. Ask Ss if they think it was the right decision to make. Tell Ss that in this class they are going to be talking about making decisions.

Vocabulary and speaking

1➤ Ss read the problem in the left-hand column of the text. In pairs Ss discuss what they think Linda should do. Ss exchange ideas with another pair.

➤ Refer Ss to the four solutions in the right-hand column. In pairs Ss discuss these solutions and decide which would be the best one for Linda. Get feedback from various pairs.

2➤ In pairs Ss discuss questions 1 and 2. Get feedback from the class.

➤ Focus Ss on the decisions in the left-hand column of the table. Check that Ss understand the vocabulary in the column. Encourage Ss to answer each others' questions if they have any problems with the words and expressions, or to look them up in their dictionaries.

➤ Ss then choose three or four of the decisions that they have made in their lives. Ss make notes in the table about these decisions. Go round and help Ss where necessary.

➤ Organise Ss into pairs, A and B. Ss A tell Ss B about the decisions they had to make. Ss B should take notes about these decisions in the right-hand column. Encourage Ss B to ask follow-up questions about the problems.

➤ Ss B now tell Ss A about their decisions and Ss A take notes about the decisions in the right-hand column of their tables.

> **OPTIONAL EXTENSION**
>
> Organise Ss into new pairs so they are working with a different student. Ss tell each other about their previous partner's decisions and whether it was an easy or difficult decision.
>
> Get feedback by asking various Ss to report to the class what they have learned about their partner's decisions. As a class, decide which of the Ss has had to make the most difficult decision.

Listening

3a➤ Tell Ss that they are going to listen to three people talking about important decisions they have taken.

➤ Play recording 8.4 and Ss write the name of the speaker and which of the decisions from Ex. 2 the speakers talk about next to their picture. Check the speakers' names and their decisions with the class.

> **Answers:** Photo A: Tunde He talks about leaving his country to go to university in Paris. Photo B: Sarah She talks about selling her house, leaving the country to start her own business in Italy. Photo C: Roger He talks about giving up work and changing his career to start his own business.

b➤ Focus Ss on the phrases 1–9 and give them time to read through them. Check that Ss understand all of the words and expressions in the phrases. Encourage Ss to answer each others' questions if they have any problems or to ask you.

➤ Play recording 8.4 again and Ss mark the phrases (*R*) if Roger says them, (*T*) if Tunde says them and (*S*) if Sarah says them.

➤ Ss compare their answers with their partners.

c➤ Refer Ss to the tapescript on page 174 so that Ss can check their answers.

> **Answers:** 1 R 2 T 3 R 4 S 5 T 6 R 7 S 8 R 9 T

d➤ Ss decide who they think had the most difficult decision to make and why. Ss discuss this with their partners. Get feedback from the whole class.

Grammar

> **OPTIONAL GRAMMAR LEAD-IN**
>
> Refer Ss back to the text in Ex. 2 on page 104. Ask Ss why Yoav Kashida was fined by two policemen. Answer: Because he fell asleep on the metro. On the board write the following jumbled sentence prompt:
> *hadn't If fallen asleep metro, Yoav on the*
> In pairs Ss unjumble and complete the sentence. Get feedback and complete the sentence in the following way: *If Yoav hadn't fallen asleep on the metro, the two policeman wouldn't have fined him.* Ask Ss what type of conditional sentence this is. Elicit/explain that it is a Third Conditional sentence and focus Ss on the form of the conditional: *If* + subject + past perfect + *would(n't) have* + past participle. Tell Ss that the order of the sentence can be inverted and write the following sentence on the board: *The two policemen wouldn't have fined Yoav if he hadn't fallen asleep on the metro.*

4a➤ Ss read the two sentences and answer the questions with their partner. Get feedback from the class.

> **Answers:** 1 No, Roger didn't stay at work. 2 Yes, he did spend time with Jack. 3 Yes, Tunde did come to France. 4 Yes, he did meet Nancy.

b➤ Ss read through the Active grammar box and choose the correct alternative to complete the rule.

> **Active grammar**
>
> Use the Third Conditional to talk about a <u>hypothetical</u> situation in the <u>past</u>.

➤ Refer Ss to Reference page 115 and give them time to read through the notes. Focus Ss on the form of the Third Conditional: *if* + past perfect + *would have* + past participle. Ask **Q: If we want to indicate possibility rather than certainty what do we use instead of *would have*?** *might/could have.* **Q: Is it possible for there to be a present result to the hypothetical past situation?** *Yes.* **Q: How does this change the form of the conditional?** *if* + past perfect + *would* + verb.

5a➤ Tell Ss to cover the sentence endings a–h. Ss read the sentence beginnings 1–8 and think of a natural way of completing the sentences. Ss compare answers with their partners. Check answers with the class and write correct sentences on the board.

➤ Ss uncover the sentence endings and match them with the beginnings. Ss compare their answers with their partners.

> **Answers:** 1 c 2 g 3 e 4 b 5 a 6 h 7 d 8 f

b➤ Play recording 8.5 so that Ss can check their answers.

6➤ Write the example sentences on the board and ask Ss to write a Third Conditional sentence using the sentences on the board as prompts. Ss look at the example sentence in blue to check their answers.

➤ With their partners Ss write Third Conditional sentences for the sentences in the prompts 1–8. Ss compare their answers with another pair. Check the answers with the class.

> **Answers:** 1 If the taxis hadn't been so expensive, we would have taken one. 2 If they had asked someone for directions, they wouldn't have got lost. 3 If the weather had been better, we would have enjoyed the holiday more. 4 If it hadn't been raining, they wouldn't have crashed the car. 5 If I had seen you when you passed me in the street, I would have said 'hello'. 6 If I had been hungry, I would have eaten lunch. 7 If I had known that Eva had to get up early, I would have woken her. 8 If I had liked my History teacher, I wouldn't have given up History.

Pronunciation

7a➤ Focus Ss on the sentence and play recording 8.6. Ss listen and mark the words which are contracted. Check students have heard that *had* and *have* are contracted.

b➤ Play recording 8.6 again and tell Ss to focus on the rhythm of the sentence and listen out for the stressed words.

8a➤ Write the sentence on the board and ask a student to come up and underline the stressed words. *If I'd <u>left</u> home earlier, I <u>would</u>n't've <u>missed</u> the <u>train</u>.* Tell Ss that the stress falls with a regular beat on the sentence. Then practise saying the sentence with individual Ss and then with the whole class.

➤ In pairs Ss read the sentences 1-3 and underline the stressed words. Ss compare their answers with their partners.

b➤ Play recording 8.7 and Ss check the words they have underlined. Ss practise pronouncing the sentences in pairs. Encourage Ss to say them with the same rhythm as on the recording.

➤ Ask a number of Ss to read the sentences aloud for the rest of the class. If they feel confident tell them they can substitute their own phrases, e.g. If I'd known ... *you needed the book today*, I would've ... *brought it in*.

> **Answers:** 1 If I'd <u>known</u> the test was to<u>day</u>, I would've done some re<u>vision</u>. 2 If I'd <u>gone</u> to bed earlier, I <u>would</u>n't 've felt so <u>tired</u>. 3 If you'd <u>asked</u> me out to <u>dinner</u>, I'd've <u>said</u> '<u>yes</u>'.

Speaking

9a➤ Tell Ss to draw two large circles in their notebooks. Tell them to label the circles *Now* and *Ten years ago*. Focus Ss on the questions 1–9 and the 'Now' circle. Ss read the questions and write short answers in the 'Now' circle.

b➤ In pairs Ss change the questions in Ex. 9a to questions in the past. Check the questions Ss have formed with the class.

> **Answers:** 1 Where were you living? 2 Who was your closest friend? 3 What did you do? 4 How did you spend your time? 5 Did you spend much time with your family? 6 Were you studying? 7 Did you play any sports? 8 What music did you enjoy? 9 What were your dreams/ambitions?

➤ Ss write answers to these questions in the 'Ten years ago' circle.

10➤ Ss show their circles to their partners and tell each other how much their lives have changed in the past ten years. Encourage Ss to ask as many follow-up questions as possible.

11➤ Ss discuss the questions 1–3 in groups of three or four. Encourage Ss to use the Third Conditional where relevant. Monitor the conversations and write important errors on the board. Get feedback and then go through the errors, asking Ss to self-correct where possible. Praise Ss for correct use of the Third Conditional.

Writing

12➤ Ss think of an important turning point in their lives and the effect this had on their lives. Give Ss time to write a paragraph to describe this event. Encourage Ss to include the Third Conditional where possible. Go round and help Ss with vocabulary where necessary.

➤ Ss in groups of three or four. Ss read out their paragraphs to the group. Encourage the Ss listening to ask follow-up questions.

➤ Get feedback from the whole class and discuss the turning points that Ss have had in their lives.

Vocabulary: Word building

In this lesson Ss look at ways of building their vocabulary by using prefixes and suffixes. Ss then speak for a minute on a topic.

OPTIONAL WARMER

Write the following adjectives on the board: *honest, faithful, legal, important*. Tell Ss to write the opposites of these words, but that they must use the stems of the words to make the opposites. Get feedback and write the opposites (*dishonest, unfaithful, illegal, unimportant*) on the board. Discuss the use of the prefixes and how we use these particular ones to make words negative.

1➤ Ss look at the examples of the prefixes and with their partners add their own examples to the table. Ss compare the prefixes they have added with another pair.

➤ Get feedback and write the prefixes Ss have added to the table on the board.

2➤ Ss complete the text using prefixes. Ss compare their answers with their partners. Check answers with the class and write the answers on the board.

Answers: 1 over 2 under 3 under 4 dis 5 in
6 in 7 dis 8 im 9 in

3➤ Ss read through the information in the table about suffixes. With their partners Ss add their own examples of suffixes to the table. Ss compare their answers with another pair.

➤ Get feedback and write the suffixes Ss have added to the table to the board.

4➤ Focus Ss on the text. Ss complete the text by adding suffixes to the words in bold. Check answers with the class.

Answers: 1 education 2 employment
3 accommodation 4 treatment 5 punishment
6 importance 7 independence 8 government
9 direction 10 difference

5a➤ Ss choose one of the topics that they feel they can talk about. Ss make notes about the topic. Go round and help Ss as necessary. Ss should use words they have previously formed with prefixes and suffixes where possible. If there is any vocabulary Ss need for their talk, encourage Ss to answer each others' questions.

b➤ Organise Ss into groups of three or four. Each student in the group speaks for about one minute on their topics, referring to their notes as necessary. Encourage the Ss listening to ask follow-up questions.

c➤ Re-organise Ss into new groups of three or four. Ss should not be in the same group as any student they were with in the original groups.

➤ Ss either talk about their original topic again or choose a new topic to talk about.

➤ Get feedback by asking Ss what they have learned about their classmates. Praise Ss for correct use of prefixes and suffixes.

Communication: Time for a change?

In this lesson Ss ask each other questions to find out if they like change or not. Ss then listen to five speakers talking about change.

1➤ Ss discuss with a partner what would be the one thing they would change in their lives if they could. Encourage Ss to ask follow-up questions.

➤ Ss change partners and discuss what they have learned about their previous partners. Get feedback from the whole class.

2a➤ Organise Ss in pairs, A and B. Refer Ss A to the questionnaire on page 114. Refer Ss B to the questionnaire on page 148. Ss add one or two more questions to the questionnaires. Go round to check the questions the Ss write.

➤ Ss ask each other the questions from their questionnaires. Encourage Ss to ask follow-up questions.

b➤ Ss report back to you about the number of questions their partner said 'yes' to.

3a➤ Focus Ss on the questions 1–5 and give them time to read through them.

b➤ Tell Ss they are going to hear five people talking about change. Play recording 8.8 and Ss write the question numbers from Ex.3 of the questions the people answer next to the photos A–E.

Answers: Photo A Question 3 Photo B Question 4
Photo C Question 1 Photo D Question 5
Photo E Question 2

c➤ Ss discuss what they think the speakers have said about change. Ss compare their answers with another pair.

➤ Play recording 8.8 again and Ss check their answers.

d➤ Ss discuss the questions in groups of three or four. Go round and monitor the conversations for errors. Get feedback from the class. Finally, write important errors on the board and discuss them with the class.

OPTIONAL EXTENSION

Write *debate* on the board and ask Ss to tell you what a debate is. If they can't tell you explain quickly how a debate normally works. Divide Ss into two groups A/B.

Group A works together to write down examples of why they think change is good for society. Group B writes down five examples of when society would have been better without change. Refer Ss back to the language in the How to … boxes on pages 106 and 107. Go round and help Ss where necessary.

Ss hold the debate, taking turns to speak about each point they have written. Encourage Ss to use language from the How to … boxes while doing so. Ss continue speaking until they have discussed all the points. Monitor and take note of errors.

The class now votes either for or against the statement: '*Change is a good thing for society*.'

Discuss with the class which group had the best arguments and give feedback, correcting any errors.

Review and practice

1►

> **Answers:** 1 If she had Dave's number, she'd call him.   2 I'd go out if I didn't have an exam tomorrow.   3 If we had enough money at the moment, we'd buy a new car.   4 They'd see the show if there was time.   5 If I had a choice, I'd live in the city.   6 We'd go swimming if the sea wasn't polluted.

2►

> **Answers:** 1 How would you feel if you got the job?   2 Which house would you buy if you had the choice?   3 What will you do if there is a train strike?   4 Where will you go if the hotel is fully booked?   5 How would you celebrate if you passed all your exams?   6 What will you wear if you're invited to the film premiere?

3►

> **Answers:** 1 I usually go to the supermarket on Saturdays.   2 Susana is so busy that I hardly ever see her anymore.   3 Steve normally drives when we go on long journeys.   4 I exercise regularly in the gym.   5 We certainly don't want to damage the relationship.   6 Personally I can't see how we can do it any other way.

4►

> **Answers:** 1 hadn't gone / wouldn't have met   2 had known / wouldn't have gone   3 had decided, wouldn't have worked in   4 hadn't listened to the radio, wouldn't have heard

5►

> **Answers:** 1 had known / would have cooked   2 had left / wouldn't have   3 had told / would have woken   4 had seen / would have been   5 hadn't drunk / would have fallen asleep   6 hadn't lost / would have taken

6►

> **Answers:** 1 subject   2 forbidden   3 pollution   4 environment   5 cure   6 give up   7 standard   8 lifestyle

Notes for using the Common European Framework (CEF)

CEF References

8.1 Can do: talk about cause and result

CEF B2 descriptor: can use a variety of linking words efficiently to mark clearly the relationships between ideas: (CEF page 125)

8.2 Can do: talk about change/lack of change

CEF B2 descriptor: can convey degrees of emotion and highlight the personal significance of events and experiences. (CEF page 76)

8.3 Can do: describe the effects of important decisions

CEF B2 descriptor: can highlight the personal significance of events and experiences, account for and sustain views clearly by providing relevant explanations and arguments. (CEF page 74)

CEF quick brief

The Common European Framework suggests that learners need more than language knowledge to communicate successfully in a language. They also need 'communicative competences' which empower the learner to actually use their knowledge. The How to boxes in Total English are designed to develop communicative competences.

Portfolio task

Download the Total English Portfolio free from www.longman.com/totalenglish.

Objective: to reinforce student autonomy in updating the Portfolio.

This task can be done in Ss' L1.

1► For homework, ask Ss to update the Passport section of their Portfolio. They might like to reassess their abilities in the different skills areas or add to their list of language learning and intercultural experiences.

2► Ask Ss to bring their Passport sections in and show them to other Ss.

Overview

Lead-in	**Vocabulary:** the working environment
9.1	**Grammar:** *make, let, allow*
	Vocabulary: work
	Can do: present ideas to the group
9.2	**Grammar:** reported speech
	Vocabulary: *-ing/-ed* adjectives
	Can do: report information
9.3	**Grammar:** past obligation/permission
	Vocabulary: job requirements
	Can do: state routine job requirements
Vocabulary	UK and US English
Com. Focus	Job advertisements
Reference	
Practice	

Summary

Lesson 1: Ss read a text about how the company Semco works and treats its employees. Ss then go on to speak about how they would set up a new company and treat their employees.

Lesson 2: Ss listen to people talking about their managers at work. Ss then go on to read a story about an engineer and a manager before listening to a job interview.

Lesson 3: Ss read and speak about a text about *Operatunity*, a TV talent show for amateur opera singers. Ss also listen to people talking about their jobs.

Vocabulary: Ss look at differences between UK and US English and write a paragraph using one of these types of English.

Communication: Ss look at different job advertisements and then conduct a job interview for one of the jobs in the advertisements.

Film bank: The ideal workplace (3'54")

A documentary explaining how Richard Sembler has created the ideal workplace at Semco in Brazil.

Richard Sembler has reorganised working life at the company he took over from his father to the advantage of all workers. Workers are now included in decision making processes connected with the work they are doing. They can question why they are doing something to ensure everything is done in the most effective way. The results are a happy and productive workforce as well as an increased annual turnover.

Possible places to use this short film are:
➤ after Lesson 1 to consolidate work vocabulary
➤ after Lesson 2 to consolidate the 'can do' statement
➤ at the end of the unit to round up the topic and language

For ways to use this short film in class, see Student's Book page 159 and Teacher's Book page 186.

Lead-in

OPTIONAL WARMER

Write a list of six jobs that you think Ss will be familiar with on the board. Check that Ss know what all the jobs are by asking various Ss what a person in each job does and what their main responsibilities are.

Organise Ss into pairs. With their partners Ss rank the jobs in order of usefulness to society; 1 being the most useful, 6 being the least useful.

Get feedback and discuss with the class why the jobs are useful for society or not.

1➤ Focus Ss on the jobs in the photos. In pairs Ss discuss if they have ever done any of the jobs shown or if they would like to do these jobs. Get feedback from the whole class.

➤ Ss discuss the questions 1–3 in groups of three or four. Get feedback from various groups.

2a➤ Ss in groups of three or four. Ss read the questions 1–12 and work out the meaning of the words in bold.

➤ Check that Ss understand the meaning of the words in bold. If there are any words or phrases that Ss don't know, encourage them to answer each others' questions within their groups or to use their dictionaries before giving an explanation yourself.

➤ Check the meaning of the words in bold with the class by asking various Ss to explain the words and phrases to the rest of the class. Ask Ss to provide one or two examples of how they would use them.

b➤ Ss pair off with a student from another group and ask and answer the questions.

➤ Encourage Ss to ask follow-up questions as this will push the speaker to develop more detailed ideas.

➤ Go round the class monitoring their coversations and making a note of any errors.

➤ After a few minutes, tell Ss to stop, change partners and repeat the exercise. Do this a number of times.

➤ Eventually Ss go back to their orginial partner and tell each other who had the most similar opinions to them.

➤ Get feedback from the whole class. Finally, write any important errors on the board and ask Ss to identify and correct the errors.

EXTEND THE LEAD-IN

Organise Ss into pairs, A and B. Student A chooses a word or expression in bold from Ex. 2a and defines it for Student B without mentioning the word or expression. Student B guesses which expression is being defined. Student B then defines a word or expression for Student A to guess. Ss continue taking turns to define the words and expressions until they have all been defined.

9.1 Democracy at work

Semco is a company which sells parts for ships. The company is organised differently from the majority of businesses. Unnecessary jobs were cut by the company boss, Ricardo Semler, with the result that even top managers do photocopying and dial the phones. Uniforms have been relaxed and employees work flexible hours. This new way of operating has proved successful for Semco.

In this lesson Ss read a text about the way Semco is run. Through this context Ss look at the grammar of *make*, *let* and *allow*. Ss then work in groups and discuss how they would set up a company. Ss then report back to the rest of the class about how their company would be run.

> **OPTIONAL WARMER**
> Ss think of a job they have done, or a job that someone they know does/has done. Ss think of the type of rules that someone doing that job has to comply with. Write the following prompts on the board to help: *timetable*, *dress*, *breaks*, *salary*, *bonuses*, *holidays*. Ss tell their partner about this job and the rules associated with it.
> In pairs Ss decide if these rules are good ones or not, and if not, how they could be changed. Get feedback and discuss how necessary rules are in different jobs.

Speaking

1a➤ Focus Ss on the quotes. Ss read the quotes and mark them (*A*) if they agree with them, (*D*) if they disagree and (*M*) if they are not sure if they agree or not.

b➤ Ss Compare their ideas with other Ss in the group. Get feedback and discuss the quotes as a class.

> **OPTIONAL VARIATION**
> Organise Ss into pairs, A and B. Tell Ss that they must not agree with their partners. Ss read the quotes. Ss A tell Ss B what they think of the first quote. Ss B must disagree and give reasons, trying to convince Ss A of their point of view. After a few minutes Ss change roles so that Ss B gives their opinion about the second quote and Ss A disagree with this opinion. Ss continue taking turns until they have discussed all the quotes.

Reading

2➤ Focus Ss on the list of tasks in the box. Check that Ss understand all of the words and phrases. If there are any words or phrases that Ss don't understand, encourage other Ss to explain them before explaining them yourself.

➤ Ss decide who normally does these tasks in a company. Ss share their ideas with their partners. Get feedback from the whole class and write the workers Ss suggest on the board.

> **Suggested answers:** wear uniforms: *policemen/hotel staff* meet guests in reception: *receptionist* decide start/finishing times/working hours: *managers* set salaries: *managers* fix equipment: *maintenance staff* do the photocopying: *secretary/PA*

3a➤ Ss read the introduction and answer the questions with their partners. Check the answers with the class.

> **Answers:** Ricardo Semler is the boss of his father's business Semco, which sells parts for ships. He had a medical problem because he was working too hard.

b➤ In pairs Ss discuss what changes they think Semler made to the way the business was run. Get feedback from the pairs.

➤ Ss read the rest of the text to find out what changes Semler made to the company. Tell Ss not to worry about any words or expressions they don't understand at this stage. Give Ss time to compare their answers with their partners.

4➤ In pairs Ss discuss the questions 1–6. Ss compare their answers with another pair. Check the answers with the class.

> **Answers:** 1 Employees set their own salaries, meet guests in reception, do the photocopying, send faxes, type letters, dial the phone and even fix equipment.
> 2 Semco has plants instead of walls, staff can decorate their own workspace so it looks different, and some of the staff wear uniforms while others wear T-shirts.
> 3 Rubin Agater is a sales manager at Semco. He is important because he knows how to fix oil pumps.
> 4 Workers can decide their own work hours and use Semco machinery. 5 Yes. Profits have increased and the company is growing. 6 Peer pressure is the strong feeling that you must do the same things as the other people around you. It is important because this is what makes people work hard at Semco.

➤ Ask Ss if there are any words or phrases that they don't understand. Encourage Ss to answer each others' questions or to use a dictionary before explaining them yourself.

5➤ Ss discuss the questions 1–3 in groups of three or four. Get feedback from the whole class.

Grammar

> **OPTIONAL GRAMMAR LEAD-IN**
> Write three sentences on the board using *make*, *let* and *allow* about what you think Ss in a language class should be expected to do. Ss discuss the sentences and decide if they think they are reasonable things for Ss to do. In pairs Ss discuss the use of *make*, *let* and *allow*.

6a➤ Ss read the example sentences a–c and complete the Active grammar box with *make*, *let* or *allow*. Ss compare their answers with their partners. Check answers with the class.

> **Active grammar**
> **Meaning**
> *Let* and *allow* mean give permission to do something.
> *Make* means force to do something
> **Form**
> *make* + person + verb (force to do)
> *let* + person + verb (give permission to do)
> *allow* + person + *to* + verb (give permission to do)
> **Use**
> Don't use *let* in the passive.

b➤ In pairs Ss find other examples of *make, let* and allow in the text.

➤ Refer Ss to Reference page 129. Give Ss time to read through the notes. Ask: **Q: what verb do we use to talk about obligation imposed by another person or a set of rules?** *make*. **Q: What do we use to talk about permission?** *let* and *allowed to*. Draw Ss' attention to the word order used with these verbs.

7➤ Ss correct the sentences 1–8 then compare their answers with their partners. Check answers with the class.

> **Answers:** 1 We're not allowed to smoke here. 2 Did you let her use my pen? 3 I made her do the washing-up. 4 He isn't allowed to leave the building. 5 My dad doesn't let me use his car. 6 The Customs Officer made me take off my shoes. 7 You're allowed to keep pets in these flats. 8 Did your teacher make you do the exam?

8➤ With their partners Ss complete the sentences with *make, let* or *(not) allowed(ed)*. Ss compare their answers with another pair. Check answers with the group.

> **Answers:** 1 let 2 allowed 3 made 4 made 5 let 6 make 7 not allowed 8 let

OPTIONAL EXTENSION
In pairs Ss discuss what they think English teachers are *let, made* and *allowed* to do. With their partners Ss make a list of these things. Ss compare their lists with another pair. Get feedback and tell the class whether their ideas are true (at least for you). Ss decide if these rules are good ones for teachers to follow.

Person to person

9➤ Ss read the statements 1–4 and decide if they agree with them and why/why not. Ss share their ideas in groups of three or four. Go around the class monitoring the conversations for correct use of *make, let* and *allow*. Make note of any errors.

➤ Get feedback about the statements, and then go through the errors with the whole class, encouraging Ss to self-correct before explaining yourself.

Listening and speaking

10a➤ Give Ss time to read through the questions 1–6. Play recording 9.1 and Ss answer the questions. Check answers with the whole class.

> **Answers:** 1 a restaurant 2 It will serve food from all over the world. 3 The chefs can chose the dishes. 4 nine; three chefs and six waiters 5 They will be able to eat for free in the restaurant. 6 World Food

b➤ Play recording 9.1. Ss take note of the phrases the speaker uses to start and finish her talk. Ss compare the phrases they have written with their partner. Check the phrases with the group.

> **Answers:** Good afternoon everybody. I'd like to tell you about … Our main idea is … The most important thing for us is … To sum up, … Thank you for listening. Are there any questions?

11➤ Ss read through the How to … box and put the phrases and sentences in the correct places. Elicit answers.

> **Answers:** 1 Good afternoon. 2 The most important thing for us is … 3 To sum up, … 4 Are there any questions?

12a➤ Ss in groups of three or four. Tell Ss they are going to set up a new company in their groups. Focus Ss on the four areas. Ss discuss these areas and decide what type of company it is. Go round and help where necessary.

b➤ When Ss have decided on the type of company they should think of how the company is going to treat its employees. Groups discuss the questions and add any extra details about how they want the employees to be treated.

13a➤ Each group fills in the profile about their company. Encourage Ss to answer each others' questions if they have any problems with vocabulary. Go round the class and check what each group is writing and correct errors where necessary.

Lifelong learning

➤ Focus Ss on the Lifelong learning box. Read through the suggestion with the class and discuss the usefulness of this advice. Point out that being well-prepared can make you sound and feel more confident.

b➤ Ss plan their presentations using the advice from the Lifelong learning box. Encourage Ss to use the expressions from the How to … box while preparing their presentations.

➤ Each group presents their ideas about their companies they prepared in Ex. 13a to the rest of the class. Tell the Ss listening to each group that they are the future employees of the company presenting itself. Encourage the Ss listening to the presentations to make notes about the companies and to ask questions.

➤ When all the companies have spoken, Ss decide which company would be the best to work for and why. Get feedback from the class.

OPTIONAL EXTENSION
Divide the class into two groups, representatives of companies who are looking for new employees and people looking for a job. Ss representing the companies can use the information they prepared in Ex. 13a. Give the Ss looking for a job time to prepare the interview situation. In the meantime the company representatives can prepare questions they want to ask in the interview. Pair Ss off so that there is one person looking for a job talking to each company. Ss conduct the interview for a specified time, e.g. five minutes. After this time Ss swap so that the people looking for a job are talking to another company. Continue until all the people looking for a job have talked to all the different companies. The companies can then tell the rest of the class who they would like to employ and why.

9.2 Good boss, bad boss

In this lesson Ss listen to people talking about their managers. Through this context Ss then look at -ing and -ed adjectives. Ss go on to read a story about a manager and an engineer. Ss use this context to analyse and practise the grammar of reported speech. Ss then listen to a job interview where someone is being interviewed for the post of manager. Ss then interview their partners to find out if they would make good managers.

> **OPTIONAL WARMER**
>
> Write the following sentences on the board: *Being a boss is easy. You just tell others what to do.* In pairs Ss discuss the sentences and decide whether they agree or disagree and why. Get feedback from various pairs.

Listening and speaking

1a➤ With their partners Ss discuss what type of boss the cartoon represents and if they have ever known a boss like the one depicted. Get feedback from various pairs.

b➤ Ss write down three things they think a good boss does and three things a bad boss does. Ss share their ideas with other Ss in the class, explaining why these things are good or bad things for a boss to do. Get feedback from the class.

2a➤ Play recording 9.2 and Ss listen to the four people talking about their managers and make notes in the table.

b➤ Ss compare their notes with their partners. Check answers with the whole class.

> **Answers:**
>
> | | Are they happy with their boss? | Why/Why not? |
> | --- | --- | --- |
> | Speaker 1 | no | She is annoying – gives you work at the end of the day |
> | Speaker 2 | yes | She's a great boss – very understanding – sent flowers and sent him home for the day |
> | Speaker 3 | no | He's aggressive – he shouts and throws things around the office – very frightening |
> | Speaker 4 | yes | He has lots of energy and enthusiasm – he has new ideas – work never boring |

3a➤ Give Ss time to read through the sentences 1–4. Play recording 9.2 again and Ss choose the correct words to complete the sentences. Give Ss time to compare their answers with their partners.

b➤ Refer Ss to the tapescript on page 175 to check their answers. Elicit answers from the class.

> **Answers:** 1 angry / annoying 2 listens and understands his feelings / understanding 3 scared / frightening 4 interesting and fun / exciting

Vocabulary

4➤ Focus Ss on the example sentences. In pairs Ss discuss the difference between the two forms of the adjectives.

➤ Ss read the rules and complete them by choosing the correct alternative.

> **Answers:** 1 We use -ed adjectives to talk about feelings. 2 We use -ing adjectives to talk about the situations that caused the feelings.

5➤ In pairs Ss read through the sentences 1-9 and choose the correct adjective. Ss compare their answers with another pair. Check answers with the whole class.

> **Answers:** 1 excited 2 exhausted 3 boring 4 frightening 5 tiring 6 depressing 7 frightened 8 relaxing 9 confusing

6➤ Write the following question words on the board: *Why? When? How long? Where? What? How often?*

➤ Ss read through the questions 1–5. Ss then discuss the questions with a partner. Encourage Ss to ask each follow-up questions, using the question words on the board as prompts. Monitor the conversations making note of any errors.

➤ When Ss have finished get feedback from the class. Finally, write any important errors you have heard on the board and ask Ss to identify and correct the errors and correct them.

> **OPTIONAL VARIATION**
>
> Ss write the answers to the questions 1–5 in a different order to the questions. Ss exchange their answers with their partners. Students guess what their partner's answers refer to: *'Do you find shopping annoying?' 'No, actually I find it relaxing because …'.* Encourage Ss to ask each other follow-up questions.

Reading

7a➤ Focus Ss on the words and phrases. With their partners Ss predict what they think the story is about, using the words and phrases to help. Ss share their answers with another pair. Get feedback from the class and decide which pair has the most likely prediction.

b➤ Ss read the story to check their predictions. Tell Ss to underline any words or expressions in the text they don't understand.

c➤ Ss discuss the questions in groups of three or four. Get feedback from the class.

➤ Ask Ss if there any words or expressions in the story they don't understand. Encourage Ss to help each other in their groups or to use their dictionaries before explaining the words and phrases yourself.

Grammar

> **OPTIONAL GRAMMAR LEAD-IN**
>
> Tell Ss to think back to Ex. 6. Give Ss time to remember and write down what their partners found confusing. On the board write *He/she said …, He/She told me …* Ask Ss to tell you what their partners said using the prompts on the board. When reporting what their partners said monitor for correct use of reported speech and write any correct examples on the board. In pairs Ss look at the examples of reported speech and discuss how we normally report things in English. Get feedback.

8➤ Ss match the sentences 1–3 with what the people actually said, a–c. Check answers with the class.

Answers: 1 b   2 c   3 a

9➤ Ss read through the Active grammar box and complete it with their partners. Get feedback and check Ss' answers.

> **Active grammar**
> He said he _would_ help me.
> She told me Carly _was_ in a meeting.
> He said he _was_ going to meet Marc.
> He told me Tom _had been_ late every day.

➤ Refer Ss to Reference page 129. Give Ss a few minutes to read through the notes. Ask: **Q: What does _will_ change to in reported speech?** would. **Q: What does Present Continuous change to?** Past Continuous. **Q: What do Present Perfect and Past Simple change to?** Past Perfect. **Q: Do time references and pronouns change in reported speech?** Yes. **Q: If what the person said is still true, do we have to shift the tense back?** No. Focus Ss on the pronoun changes and on the verb patterns for _say/tell/ask_ and the Yes/No questions.

10➤ In pairs Ss complete the sentences with the correct form of _say_ or _tell_. Check answers with the whole class.

Answers: 1 tell   2 tell   3 said   4 told   5 say
6 Tell, said   7 said   8 told

11➤ Focus Ss on the dialogues 1–8. Ss report the dialogues with their partners, then compare their answers with another pair. Check answers with the whole class.

Answers: 1 He said (that) he was the new technician.   2 Mum said (that) she would be back the next day/tomorrow.   3 Mara told us (that) she had been stuck in traffic.   4 She said (that) he wouldn't be away for long.   5 He said (that) he would carry our bags for us / my bag for me.   6 He told me (that) they were going on holiday the following week.   7 He told us (that) he had been shopping yesterday/the day before.   8 She told him (that) she was feeling better.

Listening

12a➤ Ss read the sentences 1–3. Play recording 9.3. Ss listen and choose the correct options. Elicit answers.

Answers: 1 c   2 a   3 b   4 a   5 b

b➤ Ss put the words into the correct order to form questions from the interview. Check answers with the class.

Answers: 1 Are you good at listening to people?
2 Can you usually find solutions to difficult problems?
3 What do you think are your strengths and weaknesses?   4 Do you work well under pressure?
5 Do you like working on your own?

c➤ Ss match the questions 1–5 with the reported questions a–e. Ss then complete the reported questions. Check answers with the whole class.

Answers: 1 d own   2 c   3 b   4 e   5 a
a own   b strengths / weaknesses   c solutions / difficult problems   d listening to people   e pressure

d➤ Play recording 9.3 again and Ss write down what Mr Wilkins replied. Check answers with the whole class.

Answers: 1 He said he thought so. People liked telling him about their problems and asked him for advice.   2 He said he couldn't always find solutions to problems. He usually asked other people for their ideas.   3 He said that his strengths were that he worked hard and he was good with people. His weakness was that he was disorganised and late for meetings.   4 He said that he worked well under pressure because he was calm and didn't panic, and he was happy to work all night, or early in the morning to get a job finished.   5 He said he enjoyed working with people, but that he could also work on his own.

Listening

13➤ In pairs Ss read and complete the Active grammar box. Check answers with the class.

> **Active grammar**
> We use _if_ or _whether_ to report _Yes/No questions_.
> '_Do_ you like working in an office?'
> '_What_ is your name?'

➤ Give Ss time to read through the Reference page 129. Draw Ss' attention to the pronoun and time/place reference changes as well as the word order for reported questions.

14➤ Ss write questions 1–6 in reported speech. Check answers with the class.

Answers: 1 She asked me if I was good at organising people.   2 She asked me if I enjoyed working in a team.   3 She asked me what I do when my ideas don't work.   4 She asked me whether I listened to other people's advice/suggestions.   5 She asked me what I did (do) when I have too much work.   6 She asked me what time I normally start work.

15➤ In pairs Ss correct the sentences that contain mistakes. Check the answers with the whole class.

Answers: 1 Anna **told** me that she would be back by five o'clock.   2 Correct   3 My brother asked **me** to wait for him at the station.   4 The driver **said** he was feeling sick.   5 Correct   6 Her husband **told** her that she could use his credit card.

Person to person

16a➤ Ss write five questions to ask their partners to find out if he/she would make a good manager.

b➤ Ss interview their partners, then report back to the class. When reporting back to the class, encourage Ss to use reported speech and questions.

9.3 New on the job

TV talent shows like *Pop Idol* have become everyxtremely popular over the last few years. This type of programme is a competition to find the best singer from a group of people who normally have little or no singing experience. The winners are often offered singing contracts and become famous stars. One of these programmes, *Operatunity*, offers amateur opera singers the chance to sing in competition. In 2002 the winners of *Operatunity* ended up singing at the Coliseum in Rome.

In this lesson Ss read about the TV talent show *Operatunity*. Through this context Ss look at the grammar of past obligation and permission. Ss go on to look at the vocabulary connected with job requirements and listen to people talking about their jobs. Finally, Ss describe a job and write a job description.

> **OPTIONAL WARMER**
>
> Write *opera* on the board. In pairs Ss note down anything they know about opera; the names of famous operas, singers, opera houses, musicians, etc. Get feedback from the class and write ideas on the board.

Reading and speaking

1➤ Ss discuss the questions in pairs. Get feedback.

2➤ Ss read the text quickly and answer the questions. Tell Ss not to worry if there are any words or expressions they don't understand in the text as you will be looking at them later. Check answers with the group.

> **Answers:** 1 Jane and Denise's dream was to be opera singers. 2 They achieved their dreams by participating in the TV talent show *Operatunity*. 3 Denise found waiting for the results difficult. They both found the travelling and childcare arrangements difficult as well as learning to deal with the media.

3a➤ Ss read through the text more carefully and match the headings with paragraphs a–e. Encourage Ss to underline the parts of the text that helped them choose the right heading. Check answers with the whole class.

> **Answers:** a The competition   b Their lives before
> c Living the new life   d The difficult parts   e Advice

b➤ In pairs Ss summarise each paragraph in the text in just one sentence. Ss compare their answers with another pairs. Get feedback and write interesting sentences on the board.

> **Answers:** a Denise Leigh and Jane Gilchrist entered a TV talent show called *Operatunity*, and changed from being working mothers to being opera celebrities.
> b Before their lives revolved around their families, but *Operatunity* gave them new possibilities including singing a Verdi opera at the Coliseum in Rome.
> c They have had a wonderful year recording and being 'treated like princesses'.   d They found travelling difficult, and had to learn to deal with the media.
> e Their advice to people is to try and live your dream.

4➤ Ss read the text again more carefully and find and correct the eight mistakes in the summary. Elicit answers.

> **Answers:** Jane and Denise won a **opera** singing competition on **TV**, even though Denise is blind. The competition gave them the opportunity to sing **Verdi's *Rigoletto* at the Coliseum in Rome**, and it changed their lives forever. Although they both are housewives with families – Denise has three children, and Jane has **four** – they now get the chance to travel and see the world, singing. Their new lives **have** been very exciting, and they have been treated very well. They found the travelling **difficult** because **of childcare**. They would recommend the experience to other singers, and say that if your dream is to sing, you should **try it**.

➤ Ask Ss if there are any words or expressions in the text they don't understand. Encourage Ss to answer each others' questions before explaining them yourself.

5➤ Ss discuss the question with a partner. Get feedback and discuss the questions with the whole class.

Grammar

> **OPTIONAL GRAMMAR LEAD-IN**
>
> Write six sentences on the board about when you were a child and your life at home using *had to, didn't have to, was allowed to, could, not allowed to, couldn't*. Ss discuss the sentences and decide if these were good rules for a child to follow and why/why not. Ss now write their own sentences about when they were younger using the verbs. Ss share this information with the rest of the class.

6a➤ Ss complete the rules in the Active grammar box with their partners. Check answers with the class.

> **Active grammar**
> 1 The past of *must* is <u>had to</u>.
> 2 The past of *mustn't* is <u>wasn't/weren't allowed to</u>.
> 3 *Could/couldn't* are followed by the infinitive <u>without</u> *to*.
> 4 *Had to/didn't have to* and *was(n't)/were(n't) allowed to* are followed by <u>the infinitive without *to*</u>

b➤ Focus Ss on the example sentences in the Active grammar box. Play recording 9.4. Tell Ss to pay attention to the pronunciation of the modal verbs.

➤ Ss practise saying the sentences in pairs. Ask various Ss to repeat the sentences for the class.

➤ Ask Ss to read through the Reference page 129. Check that Ss understand that *had to* is used for past obligation and *didn't have to* is used for no obligation in the past. Explain that *could* and *was/were allowed to* are used to describe things which were permitted in the past, and that *wasn't/weren't allowed to* and *couldn't* are used to describe things that were not permitted or OK in the past.

c➤ In pairs Ss discuss the meaning of sentences 1–3 and decide if there are any differences between them. Get feedback from the group.

Answers: 1 a and c have similar meaning (it was permitted) b means that they were obliged to sing. 2 a, b and c have different meanings; a We could watch TV. (it was permitted), b We had to watch TV. (it was necessary), c We weren't allowed to watch TV. (it was not permitted) 3 a, b and c have different meanings; a I wasn't allowed to study. (it wasn't permitted), b I didn't have to study. (it wasn't necessary), c I had to study. (it was necessary)

7➤ Refer students to the sentences 1–8. In pairs Ss complete the sentences with modal verbs from the Active grammar box. Check answers with the whole class.

Answers: 1 had to 2 weren't allowed 3 were allowed to 4 didn't have to 5 weren't allowed to, had to 6 had to 7 allowed to 8 didn't have to

8a➤ Ss correct the mistakes in the sentences 1–8. Check the answers with the group.

Answers: 1 I **wasn't allowed** to stay out late. 2 We **could eat** chocolate all day long. 3 **Were** you allowed to buy new clothes? 4 We **weren't** allowed to watch television. 5 I **couldn't use** the telephone, because it was too expensive. 6 We always **had** to finish the food on our plates. 7 We didn't **have** to help with the housework. 8 We had to **practise** very hard.

b➤ Ss talk to their partners and discuss if the sentences were true for them as a child. Get feedback.

Person to person

9➤ Ss in groups of three or four. Ss discuss the questions in their groups. Monitor the conversations for correct use of language of past obligation and permission.

➤ Get feedback from various groups. Write any important errors Ss have made and any correct or interesting language used by the Ss on the board and discuss them with the class.

Vocabulary

10a➤ Focus Ss on the words and phrases in the box. In pairs Ss discuss if they know the meaning of any of them.

➤ Ss match the words and phrases in the box with the meanings. Elicit the answers from various Ss.

Answers: 1 organising 2 delegating 3 prioritising 4 persuading people 5 dealing with people 6 solving problems

b➤ In pairs Ss read the sentences 1–6 and complete them using the words and phrases from the box. Tell Ss there may be more than one option. Check the answers with the class.

Suggested answers: 1 speak more than one language 2 use a range of computer software 3 give good presentations 4 work accurately 5 work under pressure 6 work irregular hours

c➤ Play recording 9.5. Ss listen and check their answers.

Listening

11a➤ Ss look at the photos of the different jobs and answer the questions in pairs. Get feedback from various pairs.

b➤ Tell Ss they are going to hear the people talking about their jobs. Play recording 9.6 and Ss match the speaker with the photos in the order they hear them and answer questions 1 and 2. Check answers with the class.

Answers:
1 D Air hostess; She still does the job now. She says she has to be good at dealing with people. When people have arguments she needs to be able to listen to people and solve their problems. She also needs to persuade people to do things they don't want to do.
2 A Office manager; She did the job in the past. She needed to prioritise and delegate. She worked under a lot of pressure and worked irregular hours. It was useful to be able to type fast, and she used a range of computer software.
3 C Medical scientist; He did this job in the past. He had to be able to work accurately, and be good with figures. Nowadays they use a lot of computer software to help solve problems.
4 B Bus driver; He does the job now. He says he needs to be able to drive well, and be patient. He has to be good at dealing with people who get angry, and he works irregular hours.

12➤ Focus Ss on the expressions in Ex. 10. Play recording 9.6 again and Ss write the number of the speaker 1–4 next to each expression. Check answers with the whole class.

Answers: dealing with people Speaker 1 solving problems Speaker 1, 3 listening to people Speaker 1 persuading people Speaker 1 languages Speaker 1 delegating Speaker 2 prioritising Speaker 2 work accurately Speaker 3 work irregular hours Speaker 2, 4 speak more than one language Speaker 1 type fast Speaker 2 drive well Speaker 4 use a range of computer software Speaker3

13a➤ Ss think about the other Ss in the class and decide who would fit the characteristics mentioned.

b➤ Ss stand up and mingle and ask questions to see if their guesses were correct. Encourage Ss to ask follow-up questions.

Speaking

14a➤ Ss choose one of the situations. Give Ss time to make notes about the situation they choose. Go round and help as necessary.

b➤ Ss describe the jobs to a partner. Go around the class monitoring the conversations and taking note of any errors.

➤ Get feedback from the class and discuss which of the jobs sounds interesting. Write errors on the board and invite Ss to come up and correct them and write the correct version. Finally, read out any language that Ss have used correctly and praise the Ss for this.

Vocabulary: UK and US English

In this lesson Ss look at some examples of the differences between UK and US English and practise using these varieties of English.

OPTIONAL WARMER

Draw two columns on the board and write *UK* at the top of one and *US* at the top of the other. Divide Ss into two groups. Each group notes down words they associate with one of the countries. Get feedback and write Ss' ideas on the board in the relevant column.

1➤ Ss look at the pictures and discuss with their partner if they know the name of the things in the pictures in US English. Get feedback and write correct ideas on the board.

2➤ Ss match the words in bold in the sentences 1–15 with their US equivalent in the box. Check answers with the group.

Answers: 1 cell phone 2 check 3 fries 4 mail
5 gas 6 freeway 7 mall 8 apartment
9 high school 10 round trip 11 subway
12 soccer 13 movie 14 vacation 15 restroom

3a➤ In pairs Ss read the sentences 1–10 and decide in each sentence if the speaker is using US or UK English. Ss then choose a word from Ex. 2 to complete the sentences.

b➤ Play recording 9.7 and Ss check their answers. Elicit answers from the whole class.

Answers: 1 high school (US) 2 bill (UK)
3 return ticket (UK) 4 freeway (US) 5 flat (UK)
6 cell phone (US) 7 movie (US) 8 subway (US)
9 restroom (US) 10 chips (UK)

4a➤ Ask Ss if they know of any differences between UK and US spelling. Get feedback then focus Ss on the table.

b➤ Tell Ss to write the words in the table in US English. Check answers and write the words with the US spelling on the board.

Answers: neighbor criticize humor
summarized theatre prioritize flavour
realized meter

5a➤ In groups of three or four Ss choose a title they would like to write a paragraph about.

➤ Divide the class into two groups, A and B. Tell group As to use as many US words seen in Exs. 2 and 4 as possible when writing their paragraphs. Tell group Bs to use as many UK words seen in Exs. 2 and 4 as possible. Go round and help Ss with their writing if necessary.

b➤ Ss exchange paragraphs so that each group A is reading a paragraph from group B and vice versa. Group As find all the examples of UK words and spellings and write these in US English. Group Bs find the examples of US words and spellings and write them in UK English.

➤ Get feedback from the whole class and check the words Ss have written.

Communication: Job advertisements

In this lesson Ss look at different job advertisements and role play a job interview.

OPTIONAL WARMER

Write the jobs from the advertisements on the board: gra*phic designer, news editor, bar/restaurant staff, tour guide, marketing manager*. Check that Ss know what the jobs are by asking Ss what people do in these jobs. Ss then discuss what characteristics a person would have to have when doing these jobs. With their partners Ss then rank the jobs in order of preference. Get feedback from various pairs.

1➤ Give Ss a few minutes to read through the five job advertisements. Tell Ss to underline any vocabulary they don't understand.

➤ Ask Ss if there are any words which they have underlined in the text. Encourage Ss to explain the words to each other if they can before using a dictionary. Check whether there are any remaining problems with new words and explain them yourself.

➤ Ss decide which of the jobs they would most like to apply for and why. Get feedback from the group then pair Ss so they are working with another student who chose the same job.

➤ With their partners Ss write a list of questions they think they could be expected to answer in a job interview. Go round and help with the questions where necessary.

2➤ With their partners Ss prepare the answers to the questions they wrote. Encourage Ss to use vocabulary seen in the unit where relevant.

3➤ Re-pair Ss so they are working with a student from another pair. Tell Ss they are going to be interviewing each other for the job they have chosen to apply for. Ss prepare a list of questions they could ask in an interview for that job.

➤ Ss perform the interviews. Go round and monitor for errors and also for correct use of vocabulary and expressions.

4➤ Get feedback from the whole class and discuss how the interviews went and if the Ss feel they would get the jobs and why/why not.

➤ Finally, write any important errors on the board and encourage Ss to correct them. Also write up any examples of language that Ss have used well and praise the Ss for using this language.

OPTIONAL EXTENSION

Ss work with another student who was interviewed for the same job. With their partners Ss make a list of tasks they think they would have to do on their first day in this job. Get feedback from the class and discuss who would have the hardest first day at work.

Review and practice

1➤

Answers: 1 let 2 make 3 are 4 made
5 don't 6 lets 7 them

2➤

Answers: 1 Jim said he had just started at
Manchester University. 2 Jim told me he was
studying Engineering. 3 Jim told me he had made
lots of new friends. 4 Jim told me that they were
going to the Lake District at the/that weekend.
5 Jim said he would call me the next/following day.
6 Jim said he had gone to a brilliant lecture that
morning. 7 Jim told me he lived in a flat with three
other students. 8 Jim said they were having a party
that/last night.

3➤

Answers: 1 She asked where the post office was.
2 He asked where he could change some money.
3 She asked if/whether I had been there before.
4 He asked me what time the meeting finished that
morning. 5 She asked if I would look after the plants
for her. 6 They asked if we had gone to the cinema
the previous night. 7 She asked what time I/we had
arrived. 8 He asked if I was meeting anyone there.

4➤

Answers: 1 couldn't 2 had to 3 weren't
allowed 4 had to 5 didn't have to
6 could 7 were allowed

5➤

Answers: 1 confused 2 deal with 3 tiring
4 delegate 5 receptionist 6 persuaded
7 annoying 8 irregular

Notes for using the Common European Framework (CEF)

CEF References

9.1 Can do: present ideas to the group

CEF B1 descriptor: can give a prepared straightforward
presentation on a familiar topic within his/her field which
is clear enough to be followed without difficulty most of
the time, and in which the main points are explained with
reasonable precision. Can take follow up questions, but
may have to ask for repetition if the speech was rapid.
(CEF page 60)

9.2 Can do: report information

CEF B2 descriptor: can synthesise and report information
and arguments from a number of sources. (CEF page 81)

9.3 Can do: state routine job requirements

CEF B1 descriptor: can give straightforward descriptions
on a variety of familiar subjects within his/her field of
interest. (CEF page 59)

CEF quick brief

There are hundreds of Can do statements in the Common
European Framework, which can make it difficult for
a learner to assess their level. To simplify matters The
CEF contains a 'self-assessment grid' containing brief
descriptions of what a learner Can do at each of the six
major levels. This grid is in the Total English Portfolio.

Portfolio task

*Download the Total English Portfolio free from
www.longman.com/totalenglish.*

Objective: to reinforce student autonomy in updating the
Portfolio.

This task can be done in Ss' own language.

1➤ For homework, ask Ss to update the Biography
section of their Portfolio. They might like to reassess their
language learning aims, history or significant experiences.
They might also like to go over the Can do statements
again and tick the new objectives at B1 and B2 level that
they can now achieve.

2➤ Ask Ss to bring their Biography sections in and show
them to other Ss.

10 Memories

Overview

Lead-in	**Vocabulary:** memories
10.1	**Grammar:** *I wish/if only*
	Vocabulary: memory
	Can do: talk about wishes
10.2	**Grammar:** review of past tenses
	Vocabulary: biographies
	Can do: say different types of numbers
10.3	**Grammar:** phrasal verbs
	Vocabulary: common phrasal verbs
	Can do: write a thank you letter
Vocabulary	The senses
Com. Focus	The memory game
Reference	
Practice	

Summary

Lesson 1: Ss read three stories about memory. They then go on to listen to two people talking about things they remember or forget. Ss then speak about skills they wish they had. Finally, Ss read and listen to a poem by Robert Frost.

Lesson 2: Ss listen to information about women who have helped shape the 20th century. Ss then read about the life of Coco Chanel.

Lesson 3: Ss read about how different companies fire their staff. Ss then listen to the song *Leaving on a jet plane*.

Vocabulary: Ss look at vocabulary connected with the senses then write a poem about the senses.

Communication: First of all Ss read the instructions to a memory game. Ss then play the game with their partners.

Film bank: Icons (3'37")

A documentary about three famous icons, Frida Kahlo, Rosa Parks and Marilyn Monroe

There are three separate extracts depicting the three icons' lives. In spite of her physical disabilities Frida Kahlo lived a full eventful artistic life and produced very original paintings. Rosa Parks is remembered for her opposition to segregation on the buses in Montgomery, USA and is known as the mother of the Civil Rights Movement. Marilyn Monroe is remembered as a female screen legend of the twentieth century. Despite being successful on screen, she didn't have a very happy life and died in mysterious circumstances.

Possible places to use this short film are:
➤ after Lesson 2 to extend vocabulary topic of biographies

➤ at the end of the unit to round up the topic and language

For ways to use this short film in class, see Student's Book page 160 and Teacher's Book page 187.

Lead-in

OPTIONAL WARMER

Tell Ss about one of your own earliest childhood memories in detail. Encourage Ss to ask you follow-up questions about the memory. Ss then tell their partners about one of their earliest childhood memories. Again encourage Ss to ask each other follow-up questions. Get feedback from the the class and decide as a group who had the most vivid childhood memory.

1a➤ Draw Ss' attention to the photos. With their partners Ss discuss the photos and decide where they are or what they represent. Get feedback from the whole class.

➤ Ss choose the correct word to complete the sentences. Check answers with various Ss.

Answers: 1 forget 2 remind us of
3 remember 4 in memory of

b➤ Ss match the sentences to the photos. Ss compare their answers with their partners. Check answers with the class.

Answers: Main photo 4 top photo 1
middle photo 3 bottom photo 2

c➤ In a monolingual class Ss discuss the questions and then tell you about the memorials in their country. In a multilingual class pair the Ss so they are working with a student of a different nationality. Ss tell each other about memorials in their countries.

2a➤ In pairs Ss discuss the differences between the pairs of words. Check the answers with the group.

Answers: a lose *not be able to find something /*
forget *not be able to remember something* b remind
me to *followed by a verb /* remind me of *followed by
a noun* c remember *think of something from the past
/* remind *tell someone something they need to do OR
make you think of something from the past*

b➤ Ss write six sentences, each using a different word or phrase. Ss compare their sentences with their partners. Get feedback from the class and ask Ss to read out their sentences to the group.

3➤ Ss discuss questions 1–3 in groups of three or four. Get feedback from the whole class and discuss any techniques for remembering things that Ss have talked about. Decide with the class which technique sounds like the most effective one.

EXTEND THE LEAD-IN

Ss write down a list of names, places, dates and phone numbers. They should have fifteen items on their lists. Ss swap their lists with their partners. Tell Ss they have thirty seconds to remember the list of items. After thirty seconds ask Ss to turn over the list and write down as many of the items as they can. Get feedback from the class and check who was capable of memorising the most items. Find out if any of the Ss used particular memory techniques to remember the items on the list.

10.1 Using and losing your memory

Authors such as Tony Buzan have claimed that it is possible to improve your memory using different memory techniques. Techniques for improving memory include associating things with places, inventing rhymes to help remember items and putting items into a surreal or absurd context.

In this lesson Ss read three different stories about memory then listen to two people talking about things they remember and forget. Using this context Ss look at the grammar of *I wish* and *if only*. Ss then talk about skills they wish they had before going on to read a poem by Robert Frost.

OPTIONAL WARMER

Write the following words taken from the texts on the board in three groups: Group 1: *unconscious, cycling, recognise, hospital.* Group 2: *hospital, documents, memory, piano.* Group 3: *journalist, perfectly-remembered facts, psychologist, secret.* Tell Ss that the words in each group are taken from a different story. Organise the Ss into groups of As, Bs and Cs. In their groups Ss try and predict what the story is about. Re-organise the groups so that there is a student A, B and C together. Ss tell the others in their groups what they think their stories might be about. Get feedback from the whole class.

Reading and writing

1➤ Ss in groups of three. In their groups Ss discuss the questions 1–4. Get feedback from the whole group.

2a➤ Focus Ss on the words and pictures from the stories about memory. With their partners Ss discuss what they think is happening in each story. Get feedback from the class.

b➤ Ss read the texts quickly to match the pictures to the stories and to check their ideas. Tell Ss that you will deal with any words they don't understand later. Check Ss' answers.

Answers: A 2   B 1   C 3

3➤ Read the statements with the whole class and then tell Ss to read the text again carefully to mark each statement (*T*) if true and (*F*) if false. Tell Ss to underline any words or phrases they don't understand in the texts. Allow Ss to compare with a partner before getting feedback.

Answers: 1 F He had forgotten four years of his life. 2 T   3 T   4 T   5 F He went to see Luria because his editor sent him.   6 F Luria tested S.'s memory thirty years after they first met.

➤ Ask Ss if there are any words which they have underlined in the text because they didn't understand them. Encourage Ss to explain the words to each other if they can.

4➤ Organise Ss into small groups. Ss work together to write titles and short endings for each of the stories. Go round and monitor what the Ss are writing and help where necessary.

➤ Ss read out the endings they have written to the rest of the class. As a group Ss decide which they think are the best titles and the most likely endings.

5➤ Refer Ss to page 149. Ss read the real endings to the stories. Ss discuss with their partners which they think is the most interesting ending to the story and why. Get feedback from the whole class.

Listening

6a➤ Tell Ss they are going to listen to two people talking about things they remember or forget. Play recording 10.1 and Ss decide what things they mention. Check Ss' answers.

Answers: appointments, meetings, faces, names, dates, birthdays, phone numbers, writers' names, names of songs, book titles

---

b➤ Play recording 10.1 again and Ss complete the sentences. Allow Ss to compare answers with their partners. Check answers with the class.

Answers: 1 had   2 didn't   3 could 4 'd remembered

---

c➤ Ss discuss if they think the people talking have good memories and if they would like to have good memories. Get feedback from the whole group.

Grammar

OPTIONAL GRAMMAR LEAD-IN

Ask Ss if they remember the song they listened to in Unit 3 by Simon and Garfunkle. If they don't remember it give them a few minutes to look back at page 37 and read through the song again. Ask: **Q: Where is the singer?** In a train station. Ask: **Q: What does he wish he was doing now?** Going home. On the board write: *I wish I _____ homeward bound.* In pairs Ss think of a word to complete the space without looking at the song. Write *was* in the space. Ask Ss what tense this is and explain that we use *I wish* + past simple to express a present wish. Tell Ss to read through the Reference page 143. Ask: **Q: What tense do we use with *wish* to talk about past wishes?** Past Perfect. Focus Ss on the fact that there is a backshift of tenses when using *wish*: for present wishes: Past Simple, for past wishes: Past Perfect. Tell Ss that this is similar to the way tenses are shifted back in reported speech which they saw in Unit 9.

7➤ Ss read through the Active grammar box and choose the correct alternatives. Check answers with the class.

Active grammar

Use *wish* + Past Simple to talk about imaginary things we would like in <u>the present</u>.

Use *wish* + Past Perfect to talk about imaginary things we'd like in <u>the past</u>.

We use *wish* + *could* to talk about <u>ability</u>.

➤ Tell Ss to read through the Reference on page 143. Answer any questions Ss may have.

8➤ In pairs Ss complete the sentences 1–8 using the phrases in the box. Get feedback from the whole class.

> **Answers:** 1 could swim 2 would be quiet
> 3 was here 4 hadn't done 5 could sleep
> 6 hadn't arrived 7 had 8 knew how

9➤ Write the first sentence on the board as an example. Tell Ss they must complete the second sentence so it has the same meaning as the first sentence and that they must use between two and three words in the space. Get ideas from the Ss and fill in the space with the answer: *I had eaten*.

➤ Ss complete the sentences 2–8. Allow Ss to compare answers with a partner before checking them with the class.

> **Answers:** 1 I had eaten 2 I was 3 you would
> 4 I hadn't 5 I could 6 you wouldn't 7 I had
> 8 could

Speaking

10➤ Draw Ss' attention to the skills in the box and give them time to read through them. If there are any words or expressions that Ss don't understand, encourage them to help each other before explaining them yourself.

➤ Ss choose five skills from the box that they wish they had. Ss discuss the skills they have chosen with their partner. Ss tell their partners why they have chosen those skills. Get feedback from various pairs.

> **OPTIONAL EXTENSION**
>
> On the board write: *I missed the plane.* Ss think of the type of regrets that someone who had missed a plane might have. As an example write *If only there hadn't been so much traffic…* on the board. In pairs Ss think of similar sentences and tell Ss to use *wish* and *if only* while doing so. Get feedback and write correct sentences on the board. Organise Ss into pairs, A and B. Each student writes a problem without showing it to their partner. Student A then makes sentences using *wish* and *If only* which somebody who had this problem might say. Student B listens to the sentences and tries to guess the problem that student A has written. When student B has guessed the problem, repeat with student A guessing what student B's problem is.

Reading

11a➤ In pairs Ss discuss what they think the man and the horse in the picture are thinking. Get feedback.

b➤ Ss decide if the picture reminds them of a time or a place in their lives. Encourage Ss to be imaginative.

➤ Ss in groups of four. Ss share their ideas with the other Ss in the group. Get feedback by asking Ss to report to the class anything they have learned about the other Ss in their groups.

12➤ Draw Ss' attention to the Robert Frost poem. Give Ss time to read through the poem on their own. Tell Ss not to worry about any words or expressions they don't understand at this stage.

➤ Ss read the poem again and answer questions 1–5. Ss compare answers in pairs. Check answers with the whole class.

> **Answers:** 1 The traveller is between woods and a frozen lake. 2 He stops to watch the snow fall in the woods. 3 The horse thinks this is strange because there aren't any houses nearby. 4 The traveller thinks what he sees is beautiful. He likes the woods because he thinks they are dark and deep. 5 He continues his journey because he has a long way still to travel.

Pronunciation

13a➤ Tell Ss they are going to hear someone read the poem. Tell Ss to read along quietly with the recording and to concentrate on the rhythm of the poem. Play recording 10.2.

b➤ Write the first line of the poem on the board and underline the stressed words in the line: *Whose woods these are I think I know*.

➤ Read the line stressing the underlined words. Ask various Ss to read the line, concentrating on the stress.

➤ In pairs Ss mark the stressed words in each line. Remind Ss that there are four stressed words in each line. Play recording 10.2 again. Ss listen and read again.

> **Answers:** The underlined parts are stressed.
> Whose <u>woods</u> these <u>are</u> I think I <u>know</u>,
> His <u>house</u> is <u>in</u> the <u>village</u> though;
> He <u>will</u> not <u>see</u> me <u>stopping</u> <u>here</u>
> To <u>watch</u> his <u>woods</u> fill <u>up</u> with <u>snow</u>.
> My <u>little</u> <u>horse</u> must <u>think</u> it <u>queer</u>
> To <u>stop</u> without a <u>farmhouse</u> <u>near</u>
> Be<u>tween</u> the <u>woods</u> and <u>frozen</u> <u>lake</u>
> The <u>darkest</u> <u>evening</u> <u>of</u> the <u>year</u>.
> He <u>gives</u> his <u>harness</u> <u>bells</u> a <u>shake</u>
> To <u>ask</u> if <u>there</u> is <u>some</u> mis<u>take</u>
> The <u>only</u> other <u>sound's</u> the <u>sweep</u>
> Of <u>easy</u> <u>wind</u> and <u>downy</u> <u>flake</u>.
> The <u>woods</u> are <u>lovely</u>, <u>dark</u> and <u>deep</u>,
> But <u>I</u> have <u>promises</u> to <u>keep</u>,
> And <u>miles</u> to <u>go</u> be<u>fore</u> I <u>sleep</u>,
> And <u>miles</u> to <u>go</u> be<u>fore</u> I <u>sleep</u>.

14➤ Ss discuss the questions in groups of three or four. Get feedback from the class and ask Ss if they read poetry in their own language or if they have read other poems in English.

Lifelong learning

➤ Ss read through the Lifelong learning box. Focus Ss on *though* and *snow* in the poem and discuss how finding words which rhyme can help when remembering the pronunciation of difficult words. In pairs Ss look for more words which rhyme in the poem.

> **OPTIONAL EXTENSION**
>
> On the board write a list of words which you have noticed your Ss find difficult to pronounce. Practise saying the words on the board with various Ss.
> In pairs Ss think of other words in English which rhyme with these words. Get feedback and write the Ss' ideas on the board if correct. Practise saying these words with the whole class.

10.2 Famous women

Among the important people in the 20th century are the following women: Mother Teresa who worked helping the sick and poor in India. Marie Curie won the Nobel Prize for Physics in 1903. Frida Kahlo, famous Mexican painter whose life was portrayed in the cinema by Salma Hayek. Marilyn Monroe, big screen star of the 1950s and 60s. Rosa Parks, the 'mother of the civil rights movement' in the USA in the 1950s and 60s.

In this lesson Ss listen to information about important women of the 20th century. Ss then read a text about the fashion designer Coco Chanel and through this context do a review of past tenses. Ss look at how different numbers are pronounced in English and practise saying these numbers.

> **OPTIONAL WARMER**
>
> In a monolingual class Ss write a list of five famous women from their country with their partners. Ss then discuss why these women have been important in shaping their country. Get feedback and ask different pairs to explain why the women they have included in their list are important. In a multilingual class Ss individually write a list of five important women from their country. Ss then pair off with a student from another country and explain to each other how these women have helped shaped their country.

Listening and speaking

1➤ Focus Ss on the pictures of the five women. With their partners Ss discuss if they know who the women are and what they know about them. Tell Ss to think about the area in which they helped to shape the 20th century.

> **Answers:** A Rosa Parks B Frida Kahlo C Mother Teresa D Marilyn Monroe E Marie Curie

2a➤ Play recording 10.3. Ss listen and write down why each of the women was famous. Ss compare what they have written with another student. Check answers with the class.

> **Answers:** Mother Teresa dedicated her life to helping street children and sick people, Marie Curie was a brilliant scientist, Frida Kahlo was a gifted painter, Marilyn Monroe was a talented actress, Rosa Parks encouraged black Americans to fight for their rights

b➤ Play recording 10.3 again and Ss complete the notes. Get feedback and check answers with the whole group.

> **Answers:** 1 forty 2 her husband, Pierre, 1911 3 paintings 4 thirty 5 prison

Vocabulary

3a➤ Focus Ss on sentences 1–8. In pairs Ss write the names of the woman next to the sentences. If necessary play recording 10.3 again to help Ss complete their answers.

➤ In pairs Ss discuss the meaning of the words in bold. Get feedback from various pairs.

> **Answers:** 1 Parks 2 Parks 3 Monroe 4 Mother Teresa 5 Kahlo 6 Curie 7 Kahlo 8 Mother Teresa

b➤ Ss match the words in bold in sentences 1–8 to the words and phrases in the box. Ss compare their ideas with another student. Check answers with the whole class.

> **Answers:** encouraged: made people want to do something brave: had courage talented: very good at something dedicated her life: spent all her time determined: never stopped trying brilliant: excellent involved: played a part in inspired: was a great example to

4➤ In pairs Ss complete sentences 1–4 with a suitable word or phrase from Ex. 3a. Check answers with the whole class.

> **Answers:** 1 inspired 2 involved in 3 determined 4 dedicated her life

5➤ On the board write the names of two of your 'heroes' of the 20th century. Encourage Ss to ask you questions about these two 'heroes' and why you think they have been important in shaping the 20th century.

➤ Ss now choose two of their own 'heroes' and tell their partners about them.

> **OPTIONAL EXTENSION**
>
> Organise Ss into pairs, A and B. Ss A think of a person who was important in shaping the 20th century and why. Ss B ask Ss A Yes/No questions to find out the identity of the person. Ss A can only answer yes or no. If after twenty questions B cannot guess who the person is, A tells B the person. Ss then change roles so that Ss A guess the identity of Bs' important person.

Reading

6a➤ Focus Ss on the pictures. With their partners Ss guess who the text is about and what type of life she might have had. Get feedback from the whole class.

➤ Tell Ss they are going to read a text to find out who the famous woman is. Tell Ss that if there are any words or phrases in the text that they don't understand they should underline them and that you will deal with them later.

➤ Ss read paragraph number 1. With a partner Ss discuss the question at the end of the paragraph and decide what would be the best answer, a, b or c.

➤ Ss then read the next paragraph signalled at the end of the first paragraph (paragraph 5) and discuss the questions at the end of the paragraph. Ss continue until they have read all the paragraphs.

b➤ When Ss have decided who the famous person is they can write her nickname in the title. Check the Ss' answers.

> **Answer:** Coco (Chanel)

➤ Check if there are any words or expressions in the text the Ss don't understand. Encourage Ss to answer each other's questions before asking you.

Listing

7➤ Tell Ss they are going to hear a summary of Coco Chanel's life but that there are three mistakes in what they are going to hear.

➤ Play recording 10.4 and Ss write down the three facts which the speaker gets wrong. Check answers with the class.

Answers: Her mother, not her father, died. In her first shop, she sold hats, not perfume. She went to Switzerland, not Hollywood.

8➤ Give Ss time to read through the numbers and dates in the box. In pairs Ss retell the story of Coco Chanel's life using the numbers and dates as prompts.

➤ Go round and monitor and take note of any errors Ss make while saying the numbers and dates. Keep note of these errors for Ex. 11a below.

Grammar

OPTIONAL GRAMMAR LEAD-IN

Think of a traditional story such as a fairy tale to tell the class. Before telling the story to the Ss, tell them they are going to hear a story and that they must try and pay attention to the structures used in the story. When telling the class the story, include examples of the Past Simple, Past Continuous and Past Perfect. Ss note down examples of tenses used in the story. Ss compare these structures with their partners. Get feedback and write examples of the Past Simple, Past Continuous and Past Perfect on the board.

9a➤ In pairs Ss underline the different tenses used in the text to describe Coco Chanel's life. Get feedback and write examples of the Past Simple, Past Continuous and Past Perfect on the board.

b➤ Focus Ss on the Active grammar box and give them time to complete the rules using the Past Perfect, Past Continuous and/or Past Simple.

Active grammar
1 Past Simple
2 Past Perfect
3 Past Continuous
4 Past Continuous / Past Simple
5 Past Simple / Past Perfect

➤ Refer Ss to Reference page 143. Give Ss time to read through the notes. Ask: **Q: What structure do we use for the main completed events in a narrative?** Past Simple. **Q: What structure do we use if we want to show that one action happened before another action?** Past Perfect. **Q: What structure do we use for an action in progress over a period of time?** Past Continuous.

10a➤ Draw Ss' attention to the text about Gianni Versace. In pairs Ss put the verbs in brackets into the correct tense. Tell Ss that there is one verb in the passive form. Ss compare their answers with another pair. Check answers with the class.

Answers: 1 was growing up 2 moved 3 opened 4 presented 5 had already designed 6 were 7 brought out 8 was walking 9 was shot 10 had become

b➤ Ss find three things Gianni Versace had in common with Coco Chanel. Ss compare their answers with another student. Get feedback from the whole class.

Answers: Both Coco Chanel and Gianni Versace opened shops. They then both started designing women's clothes. They both brought out perfumes.

Pronunciation

11a➤ Ss read the How to … box. Refer Ss back to the numbers and dates in Ex. 8. Ss read through the numbers with their partners. Ask various Ss to read different numbers aloud.

b➤ In pairs Ss practise saying the different numbers a–f. Monitor and correct Ss where necessary. Ask various Ss to say the numbers for the class.

c➤ Play recording 10.5 and Ss check the pronunciation of the numbers. In pairs Ss decide when we use *and* and when we use *the*. Get feedback from the class.

Answers: We use *and* before the smallest part of a big number (one thousand *and* ten, ten million, six hundred *and* forty), and between whole numbers and fractions (three *and* a half, nine *and* three-quarters). We use *the* before dates (*the* fourth of June) and time periods (*the* fifth century, *the* nineteen seventies).

12➤ Ss in two groups, A and B. Ss A look at the sentences on page 147. Ss B look at the sentences on page 150.

➤ In their groups Ss think of questions they can ask to find out the missing numbers. Go round and check the questions Ss write.

➤ Pair Ss off so that Ss A are working with Ss B. Ss ask each other the questions they have made to fill in the gaps in their sentences with numbers.

➤ Monitor the conversations and take note of any errors Ss make with the numbers. Get feedback from the group and check answers. Finally, write any numbers Ss have made errors with on the board and practise saying them with the class.

Speaking

13a➤ Write five numbers that are important to you on the board. Include dates, years, numbers, etc. In pairs Ss discuss the numbers and decide why they might be important for you. Get feedback from various pairs in the class.

b➤ Individually Ss think of five numbers that are important to them and write them down. Ss swap their numbers with a partner.

c➤ Ss Ask each other questions to find out why each number is important. Encourage Ss to ask follow-up questions where relevant. Monitor the conversations for errors. When Ss have finished, write any errors on the board and ask Ss to correct them. Finally, praise Ss for correct use of numbers.

10.3 Saying goodbye

There are many ways of saying goodbye in English: *Goodbye*, *Bye*, *See you later*, *See you*, *Later*, *Bye for now*, *Catch you later* are just a few.

In this lesson Ss listen to people saying goodbye in four different situations. They then read a text about how different companies fire their staff. Using the context Ss look at the grammar of phrasal verbs and then practise using some phrasal verbs. Ss then listen to the song, *Leaving on a jet plane*. Finally, Ss look at some 'thank you' letters and then write their own 'thank you' letter.

> **OPTIONAL WARMER**
>
> Tell Ss to think of places where they could say goodbye to someone. With their partners Ss write a list of places and discuss who they could say goodbye to in these places. Ss swap partners and tell each other about the places and people they have written down. Ss then make a list of ways of saying goodbye in English that they know. Get feedback from various pairs.

Listening

1➤ In pairs Ss discuss what type of goodbye is being shown in the photos and if they have ever been in these situations themselves. Get feedback from the whole class.

> **Suggested answers:** A seeing someone off at the airport B Sending a footballer off the pitch (showing the red card) C seeing someone off on a train D seeing a boat (cruise ship) leaving port

2a➤ Tell Ss they are going to hear people saying goodbye in different situations. Give Ss time to read the situations a–d. Play recording 10.6 and Ss number the situations in the order they hear them. Check answers with the whole class.

> **Answers:** a 2 b 4 c 1 d 3

b➤ Ss read through the situations 1–4. Play recording 10.6 again and Ss number the situations. Ss check their answers with their partners.

c➤ Refer Ss to the tapescript on page 176 so they can check their answers.

> **Answers:** 1 4 2 1 3 3 4 2

Reading and speaking

3➤ Ss read the introduction to the texts and answer the questions with their partners. Get feedback from various pairs.

> **Answers:** 1 The text is about (good and) bad ways to say goodbye. It is (b) a little bit funny. 2 How to leave your partner and how to fire your staff.

4➤ Ss in two groups, A and B. Ss A read the text on page 138 and Ss B read the text on page 150. With another student from their group Ss answer the questions 1–5.

➤ Go round and help Ss with any words or phrases they don't understand in the text. Encourage Ss to answer each others' questions or use a dictionary where possible.

> **Answers:** 1 Ss A's text is about saying goodbye to your staff. Ss B's text is about saying goodbye to a partner. 2 One company sent texts to its employees; another made sure the employees' security cards didn't work; another invited employees to a conference and put all the people who were fired into one room. One actor sent his pregnant girlfriend a fax to say he was leaving her; another split up with his partner on live TV; another got married without telling his girlfriend, and a king killed some of his wives. 3 It's impossible to fire someone nicely, but managers should show respect for the employee. In relationships, men have always seemed a bit insensitive when it's time to say goodbye. 4 Ss' own answers. 5 Both texts suggest you should show respect to others.

5➤ Ss pair off with a student from the other group. Ss explain their texts to each other, using the answers from Ex. 4 to help. Ss then read each other's texts quickly to check.

> **OPTIONAL EXTENSION**
>
> In pairs Ss decide which of the ways of firing people mentioned in the text on page 138 is the worst and why. Get feedback from the whole class and discuss Ss' ideas. Ss then decide which of the ways of splitting up with someone mentioned in the text on page 150 is the worst and why. Discuss Ss' ideas with the whole group.
>
> Ss in small groups then decide what would be the best way to fire someone and what would be the best way to split up with someone. Get feedback from each group.

6➤ Ask Ss what a phrasal verb is. Elicit/Explain that a phrasal verb is a verb with one or two particles.

➤ Focus Ss on the words in the box. In pairs Ss read both texts again to find the phrasal verbs which have the meaning of the verbs in the box. Get feedback from the class and write the phrasal verbs on the board.

> **Answers:** Text A find out: *discover* came back: *returned* going on *happening* turned up: *arrived* come up with: *think of/invent* Text B split up: *finished a relationship* carry on: *continue* called off: *cancelled* went through: *experienced (something bad)* put up with: *tolerate*

Grammar

7➤ Give Ss a short time to read through the Active grammar box. Ss look back at the phrasal verbs in the texts and decide with their partners what type of phrasal verb each one is. Ss then compare their answers with another pair. Check answers.

> **Answers:** Type 1: find out, come back, go on, turn up, split up, carry on Type 2: call off Type 3: go through Type 4: come up with, put up with

➤ Refer Ss to Reference page 143. Give Ss time to read through the notes. Check they understand the notes.

8➤ Focus Ss on the jumbled sentences 1–10. With their partners Ss put the words in the correct order to make correct sentences. Ss compare their answers with another pair. Check answers with the class and ask Ss to read out the correct sentences.

> **Answers:** 1 I split up with my girlfriend.
> 2 We didn't find out until later. 3 When are you coming back? 4 I couldn't carry on because I was tired. 5 She always turns up late. 6 Did they come up with any good ideas? 7 What is going on here?
> 8 The match was called off because of rain.
> 9 The company is going through a difficult period.
> 10 I can't put up with him any more.

9➤ Ss read the gapped sentences 1–9 and think of phrasal verbs that might fill these gaps. Ss discuss their answers with their partners. Get feedback and write any correct possibilities on the board.

➤ Ss complete the sentences with phrasal verbs using the words from boxes 1 and 2. Tell Ss they have to use verb tenses which fit the context of the sentences.

➤ Get feedback from the class and check answers. Write the phrasal verbs on the board.

> **Answers:** 1 put up with 2 find out about
> 3 carry on 4 turned up 5 going on
> 6 went through 7 split up 8 coming back
> 9 come up with

10➤ With their partners Ss decide which phrasal verbs are illustrated by the pictures. If Ss need extra help refer them to Ex. 9. Get feedback from the group.

> **Answers:** A split up B put up with C called off
> D come back E find out F come up with

> **OPTIONAL VARIATION**
> Before looking at the gapped sentences in Ex. 9, focus Ss on the pictures in Ex. 10. Write the following sentence on the board: *Today's concert was called off because of bad weather*. In pairs Ss decide which of the pictures is being described by this sentence. Ss then write five sentences to describe the other pictures. Ss read their sentences to their partners who decide which picture each sentence is describing. Ss then complete the gaps in the sentences in Ex. 9 using the words from boxes 1 and 2. Ss then compare the sentences they wrote about the pictures with the sentences in Ex. 9.

Listening

> **OPTIONAL LEAD-IN**
> Write the following questions on the board: *Have you ever travelled by plane? Where did you go? When was the last time that you travelled somewhere? Did you leave someone behind when you left? Who?* In pairs Ss discuss these questions. Get feedback from the class by asking various Ss about their travel experiences.

11a➤ Focus Ss on the photos. Tell Ss that they are going to listen to a song and that the photos are connected to the song. In pairs Ss talk about what they think the song is about. Get feedback from the class and discuss Ss' ideas.

b➤ Tell Ss to cover the words to the song. Play recording 10.7. Ss listen and write down any words they hear.

➤ Ss compare the words they have written with their partners. Get feedback from the class and write any words from the song that Ss have heard on the board.

c➤ Ss in groups of three or four. Ss discuss what they think the song is about using the words they have written down to help them. Get feedback form the whole class.

d➤ Ss uncover the song and read through the lyrics. With their partners Ss predict which words could go in the gaps.

➤ Play recording 10.7 again and Ss listen and fill in the gaps. Ss compare their answers with another pair. Elicit the answers from various pairs.

> **Answers:** 1 go 2 wake 3 horn 4 wait
> 5 back 6 down 7 played 8 come 9 leave
> 10 way

➤ Ss discuss the questions 1–3 with their partners. Get feedback form the whole class and discuss the answers.

> **Answers:** 1 The song is about a man leaving his partner to go on a tour. 2 He will be happy to return to her. 3 his partner

12➤ In pairs Ss find the phrasal verbs in the song which match the meanings 1–5. Check answers with the class.

> **Answers:** 1 wake up 2 let go 3 let
> down 4 play around 5 come back

Writing

13a➤ Refer Ss to the Writing bank on page 162. Ss read through the two thank you letters and answer the questions 1-4. Ss compare their answers with their partners. Check answers with the class.

> **Answers:**
> **1** 1 Because she stayed with Andrea and wants to say thank you. 2 They visited the city and saw many things. 3 To thank Ms Jenkins for hosting a conference. 4 Yes. Several participants commented on the excellent organisation.
> **2a** The second letter is formal. 1 full verb forms (F) 2 contractions (I) 3 the passive (F) 4 exclamation marks (I) 5 abbreviations (I)
> **2b** 1 I am 2 I'll 3 Your efforts were appreciated by all … 4 Keep in touch! 5 Enjoy …

b➤ Ss write a thank you letter to another student, to you or to someone else at the school. Ss could plan how they are going to write the letter with a partner and finish writing it for homework.

Vocabulary: The senses

In this lesson Ss look at vocabulary related to the five senses.

1a➤ With their partners Ss discuss which senses they associate with each photo. Go round the class helping Ss with any necessary vocabulary. Get feedback from various pairs.

b➤ Ss decide what sense they associate with the words in the box. Draw five columns on the board and write a sense at the top of each one. Allow Ss to compare their answers before eliciting from the Ss. Write the words into the columns as the Ss give you their answers. There are no correct or incorrect answers as it depends on how Ss feel about the words.

c➤ Ss complete the phrases with any words they want to. Ss share their ideas with other Ss in the group.

d➤ Ss talk about the things that they like and dislike with their partners. Monitor the conversations and take note of errors. Then get feedback from the class. Finally, write the errors on the board and encourage Ss to self-correct.

2a➤ Ss read through the table. Focus Ss on the word order of the verbs + adjective and the verb + *like* + noun phrase.

b➤ Ss cover column B of the table. In pairs Ss think of responses to the sentences and questions in column A. Ask various pairs for their ideas.

➤ Ss uncover column B and match the phrases in B to the ones in A. Check answers with the class.

> **Answers:** 1 d 2 e 3 g 4 f 5 a 6 b 7 h 8 c

c➤ Ss cover the dialogues in Column B and practise saying the dialogues in pairs.

d➤ Play recording 10.8 and Ss decide what has just happened. Check answers with the class.

> **Suggested answers:** 1 A woman is cooking. She's just burned her hand. 2 He's eaten something disgusting 3 Some birds have just started singing and the person wants to hear them. 4 She's just eaten something delicious. 5 She's just smelled something horrible.

3a➤ Ss discuss the difference between the words with their partner. Check the answers with the class.

> **Answers:** 1 see: either a long time or a short time / look at: usually for a short time / watch: for a long time deliberately (e.g. a TV programme) 2 listen to: deliberately / hear: probably by chance 1 touch = for one moment; hold = for a long time

b➤ Ss write a sentence for each word using their own ideas.

4➤ Ss complete the sentences 1–7 with the words and phrases from Ex. 3. Check answers with the group.

> **Answers:** 1 hold 2 seen 3 hear 4 touch 5 looking at 6 listen to 7 watch

5a➤ Ss read the poem then write their own version using the model. Help Ss with vocabulary where necessary.

b➤ Ss read their poems to other Ss.

Communication: The memory game

In this lesson Ss read instructions about how to play a memory game. Ss then use these instructions to play the game in groups of three or more. To play the game you will need counters and a dice for each group.

> **OPTIONAL WARMER**
>
> In pairs Ss discuss any table games that they play or have played. Get feedback and ask Ss to explain how these games are played. In a monolingual class ask Ss to tell you the rules of any typical table games played in their country. In a multilingual class form small groups and ask Ss to explain to each other how typical table games from their countries are played.

1a➤ Focus Ss on the questions on the board. Ss read through the questions and check they understand all of them. Encourage Ss to use a dictionary if there are any words or phrases they don't understand or to answer each others' questions.

➤ Ss then read the instructions. Check that Ss have understood the instructions by asking: **Q: Where do you put your counters to start the game.** On the START box. **Q: How do you move round the board?** By rolling the dice and moving the correct number of squares. **Q: What do you have to do when you land on a square?** You have to talk about the topic in the square. **Q: Who is the winner of the game?** The first person to reach the FINISH.

b➤ Ss play The Memory Game in their groups. As the Ss are playing, monitor carefully to offer help where needed. Take note of errors that Ss make as well as any examples of good language and expressions that Ss use.

➤ When Ss have finished the game get feedback from each group by asking the Ss to report to the rest of the class something they have learned about the other Ss in the group.

➤ Finally, write any important errors on the board and invite Ss to come up and correct them on the board. Congratulate Ss on any good language and expressions they have used in the class and praise them for their efforts throughout the course.

> **OPTIONAL EXTENSION**
>
> When Ss have finished the game in their groups organise the class into new groups so that the Ss are all working with different partners. Ss choose one of the squares that they haven't landed on and prepare a three-minute talk about the topic. Go round and monitor and help as necessary. When Ss are ready they give the talk to the other Ss in their group. Monitor carefully and take note of errors as well as use of correct or interesting language. When all the Ss have finished giving their talks, write up any errors on the board. In their groups Ss decide how to correct the errors. Get feedback and ask Ss from each group to come up and write the correct forms on the board. Finally, write examples of correct or interesting language that Ss have used on the board and congratulate Ss on its use.

Review and practice

1➤

> **Answers:** 1 wasn't 2 hadn't eaten
> 3 had gone 4 had 5 could work
> 6 had shown 7 could play 8 were

2➤

> **Answers:** 1 were you doing 2 was listening
> 3 didn't hear 4 Did you have 5 went
> 6 had stopped 7 didn't you go 8 had got back
> 9 was visiting

3➤

> **Answers:** 1 She had changed a lot. 2 I had never
> read it before 3 At 6.30 he was swimming.
> 4 He was sleeping in his room at midnight. 5 I had
> lost my passport. 6 She was looking for a job.

4➤

> **Answers:** 1 (a) after many years ✔ (b) because we
> argued a lot ✔ (c) my husband ✗ 2 (a) a difficult
> time ✔ (b) hell ✔ (c) a nice month ✗ 3 (a) on time ✔
> (b) very well ✗ (c) to watch the match ✔ 4 (a) the
> party ✔ (b) my friends ✗ (c) our arrangement ✔
> 5 (a) the excellent service ✗ (b) the press ✔ (c) those
> stupid comments ✔ 6 (a) if we don't tell him ✔
> (b) about the money ✔ (c) of the story ✗
> 7 (a) wrong ✗ (b) here ✔ (c) today ✔ 8 (a) working ✔
> (b) playing next year ✔ (c) to watch the film ✗

5➤

> **Answers:** 1 reminds 2 horses 3 turned up
> 4 woods 5 dedicated 6 encouraged
> 7 found out

Notes for using the Common European Framework (CEF)

CEF References

10.1 Can do: talk about wishes

CEF B1 descriptor: can describe dreams, hopes and ambitions. (CEF page 59)

10.2 Can do: say different types of numbers

CEF B1 descriptor: can initiate, maintain and close simple, face-to-face conversation on topics that are familiar or of personal interest. (CEF page 86)

10.3 Can do: write a thank you letter

CEF B2 descriptor: can write letters conveying degrees of emotion and highlighting the personal significance of events and experiences. (CEF page 83)

CEF quick brief

One of the implications of the Common European Framework and the Can do statements is that Ss are assessed in terms of how well they can achieve a communication objective. The aim is not to perform the task with perfect accuracy but to perform well enough at that particular reference level. The Can do statements set appropriate objectives for each reference level.

Portfolio task

Download the Total English Portfolio free from www.longman.com/totalenglish.

Objective: to reinforce student autonomy in updating the Portfolio.

This task can be done in Ss' own language.

1➤ For homework, ask Ss to update the Dossier section of their Portfolio. They might like to add another piece of work to their folder or choose another task to work on with the aim of adding it to their Biography.

2➤ Ask Ss to bring their Biography sections in and show them to other Ss.

photocopiable worksheets

contents

Who am I thinking about?
Part A

Read the description below.

Guess what relationship there is between the writer and the person being described.

I have known this person for about six years. She's about forty and very nice. We don't really have the same sense of humour, but we get on quite well. I normally see her every day during the week, but some days we don't get the chance to speak much. We're both too busy. We don't keep in contact during the holidays as we don't enjoy each other's company socially.

Work in pairs. Think of questions to ask about a person using the ideas below.

How/old	Male/Female	What/like	What/job	Where/live	Same sense of humour
How long/know		Get on with this person		Spend a lot of time together	Keep in touch

Can you think of any other useful questions?

- -

Part B

Student A

Choose 4 of the following people and write their names in the spaces below.

MOTHER OR MOTHER-IN-LAW

BOSS

BOY/GIRLFRIEND

AQUAINTANCE

SISTER OR BROTHER

1 _____

2 _____

3 _____

4 _____

Now ask your partner questions in order to guess the relationship he or she has with the people whose names they have written.

Student B

Choose 4 of the following people and write their names in the spaces below.

CLOSE FRIEND

FATHER OR FATHER-IN-LAW

HUSBAND OR WIFE

COLLEAGUE

AUNT OR UNCLE

1 _____

2 _____

3 _____

4 _____

Now ask your partner questions in order to guess the relationship he or she has with the people whose names they have written.

Which question am I answering?

Student A

Write a complete answer for the following questions.

1   What food do you hate?
_____

2   What foreign countries have you visited?
_____

3   What did you do last night?
_____

4   How often do you go to the cinema?
_____

5   Who is your favourite actor?
_____

6   Where do you usually spend your holidays?
_____

7   What have you done today?
_____

8   How many brothers and sisters have you got?
_____

9   What type of music do you like the most?
_____

10 What did you do last weekend?
_____

Listen to your partner's answer and choose an appropriate question below. Add an auxiliary verb to complete it.

1   Where _____ you study or work?

2   What time _____ you usually get up during the week?

3   Who _____ your favourite singer/group?

4   What _____ you eaten today?

5   How many English teachers _____ you had?

6   What type of music _____ you like?

7   How often _____ you do sport?

8   What _____ you do last summer?

9   How much _____ you usually spend at the weekend?

10 What _____ the last thing you bought?

Student B

Write a complete answer for the following questions.

1   What have you eaten today?
_____

2   How often do you do sport?
_____

3   What type of music do you like?
_____

4   What did you do last summer?
_____

5   Where do you study or work?
_____

6   How much do you usually spend at the weekend?
_____

7   How many English teachers have you had?
_____

8   What was the last thing you bought?
_____

9   Who is your favourite singer/group?
_____

10 What time do you usually get up during the week?
_____

Listen to your partner's answer and choose an appropriate question below. Add an auxiliary verb to complete it.

1   Who _____ your favourite actor?

2   What _____ you do last night?

3   Where _____ you usually spend your holidays?

4   What _____ you done today?

5   What food _____ you hate?

6   How often _____ you go to the cinema?

7   What foreign countries _____ you visited?

8   What _____ you do last weekend?

9   What type of music _____ you like the most?

10 How many brothers and sisters _____ you got?

I think or I'm thinking?

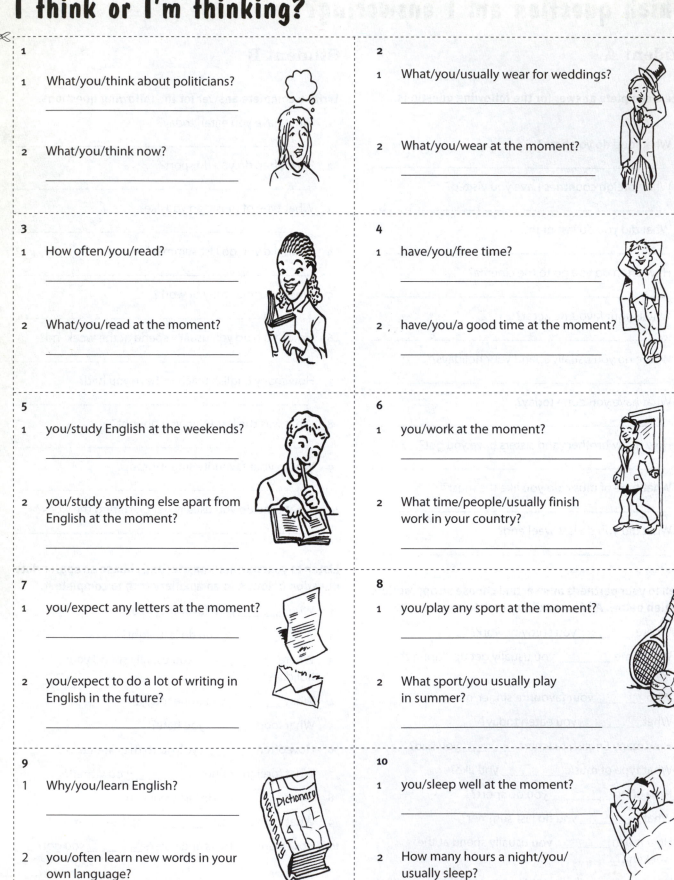

1

1 What/you/think about politicians?

_____

2 What/you/think now?

_____

2

1 What/you/usually wear for weddings?

_____

2 What/you/wear at the moment?

_____

3

1 How often/you/read?

_____

2 What/you/read at the moment?

_____

4

1 have/you/free time?

_____

2 have/you/a good time at the moment?

_____

5

1 you/study English at the weekends?

_____

2 you/study anything else apart from English at the moment?

_____

6

1 you/work at the moment?

_____

2 What time/people/usually finish work in your country?

_____

7

1 you/expect any letters at the moment?

_____

2 you/expect to do a lot of writing in English in the future?

_____

8

1 you/play any sport at the moment?

_____

2 What sport/you usually play in summer?

_____

9

1 Why/you/learn English?

_____

2 you/often learn new words in your own language?

_____

10

1 you/sleep well at the moment?

_____

2 How many hours a night/you/ usually sleep?

_____

What have we got in common?

Write a short answer for each point below.

	QUESTION	YOU	OTHER STUDENTS
1	A film you have seen recently.		
2	A place you went last weekend.		
3	Something you have eaten today.		
4	A foreign country you have visited.		
5	The time you went to bed last night.		
6	A group or singer you have seen live.		
7	The last English text book you used.		
8	Something you watched on TV last night.		
9	A feeling you have felt recently.		
10	A school subject you liked when you were a child.		
11	A sport you have done recently.		
12	The number of phone calls you made yesterday.		
13	A job you wanted to do when you were a child.		
14	The number of times you have been ill this year.		

Ask questions and try to find two other students in the class who have the same answer as you. Write their names in the space provided.

Have you ever visited France?

Yes, I went to Paris about two years ago.

Beginnings and endings

1st halves	2nd halves
The teacher tells the students off	because he's so intelligent.
My grandmother brought me up	for not doing their homework.
I usually ask my neighbours	can be a very difficult process.
I really look up to my brother	we are both ambitious and hard-working.
My family don't get on very well	and we're always arguing.
I'm going to carry on	for staying out later than they said.
I grew up	because my mother and father went to find work in another country.
I take after my mother physically,	studying English for the next few years.
My parents used to tell me off	in the countryside.
I take after my father in personality,	living with their parents until they get married.
I sometimes have to look after	gets on very well together.
Everybody in my class	my sister's children at the weekend.
Most people in my country carry on	to look after my plants when I go on holiday.
I think growing up	we are both tall and slim.

A good friend is …

Mm, you look really nice …

Read the following statements and tick the column that best reflects your opinion.

	TRUE	FALSE	DEPENDS
1 You can predict which people will become your friends from your first impressions.			
2 Best friends should like everything about each other.			
3 Good friends always have a lot in common.			
4 Best friends must have similar characters.			
5 Friendship doesn't last unless you keep in touch.			
6 It's impossible to have a good friend of the opposite sex.			
7 It's difficult to be friends with an ex-boyfriend or ex-girlfriend.			
8 You can depend on members of your family more than you can depend on your friends.			
9 Most friends have fallen out with each other at some time.			
10 A good way of making friends is through Internet chat rooms.			
11 Good friends are normally keen on doing the same kinds of things.			
12 You can only have a few really close friends.			
13 You normally get on with your friend's friends.			
14 Close friends should never lie to each other.			

Now discuss the statements in small groups. Explain your opinion, giving examples.

Media crossword

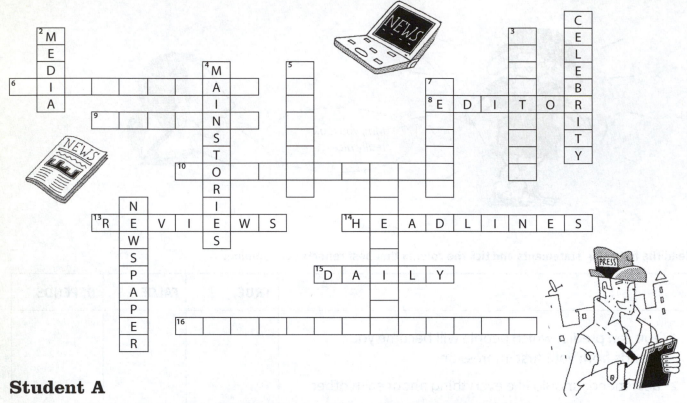

Student A

Give your partner a clue for the words given in the crossword. e.g., Number 4 down is a written account about something which is happening in the world.

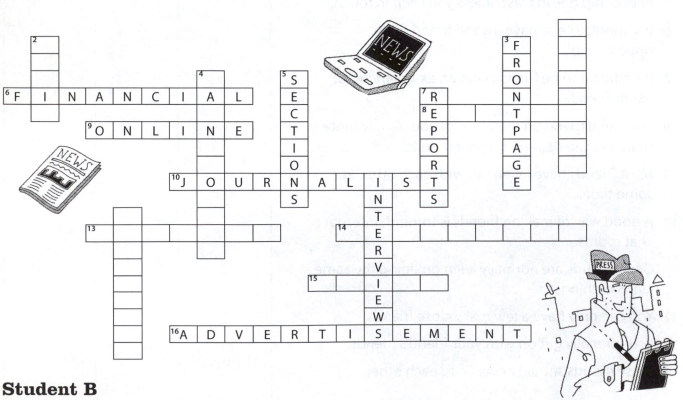

Student B

Give your partner a clue for the words given in the crossword. e.g., Number 9 across is related to the Internet. When you are connected you are this.

Sentence auction

Read the following sentences and decide if they are grammatically correct. Decide with your team how much to bet on each one (minimum £10 and maximum £100).

	BET	WIN	LOSE
1 Famous people is often interviewed on the TV and radio.			
2 The news is normally broadcast at midday and in the evening.			
3 Handwritten newspapers were circulated as early as 59BC in ancient Rome.			
4 The ballpoint pen was invent by the Biro brothers in 1938.			
5 Children should been supervised when they are surfing the net.			
6 Some pop videos have been prohibited because of the images they contain.			
7 Lots of mobile phones have been stealed this year in the UK.			
8 The idea of *Big Brother* was originally create by George Orwell in his novel *1984*.			
9 Many journalists are sent to live in foreign countries to report what is happening there.			
10 Jobs are usually advertised in local and national newspapers.			
11 Mobile phones must recharged every couple of days.			
12 An estimated $250 million were spend on the rental and purchase of the *Titanic* video in the first 6 days after its release.			
13 Sales of CDs have been affected by people who download songs on the internet.			
14 Coca-Cola is known for its clever advertising campaigns.			
15 Home videos have mostly replaced by DVDs.			

Shh! Don't say that word!

HOSPITAL doctor ill medicine	**ACTOR** film to act theatre	**TOAST** bread breakfast to eat	**CHRISTMAS** December presents Santa Claus
SUPERMARKET to buy food shop	**TEACHER** to teach school student	**CAR** transport to drive road	**MORNING** to get up early afternoon
BEACH sea coast to sunbathe	**MOTHER** father child to give birth	**PEN** to write pencil paper	**BIRTHDAY** presents born to celebrate
CITY town busy to live	**PILOT** to fly plane airport	**TABLE** to study to eat wood	**WEEKEND** to work Saturday Sunday
BEDROOM bed to sleep wardrobe	**NURSE** to look after hospital job	**BALL** game round to throw	**SUMMER** hot holidays beach
LONDON England Big Ben rain	**JOURNALIST** newspaper to write report	**MOBILE PHONE** to ring to talk communication	**WINTER** season cold Christmas

What was going on when …?

Match the pairs of verbs to the pictures.

WAIT/STEAL	DRIVE/JUMP	COOK/ARRIVE	SAIL/APPEAR
RUN/BITE	LAND/RAIN	EAT/BREAK	PLAY/GET BROKEN
HAVE/RING	SUNBATHE/STING	ESCAPE/SLEEP	CLEAN/FALL

Say what is happening in each picture.

Now think of an important event that has happened over the last few years. Interview your classmates to find out what they were doing when that event happened.

Verb collocations noughts and crosses

1	2	3	4
5	6	7	8
9	10	11	12
13	14	15	16

INSTRUCTIONS

Choose a rectangle and listen to your partner's sentence. Is it right or wrong? If it's wrong, correct it. If you choose correctly, put a cross or a nought in the square.

Now it's the other team's turn.

The winner is the one with the most noughts or crosses at the end. You get an extra point for 3 noughts or crosses in a row.

Sentences A

1 Scientists make many important discoveries. (✓)

2 You can make a good job after university. (✗ – get/find)

3 My cousin came into a lot of money last year. (✓)

4 They got a cup for committing a race. (✗ – winning)

5 More people commit suicide in winter. (✓)

6 We do business with a Japanese company. (✓)

7 She's very good at making ideas. (✗ – developing)

8 Parents have a duty to their children. (✓)

9 He performed the song very well. (✓)

10 I can't cause enough time to do all my work. (✗ – find)

11 The children are always performing trouble at school. (✗ - causing)

12 Why do you keep breaking your promises. (✓)

13 The shop has developed prices by 10%. (✗ – increased)

14 Sally got lost when she was in London. (✓)

15 The woman had to make the child first aid. (✗ – give)

16 She moved in with her boyfriend last year. (✓)

Sentences B

1 That business performed a big profit last year. (✗ – made)

2 Short skirts have come into fashion recently. (✓)

3 Those boys have won a football team. (✗ – joined/formed)

4 She won the competition in the end. (✓)

5 Many crimes have been committed here recently. (✓)

6 She develops the news in the local area. (✗ – reports)

7 The company has performed a new product for adults. (✗ – developed).

8 Many stars have plastic surgery. (✓)

9 They performed the match very well. (✗ – played)

10 A play has just been performed at the theatre. (✓)

11 He was driving so fast that he committed an accident. (✗ – caused)

12. The athlete made a record in the last race. (✗ – broke)

13. The driver took a wrong turn in that street. (✓)

14 The vandals made damage to the building. (✗ – caused)

15 All workers need to perform a break. (✗ – take/have)

16 They will return home after the course. (✓)

Newspaper headlines

Write newspaper headlines for the stories presented in the following pictures.
Use your imagination!

1 	2 	3 
4 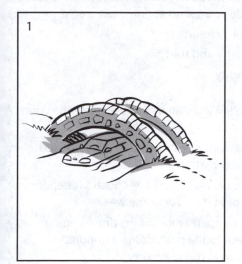	5 	6 
7 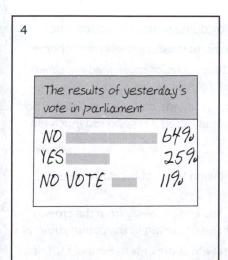	8 	9 

4 — The results of yesterday's vote in parliament
NO 64%
YES 25%
NO VOTE 11%

Read your headlines to a partner, but not in order. Your partner must guess the right picture.

Choose one of the headlines and invent the complete story with a partner. Prepare it as if it were a news broadcast. Tell your stories to the rest of the class.

What kind of lifestyle do you prefer?

Ask and answer the questions in pairs.

1 What does the word 'home' suggest to you?

   a It's really important, and everything that's in it. It's the place where I feel happy and safe.

   b It's important, but not as much as my job or friends.

   c It's a place to sleep and sometimes eat, but if I had to sleep and eat somewhere else, it wouldn't bother me.

2 Which of the following would you choose to have?

   a A big spacious detached house with high ceilings, wooden floors and a fireplace but no money left to spend on holidays, going out, little luxuries etc.

   b A medium-sized flat on the third floor, with quite a good view but noisy neighbours and a bit of extra money to spend on going out sometimes.

   c A cramped apartment on the first floor and lots of extra cash to spend on yourself.

3 Which of the following statements best describe your house or flat?

   a It's always in very good condition and clean and tidy as I spend a lot of time looking after my home.

   b It's in fairly good condition and usually quite clean and tidy although sometimes I don't look after my home as much as I should.

   c It's in quite bad condition and usually untidy.

4 Where would you prefer to live?

   a In the countryside or a very quiet residential area.

   b In a lively suburb, but one with plenty of shops, restaurants and pubs.

   c Right in the centre of town where everything's happening.

5 On average, how much of your free time (when you're not sleeping) do you spend at home per week?

   a More than thirty hours.

   b Between twenty and thirty.

   c Less than twenty.

6 Which of the following statements best describe your lifestyle?

   a Quiet. I take things calmly and don't get stressed about everyday matters.

   b Sometimes quiet and sometimes hectic. It depends on the time of year or day of the week.

   c Usually hectic. I spend most of my time running from one place to the next, doing a hundred different things at the same time.

7 What do you enjoy doing most in your free time?

   a Reading, listening to music and relaxing at home.

   b A mixture of things, a bit of sport, reading, cinema and occasionally clubbing.

   c Being out with my friends, clubbing, socialising and keeping busy. I get bored if I spend too much time alone at home.

8 Which of the following types of holiday would you prefer?

   a Rural tourism. You can get away from the crowds and relax, walking or cycling in the countryside.

   b A tourist resort with some entertainment facilities, but reasonably quiet and relaxing.

   c A busy, lively tourist resort, where I can go clubbing all night long.

Calculate how many A, B and C answers you have got. Read the results below.

Mostly As

What a quiet, relaxed life you lead. Home is definitely where the heart is for you. Your idea of paradise is a little cottage in the country, far away from the stress of the big city. Don't forget, though, there may be something else out there that's interesting.

Mostly Bs

Well, you seem to have a very balanced approach to life. You like doing exciting things but you also know when to relax and take it easy. You value your home, but not too much as other things interest you too.

Mostly Cs

What a life! You love to be in the centre of it all, running around and socialising. Do you remember where your home is? It sounds fun, but be careful not to get too stressed. Everybody needs to relax sometimes.

What the future holds

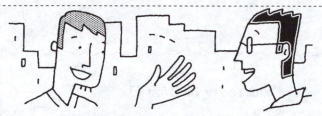

Find out how many people are meeting a friend after class. (*Ask who and where*)

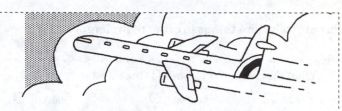

Find out how many people are going to travel abroad at some time this year. (*Find out where and why*)

Find out how many people are going to study English again next year. (*Find out where and why*)

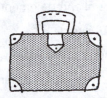

Find out how many people are going away next weekend. (*Find out where and who with*)

Find out how many people are going to study later today. (*Find out what and where*)

Find out how many people will help you with your English homework in the future. (*Find out why or why not*)

Find out how many people think they are going to be rich in the future. (*Find out why or why not*)

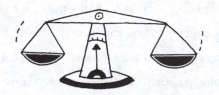

Find out how many people think the world will be a fairer place in the future. (*Find out why or why not*)

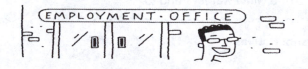

Find out how many people think they are going to start work or change their job in the near future. (*Find out when and where*)

Find out how many people are going out tonight. (*Find out where and who with*)

Find out how many people are going to do some kind of sport in the next few days. (*Find out what and where*)

Find out how many people think they will have children in the future. (*Find out how many*)

Preferences

Put the following things in order of preference.

1   What do you prefer to have for breakfast?

   a fruit ☐   **b** toast ☐   **c** cereal ☐   **d** a full English breakfast ☐

2   Which of these cities would you prefer to visit?

   a Tokyo ☐   **b** Sydney ☐   **c** Buenos Aires ☐   **d** Moscow ☐

3   Which of these forms of entertainment do you prefer?

   a theatre ☐   **b** cinema ☐   **c** live pop concerts ☐   **d** opera ☐

4   Which of the following singers do you prefer?

   a Frank Sinatra ☐   **b** Britney Spears ☐   **c** Elton John ☐   **d** Madonna ☐

5   Which of these subjects did you prefer when you were at school?

   a Maths ☐   **b** English ☐   **c** Physics ☐   **d** History ☐

6   In which of the following places would you prefer to live?

   a in the middle of the countryside ☐   **b** a small village ☐   **c** a town ☐   **d** a big city ☐

7   Which of the following animals would you prefer to have as a pet?

   a cat ☐   **b** dog ☐   **c** snake ☐   **d** fish ☐

8   Which of the following jobs would you prefer to do?

   a doctor ☐   **b** plumber ☐   **c** politician ☐   **d** teacher ☐

9   Which way of socialising do you prefer?

   a clubbing ☐   **b** going to the pub ☐   **c** having lunch/dinner in a restaurant ☐   **d** going for a walk ☐

10   Where would you prefer to stay on holiday?

   a a camp site ☐   **b** a 5 star hotel ☐   **c** a caravan ☐   **d** a holiday flat ☐

11   How would you prefer to travel between London and Edinburgh?

   a by plane ☐   **b** by train ☐   **c** by coach ☐   **d** by car ☐

12   Which of the following adventure sports would you most like to do?

   a parachuting ☐   **b** bungee jumping ☐   **c** deep sea diving ☐   **d** white water rafting ☐

Explain your preferences to a partner using comparatives and superlatives.

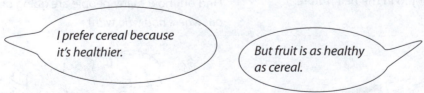

I prefer cereal because it's healthier.

But fruit is as healthy as cereal.

The Multiplex Centre

A recent proposal has been made by a group of businessmen to build a Multiplex Centre in the residential area of Little Hortunn. The centre will have a ten-screen cinema, restaurants, shops, a bowling alley and a nightclub in the basement, and it will be situated where Hortunn park is currently located. The businessmen have also considered buying the library and the community centre, knocking them down and using this land too. Local residents have mixed feelings about these plans and a meeting has been called in the Community Centre to discuss the advantages and disadvantages of the proposed multiplex centre.

1 Sam Brown – businessman/woman

You are one of the associates who want to build the Multiplex Centre. You must try to convince the others that it will be beneficial for the area and the residents. You think that it will certainly increase house prices in the area and that it will definitely provide entertainment for the local residents. Some local residents will probably also be able to get jobs in the centre and there might also be opportunities for locals to open businesses within the centre. It definitely won't cause problems of parking or noise because there will be a car park on the top floor and the building will be sound-proofed.

2 Paul/Paula Jones – 19-year-old student

You really like the idea of the Multiplex Centre as you live in this residential area with your parents and you think it's really boring. You think that all the facilities will definitely be really good fun. You will certainly go to the cinema once a week and you'll probably go to the club quite often as you'll be able to walk home afterwards instead of getting a taxi. You think you might be able to get a Saturday job in one of the shops, which would give you a bit of extra money because as a student you are quite poor. You think it will probably make the area more fashionable and that it will attract more interesting people to the area.

3 Edward/Edwina Bowles

You are a pensioner who has lived in this area for some time and you really don't like the idea of the Multiplex Centre. You think it will definitely make the area noisier and there will certainly be more traffic. At the moment you enjoy peaceful walks in Hortunn Park and in the future you definitely won't be able to do this. You think that the business associates who are building the multiplex might also buy the Community Centre and the local library where you often go during the day to read and do other activities that are organised there. Furthermore, you think you probably won't use any of the facilities and therefore it will have no use at all for you.

4 John/Jean Siles

You are in your 40s, a police officer and parent of two teenage children. You have a lot of doubts about the Multiplex Centre as you think that it definitely won't be a good thing for your children. You've seen in other areas how children tend to spend all day in these places and you think that it might stop your children from studying. You also believe that it might attract other, not very well behaved, teenagers to the area and this could be a bad influence on your kids. The club might also bring problems of people making noise in the streets at 2 or 3a.m. On the other hand, you think it will probably increase house prices, which you would be happy about.

How do you say …?

FUL   UN   LESS   Y   RE   EX

START	**1** a person who has nowhere to live (8 letters)	**2** a confusion about what something means (15 letters)	**3** write a critical article about a film or book (6 letters)
4 a thing that has no purpose (7 letters)			
5 the woman you divorced (6 letters)	**6** when you have a different point of view from someone (8 letters)	**7** the adjective of week (6 letters)	**8** a person who doesn't usually remember things (9 letters)
9 when you don't fail, you are this (10 letters)			
10 when you say something with the wrong phonetic sound (12 letters)	**11** when there is no justice (6 letters)	**12** something that never finishes (7 letters)	**13** a place that lots of people visit on holiday (8 letters)
14 a place which has not been developed for tourism (8 letters)			
15 the adjective of create (8 letters)	**16** if something makes you have a good time, it is this (9 letters)	**17** a thing that doesn't interest you (13 letters)	**18** something that isn't common (7 letters)
19 if you organise a meeting again you do this (9 letters)			
20 the adjective of air (4 letters)	**21** when you have listened to something wrongly (8 letters)	**22** the opposite of cheap (9 letters)	**23** if you do something without paying enough attention (8 letters)
24 the opposite of clean (5 letters)			
25 the opposite of hectic or noisy (8 letters)	**26** something fragile like a glass (9 letters)	**27** an untidy person or place (5 letters)	**28** handsome or pretty, in your opinion (10 letters)
29 a person who chats to others and gets on with people (8 letters)			
30 if you go back to a place again (7 letters)	**31** one minute you are here, and the next you're not (9 letters)	**32** something which you can understand easily (14 letters)	**33** a person who helps a lot (7 letters)
FINISH			

MIS   DIS   IVE   ABLE   IBLE

Estate agents

Estate agent

Try to sell this house.

Price: £190, 000

Location: Residential area in the suburbs with several local schools and shops. 7 miles from the city centre, with good transport links.

Description: On the ground floor there is a large living room and a kitchen. On the first floor there is a bathroom, two large bedrooms and a small bedroom. The fourth bedroom is in the attic. The house has central heating, but no air conditioning or burglar alarm. It has a garage with space for one car and access via the drive and a fairly large garden. It's about 30 years old and needs some work done in the kitchen and bathroom.

Estate agent

Try to sell this house.

Price: £160,000

Location: In the countryside, about 2 miles from the outskirts of the city and 10 miles from the city centre. There are no local schools but there is a little shop 10 minutes walk away. There is a bus to the city centre that passes once every 2 hours.

Description: This cottage is about 150 years old but has been modernised and is in very good condition. It has only one floor, but it has a large living room, a good size dining room, a kitchen, 3 large bedrooms and 2 bathrooms. There is no garage but because the area is so quiet, there are no parking problems. It doesn't have central heating or air conditioning but it has an open fireplace in the living room and dining

Estate agent

Try to sell this house.

Price: £210,000

Location: Near to the city centre. There are lots of shops of all kinds and public transport to all parts of the city is excellent. It's 4 miles to the nearest school.

Description: This flat is new and extremely modern. It has central heating, air conditioning and a burglar alarm. It has two large bedrooms, two on-suite bathrooms, an enormous living room with a large balcony with views of the city centre. It also has a large kitchen with its own dining area and a small office. There is a parking space available at a little extra cost in the basement.

Buyer

BIGGER AND BETTER
ESTATE AGENTS

You are looking to buy a house. Visit three estate agencies and decide which of the three houses you would like to buy.

You are 28 and single with a girl/boyfriend. You think you might get married in a couple of years and have children. You work as a lawyer in the city centre and have a BMW car. Your girl/boyfriend also has a BMW, so it's important that there is somewhere safe to park the other car too. You love meeting people, going out and clubbing. You also go to the gym most evenings and you like to be near to some green areas where you can go running. You like modern things, but they have to be original and special. You can afford about £180,000, but if there were something you really liked you would be prepared to spend a bit more.

Buyer

MY KIND OF PLACE
ESTATE AGENTS

You are looking to buy a house. Visit three estate agencies and decide which of the three houses you would like to buy.

You are 55 and divorced. You have three children but they are all living away from home, although they sometimes come to visit you. You work as an administration assistant in the centre of town and you don't have a car. You can drive, however, and if you needed to buy a car you would. You love gardening and you'd like to live in a peaceful area of town or in the countryside. You'd like to have all modern appliances like central heating and air conditioning. You want to be able to get into the city centre easily because you meet your friends there at the weekend. You can afford about £180,000, although you would pay a little more if necessary.

Buyer

HOME SWEET HOME
ESTATE AGENTS

You are looking to buy a house. Visit three estate agencies and decide which of the three houses you would like to buy.

You are 38 and married with two small children. You might want to have another child in the future. You are a computer programmer and work from home, so it's very important for you to have a study area. You prefer to be near the city centre because you don't really like the countryside although a garden would be nice for the children. You don't want to buy anywhere that needs work doing to it. You think it's very important to have schools and shops nearby, but as you and your partner have cars, you could take the children to school by car if it was necessary. You'd also like a quiet location. You can afford about £200,000.

Money problems

Student A

Situation 1: You have just started a holiday travelling around Europe with a friend. You have a limited amount of money and you have to spend it wisely. You'd like to stay in 3 or 4 star hotels because you think they are good value for money and that way you'll sleep well and have lots of energy for visiting different places. You can save money by buying food from supermarkets and eating it in the streets or hotel room. If you run out of money, you know your friend has a visa card and could get some cash to lend you and you would pay it back when you get home.

Situation 2: You know that your partner is about to inherit some money from an aunt. You don't know how much it's going to be, but if it's more than £2,000, you would like to go on a trip around the world. You and your partner have been working very hard recently and you still haven't got too many responsibilities, as you are only 25 and live in rented accommodation. You think this will be an opportunity to do something that you will never be able to do again, and you have the rest of your lives to save and spend wisely.

Situation 3: You are the boss of a small design company that makes clothes for shops in the local area. You aren't making a lot of money at the moment because there is a lot of competition, and the money you make is usually invested in new equipment and expansion of the company. You also think one of your staff is stealing, but you are not sure who it is. You've decided to speak to an employee who has worked for you the longest to ask him/her to spy on the others in order to find out who it is.

Student B

Situation 1: You have just started a holiday travelling around Europe with a friend. You have a limited amount of money and you have to spend it wisely. You think that the best idea would be to stay at campsites because they are very good value for money and cheaper than hotels. This way you would have some spare money to spend on eating in local restaurants and buying souvenirs. You don't want to waste your money on hotels. You have a visa card, but you don't want to use it because they charge a lot of commission and you need the money you have in the bank when you get home.

Situation 2: You have just inherited £3,000 from an aunt. Tell your partner and suggest ways of spending the money. You think that you should spend the money wisely and not waste it on things that aren't necessary. You would like to invest a little of it, about £500, and put the rest in the bank in order to start saving to buy a house. You think this is a good time to start thinking about the future. You have never had enough money to do this before and you haven't got time or money to spare as you are 25 and need to be responsible.

Situation 3: You work in a small design company that makes clothes for shops in the local area. You have worked there for a very long time (longer than any other employees) and have earned the same amount of money for the last 5 years. Your boss has asked to see you and you are very pleased because it will give you the opportunity to tell him/her that you would like to earn more money. At the moment, you never have any money to spare at the end of the month and if he doesn't give you a rise, you think it's not worth continuing in the company.

How well do I know my classmates?

Write the name of one or more of your classmates who correspond to the sentences below.

1 _____ doesn't have a very healthy lifestyle.

2 _____ travelled abroad more than 4 times.

3 _____ is feeling quite tired at the moment.

4 _____ can work out what 5% of 175 is in his/her head.

5 _____ has had more than 4 girl/boyfriends.

6 _____ has been to the cinema this week.

7 _____ can ski.

8 _____ studies almost every day.

9 _____ wouldn't like to go bungee jumping,

10 _____ spends his/her money wisely.

11 _____ hasn't got a mobile phone.

12 _____ lives in a big house or flat.

13 _____ is afraid of snakes.

14 _____ would like to live in another country in the future.

15 _____ is ambitious.

16 _____ went to bed early last night.

17 _____ hasn't studied English for more than three years.

18 _____ has met somebody famous.

19 _____ didn't do any sport when he/she was a child.

20 _____ is interested in music.

Ask your classmates using question tags to find out if you were right.

Utopia

What is your idea of Utopia? Read the following rules and put a (✓) if they fit your idea of a perfect world. Change the rule if you don't agree with it.

Everybody should go to university. .... ❏

Children over the age of 12 don't have to go to school if they don't want to. .... ❏

People mustn't smoke in any public places. .... ❏

People shouldn't tell lies under any circumstances. .... ❏

Politicians must take very difficult exams before they can stand for election. .... ❏

Young people have to spend at least one year living in a foreign country. .... ❏

People shouldn't make sexist or racist comments or jokes. .... ❏

People don't have to pay taxes. .... ❏

Holidays should be a lot longer than they are now. .... ❏

Governments shouldn't spend money on weapons. .... ❏

People don't have to show identification when passing from one country to another. .... ❏

Factories shouldn't pollute the atmosphere under any circumstances. .... ❏

Everybody has to take turns in looking after the children and old people in a community. .... ❏

Drivers shouldn't use their cars more than twice a week. .... ❏

People mustn't eat or drink more than they need. .... ❏

Everybody must earn the same amount of money if they work for the same number of hours. ❏

Wealth must be divided equally between countries. .... ❏

English should be the international language. .... ❏

Now discuss the rules in small groups, saying why you agree or disagree.

Can I sell you this?

Student A

1

If you buy this car ………….

………………….. as soon as you drive this car.

When you show this car to your friends …………….

…………………. unless you buy this car from me.

2

If you buy this computer ……………

………………………. as soon as you use this computer.

When you compare this computer to other computers
……………….

……………………. unless you are fully satisfied.

3

If you book this holiday ………….

……………………….. as soon as you arrive at the hotel.

When you are there ………………………

……………………….. unless you decide today.

Student B

1

If you buy this mobile phone ………….

………………………… as soon as you switch it on.

When you run out of credit………………

……………………….. unless you buy it today.

2

If you do this English course …………

……………………………. as soon as you pay.

When you finish this course …………….

……………………………... unless you fail the exam.

3

If you come to our clinic ……………

………………………… as soon as you have the
operation.

When you leave the clinic ………………

BLEEP: Which word was that?

Last year I BLEEP to New York on a plane. (*travelled*)	The local bank was BLEEP last weekend. (*robbed*)	I had my purse BLEEP when I was shopping. (*stolen*)	My son is going on a school BLEEP next week to the coast. (*trip*)
BLEEP to other countries makes you more tolerant of other cultures. (*travelling*)	The party I went to was really good BLEEP. (*fun*)	That new comedy was the BLEEP thing I've seen in a long time. (*funniest*)	My teacher BLEEP us to be quiet. (*told*)
Can you tell me what the teacher BLEEP? I didn't hear her. (*said*)	I'd like to get a BLEEP as a waitress in the summer. (*job*)	I can't go out. I've got to much BLEEP to do. (*work*)	Paul is BLEEP as a waiter in his father's restaurant at the moment. (*working*)
The bank normally BLEEP people money to buy a house. (*lend*)	She BLEEP my bike and never gave it back. (*borrowed*)	I never BLEEP my mother's birthday and she gets angry. (*remember*)	Could you BLEEP me to buy some milk later. (*remind*)
I don't know this vocabulary because I BLEEP the class. (*missed*)	She has BLEEP a lot of weight since she started the diet. (*lost*)	BLEEP the truth now or you will be punished. (*tell*)	My father was often away on business BLEEP when I was young. (*trips*)
You can't BLEEP a book without identification. (*borrow*)	That joke really wasn't very BLEEP. I didn't laugh at all. (*funny*)	She BLEEP me her mobile to phone home. (*lent*)	I really BLEEP my family when I go abroad. (*miss*)

BLEEP: Which word was that?

Which would you buy?

Some very similar products often have very different prices. Look at the following adverts with a partner and discuss.

a What are the main differences between the two products?

b Is it worth paying for the most expensive one or would you be wasting your money?

c Which would you buy?

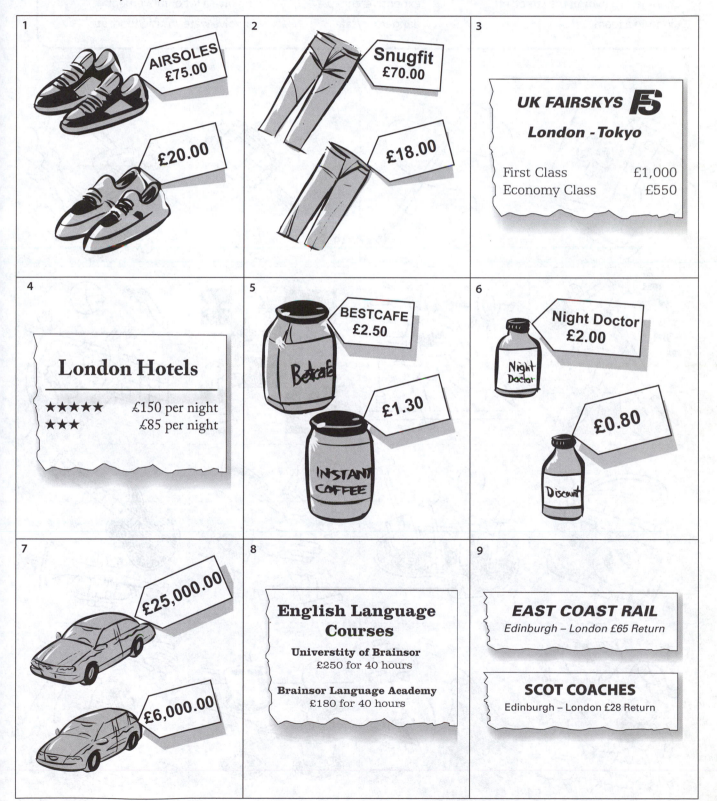

Which leisure activity?

inside/outside	difficult/easy	win the game
special clothes	special equipment	energetic
at home/in a gym/in the street, etc	expensive/cheap	involve a lot of movement
alone/in a team	dangerous/safe	involve water/music/food, etc

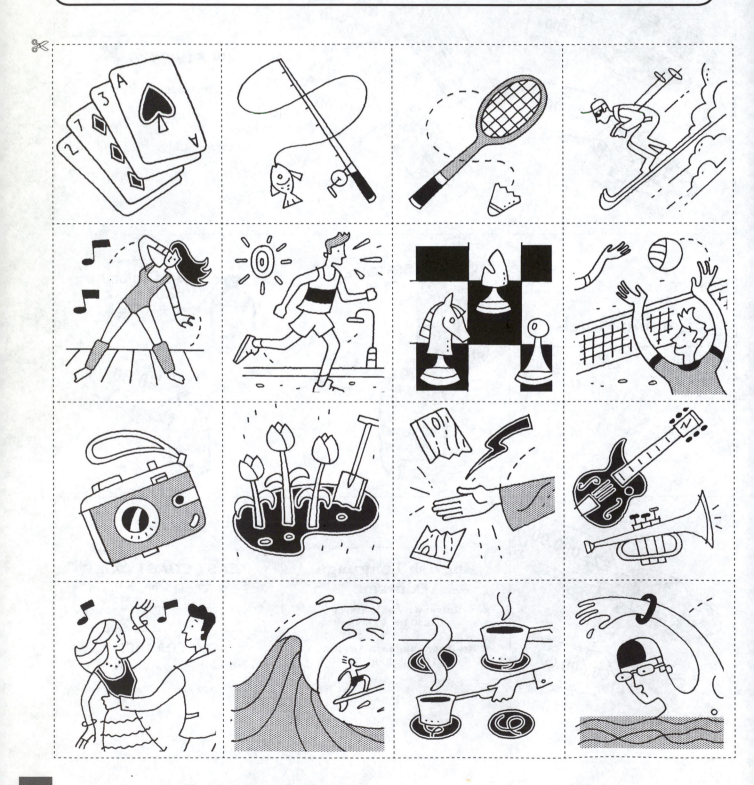

What have they been doing?

Match the words in the box to the pictures in pairs.

Student A

lift weights/hurt one's back

punish/fight

run/miss the train

make a cake/cook

cut one's finger/chop onions

cry/break one's arm

Student B

garden/find a frog

drop a bucket/clean windows

steal a lot of money/rob a bank

run in the rain/catch a cold

pick a flower/cycle in the countryside

play tennis/win a cup

Now explain with a partner what has been happening and what has happened in each picture using the words from the box.

Has anything similar happened to you? Explain to your partner what happened.

Find somebody like you

Complete the sentences with a verb in the correct form (gerund or infinitive) so that they are true for you.

NAME: [   ]

When I was a child I couldn't stand ....

I love .... at the weekends.

My friends usually help me ....

Recently, I have stopped ....

Next year I want ....

I enjoy .... during the holidays.

My parents didn't allow me .... when I was a teenager.

I would like to continue .... next year.

I expect .... in the near future.

My teachers at school advised me ....

I'm always forgetting ....

I hate .... at home.

I remember .... when I was very little.

At the moment I'm looking forward to ....

I started .... a few years ago.

Now ask questions to your classmates and find one person who is like you. Write their name next to the sentence.

Could you stand eating lentils when you were a child?

Yes, I could. I loved eating lentils!

Find the difference

Student A

Find 12 differences between your picture and your partner's picture by asking questions or describing. Use the words in the box.

| some | (not) any | many | much | a few | a couple | a little | lots of | a lot of |

Student B

Find 12 differences between your picture and your partner's picture by asking questions or describing. Use the words in the box.

| some | (not) any | many | much | a few | a couple | a little | lots of | a lot of |

What word am I explaining?

Student A

Match the words in the box to the definitions below.

> CARPET   FORK   MEDICINE   ELEPHANT   SHARPENER
> EGG   JOGGING   DESSERT   PILLOW   CREAM

1   It's a kind of dish that you have after your main course. It's sweet.

2   It's a type of animal that is normally huge, heavy and grey. It can be found in Africa and has a trunk.

3   It's the stuff you put on desserts like strawberries to make it sweeter. It's thick and smooth.

4   It's something English people put on the floor. It comes in different colours and it can be smooth or rough.

5   It's a thing you use for making your pencil pointed at the end so that you can write with it.

6   It's very soft and you use it when you are sleeping for your head.

7   It's a smooth, oval thing that you can eat; fried, boiled or scrambled.

8   It's usually made of metal and it has a narrow handle. You use it for eating, but not cutting.

9   It's a type of sport that you can do anywhere. It's like running but slower.

10   It's stuff that you take when you are feeling ill.

Now read out the definitions to the other team. They score 1 point for each word they guess correctly.

- -

Student B

Match the words in the box to the definitions below.

> DUB   CORRIDOR   REMOTE CONTROL   COURT   FEATHER
> MOTORWAY   PALACE   FRYING PAN   COLLEAGUE   CHOCOLATE

1   It's a rectangular area where people play tennis or volleyball.

2   It's sweet, brown, sticky stuff that is made from cocoa.

3   It's a very wide road where cars can drive very fast between different cities.

4   It's a thing that they do to films when they change the original language.

5   It's a person who you work with or who has the same profession as you.

6   It's a hard, round thing you can find in the kitchen. It's used for frying things.

7   It's a huge, beautiful building where royal families traditionally lived.

8   It's a narrow space between rooms in a house where you can walk to get from one place to the other.

9   It's very light and soft and it comes from the birds.

10   It's rectangular and made of plastic and it's used for changing the TV channel.

Now read out the definitions to the other team. They score 1 point for each word they guess correctly.

Trivia quiz: How much do you know?

> **RULES**
>
> Choose a square. Listen to the other team's question. If you get it right, you win the square and 1 point, and you can have another turn. If you get it wrong, it's the other team's turn.
>
> The squares are as follows: H=History, G=Geography, Sc=Science, A=The Arts, Sp=Sport, F=Famous People
>
> Score 1 extra point if you get both squares in any one category..

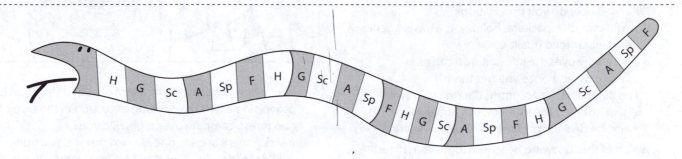

Team A

History

1 Where was Alexander the Great originally from? (*Macedonia*)

2 In which century did the French Revolution take place? (*18th century*)

Geography

1 Which gas makes up 78% of the world's atmosphere? (*nitrogen*)

2 In which two countries can you find Mount Everest? (*China and Nepal*)

Science

1 What is the scientific study of plants called? (*Botany*)

2 Which planet is nearest to the sun? (*Mercury*)

The Arts

1 In which country did the impressionist movement originate? (*France*)

2 Who wrote *Alice in Wonderland*? (*Lewis Carroll*)

Sport

1 What is the most important game of the season in American football? (*Superbowl*)

2 When was the first world cup held? (*1930*)

Famous people

1 Which Greek philosopher lived between 384 and 322 BC? (*Aristotle*)

2 Which Swedish actress starred in *Casablanca*? (*Ingrid Bergman*)

Team B

History

1 Which civilization, the Maya or the Aztec, is the oldest? (*the Maya civilization*)

2 In which century did the Russian Revolution take place? (*20th century*)

Geography

1 Which is the largest continent in the world? (*Asia*)

2 At what distance from the Equator can you find the tropics? (*23.5 degrees*)

Science

1 What is the chemical symbol for magnesium? (*Mg*)

2 In which year did an American team of astronauts first land on the moon? (*1969*)

The Arts

1 What is a 'fresco'? (*painting directly painted on a wall*)

2 Which Jane Austen book was made into a film starring Emma Thompson? (*Sense and Sensibility*)

Sport

1 When were the first modern Olympic Games held? (*1896*)

2 Which country won the World Cup in 1958, 1962 and 1970? (*Brazil*)

Famous people

1 Where was the revolutionary Che Guevara from? (*Argentina*)

2 What was Einstein's first name? (*Albert*)

133

Are you an adventurous holiday-maker?

Ask and answer the following questions with a partner.

1   Where do you normally choose to go on a holiday?
   a To a different country every year so that you can experience lots of different cultures.
   b To the same place every year. New sensations are not for you.
   c It depends. Sometimes to a place you already know and sometimes somewhere new.

2   What and how do you usually book?
   a An all-inclusive package holiday at a travel agent's with guaranteed quality.
   b Flight only over the Internet. You can plan everything else once you get there.
   c The flight and the accommodation at a travel agent's or over the Internet, but not always a package deal as it's nice to have some freedom.

3   Which of the following beaches would you prefer?
   a You don't like the beach. The hotel swimming pool is much warmer, safer and has waiter service.
   b Not too busy, but near the hotel, shops and cafés so that you can get drinks or food to eat when you want.
   c One that you can't get to by car, so there are normally no other people there.

4   What do you think about the food when you go abroad?
   a You try some of it, but nothing too strange. It depends really what it is.
   b You never try any of it. Better to eat the hotel food or take it with you from home.
   c You'd try anything; fried insects, spicy curries, strange animals. It's all part of the experience.

5   You meet a local couple on holiday abroad who suggest you go with them to explore the area. What do you decide?
   a No way. You're staying in the hotel complex. You never know what's out there.
   b You think twice about it. It would probably be better to hire a car and go alone. You don't really know what this couple is like.
   c Jump at the chance. Local people always show you the most interesting sights and landmarks.

6   You are on holiday in Central America and the hotel is organising a two-day walking excursion in the tropical rain forest, camping over night. Do you?
   a Ask if there are any one-day excursions. You quite like the idea, but feel afraid about sleeping in the rain forest.
   b Put your name down immediately. It sounds great!
   c Think 'I can't imagine anything worse'.

7   You arrive at your holiday destination and are informed that there has been a political crisis and the government of the country can't guarantee the safety of tourists. What do you do?
   a Ignore it. You've paid for the holiday and you are going to stay.
   b Stay, but worry and watch the news. If things get any worse, you will leave.
   c Get the next flight home.

8   Your friend has won a round-the-world air ticket for two and asks you to accompany her. You know you haven't got a lot of spending money, so you will need to be careful.
   a Pack your bags straight away and go camp at your friend's in case she changes her mind.
   b Sit down and calculate exactly how much money you've got and then make a decision.
   c Decide not to go. There are lots of countries you don't want to visit and especially without much money.

Results

1 a3 b1 c2   2 a1 b3 c2   3 a1 b3 c3   4 a2 b1 c3
5 a1 b2 c3   6 a2 b3 c1   7 a3 b2 c1   8 a3 b2 c1

8–13

You really aren't very adventurous when it comes to holidays, are you? Maybe you are right to worry about some of the risks you face when you face away from home, but relax a little. If not, then you should probably just stick to package holidays in your own country.

14–19

Well, there is some spirit of adventure in you somewhere, although you don't do things without thinking about them first. You probably enjoy different types of holidays and you probably have a lot of fun without getting yourself into too many dangerous situations.

20–24

Rainforests, wild animals, political crises, nothing worries you, does it? Holidays are about adventures, new sensations, excitement and anything else that is on offer. Just remember, however, not all adventures are safe and there is life after the holidays!

Are you lying to me?

> MOVE HOUSE   HAVE A JOB   LEARN TO SWIM
>
> TRAVEL ABROAD   LEARN TO DRIVE   HAVE A BOYFRIEND/GIRLFRIEND
>
> STAY OVERNIGHT IN HOSPITAL   STUDY A FOREIGN LANGUAGE   LEARN TO PLAY A MUSICAL INSTRUMENT

Match the expressions in the box above to the pictures below.

By the time you were 6

By the time you were 11

By the time you were 18

Now choose 1 picture from each row and put a X through it. Don't show your partner!

Ask your partner about the activities above. Ask follow-up questions to guess if he or she is telling the truth.

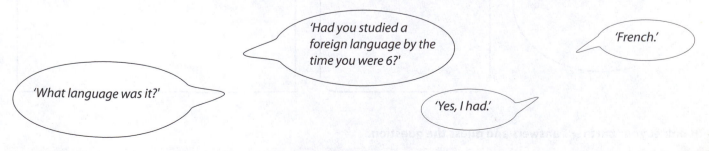

What question was that?

Write short answers to ten of the following questions in the shapes below. Don't do it in order.

1 What food do you like the most?

2 Which country would you like to visit in the future?

3 Who do you look like the most in your family?

4 What's the weather like today?

5 What does curry taste like?

6 What do you like doing in your free time?

7 What does heavy metal sound like?

8 What would you like to change about your physical appearance?

9 What is London like?

10 What does Britney Spears look like?

11 What kind of TV programmes do you like?

12 What jobs around the house don't you like doing?

13 What was the last film you saw like?

14 Where would you like to live in the future?

15 What does Spring smell like?

16 Which other student in the class looks the most like you?

Look at your partner's answers and guess the question.

The article race

Student A

Correct your partner's sentences, which all contain a grammar mistake. If you get it wrong, you miss a turn.

	START
1	I went to shop where I bought the book and spoke to a shop assistant about changing it. (*the shop*)
2	The boy who sits next to me is fastest runner in the class. (*the fastest*)
3	I was standing on bridge that crosses the River Thames. (*a bridge*)
4	The violence in the United States is getting worse all the time. (*Violence with no article*)
5	My brother lives in a big house in south of France. (*the south of France*)
6	I had the dinner in a small restaurant in the centre of the city. (*dinner with no article*)
7	Swedish are usually very fair and quite tall. (*The Swedish*)
8	The last weekend we went to the countryside to camp. (*Last weekend with no article*)
9	I had a apple and a banana after lunch. (*an apple*)
10	There's boy in my class who I don't really like. He's a history student. (*a boy*)
11	We stayed in a small hotel in the southern Italy. (*southern Italy with no article*)
12	I like the music she played at the beginning of night but not at the end. (*the night*)
13	I was chased by dog on my way home from school. (*a dog*)
14	It's possible to swim in Mediterranean sea even in winter. (*the Mediterranean*)
15	I went shopping on bus but I got a taxi to get back home again. (*the bus*)
	FINISH

Student B

Correct your partner's sentences, which all contain a grammar mistake. If you get it wrong, you miss a turn.

	START
1	Himalayas are a mountain range in Asia. (*The Himalayas*)
2	There wasn't any furniture in the new house except fridge in the kitchen. (*a fridge*)
3	I'd like to get job as nurse in a big hospital in the future. (*a nurse*)
4	Sahara desert is an extremely hot and dry place. It's also very big. (*The Sahara*)
5	I met my first boyfriend at club when I was on holiday in the south of France. (*a club*)
6	I love the dancing, especially when I go out to a club with my friends. (*dancing with no article*)
7	Last night I saw ghost, but it wasn't the same ghost as I saw the night before. (*a ghost*)
8	President of the United States is probably the most powerful person in the world. (*The President*)
9	The River Seine runs through centre of Paris and it's very important to the city. (*the centre*)
10	The travel makes people more tolerant and open-minded. (*Travel with no article*)
11	I'm going to play a tennis match with my cousin the next weekend. (*next weekend with no article*)
12	She was the stronger than the others so she won the game. (*stronger with no article*)
13	We study at very old university which has a very good academic tradition. (*a very old*)
14	When I want a break from work I take a few days to go to coast and relax. (*the coast*)
15	Jamaica is in West Indies. I went there for a few weeks on holiday last year. (*the West Indies*)
	FINISH

Getting information

1  Find out how your classmates get around town. Do they always do the same thing?	**2**  Find out if your classmates think their English is getting better. In what way specifically?	**3**  Find out when was the last time your classmates got ill and what the problem was.
4  Find out what your classmates normally do as soon as they get home in the evening or at night.	**5** Find out who your classmates get on with in their family and why?	**6**  Find out at what time of day your classmates usually get hungry.
7  Find out how often your classmates get a taxi. Why do they get a taxi on these occasions?	**8**  Find out how many of your classmates think they will get married (again) in the future. If not, why not?	**9**  Find out how many of your classmates have got lost at some time in their lives. Ask where and when this happened.
10  Find out how many of your classmates have got something in the post this week. Find out what it was.	**11**  Find out what was the best present that your classmates have ever got. Find out who it was from and why they got it.	**12** 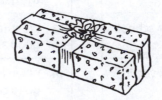 Find out how long it takes your classmates to get ready in the morning. And to go out on a special occasion?

Around the world tourism quiz

Answer the questions in your teams.

1   Where would you go if you wanted to see one of the world's most important international Film, Music, Theatre and Fringe Festivals in August?

2   Which city do you need to visit if you want to cross the Golden Gate suspension bridge?

3   If you were travelling around the Alps, which 6 countries might you be in?

4   Which country would you have to visit to see the ruins of the great Inca city, Machu Picchu?

5   If you were sightseeing in the capital city of Wellington, which country would you be in?

6   On which border are the Niagara Falls, one of the world's most spectacular waterfalls, situated?

7   Which two South America countries could you visit in order to explore the Patagonia desert?

8   In which ocean can you find Christmas Island?

9   Which city would you have to visit to go to the Prado art gallery?

10 What ruined temple is Athens famous for?

11 In which city can you simply cross a river and travel between two continents?

12 In which country can you see the beautiful Lake Geneva?

13 In which city can you find the remarkable landmark, the Alhambra Palace?

14 In which European capital city could you enjoy a traditional pint of Guinness?

15 In which country would you be if you were looking at a palace called the Taj Mahal?

Educational issues: agree/disagree

Mark one of the columns with an X for the ten statements you hear.

	TOTALLY AGREE	PARTIALLY AGREE	DEPENDS	PARTIALLY DISAGREE	TOTALLY DISAGREE
1					
2					
3					
4					
5					
6					
7					
8					
9					
10					

✂ ---

Statements

1 You should always plan first what you are going to say in English in order to avoid making mistakes when you speak.

2 Governments should spend more money on scientific research.

3 Everybody should be given the opportunity to do a university degree.

4 Some subjects like religion or physical education should never be obligatory.

5 It's a good idea to take a sabbatical year after graduating from university and before looking for a job.

6 If a student always gets good marks it shows that he or she is intelligent.

7 It is better to evaluate students on coursework and participation in class rather than make them do exams.

8 When you take notes, you should try to write down everything the teacher says.

9 Students learn more when they go to small classes or tutorials rather than when they attend big lectures.

10 The best way of making progress in a language is to live in a country where it is spoken.

Fact or fiction?

Student A

Read the following sentences and think of a question to ask to find the missing information.

1 Pablo Picasso was born in Barcelona and painted many famous paintings including *La Guernica, Woman with a Crow* and *Sunflowers*.

2 Charles Darwin was born in _____ in 1809 and wrote *On the origin of the species* in 1859.

3 The famous writer Oscar Wilde was born in Dublin in 1905 and died in France in 1949.

4 _____ ruled Great Britain for 40 years.

5 Penguins can jump almost 6 feet in the air.

6 _____ is the only animal with four knees.

7 The Hundred Years war actually lasted 200 years.

8 President Roosevelt was extremely superstitious and never _____ on a Friday.

9 The only nation whose name begins with an 'A', but doesn't end in an 'A' is Afghanistan.

10 _____ shot and killed John Lennon in New York in December 1980.

11 The original version of the film *King Kong* was first released in 1949.

12 The first *Star Wars* film was released in 1987 and won _____.

Now guess with your partner which 6 sentences are false.

✂ --

Student B

Read the following sentences and think of a question to ask to find the missing information.

1 _____ was born in Barcelona and painted many famous paintings including *La Guernica, Woman with a Crow* and *Sunflowers*.

2 Charles Darwin was born in England in 1809 and wrote *On the origin of the species* in 1859.

3 The famous writer Oscar Wilde was born in Dublin in 1905 and died in France in _____.

4 Queen Victoria ruled Great Britain for 40 years.

5 Penguins can _____ almost 6 feet in the air.

6 The elephant is the only animal with four knees.

7 _____ actually lasted 200 years.

8 President Roosevelt was extremely superstitious and never started a journey on a Friday.

9 The only nation whose name begins with an 'A', but doesn't end in an 'A' is _____.

10 Mark David Chapman shot and killed John Lennon in New York in December 1980.

11 _____ was first released in 1949.

12 The first *Star Wars* film was released in 1987 and won 6 Oscars.

Now guess with your partner which 6 sentences are false.

What's happened to me?

You've just graduated from university. 	You've just become an ecologist. 	You're an astronaut and you've just flown into space. 	You've just become a vegetarian. 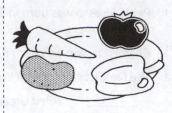
You've just started going out with a famous actor/ actress. 	You've just broken your leg. 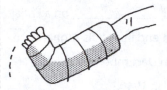	You've just got divorced. 	You started body building at the gym. 
You've moved to England. 	You've started smoking. 	You've just had twins. 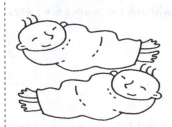	You've just sold your car. 
You've started meditating and doing yoga. 	You've just bought your first mobile phone. 	You've just retired. 	You've started work in a nightclub. 
You've won the lottery. 	You've learned to speak English very well. 	You've been elected President of the USA. 	You've just started a diet. 

How many people …?

Find out how many people in the class

a   can speak more than two languages. (*Ask which*)

b   can't drive a car. (*Ask why they haven't learned*)

Find out how many people in the class

a   could use a computer as a small child. (*Ask when and how they learned*)

b   couldn't see their relatives very often as a child. (*Ask why*)

Find out how many people in the class

a   managed to achieve an important objective last year. (*Ask what*)

b   didn't manage to get up at the time they planned this morning. (*Ask why*)

Find out how many people in the class

a   were able to pass all their exams at school. (*Ask how*)

b   weren't able to do everything they wanted to do yesterday. (*Ask what they didn't do*)

Find out how many people in the class

a   can tell a joke in English. (*Ask which one*)

b   can't eat a certain kind of food. (*Ask which and why*)

Find out how many people in the class

a   could ski when they were a child. (*Ask where they learned*)

b   couldn't understand a school subject at all. (*Ask which*)

Find out how many people in the class

a   were able to meet somebody famous when they were growing up. (*Ask who*)

b   weren't able to do everything they wanted as a teenager. (*Ask what*)

Find out how many people in the class

a   managed to save some money last year. (*Ask how*)

b   didn't manage to do their last piece of English homework. (*Ask why*)

Find out how many people in the class

a   can lose weight easily. (*Ask how*)

b   can't see their friends as much as they would like at the weekends. (*Ask why*)

Find out how many people in the class

a   were able to travel abroad a lot as a child. (*Ask why*)

b   weren't able to do sport when they were at secondary/any school. (*Ask why*)

All about learning and knowing

Student A

Replace the <u>underlined</u> expression(s) with an appropriate idiom in the correct form. Make other changes if necessary.

1   Are there any people that you know <u>very well</u>? Why do you think this is?

_____

_____

2   When travelling abroad, have you ever <u>learned</u> any foreign words <u>by chance</u>? Do you still remember them? What were they and what did they mean?

_____

_____

3   When you were a child, did you use <u>to help</u> your parents to do things around the house? What things did you do and do you think you learnt a lot from this experience?

_____

_____

4   If you were in an exam and you had no idea of the answer, would you <u>invent an answer without thinking about it too much</u>? Have you done this often? Were you successful?

_____

_____

5   What things would you like to <u>study again in order to remember better</u>? How could you do this?

_____

_____

6   If you <u>have no idea</u> about how to say something in English when you are in class, what do you do? What would you do if you were in an English speaking country?

_____

_____

Student B

Replace the <u>underlined</u> expression(s) with an appropriate idiom in the correct form. Make other changes if necessary.

1   When you were at school, which subject did you not <u>know anything about</u>? Why was this?

_____

_____

2   Who normally <u>helps</u> you if you have problems doing your homework? Do you ever <u>help</u> anybody else with their homework?

_____

_____

3   Have you ever <u>read a lot of books</u>? Do you think children tend to <u>read a lot of books</u> these days?

_____

_____

4   Do you think it's better to <u>memorise</u> things before an exam? Does it depend on the subject you are studying?

_____

_____

5   If you were in a job interview and the interviewer asked you a question you didn't know the answer to, would you <u>invent the answer without thinking</u>? Why is this a bit risky?

_____

_____

6   Do you think the teacher's <u>favourite student</u> is always one of the most intelligent people in the class? What other characteristics do teachers really like?

_____

_____

Those were the days!

Match the expressions from the box with the pictures.

GET GOOD MARKS   DO RESEARCH IN SCIENCE   HAVE STRICT, FRIGHTENING TEACHERS
WEAR UNIFORMS   WORK IN GROUPS   GO ON SCHOOL TRIPS
HAVE (HORRIBLE) SCHOOL DINNERS   PLAY SPORTS   BE PUNISHED

Talk in small groups about the pictures in relation to your school days. Did you have a similar experience? In what way was it similar and in what way was it different?

Guess the change expression

You agreed to meet your friend this afternoon at 6 o'clock, but now you can't arrive until 7. You phone her to see if you can come to a different agreement. What do you say?	You're in a restaurant and you've just told the waiter that you want soup for starters. Now, you suddenly think that you'd prefer salad. What do you say to the waiter?	You went out for a walk on a sunny day and suddenly it began raining very heavily. What should you do when you get home?
Can we change the arrangement?	*I've changed my mind.*	*Change your clothes.*
You are living in England and all winter it has been very cold, cloudy and it has rained a lot. One morning you wake up and it's sunny and warm. What do you say?	You've been working in your present job for the last 10 years. You're reasonably happy but it's getting a little boring and you'd like to do something different. What do you say?	Ten years ago you went on holiday to a small, quiet fishing village in the south of Spain. You've just gone back there and now there are lots of hotels, bars and clubs. What do you say?
That makes a (nice) change!	*It's time for a change.*	*There have been some major changes.*
You've just got off the plane in a foreign country and you realise that you haven't brought any of the local currency. You only have money from your country. What do you need to do?	You're in a café with some friends and one of them starts talking about love problems. You know that your other friend has just broken up with her boyfriend and it's not a good idea to talk about this. What do you need to do?	Everyday you go to work with a friend by car. It's not very far and you'd really like to get a bit more exercise. What do you say to your friend?
You need to change some money.	*You need to change the subject.*	*Let's walk for a change.*
Your friend has not been to the hairdresser's for a couple of years and she doesn't look very modern or attractive. Tonight she has a date. What do you say to her?	You work in an office with a lot of other people. One day you discover that somebody has been using your computer and looking at your personal files. What do you need to do?	You have been working as a model for several years but have now reached an age where it is difficult to find work. What do you need to do?
You should change your hairstyle.	*You need to change your password.*	*You need to change your career.*

In what circumstances would you?

RULES
Put your counters on start. Throw the dice and move. Talk about circumstances in which you will or would do the thing written in the square. On the ? square, listen to the sentence another classmate says and say if it is right or wrong. If it's wrong correct it. If you don't do this correctly, miss a turn.

START	Have cosmetic surgery	Get angry with your teacher	?	Leave a restaurant without paying	?
Change your job	Stay at home all next weekend	?	Fail your English exam	Lie to your best friend	Steal from a shop
Lend a lot of money to a friend	?	Hitchhike	Sleep in the street	Not eat for a whole day	?
?	Kiss one of your classmates	Cheat in a game	Start studying another language	?	Hit somebody
Break a window	Stay up all night	?	Become a vegetarian	Commit a crime	Do a striptease
Go on holiday abroad	?	Cry	Appear on TV	?	FINISH

If am tired, I'd go to bed. (✗) (*If I were or was*)	If I could, I'd travel the world. (✓)	If they would be quiet, we could continue. (✗) (*If they were*)
Peter would play better if he practised more. (✓)	You'll get a good mark if you studied. (✗) (*You would*)	People might be happier if they had more money. (✓)
If she might see him, she'll tell him. (✗) (*If she sees him*)	I'd lend him a pen if I had another. (✓)	If I can drive, I'd buy a car. (✗) (*If I could drive*)

Adverb bingo

QUIETLY	CAREFULLY	USUALLY	PROBABLY
REALLY	COMPLETELY	SURPRISINGLY	ACTUALLY
WELL	QUICKLY	HARD	GENTLY
UNFORTUNATELY	DEFINITELY	HARDLY EVER	BASICALLY

1 I (really/definitely) want to see Peter tonight. There's something important I need to tell him.

2 She did the exam very (well) and the teacher gave her a good mark.

3 I (hardly ever) see my family as they live in another country.

4 She drives very (carefully). She's never had an accident.

5 I (usually) have a piece of toast for breakfast. In fact, every day during the week, but at weekends I have something else.

6 She was (completely) exhausted after walking all day in the countryside.

7 If you work (hard), you should pass all your exams without any problems.

8 She speaks very (quietly) and it's very difficult to hear what she's saying.

9 (Surprisingly), the worst student in the class got the best mark.

10 We'll (probably) arrive around 6 o'clock but I can't be sure.

11 Peter said it started at 6, but (actually) it starts at 6.15.

12 If we walk (quickly) we should get there on time.

13 If you touch the animals (gently/carefully), they won't hurt you.

14 (Unfortunately), I said something that I shouldn't have said and my friend felt very upset.

15 (Basically), all you need to do is bring some warm clothes and a packed lunch.

What could have been different?

Student A

1 You are the parent of a teenager. Recently you have been having problems with him/her because he/she has not been studying very hard and failed most of the end of term exams. He/she asked for permission to go to a concert with friends last week and you said no because you were angry, but he/she went anyway. Now you have decided to tell your son/daughter that as a punishment, he/she cannot go out for the next two weeks.

2 You and your partner have just bought a new flat. You wanted to buy a smaller place because you thought that you wouldn't be able to afford the mortgage on the place you've actually bought but your partner convinced you. You also wanted a new car and spent a lot of money on that and your partner spent a lot of money on a holiday with his/her friends. You now have serious money problems and need to discuss the situation with your partner.

3 You used to have a very good relationship with your neighbour but now you are having problems. She/he used to come round to your house to chat but then she/he started gossiping with other neighbours about you, so you got a little angry. You had a party last week and didn't invite your neighbour, and he/she called the police because of the noise. Now you play your music very loud on purpose to annoy your neighbour. She/he comes to complain. Discuss your problems.

Student B

1 You are a teenager. You have been having problems with you mother/father recently. You have failed a lot of exams but you found it difficult to study because it was always so noisy in the house. The exams were also very difficult and your teachers were not very good at explaining. You went to a concert with your friends last week although your mother/father had said you couldn't go, but he/she didn't listen to you when you tried to talk about the matter. Now, you are going to be punished.

2 You and your partner have just bought a big, new flat and you now have money problems because you can't afford the mortgage. You know that your partner wasn't happy about buying the flat you bought, but he/she didn't talk to you about why. He/she also spent a lot of money on a new car when you thought that it wasn't necessary. You spent a lot of money on a holiday with your friends because you were angry about the car. You now have to discuss the situation.

3 You used to have a very good relationship with your neighbour but now you are having problems. You used to go to her/his house to chat but then he/she got angry. You think it's because you talked to other neighbours about your conversations but she/he didn't tell you that they were secret. He/she had a party and didn't invite you so you called the police because of the noise. Now he/she plays loud music all the time and you decide to go and talk about the problems.

Word building crossword

Student A

Give your partner a clue for the words given in the crossword.

Tell them if it is a noun, an adjective or a verb and what it means. Don't use any part of the word!

Across:
3. PUNISHMENT
7. UNDERVALUED
11. CREATION

Down clue letters visible:
1. DISAPPER (D I S A P P E R)
4. UNDERPAID (U N D E R P A I D)
9. OVEROOK / OVERCOOK (O V E R C O O K)

✂ -

Student B

Give your partner a clue for the words given in the crossword.

Tell them if it is a noun, an adjective or a verb and what it means. Don't use any part of the word!

Across:
8. DARKNESS
10. UNDERDEVELOPED

Down letters visible:
2. EMPLOYMENT (E M P L O Y M E N T)
5. ACHIEVEMENT (A C H I E V E M E N T)
6. INHUMAN (I N H U M A N)
3. P
Across: DISHONEST (D I S H O N E S T)

A change for the better?

Look at the following pictures and discuss in pairs.

a What can you see? Match the words in the box.

b What type of changes have these things caused in our society?

c Are there any negative consequences of these changes?

REALITY TV	INTERNET	FEMINIST MOVEMENT
MASS AIR TRAVEL	SKYSCRAPERS	GENETICALLY MODIFIED FOOD
EMBRYONIC RESEARCH	MOBILE PHONES	INCREASE IN NO SMOKING AREAS

Perks and promotions

What jobs can you see in the pictures below?

Answer the following questions in small groups.

In which jobs …

a   Is there a lot of unemployment?

b   Do people sometimes work after the official retirement age?

c   Do people need a lot of qualifications? Do people usually need experience?

d   Do people usually work 9–5, flexitime or overtime?

e   Are there a lot of perks?

f   Do you think people find it rewarding?

g   Do you think people face the biggest challenges?

h   Do people earn the most?

i   Are there many chances of promotion?

Jumbled questions

Student A

Order the following words to make questions.

1 help your teenager parents housework did were a you the make you when with ?

   _____

   _____

2 go late parents did were 15 you your let you when out ?

   _____

   _____

3 many in allowed places your smoke are you to public country in ?

   _____

   _____

4 politician would taxes if you make higher people you were a pay ?

   _____

   _____

5 should you wear clothes allowed think do school to normal to be children ?

   _____

   _____

6 let go would teenager 16 alone of a you holiday on ?

   _____

   _____

Student B

Order the following words to make questions.

1 activities did child make were when your extra-curricular do you parents you a any ?

   _____

   _____

2 were let child did parents a when up stay late you your you ?

   _____

   _____

3 the country maximum what your is are allowed drive speed you in to ?

   _____

   _____

4 were make students if you would a exams do lot of you teacher a ?

   _____

   _____

5 people should vote 16 allowed do at to be think you ?

   _____

   _____

6 the government do think hours 24 let open shops a day should you ?

   _____

   _____

Find someone who ... and report back!!

	NAME	EXTRA INFO
1 went to the cinema last week. (*Ask what they saw and their opinion*)		
2 has been ill this year. (*Ask what the illness was*)		
3 is going away next weekend. (*Ask where*)		
4 thinks they will be rich one day. (*Ask why*)		
5 is afraid of some kind of animal. (*Ask which*)		
6 is going to do something exciting after class. (*Ask what*)		
7 went abroad last year. (*Ask where*)		
8 has studied another foreign language. (*Ask which*)		
9 did a part-time job when they were a student. (*Ask what*)		
10 is missing somebody at the moment. (*Ask who*)		
11 has some type of allergy. (*Ask what*)		
12 went out for a meal last week. (*Ask where*)		
13 can do a sport very well. (*Ask what*)		
14 is planning to start a new job in the near future. (*Ask what*)		

Work in small groups. Report back to your group about the things you found out.

Pablo told me that he was going to London next weekend.

Mustafa said he was allergic to peanuts.

Past rules and regulations

Student A

Ask your partner questions to complete the rules.

1   In Switzerland, women were not allowed to vote until 1971.

2   Until recently, pubs in Great Britain had _____ every night.

3   In Italy, everybody had to go to church on Sunday until 1981.

4   During the rule of General Franco in Spain, women couldn't have _____.

5   Before 1947, children didn't have to go to school in Great Britain after they reached the age of 14.

6   The Germans weren't allowed _____ until 1975.

7   Doctors in the Netherlands were first allowed to carry out euthanasia legally in 2002.

8   Men could _____ in Russia after the Russian Revolution.

9   Americans couldn't drink alcohol legally between 1950 and 1965.

10   Until 1976 London taxis had to carry _____ by law.

Now discuss with your partner which 4 rules you think are false.

Student B

Ask your partner questions to complete the rules.

1   In Switzerland, women were not allowed _____ until 1971.

2   Until recently, pubs in Great Britain had to close before 11p.m. every night.

3   In Italy, everybody had _____ until 1981.

4   During the rule of General Franco in Spain, women couldn't have their own bank accounts.

5   Before 1947, children didn't have _____ in Great Britain after they reached the age of 14.

6   The Germans weren't allowed to buy more than one car until 1975.

7   Doctors in the Netherlands were first allowed _____ in 2002.

8   Men could have more than one wife in Russia after the Russian Revolution.

9   Americans couldn't drink _____ between 1950 and 1965.

10   Until 1976 London taxis had to carry some hay and a sack of oats by law.

Now discuss with your partner which 4 rules you think are false.

Pelmanism

CELL PHONE	MOBILE PHONE	BILL	CHECK	CHIPS
FRIES	POST	MAIL	PETROL	GAS
MAIN ROAD	HIGHWAY	SHOPPING CENTRE	MALL	FLAT
APARTMENT	SECONDARY SCHOOL	HIGH SCHOOL	RETURN TICKET	ROUND TRIP
UNDERGROUND	SUBWAY	FOOTBALL	SOCCER	FILM
MOVIE	HOLIDAY	VACATION	TOILET	RESTROOM

Choosing the right career

Choosing a career can be difficult. You have to think about what you are good at, your qualifications, your interests and hobbies, the type of person you are and the type of working life you want. Interview your partner using the following questions and see if you can think of a job that would be suitable for him or her.

1   What were your best subjects when you were at school?

2   Have you studied or are you studying at university? What subject?

3   Have you ever had a job before? What was it? What did you like about that job and what did you dislike about it?

4   Do you like working with your hands or do you prefer working with your mind?

5   Can you use a computer well?

6   Do you prefer working alone or as part of a team?

7   Do you like the outdoors?

8   Do you react well under pressure or do you get very nervous?

9   How would you describe your personality?

10   Is it important for you to earn a lot of money or would you prefer to have less money and more free time?

11   Are you very ambitious or are your family and friends more important than your job?

12   Do you like being with people?

13   How many languages do you speak?

14   Can you drive and do you like driving?

15   Would you say you were creative? In what way?

Talking about memory

Student A

Complete the questions with an appropriate expression/word from the box in the correct form. One word is extra.

> remember   forget   remind you to   remind you of   lose   miss   in memory of

1   Do you ever _____ to do your English homework?

2   What does the word 'summer' _____?

3   Are there any statues or monuments in your town that were built _____ a famous person or an important event?

4   Have you ever _____ your wallet or some money? Did you find it again?

5   What do you think you would _____ the most if you went to live abroad?

6   Can you _____ what you were doing during the Millennium celebrations?

✂ -

Student B

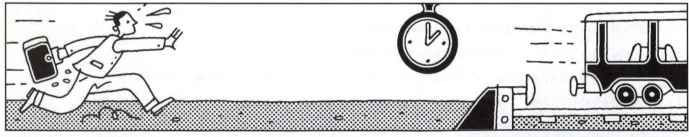

Complete the questions with an appropriate expression/word from the box in the correct form. One word is extra.

> remember   forget   remind you to   remind you of   lose   miss   in memory of

1   Have you ever _____ to take something important with you when travelling?

2   What techniques do you use to _____ do all the things that you have to do during the week?

3   Can you _____ any things that happened to you when you were 5 or 6 years old?

4   Have you ever _____ a flight, train or coach? What happened next?

5   What does the word 'winter' _____?

6   Have you ever got _____ in a big city? What happened?

If things were different!

Read the following sentences and put a (✓) if you agree and a (✗) if you disagree.

I wish I were rich.

I wish I had listened more to my parents.

I wish my English teacher would give us

more homework.

If only I had more free time.

I wish my friends would go out
more often.

If only it were summer all year round.

I wish I had studied something different.

I wish I lived somewhere different.

I wish my family wouldn't interfere
in my life so much.

I wish I could speak another language.

If only people didn't use their cars so much.

I wish I had studied harder when I was at school.

I wish my neighbours wouldn't make so much noise.

If only I could give up smoking.

I wish the world were a fairer place.

Work in small groups and compare your answers. Discuss why you agreed or disagreed with the sentences.

I wish I had more time because I'm very busy and if I had more time I'd …

A tale with a twist!

Work in pairs to tell the story of John and Claire Stevens. Include the words given under each picture.

1

last Saturday/have a party/invite friends/get a new job

2

while/have fun/steal

3

leave the party/say goodbye/realise/disappear

4

call/explain/happen/write down/investigate

5

next morning/go out/realise/appear

6
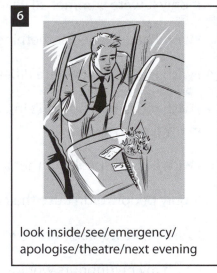
look inside/see/emergency/apologise/theatre/next evening

7

call/explain/stop the investigation

8
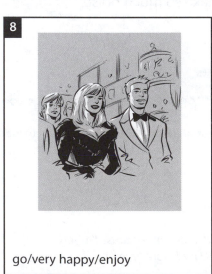
go/very happy/enjoy

9

while/leave/mobile/neighbour/shocked

What do you think the neighbour told John? Finish the story with a partner.

Phrasal verb survey

Ask your classmates the following question and make notes about their answers.

What would you do if you found out that your boyfriend/ girlfriend was fooling around?

Ask your classmates the following question and make notes about their answers.

What do you normally do when you come back home after a long day working or studying?

Ask your classmates the following question and make notes about their answers.

What is going on in the national and international news at the moment?

Ask your classmates the following questions and make notes about their answers.

Do you normally turn up late for things? Does it depend on what it is?

Ask your classmates the following question and make notes about their answers.

What ideas can you come up with for raising money for a class trip?

Ask your classmates the following question and make notes about their answers.

For what reasons do couples normally split up?

Ask your classmates the following questions and make notes about their answers.

Are you going to carry on studying English next year? Where are you going to study?

Ask your classmates the following questions and make notes about their answers.

Have you ever had to call off a trip or journey? Why did this happen?

Ask your classmates the following questions and make notes about their answers.

How can you help a friend who's going through a bad time? Have you had to do this recently?

Ask your classmates the following questions and make notes about their answers.

What do the people you live with do that you can't put up with? And the people you work or study with?

What am I describing?

Read the following descriptions with a partner and guess what is being described.

> It feels hot and nice on your skin. It looks round and quite near, although it's really very far away. You can't touch it or hear it but you can look at it in the sky, if you protect your eyes.

> It looks like a bird but it sounds like something mechanical. Some people don't like the feeling of being inside this thing and some people love it. You can hear and see them when they are low.

PERFUME	CHEESE	STORM	MOUSE
HEAVY METAL	SNOW	CURRY	WINE
WHALE	MOTORBIKE	FIRE	SHOWER
COMPUTER	FIREWORKS	WATERFALL	A KISS

MEDICINE	FRESH BREAD	CAT	SWIMMING POOL

Test your memory!

What have you learned about your classmates during this course? Do you remember what they have talked about in class? Write one or two names next to each of the sentences below.

SOMEBODY WHO ...	NAME(S)
1 is a little bit younger than you.	
2 has turned up late for a lot of classes.	
3 enjoys travelling to exotic places and experiencing different cultures.	
4 has a hectic lifestyle.	
5 regularly plays some kind of sport.	
6 lives in a lively suburb.	
7 has got ill at some time during the course.	
8 gets on very well with his or her mother-in-law.	
9 was brought up in a different place from where he or she was born.	
10 managed to achieve an important objective last year.	
11 met somebody famous when they were growing up.	
12 revises a lot before exams.	
13 hasn't got a clue about computers.	
14 has experienced major changes in his or her life recently.	
15 was made to do housework when they were younger.	
16 had a part time job when they were studying.	

Now ask your classmates to find out if you were right. Do you know each other very well?

Teacher's notes
Photocopiable worksheets

Teacher's notes

UNIT 1 Vocabulary 1
Who am I thinking about?

Procedure

Give a copy of part A of the worksheet to each student. Tell them to work in pairs to read the description and guess the relationship between the writer and the person being described.

Now tell students to use the cue words given to think of questions to ask in order to guess the relationship between two people. Tell them to write down any questions that they have difficulty with. Go around the class, checking the structure of questions.

Ask students to add any extra questions and get feedback from the whole group.

Arrange students in different pairs and give a copy of part B, student A to one and student B to the other. Students write the names of three of the people suggested.

Students ask each other questions in order to guess the relationship each has with the person whose names they have written. Point out before you begin that the students have different lists of relationships to choose from.

Answer

The woman being described is her boss.

UNIT 1 Grammar 1
Which question am I answering?

Procedure

Put the students into pairs and give a copy of worksheet A to one and worksheet B to the other. Ask them to answer the questions on the left, writing complete answers on a separate sheet of paper. Tell them not to speak to their partner yet.

Tell the students to work with their partner. Ask the students to keep their paper hidden from their partner so they can't copy the auxiliary verbs. Each student reads out the answers they have written and their partner must guess the correct question, completing it with the appropriate auxiliary verb as they say it.

Get feedback from the whole class about some of the things they found out.

UNIT 1 Grammar 2
I think or I'm thinking?

Procedure

Give a card to each student. Tell them to write one question in the Present Simple and one in the Present Continuous. Go around the class checking that the questions are correct.

Tell the students to mingle, asking and answering each other's questions. Students don't need to write down the answers but ask them to try to remember what other students have said.

Ask each student to report back on the answers they were given. If you have more than ten students, allow students with the same card to confer previous to the feedback stage.

UNIT 1 Grammar 3
What have we got in common?

Procedure

Give a copy of the worksheet to each student and tell them to write an answer in the first column for each of the fourteen points.

Now tell them to mingle with other students asking questions in the Present Perfect or Past Simple in order to find two other students who have the same answer as they have. If you think students will have problems forming the questions, brainstorm them as a class first. Encourage students to discuss their answers when they find somebody with the same answer.

Get feedback from the whole class about the things they found they had in common.

UNIT 1 Vocabulary 2
Beginnings and endings

Procedure

Cut up a copy of the worksheet for each pair or group of three students.

Give the students the cut up sentences and tell them to read through each one and arrange them in a logical way. Check the answers with the whole class.

Now ask students to comment on each sentence to say if it is true for them. Encourage them to explain why or why not, giving alternative sentences with the same phrasal verb where appropriate.

UNIT 1 Communication
A good friend is …

Procedure

Give a copy of the worksheet to each student and tell them to read the statements and tick the appropriate column. Go around the class, helping with any structures or vocabulary they don't understand.

Now organise the class into small groups of three or four. Tell them to compare their opinions, giving examples with their friends.

Get feedback from the whole class.

UNIT 2 Vocabulary 1
Media crossword

Procedure

Divide the class into two groups, A and B, and give copies of worksheet A to group A and a copy of worksheet B to group B.

Have the students check they understand all of the words written in their crossword in pairs, helping them with any problems they might have.

Now rearrange the students so that a student A is with a student B. Tell them not to look at each other's paper. Focus the students' attention on the example sentence and tell them to give each other clues for the rest of the words. Write *down* and *across* on the board so that students can identify the direction of the words.

UNIT 2 Grammar 1
Sentence auction

Procedure

Organise the class into pairs or groups of three and give each team two copies of the worksheet.

Tell them to read the sentences and decide if they are right or wrong and why. They must bet between £10 and £100 for correct sentences, depending on how sure they are, writing their bet on both copies.

When they have finished, take in one of the copies from each team and give them to a different team to check. Go through the sentences one by one, asking the students how much they have bet and whether they think it is correct or not and why. If the students have bet on a correct sentence, those correcting write the amount in the win column. If they have bet on an incorrect sentence, those correcting write it in the lose column. At the end, students add up the win column and the lose column and then subtract the lose column from the win column. The team with the most money is the winner.

Answers

Sentences 1, 4, 5, 7, 8, 11 and 12 are incorrect. **1** are often interviewed **2** was invented by **5** should be supervised **7** have been stolen **8** was originally created **11** must be recharged **12** was spent

UNIT 2 Grammar 2
Shh! Don't say that word!

Procedure

Organise the class into groups of four. Give one set of cut up cards to each group.

Write the following on the board: *It's a person who/ whose … It's a place where … It's a thing which … It's a time when …*

Write the following example card on the board:

> **MILLIONAIRE**
> *money*
> *rich*
> *luxury*

Give an example of how to play. Students must define the word using relative clauses but without saying the words stated, e.g. *It's a person who can spend a lot. It's a person whose bank account contains many thousands of pounds.*

Organise the students so that they are sitting in groups of four to six. Within the groups they divide into two teams. Each student has a maximum of one minute to explain as many words as possible to the other team member(s), while a member of the other team looks at the same cards to check that they don't say any of the prohibited words. For each word guessed the team scores one point. For each prohibited word said, the other team scores a point.

UNIT 2 Grammar 3
What was going on when …?

Procedure

Give a copy of the worksheet to each pair of students and tell them to match a pair of words from the box with a picture. Check with the whole class, making sure they understand the words.

Ask the students to discuss in pairs which of the verbs are irregular and check with the whole class.

Now students say sentences in pairs for each picture using the Past Simple and Past Continuous. Get feedback from the whole class.

Students then think of an important event that has happened recently and mingle, asking their classmates what they were doing when that thing happened.

Answers

1 escape/sleep **2** land/rain **3** play/get broken **4** have/ring **5** cook/arrive **6** sail/appear **7** sunbathe/sting **8** wait/appear **9** clean/fall **10** run/bite **11** eat/break **12** drive/jump

UNIT 2 Vocabulary 2
Verb collocations noughts and crosses

Procedure

Divide the class up into groups of four and divide each four into two teams of two. If you have odd numbers make some teams of one or three. Give each team a copy of the grid and explain the title *noughts and crosses*. Read through the instructions with the students and check that they understand how to play the game.

Give a copy of sentences A to one team and sentences B to another team. Each team must decide whether to be noughts or crosses.

Tell the students to take it in turns to choose a number and the other team will read them the sentence. If they decide right or wrong correctly they put the symbol in the square. Now the other team plays.

At the end, the students count how many noughts and crosses they have and add an extra point if they have three in a row. The winner is the team with the most points.

Unit 2 | Communication
Newspaper headlines

Procedure

Give a worksheet to each student and put them in pairs. Tell them to look at the pictures and invent a headline for each one, writing it under the picture. Point out that newspaper headlines often don't use articles (*the, a*) or the verb *to be* in passives. Tell them to look at the headlines in Ex. 2a on page 30 for reference and ask them to use their imagination.

Go around the class, helping with vocabulary and correcting any errors.

When they have finished, organise the students in different pairs. Tell them to take it in turns to read out their headlines, but not in the correct order. The other student must guess which picture it goes with.

Unit 3 | Vocabulary 1
What kind of lifestyle do you prefer?

Procedure

Give a copy of the worksheet to each student. Tell them to work in pairs to ask and answer the questions. While the first student asks question 1, the other one doesn't look at the sheet and simply listens and chooses an option to increase listening practice. After they have chosen, they can then look at the sheet and mark the option. The second student then asks question 2, following the same procedure.

Go around the class, helping with any problematic vocabulary or expressions.

When they have finished, get them to count up A, B and C answers. Get feedback from the class about who is mostly which letter. Read through the results with the whole class and see if students agree with the analysis.

Unit 3 | Grammar 1
What the future holds

Procedure

Cut up the worksheet and give one card to each student. Tell the students to read the card and check they understand. Explain that they have to ask a question to all the other students in order to find out the information. Remind them that they must use the future tense given on the card.

Students mingle asking and answering questions. Mingle with them, checking that they are using appropriate questions and answering in the appropriate tense.

Get feedback from each student. Ask them to tell you the questions they asked and the answers they were given. Elicit from the whole group the tense that was used and why.

Unit 3 | Grammar 2
Preferences

Procedure

Give a copy of the worksheet to each student and tell them to read the question and order the items according to their preferences (number 1 for what they prefer the most). Tell them if there are two items they consider to be equal, then they can put the same number for both.

Read the example at the bottom of the page with the whole class and tell them to discuss in pairs their preferences using comparatives and superlatives. Go around the class correcting and helping with any vocabulary they need.

Get feedback from various members of the class.

Unit 3 | Grammar 3
The Multiplex Centre

Procedure

Give a copy of the top part of the worksheet to each student and read through the text with the whole class, referring to the map where necessary.

Now organise the class into groups of four, and give a role card to each student. If you have odd numbers, some groups can be made up of five students and two students can be given the same role card, pretending they are either brother and sister or husband and wife. Allow students time to read through the information and check they understand.

Explain that they are going to discuss the proposal for the Multiplex Centre, from the point of view of their role. Encourage them to add any more arguments they think are relevant. Go around the class monitoring the activity and making a note of any mistakes they make.

When they have finished, have a class vote about the proposal. Tell students to imagine they really live in the area and to vote according to their real point of view.

Unit 3 | Vocabulary 2
How do you say …?

Procedure

Organise the class so that students are sitting in small groups of three or four. Give each group a set of counters and a dice and a copy of the worksheet. Read through the instructions with the whole class and check that students understand.

Students throw the dice to see who starts, and then play the game in their groups. The groups decide if the answer is correct or not, consulting with you where necessary.

Answers

1 homeless **2** misunderstanding **3** review **4** useless **5** ex-wife
6 disagree **7** weekly **8** forgetful **9** successful **10** mispronounce
11 unfair **12** endless **13** touristy **14** unspoilt **15** creative
16 enjoyable **17** uninteresting **18** unusual **19** rearrange **20** airy
21 misheard **22** expensive **23** careless **24** dirty **25** peaceful
26 breakable **27** messy **28** attractive **29** friendly **30** revisit
31 disappear **32** comprehensible **33** helpful

UNIT 3 Communication
Estate agents

Procedure

Organise the class into groups of six and give a role card to each one. With odd numbers, double up the buyers so that they are husband and wife, boyfriend and girlfriend or friends. Tell students to read through the information on the card and check they understand.

Now elicit from the students how the conversation between an estate agent and a buyer might start, e.g. *Good morning, how can I help you? What are you looking for?* Etc.

Each buyer then has to visit each estate agent in their group and the estate agent has to try to convince the buyer to buy the house they are selling. When they have visited all three, get feedback from the buyers and find out who has been the most successful at selling houses and why.

UNIT 4 Vocabulary 1
Money problems

Procedure

Organise the class into pairs and give a copy of worksheet A to one of the students and a copy of worksheet B to the other.

Tell them they are going to role play a number of money problems, and that they have to try to reach an agreement. Give students a minute to read through situation 1. Allow them to use dictionaries to look up any words they don't understand, or they can ask you. Now have them role play the situation. When they have finished, get feedback from the class to see if any of the students found a solution and what it was.

Now do the same with situations 2 and 3.

UNIT 4 Grammar 1
How well do I know my classmates?

Procedure

Give a copy of the worksheet to each student and tell them to think which students in the class might correspond to the sentences. Tell them they have to write at least one name for each, but they can write more if they want.

When they have finished, tell them to mingle, checking to see if they were right by saying the sentences with a question tag. Remind them that they must say the sentence in the 2nd person singular. Tell them to tick or cross the sentence.

Get feedback from the whole class about which sentences they got right and any surprising information they found out.

UNIT 4 Grammar 2
Utopia

Procedure

Give a copy of the worksheet to each student and tell them to work individually to decide if they agree with the rules or not. If they agree, they tick them and if they don't, they change the sentence so that it fits their idea of the perfect world.

When they have finished, arrange them into small groups of three or four and tell them to compare their sentences, justifying why they think one thing or another. Go around the class, monitoring their conversations.

Get feedback from the whole class. As an extension, you can ask them to think of some more rules for a perfect world in their groups.

UNIT 4 Grammar 3
Can I sell you this?

Procedure

Organise the students into pairs, A and B. Give a copy of worksheet A to both students in pair A, and a copy of worksheet B to both students in pair B. Tell them to look at the three things they have to sell and write sentences with the cues given to help them sell those products. Go around the class, helping with vocabulary and correcting any mistakes the students make.

When they have finished, reorganise the class so that there are two A students from different pairs, and two B students from different pairs working together in groups of four. The A students begin, taking it in turns to sell their items, including the sentences they have written. The B students have to decide which of the two A students is most convincing. Then the B students try to sell their items to the As.

Teacher's notes

Get feedback from the class to find out who were the most successful salespeople and why.

Unit 4 | Vocabulary 1
BLEEP: Which word was that?

Procedure

Organise the students into groups of four and give one set of cut up cards to each group. Within the groups, students divide themselves into two teams. If you have odd numbers, use groups of five.

Write the word *BLEEP* on the board and tell the students that on each card there is a sentence that contains BLEEP instead of a word. Each team takes it in turn to take a card and read out the sentence. The other team must guess the correct word in the correct tense. If they get it right, they score one point.

The winner is the team with the most points at the end.

Unit 4 | Communication
Which would you buy?

Procedure

Organise the class into pairs and give a copy of the worksheet to each pair. Read through the questions at the top of the page with the whole class. Pre-teach or elicit 'brand name'.

Students look at the different pictures and answer the questions orally. Go around the class monitoring their conversations.

Get feedback from the whole class about whether it's worth paying more for 'the name' or whether it's a waste of money.

Unit 5 | Vocabulary 1
Which leisure activity?

Procedure

Give a copy of the first part of the worksheet to each student and tell them to work in pairs to think of questions they could ask using the cues in the box (or their own ideas) to guess a leisure activity. Point out that the answer can only be 'yes', 'no' or 'it depends'.

Get feedback from the class, writing any difficult questions on the board.

Now choose a leisure activity yourself (*football*). Have the students ask you ten questions in order to discover the activity.

Divide the students up into small groups of three or four and give each group a set of cards. The students take it in turns to pick up a card and the others have to ask ten questions to guess the activity. They continue until all the cards have been used.

Unit 5 | Grammar 1
What have they been doing?

Procedure

Divide the class into two groups, A and B, and give copies of the cue words for student A to one group and the cue words for student B to the other group. Give a copy of the pictures to all the students and tell them to work in pairs to match the cue words in the box with six of the pictures. Tell them to imagine what is happening in the other six pictures.

Now rearrange the students so that an A student is working with a B student. Students explain what they guessed was happening in the six pictures for which they had no cues and the other student tells them if they were right or wrong.

Now tell students to talk about each picture, saying what has been happening and what has happened in each picture. Remind them that they are using the Present Perfect Simple and the Present Perfect Continuous to contrast a short action or result with a longer or unfinished action.

Get feedback from the whole class. In pairs, students now talk about whether these things have ever happened to them. Get further feedback.

Unit 5 | Grammar 2
Find somebody like you

Procedure

Give a copy of the worksheet to each student and tell them to complete the sentences so that they are true for them. Remind them to complete with verbs and tell them to use the Reference on page 73 if they are not sure which form to use. Students write individual answers but they can confer with a partner over verb forms and to share ideas. Go around the class, checking their sentences.

Focus the students on the example sentences at the bottom of the page, and tell them to mingle, asking questions to find a student who agrees with their sentence. Tell them to write the name of that student in the column provided.

Get feedback from the class, finding out what different students have in common.

Unit 5 | Grammar 3
Find the difference

Procedure

Divide the class into pairs and give a copy of worksheet A to one of them and worksheet B to the other. Tell the students not to look at each other's paper.

Read the instructions with the whole class and students ask questions and describe their pictures, using quantifiers, in order to find twelve differences. Go around the class, helping with any vocabulary they need and correcting errors.

When they have finished, get students to report back on the differences.

Answers

The differences are: **1** number of tables **2** number of customers **3** amount of hair the man has **4** amount of meat **5** pasta/soup **6** number of napkins **7** number of glasses **8** amount of wine **9** number of waiters **10** the advice of the waiter **11** information on the notice board **12** number of bottles of water

UNIT 5 | Vocabulary 2
What word am I explaining?

Procedure

Divide the class into half and give a copy of worksheet A to one half and worksheet B to the other half. Tell them to work with a partner to match the definitions to the words in the box. Go around the class, checking that their answers are correct.

Now reorganise the class so that two student As are working with two student Bs. If you have odd numbers, form some groups of three. Each pair makes a team and the teams take it in turns to read out the definitions while the other team has to guess the word. Each correct word is worth one point. The winner is the team with the most points at the end.

UNIT 5 | Communication
Trivia quiz: How much do you know?

Procedure

Organise the class into groups of four and divide each group into two teams, A and B. Give a copy of the top part of the worksheet to each team and read through the instructions with the whole class.

Now give a copy of team A questions to one pair and team B questions to the other pair. Ask some general vocabulary questions to see which team in each group goes first, e.g. *What do we call this in English?* (pointing to things around the class).

Students play the game until all the squares have been won or all the questions have been asked. Students mark the squares they win with a symbol. At the end, students work out their teams score by adding up the squares they won plus an extra point for each time they have won both squares belonging to one category.

UNIT 6 | Vocabulary 1
Are you an adventurous holiday-maker?

Procedure

Organise the class into pairs and give a copy of the

worksheet to each student. Tell the students to take it in turns to ask each other the questions and read out the options. While one student is asking, tell the other not to read the sheet in order to increase listening practice. When they have chosen an option, they can then look at the sheet and mark their answers. Go around the class, helping with any difficult vocabulary or expressions.

When they have finished, students work out their scores. Ask the students which category they fall into and read through the results together as a class. Ask the students if they agree with the analysis.

UNIT 6 | Grammar 1
Are you lying to me?

Procedure

Give a copy of the worksheet to each student and tell them to work in pairs to match the expressions from the box to the pictures.

Now tell the students to randomly cross out one of the pictures in each row without their partner seeing which it is. Tell them that they have to lie when they answer the question about the crossed out picture and tell the truth when they answer the questions about the other pictures. Focus on the example at the bottom of the sheet and brainstorm some follow up questions that students could ask, e.g. *What language was it? Where did you study it?*

Students work in pairs to do the exercise and at the end, try to guess when their partner was lying.

UNIT 6 | Grammar 2
What question was that?

Procedure

Give a copy of the worksheet to each student and focus their attention on the questions. Tell them they have to work individually to write short answers to ten of those questions in the shapes in the second part of the sheet. Remind them not to do it in order.

Now tell them to tear off the second part of the sheet and exchange it with a partner. Looking at each other's answers they have to guess the question, without looking back at the original questions. When they guess correctly they cross out the answer. This continues until students have crossed out all the answers.

Get feedback from the whole class by having students read out some of their answers and eliciting the question from the whole class.

UNIT 6 | Grammar 3
The article race

Procedure

Organise the class into pairs and give a copy of worksheet A to one of the pairs and worksheet B to the other. Explain that they are going to have a race to see who can correct the most incorrect sentences first.

Read through the instructions and check the whole class understands. Hide something in one of your hands and ask each pair to guess which hand it is to see who goes first. Students read out the incorrect sentences to their partners, repeating once if necessary. The partner tries to correct the sentence. If they fail they miss a turn. The winner is the first to get to the finish.

Unit 6 Vocabulary 2
Getting information

Procedure

Cut up the question cards and give one to each student. If you have more than twelve, organise the students into pairs and give them the same card. Allow students to read the card, and check they understand. Tell them they must ask as many students as possible (making questions in the 2nd person singular) and remember the answers in order to report back to the class about their findings.

Students mingle, asking and answering their questions. Mingle with them monitoring language.

Get feedback from all the students about what they found out. If two students had the same card, allow them to confer first.

Unit 6 Communication
Around the world tourism quiz

Procedure

Organise the students into groups of three or four and tell them they are going to do a quiz about world tourism. Don't give out the sheets yet, but read out the questions (to give the students extra listening practice and have them discuss their answers without writing them down.

When you have finished, give out the sheets and tell them they have a few minutes to write down their answers.

Collect in a sheet from each team, and give it to another team to correct. Read through the questions again, eliciting answers and giving the correct ones if necessary. Students score one point for each correct answer. The winning team is the one that has most points at the end.

Answers

1 Edinburgh **2** San Francisco **3** Switzerland, France, Germany, Austria, Slovenia, and Italy (0.5 points for each country) **4** Peru **5** New Zealand **6** USA and Canada **7** Chile and Argentina **8** Indian **9** Madrid **10** The Acropolis **11** Istanbul **12** Switzerland **13** Granada **14** Dublin; **15** India.

Unit 7 Vocabulary 1
Educational issues: agree/disagree

Procedure

Cut the worksheet in two and give a copy of the top part to each student. Check the students understand partially agree and pre-teach *evaluate* and *sabbatical* if you feel it is necessary. Tell the students to listen to the statements that you read out and mark a column for each one according to how much they agree or disagree with each statement.

Read the statements from the second part of the sheet, repeating each one several times and if necessary rephrasing it to make sure that the students understand.

When you have read all ten and the students have filled in the table, organise the class into small groups of three or four. Distribute copies of the statements, and have the students discuss each one, comparing the way in which they had filled out the agree/disagree table.

Unit 7 Grammar 1
Fact or fiction?

Procedure

Organise the class into two groups, A and B, and give copies of worksheet A to group A and worksheet B to group B. Tell the students to work in pairs to think of a question that they could ask to find out the missing information in six of their sentences. Remind them to pay attention to subject and object sentences. Go around the class monitoring their work.

Now reorganise the class so that a student A is working with a student B. Tell them to ask each other their questions and to complete the missing information. When they have finished, check the complete sentences with the whole class.

Now tell them that six of the sentences are false. Students work together to guess which they are. Check with the whole class. Students score a point for each false sentence they guess. The winners are those who guessed the most false sentences.

Answers

1 F (Van Gogh painted Sunflowers) **2** T **3** F (Oscar Wilde was born in 1854) **4** F (Queen Victoria ruled from 1837 to 1901, almost 64 years) **5** T **6** T **7** F The Hundred Years War lasted from 1337 to 1453, 116 years) **8** T **9** T **10** T **11** F (King Kong was released in 1933) **12** F (Star wars was released 1977)

UNIT 7 | Grammar 2
What's happened to me?

Procedure

Organise the class into groups of four (or three) and give each group a copy of the cut up cards. Tell them to share the cards out equally (if there are some cards left over, it doesn't matter).

Explain that each card tells them about a change that has happened in their lives and that they have to think of sentences using *used to/didn't use to/would/wouldn't* that demonstrate that change. Give the students time to look at their cards (without showing the others) and think about what they are going to say, asking you for any vocabulary they might need.

Students now play the game. They take it in turns to say sentences with the above structures about each card and the other students in the group have to guess the change. The first student to guess the change wins the card. If no student can guess initially, they can ask questions until somebody guesses. The winner is the student with the most cards at the end.

Get feedback from the whole group about some of the sentences they made.

UNIT 7 | Grammar 3
How many people …?

Procedure

Give one card to each student and allow them time to read it. (If there are more than ten students, use some of the cards twice or three times.) Tell the students that they have to ask other members of the class a question to find the information stated. Remind them that they must form the question in the second person singular and that the second question would also be formed in the affirmative (we don't normally make questions in the negative), but that they are looking for students who answer 'no'.

Students mingle asking and answering questions. They can either write down the names of the students they find, or make a mental note of what they are told.

Get feedback from the whole class about what they found out. If you had more than ten students, allow those with the same card to confer first about the information.

UNIT 7 | Vocabulary 2
All about learning and knowing

Procedure

Organise the class into two groups, A and B, and give a copy of worksheet A to the As and worksheet B to the Bs. Tell them to work in pairs to substitute the underlined

parts of each question with an idiom in the correct form. Go around the class checking their work.

Now reorganise the class so that a student A is with a student B. Tell the students to ask and answer each other's questions. Remind them not to look at each other's sheets as they do this to increase listening practise. Go around the class monitoring their interaction.

Get feedback from the whole class about their answers.

UNIT 7 | Communication
Those were the days!

Procedure

Give a copy of the worksheet to each student and tell them to match the expressions from the box to the pictures in pairs. Check with the whole class.

Arrange the students into small groups and tell them to talk about each picture with respect to their own school days. Tell them that they can talk about both primary and secondary school and encourage them to give as much detail as possible. Go around the class monitoring their conversations.

Finally, get feedback from the whole class about their experiences.

UNIT 8 | Vocabulary 1
Guess the change expression

Procedure

Organise the class so that students are sitting in small groups of three or four. Give each group a set of cut up cards and tell them to share them out evenly among the members of the group.

Allow students to read through their own cards and ask you any vocabulary questions. Now tell them to take it in turns to read out the situation to the person on their right. This person has to try to guess the expression with change. If they guess correctly they keep the card. If they don't, the next person has a chance to guess. The winner is the student with the most cards at the end.

UNIT 8 | Grammar 1
In what circumstances would you?

Procedure

Organise the class so that they are sitting in groups of three and give one copy of the board game, one set of cut up cards and dice and counters to each group.

Read through the rules with each group and make sure they understand. Tell the students to throw the dice to see who goes first. As they play the game, go around the classroom monitoring their work.

UNIT 8 | Grammar 2
Adverb bingo

Procedure

Give a copy of the bingo sheet to each student and have them look at the adverbs in pairs, checking that they understand the meaning of all of them.

Before you begin reading the sentences, tell them put a cross through eight of the adverbs of their choice. Read out the sentences in order, substituting the adverb for 'beep'. The students put a different symbol (e.g. a circle) around the adverbs if they think they fit the sentence. The first student to circle all the adverbs, shouts 'bingo'. Check that the bingo is correct, by reading the sentences again and having the student tell you the correct adverb.

Give the students another bingo sheet (or have them copy it) and play again with the rest of the sentences or sentences that you invent. This could also be played in small groups, with students writing their own sentences (especially for revision) and reading them for other members of the group to play bingo.

UNIT 8 | Grammar 3
What could have been different?

Procedure

Divide the class into two groups, A and B, and give copies of worksheet A to group A and worksheet B to group B. Tell the students to work in pairs or small groups to read through the situations and write a number of sentences in the Third Conditional that they could say about each one. Go around the class helping with any difficult vocabulary and checking the sentences they write.

Now put a student A with a student B to role play the situations. Tell them to try to resolve the problems, including the Third Conditional sentences in their conversations.

Get feedback from the whole class about the sentences they constructed and who they feel is to blame in each situation.

UNIT 8 | Vocabulary 2
Word building crossword

Procedure

Divide the class into two groups, A and B, and give copies of worksheet A to group A and of worksheet B to group B.

Have the students check they understand all of the words written in their crossword in pairs, helping them with any problems they might have. Tell them to decide if each word is a verb, noun or adjective.

Now rearrange the students so that one student A is with one student B. Tell them not to look at each other's paper. Read the instructions with the whole class. Write *down*

and *across* on the board so that students can identify the direction of the words.

UNIT 8 | Communication
A change for the better?

Procedure

Give a copy of the worksheet to each student or pair of students and tell them to work in pairs to say what they can see in the pictures, using words from the box. Check with the whole class.

Now get the students to discuss the effects of these changes for society and to talk about whether there were any negative consequences. Go around the room, monitoring their conversations.

Answers

1 Mobile phones **2** Internet **3** Mass air travel **4** Skyscrapers
5 Genetrically modified food **6** Increase in no smoking areas
7 Feminist movement **8** Embryonic research **9** Reality TV

UNIT 9 | Vocabulary 1
Perks and promotions

Procedure

Give a copy of the worksheet to each student or pair of students. Tell them to name the jobs they can see in the pictures. Check with the whole class.

Now read through the questions with the whole class, checking that they understand all the vocabulary. Organise the class into small groups of three or four and tell them to discuss the questions in relation to the jobs they can see in the pictures. Go around the class, monitoring their conversations.

Get feedback from the whole class.

UNIT 9 | Grammar 1
Jumbled questions

Procedure

Divide the class into two groups, A and B, and give a copy of worksheet A to one group and worksheet B to the other. Tell the students to work together to order the words to make questions. Go around the class, checking that students have appropriate questions.

Now reorganise the class so that one student from group A is working with one from group B. Students ask and answer each other's questions (tell them not to look at each other's papers in order to increase listening practice).

Get feedback from the whole class.

Answers

Student A

1 Did your parents make you help with the housework when you were a teenager?

2 Did your parents let you go out late when you were 15?

3 Are you allowed to smoke in many public places in your country?

4 If you were a politician, would you make people pay higher taxes?

5 Do you think children should be allowed to wear normal clothes to school?

6 Would you let a teenager of 16 go on holiday alone?

Student B

1 Did your parents make you do any extra-curricular activities when you were a child?

2 Did your parents let you stay up late when you were a child?

3 What is the maximum speed you are allowed to drive in your country?

4 If you were a teacher, would you make students do a lot of exams?

5 Do you think people should be allowed to vote at 16?

6 Do you think the government should let shops open 24 hours a day?

UNIT 9 Grammar 2
Find someone who... and report back!!

Procedure

Organise the class into small groups of four (use groups of three if necessary). Hand out the worksheets and tell students they have to mingle with students from other groups in order to find somebody who corresponds to their sentences, asking and noting down extra information when they do find someone.

When they have finished students sit down in their original groups. They take it in turns to report back, using reported speech, about what they have found out without saying the student's name, e.g. *Somebody told me that…* The other students in the group must guess who said each thing, scoring one point if they guess correctly. The winner is the student with the most points at the end.

UNIT 9 Grammar 3
Past rules and regulations

Procedure

Divide the class into two groups, and give copies of worksheet A to one group and worksheet B to the other. Tell students to work in pairs to read through the sentences, checking with you any vocabulary they don't know, and writing questions for those sentences that have gaps in them. Go around the class checking the questions.

Now put a student A with a student B. Tell them to ask each other the questions to complete the sentences, without looking at each other's paper.

Check all the sentences with the whole class, and then

tell them that four are false. Students discuss with their partner which four are false. Get feedback from the whole class, with their reasons.

Answers

Numbers 3, 6, 8, and 9 are false. Numbers 3, 6 and 8 are completely invented and number 9 was true but during the period 1920–1932.

UNIT 9 Vocabulary 2
Pelmanism

Procedure

Organise the class so that the students are sitting in groups of three or four, and give a set of cut up cards to each group. Tell the students to put the cards on the desk face down and spread out.

Explain the rules of the game. Each student takes it in turn to turn over two cards. If the cards match (i.e. the word means the same), that student takes the two cards and explains the meaning and says which one is American and which one is British English. They then have to define the words, e.g. *Petrol is something you put in your car to make it work*. The rest of the group checks that this is correct and if there is any dispute, they consult with you. If the student does this correctly they keep the cards and if they do it incorrectly, they put them back down on the table and mix up all the cards. The winner is the student with the most cards at the end.

Go around the class, monitoring the students' sentences.

UNIT 9 Communication
Choosing the right career

Procedure

This activity will probably work best before doing the Communication page of the Student's Book.

Organise the class so that the students are sitting in pairs. Tell them they are going to do an activity that simulates going to a Careers Advice Centre. Ask students if they have ever been to one of these and what experience they had.

Give a copy of the worksheet to each student and read the introduction with the whole class. Give them a few minutes to read through the questions to check that they understand.

Students now take in turns to interview each other. Tell them to make brief notes of the answers they hear. When they have finished the interviews, they decide what type of job would be suitable for their partner. Get feedback from the whole class about these jobs, with students giving reasons for their choice and their partners saying whether they had thought of doing this job or not.

Teacher's notes

UNIT 10 Vocabulary 1
Talking about memory

Procedure

Divide the class into two groups and give copies of worksheet Student A to one group and worksheet Student B to the other. Tell the students to work in pairs to complete the questions with the correct expression from the box in the correct form. Go around the class monitoring their work.

Now reorganise the class so that a student A is working with a student B. Tell them to ask and answer each other's questions (without looking at each other's papers in order to increase listening practice).

When they have finished get feedback from the whole class about their answers to the questions.

UNIT 10 Grammar 1
If things were different!

Procedure

Give each student a copy of the worksheet and tell them to read through the sentences and put a tick or a cross depending on whether they agree or disagree with each one. Go around the class helping them with any vocabulary or sentences they don't understand.

Now organise the students into small groups of three or four and tell them to compare what they have put, giving reasons for agreeing or disagreeing with each one.

Get feedback from the whole class.

UNIT 10 Grammar 2
A tale with a twist!

Procedure

Give each student or pair of students a copy of the worksheet. Read the title and explain that 'a tale with a twist' is a story with a surprise ending. Tell the students to work in pairs to tell the story, paying attention to the correct use of past tenses, and including the words that are given under each picture. Ask them to make at least two sentences per picture. Go around the class, monitoring their work.

Now have the whole class retell the story, checking for any variations there might be among the pairs of students. Ask each pair to discuss what they think happens at the end of the story and get feedback from the whole class. If nobody has guessed, give them the correct answer.

Answer

While they were at the theatre, the thief who had stolen the car burgled their house.

UNIT 10 Grammar 3
Phrasal verb survey

Procedure

Cut up the cards and give one card to each student. Allow the students time to read the question and check that they all understand. Students stand up and mingle, asking their questions and making brief notes about the answers they are given. If you have more than ten students, double up the cards and tell the students to work together, interviewing only some of their classmates.

Get feedback from the whole class about what they found out.

UNIT 10 Vocabulary 2
What am I describing?

Procedure

Give a copy of the top section of the worksheet to each student or pair of students and tell them to read the descriptions and guess what is being described. Elicit suggestions from the whole class (**1** the sun **2** a plane).

Organise students into groups of three or four and give them a set of cut up cards (the second half of the sheet). Tell them to share them out equally and ask each student to look at their cards without letting any of the other students see them. Give them a few minutes to think of ways of describing the words on their cards in a similar way to the ones the read earlier. At this point allow them to ask you for any vocabulary they might need.

Students now play the game. Each student takes it in turn to describe their words and the first of his or her group mates to guess, wins the card. The winner at the end is the one with the most cards.

UNIT 10 Communication
Test your memory!

Procedure

Give a copy of the worksheet to each student and read through the instructions with the whole class. Students then write one or two names next to each sentence (if they can). Include yourself if you want.

Students mingle, asking each other questions to check if they were right or not. Get feedback from the whole group as to how much they know about each other.

As an extension to this activity, distribute the names of all the students so that each one has a name that is not their own. Tell students to write three or four things about this person they have found out during the course. Students then read out this information and the rest of the class guess who it is.

DVD worksheets

Before watching

1   Match the words and phrases from each column to form sentences.

1	I love	a	in touch with my friends
2	I get on with	b	to run my own business in the future
3	I prefer	c	lots of different people
4	I want	d	finding out about new places
5	I hate	e	to work in another country next year
6	I hope	f	not having anything to do
7	I like to keep	g	beach locations to mountain locations

2   Discuss.

If you visited another country for a holiday or work, what might make you want to live there? What could tempt you away from your home country?

While watching

3   Watch the first extract and answer the questions.

1   The man tells his friend that he may lose his job if he doesn't go back home and the man replies: *So what?* What does he mean by this reply?

2   What are the two men drinking? How do you know they are sharing?

3   Fill in the gaps of the following rhyme Ollie wrote.

Roses are ___

Candy is ___

This is something I sent you to ___

4   Watch the second extract and answer the questions.

1   The man suggests that the only way to get the ball is by climbing up:

a   *a tree*?

b   *a drainpipe*?

c   *a wall*?

2   One of the boys says '*I'll tell me brother*' if the men don't retrieve the ball. And then another boy says: '*His brother's bigger than you!*'. Why do you think the men then quickly agree to get the ball?

3   The two men have to decide who is going to get the ball, so one says:

a fair's good   b fair's fair   c fair's best

4   As the man is rescued, a bystander says: '*S _____ was it?*' What is the missing word? Why do you think he suggests this?

5   The other man replies to no 4. '*It might be later when he gets home to the wife!*'. What do you think the wife's reaction might be to her husband's escapade?

After watching

5   Discuss.

Do you agree with the man's reasons for wanting to stay in Paris in the first extract? Do you think his reasons are good ones? Why/Why not? If you had been the man in the second extract, would you have gone up the drainpipe? How would you have resolved the situation?

Before watching

1 Complete the sentences using a word or phrase from the box below.

> reviews   journalists   broken the record
> headlines   online news   main stories

a   The _____ in the newspapers are often very depressing.

b   The _____ on the front of today's paper really shocked me.

c   I enjoy reading film and book _____ in the papers.

d   If I'm in the office, I usually read the _____ on my computer.

e   I was interested to see that someone had _____ time for running a marathon.

f   The national newspapers have _____ who report from all over the world.

2 Discuss.

Which important items of world and local news have really affected you during your life?

While watching

3 Watch the first news report and answer the questions.

1   Fill in the gaps:
    Berliners linked hands and _____ round their _____ territory.

2   Does the newsreader say that the people *clambered* or *climbed* playfully up and down the Berlin Wall itself?

3   What is no longer needed to pass between East and West Berlin?

4   The Berlin Wall is described as the most *potent* symbol of division in Europe? What does the newsreader mean by *potent*?

4 Watch the second news report and answer the questions.

1   What type of election is this?

2   How long have some people waited to vote?

3   Which of the following does Nelson Mandela swear to be to the Republic of South Africa?
    a committed   **b** faithful   **c** true

4   What type of birds was released as a peace symbol?

5 Watch the final news report and write *T* (*true*) or *F* (*false*) next to the following statements.

1   At 11:11 on the 11th month the first rays of the sun disappeared. ___

2   The eclipse was felt because the light went very quickly and the temperature dropped. ___

3   The heavens promised little and delivered more. ___

4   This will only happen once in our lives. ___

After watching

6 Choose one of the items of news that you discussed in Ex.2. Imagine you are a newscaster and write a brief paragraph describing events.

7 Exchange your paragraph with your partner's and read through each others correcting any mistakes you find.

Before watching

1   Which of the words and phrases in the box do you associate with the city and country? Fill in the chart below.

music venues	museums	stress free	cottage	clubs
rural	theatres	big nights out	no noise	everything at
slow pace of life	fresh air	wildlife	relaxation	your fingertips

City	Country

While watching

2   Watch the film and answer the questions.

1   Speaker 1 says that the main thing he likes about living in Leeds *is easy_____ to a lot of things*. Which word does he use here?

2   How can living in Leeds feel at first?

3   In the speaker's opinion which group of people does Leeds really appeal to?

4   Why might speaker 1 move to London in the future?

5   Speaker 2 describes his country setting as _____ ?

6   What's great about looking out of the window for speaker 2?

7   Speaker 2 says that outings such as going to the cinema can't be done '*on the _____ of the _____* ' What does he mean by this phrase?

8   How does everything seem for speaker 2 when he goes to cities now?

9   Are the following statements from speaker 3 true or false?

   a   her flat is the upper half of a house that's been converted. ___

   b   the trains that run nearby her flat make a lot of noise during the day and at night. ___

   c   There's not enough nice things to do and see in the city. ___

   d   She doesn't go to the museums and theatres as much as she used to. ___

10   Which one of the following does speaker 4 *not* mention about living in the country?

   freedom   fresh air   no noise   wildlife

11   Does she have next door neighbours?

12   How does speaker 4 describe her journey home?

13   Fill in the gaps in speaker 4's final sentence:

   '*I _____ going back to a town.*'

After watching

3   Discuss.

All the speakers feel that when they are older they'll live in the country (if they aren't already). Why do you think this is?

Before watching

1 <u>Underline</u> the correct word in the following sentences:

a I *don't get/have* enough money to go away this weekend.

b I've been advised to *use/have* my money wisely.

c That coat is great *value/worth* for money.

d He *ran/walked* out of money last night.

e I want to have a job where I can *make/do* lots of money.

f We *invested/developed* some money in the stock exchange.

2 Discuss.

Do you know anyone that was very poor and became very rich? What sort of jobs or activities do people need to do to get very rich? List three of your ideas below:

1 _____

2 _____

3 _____

While watching

3 Watch the film and complete the sentences.

a Racing's not quite _____ out here.

b Fate _____ me the one _____ essential to the _____ of all my plans.

c _____ merely a_____ among all those 1000s who _____ every morning into the city.

d I was in the _____ position of having a fortune literally_____ my _____ .

4 Watch the film and correct the factual mistakes in the sentences below.

1 It's the visitor's second visit to South America and he doesn't want to stay any longer.

2 The man thinks it's a pity his companion can't stay until Saturday as he has a horse in the Jockey Club stakes.

3 The man describes his year as one super year.

4 He was beginning to think he might achieve it.

5 He lost sight of his goal.

6 Most men who long to be rich believe they will achieve it.

After watching

5 The main character supervised the deliveries of bullion from the gold refinery to the bank. How do you think this job helped him to get rich? Compare your ideas with your partner.

6 If you were very rich, is there another country you'd choose to live in because of the lifestyle? Compare your ideas with your partner.

Before watching

1   Match each definition below with a word or phrase from the box.

> sequel   was dubbed   chapter
> was written by   soundtrack   plot

a   the set of connected events that a story/film is based on   ____*plot*____

b   a book, film or play that continues the story of an earlier one _____

c   the original spoken language of a film or television programme was changed into another language _____

d   was created by _____

e   the recorded music from a film _____

f   one of the parts into which a book is divided _____

2   *Casablanca* is described by one of the speakers as a 'classic' film. What makes a film a 'classic'? With your partner, list four other classic films.

While watching

3   Watch the first part of the film and complete the sentences below.

1   It's set in World War II and there's lots of political _____ .

2   It's set in the 1940s in a _____ in_____ .

3   It's a _____ drama.

4   I think probably the most _____ _____ are … .

5   'Is that cannon fire or is it my _____ _____ ?'

6   There is a wonderful time when a girl _____ to _____ with the Humphrey Bogart character … .

7   'That was so _____ I can't _____ .'

8   'That's so far into the future I _____ make _____ .'

4   The following sentences all appear in the film trailer. Number them 1–8 according to the order you hear them.

a   Isn't it about time we play it again?   ___

b   Ingrid Bergman is Ilsa, the last woman he ever expected to see.   ___

c   If you knew how much I loved you, how much I still love you.   ___

d   He's travelling with a lady.   ___

e   You have to think for both of us. For all of us.   ___

f   I stick my neck out for nobody.   ___

g   There is a man arrived in Casablanca on his way to America.   ___

h   That is my least vulnerable spot.   ___

After watching

5   Think of a film you have seen recently, and use some of the phrases from Ex.3 to describe it to your partner, without using the film's name.

Before watching

1   Complete the sentences with a word or phrase from the box.

> package holidays   cruise   unforgettable journey
> local culture   safari   sightseeing tours

a   I'd never go on a _____ because I get seasick very easily.

b   I'd love to go on a _____ to see animals in their natural habitat.

c   We think _____ _____ are great because everything is organised for you.

d   _____ _____ are a great way to see local places of interest.

e   It's wonderful to experience _____ _____ on holiday.

f   My trip to the Pyramids in Egypt was a truly _____ _____ journey.

2   Discuss in pairs.

   1   *Who would be your ideal companion for your dream holiday?*

   2   *Why have you chosen this person?*

   3   *Where would you go with your ideal companion?*

   4   *What type of holiday would you choose?*

While watching

3   Watch the film and mark the sentences below *T* (*true*) or *F* (*false*). Correct the sentences which are false.

   1   One of the fastest growing holiday activities is diving. ___

   2   In the Maldives, you can train to be a scuba diver in less than two weeks. ___

   3   In a single dive you can see fish in every colour of the rainbow. ___

   4   In New Zealand hiking is called tramping. ___

   5   You can follow trails in New Zealand across the magnificent Northern Alps. ___

   6   Paths lead through recently developed forests and around deep lakes. ___

   7   Travelling south down the River Nile is like sailing back in time. ___

   8   The scenery along the river bank has changed a lot in thousands of years. ___

   9   *Falukas* carry silks, spices and tourists to the Egyptian markets. ___

   10 You can watch the sun rise across the Sahara. ___

After watching

4   Choose one of the places described in the film.
Imagine you are on holiday there and write a short postcard to a friend at home describing the area and what you're doing. Write five or six sentences.
Exchange postcards with your partner. Does the holiday sound like fun?

Before watching

1 Replace the <u>underlined</u> word in the phrases a–h below with a word from the box.

> only   busy   stayed   saying   free   aim   notable   concentrated

a most <u>distinctive</u> buildings

b has <u>remained</u> as it would

c <u>strictly</u> for male students

d very <u>intense</u> course

e there's an <u>expression</u>

f <u>spare</u> time

g social life is very <u>active</u>

h its <u>purpose</u>

2 Discuss the following questions in groups. Give reasons for your answers.

1 *Are there any notable buildings in your country? What is the oldest university?*

2 *Are any of the university colleges in your country for males or females only? Are they popular? Do you think they are a good idea?*

3 *Why is it a good idea for students to have enough free time?*

While watching

3 Watch the first part of the film and choose the correct alternative in the following sentences.

1 Corpus Christi was founded in *1352/1370*.

2 Corpus Christi decided to admit women students in *1980/1988*.

3 All the other courts have *been rebuilt in current style/remained in medieval style*.

4 Christopher Marlowe was a *playwright/poet*.

4 Watch the film and answer the following questions.

1 Are there more men than women studying at Cambridge today?

2 The first student to talk about Cambridge says that it has a very good _____ reputation. What's the missing word?

3 Which subject does student two say Cambridge is the best university for?

4 What does student three think is the advantage of the college structure?

5 Student four is working hard studying management studies for one year on a very intense course. What helps him get through the year?

6 What is the expression which applies to Cambridge according to one of the towns people?

7 What are some of the high tech subjects taught at the new colleges?

8 What is the name of the river that flows through Cambridge?

9 What else is there apart from the work for students in Cambridge?

10 The narrator ends by saying that Cambridge still has the same purpose as it did centuries ago? What is this?

After watching

5 Discuss the following questions with your partner.

1 *Have you been/would you like to go to university? What did/would you study?*

2 *How important is a balance between academic life and social activities at university?*

Before watching

1 Choose the correct alternative in each of the following sentences.

   a It *makes/time for* a change to have a day out.

   b Shall we do something different *make a change/for a change*?

   c We had a change of *heart/head* over our plans to move.

   d It's time *for/to* a change I think.

   e The situation is worse. It has *improved/deteriorated*.

   f Things are *still/even* the same.

2 Guess the answers to the following questions before you watch the film.

   1 *How much time in total will we spend eating during our lifetime?*

   2 *How often will we learn a new word in the first ten years of our lives?*

   3 *By the age of twenty-one, how many people can each of us name?*

   4 *How many times will each of us fall in love?*

   5 *How much time in total will each of us talk for during our whole life?*

While watching

3 Watch the film and answer the questions.

   1 How many eggs and how much chocolate will Charlotte consume?

   2 How far will she crawl before she reaches the age of two?

   3 How many times will her heart have beaten by the time she's ten?

   4 Will she grow twenty-eight or thirty-eight metres of fingernails?

   5 At 21, will she have breathed 3.5 million or billion balloons of air?

   6 Everyday she'll produce 20 billion new red blood cells. True or false?

   7 How many grandchildren will she have?

   8 Will two or three of her eight great grandchildren remember her name?

   9 What is the life expectancy in France, North America and Africa?

   10 When she dies, how many kilometres will she have walked?

After watching

4 What is the noun form of the following verbs? Use your monolingual dictionary to help you.

   1 achieve _____   4 breathe _____

   2 consume _____   5 produce _____

   3 grow _____   6 marry _____

5 Think about your own life. Write a sentence about yourself using each verb from Ex.5. Use future forms to express hopes for the future.

Before watching

1 Discuss.

What is your ideal job working environment? Think about the following – manager, clothes, working hours, colleagues, training – and write a few sentences to summarise your views.

While watching

2 Watch the film and answer the questions.

1 Where is the ideal workplace in the extract located?

2 In the opening line of the extract which word is used to describe the type of workplace that Richard Semler has created?

3 Friday is described as a 'good example' of the way the office works. Why?

4 What exactly is Richard buying from his employees?

5 Which of the following phrases is used to describe the employees?

   a *grown down*   b *grown up*   c *grown to*

6 Employees can start work when they want to. True or false?

7 They aren't allowed to choose their bosses or set their own pay. True or false?

8 How does Richard think the employees should see their working lives?

9 Is what Richard is doing described as new stuff or old stuff?

10 What is revolutionary about what Richard is doing?

11 How much does the company turn over a year these days?

12 What type of control was operated when Richard took over from his father? How do you think this is different to how the company is run now?

13 Richard reorganised the workforce into small autonomous teams. What do you think autonomous means here?

14 The autonomous teams were divided into teams of a dozen. How many in a dozen?

   a 10   b 12   c 14

15 Richard started his new approach by giving employees choices on simple things such as?

After watching

4 Match the verbs to their correct meanings.

1	Turn over (money)	a	expand your viewpoint
2	Take (sth) over	b	manage (sth)
3	Reorganise	c	make someone answerable for something
4	Give someone responsibility	d	change of leadership
5	Broaden your way of thinking	e	the money a company makes

5 Now use the verbs to write a paragraph describing how you would manage a small team of designers. You are their new boss! Be as creative and imaginative as you like and list some of the goals you would have.

Before watching

1   Think of your modern day icon. What field does this person work in? Why do you think they are an icon? Use at least five of the words in the box below to describe your icon and reasons for choosing this person.

> determined   encourage   inspire   be involved in
> talented   brilliant   brave   dedicate (one's life)

2   Discuss in groups.

1   *Do you like modern art? Have you seen any of Frida Kahlo's paintings or seen the Hollywood film of her life story? What did you think?*

2   *Rosa Parks spoke publicly against injustice and by doing so segregation on buses was banned. Are there any injustices in today's world, in your country, town that you would like to see disappear? Why?*

While watching

3   Watch the film and complete the sentences.

1   Frida Kahlo was the subject of a _____ Hollywood film.

2   Her works are _____ by Madonna.

3   But Frida had incredible _____ .

4   She developed a _____ personal style.

5   Frida produced _____ paintings.

6   Rosa refused and was _____ $14.

7   The black population of Montgomery_____ to use the buses and _____ to work or got _____ from friends.

8   Martin Luther King helped organise the _____ .

9   … both he and Rosa became national _____ .

10   After thirteen months the _____ of segregation on buses was defeated.

11   Marilyn Monroe was _____ that because of her looks no one would take her seriously.

12   But during her _____ , she became the _____ movie star.

13   _____ and then appeared in _____ films.

14   Her mother had mental problems and she was _____ in foster homes and orphanages.

15   Marilyn was a celebrity who suffered from the _____ of her privacy.

After watching

4   Discuss the following with your partner

1   *Marilyn Monroe's privacy was affected by her celebrity status. Do you think celebrities' privacy in the 21st century has improved or become worse? Give some examples.*

2   *In the world of politics, the arts, business, sport, charity or media can you think of anyone today who could be described as an icon? Why would you describe this person as an icon?*

Teaching notes

Unit 1   Best friends

Before watching

1➤   Ss work in pairs, matching the phrases. Check the answers with the class.

Answers:
1 d   2 c   3 g   4 e   5 f   6 b   7 a

2➤   Ss discuss the questions with a partner. Get feedback.

While watching

3➤   Give Ss a short time to read the questions. Then play the first film extract and allow Ss to take notes.

➤   Ss watch the extract again, pausing where necessary, to check their answers. Elicit the answers from the class.

Answers:
1 *So what?* – the man means who cares? This doesn't matter, it's not important.   2 They're drinking milk and they're sharing because they only have one glass with two straws.   3 *Roses are red, candy is sweet, this is something I send you to eat.*

4➤   Give Ss time to read the questions. Then play the second extract, pausing for Ss to answer the questions.

➤   Watch the extract again for Ss to check their answers. Elicit the answers from the class.

Answers:
1 b   2 The fact that the boy says his brother is bigger than the two men is suggesting that the brother might physically harm the men if they don't get the ball.
3 b   4 Suicide. He suggests this because people can commit suicide by jumping from a high building.
5 His wife might be furious that he took such a risk climbing up to get the ball, and she might get so angry that he actually does feel like committing suicide!

After watching

5➤   Ss discuss the questions in small groups.

➤   Encourage Ss to think about how they would react in both situations. Get feedback from the whole class.

Unit 2   Breaking news

Before watching

1➤   Ss work in pairs to complete the sentences with the words or phrases in the box. Check answers with the class.

Answers: a main stories   b headlines   c reviews   d online news   e broken the record   f journalists

2➤   Ss discuss the questions with a partner. Get feedback.

While watching

3➤   Ask Ss to read the questions.

➤   Watch the first report, pausing for Ss to find the answers.

Answers: 1 danced/liberated   2 clambered
3 visa   4 It is a powerful and effective symbol, both physically and psychologically

4➤   Give Ss time to read the questions in pairs. Encourage them to help each other with any difficult vocabulary.

➤   Watch the second report, pausing for Ss to find the answers. Then replay the extract again for Ss to check answers.

Answers: 1 democratic   2 all their lives   3 b
4 The dove

5➤   Ss read the statements 1–4 and decide if they are true or false. Ss then mark the statements (*T*) if true and (*F*) if false.

➤   Watch the final report for Ss to check answers.

Answers: 1 F The *last* rays of the sun disappeared
2 T   3 F The heavens delivered *much less than expected* thanks to the weather   4 T

After watching

6➤   Ask Ss to write their own paragraph describing a piece of news they discussed in Ex. 2, using the reports they have just seen as a model. If you have time, replay the film to help.

7➤   Encourage them to exchange stories at the end and read each other's through, correcting where necessary.

Unit 3 City or country?

OPTIONAL WARMER

Write *city* and *country* on the board. Ask Ss which kind of people they think prefer the city and which kind prefer the country. Ask for class feedback.

After Ss have watched the film, ask them if they think the speakers seem like typical country or city types.

Before watching

1➤ Give Ss a short time to study the words. Then in pairs Ss fill in the chart. Check the answers with the class.

➤ Add to the list any extra vocabulary from the Ss, and encourage them to record this too.

Suggested answers:
City – music venues, everything at your fingertips, big nights out, clubs, museums, theatre
Country – rural, slow pace of life, cottage, wildlife, fresh air, no noise, relaxation, stress free

While watching

2➤ Give the Ss a short time to read the questions.

➤ Play the film stopping at the end of each speaker.

➤ Replay the film to allow Ss to check answers.

Answers: 1 access   2 quite overwhelming
3 students   4 it has a more diverse population
5 idyllic   6 seeing wonderful birds and mammals
7 on the *spur* of the *moment;* he means that decisions to go to the cinema etc have to be made in advance, not spontaneously/on the spur of the moment
8 everything seems very fast   9 a F It's lower
b T   c F There's just lots of nice things to do and see
d T   10 wildlife   11 No, she is surrounded by fields, and lives quite a way off the village.   12 stress free   13 I *can't see myself* going back to a town.

After watching

3➤ Ss discuss the questions. Get feedback from the class.

OPTIONAL EXTENSION

Writing activity: A very stressed group of city workers seriously need a good relaxing weekend break. They are all friends – there are three women and two men. Plan a relaxing weekend for them in the country.

Ss decide on the type of accommodation they stay in, the food they eat and the activities and pursuits they can enjoy to wind down.

This can be homework if time is short or a fun classroom activity with Ss working together to plan the weekend.

Unit 4 From rags to riches

OPTIONAL WARMER

Ask Ss what they would do if they suddenly got rich. Which three things about their life would they change?

Before watching

1➤ Ss read the sentences and work with a partner to select the correct word. Check the answers with the class.

Answers: a have   b use   c value   d ran
e make   f invested

2➤ Ss discuss the questions. Elicit some of the ideas from the Ss and write them on the board.

While watching

3➤ Ask Ss to predict words they think could fit in the gaps

➤ Play the film through allowing Ss to make notes.

Answers: a straight   b denied / contact / success
c nonentity / flock   d unique / within / grasp

4➤ Give Ss time to read the incorrect statements.

➤ Watch the film, pausing where necessary for Ss to make their corrections to the sentences.

➤ Replay the film for Ss to check their answers to Ex. 3 and Ex. 4. Elicit answers from Ss.

Answers: 1 It's his *first* visit to South America and he wishes he *could* stay longer.   2 He thinks it's a pity his companion can't stay until *Sunday* as he has a horse in the jockey club stakes.   3 He describes his year as one superb year.   4 He was beginning to think he'd *never* achieve it.   5 He never quite lost sight of his goal.   6 Most men who long to be rich know inwardly that they will *never* achieve their ambition.

After watching

5➤ At the end of the film, Ss are left not knowing but perhaps having a few ideas as to how the main character achieved his wealth. Ask Ss to think about how this job enabled him to get so rich. Give Ss time to compare their ideas in pairs before asking them to share their views with the class.

6➤ Ss discuss the questions in pairs. Get feedback from the whole class.

OPTIONAL EXTENSION

Ss did some work on opposites in Lesson 4.3. List the following adjectives from the film and ask Ss to use their monolingual dictionary to find the opposites: pleasant, generous, superb, success, unique, essential, believe, inwardly.

Unit 5   Favourite films

OPTIONAL WARMER
Write *Casablanca, film, Ingrid Berman, Humphrey Bogart* on the board. Elicit other words Ss associate with the film and write them on the board. Divide Ss into groups and ask them to write three short sentences promoting the film using some of the words on the board. Ask each group to read their best sentence to the rest of the class.

Before watching

1➤ Ss work in pairs to match the definitions with the words.

Answers: a plot b sequel c was dubbed
d was written by e soundtrack f chapter

2➤ Ss work in pairs to define a classic. Ss then list four examples of classic films. Check answers with the class.

Suggested answers: Definition: a *classic* is a film that is important and has been popular for a long time. Other classics are: *Chitty Chitty Bang Bang, Spartacus, Ben Hur, The Magnificent Seven, The Good, the Bad and the Ugly, The Great Escape, Titanic, Gone with the Wind.*

While watching

3➤ Give Ss to read through the sentences, thinking about what might fit into the gaps.

➤ Play the film to the end of the four speakers talking, pausing for Ss to complete the sentences.

➤ Replay the same film section without pausing, for Ss to check their answers. Elicit answers from the whole class.

Answers: 1 goings on 2 bar, Morocco 3 romantic
4 famous lines 5 heart pounding 6 comes, meet
7 long ago, remember 8 never, plans.

4➤ Divide the class into pairs and ask Ss to order the sentences in the sequence they appear in the film trailer.

➤ Play the second clip (the film trailer) through once for Ss to order the sentences.

➤ Watch this part of the film again to check the answers.

Answers: a 8 b 4 c 5 d 3 e 6 f 1 g 2 h 7

After watching

5➤ Ask Ss to write a description of a film they have seen recently using phrases from Ex. 2 and Lesson 5.2.

➤ Ss take turns to read their descriptions to their partner who tries to guess what the film is.

OPTIONAL EXTENSION
Ask Ss to prepare a mini film review using their notes from Ex.5 as a starting point. In the next class, form groups and have Ss tell each other their film reviews.

Unit 6   Dream holidays

OPTIONAL WARMER
Write the table on the board and ask Ss to fill in five places for each column. One place can appear in more than one column. Ask Ss to compare their results. Get class feedback.

Beach holiday destinations	Historical and cultural holiday destinations	Hills, mountains, lake and forest destinations

Before watching

1➤ Ss work in pairs to complete the sentences with the words or phrases in the box. Check answers with the class.

Answers: a cruise b safari c package holidays
d sightseeing tours e local culture
f unforgettable journey

2➤ Ss discuss the questions with a partner. Get feedback.

While watching

3➤ Ss read the statements 1-10, and decide if they are true or false.

➤ Play the film through without pausing for Ss to mark the statements (*T*) if true or (*F*) if false.

➤ Replay the film for Ss to check answers and correct the false sentences.

➤ Give Ss time to compare their answers in pairs before checking the answers with the class. Encourage Ss to explain any difficult vocabulary to each other before doing so yourself.

Answers: 1 T 2 F less than a week 3 T
4 T 5 F Southern Alps 6 F paths lead through ancient forests 7 T 8 F the scenery has changed surprisingly little 9 T 10 F you can watch the sun go down across the Sahara

After watching

4➤ Ss choose their favourite holiday destination from the film. Ss look back at unit 6 from the SB for descriptive vocabulary to help with their postcards. Give Ss time to write the postcards. Go around the class, correcting errors.

➤ Ask Ss to exchange their postcards with their partner's. Ss read the new postcard and ask follow-up questions.

OPTIONAL EXTENSION
Ss choose a place in their own country and note down five or six reasons why it would make a good holiday destination. Does it have dream holiday potential? This can be an oral activity rather than a written one to give Ss practice describing places orally.

Unit 7   Cambridge

Before watching

1➤ Ss read the phrases and replace the underlined word with a word in the box. Check the answers with the class.

Answers: a notable   b stayed   c only
d concentrated   e saying   f free   g buy   h aim

2➤ Ss discuss the questions in groups of three or four. Encourage them to give reasons for their answers. Then get feedback from the whole class.

While watching

3➤ Ss read the statements. Encourage Ss to explain any difficult words first, before doing so yourself.

➤ Play the film through to the end of the first speaker, pausing if necessary for Ss to circle their answers.

➤ Play this section again for Ss to check their answers.

Answers: 1 1352   2 1980
3 have been rebuilt in current style   4 playwright

4➤ Give Ss time read the questions.

➤ Play the film without pausing, allowing Ss to make notes.

➤ Play it through once again for Ss to check their answers.

➤ Give Ss time to compare their answers before checking them with the whole class.

Answers: 1 No, it's more or less equal
2 international   3 medicine   4 The colleges are quite small so it's easy to get to know everyone. Also the colleges arrange all tuition for the students
5 The fact that there are lots of holidays
6 town and gown   7 Molecular Biology, Physics and Computing   8 Cam   9 an active social life; sport, drama, university societies   10 to provide the best possible education to its scholars.

After watching

5➤ Ss discuss the questions. Get feedback from the class.

Unit 8   From cradle to grave

Before watching

1➤ Ss read the sentences and choose the correct alternative. Elicit answers from the class.

Answers: a makes   b for a change   c heart
d for   e deteriorated   f still

2➤ Ss guess the answers to the questions 1–5. Ask Ss to compare their answers with a partner. Get feedback.

➤ Write some of their figures on the board so Ss can compare their predictions with the facts in the extract.

Answers: 1 3.5 years   2 a new word every 2 hours
3 2,000 people   4 twice   5 12 years

While watching

3➤ Play extract through pausing a couple of times so Ss can absorb the figures as some figures closely follow each other. Play the whole extract for Ss to check their answers.

Answers: 1 7,300 eggs and 160kg of chocolate
2 150km   3 368 million times   4 28 metres
5 3.5 million   6 False. She'll produce 200 billion new red blood cells everyday   7 4   8 2   9 82, 80 and 55 respectively   10 22,000km

After watching

4➤ Ask Ss to form the nouns from the verbs 1–6. Tell Ss they can use their he monolingual dictionaries or the word building lists from the vocabulary page in unit 8. Elicit the answers.

Answers: 1 achieve / achievement   2 consume / consumer   3 grow / growth   4 breathe / breath
5 produce / production   6 marry / marriage

5➤ Ss write sentences about their lives using the verbs and nouns from Ex. 5. Tell them they must use a verb or noun from each number. Go around the class, correcting any errors.

➤ Allow Ss to compare answers before getting feedback.

Unit 9   The ideal workplace

Before watching

1➤ Ss discuss Ex.1 in groups. Go around the class correcting any errors. Get feedback by asking each group to present a summary of their discussion.

While watching

2➤ Give Ss time to read the questions 1–5. Ask Ss to predict the answers with a partner.

➤ Play the film through until … 'choose what uniform', pausing if necessary for Ss to make notes.

➤ Replay the same section of film for Ss to check answers.

Answers: 1 It's in the 3rd largest city on earth
2 unusual   3 half the office is empty and this shows flexibility   4 talent   5 b   6 true   7 false; they can choose their own bosses and set their own pay.
8 as seven-day weekends   9 old stuff
10 There is nothing revolutionary about what he's doing; what's revolutionary is the fact that he's actually *doing* it.   11 over a 100 million pounds
12 There was a stern top-down control i.e. the employees had to do what they were told by their managers/bosses without discussion. Richard has created an open atmosphere where employees have more control over their working conditions.
13 Teams now have responsibility for running everything in their area as they see best.
14 b   15 choosing what uniform they wanted to use

After watching

4➤ Ss match the verbs 1–6 with the meanings a–f. Allow Ss time to compare their answers with a partner before eliciting answers. Encourage Ss to self-correct before doing so yourself.

Answers: 1 e   2 d   3 f   4 c   5 a   6 b

5➤ Ask Ss to read the task and give them a few minutes to prepare. Tell them to imagine themselves in a practical work situation.

➤ Ss work in pairs to compile a paragraph describing how they would manage a small team of designers.

➤ Regroup the Ss so two pairs are working together. Ask Ss to compare their ideas before getting feedback from the class.

Unit 10   Icons

Before watching

1➤ Ss decide on their modern-day icon from any field of their choice.

➤ Give Ss time to write a few sentences describing their icon using the vocabulary listed. Ask Ss to compare descriptions with a partner. Encourage Ss to correct each other's work before doing so yourself.

2➤ Ss discuss the questions 1–3 in pairs. Get feedback from the whole class.

While watching

3➤ Get Ss to read the questions and predict what the missing words could be.

➤ Play each film extract and pause after each icon so the Ss can make notes.

➤ Play the film through once again so that Ss can check their answers.

Answers: 1 major   2 collected   3 courage
4 unique   5 unforgettable   6 fined
7 refused / walked / lifts   8 protests   9 heros
10 policy   11 worried   13 lifetime / biggest
13 thirty   14 brought up   15 invasion

After watching

4➤ Ss discuss questions 1–2 with a partner.

➤ Encourage Ss to think of the ways being an icon can affect people's private lives using Marilyn Monroe's life as an example.

➤ Get class feedback on question 2 and write a list on the board of the class's choice of modern-day icons.

Tests

Test A Units 1-5

Grammar

auxiliary verbs

1 Put the words in correct order to make sentences.

hasn't cinema time for to long he a been the.
He hasn't been to the cinema for a long time.

1 do what summer you did last?
_____ ?

2 home at cook do normally you?
_____ ?

3 place been this ever you to have?
_____ ?

4 nights go does friend Friday best on your where?
_____ ?

[2 points]

Present Perfect Simple and Past Simple

2 Complete the text with the correct form of the verbs in brackets.

Six years ago I *went* (go) to Düsseldorf in order to work as an au pair because I (1) _____ (always enjoy) working with children. At that time I (2) _____ (cannot) speak any German but I (3) _____ (learn) it in a short time thanks to the family I was living with. My stay in Germany was a long one and, ever since I (4) _____ (return) to England, I (5) _____ (work) as a translator. I (6) _____ (have) this job for six months now.

[3 points]

the passive

3 Complete the following sentences in either the active or passive form using a suitable tense of the verb in brackets.

This book was published (publish) only two months ago.

1 This shop _____ (rob) at least three times since the beginning of the year.

2 Every year natural disasters _____ (cause) terrible damage to the world.

3 This law _____ (change) by the government last month.

4 My friend _____ (offer) a promotion three times but prefers her present job.

5 This type of thing _____ (do) by our workers all the time.

6 The secretary _____ (organise) the last managers' meeting.

[3 points]

relative clauses

4 Underline the correct relative pronoun to complete these sentences.

This is the small town _____ I was brought up.
(a) which (b) where (c) that

1 Would the person _____ car is parked in front of the door kindly move it?
(a) who (b) which (c) whose

2 That was the moment _____ he started to feel really nervous.
(a) where (b) that (c) when

3 She always helps people _____ are less fortunate than herself.
(a) who (b) whose (c) which

4 It is a machine _____ is used for cutting paper.
(a) where (b) that (c) who

[3 points]

talking about the future

5 Complete the sentences using the correct future form.

Did you know that we <u>are going to buy</u> a new house in the suburbs?

1 A couple from Leeds _____ (buy) our old cottage. It has all been arranged.

2 That's the doorbell. I _____ (answer) it.

3 Some time next year we _____ (build) a new fireplace for the living room.

4 Good lord! Is that the time? I'm sorry but I _____ (have) to go.

5 It's our anniversary tomorrow and we _____ (have) a big party at home. We have invited a lot of people.

6 We have quite a few problems to solve but I think everything _____ (be) okay.

(**3 points**)

comparatives and superlatives

6 Complete the text using a comparative or superlative form of the words in brackets.

> I feel a lot *more relaxed* (relaxed) after my trip to Prague. In fact, it has probably been
> (1) _____ _____ (good) holiday I've had for a long time. This city has (2) _____ _____ (picturesque) architecture than most other places, although perhaps it is not (3) _____ _____ (easy) to live in as other parts of the country where life is (4) _____ _____ (peaceful). Although Prague can be a bit noisy with so many tourists, it is still a really fantastic place to visit.

(**2 points**)

modal verbs of obligation and prohibition

7 Complete the sentences using *must(n't), should(n't)* and *don't (doesn't) have to.*

You <u>don't have to</u> work long hours if you don't want to in this job and timetables are quite flexible.

1 You really _____ be good with people in order to be a good seller.

2 I know that your job is quite hectic so you _____ try to relax more at home.

3 You _____ come in here with your dog because it is strictly forbidden.

4 One of the best things about my job is that I _____ get up early every day.

5 As you have a headache, you _____ go out tonight.

6 We _____ wear a shirt and tie every day at work because our boss expects us to look smart.

(**3 points**)

First Conditional with *if/when/unless/ as soon as*

8 <u>Underline</u> the correct option in these sentences.

<u>If</u> /When you don't help me with this right now, I'll be annoyed.

1 I'll learn lots of Spanish *when/as soon as* I travel to Mexico next year.

2 I won't buy any food *unless/if* I start to feel hungry.

3 *As soon as/If* I get home this evening I'll call you.

4 *Unless/If* they run out of money, they will try to borrow some.

(**2 points**)

Present Perfect Simple and Present Perfect Continuous

9 Complete the sentences with the correct form of the verbs in brackets (Present Perfect Simple or Continuous).

I have called (call) three clients today.

1 Michelle _____ (work) hard all afternoon and now she is exhausted.

2 How long _____ Derek _____ (play) badminton?

3 Now that I _____ (finish) my report, I think I can relax a little.

4 Ron _____ (have) an accident and that's why he wasn't in when you phoned.

5 I _____ (try) to contact her all day but it is impossible. Her line is always busy.

6 Cathy _____ (not speak) to Maria yet but she will as soon as she gets the chance.

(**3 points**)

gerunds and infinitives

10 Fill the gaps in the text with either the gerund or the infinitive form of the verb in brackets.

Although she can't stand *getting* (get) up early on Saturdays, Anna agreed (1) _____ (make) an exception and go mountaineering with us. I reminded her (2) _____ (set) the alarm clock as we all had to be up before 5a.m. We were all feeling excited about the trip, however, because we adore (3) _____ (be) out in the fresh air and we expected (4) _____ (see) some spectacular views.

(**2 points**)

Total: 20 points

Pronunciation

1 Underline the verb that is stressed (main verb or auxiliary) in these sentences.

Tony was bitten by a dog the other day.

1 Work on this project must be finished before the end of the month.

2 This criminal will be arrested soon.

3 These chairs are made in Italy.

4 This is proof that advertisements of this type can be effective.

5 These main headlines have been heard many times on the radio.

6 These ideas for new products were developed by two different companies.

(**3 points**)

2 Underline the stressed syllable in the following compound nouns.

double glazing

air conditioner	washing machine
mobile phone	central heating
alarm clock	answer phone

(**3 points**)

3 Put the words into the correct column in the table below.

take	band	bag	card	gate	heart
park	cap	mail	paint	farm	camp

/æ/	/eɪ/	/ɑː/
land	game	hard
_____	_____	_____
_____	_____	_____
_____	_____	_____
_____	_____	_____

(**4 points**)

Total: 10 points

Vocabulary

1 Complete the sentences with the correct preposition from the box.

in	on	about	at	for	to

I'm very worried <u>about</u> these exams.

1 I spent a lot of money _____ my car last year.

2 I am reading _____ the history of Russia at the moment. It's really interesting.

3 Janice is very good _____ playing tennis.

4 What is this machine used _____ ?

5 Michael is very interested _____ contemporary art and literature.

6 Our small society belongs _____ a much larger national association.

(**3 points**)

2 Complete the sentences by choosing the correct option (a, b or c).

He made <u>up</u> a good excuse for being late for the weekly meeting.
<u>(a) up</u> (b) of (c) with

1 After my holidays, I had to catch _____ a lot of work.
(a) up (b) with (c) up with

2 When I was a boy, I picked _____ a lot of useful things about carpentry from my father.
(a) out of (b) up (c) out

3 After two hours of hard thinking, Mary finally worked _____ the solution to the problem.
(a) out of (b) out (c) up

4 She told me that she had broken _____ her boyfriend last week.
(a) up (b) up from (c) up with

5 At the party we ran _____ food and drink so we had to buy some more.
(a) out of (b) up with (c) out from

6 We were talking for such a long time that we ended _____ missing the film.
(a) out (b) up with (c) up

(**3 points**)

3 Write the opposites of the following words.

lend/<u>borrow</u>

1 punishment/_____

2 buyer/_____

3 success/_____

4 produce/_____

(**2 points**)

4 <u>Underline</u> the correct option in these sentences.

When I was at the disco, someone <u>stole</u>/robbed my jacket.

1 Jerome *remembers/reminds* me of a famous American actor.

2 This evening I have to prepare for my *trip/travel* to London because my flight leaves at 7.45a.m.

3 I was at a party the other night and I enjoyed myself a lot. It was *fun/funny*.

4 She *told/said* me that I had to send my report by email to the office in Barcelona.

(**2 points**)

Total: 10 points

Test A Units 1-5

Reading

1 Read the following newspaper article.

SCREAM STOLEN IN OSLO

Armed robbers stole *The Scream* and another masterpiece, *Madonna,* by the Norwegian artist Edvard Munch on Sunday during the daytime in an Oslo museum packed with terrified tourists.

A pair of masked robbers ran into the Munch Museum, threatened staff members with a handgun and forced people to lie down before grabbing both *The Scream* and *Madonna.*

Shocked tourists said they thought they were victims of a terror attack. The men pulled the masterpieces from the wall, walked out the front door and escaped in a black Audi driven by a man who had been waiting outside, police said.

'We're busy looking for clues,' Chief Inspector Kjell Pedersen said at a news conference. 'We don't know who did this.' The paintings were later cut from their frames, which were found smashed into pieces in an Oslo street. The car was separately found abandoned a few kilometres away.

Munch, a founder of modern expressionism who lived from 1863 to 1944, painted both works as part of a series about love, anxiety and death.

The paintings are among Munch's best-known and are worth millions of dollars. He actually produced several similar versions of both.

Art experts speculated that the thieves might demand a ransom from the government because the works were too well known to be sold on the open market. But Pedersen said, 'We have heard nothing'.

The police blocked off the museum, informed Interpol and alerted airports and border crossings. One of the thieves spoke during the robbery in the local tongue. No shots were fired; one guard was treated for shock.

'I saw one of the men put a gun right behind a guard's head,' said one of the witnesses, a sixty-three-year-old Texas businessman visiting Oslo. 'It took quite a while for the police to come.' Anna Lieherr, a twenty-two-year-old German student, was also a witness. 'Some people were lying on the floor,' she said. 'I don't know if they were forced to or were just scared.'

Another and perhaps better known version of *The Scream* was stolen from Norway's National Gallery in a break-in in February 1994 on the opening day of the Winter Olympics in Lillehammer. The government refused to pay a ransom, and the police caught the thieves a few months later, recovering the painting. Those thieves, including one who stole another Munch painting in 1988, were later released from jail.

One Norwegian art expert estimated that the version of *The Scream* stolen on Sunday would cost $60 million to $75 million if legally sold, and *Madonna* about $15 million.

2 Mark the following statements true (T) or false (F)?

There weren't very many people in the museum when the crime was committed. <u>F</u>

1 It was possible to describe the robbers' faces. ___

2 Four men participated in the criminal operation. ___

3 The thieves decided to keep the frames to protect the paintings. ___

4 Munch was one of the first ever expressionist painters. ___

5 The men responsible for the crime had demanded a lot of money from the government. ___

6 The police arrived at the scene immediately. ___

7 A 'witness' is a person who sees a crime being committed. ___

8 The people who were guilty of the 1994 robbery are still in prison. ___

(**8 points**)

3 Answer these questions.

Why were some tourists so frightened?
<u>They thought that the robbers were terrorists.</u>

1 Which word in the text means 'exceptional works of art'?

2 Why might the criminals want to demand a sum of money from the government for the paintings?

3 What did the police do after the crime?

4 Where do you think the thieves were from and why?

5 Who needed medical attention and why?

6 Why were people lying on the floor during the robbery?

(**12 points**)

(**Total: 20 points**)

Listening

1 Mark these statements true (T) or false (F)?

The cottage's cellar will be used for storing wine. _T_

1 Mark's new cottage is in the centre of a town. ___

2 It won't be a big problem to travel to and from London for him. ___

3 He loves the scenery near the cottage. ___

4 He doesn't like the nightlife in London because it is too noisy. ___

5 Sylvia is quite happy to continue with her present lifestyle. ___

6 In the future she wants to invest money in property. ___

7 She doesn't like the idea of working long hours as she needs to have spare time. ___

8 She has an interview with a company that makes furniture for houses. ___

(**8 points**)

2 Answer these questions.

Which word does Mark use to describe the countryside near his new home and the lifestyle in big cities?
The countryside is unspoilt and the city lifestyle is hectic.

1 What is Mark's profession and what type of atmosphere does he need in order to work well?

2 In his opinion, what are the two main problems of living in a big city?

3 What expression does Mark use which means "I like it much more?"

4 What happened with Sylvia's boyfriend and when did it happen?

5 In Sylvia's opinion, what two aspects of someone's personality are necessary to be a salesperson?

6 When did she respond to the ad and when will her interview be?

(**12 points**)

Total: 20 points

Writing

Choose ONE of the following topics and write a composition of about 250-300 words.

1 In your opinion, what qualities must a person have to become a very good friend of yours? You can give examples of people you know.

2 Do you think that the media has too much power and influence in people's lives? Give examples.

3 If you could live in a different place, which city in the world would you choose and why?

4 Do you think people in today's society think too much about money and wealth? How important is this in our lives compared to other things?

5 What things do you like doing most in your spare time and why? Are there any new hobbies that you would like to take up?

(**15 points**)

100 points

Test B Units 1-5

Grammar

Present Simple and Present Continuous

1 Complete the sentences with the correct form of the verbs in brackets. Choose either the Present Simple or Present Continuous.

I don't understand (not understand) this lesson very well.

1 I can't speak to you now because I _____ (work) on a very urgent document at the moment.

2 Yes, now I _____ (remember) exactly what happened.

3 From time to time we _____ (climb) mountains to the north of our city.

4 I definitely _____ (not want) to lose touch with my ex-classmates.

5 Mary _____ (do) a computer course because she needs it for her job.

6 I _____ (think) that Hitchcock was a truly wonderful film director.

(**3 points**)

Present Perfect Simple and Past Simple

2 Complete the sentences with either the Present Perfect Simple or the Past Simple using a suitable verb of your choice.

When he was alive, my grandfather made some beautiful wooden ornaments.

1 All my life I _____ to Rolling Stones records. They're the best.

2 The other day I _____ a window in my house and my dad was furious.

3 Paul _____ volleyball since he was a small child.

4 We _____ in Canada for six years but last month we came back to Britain permanently.

(**2 points**)

relative clauses

3 Complete the text with an appropriate relative pronoun.

This is the place *where* the crime was committed. At the time (1) _____ the body was found by two joggers, the police were quickly informed. Three suspects (2) _____ were seen in the area late yesterday evening are being questioned. The woman (3) _____ husband was killed is being comforted by relatives and the weapon (4) _____ was used to murder the victim still hasn't been found.

(**2 points**)

Past Simple and Past Continuous

4 Complete the sentences with the correct form of the verbs in brackets. Choose either the Past Simple or the Past Continuous.

1 I _____ (meet) my wife for the first time when I _____ (live) in Belgium.

2 While I _____ (walk) along the road last night, I _____ (see) a terrible car accident.

3 Then he _____ (sit) down at the table and _____ (open) the newspaper.

(**3 points**)

comparatives and superlatives

5 Complete the sentences using the information below.

James: 66kg Gordon: 63kg Don: 66kg Ken: 81kg

Gordon is not as heavy as Don.

1 Ken is _____ _____ James.

2 Gordon is _____ _____ of the four men.

3 Ken isn't as _____ _____ the others.

4 James is as _____ _____ Don.

(**2 points**)

future possibility

6 Rewrite the sentences using the words in brackets without changing the meaning.

It is possible that I won't be able to go to the party tonight. (might not)
I might not be able to go to the party tonight.

1 Mr. Peterson is certain to become the new sales manager.

(will definitely)_____

_____.

2 I possibly won't arrive on time because I am very busy.

(may not) _____

_____.

3 I'm almost 100 percent certain that it will rain later this evening.

(probably) _____

_____.

4 A friend of mine has a reasonable chance of becoming the university chess champion in the future.

(could) _____

_____.

5 It's quite possible that I will have to take the bus to get to work tomorrow.

(might) _____

_____.

6 My aunt's horse 'Bad Boy' is a strong favourite to win this race.

(will probably) _____

_____.

(**3 points**)

question tags

7 Use the correct question tag to complete these sentences.

Perry Como was a very famous singer, <u>wasn't he</u>?

1 Jennifer goes swimming twice a week, _____ ?

2 You couldn't finish that last job on time, _____ ?

3 They must get up at six o'clock every morning, _____ ?

4 You didn't go out last night, _____ ?

5 We have run out of money, _____ ?

6 They will arrive there before ten o' clock tonight, _____ ?

(**3 points**)

First Conditional with *if/when/unless/ as soon as*

8 Fill the gaps in this telephone dialogue using *if, when, unless* or *as soon as*.

Jane: <u>If</u> you have time, Alan, can you pick up some bread from the bakery?

Alan: I'll try to darling but I'm extremely busy. (1) _____ I've prepared these documents, I have a meeting with my boss about a very urgent matter.

Jane: Okay. (2) _____ I get home I'll start preparing the dinner (3) _____ , of course, you arrive before me. We're having spaghetti this evening.

Alan: That sounds good. (4) _____ my meeting is short, I'll be home some time before you and you'll have a nice, hot dinner waiting for you.

Jane: That's great darling. I have to go now. Good luck with your meeting.

Alan: Thanks darling. Bye.

Jane: Bye.

(**2 points**)

gerunds and infinitives

9 Underline the correct option in the following sentences.

He forgot taking/to take his umbrella with him.

1 We usually manage *to finish/finishing* our dinner before our favourite TV programme starts.

2 I would really love *to go/going* to the theatre tonight.

3 She refused *accepting/to accept* the job offer because the salary was quite low.

4 I usually hate *travelling/to travel* to work on a Monday morning.

(**2 points**)

countable and uncountable nouns

10 Complete the sentences by choosing the correct option for these sentences (a, b or c).

We already have a lot of washing-up liquid at home so there is no need to buy more.
(a) much (b) a lot of (c) a few

1 I heard _____ news that petrol prices will continue to go up.
(a) a (b) any (c) some

2 I can't lend you any money now because I only have _____ left for myself.
(a) a few (b) not much (c) a little

3 She inherited _____ enormous amount of money.
(a) a (b) an (c) some

4 We are afraid we don't have very _____ information at the moment.
(a) much (b) much of (c) lots

5 My friend gave me _____ useful advice.
(a) a (b) an (c) some

6 It looks like we don't have very _____ time to finish the job.
(a) much (b) little (c) few

(**3 points**)

Total: 25 points

Pronunciation

1 Put these regular verbs in the past tense into the correct column in the table below.

stopped	needed	delivered	watched
pushed	committed	breathed	failed
defended	asked	pulled	waited

/t/	/d/	/ɪd/
liked	*loved*	*wanted*
_____	_____	_____
_____	_____	_____
_____	_____	_____

(**4 points**)

2 Underline the stressed syllables in the following sentences.

We don't have to come.

1 You have to read this book.

2 We must see this film.

3 You shouldn't go out tonight.

(**3 points**)

3 Underline the syllable stress in these words.

punishment

consumer buyer reward

produce pollution success

(**3 points**)

Total: 10 points

Vocabulary

1 Choose the correct option for these expressions.

To move/get lost

1 To *give/cause* damage.

2 To *return/take* to the sea.

3 To *take/give* first aid.

4 To *give/move* in with someone.

5 To *take/return* a break.

6 To *cause/take* a wrong turn.

(3 points)

2 Choose the most appropriate word (a, b or c) to complete the following sentences.

Sydney is a very modern city with many new buildings and very wide avenues.
(a) modern (b) quiet (c) cramped

1 I saw some really _____ views when I was driving through a mountainous region last weekend.
(a) lively (b) picturesque (c) enormous

2 Edinburgh is a really _____ city with its castle, palace and other beautiful old buildings.
(a) historical (b) unspoilt (c) dull

3 This small village has some very _____ but attractive customs and traditions. For example, the people always use an open fire to cook their meals.
(a) peaceful (b) old-fashioned (c) noisy

4 This seaside town is extremely _____ .
Thousands of people from many different countries visit it every summer.
(a) mediocre (b) cramped (c) touristy

5 The room we rented was _____ . In fact, it was so small that the bed nearly filled the room.
(a) tiny (b) spacious (c) cosy

6 The pubs in this city are very _____ with bands playing live music and lots of people dancing.
(a) energetic (b) dull (c) lively

(3 points)

3 Fill the gaps in these sentences with a suitable word of your choice.

1 I've nearly finished this book. I'm already on the tenth _____ .

2 Spaghetti Bolonese is the most well-known _____ from Italy.

3 We were so happy with the quality of the service and food that we gave the waitress a generous _____ .

4 The _____ of this film contains music from several famous pop and rock groups from the nineties.

5 It is not very common that the _____ is better than the original film.

6 The best part of this film is the _____ . It is a fascinating story about how a young man investigates the mysterious disappearance of his father.

7 I saw some excellent acting at the Principal Theatre the other night. It was a great _____ .

8 In the restaurant last night, I felt so full after the main course that I couldn't eat a _____ .

(4 points)

Total: 10 points

Reading

1 Read this text about a famous confidence trickster and answer the questions.

Joseph 'Yellow Kid' Weil was arguably the greatest conman in American history. He had a great understanding of human nature and was a genius for inventing elaborate schemes and games. He was a kind of Robin Hood who robbed the greedy and corrupt and gave to the people who could enjoy spending the money: himself and his friends.

Weil, whose nickname 'Yellow Kid' came from a cartoon character he loved, was the son of German-American grocers in Chicago. He dropped out of high school and his first job was as a messenger in a company full of dishonest people. When he asked them about their activities, they paid him to keep quiet. Many years later, he said the job taught him that cleverness and dishonesty paid a lot better than leading an honest life. He began to cheat people at an early age by selling bottles of fake 'miracle medicine' as well as fake gold-framed glasses at expensive prices. As his confidence grew, he gradually developed more ways to cheat people using some very original ideas. At the horse races, for example, he worked with a made up brother-in-law, who was naturally also a conman, to gain people's confidence. Weil's racetrack victims were Chicago businessmen who were thought to have full knowledge of what they were getting into and the 'Yellow Kid' benefited from this legal situation.

Some years later, he became a self-made millionaire through dishonest dealings during the Florida land boom of the 1920s. After this he began to put adverts in newspapers to trick people across America promising to give people back $1,000, if they invested $100. As criminal law related to con artists was changing in Chicago, he did not advertise in local papers.

Later he opened a real bank which made enormous illegal profits by using false documents. Weil's bank manager escaped the anger of the victims by saying that a dishonest secretary had disappeared with all the money. He once said: 'the men I cheated were wealthy and also had a strong desire to gain money and didn't care how they got it.'

In his whole life he went to prison only twice and he completely reformed when he was around seventy as he didn't want to go back there again. In his old age, he had a very dignified and friendly manner although the police still didn't trust him. He lived to be very old and there is a photo of him at his 100th birthday party in which he looks rather skinny but extremely well-dressed. He finally died in 1976 and everyone agreed that the self-taught, endlessly imaginative and incredibly successful 'Yellow Kid' was a unique genius. The crime world will not see someone like him again.

2 Choose the correct option (a) or (b).

Weil was (a) definitely (b) possibly the greatest con artist in American history.

1 (a) He didn't finish his school education. (b) He obtained good school qualifications.

2 The glasses he sold were made of (a) gold (b) something that looked like gold.

3 In Chicago after the 1920's, it became (a) easy (b) difficult for Weil to cheat people out of money with confidence tricks.

4 He retired from crime because he (a) felt too old (b) didn't want to return to jail.

5 After he had stopped cheating people, the police (a) thought he was a nice person (b) continued thinking that he had criminal intentions.

6 When he was very old, he was (a) too thin (b) too fat.

6 points

3 Answer these questions using your own words if possible.

Why was Weil a popular figure? *He robbed corrupt or greedy people and was generous to his friends.*

1 Why was he called 'The Yellow Kid'?

2 Why did the people in his first job pay Joseph extra money?

3 At what moment in his life did Joseph Weil think that he would be better off being dishonest?

4 How did he make money dishonestly when he was young?

5 What excuse was given to customers in Weil's bank to explain why they had lost money?

6 Did he sometimes feel guilty about the people he cheated? Why/Why not?

7 Who taught him to become a confidence trickster?

14 points

Total: 20 points

Listening

1 Mark the following statements true (T) or false (F).

Tracy and Geoff have similar hobbies. *F*

1 Tracy isn't very interested in her social life. ___

2 She does karate and goes jogging. ___

3 Geoff doesn't think he spends enough time with his daughters. ___

4 Tracy isn't married. ___

5 She thinks that she will possibly change in the future. ___

6 Geoff doesn't usually send emails. ___

7 He was visiting a website when he had a problem with the computer. ___

8 Geoff and Tracy feel that sometimes they don't have enough things to talk about. ___

8 points

2 Answer these questions.

How does Geoff describe himself as a person?
He is someone who needs to be with people.

1 Why does he speak a lot on the telephone?

2 Name two activities that Tracy likes doing at weekends.

3 Name two things that Geoff would like to do if he had more spare time.

4 When is the only time that Tracy reads anything?

5 What exactly happened to Geoff's computer and what does he plan to do?

6 What exact words does Geoff use to mean 'I think that is true'?

12 points

Total: 20 points

Writing

Choose ONE of the following topics and write a composition of about 250-300 words.

1 In your opinion, what qualities must a person have to become a very good friend of yours? You can give examples of people you know.

2 Do you think that the media has too much power and influence in people's lives? Give examples.

3 If you could live in a different place, which city in the world would you choose and why?

4 Do you think people in today's society think too much about money and wealth? How important is this in our lives compared to other things?

5 What things do you like doing most in your spare time and why? Are there any new hobbies that you would like to take up?

15 points

100 points

207

Test A Units 6-10

Grammar

Past Perfect Simple

1 Choose the correct option to complete the sentences.

I didn't go to the cinema to see that film because I saw/ had seen it before.

1 Then she *entered/had entered* the room and switched on the light.

2 We all got a surprise when the boss suddenly *appeared/had appeared*.

3 I went sightseeing in the city after I *checked/had checked* into my hotel.

4 When I got back to the pub I discovered that all my friends *went/had gone*.

5 She told me that she *was/had been* ill and that's why she didn't go on holiday last year.

6 We *arrived/had arrived* at the art gallery and then we began taking some photos.

3 points

articles

2 Fill the gaps in this text with *a, an, the* or leave the space blank (-).

One of *the* best holiday experiences I have ever had was when we went to Tikal in (1) _____ northern Guatemala three years ago. We met a very interesting American woman there who is (2) _____ archaeologist and she gave us a fantastic free guided tour of (3) _____ famous ruins, which included some impressive temples. The wildlife in the region is fascinating too and one of the first things we saw when we arrived was (4) _____ spider monkey happily swinging in the trees.

2 points

used to and would

3 Choose the correct options to complete the text.

When we were kids we *used to/would be/used* have a great time during our school summer holidays. We would (1) *go cycling/to cycle/cycling* in the countryside every morning and then we (2) *would having/would have/used to having* a picnic lunch. It was great to get home again in the afternoon, however, as I (3) *used to/got used to/would to* enjoy playing with my dog Sandy for hours and hours. In fact, at that time we (4) *would/used be/used to* have one dog and three cats.

2 points

modals of ability

4 Choose the correct option to complete the sentences.

I repeated that exam I failed and I could/managed to/ could to pass it this time.

1 The wild animal attacked him but fortunately he *was/was able/could* to escape.

2 When I was very small I *managed to/was able to/couldn't* get good marks because I was easily distracted.

3 My mother has a great memory and when she was at school she *could to/knew to/managed to* learn very long texts by heart.

4 I *wasn't able to/can't /couldn't to* go to the party last night because I was feeling ill.

5 He tried very hard but he *was able to/managed to/ didn't manage to* qualify for the semi-final.

6 Both of them are fast runners. Yesterday they *could/ were able to/managed* complete 1,500 metres in less than four minutes.

3 points

Second Conditional

5 Use the verbs in brackets to make Second Conditional sentences.

If you <u>decided</u> (decide) to retire early, you <u>would be able to</u> (be able to) relax and enjoy life for longer.

1 If you _____ (change) the password on your computer, you _____ (feel) safer.

2 There _____ (be) less starvation in the world if wealthier nations _____ (help) poorer countries more.

3 If you _____ (leave) your job, you _____ (have) no guarantees of finding another one quickly.

4 I _____ (travel) around the world if I ever _____ (win) a fortune.

5 If we all _____ (think) a bit harder, I'm sure we _____ (find) some solutions to these problems.

6 You _____ (have) a more tranquil life if you _____ (buy) bought a house in the country.

(**3 points**)

Third Conditional

6 Make Third Conditional sentences by combining the following pairs of sentences.

I didn't train well. I didn't win the match.
<u>If I had trained well, I would have won the match.</u>

1 Sharon ate too much chocolate. She felt bad later.

2 I said something terrible. My girlfriend stopped talking to me.

3 We didn't follow the signs. We got lost.

4 I shouted a lot to my friends inside the discotheque. I lost my voice.

(**2 points**)

reported speech

7 Convert the following into reported speech. Remember to use a pronoun after the verb *to tell*.

Ruth: 'My new job offers me a lot of perks.' (tell)
<u>Ruth told us that her new job offered her a lot of perks.</u>

1 Tony: 'Do you work a lot of overtime?' (ask)

2 Anne: 'I'm working some very irregular hours these days.' (tell)

3 Darren: 'We have been unemployed for nearly three months.' (say)

4 Lynn: 'I think they will win the elections.' (tell)

5 Scott: 'Did you get a pay-rise yesterday?' (ask)

6 Cathy: 'I must get a couple of good references before I can apply for this job.' (say)

(**3 points**)

past obligation/permission

8 Choose the correct option to complete the sentences.

We could/<u>had to</u>/were allowed to work very hard when we were younger. (It was necessary)

1 We *couldn't/hadn't to/didn't have to* wear jeans to school. (It was not permitted)

2 In my last job I *wasn't allowed to/couldn't/didn't have to* get the bus every morning because my colleague had a car. (It wasn't necessary)

3 When I was a kid, I *could to/was allowed to/had to* cook some simple dishes in the kitchen. (It was permitted)

4 She *had to/could/must* be good with figures in order to get that job last year. (It was necessary)

(**2 points**)

209

I wish/if only

9 Complete the sentences with the correct form of the verb in brackets.

I wish I could (can) remember more things about my childhood.

1 If only he _____ (not talk) so much all the time. It's so annoying!

2 I wish I _____ (phone) her last night but I completely forgot to.

3 If only we _____ (have) more free time to do all those things!

4 I wish they _____ (hurry) up and finish the job because it's getting late.

[**2 points**]

phrasal verbs

10 Fill the gaps in this text with a suitable particle (or particles).

The other night more than a hundred people turned *up* for a concert at our local pub only to discover that the it had been called (1) _____ . Everyone wanted to know what was going (2) _____ and we soon found (3) _____ that the cancellation had been due to a technical problem. It didn't take us long, however, to come (4) _____ _____ another plan. We decided to go to another good pub in the area and buy Gerry a couple of drinks to cheer him up. He has been going (5) _____ a bad time since he split (6) _____ with his last girlfriend.

[**3 points**]

[**Total: 25 points**]

Pronunciation

1 <u>Underline</u> the stressed syllables in these sentences.

<u>May</u> I ask you what <u>time</u> it is?

1 When can you come to the office?

2 Can you tell me the way to the station?

3 Do you know if there is a supermarket near here.

[**3 points**]

2 <u>Underline</u> the stressed words in these Third Conditional sentences.

If they'd <u>turned</u> up <u>earlier</u>, they could've <u>eaten</u> with us.

1 If we hadn't missed that last bus, we would've arrived on time.

2 If they hadn't interrupted me, I would've finished by now.

3 If she'd called me before seven, I'd have gone out with her.

[**3 points**]

3 Write the following figures and dates in words.

82½: eighty-two and a half

1 126.8: _____
_____

2 30/1/04: _____
_____

3 $149.68: _____
_____

4 71.5%: _____
_____

[**4 points**]

[**Total: 10 points**]

Vocabulary

1 Complete the sentences using the correct form of the words/phrases in the box.

have good relations	buy	obtain
collect	inspire	return	become

I <u>got</u> a birthday present from my grandmother yesterday. <u>obtained</u>

1 Sandra has just <u>got back</u> from her trip to Uruguay. _____

2 I'll be right back. I'm just going <u>to get</u> some bread at the baker's. _____

3 I think I'll put on my sweater because it's <u>getting</u> quite cold. _____

4 When you arrive at the train station tomorrow, I'll come and <u>get</u> you and then we can have breakfast together. _____

5 He was <u>a great example to</u> his students. They all wanted to do well. _____

6 I used to <u>get on well</u> with one of my neighbours but not anymore. _____

(**3 points**)

2 Complete the sentences by choosing the correct option (a, b or c).

I enjoy teaching María because she is a <u>fast</u> learner.
(a) fast (b) steep (c) deep

1 When I was at school, we had to learn a lot of poems by _____ .
(a) memory (b) heart (c) perfection

2 When I started the course, I was the only one who knew nothing about computers so I felt I had been thrown in at the _____ end.
(a) deep (b) hard (c) steep

3 I picked _____ a lot of my French by simply watching films and TV programmes.
(a) out (b) on (c) up

4 We felt obliged to study hard because we had a very _____ teacher.
(a) perfect (b) strict (c) steep

5 Practice makes _____ .
(a) learning (b) good (c) perfect

6 I was _____ up to speak to people very politely.
(a) brought (b) picked (c) taken

(**3 points**)

3 Unscramble the letters to make words/phrases related to global issues.

hte temvrinenon : <u>the environment</u>

1 essadie : d _____

2 drtasand fo gnivil : s _____ ____ l _____

3 neamfi : f _____

4 meirc : c _____

5 gvepoldein siurctone : d _____ c _____

6 lnutpoilo : p _____

7 ctseyiru : s _____

8 ntrastivao : s _____

(**4 points**)

Total: 10 points

Reading

1 Read this text about Malta and answer the questions.

Malta is a truly wonderful country whose towns are populated with baroque palaces and its countryside <u>abounds</u> <u>with</u> the oldest known human constructions in the world. The best time to visit is spring or autumn as it is still hot enough to get a suntan and hotel prices come down significantly. The weather, sea and sandy beaches are a <u>bonus</u>, however. The main attractions are definitely the island's antiquities and the Baroque architecture.

There are an <u>amazing</u> number of things to discover as you explore 7,000 years of history. In fact, the Maltese Islands have been described as one big open-air museum. Wherever you go, the scenery on the islands and the architecture are <u>truly spectacular</u>.

Malta is the ideal place <u>to get away from it all</u> with its rocky coastlines, narrow and tranquil village streets, marinas and fishing villages, etc. But, the best thing about a stay here is that you can experience several holidays in one and there are <u>endless</u> things to do. For people who are physically fit, it is a great place for rock-climbing, trekking and several types of water sports. You can enjoy a busy calendar of cultural events all year round, as Malta is also a bilingual country which has strong historical and cultural links to Britain. It is also an enjoyable place to learn and practise English, so English courses are available in several language schools and English language newspapers, books and magazines are sold everywhere. People even drive on the left here! The capital of the country is Valletta, which is less than two kilometres in length so it is possible to explore this beautiful city in a relatively short time. It has many interesting squares that are surrounded by palaces and other historical buildings. Another important tourist attraction is Gozo, which is separated from the mainland by three kilometres of sea. The island has a spectacular rocky coastline and also has a relaxing, rural atmosphere. The cuisine has Italian, French and Maltese influences. <u>Standards are generally high</u> and fresh fish is a favourite in local restaurants and bars. Many species of seafood are consumed all year round and this is what Maltese restaurants do best. Several dishes with rice, meat and vegetables are also popular, however.

Malta's hot, dry summers can be uncomfortable but they are normally very pleasant and the <u>mild</u> winters are also nice. The rain is heaviest in winter but is still only moderate. In <u>the high season</u>, the most economical option is a package tour that includes the flight and seven nights in a two or three star hotel as this will cost under £500. Whether you end up choosing a package tour or <u>travelling independently</u> in Malta, you are guaranteed to have an unforgetable experience.

1 Choose the correct definition for these words and expressions. They are underlined in the text so look at them carefully in their context before answering.

abounds with means (a) to be full of (b) to have a few of (c) to be decorated with

1 <u>bonus</u> means (a) the best thing (b) an extra or added benefit (c) a nice surprise

2 <u>amazing</u> means (a) incredible (b) useful (c) interesting

3 <u>to get away from it all</u> means (a) to have fun (b) to escape from the pressures and routines of daily life (c) to have an adventure

4 <u>endless</u> means (a) fantastic (b) with limitations (c) without limits

5 <u>Standards are generally high</u> means (a) the food has a lot of variety (b) the food is normally expensive (c) the quality of the food tends to be good

6 <u>mild</u> means (a) variable (b) very cold (c) gentle or soft, i.e. not too cold

7 <u>the high season</u> means (a) the most popular time of the year for tourists (b) the time of the year with the highest temperatures (c) the festival period

8 <u>travelling independently</u> means (a) travelling on your own (b) arranging your own travel (c) arranging travelling without dependents

⟨ **8 points** ⟩

2 Answer these questions in your own words if possible.

What two aspects make Malta a wonderful country?
<u>Its baroque palaces and the most ancient man-made constructions in the world.</u>

1 Why is spring or autumn the best time to visit?

2 Why do you think Malta has been described as 'a big open-air museum'?

3 What type of physical outdoor activities can people do in Malta?

4 Why is English spoken so well here?

5 What would you notice about traffic in Malta?

6 What type of food does Malta specialise in most?

⟨ **12 points** ⟩

Total: 20 points

Listening

Listen to two young men speaking about their school and university days.

1 Select the correct option.

The first speaker (Phil) <u>(a) thinks that school days are the happiest days your life</u> (b) doesn't think that school days are the happiest days your life (c) doesn't have an opinion on this.

1 Wayne (a) was happy with all of his teachers (b) was happy with one or two of them (c) didn't like a couple of them.

2 Wayne and most of his classmates (a) did well in their exams (b) did badly (c) felt very nervous because of their maths teacher.

3 The best adjective to describe Phil's old French teacher is (a) understanding (b) frightening (c) boring.

4 At first, Wayne found biology at university (a) easy (b) difficult (c) neither easy nor difficult.

5 Phil thinks that (a) university prepares you well for other things as well as for a job (b) university life can be frustrating (c) the social life at university is terrible.

6 Phil is interrupted by (a) a person in the street (b) a call from his wife (c) a call from his boss.

> **6 points**

2 Answer the following questions.

What negative aspect about school exams does Wayne mention? <u>There was a lot of pressure to pass them.</u>

1 What expression does Phil use to agree with Wayne's negative opinions about school?

2 What did Phil use to do sometimes before important exams?

3 Wayne didn't like his maths teacher but mentions one positive quality. What was it?

4 Why did Phil like his English teacher?

5 What advantage and what disadvantage does Phil mention about his history course?

6 When Wayne started at university what did he have to get used to?

7 What is Wayne's cousin's job and what did he do for Wayne?

> **14 points**

> **Total: 20 points**

Writing

Choose ONE of the following topics and write a composition of about 250-300 words.

1 What type of holiday do you like most and why? Give examples from your own experience.

2 Is discipline a problem in the schools of today? What do you think are the best ways for a teacher to punish problematic children and get respect from everyone in the class?

3 What do we need to do to preserve our environment and try to reduce the ecological problems of our planet?

4 If you could change your profession, what kind of job would you most like to do and why?

5 Write in detail about one of the most special memories that you have from the past. Why is it so important to you?

> **100 points**

Test B Units 6-10

Grammar

uses of like

1 Write questions for these answers using the word *like*.

A: *What does she look like?*

B: *She is tall with fair hair and blue eyes.*

1 A: _____?

B: No, they are completely different. Sam is reserved and shy while Mathew is very sociable and friendly.

2 A: _____?

B: Tonight? I don't know really. Maybe go out and see a film or perhaps just relax at home.

3 A: _____?

B: Oh, Rome is special. It's a fascinating historical city.

4 A: _____?

B: Yes, very much. In fact, I think spaghetti is one of my favourite dishes.

(**2 points**)

articles

2 Fill the gaps in this text with *a, an, the* or nothing (-).

Last summer, I went on <u>a</u> special tour of a range of mountains in (1) _____ north of Mexico to observe and photograph some wild cats in their natural habitat. I think (2) _____ wild cats are fascinating animals and I have studied them all my life.

While we were climbing up a steep hill, (3) _____ tour guide suddenly shouted that he had just seen (4) _____ enormous snake. Everyone was terrified for a moment but fortunately (5) _____ snake disappeared into the trees. Apart from this little shock, everything else on the tour was fine and our guide gave us (6) _____ very interesting and useful information about the area.

(**3 points**)

subject and object questions

3 Write questions for these answers.

A: *Which car did Tim choose?*

B: *Tim finally chose the Renault.*

1 A: Who _____?

B: Curtis Hanson directed the film *LA Confidential*.

2 A: When _____?

B: Fleming discovered penicillin in 1928.

3 A: Which _____?

B: A 500cc Suzuki won the motorcycle race.

4 A: What _____?

B: Someone's hand touched Fred on the shoulder.

5 A: Where _____?

B: Carol saw the concert in Leeds.

6 A: How many _____?

B: Tanya bought three books.

(**3 points**)

modals of ability

4 Complete the text using four of the words from the box.

| can | can't | could | couldn't | able | manage |

Now I *can* use computers well for most applications but only five years ago I (1) _____ understand anything about them. I remember one day at work when I didn't even (2) _____ to send an email correctly and I wasn't (3) _____ to use the Word programme very well either. I did a couple of computer courses, however, and made good progress. Only six months after that I (4) _____ do all of the things that were necessary for my job.

(**2 points**)

adverbs

5 Choose the most appropriate adverb to complete these sentences.

I'm sorry for forgetting the book. I promise that I'll _____ *bring it tomorrow.*
a) hopefully b) actually c) definitely

1 He is normally not a punctual person but _____, today he arrived very early.
a) surprisingly b) obviously c) usually

2 I _____ believe that all politicians should think more about the environment.
a) carefully b) personally c) surprisingly

3 He lost his job for spending too much time on the Internet. That's what _____ happened.
a) fortunately b) hopefully c) actually

4 She drove _____ because the roads were in bad condition.
a) naturally b) quietly c) carefully

5 I think my brother will _____ win this squash match.
a) completely b) probably c) personally

6 The pay was too low. That's _____ the reason why I left my job.
a) interestingly b) basically c) completely

(**2 points**)

Third Conditional

6 Make Third Conditional sentences using the verbs in brackets.

If you <u>hadn't forgotten</u> *(not forget) to take your coat, you* <u>wouldn't have been</u> *(not be) so cold.*

1 If they _____ (take) a taxi, they _____ (arrive) much earlier.

2 If you _____ (come) to the party last night, you _____ (have) a great time.

3 They _____ (not feel) so tired this morning if they _____ (not stay) up so late last night.

4 She _____ (hear) you if you _____ (shout) louder.

(**2 points**)

make, let, allow

7 Choose the correct option to complete the sentences.

They allowed us enter/<u>to enter</u> *the flat.*

1 They made us *working/work* long hours last week.

2 We weren't *allowed/let* to wear jeans in this place.

3 The teacher made me *repeat/to repeat* the exercise.

4 You are allowed *using/to use* the library whenever you want.

5 I let my son *stay/to stay* up late last night to see the match on TV.

6 Why did you let the cat *coming/come* into the house?

(**3 points**)

reported speech

8 Convert these reported statements into direct speech.

She asked me if I liked travelling.
<u>'Do you like travelling?'</u>

1 He told me that he had visited Paris many times in his life.
_____ .

2 She said she had to do something important the following day.
_____ .

3 He asked me what I had done that day.
_____ .

4 She told us that she would travel to New York some time in the future.
_____ .

(**2 points**)

review of past tenses

9 Fill the gaps with the correct form of the verbs in brackets. Choose the Past Simple, Past Continuous or Past Perfect Simple.

I remember a very talented friend called Brigitte who _could_ (can) speak several languages. She (1) _____ (be) born in Paris to a Spanish mother and an English father, so she (2) _____ (learn) to speak all three languages before she started school. While she (3) _____ (study) at secondary school, she (4) _____ (begin) to learn Japanese, German and Italian. She was a determined and brilliant student. After Brigitte (5) _____ (finish) her school studies, she travelled and worked in four different countries before starting university. The last time I saw her, she told me that she (6) _____ (prepare) for a master in Russian!

3 points

phrasal verbs

10 Underline the correct option. If the two options are correct, underline both sentences.

We are going through a bad time / We are going a bad time through.

1 I had to put up the inconvenience with / I had to put up with the inconvenience.

2 I woke up my friend early / I woke my friend up early.

3 I got off the bus in Blackpool. / I got the bus off in Blackpool.

4 I'll pick him up from the station / I'll pick up him from the station.

2 points

Total: 25 points

Pronunciation

1 Underline the long vowel sounds that give extra emphasis to these expressions.

Really?

That's amazing!   Oh no!

How awful!   My goodness!

You're joking!   How incredible!

3 points

2 Put these words into the correct column in the table below.

history   sight   island   strict
practice   live (v)   life   environment
direct   chips   miss   remind

/ɪ/	/aɪ/
split	_revise_
_____	_____
_____	_____
_____	_____
_____	_____
_____	_____
_____	_____

4 points

3 Underline the stressed syllable in these words.

adventure

package   abroad   cultural

historical   newspaper   degree

research   lifestyle   unemployed

3 points

Total: 10 points

Vocabulary

1 Choose the correct option to complete the sentences.

I can't do this exercise. Can you give me a heart/<u>a hand</u>/a favour, please?

1 Ralph is always reading books. He's a real *library rat/ reader's pet/bookworm*.

2 I know this subject *inside out/outside in/like the palm of my hand*.

3 I'm travelling to Paris on business next week so I'll have to *clean up/brush up on/polish on* my French before I go.

4 I'm good at arts and languages but with science subjects I haven't got *an idea/a guess/a clue*.

5 I'm very pleased with the computer course I'm doing because I have *picked up taken up/given up* many useful things.

6 I don't know the answer to this question but I think I'll make a wild *try/guess/effort*. Who knows? I might be right.

3 points

2 Make nouns from the following verbs and adjectives by adding the correct suffix.

independent : independence

punish: _____   ignore: _____

dark: _____   employ: _____

create: _____   intelligent: _____

3 points

3 Choose the best word from the box to complete the sentences.

tired/tiring	exhausted/exhausting
excited/exciting	annoyed/annoying
bored/boring	confused/confusing
relaxed/relaxing	depressed/depressing

I saw that Dracula film last night and it was really <u>frightening.</u>
frightened/frightening

1 When I don't have anything to do I start to feel really _____ .

2 Climbing that mountain was an _____ experience. When we finally got to the top, most of us literally collapsed.

3 Listening to classical music or sitting on the sofa with a nice cup of tea are two things that I find really _____ .

4 When I listened to one tragic story after another, I began to feel very _____ .

5 Celia can't wait to go on holiday to Canada in two months time. She already feels really _____ about it.

6 People interrupting me when I am speaking is a habit which I find quite _____ .

7 Can you explain that again? I'm a bit _____ .

8 It is very important for me to get enough rest every day because my job is quite _____ as I have to drive long distances to visit potential clients every day.

4 points

Total: 10 points

Reading

1 Read the following text about famine in Africa and answer the questions.

Nearly 30 million Africans could soon be facing famine. The immediate cause is drought, which has destroyed crops and left people and livestock without food and water. But this is not the only reason why Africa suffers regularly from famine. Most African countries do not produce enough food and depend very much on imports and on having the income to pay for them.

There are also other contributory factors; war, corruption and bad management of food supplies, environmental problems, natural disasters, the long-term effects of Aids and other diseases, as well as plagues of locusts which eat up enormous areas of vegetation.

Famine is caused by not enough food being produced or people not being able to obtain it. This may be because there is not enough water or because people can't afford to buy food. Even in famine-free years, it is common across Africa for people to not have sufficient food, especially in rural areas. The United Nations estimates that the situation in sub-Saharan Africa is worse today than it was thirty years ago. Growing poverty in Africa has left the continent with a population that has the biggest food problems in the world.

Interestingly, East and South Asia, where there have been enormous increases in agricultural production and significant economic growth have reduced the number of people who are not properly fed from forty-three percent to thirteen percent but sub-Saharan Africa has not managed to get the rate below the 1969 figure of thirty-four percent of the population.

The Nobel Prize-winning economist Amartya Sen has argued that hunger and famine are caused mostly by poverty and not just a country's ability to grow enough food. People in poverty often go hungry because they do not have enough money to buy food when they have not been able to produce enough themselves. So when there is a drought or something similar they become the first victims of famine. Professor Sen argues that if countries in Africa could make sufficient income, they would be able to avoid hunger, as they could afford to import food to make up for any food they don't produce themselves. At the moment, however African farmers can only get low prices for the products they want to export to other countries and so cannot compete on world markets.

War and terrible diseases are making some countries lose a high number of the economically-active population and there are now many children who have lost their parents and elderly people with no means of support. Natural disasters frequently happen, but it is when they hit countries that are already suffering from the effects of other problems that famine becomes inevitable.

2 Choose the correct definition for these words and expressions. They are underlined in the text so look at them carefully in their context before answering.

drought means (a) a large forest fire (b) the problem of having little or no water (c) pollution

1 livestock means (a) possessions (b) food (c) farm animals

2 income means (a) money received through work or other commercial activity (b) effort (c) transport

3 long-term effects are (a) immediate results (b) results that happen in the distant future (c) important results

4 locusts are (a) large insects that destroy crops (b) diseases (c) climatic problems

5 to afford means (a) to want (b) to try (c) to have enough money or other resources to do something.

6 to make up for means (a) to add to (b) exchange for (c) compensate for

7 economically-active means (a) rich (b) being at the right age to work (c) having studies in economics

8 elderly means (a) poor (b) ill (c) old

(8 points)

3 Answer these questions in your own words if possible.

What is one of the most important reasons for famine in Africa? There isn't enough water.

1 Why do many African countries rely on imports so much?

2 In what type of regions are the biggest food problems to be found?

3 How does the food situation in sub-Saharan Africa compare to the past?

4 Why is the situation less extreme in Asia?

5 Why does Professor Sen think that being poor is a bigger problem than not growing enough food?

6 Apart from famine, what has caused many children and elderly people to lose their economic support?

(12 points)

Total: 20 points

Listening

Listen carefully to this job interview and answer the questions.

1 Choose the correct answer.

How does the interviewer feel about Tamara's CV? (a) excited <u>*(b) impressed*</u> *(c) confused*

1 What type of job has Tamara applied for?
(a) sales manager (b) sales person (c) receptionist

2 Tamara (a) sometimes leaves jobs unfinished
(b) always likes to do jobs well (c) says that it is sometimes impossible to do certain jobs well.

3 The interviewer says that (a) driving long distances
(b) selling things (c) working long hours in the office can be very tiring.

4 Tamara says she is persuasive because of her
(a) training and motivation (b) motivation and experience (c) training and experience.

5 She (a) wants to be promoted as soon as possible
(b) isn't interested in promotion (c) wants more experience first.

6 The company runs training courses in (a) selling techniques, computer skills (b) selling techniques, driving skills (c) managing techniques, computer skills and foreign languages.

> **6 points**

2 Answer these questions.

What expression does the interviewer use to ask Tamara to sit down? <u>*Have a seat.*</u>

1 Why is Tamara interested in the job?

2 What were the two main things she had to do in her previous job?

3 What does Tamara see as her main strengths?

4 Why is working long hours not a problem for Tamara?

5 Why does Tamara not mind working on commission?

6 What could be a possible disadvantage of being promoted to regional sales manager?

7 What two things does the possibility of offering training courses depend on?

> **14 points**

> **Total: 20 points**

Writing

Choose ONE of the following topics and write a composition of about 250-300 words.

1 What type of holiday do you like most and why? Give examples from your own experience.

2 Is discipline a problem in the schools of today? What do you think are the best ways for a teacher to punish problematic children and get respect from everyone in the class?

3 What do we need to do to preserve our environment and try to reduce the ecological problems of our planet?

4 If you could change your profession, what kind of job would you most like to do and why?

5 Write in detail about one of the most special memories that you have from the past. Why is it so important to you?

100 points

219

Answer key

Test A Units 1-5

Grammar

1 auxiliary verbs
1 What did you do last summer?
2 Do you normally cook at home?
3 Have you ever been to this place?
4 Where does your best friend go on Friday nights?

2 Present Perfect Simple and Past Simple
1 have always enjoyed   2 could not (couldn't)
3 learnt   4 returned   5 have worked   6 have had

3 The Passive
1 has been robbed   2 causes   3 was changed   4 has been offered   5 is done   6 organised

4 relative clauses
1 (c)   2 (c)   3 (a)   4 (b)

5 Talking about the future
1 are buying   2 will ('ll) answer   3 are going to build
4 will ('ll) have   5 are having   6 will be

6 comparatives and superlatives
1 the best   2 more picturesque   3 as easy   4 more peaceful

7 modal verbs of obligation and prohibition
1 must   2 should   3 mustn't   4 don't have to
5 shouldn't   6 have to

8 First Conditional with *if/when/unless/as soon as*
1 when   2 unless   3 As soon as   4 If

9 Present Perfect Simple and Present Perfect Continuous
1 has been working   2 has Derek been playing   3 have finished
4 has had   5 have been trying   6 has not (hasn't) spoken

10 gerunds and infinitives
1 to make   2 to set   3 being   4 to see

Pronunciation

1
1 must   2 arrested   3 made   4 can   5 heard   6 developed

2
air conditioner   washing machine
mobile phone   central heating
alarm clock   answer phone

3

/æ/	/eɪ/	/ɑː/
land	game	hard
band	take	card
bag	gate	heart
cap	mail	park
camp	paint	farm

Vocabulary

1
1 on   2 about   3 at   4 for   5 in   6 to

2
1 (c)   2 (b)   3 (b)   4 (c)   5 (a)   6 (c)

3
1 reward   2 seller   3 failure   4 consume

4
1 reminds   2 trip   3 fun   4 told

Reading

2
1 False   2 False   3 False   4 True   5 False   6 False
7 True   8 False

3
1 masterpieces
2 The paintings are too famous to be sold in the open market.
3 They blocked off the museum, informed Interpol and alerted airports and border crossings.
4 Norway because one of them spoke in Norwegian during the robbery.
5 One security guard because he was suffering from shock.
6 Possibly they were forced to do this or maybe they were frightened.

Listening

Tapescript
S=Sylvia   M=Mark
S: So I hear you've just bought a new house in the country, Mark.
M: Yeah, it's great! It's quite a large cottage with a garden, three bedrooms, an attic and a wine cellar.
S: But you won't be too far away from London, will you?
M: Not really. It's actually on the outskirts of a town about forty minutes drive from the centre of London. That's if there are no traffic problems, of course…
S: Mm… It sounds really nice.
M: Yeah, well, I like it. It's really picturesque actually. There are some great views of hills, forests and some lovely unspoilt countryside. As a writer, I really need peace and quiet in order to think clearly.
S: I know what you mean, but won't you miss London?
M: Well, I know that London's exciting and I'll miss that but a healthy life away from the noise and pollution appeals to me more. Anyway, what about you Sylvia? I hear you're looking for a new job.
S: Yes, since I broke up with my boyfriend a couple of weeks ago, I've decided to make some changes in my life. Like you, I'm interested in buying a house or a flat, so I guess I need to earn and save a lot of money in the next few years.
M: You'll have to work hard then because it isn't exactly cheap to buy property these days.
S: I know, but I'm ambitious and really don't mind working long hours.
M: What type of job are you looking for?
S: I'd like a job as a sales rep. because I think I have the right type of personality. I'm good with people and I've got a sense of humour.
M: Have you had any luck yet?
S: Well, I responded to an advert yesterday and I've got an interview next Tuesday.
M: Great! What type of company is it?
S: It's a furnishing company which manufactures office equipment.
M: Sounds interesting. Well, best of luck on Tuesday.
S: Thanks a lot, Mark.

1
1 False   2 True   3 True   4 False   5 False   6 True
7 False   8 False

2
1 He is a writer and he needs peace and quiet.
2 The noise and the pollution.
3 It appeals to me more.
4 They broke up (separated) a couple of (two) weeks ago.
5 To be good with people and have a sense of humour.
6 She responded yesterday and the interview will be next Tuesday.

Test B Units 1-5

Grammar

1 Present Simple and Present Continuous
1 am working 2 remember 3 climb
4 do not (don't) want 5 is doing 6 think

2 Present Perfect Simple and Past Simple
1 have listened 2 broke 3 has played
4 lived

3 relative clauses
1 when 2 who (that) 3 whose 4 which (that)

4 Past Simple and Past Continuous
1 met / was living 2 was walking / saw
3 sat / opened

5 comparatives and superlatives
1 heavier than 2 the lightest 3 as light as
4 heavy as Don

6 future possibility
1 Mr Peterson will definitely become the new sales manager.
2 I may not arrive on time because I am very busy.
3 It will probably rain later this evening.
4 A friend of mine could become the university chess champion in the future.
5 I might have to take the bus to get to work tomorrow.
6 My aunt's horse "Bad Boy" will probably win this race.

7 question tags
1 doesn't she 2 could you 3 mustn't they
4 did you 5 haven't we 6 won't they

8 First Conditional with *if/when/unless/as soon as*
1 As soon as/When 2 When/as soon as 3 unless 4 If

9 gerunds and infinitives
1 to finish 2 to go 3 to accept
4 travelling

10 countable and uncountable nouns
1 (c) 2 (c) 3 (b) 4 (a) 5 (c) 6 (a)

Pronunciation

1

/t/	/d/	/ɪd/
liked	loved	wanted
stopped	delivered	needed
watched	breathed	committed
pushed	failed	defended
asked	pulled	waited

2
1 You <u>have</u> to read this <u>book</u>.
2 We <u>must</u> see this <u>film</u>.
3 You <u>should</u>n't go out to<u>night</u>.

3
con<u>su</u>mer <u>buy</u>er re<u>ward</u> pro<u>duce</u> pol<u>lu</u>tion suc<u>cess</u>

Vocabulary

1
1 cause 2 return 3 give 4 move 5 take 6 take

2
1 (b) 2 (a) 3 (b) 4 (c) 5 (a) 6 (c)

3
1 chapter 2 dish 3 tip 4 soundtrack 5 sequel
6 plot 7 performance 8 dessert

Reading

2
1 (a) 2 (b) 3 (b) 4 (b) 5 (b) 6 (a)

3
1 He took the name from one of his favourite cartoon characters.
2 They didn't want him to tell anyone about their illegal activities.
3 During his first job.
4 By selling fake miracle medicine and gold-framed glasses at high prices.
5 The secretary had gone away with their money.
6 No, because he felt that his victims were rich and also dishonest.
7 He taught himself.

Listening

Tapescript
T=Tracy G=Goeff
T: Isn't it strange Geoff... we're such good friends but don't have much in common. Our hobbies are completely different...
G: You're right, Tracy. I'm the sort of person who needs to be with people a lot, but unlike you I've never been good at sport. I like spending time with my family and I use the phone a lot because I don't want to lose touch with my friends.
T: Well, social life means a lot to me too and I like getting to know new people. But, I spend most of my spare time going to karate classes and jogging. I'm also keen on going away at weekends; climbing mountains, sailing, that kind of thing.
G: Oh, that's not for me at all! However, I'd like to have time to read more and eat out in restaurants. Unfortunately, bringing up two small daughters means I have to give up some of the luxuries in life.
T: Hmm, I'm a bit younger than you and still single so I might change a little one day but I can't stand reading apart from when I'm surfing the net.
G: Well, I sometimes use the Internet as well but usually for sending emails. It's normally very convenient. Unfortunately though, my computer shut down completely while I was downloading an important file last week and now I'll have to spend quite a lot of money on a new one.
T: Oh, you poor thing! Well, I'm sure you can afford it.
G: I suppose so. You know, the good thing about you and me, Tracy, is that although we're very different in many ways, I really enjoy your company – we've got the same sense of humour.
T: I agree, Geoff. We always have a lot to talk about too.

1
1 False 2 True 3 False 4 True 5 True 6 False
7 False 8 False

2
1 He doesn't want to lose touch with his friends.
2 Climbing mountains and sailing.
3 Reading and eating out in restaurants.
4 When she is surfing the (Inter)net.
5 It shut down completely and he will have to buy a new one.
6 I suppose so.

Test A Units 6-10

Grammar

1 Past Perfect Simple
1 entered   2 appeared   3 had checked
4 had gone   5 had been   6 arrived

2 articles
1 (-)   2 an   3 the   4 a

3 *used to* and *would*
1 go cycling   2 would have   3 used to   4 used to

4 modals of ability
1 was able   2 couldn't   3 managed to   4 wasn't able to
5 didn't manage to   6 were able to

5 Second Conditional
1 changed/would feel   2 would be/helped   3 left/would have   4 would travel/won   5 thought/would find
6 would have/bought

6 Third Conditional
1 If Sharon hadn't eaten too much chocolate, she wouldn't have felt bad later.
2 If I hadn't said something terrible, my girlfriend wouldn't have stopped talking to me.
3 If we had followed the signs, we wouldn't have got lost.
4 If I hadn't shouted a lot to my friends inside the discotheque, I wouldn't have lost my voice.

7 reported speech
1 Tony asked (me) if I worked a lot of overtime.
2 Anne told me/us that she was working some very irregular hours those days.
3 Darren said that they had been unemployed for nearly three months.
4 Lynn told me/us that she thought they would win the elections.
5 Scott asked me if I had got a pay rise the previous day (the day before).
6 Cathy said that she had to get a couple of good references before she could apply for that job.

8 past obligation/permission
1 couldn't   2 didn't have to   3 was allowed to   4 had to

9 *I wish/if only*
1 wouldn't talk   2 had phoned   3 had
4 would hurry

10 phrasal verbs
1 off   2 on   3 out   4 up with   5 through   6 up

Pronunciation

1
1 <u>When</u> can you come to the <u>office</u>?
2 Can you <u>tell</u> me the way to the <u>station</u>?
3 Do you <u>know</u> if there is a <u>supermarket</u> near here.

2
1 If we <u>hadn't</u> missed that last <u>bus</u>, we would've arrived on <u>time</u>.
2 If they <u>hadn't interrupted</u> me, I would've <u>finished</u> by now.
3 If she'd <u>called</u> me before <u>seven</u>, I'd have gone <u>out</u> with her.

3
1 one hundred and twenty-six point eight.
2 the thirtieth of January, two thousand and four.
3 one hundred and forty-nine dollars sixty-eight cents.
4 seventy-one point five percent.

Vocabulary

1
1 returned   2 to buy   3 becoming
4 collect   5 inspired   6 have good relations

2
1 (b)   2 (a)   3 (c)   4 (b)   5 (c)   6 (a)

3
1 disease   2 standard of living   3 famine
4 crime   5 developing countries
6 pollution   7 security   8 starvation

Reading

2
1 (b)   2 (a)   3 (b)   4 (c)   5 (c)   6 (c)   7 (a)   8 (b)

3
1 The weather is still good and hotels are less expensive.
2 You can see beautiful scenery and historical architecture outside. You don't have to enter any museum.
3 You can climb rocks, go trekking and do water sports.
4 It has close historical and cultural connections with Britain.
5 People drive on the left.
6 Fresh fish and seafood.

Listening

Tapescript
P=Phil   W=Wayne

P: You know, Wayne, many people say that school days are the happiest days of your life and I think they're probably right.
W: I'm not so sure, Phil. It's easy to say that now but when you look back, we didn't enjoy the discipline… One or two of my teachers weren't exactly, you know, the nicest people you could meet. We also had heaps of pressure to pass exams.
P: I suppose you've got a point. We used to get quite nervous especially before important exams and we'd sometimes stay up all night revising! I didn't like some of my teachers very much either… but most of them were pretty good, I suppose.
W: Hmm, I'm not so sure about that… We had one who taught us maths and he was absolutely useless! He was very knowledgeable but he couldn't explain things and some of us got completely lost. In spite of it all, most of us managed to pass our exams in the end.
P: Our French teacher was really strict and used to lose her temper a lot. We were frightened to make a single mistake in class! Our English teacher was great though. She was really open-minded and we'd pick up a lot of interesting and useful things from her classes.
W: What did you do at university, Phil?
P: I studied history, which was very interesting but not the best thing to get you a good job. What about you, Wayne?
W: I did a biology course. It was hard at first and it felt strange when I had to go to lectures and take notes instead of being told what to do all the time. I failed a couple of exams in the beginning but my cousin's a biologist and he gave me a hand. I think I'm quite a fast learner so I ended up making good progress.
P: Good for you! I suppose university's very good preparation for the professional world and for life in general… the social life isn't bad either. Oh no! That's my boss calling me on my mobile. I've got to go. See you later, Wayne.
W: See you then, Phil.

1
1 (c)   2 (a)   3 (b)   4 (b)   5 (a)   6 (c)

2
1 I suppose you've got a point.
2 Stay up all night revising.
3 He was very knowledgeable.
4 She was open-minded and they learnt a lot of interesting and useful things in her classes.
5 It was very interesting but not ideal for finding a good job.
6 He had to take his own lecture notes without being told what to do.
7 He is a biologist and gave Wayne a hand when he was at university.

Test B Units 6-10

Grammar

1 uses of *like*
1 Is Sam like Mathew? 2 What would you like to do tonight?
3 What is Rome like? 4 Do you like spaghetti?

2 articles
1 the 2 (-) 3 the 4 an 5 the 6 (-)

3 subject and object questions
1 Who directed the film *LA Confidential*?
2 When did Fleming discover penicillin?
3 Which motorcycle won the race?
4 What touched Fred on the shoulder?
5 Where did Carol see the concert?
6 How many books did Tanya buy?

4 modals of ability
1 couldn't 2 manage 3 able 4 could

5 adverbs
1 a) 2 b) 3 c) 4 c) 5 b) 6 b)

6 Third Conditional
1 had taken/would have arrived
2 had come/would have had
3 wouldn't have felt/hadn't stayed
4 would have heard/had shouted

7 make, let, allow
1 work 2 allowed 3 repeat 4 to use 5 stay 6 come

8 reported speech
1 'I have visited Paris many times in my life.'
2 'I have to do something important tomorrow.'
3 'What have you done today?'
4 'I will travel to New York some time in the future.'

9 review of the past tenses
1 was 2 had learnt 3 was studying 4 began
5 had finished 6 was preparing

10 phrasal verbs
1 I had to put up with the inconvenience.
2 I woke up my friend early / I woke my friend up early.
3 I got off the bus in Blackpool.
4 I'll pick him up from the station.

Pronunciation

1
That's am<u>a</u>zing! Oh n<u>o</u>!
How <u>aw</u>ful! My g<u>oo</u>dness!
You're j<u>o</u>king! How incr<u>e</u>dible!

2

/ɪ/	/aɪ/
split	revise
history	sight
strict	island
practice	life
live	environment
chips	direct
miss	remind

3
<u>pa</u>ckage a<u>broad</u> <u>cul</u>tural
his<u>to</u>rical <u>news</u>paper de<u>gree</u>
re<u>search</u> <u>life</u>style unem<u>ployed</u>

Vocabulary

1.
1 bookworm 2 inside out 3 brush up on
4 a clue 5 picked up 6 guess

2
punishment   ignorance
darkness   employment
creation   intelligence

3.
1 bored 2 exhausting 3 relaxing
4 depressed 5 excited 6 annoying
7 confused 8 tiring

Reading

2
1 (c) 2 (a) 3 (b) 4 (a) 5 (c) 6 (c)
7 (b) 8 (c)

3
1 Because they cannot produce enough food for themselves.
2 In the countryside.
3 It is much worse now than 30 years ago.
4 They have been producing a lot more food from agriculture than before and their economy has become stronger.
5 People who are very poor and have very little food will be the first ones to suffer in years of drought or other problems.
6 War, terrible diseases and natural disasters.

Listening

Tapescript
M=Melanie T=Tamara
M: Please come in and have a seat.
T: Thank you.
M: Well, Tamara. I've seen your CV and I'm very impressed. The first thing I'd like to ask is: Why have you applied for this job?
T: Erm, well, mainly because T.S.A. is a company with an excellent reputation. I see selling computer software as... err... an exciting new challenge.
M: Can I ask you what you had to do in your last job? What were your responsibilities exactly?
T: Well, as a sales rep. for Ben Shi, a Chinese company, I had to sell office furniture to companies and offer after-sales service to existing clients.
M: What do you think are your strengths and weaknesses?
T: Um... I'm a highly motivated, hard-working person and I think that I'm good with people too. Weaknesses? Mmm, I don't know if it's a weakness exactly but I think that I'm possibly a bit of a perfectionist. I don't like to see jobs only half-finished or badly done. They have to be done really well.
M: So you don't mind working long hours? After all, you'd sometimes have to drive long distances and this can be very tiring, you know.
T: I'm used to that because of my previous jobs.
M: Are you good at persuading people to buy from you?
T: I think so. I have had a lot of training and I've learnt through experience, of course.
M: Would working on a commission only basis be a problem for you?
T: Oh no, not at all. This would motivate me more and I love a difficult challenge.
M: What are your ambitions for the future?
T: Well, after getting another two or three years' experience in sales, I'd like to become a sales manager.
M: OK, thank you very much Tamara. Now, are there any questions that you'd like to ask me?
T: Yes. What are the possibilities of getting promoted in the company?
M: There are very good opportunities for the right people. There are often new positions for regional sales managers but you might have to work in a different part of the country.
T: Mm... What sort of training does the company offer?
M: Well, we run all types of courses including ones on selling techniques, computer skills and foreign languages. It all depends on the employees' needs and our economic situation.
T: Oh, great. That all sounds very interesting.
M: I'm glad you think so. Well, thank you for coming to this interview Tamara. We'll be in touch soon.

1
1 (b) 2 (b) 3 (a) 4 (c) 5 (c) 6 (a)

2
1 The company has an excellent reputation and the job would be an exciting new challenge.
2 She had to sell office furniture to companies and offer after-sales service.
3 She is highly motivated, hard-working and good with people.
4 She is used to that because of her previous jobs.
5 This would motivate her and she loves a difficult challenge.
6 It might be necessary to work in a different part of the country.
7 The economic situation of the company and the needs of the employees.

Pearson Education Limited,
Edinburgh Gate, Harlow
Essex, CM20 2JE, England
and Associated Companies throughout the world

www.longman.com

The right of Will Moreton, Diane Naughton, Alison Bewsher and John Pebbles to be identified as authors of this work has been asserted by them in accordance with the Copyright, Designs and Patents Act 1988.

First published 2006

Designed by Pentacor

Illustrated by Andy Robb, Clive Goodyer, Peter Richardson, Phil Garner (Beehive Illustration)

Set in Myriad Pro 9pt
Printed in UK
by Anthony Rowe Ltd

ISBN-13: 978-0-582-841857 (Teacher's Resource Book)
ISBN-10: 0-582-84185-2

ISBN-13: 978-1-405-843058 (Test Master CD-ROM for pack)
ISBN-10: 1-405-84305-5

ISBN-13: 978-1-405-843218 (Teacher's Resource Book and Test Master CD-ROM for pack)
ISBN-10: 1-405-84321-7

LEARNING SKILLS SERIES

HOW TO STUDY EFFECTIVELY

Richard Freeman and John Meed

NATIONAL
EXTENSION
COLLEGE

Collins Educational
An imprint of HarperCollinsPublishers

Published by
Collins Educational Ltd
77-85 Fulham Palace Road
Hammersmith
London W6 8JB

First published in 1993
Reprinted 1994, 1995 (twice)

The National Extension Collge (NEC) is an educational trust with a distinguished body of trustees. Since it was established in 1963, it has pioneered the development of flexible learning for adults. NEC is actively developing innovative materials and systems for distance learning on over 100 courses, from basic skills to degree and professional training. Working in partnership with Collins Educational, NEC can now offer the best in flexible learning materials to the widest possible audience and further its aim of extending educational opportunities for all.

About the authors:

Richard Freeman has been developing and running self-study materials for adults for over twenty years, first at the National Extension College and more recently at the Open College. He now works as a freelance training consultant in open learning.

John Meed is a writer and researcher of learning materials. He works on a range of training and open-learning projects designed to help people take control of their own learning. He was previously Assistant Director of the National Extension College, Cambridge.

The publishers wish to thank Tim Burton for his invaluable editorial expertise.

British Library Cataloguing-in-Publication Data

A catalogue record for
this book is
available from the
British Library.

ISBN 0 00 322345 0

Typeset by Graham Hiles. Cover design by Information Design Worskshop. Printed in Great Britain at Redwood Books, Trowbridge, Wiltshire.

Contents

INTRODUCTION

About this book

How to Study Effectively is designed for students who are learning on their own. It is a fully revised version of one of the most successful introductions to study skills. Over 100,000 students have already been helped by *How to Study Effectively*, and typical comments include:

> *After reading the book I felt more confident as it offered very practical advice on each area of study, making it much easier than I imagined.*

> *I would like to say how much I have enjoyed the book. I would certainly recommend it as money well spent to anyone returning to learning.*

> *An excellent, enjoyable book which has given me confidence and fills me with enthusiasm for further learning.*

> *It has been and is continuing to be an exciting time for me.*

The text has now been updated in the light of student and tutor comments, and reflects the latest ideas and research about learning.

Purpose

There is a good chance that you haven't studied recently. You may indeed feel nervous about it. And you probably have many other commitments on your time. You may have a job, a family to look after or other responsibilities.

This book will help you to become a more confident and efficient learner, so that when you are studying you are also learning. In more detail, the book will help you to:

- analyse how you learn most effectively;
- identify techniques that will help you learn;
- read effectively;
- keep useful notes;
- write effectively;
- prepare for assessment;
- make the most of your resources.

Using the book

The book is divided into six units. You should be able to complete a unit in three hours or so, though you may want to spend more time on any units that you find especially helpful. The units contain a number of features that will help you learn effectively. Each feature is accompanied by a symbol, as follows:

What this unit is about

Each unit begins with an introduction. This describes what you will get out of the unit. It gives you a clear idea of what you will learn, and you can check with it at the end of the unit to make sure you have understood everything.

Activity

All the units are based on a series of activities. Research into learning shows that people learn better when they are doing something. It is much harder to learn just from reading or listening. So the activities suggest what you should do to achieve the objectives.

Activities may ask you to think about something, to write something down, or to find something out.

After every activity there is comment on what you may have done, plus extra ideas and suggestions.

Action plan

At the end of each unit is a summary and action plan which suggests how you can put the ideas in the unit into practice.

UNIT 1

HOW DO YOU LEARN?

What this unit is about

You have purchased this book because you want to learn as effectively as possible. You may feel that you are not very good at learning at the moment. You may feel that you are out of practice, or rusty. Most people feel this way at some time.

However, this book will show you that learning is a skill – in fact a number of skills – that you can improve and develop. And this unit will show you that in fact you are learning all the time. It will also help you to get to know yourself as a learner, so that you can find out which style of learning suits you best, and to set realistic goals for your study.

The rest of your work will then be devoted to maximising your own strengths and abilities, and developing the skills you need to succeed.

This unit will help you to:

➔   analyse how you learn;

➔   identify your strengths as a learner;

➔   describe how you feel about studying;

➔   list your reasons for studying;

➔   identify your study goals;

➔   plan your study.

How you feel about learning

You may feel that learning is something that takes place only at school or college, in a classroom, with a tutor. In fact, you learn all the time. You have learnt to do some or all of these things:

■   how to do things round the house, like changing a plug or cooking a meal;

■   how to play a sport;

■   how to do a job;

■   how to drive a car or ride a motorcycle;

■   how to manage your money;

■   how to carry out a particular hobby or interest.

In any of these examples you will have used special skills. In driving or housework these may be practical – using the steering wheel or operating the cooker. In managing your money they will be mental – for example, doing arithmetic. Often, as with playing a sport, you use both practical and mental skills, and perhaps your emotions as well! You have probably learnt all these skills either on your own, or with the help of someone who is not a school or college teacher.

Formal learning, or study, is just another kind of learning. It has its own particular skills, such as reading or writing, which we will look at in detail in this book. But it is still only learning. And one thing is sure: you will have learning strengths that you can build on.

1 Think of some things you have learned. You could include examples both of:

■ formal learning – things you learnt at school or college;

■ informal learning – things you learnt at home or work.

2 Select three things that you have enjoyed learning, or which you feel have been successful, and three things you have not enjoyed learning, or where you have felt unsuccessful.

3 Fill in the boxes in the table that follows to show why you feel each learning experience was positive or negative. Was it because of:

■ how easy or difficult you found the learning?

■ whether you were interested in what you were learning or not?

■ whether you liked what you were learning?

■ the kind of help you had or did not have?

Note your answers in this box.

What you learnt	Why was this?
Enjoyable/successful	
Example 1	
Example 2	
Example 3	

(continued opposite)

Unenjoyable/unsuccessful	
Example 4	
Example 5	
Example 6	

Many learners find that the following factors affect how well they learn:

Positive factors	Negative factors
I want to learn	Other people tell me to learn
I am interested in the subject	I find the subject boring
I have good support from other people	I have poor support
I learn effectively	I learn ineffectively
I have enough time	I am short of time

It makes sense to build on the things you enjoy and do well.

Ways of learning

The last activity asked you to think about ways in which you learn best. This section will take this further. Everyone has their own learning style, and while one style is ideal for one person, another person will learn the same thing in a different way.

For example, you may prefer to:

■   be told what to do, or to decide what to do yourself;

■   be left alone to do something, or to work with someone else;

■   be very tidy, or quite disorganised.

11

This activity will help you find out what learning style suits you best.

2 Which style suits you best?

1 Look through each of these pairs of statements.

2 For each pair, decide whether Statement A or Statement B is closest to your own feelings. Tick the box nearest that statement.

3 If you really are not sure, tick the middle box.

Statement A				Statement B
I like detailed instructions	❑	❑	❑	I like to try things on my own
I enjoy reading around a subject	❑	❑	❑	I enjoy learning by doing
I prefer my tutor to tell me what to do	❑	❑	❑	I prefer to negotiate what I will do with my tutor
I like to work on my own	❑	❑	❑	I like to work with others
I like to do one thing at a time	❑	❑	❑	I like to have several things on the go at once
I prefer everything to be tidy and organised	❑	❑	❑	I can cope with things being untidy
I need the discipline of a timetable	❑	❑	❑	I can motivate myself to do things
I think exams reflect my abilities well	❑	❑	❑	I like my progress to be checked as I go along
I need to be prodded into action regularly	❑	❑	❑	I am good at keeping myself motivated
I like to work steadily	❑	❑	❑	I need a challenge
I need a good reason for taking a course	❑	❑	❑	I find out about the course as I go along

None of these statements is good or bad – they are all strategies for learning that some people use effectively. Some people must keep everything tidy and organised, while others thrive on what looks like chaos. However, you can draw three lessons from what you ticked:

- In some cases, you will have a tried and tested way of learning that you know works for you – you need to make the most of this.

- In other cases, you may like to try using a different approach – you may be surprised at how well it suits you.

- Finally, in some cases you will have to adopt an approach that doesn't suit you – for example you may have to take exams even if you find them stressful. You need to decide what you can do to overcome these problems. This book will help in some cases. And you can always discuss it with your tutor. Or you could talk it over with any friends who are on, or have been on, similar courses to the one you're having problems with.

Research that has been carried out with other learners does suggest that some approaches to learning may be more effective than others.

- You are more likely to succeed if you take an active approach to learning, question what you do and try to understand it.

- You are less likely to succeed if you are more passive, do only what other people tell you, and concentrate on remembering things rather than understanding them.

Unit 2, *Learning effectively*, will help you to understand learning better, and to develop strategies that will help you to learn effectively. The section on *Getting support* in *Extra resources* on page 73 will help you if you feel you need more help from other people.

Here is what other readers of *How to Study Effectively* have said:

> I need to talk things over with someone or else I just come to a halt. That was the worst problem when I started. It's easy to feel isolated. But now I've found a friend who is very good at listening and I meet with her regularly to talk things through.

> I always used to work in a muddle, and I honestly felt this suited me best. However, when I tried keeping my desk tidy, I found it actually helped me work more effectively. I wouldn't say I have become fanatical about tidying things up, but I make more of an effort now.

Reasons for study

There are many different reasons for wanting to study. Some will be your own – to get qualifications, to go to university. Others will be other people's reasons – because your tutor asks you, for example. It is very important to make the most of your own reasons, as these will keep you motivated for longer.

Your own reasons may be:

- vocational – related to qualifications;

- academic – for example, to prepare for further study;

- personal – for example, to raise your self-esteem or to make better use of your time.

3 Think about what you are studying or planning to study. What are your reasons for doing this? Tick any of the reasons below, and add any other factors that may motivate you:

☐ getting qualifications for your job or career;

☐ getting more pay;

☐ feeling more self-confident;

☐ playing a greater part in the community;

☐ learning something you enjoy;

☐ doing something you have always wanted to do;

☐ going on to further study;

☐ impressing your family;

☐ other:

☐ other:

☐ other:

☐ other:

Try to find ways of making these reasons work for you. For example, you could write them down on a poster above the place you study. Tell other people about them, so that they can back you up.

If you found it difficult to list your reasons for studying, what can you do about this? Good motivation is always tied up with interest in the subject. There are many ways of livening up an area of study.

■ Look out for films, and television and radio programmes connected with the subject.

■ Find out how it comes into everyday life.

■ Try reading a book on its history.

■ Try to find out how your subject relates to other subjects.

All these approaches can stimulate your interest and increase your motivation.

If you still find it hard to convince yourself that you have good reasons for studying, talk this over with your tutor or with a friend. It may be that now is not the best time for you to study, or that you have chosen the wrong course. It may be better to reconsider what you are doing now rather than later.

Setting goals

Once you are clear about why you are learning you will have a clear motivation for studying. You know that, as long as these reasons don't change, your learning will be worth the effort. However, your reasons are likely to be quite distant and long term. It may take you several months or even years to achieve them. And it's easy to get dispirited along the way.

So it makes sense to set shorter-term goals which will help to keep you going on a day-to-day basis. Most courses are divided up into several modules or units, because most students like a regular sense of getting somewhere. So goals you could set yourself might include:

- completing a short course or one part of a longer course;

- completing a unit or project.

Goals like this are like milestones during a long walk – they give you something to aim at soon, and they give you a regular sense of achievement.

4

1   Begin with this book. When, ideally, would you like to finish it? Note this down in the box below.

2   In the light of this, can you set yourself some shorter-term targets? How quickly will you aim to complete each unit? For example, if you want to complete your work on the book in four weeks, you will need to work through about one unit a week, or two every fortnight. Again, note these in the box below.

Target date for completing work on *How to Study Effectively*:

Target date for completing Unit 2:

Target date for completing Unit 3:

Target date for completing Unit 4:

Target date for completing Unit 5:

Target date for completing Unit 6:

---

3   Obtain a calendar or wall chart, or a filofax planning sheet, and mark your goals on this.

Don't feel that you have to get this exactly right now. You can always revise your goals later.

Check that your goals take account of times you will be unable to study, such as holidays, weekends away, times when you are likely to be very busy with other work or social activities.

A typical month on your study calendar might look like this:

M	T	W	T	F	S	S
						Weekend in Devon
1	2	3	4	5	6	7
	Start Unit 2		Swimming gala		Finish Unit 2	
8	9	10	11	12	13	14
Start unit 3	Birthday		Maths assessment			
15	16	17	18	19	20	21
Finish Unit 3	Start Unit 4			Begin history project		
22	23	24	25	26	27	28

If you are taking one or more courses at the moment, you should set yourself similar goals for them. Note these in the action plan on page 19.

Planning your work in this way has the following advantages:

■ You ensure that you put in work regularly.

■ You don't panic because you have left your work until the last minute.

■ Once you have completed the work that you planned for a particular number of days, the rest of the days are free from the worry of not getting your work done.

■ By allowing a span of days rather than one day to do your work, you can then cope with unforeseen interruptions.

Being realistic

Your goals will only help you if they are realistic. In particular, they need to reflect your learning style; if you are someone who needs a deadline to get you going, make sure you have regular deadlines; if you are someone who likes a challenge, make sure your goals will stretch you enough; and if you are someone who likes being prodded, agree your goals with your tutor or a friend.

Good goals are also:

■ achievable – you know you will be capable of meeting them;

■ reasonable – if you set goals that you cannot meet, they will reduce rather than increase your motivation;

■ flexible – it is always worth building in some additional time in case something unpredictable happens, like an illness;

■ sufficient – at the same time, your goals must ensure that you achieve what you want to do.

It is also important to make the most of your study sessions, and to choose study times that reflect your learning style; if you work best in the morning, try to plan morning study sessions. Allow enough time to do something useful each time you study and make the most of the times you set aside; if you tire after one hour, is it really worth setting aside two hour study periods?

When you study, build in variety; if you blend reading, writing, thinking, research and doing, you can concentrate for longer.

Ask yourself whether each of these questions is true for you.

Is this true for you:	Always	Some-times	Rarely
Do you achieve what you want to achieve in each study session?	❑	❑	❑
Can you cope if something unexpected happens – for example, illness?	❑	❑	❑
Are you allowing enough time to do something useful each time you study?	❑	❑	❑

(continued opposite)

Are you sure you can make the most of the times you set aside?	❏	❏	❏
Are you building in variety?	❏	❏	❏
Do you study at a good time of day?	❏	❏	❏

Many people motivate themselves to study by deciding on a goal for a particular day (or evening) and promising themselves a reward when they have finished. This really helps you to get started, and not to become easily distracted. Most people find it very hard to study, so do not worry if it is difficult for you. The great Italian dramatist, Alfieri, even made his servant tie him to the study table!

Timetables are great aids to efficiency. They enable you to analyse the use you are making of your time. Is it the most effective scheme? Are the hours allocated to study the best ones? A timetable also takes a load off your mind; without a timetable you will have to make a hundred decisions each week as you try to fit everything in. Timetabling the day's or week's routine ensures that you take all the decisions in advance.

One part-time student found it helpful to produce a weekly study plan, like this:

Tasks – week beginning 7 March	Time and place
Preview Unit 3	On the train Monday
Do Unit 3 activities	7–9 p.m. Tuesday
Background reading	Lunch hour Wednesday
Preview Unit 4	7–8 a.m. Thursday
Extra times in case of unforeseen interruptions:	Thursday evening Lunch hour Friday

Note down here your study plan for next week.

Tasks – week beginning	Time and place

Summary

Key points from this unit:

- You are learning all the time.

- You should build on the things you enjoy and do well.

- Different people can use different learning styles successfully.

- You are more likely to succeed if you take an active approach to learning, question what you do and try to understand it.

- Make sure you have your own reasons for studying, as these will keep you motivated.

- Get a clear view of your course and set yourself goals and targets.

- Make the most of your study sessions by studying at a good time of day, for the right amount of time.

You may like to note down here the main points you have found out.

I learn best by:

I find the following things difficult:

I will try out the following approaches to see if they suit me better:

I will review my learning style by the following date:

(continued opposite)

Summarise your main goals for the next six months here.

Date	Course	Target

LEARNING EFFECTIVELY

What this unit is about

Although much research has been done into learning, we still know surprisingly little about what it involves. And as we said in Unit 1, you are the person who knows most about how you learn. However, experts on learning have highlighted a number of skills and strategies that help us to learn effectively. This unit explores each of these skills in turn and suggests strategies for developing and using them.

This unit will help you to:

→   concentrate on what you are learning;

→   use your existing knowledge and experience;

→   ask questions to help you understand;

→   be creative and come up with your own ideas;

→   tackle your study problems;

→   identify opportunities to use these skills;

→   plan how you will develop these skills.

The main skills and strategies that we focus on in this unit are:

■   being able to **concentrate** on what you are learning; you will encounter a range of ideas and facts and you need to be able to focus your attention on these fully, and select what is most useful;

■   linking new ideas and facts to your **existing knowledge and experience** will help you to learn them; you are more likely to be able to remember or apply something if you learn it in context than if you learn it in isolation;

■   you must work actively on what you are learning; it's important to **ask questions** and seek your own understanding if you are to remember;

■   you also need to allow time to **be creative**, and to come up with your own ideas; it may well be that some important learning takes place as a result of insights;

■   finally, adopting a **problem-solving** approach where possible can increase your ability to learn.

The following diagram shows how these skills and strategies can work together to help you learn effectively.

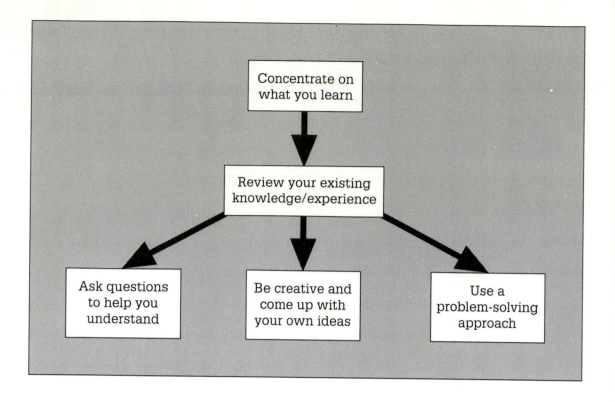

Concentrating

Being able to concentrate is a vital first step in learning. If you are constantly distracted, or if your attention wavers, you will find it hard to get going.

Concentration involves a number of things:

- reducing **interruptions** to a minimum; interruptions come from other people; they could include the television being on in the same room, friends or family asking questions or the telephone ringing; few people can concentrate effectively under pressures like these!

- clearing your own mind of **distractions**; distractions come from yourself; they could include other things you have to do, or other activities that you would enjoy doing; you may be tempted to do these rather than to study;

- being able to **focus your attention** clearly on what you are learning; knowing why you are learning something, and what you want to get out of it.

1   What may be stopping you concentrate effectively on your learning? Note down here:

- any regular interruptions to your studying;

- distractions that make it hard for you to keep going;

- anything else that stops you focusing fully on your learning.

2   Then think about each item and try to suggest a solution. For example, could you:

- find somewhere else to study?

- make a list of tasks to do each day?

(continued opposite)

What stops you concentrating	What you might be able to do
Interruptions – from others:	
Distractions – from yourself:	
Anything else:	

Here are some ways of tackling interruptions and distractions:

- Can you negotiate study times with other members of the family?

- Could you study elsewhere – for example, in a different room or in a library?

- Can you timetable the tasks that get in your way, so that you know you will do them?

- Can you promise yourself time doing the things you really enjoy?

- Can you use a desk or table where you can leave your books undisturbed, so that it's easy to get started again?

The key to focusing your attention is making sure you are interested in what you are learning. Your reasons for study and your targets (see Unit 1, *How do you learn?*) should help you to do this. So will the other ideas in this unit.

Using existing knowledge and experience

It's unlikely that much of what you learn will be completely new to you. If you study a subject like history or economics you can draw on your general knowledge; if you are learning a practical skill you will be influenced by other similar things you can do; and even if you are tackling an abstract topic in maths, you are likely to use operations you have already learnt.

Research suggests that this is a very good way to learn. For example, one research project found that people learnt about Buddhist ideas much more easily if they linked them to what they already knew about Christianity. It seems that you can understand and remember new facts and ideas far better if you 'attach' them like this to other things you know about and understand already.

However, it's not always obvious how to make the links with what you know or have done already. So how can you do this?

2 Imagine that you have to start learning a new topic now – perhaps 'inflation' on an economics course. Can you suggest at least three ways in which you could link this new topic to what you already know?

Here are some possible ideas:

■ When you start a new topic, write down everything you already know about it. Just reviewing your existing knowledge will help make your mind more receptive to the new material you will meet. For example, if you were learning about inflation as part of an economics course, you might be surprised at how much you know about the subject already – things like price rises and wage increases.

■ Early on in a topic, aim to get an overall view of what it is about. You can fit the details into this later. You could try drawing a map of the topic with a key idea in the middle and all the other ideas round the outside. Unit 4, *Keeping notes*, may be helpful here.

■ Try to think of examples of what you are learning. For inflation, you could try to find relevant articles in your newspaper or in television news reports; and what about the effect it has on your own spending power?

■ Discuss a topic with other learners and share existing ideas and facts. Try to identify examples together.

■ Ask your tutor which topics you have already studied relate to each new topic, and review your notes on these first.

■ Try to choose textbooks that give good introductions, summaries and regular headings. (See Unit 3, *Reading*.) You may well find it then helps to look at these parts of any chapter first, to help you gain an overview.

In fact, this activity was itself an example; just thinking about the question before reading my comment will have helped your mind take in some of the ideas.

Asking questions

All effective learning is active learning. Even if you're reading a book or listening to a talk you need to be active to make the most of it. The key to active learning is asking questions. And you can learn more actively by becoming better at asking questions. Some of the most useful question words are *what, why, how, who, where* and *when*.

You can use questions in all kinds of circumstances. For example:

■ to focus your approach to a topic;

■ to help you plan a piece of work;

■ as headings for notes;

■ as the basis for an interview with another person such as your tutor;

■ as the structure of a report or essay plan.

Here are the questions that one history student wrote as she prepared to study Chamberlain's policy of appeasement in the 1930s:

> *What was appeasement?*
>
> *What was the background to appeasement?*
>
> *What other points of view were there at the time?*
>
> *Why did Chamberlain adopt this policy?*
>
> *How did he carry out the policy?*
>
> *How did the policy change?*
>
> *Who supported Chamberlain's policy? Who opposed him?*
>
> *When did appeasement start?*
>
> *When did it become clear that it was not working?*

3 Choose a topic that you are studying or planning to study. Aim to write down at least two questions beginning with each of the following words in the box below.

What…
What…
Why…
Why…
How…
How…
Who…
Who…
Where…
Where…
When…
When…

How easy it was to find questions may depend on the topic. In the history example we looked at it was harder to find Where? questions than What? questions. So don't worry if you found it easier to think of some questions than others.

Once you have thought of the questions, the next stage is of course to answer them. Some you will already know the answer to, or have some ideas about. In other cases you will need to do more research, perhaps by asking someone else, or by reading about it.

You may like to go back to the questions you wrote down and tick the ones you can answer now. Beside the others, write in the name of someone you could ask, a place to visit or a book to consult.

Being creative

Learning, like most things, usually involves 10% inspiration and 90% perspiration. However, that 10% of the time when you need to be inspired and creative will be critical to your success the other 90% of the time. You may need to be creative when:

- you begin to plan a project;

- you are starting a piece of writing;

- you feel dissatisfied with what you are doing;

- you get stuck.

It's easy to think that you are not a creative person, but in practice *everyone* can be creative. Being creative isn't simply about writing plays or music; it's also about enriching the quality of your learning and experiences by being able to:

- stand back from your day-to-day tasks and routines;

- put your preconceptions out of your mind;

- examine things from different perspectives;

- welcome strange ideas;

- cope with being uncertain for a time.

One of the best ways of being creative is brainstorming. To brainstorm, you write down a word or phrase (it could be an assessment question) on a piece of blank paper, and spend a few minutes writing down all the ideas that come into your mind about this word or phrase.

Brainstorming is often used by groups of people, and if you can do it with someone else, great. But you can also do it on your own. This activity will show you how to do it. You'll be amazed at how many ideas you can come up with.

You can brainstorm about absolutely anything. Common examples used in management training include uses of a brick or a paperclip. I suggest you brainstorm all the things that will help you study effectively – though you could choose something else that is more important to you now.

Here are the rules:

1   Make sure you won't be interrupted.

2   Spend 10–15 minutes thinking of absolutely anything that could help you study effectively.

3   Write down all your ideas in the space below, even if they seem ridiculous – they may spark off other, useful ideas.

4   If you run out of ideas, try something different – like changing your position in the room or imagining you are someone else.

(continued opposite)

Here is the result of my own brainstorm about this topic.

be organised   find out what you   get a dictionary
                need to know

make the most of   be creative   make sure you
your strengths   enjoy it

think ahead   to study   have good reasons
                     effectively   for learning

don't be afraid to   make sure you
ask for help   find the time
                   read effectively

use the library   be disciplined
                plan your writing

When you have finished your brainstorm, leave it for a while. Then come back and highlight or underline all the ideas that seem useful.

Solving problems

It's normal to run into problems from time to time during your study. The vital thing is to have a good problem-solving procedure so that you can clear them up quickly and make sure they do not become worse.

The key stages of problem solving are:

1 **Analyse the problem**. The first stage is to spend time thinking the problem through.

   Ask yourself:

   ■ What exactly is it that you have to solve?

   ■ Is it your problem?

   ■ What do you want to achieve?

2 **Obtain information** you need in order to solve it. The next stage is to make sure that you have the relevant details. Just obtaining information can sometimes solve the problem.

Ask yourself:

■ Which books or other resources might help?

■ Who can you ask for advice?

3 **Consider alternative solutions** and evaluate each one. When you're faced with a problem, the choices often seem stark. But there may be other possible ways of looking at it, and one way is likely to be more appropriate than the others.

Ask yourself:

■ What will be the advantages of each?

■ What would be the drawbacks?

■ Which will be most appropriate?

4 **Implement the best solution**. Once you have decided, act on it at once, before the problem gets worse.

5 Think of any problem you have at the moment, in your study, your work, or elsewhere in your life, and practise solving it now.

In the box that follows:

1 describe the problem;

2 note down what information would help you to solve it;

3 list some possible solutions;

4 decide which you feel is the best solution.

Statement of problem:		
Information required: *Resources:* *People:*		
Alternative solutions:	Advantages:	Drawbacks:
1		
2		
3		
Chosen solution: Action:		

Here is the response from one learner:

Statement of problem:	*I am concerned that I will not complete all the course in time and will therefore perform poorly in exam*	
Information required:		
Resources:	*obtain copies of syllabus and past exam papers*	
People:	*talk with tutor*	
Alternative solutions:	**Advantages:**	**Drawbacks:**
1 Defer exam to next year	*Time to prepare Reduced stress*	*Time lost Extra cost*
2 Concentrate on key topics	*Stay on schedule Meet other commitments*	*Fewer questions to choose from Likely lower grade*
3 Increase time devoted to study	*Full range of questions to answer Stay on schedule*	*Increased stress Less time for social life*
Chosen solution:	*Concentrate on key topics*	
Action:	*Discuss further with tutor*	

Summary

Key points from this unit:

- To learn effectively you must concentrate on what you are learning.

- Aim to link new ideas to existing knowledge.

- Ask questions to help you understand.

- Everyone can be creative.

- A problem-solving approach can increase your ability to learn.

In this unit you have thought about and practised a number of key learning skills. Using these regularly will greatly increase your success as a learner. However, they are all skills that you can develop and improve. This action plan asks you to identify opportunities to practise and develop them in your study.

Beside each of the skills in the box on page 30, think of at least one occasion when you will need to use it. For example:

- you may wish to organise your resources for a forthcoming project;

- you could draw up a list of questions for your tutor;

- you may need to be creative when you write an essay;

- you may need to practise problem solving if you find you are short of time to study.

(continued overleaf)

Note your example in the box below. Then review this over the coming days or weeks and tick each skill as you practise it.

Skill	Occasion	Tick
Concentrating		❑
Using existing knowledge and experience		❑
Asking questions		❑
Being creative		❑
Solving problems		❑

UNIT
3

READING

What this unit is about

Reading is a central task for many learners. The key to successful reading is to decide what to read, to know why you are reading it, and then to select an appropriate strategy for reading it.

This unit will help you to practise a number of strategies so that you learn to read more efficiently.

This unit will help you to:

→ list the kinds of reading you will do;

→ identify the purpose of your reading;

→ identify different reading strategies;

→ select appropriate strategies;

→ apply appropriate strategies.

Reasons for reading

During your study you may draw on various publications, including:

■ textbooks;

■ reference books such as directories, dictionaries and manuals;

■ newspapers, magazines and journals;

■ literature, including novels, plays and poems;

■ other sources such as maps or historical information.

You are likely to consult different publications for different reasons. You might wish to look up a piece of information in a reference book, or you might use a textbook to find the answer to a question that is raised during your course. Your reasons for reading will have a major impact on how you read.

1 Note down six things you read recently. If possible, include some items connected with your study. Beside each item, note down why you were reading it.

Item of reading	Your reason for reading it
1	
2	
3	
4	
5	
6	

It's likely that you had a variety of reasons, which could have included:

- obtaining a particular piece of information – for example, the price of an item in a catalogue, the meaning of a word in a dictionary, or the date of a historical event;

- finding the answer to a question – for example, how to highlight a word in your wordprocessing program, or which character gave a particular speech in a play you are studying;

- gaining more detailed information – for example, the day's news in the paper, or a list of factors affecting bacterial growth;

- trying to understand something – for example, a scientific theory or the reasons why the world went to war in 1914;

- pleasure – for example, a novel or magazine.

Your purpose will affect the way you read. You might read a novel from cover to cover, you might look for particular articles in a newspaper, and you might just look for one word in a dictionary. We shall explore different ways of reading next. *Choosing what you will read* in the section on *Extra resources* may also be helpful.

How will you read?

Skilled readers vary their reading speed and method to suit both the material they are reading and their purpose in reading it. You 'read' a telephone directory rather differently from a novel. In your learning, you should seek to use a similarly varied approach to reading. Here are some of the main techniques you can use:

■ **Skimming**: this involves looking quickly through the book and reading only things like contents, headings, introductions and conclusions. It is a quick and efficient way of familiarising yourself with a publication and is useful if you wish to check whether a book is relevant or for finding particular information or ideas quickly.

■ **Scanning**: this is a very rapid search for some important point. It may be a page number, a title or a key word. The essential thing is that you deliberately ignore everything except the one item for which you are scanning. You use scanning when you look up a number in the telephone directory.

■ **Reading to understand:** this involves detailed study of a chapter, passage or article in order to absorb all the major facts and ideas. You may read it more than once, and take notes to summarise what you have read.

■ **Word-by-word reading**: very occasionally, you actually need to read every word extremely carefully; for example, when reading an exam question or following a set of instructions.

■ **Reading for pleasure**: this is the reading you do to relax and enjoy, as with a novel.

2 Look back to the items you mentioned in the first activity in this unit, and your purpose for reading them. Which of the techniques we have just mentioned would be most suited to each one?

Item	Technique to use

Skimming is particularly useful for finding your way round a publication. You may skim the newspaper to find the articles you want to read, or a textbook to identify a relevant chapter.

Scanning is useful when you want to identify a particular piece of information – for example, in finding a telephone number or a football result.

Reading to understand is useful when you want to study something thoroughly.

You will probably rarely need word-by-word reading, unless you frequently refer to technical manuals or scientific formulas.

Reading for pleasure could cover any reading – books, newspapers, magazines etc. – which you do for relaxation.

To study efficiently you must learn to vary your reading style to suit both the material in front of you and your reason for reading that material. You must first become proficient at each type of reading in your studies and, if speed is important to you, in leisure reading.

By developing the ability to switch from one method of reading to another, you will vastly increase your efficiency. You will be able to search for specific items by scanning, to assess a passage quickly by skimming, and then to read it closely to understand it.

The next three sections look in more detail at skimming, scanning and reading to understand.

Skimming

As we have seen, skimming involves looking quickly through a publication to familiarise yourself with its contents. This activity will help you to practise skimming.

3

1 Practise skimming on this book. Spend up to ten minutes skimming the remaining units, and aim to find out as much about them as you can. You can check:

- the contents;

- the introductions and summaries;

- headings and sub-headings in the text;

- first and last paragraphs (or sections) of units; first and last sentences of paragraphs;

- figures and diagrams.

2 Note down here what you have found out about the book.

Your skim should have given you a good idea of what each unit was about – the contents, introductions and objectives will have highlighted what you will get out of each unit, and the headings will have described the ground that each unit covers.

After skimming material in this way you have three choices:

■ Decide the publication is not suitable.

■ Decide that certain sections are appropriate to your needs.

■ Decide that you need to read all of it. Even in this case your skimming has still been useful as it has given you an overall view of the material.

Scanning

Scanning involves looking through a publication for a particular piece of information. You may have to scan books or notes for a point to include in your writing, or you may have to scan journals and indexes for subjects which are important to your studies.

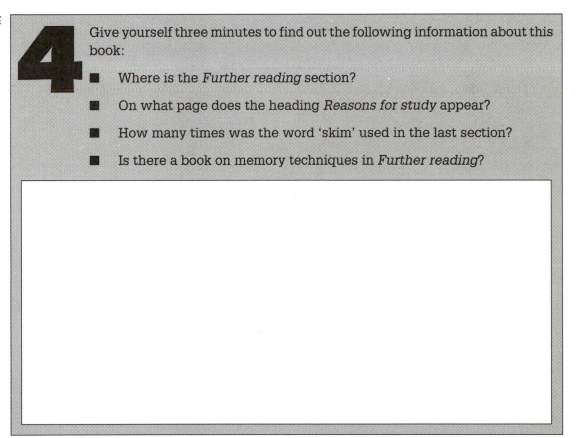

4 Give yourself three minutes to find out the following information about this book:

■ Where is the *Further reading* section?

■ On what page does the heading *Reasons for study* appear?

■ How many times was the word 'skim' used in the last section?

■ Is there a book on memory techniques in *Further reading*?

Effective scanning involves:

■ using references – the contents page, and the index, if the book has one, will help you find something quickly – you probably used the contents to check where *Reasons for study* appeared;

■ moving round the book quickly – just flicking through the book, looking at headings and sub-headings, may help you locate the information you need – this may well be the technique you use to find the weather page in the newspaper;

■ using your experience – you may well have expected that the *Further reading* section was at the back, and you were probably able to find the section on *Skimming* without checking the contents page.

Reading to understand

When you need to study something in depth, try using a technique called SQ3R. This stands for:

- Survey;

- Question;

- Read;

- Recall;

- Review.

It is a useful method of approaching a passage, such as a chapter of a book, which you want to study. The idea is that your reading of the passage is broken down into five stages. The details of each stage are as follows:

Survey

This is rather like the skimming process. You look at:

- the title, author, date of first publication and date of this edition, to check that it is relevant to you and up to date;

- the contents and chapter headings to identify which parts to concentrate on;

- the introduction, to understand the author's intention in writing the publication;

- the index and bibliography.

Question

Before embarking on detailed reading of all or part of the publication, ask yourself what you expect to gain from it. Why are you reading it? What points are you particularly interested in? These sorts of question ensure that you read with a purpose.

You might even ask, 'Is it worth reading?' To answer this, read its first and last paragraphs, then its first and last sections or chapters. This should help you decide whether it is worth studying.

Read

Begin by getting a clear picture of what the passage is about. You may wish to read a chapter at least twice at a fair speed. At this stage you want to find out:

- What is the author's general stance for this passage?

- What is the basic idea in each paragraph?

- Do you understand everything the author is saying?

Then look at the detail:

- Which parts are factual? Are all the facts you need provided?

- Which parts give the author's ideas? What evidence does the author produce to back up his or her ideas?

- Look at the examples, diagrams and illustrations. Why did the author choose these examples? What points do they illustrate? Can you think of any contrary examples?

Then form an overall judgement on the passage:

- Is the passage convincing?

- Are there alternative theories which would do just as well in the circumstances?

- What consequences flow from the author's theory? What consequences flow from your alternative theories?

You will notice that at the beginning of the **READ** stage, you are simply trying to grasp what the author says, to understand his or her arguments. Only when you completely follow the author's case do you turn to criticising it. If you criticise too soon, you may not take in everything the author has to say.

Recall

This stage may follow the **READ** stage for the whole passage, or, if the passage is rather lengthy or complex, it may follow the **READ** stage for sections of the passage.

The **RECALL** stage involves trying to recall all the main ideas in the section you've just read. You may like to write them down in note form (see Unit 4, *Keeping notes*).

Review

The **REVIEW** stage is the checking which follows recall. Look back over the passage and check that your recall was correct. Make a special note of any important points which you failed to recall, or which you wrongly recalled.

To help you in your reading, it is useful to know something about how writing is usually structured. In particular, this will help you to find your way around paragraphs quickly and identify which paragraphs are relevant to you.

Paragraphs generally cover one main idea, and you can usually find this idea in what is called a 'topic sentence'. For example, the sentence you have just read is the topic sentence of this paragraph, and the main idea is 'paragraphs generally cover one idea'. All the other sentences are likely to support this main idea, perhaps by giving examples or extending the idea further.

Look back to the section *Being creative* in Unit 2. There are five paragraphs in the introduction to this section. Can you identify the main idea and the topic sentence in each paragraph?

Paragraph 1:

Paragraph 2:

Paragraph 3:

Paragraph 4:

Paragraph 5:

The main idea in the first paragraph is that creativity is important in learning. So the topic sentence is the second one which begins 'However, that 10% of the time…'. The rest of the paragraph just gives examples.

The main idea in the second paragraph is that everyone can be creative, so the topic sentence this time is the first one, beginning 'It's easy to think…'.

In the third paragraph the first sentence is again the topic sentence and the main idea is that brainstorming is a good way to be creative.

I think the main idea of the fourth paragraph is that the activity will show you how to do it – in which case the topic sentence is the third one beginning 'This activity will…'. But you might argue that the fact that brainstorming can be done in groups is the main idea.

Finally, the first sentence of the last paragraph is again probably the topic sentence, and the main idea is that you can brainstorm almost anything.

This activity should have helped you identify the key ideas in paragraphs. It has also shown that the topic sentence is often the first one.

Try practising the SQ3R technique on a passage you are studying. It could be a chapter from a book or an article from a journal or magazine. Or you can use the newspaper article on the next page.

Apply the SQ3R technique to the passage as follows:

1   Survey the passage.

2   Question. Write down the questions you hope to be able to answer by reading the chapter.

3   Read.

4   Recall. Jot down the answers to your questions.

5   Review what you have jotted down by referring back to your questions.

Sample article for reading practice

You're an old cow, Miss

How should teachers deal with bad behaviour in the classroom? Judith Judd reports on a new study in discipline

WHAT does a teacher do if a pupil calls her "an old cow"? Parents put discipline near the top of their list when they choose a school, but strategies for keeping order are a subject of keen debate. An Exeter University study to be published in full next year reveals an intriguing variety of approaches to controlling children.

Allyson Trotter and Ted Wragg talked to 20 supply teachers as part of their research into classroom management. They say the insights of supply teachers are particularly useful because their discipline problems are even greater than those of permanent staff, who know the pupils and usually receive more respect from them. Teachers in the survey, which was funded by the Leverhulme Trust, had to look at four pictures, study a storyline which accompanied them and say what they would do.

One of the trickiest situations, and the one which caused most debate, was the case of a girl who called her teacher an old cow. The teachers had to decide what to do on the basis of this description: "In the afternoon you caught this girl scribbling on someone else's book. You tell her off in front of the rest of the class and much to your surprise she mutters, 'Old cow' under her breath. You do not think the majority of the rest of the class heard it but those sitting nearby start to snigger."

One teacher's initial reaction was: "Panic". All felt this was a particularly awkward decision to take because any action might make matters worse. Five out of the 20 taking part in the survey felt they could ignore the incident but for different reasons.

However, their reaction was untypical. The 15 other teachers felt it was important to take action. One said: "You simply have to give her a firm punishment to show the rest of the children she couldn't get away with either the scribble or the 'old cow'. She's taking you on." Another would warn that further use of such language would be punished.

In the three other situations, teachers were much more emphatic that something had to be done. These included two children not getting on with their work, children making a lot of noise and paper aeroplanes when the teacher returned to the class after a brief absence, and a class arriving for a lesson in an unruly manner. The reseachers described the final incident thus: "It is time for the second half of the morning on your first day with this class. They come running into the room, pushing each other and squealing and laughing."

This time all the teachers decided that action was necessary. One said: "March them all out and get them to line up." Seven of the 20 adopted a low-key approach and did not send the children out. Instead they told them off or talked to them about their behaviour. They played down the incident and got on with the lesson.

Is there a right answer to the questions posed by the researchers? Professor Wragg says there is not: it all depends on the circumstances and the child. "Is he or she shy or a known troublemaker? Is the pupil 6ft 4in and a karate expert? Are you in the middle of a science experiment that you cannot safely stop?" He added that teachers would need to act urgently if the rest of the class was laughing uproariously.

The Exeter research, which has so far examined 1,000 hours of lessons taken by teachers of all types, including students, shows that few teachers ignore misbehaviour. Equally, they have little time to decide what to do. Most disciplinary decisions are made in less than one second. Despite lurid headlines, serious disruption is rare, accounting for only about 1 per cent of incidents. The most common type of indiscipline is talking in class.

Yet the researchers' conversations with children show what an important part discipline plays in their perception of school. Professor Wragg says the research shows that most children are prepared to accept punishment provided they believe it is justified. "Children have a very keen notion of fairness. Most children prefer teachers who are slightly strict and they accept suitable punishment provided it doesn't involve sarcasm or humiliation." The sense of injustice may last for life. A Nottingham University study showed that people in their eighties could remember in detail being told off at school for something which was not their fault, even though the incident occupied only about 20 seconds.

Reading quickly

Reading quickly is much less important than reading effectively. Many people who feel they read slowly actually use the wrong reading strategies – they may read right through a book without concentrating on the parts that matter. If you practise skimming, scanning and SQ3R, you will become an efficient reader and you will also start to read more quickly.

However, you may wish to improve your reading speed still further. There are many exercises which can be used to increase reading speed (see the *Further reading* list for some of these). However, it is very difficult to get a reliable indication of the speed at which you read. If the material is familiar, if the vocabulary is simple, and/or if you are interested, you tend to read faster. And beware of speed-reading teachers who simplify the material in order to produce good results in their students!

If you wish to get a rough indication of your reading speed try the following activity.

1   Find a passage of familiar material (the article on page 39 would be suitable) .

2   Read from the start at your normal speed (not aloud) for one minute.

3   Count the number of words you have read.

4   Repeat steps 2 and 3 twice, starting at different points.

If your reading speed is below 200 words per minute you may be able to increase it as follows:

■   Decide on your purpose before you start and concentrate on this.

■   Always skim new material first and scan for key words and ideas.

■   Train your eyes to see more in each eye movement. Instead of moving them along each line of print concentrate on the centre of each line.

■   Do not look back after you have read a difficult sentence. Keep going and see if the meaning becomes clearer. If necessary, go back when you have finished the section.

■   Avoid mouthing the words. The way to overcome this is to read faster than you can speak.

■   *Extending your vocabulary* in the section *Extra resources* may also be helpful.

Summary

Key points in this unit:

■   Reading is a central task to most learners.

■   Your purpose for reading should influence how you read.

■   You should adopt different reading methods.

■   You don't always have to read every word – skimming and scanning are also useful techniques for obtaining information.

■   A useful method for reading to understand is SQ3R – survey, question, read, recall and review.

■   Reading effectively is more important than reading quickly.

Summarise your work on this unit here. Note down:

■   what you need to read for your course;

■   why you need to read it;

■   how you will read it.

What you need to read	Why you need to read it	How you will read it

UNIT 4

KEEPING NOTES

What this unit is about

Your own notes can be some of the most useful aids to your study. They can help you to understand what you are learning, and to remember it later.

In this unit we look at why you might need to make notes, and at how useful your existing note-making is. We then go on to examine different methods of note-making, and to consider ways of storing your notes.

This unit will help you to:

➔ list the kinds of notes and other records you should keep;

➔ identify the purpose of your notes/records;

➔ identify different ways of making notes;

➔ analyse your notes;

➔ make effective notes.

Why take notes?

You may need to take notes for a number of reasons:

■ to help you **remember** something – you can't hope to retain a whole lecture, book or discussion permanently in your memory, so instead you make notes of the most important items and use the notes for revision and reference;

■ to keep a **permanent record** of something – if you attend a lecture or visit somewhere as part of your course, your notes may be your only record of what took place;

■ to help in your **planning** – notes can be a good way of starting off a project or a piece of writing; you can note down the main things you need to do, the books you will read, and so on;

■ to **re-order material** – making notes is one of the most useful opportunities for rearranging material in whichever form is most convenient to you;

■ to help you **understand** what you are learning – writing things down yourself forces you to think them through properly and is one of the best ways of remembering them;

■ to help you to **concentrate** – if you are listening to someone talking, your mind may easily wander; making notes helps to keep you active and involved;

■ to **show other people** – you may want other learners to benefit from the notes you have made.

1 Look through three examples of notes you have made for your study. Note down here what they were about, and why you made them.

Notes	Why you made them

Your reasons for taking notes are very important. For example, if other people will read your notes, they may need to be more detailed or tidy than if you are the only person who will read them. If they will be your only permanent record, they will need to be self-contained, whereas if they are based on a book you own, you can always cross-refer to particular passages in the book.

Your reasons will also affect the way you make notes. You may well wish to concentrate on written notes; most learners do. Written notes are easy to make, and you can easily access them later. But bear in mind:

■ If you have a wordprocessor, could you use this? It would have the advantage that you could easily modify notes, and rearrange them.

■ Could you use a tape recorder in some circumstances? It might be a useful way of recording your first ideas. Bear in mind that if you record what someone else says, it is wise to ask their permission.

Finally, the purpose of your notes may affect the kind of notes you take. We will look at different types of notes later in the unit.

How useful are your notes?

Notes are usually a personal learning aid, so the most important thing about them is that they suit your learning style and your reasons for taking them.

Above all, notes should be:

■ brief and clear: if they are too long, you will find it tedious to wade through them, either to look for a specific point, or to refresh your memory;

■ easy to read and understand: if you cannot quickly read through them to refresh your memory, they will fail in their purpose;

■ organised to suit the way you learn and your reasons for learning: if they are not relevant to you, you will never look at them again.

2 Look at each of the sets of notes you used in the previous activity, and tick whether they are:

Easy to read	❏	❏	Difficult to read
Brief	❏	❏	Long
Clear	❏	❏	Unclear
Easily understood	❏	❏	Difficult to understand
Organised the way you learn	❏	❏	Organised in some other way
Relevant to your needs	❏	❏	Not relevant to your needs

Have you given yourself lots of ticks in the left-hand column? If you have, then your note-taking system is already excellent. But if you have lots of ticks in the right-hand column, then you need a new approach to note-taking.

The next two sections look at some of the specific points to bear in mind when taking notes from books, articles and speech – talks, lectures, television programmes, interviews, visits, etc.

Taking notes from books

When taking notes from books remember the following points:

Checklist

1 Prepare yourself by asking yourself what you want to get out of the book, and checking that the book will help you answer these questions.

2 Label your notes clearly. Write down:

- ■ title;

- ■ author;

- ■ publisher and place of publication;

- ■ ISBN number and date.

If it is from a library, also write down the classification number (printed at the base of the spine) for future reference.

3 Get an overall sense of what the book is about, by skimming to see which parts of the book are most relevant. Use the SQ3R technique (see Unit 3, *Reading*) to find out the main points in the chapters.

4 Make notes in your own words. The process of converting the ideas into your own language also ensures that you understand the material. In making permanent notes you will want to do your own rearranging of the material, and possibly you will want to add your own comments and cross-references to other notes.

5 Record the main topics and then note the important points under each topic. These will tend to be headings or brief statements. Where an argument, proof or sequence of reasoning is presented, try to note down the main steps, but don't leave out so much that you can't restate the missing processes.

You should also record the major conclusions or results of each chapter. Thus your framework might be something like this:

- ■ chapter heading;
- ■ important points;
- ■ illustrations and arguments to support points;
- ■ result/conclusions.

Of course, you shouldn't regard this as a skeleton outline for all note-taking, but it does illustrate the *type* of organisation you should be aiming at when making notes.

6 Record the page numbers of the sections you are noting. For instance 'Brown – 27' means that the notes came from page 27 of Brown's book. In this way you can double-check a point subsequently if you need to. Always remember to put quotation marks around material which you copy exactly from a book. You can then use your quotation (with an appropriate acknowledgement) in your writing without having to return to the original page to check details. This can save you a lot of time.

Taking notes from speech

Another common occasion for taking notes is to record what someone else has said, perhaps in a talk, lecture or television programme, or during a visit or interview. These notes will be different from notes from print because you are likely to have just one opportunity to make them, whereas you can read a book at your own pace. So you may have to make hasty notes that you revise afterwards – unless you can tape record what is said (and you will need the speaker's permission to do this).

Checklist

1 Prepare yourself beforehand by finding out about the topic. This will make it easier to understand and help you to recognise the main points. Note down questions that you want answers to. Make sure you can see and hear the speaker(s) easily.

2 Label your notes clearly. Write down:

- ■ the subject;
- ■ the speaker's name;
- ■ the date.

3 Try to get a good overall picture of what is being said. Concentrate on understanding first – don't let taking notes get in the way of grasping what is being said. If in doubt, concentrate on listening rather than writing.

4 People do not always talk in a logical order, and you may have to try to do this for them by using headings in your notes, so that you can always go back to an earlier part of your notes.

5 Be prepared to ask questions if you do not understand every point, or if you need further information.

6 Go over your notes as soon as possible afterwards, before the detail fades from memory. If your notes are still confused, talk about them to another student. This may help to clarify them.

If your course involves lectures, and you find that two or three of you are confused, go to see the lecturer concerned. You may be embarrassed about doing this, but your study is too important to be ignored. Provided you are reasonably courteous, this strategy often results in the lecturer agreeing to put headings on the chalkboard or use transparencies to clarify important points.

Different types of notes

There is more than one way of making notes, and it makes sense to choose a method or methods which you feel at ease with and which suits your purpose.

Two commonly used methods are:

■ sequential notes;

■ nuclear notes.

Sequential notes

Sequential notes involve listing the key points under a series of headings and sub-headings. With this method you can:

■ number the points;

■ emphasise material by underlining, using different colours or capital letters, though this slows some people down and so may not be appropriate for notes taken from lectures or TV or radio programmes;

■ use abbreviations, though be careful that you are consistent and can remember what the abbreviations mean.

Nuclear notes

Nuclear notes are more visual. With this method you:

■ write the main topic in the centre of the page;

■ write related ideas around it and link them up to show their relationship to the main idea;

■ add links around the edges to show relationships.

3 Both methods have their advantages. Try out both methods by making notes on Unit 3, on reading.

1   Make one set of sequential notes, making a list of the main points and including headings and sub-headings.

2   Make another set of nuclear notes, writing the word 'reading' in the middle of a blank sheet of paper and then writing the other points around this.

Glance at my examples on the next two pages if you need a clearer idea of what the notes should look like.

3   Then note down here which method you found most useful, and why.

Nuclear notes can be very useful if you want to generate ideas – perhaps for an essay or during brainstorming (see Unit 2). They also have the advantage that you can show links between ideas which can help you to understand and remember them.

Sequential notes are useful when a topic is easily subdivided under a number of headings, or when a book or talk is ordered in a way that is easy to follow.

You may find that one method suits you best. I use both, depending on the circumstances.

Here are my example notes on Unit 3. Don't feel your notes must be identical – you are making them for a different purpose and you may want more or less detail, or to highlight other points.

Example 1: Sequential notes

How to study effectively

Richard Freeman and John Meed

Unit 3: Reading (pp 31-41),

Reasons for reading:

- obtaining a piece of information
- answering a question
- gaining detailed information
- trying to understand something
- pleasure.

Ways of reading:

- skimming – looking through a book quickly
- scanning – searching for a particular point – involves:
  - using references
  - flicking through the pages
  - using your experience
- reading to understand – detailed study
- word-by-word reading – rarely needed
- reading for pleasure – e.g. a novel

SQ3R:

- survey – like skimming
- question – ask questions before you read
- read – look for answers to your questions; form a judgement of the passage
- recall – check you can remember the main ideas
- review – was your memory right?

Example 2: Nuclear notes

I found that when I made these notes I was able to jump around the unit more quickly. I also found quite a few links between parts of the unit.

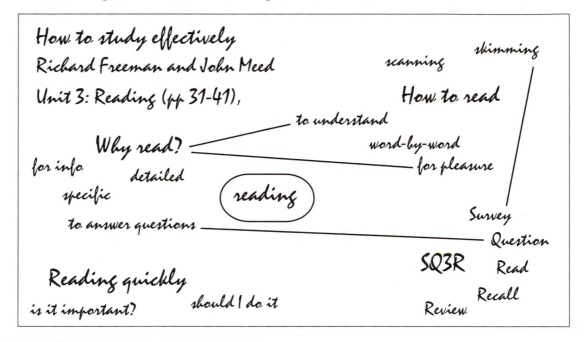

How will you store your notes?

You will want to store your notes so that you do not lose them, and can find them again easily, perhaps for some coursework or for revision. So you will need to design a good filing system.

There are two aspects to a filing system:

■ what you use to store the notes in;

■ how you classify the notes.

Ways of storing notes

This table compares some of the commoner ways of storing notes.

Method	Implications
Loose-leaf folders	Easy to subdivide and add to later.
Ring binder	Also easy to add to: sheets less likely to fall out. Material could be kept in plastic pockets.
Filing cards	Easy to shuffle and reorganise. Good for project, essay or report plans.
Notebook	Convenient to carry. Pages cannot fall out.
Concertina file	Has ready-made subdivisions.
Wordprocessor	Easy to edit material and to reuse for other writing. Remember to make back-up copies.
Tape recorder	Good if you find it easier to say things than write them down. Useful for recording speech too.

Ways of classifying notes

Within your filing system, you need to organise your notes so you can find them again.

Method	Implications
By date	May be useful for a series of lectures. You may forget when you made notes, though.
By first letter	A simple system to use. May let you down if you make a lot of notes.
By topic	Often the best system as it is easy to add to as you go along. But you need to choose topics that are easy to file under.
A mixture	For example, alphabetically within topics.

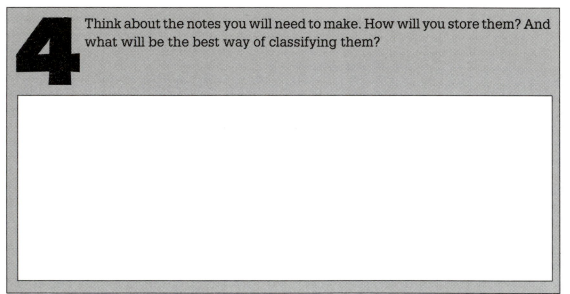

Think about the notes you will need to make. How will you store them? And what will be the best way of classifying them?

Whichever system you adopt, make sure that:

■ it is easy to decide where you will put new notes – if you can't decide where to put something, this may mean that your categories are not working;

■ it is easy to find them later – consider using an index if this helps;

■ it is easy to identify individual notes – they should all have clear headings.

Summary

Key points from this unit:

■ Your purpose for taking notes will influence how you take them.

■ Notes must be easy to read, brief, clear, easy to understand, organised the way you learn and relevant to your needs.

■ There are particular points to bear in mind when taking notes from books or from speech.

■ Nuclear and sequential notes can both be useful.

■ Your method of storing notes should make it easy for you to file notes and to find them again later.

Note down here:

■   which methods you will try out for making notes;

■   how you will store your notes;

■   how you will classify your notes.

Methods to try out:

How you will store notes:

How you will classify notes:

UNIT 5

WRITING

What this unit is about

Most learners need to write from time to time during their courses; and many will need to write extensively.

Writing, particularly in academic subjects, can be daunting. You may have to use particular formats – like essays, reports or memos. And you may have to adopt a more formal style than you use in everyday life for letters or notes. Many people find the idea of sitting down with a blank sheet of paper one of the most difficult aspects of studying.

However, there are skills and strategies you can learn which will help you to write more effectively. In particular, this unit will show you how to focus your writing, how to plan it, how to do it and how to check that it is good.

This unit will help you to:

→   list the kinds of writing you will have to do;

→   identify the purpose of your writing;

→   identify the audience for your writing;

→   collect the information you will need;

→   plan what you will write;

→   write clear paragraphs;

→   draft and edit what you write.

The writing process

All writing involves a number of stages:

■   identifying what kind of writing you must do (the task), and who it is for (the reader);

■   deciding how to tackle it – this can involve choosing a topic or analysing a question;

■   collecting information you will need – this may involve doing research or reading;

■   preparing an outline for what you will write;

■   writing a first draft;

■   editing and redrafting to refine it;

■   giving a final check before handing or sending it to the reader.

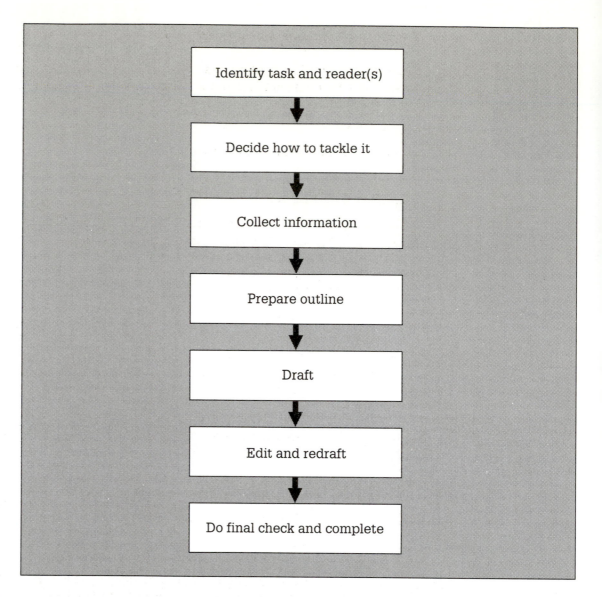

Identify task and reader(s)

Decide how to tackle it

Collect information

Prepare outline

Draft

Edit and redraft

Do final check and complete

1 As you work through the rest of this unit we would like you to practise writing an essay of your choice. If possible you should pass this to a tutor or friend for comment when you have completed the unit, together with the plans and drafts that we will ask you to prepare.

If you are working on a course at the same time as *How to Study Effectively*, you may like to choose a piece of written work you must do anyway. If not, you should choose **one** of the titles that follow:

1   Do a short project about how people learn. Talk to at least three friends or members of your family and ask them what they find difficult and how they try to overcome these difficulties. Draw conclusions about what can help people learn.

2   Write an essay for this title: 'All tobacco advertising should be banned – discuss.'

3   Write an essay for this title: 'Mothers should always get custody of children after a divorce – discuss.'

4   Write a letter to your newspaper in response to one of the articles published in today's edition.

What will you write?

Traditionally, most student writing has involved essays. And you may well have to do some essays in your own learning. But it is also possible that you will do other kinds of writing. These could include:

■ letters or memos;

■ reports – of experiments, tasks or visits;

■ projects;

■ assignments for your tutor.

You will probably be writing for more than one person. Your notes may just be for your reading, or for other learners. An essay may be for your tutor or an examiner. A report might be for someone at work to read. It is very important to be clear about who the reader or readers will be – they may expect you to say certain things, and they will certainly expect to be able to read your writing!

In addition, some kinds of writing have particular requirements and conventions, so it is very important to be clear about exactly what you will be asked to do.

This activity asks you to think about what you may have to write in your learning. If you are not sure about what your writing may involve, ask your tutor for guidance. If necessary, just look through the activity, comment quickly now and come back to it later.

2

1   Look through the following list and tick those kinds of writing you may have to do in your learning:

☐ notes	☐ memos	☐ letters
☐ projects	☐ reports	☐ assignments
☐ essays	☐ summaries	☐ exams
☐ coursework	☐ projects	☐ other.

2   Then, in the box below, note down each kind of writing you ticked and decide which person or people will read it.

3   Finally, note down special features of each kind of writing – for example, whether you should use certain headings, whether you should write in sentences and paragraphs or whether notes will be acceptable. Again, check with your tutor if necessary.

Type of writing	Who will read it?	Special features

Key questions you may need to check include:

- How long should it be? Many essays specify lengths.

- Should you use headings? Essays do not usually use headings, while reports often use standard headings like Introduction, Method, Results and Conclusions.

- Should you include other people's ideas, from your reading? In much academic writing you will be expected to quote what other writers have said, and to illustrate different views. In some cases you may be asked to list the reading you carried out at the end.

- Should you include your own ideas? In many essays or reports you should finish up with your own conclusions or recommendations.

- Should you include evidence from your research? This would be necessary if you were writing up a scientific experiment or the results of a survey.

There may also be points of style and presentation:

- Should you write in paragraphs or in note form?

- Should you use an impersonal style (it could be argued that…) or a personal style (I feel that…)?

- Should you type or wordprocess, or would handwriting be acceptable?

- Should you write on one side or both sides?

- Should you use single or double spacing?

- Where should you put details like your name and the title?

You can check these points by looking at your syllabus or past papers, or asking your tutor.

How will you tackle it?

You will probably have some choice over what to write. In some cases you will have a wide choice – for example, if you are doing some research. In other cases, as in an exam, you may have to choose between a few topics or questions. It makes sense to choose a topic which you know and understand well rather than something new and unfamiliar.

If you have no choice and find yourself committed to an unfamiliar topic, find out about it before you even begin to plan your writing. If you can't understand a topic before you write on it you will be unable to select material for inclusion or develop a logical argument around the material you select.

To help yourself analyse a question or topic it is a good idea to underline the key words. These can be described as the important words, the ones that give the essential information. They can:

- tell you how to proceed;

- help you to collect material which is relevant.

The following activity illustrates this point.

3 Here are three topics for writing. Look at each one and underline what you think are the key words.

1. **Essay**: Discuss whether the Japanese should be allowed to kill dolphins in Japanese waters.

2. **Report**: Investigate recent returns from customers. List the main reasons for returns and make recommendations for reducing the rate of returns.

3. **Project**: Investigate child care provision for the under-5s in your area. Talk with parents you know and ask them how much this provision meets their needs. Write up what you find out.

The words I underlined are:

1. **Essay**: <u>Discuss</u> whether the <u>Japanese</u> <u>should be allowed</u> to <u>kill dolphins</u> in <u>Japanese</u> <u>waters</u>.

2. **Report**: <u>Investigate recent returns</u> from <u>customers</u>. <u>List</u> the main <u>reasons</u> for returns and <u>make recommendations</u> for reducing the <u>rate</u> of returns.

3. **Project**: <u>Investigate child care provision</u> for the <u>under-5s</u> in <u>your area</u>. Talk with <u>parents</u> you know and ask them <u>how much</u> this <u>provision</u> meets their <u>needs</u>. <u>Write up</u> what you find out.

Collecting information

Collecting information involves a number of possible tasks:

■ writing down what you already know on the subject;

■ asking questions to which you hope to find answers in your reading or research (see also Unit 2, *Learning effectively*);

■ finding answers to the questions;

■ recording what you find out.

4 Look again at this question:

'Discuss whether the Japanese should be allowed to kill dolphins in Japanese waters.'

Note down here:

■ what you already know about this;

■ what questions you would wish to answer;

■ where you might be able to find the answers to your questions.

What you know already:

(continued overleaf)

```
Questions to answer:




Sources of information:
```

Known information might include:

- Dolphins are a protected species in most parts of the world.

- There is a strong lobby group in America and Europe whose aim is to protect dolphins.

- The Japanese fishermen are poor and kill the dolphins because they eat their fish.

Questions to answer might include:

- Are dolphins an endangered species or are their numbers on the increase?

- How far do Japanese waters extend?

- Are there international rules about killing dolphins?

- Are there unusually high concentrations of dolphins in Japanese waters?

Possible sources of information to answer these questions include:

- your own notes;

- your reading list or tutor's recommendations;

- the library index – the subject catalogue for the topic should list any books on this topic; you could look up possible authors from your reading list in the author catalogue; and you could also look up the periodicals indexes to find a recent article on this topic.

Use all available sources of information. Don't forget that there are sources other than books and periodicals (e.g. radio and television programmes). Discussions with others doing the same course may be useful too.

Recording information

If you are writing something long, like a project or an essay, you will need to record the information you collect. You will need to choose one of the note-taking methods described in Unit 4, *Keeping notes*. You may find it helpful to:

- use index cards to record useful quotations – on one side of the card you can write the quotation and on the other side the reference to where it came from;

- use separate sheets of paper to answer each of your questions, and record any relevant quotations or ideas on each one.

When you record a quotation from a book, make sure you include a full reference of chapter and page number together with the author, the publisher and possibly the ISBN number.

Preparing a plan

A plan is a series of headings with an idea or two under each heading. The headings should do no more than cover the points you intend to write about.

The priority in the plan is logical order. This does not mean that there is one and only one order which you can consider but it does mean that your final order must justify itself and be clear to the reader.

One way of doing this is to look at the material you have collected and decide which are the main points you wish to cover. Your plan would then look like this:

- Introduction: define your terms and indicate how you intend to tackle the topic.

- Main sections.

- Summary or conclusion: recall the issues raised in the introduction, draw together the points you made in the main sections and explain the overall significance of your conclusions.

5 Look back at Unit 4, *Keeping notes*. Then write out a plan for this unit in the box below.

Introduction:

Main sections:

Summary/conclusion:

My plan looks like this:

Introduction
Main points to cover
Objectives

Section 1: Why take notes?
Main reasons: to help remember something, to keep a record, to help planning, to re-order material, to help understanding, to aid concentration, to show other people
Activity – why you make notes

Section 2: How useful are your notes?
Notes should be easy to read, brief, clear, easily understood, organised the way you learn and relevant to your needs
Activity – analyse your notes

Section 3: Taking notes from books
Key points to bear in mind

Section 4: Taking notes from speech
Key points to bear in mind

Section 5: Different types of notes
Sequential and nuclear notes
Activity – try them out and compare them

Section 6: How will you store your notes?
Different methods: loose-leaf folders, ring binder, filing cards, notebook, concertina file, wordprocessor, tape recorder
Classifying notes: by date, first letter, topic
Activity – think through which method will suit you

Summary/conclusion
Key points/action plan/assignment

Length

A limitation on your outline is length. If you are set a limit of 2,000 words you will have to be far more selective than for 5,000 words. Make sure that you take this into account at the outline stage. If you don't you will have to replan in the middle of writing.

If you are given a limit of 2,000 words you might split it up like this:

- Introduction   250 words or less
- Main sections   1,200–1,400 words – say 250 per section
- Summary/conclusion   500 words or so.

6 Plan what you will do for the essay you chose in Activity 1.

Drafting

Once you have collected the information you need and prepared a plan, you are ready to start writing. Very few writers get it right first time, and most good writers begin with a first draft which they then revise. As I write this introduction, I am doing just that.

Advantages of drafting include:

■ you don't have to get it right first time, and this sometimes makes it easier to start writing;

■ you don't have to start at the beginning – the introduction can be difficult to write, so it might make sense to start in the middle;

■ you can change the order of things if they don't work in practice;

■ you don't have to worry about getting your style and spelling right first time – you can come back and correct later.

Key points during the drafting stage include paragraphing, using ideas and evidence, and using illustrations. We will explore these in more detail now.

Paragraphs

At the first draft stage you should aim to write one paragraph (or more) for each of the headings in your outline. We have already met some of the rules for good paragraphs in Unit 3, *Reading*:

■ each paragraph should contain one main idea – from your outline;

■ the first sentence should, if possible, introduce this idea;

■ other sentences should support the main idea by explaining it more, giving examples or linking it to other paragraphs;

■ it is very dangerous to introduce a second idea as this will almost certainly confuse the reader.

Ideas and evidence

In most kinds of writing, you will wish to put forward your own and other people's ideas. Make sure that you:

■ express ideas clearly and concisely;

■ back them up with evidence, whether from your own research or as quotations from your reading;

■ give credit where it's due – for example, if you quote from a book, give the title, author and publisher.

Illustrations

Also at the first draft stage, you should be thinking about whether, and how, you should illustrate what you write. Depending on what you are writing, you may wish to draw your own pictures – diagrams, charts, maps, graphs or tables – or to include copies of pictures from other sources.

Any illustrations should:

- be relevant to what you are saying;

- be clear and simple to understand;

- add usefully to what is already there;

- be clearly labelled and, if from another source, fully referenced.

Getting started

It's often difficult to get started on writing. Here are some ideas:

- Remember it's only a first draft.

- Start with an easy part.

- Try a brainstorming exercise (see Unit 2, *Learning effectively*) to clear your mind and get you going.

- Rewrite your outline over two or three pages with headings and lots of white space, and then start filling in the gaps.

 **7** Prepare a first draft of your essay, drawing on the plan you have prepared.

Editing and redrafting

When your first draft is complete, edit and redraft it. Editing involves reading through and checking what you have written; redrafting means revising in the light of your editing comments.

Editing

As you read through what you have written, you can write your comments on the draft itself. Minor changes (say to spelling) you can correct on the spot. For more major problems you may wish to write the comment in the margin and think about how to improve it. You could ask someone else to help with the editing process. They may spot things that you miss, and tell you the things they like about it!

 **8** What kinds of things might you look for as you edit something you have written? Note down your thoughts here. If possible, look at something you have written recently to give you some ideas.

Some of the things you might check for include:

Coverage

- Have you answered the question/followed the instructions?

- Have you included all the points from your plan?

- Is everything relevant to the question or topic?

- Is there anything you need to add?

- Is there anything you can delete?

- Is the order right?

Approach

- Have you backed up all your ideas with evidence?

- Is the balance between points right?

- Does the introduction give a clear idea of what is to come?

- Is the conclusion strong enough?

Style

- Is each paragraph limited to one main idea?

- Is it easy to read and understand?

- Could you say anything just as well in fewer words?

- Does the grammar, punctuation and spelling need correcting?

Redrafting

How you implement your changes in a redraft will depend on how you are working:

- if you have a wordprocessor, you can make all your changes and then print it out again;

- if you are writing or typing you will have to decide whether whole pages need rewriting, or whether you could make changes to the draft without it looking too messy.

Always bear in mind who will read it. If you are submitting a piece of work for someone you don't know (like an examiner), you will want to aim at a high quality of presentation. But if, say, it is a draft of a piece of coursework that you will revise in the light of your tutor's comments, all that really matters is that it is easy to read. And if the reader is just you – perhaps because you plan to edit it again – you can probably get away with murder!

Edit and redraft your essay now. When you have finished, ask your tutor, or a friend, to read through it and comment. If you choose a friend, pick someone whom you can trust to make constructive comments; explain to them that you have written the essay as part of a project to develop your study skills.

Completing your writing

You have now done the hard work. You should have an edited and redrafted piece of writing which you feel conveys well what you wanted to say.

It is wise to check it one last time, making sure in particular that:

■   spelling and punctuation are accurate;

■   presentation and appearance are good enough;

■   your name and any other essential information are included.

You can then send or give it to the reader. Bear in mind that you can always include a covering note, to explain what it is and to mention any points you would like the reader to comment on, if this is appropriate.

Summary

Key points from this unit:

■   The writing process involves a number of stages.

■   Different types of writing may need to be tackled differently.

■   Always analyse the question, topics or instructions.

■   Collect the information you need.

■   Produce a plan before you start writing.

■   Writing involves drafting, editing and redrafting – you can afford to make mistakes first time provided you check it carefully.

Note down any aspects of your writing that you will try to work on.

UNIT
6

ASSESSMENT

What this unit is about

Assessment is the way in which your success at learning will be measured, and the way your achievement will be recognised.

Doing well in assessment is, again, a special skill. It's not just a matter of hoping that your skills and knowledge will come across automatically; you need to present them effectively. And this involves:

■ being clear about how exactly you will be assessed;

■ planning your approach to assessment;

■ preparing effectively for your assessment.

This unit looks at these points in turn, and concludes with a section on how to tackle exams.

This unit will help you to:

→ find out how you will be assessed;

→ plan how to tackle your assessment;

→ plan your revision;

→ develop suitable exam strategies.

How will you be assessed?

Assessment has changed rapidly in recent years. Exams are no longer seen as the best way of testing much that is learnt, and while they are still important, particularly on 'A' level courses, in most other areas other forms of assessment are used as well or instead.

Two methods of assessment have become particularly important:

■ assessment of **coursework**, i.e. what you do during your course, including projects, assignments and practical work;

■ assessment of **competence**, i.e. what you do at work, the skills and abilities that you use every day.

The first step in preparing for assessment is to be clear about exactly how you will be assessed and what the assessor expects of you. This activity will guide you through this process. If you do not know the answers to some of these questions now, arrange to talk it over with your tutor, or to look at a copy of your course syllabus.

Look through the following list of types of assessment, and tick those which will apply to you. Then find out:

■ what you will be asked to do; e.g. a choice of four essay questions out of 20, a paper of 50 compulsory multiple choice questions, or a project of 2,000 words with Introduction, Method and Conclusions, illustrated with diagrams or photographs;

■ what the 'assessment criteria' for the course are – in other words, what you will be assessed on.

Assessment	Tick	Assessment	Tick
Exam	❑	Assignment/essay	❑
Project	❑	Practical work	❑
Interview	❑	Competence	❑
Other:	❑	Other:	❑

Assessment	What you have to do	Assessment criteria

These are the assessment methods for three typical courses:

An 'A' level syllabus

Two exam papers, each three hours long and each contributing 50% of the total marks:

■ *Paper 1: Four essay questions out of a possible choice of 16 titles, each receiving 25 marks.*

■ *Paper 2: Four questions: two compulsory questions (with a total of 50 marks) and two other questions out of a choice of seven, each receiving 25 marks.*

The assessment criteria in the syllabus are very general, and described as assessment objectives, for example, 'to evaluate and interpret source material as historical evidence' or 'to present a clear, concise, logical and relevant argument'. I would want to ask my tutor for more detail about how they are applied in practice.

A GCSE syllabus

Coursework (40% of the marks) and 2 two hour exam papers (each 30% of the marks).

■ *Coursework: two to four short assignments of 1,250–2,000 words each, plus two or three longer assignments of 2,000–3,000 words each.*

■ *Paper 1: 15 source-based questions, all of which must be answered.*

■ *Paper 2: four questions from a choice of ten.*

The assessment criteria are more detailed than in the 'A' level example.

A Certificate of Management Studies course

> *There are two main components:*
>
> ■ *Using a learning contract and a personal development journal to record progress and evidence of competence.*
>
> ■ *A project, based on two assignments, which can demonstrate the learner's knowledge and application.*
>
> *Detailed assessment criteria are provided.*

Planning for assessment

Planning is important for all assessment. It is particularly so for exams – if you leave all your exam revision to the last minute you are unlikely to be able to do it well.

Ideally, you should plan for assessment as part of your overall plan for study. It is worth revising what you do from time to time in any case as this helps you to consolidate your learning. However, you are likely to need to start actively working on assessment six to eight weeks before you are due to take it.

Draw up your assessment plan and timetable in the *Action plan* at the end of this unit.

■ List all the pieces of assessment you must do in the left-hand column.

■ Note down beside each one how you will prepare for it.

■ In the next column note down the date when you will start preparing for each one.

■ In the right-hand column, note down the date of the exam or the due date for the coursework, project or assignment.

As you approach the time to start preparing, make sure you:

■ know exactly what you must do – check with the syllabus or your tutor; past papers are useful for checking what is required in exams;

■ have all the resources you need – your notes plus any reading.

Preparing and revising

Revising is particularly associated with exams. However, you may need to revise for other types of assessment, and regular revision in any case will help you to refresh and deepen your learning.

One particularly important aspect of preparing for assessment is checking how you are doing against the assessment criteria for your course. You should have found out what your assessment criteria are in the first activity in this unit. There are three ways you can make use of them:

■ get together with another learner who is tackling the same course, try marking a piece of each other's work against the criteria, and then talking about how you did it;

■ try assessing your own work against the criteria;

■ ask your tutor to use the criteria on a piece of your work, and to explain to you how he or she did this.

Make sure you try out one of these methods. If the assessment criteria are not clear or detailed for your course, ask your tutor to explain what he or she thinks really matters.

Other ways in which you can revise include:

■ making notes from your notes – this will help you check that you understand everything, and will also help you to remember things;

■ preparing outline answers – it also helps to prepare other possible answers in outline form; this way you reorganise material and understand it better;

■ working with other people – if you can work with other learners, there is a lot of value in revising together; that way you can share topics out between you and check each other's work.

3 Note down here the revision techniques you might try.

Here is what other learners have suggested:

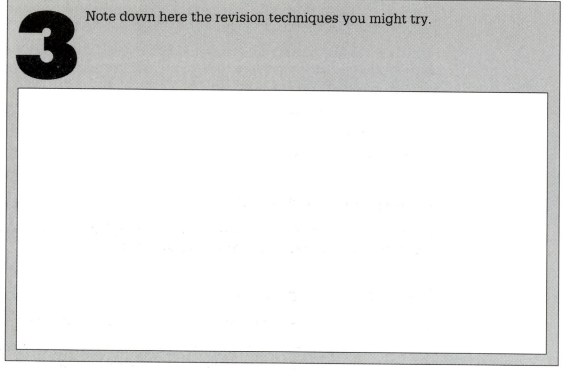

In the last term five friends and I worked closely together. We divided up the course between us and each person prepared one topic and gave a seminar about it. I honestly feel I learnt more in this time than in the previous two years of this course, and we all did well in the exam.

I worked out a timetable for my revision. I spread the topics I had to revise over the six weeks before the exams, so that I had so much to do each week. I allowed at least one free day each week to relax, and I made sure I stopped two days before each exam itself.

Tackling exams

If you do have to tackle an exam, it pays to plan. Use these checklists to help you.

The day before

Check, and tick off when you've done so:

❑ The place of the exam. (Be sure you know how to get there.)

❑ The starting time.

❑ Your candidate number.

❑ Your equipment:

    ❑ pens – including cartridges or a refill;

    ❑ pencil;

    ❑ rubber;

    ❑ watch;

    ❑ paper (if needed);

    ❑ calculator;

    ❑ other equipment:

In the examination room

If you have a chance, choose an area where there is plenty of light and where you can see the clock clearly. Check your watch with the clock.

Tackling the paper

1   Check that it is the correct one (there may be other exams taking place in the room).

2   Fill in your personal details. Put your name, candidate number and any other details required on your first sheet, and on any other sheets as required.

3   Read the instructions carefully:

    ■ How many questions are you asked to do?

    ■ Are any or all compulsory?

    ■ Do different sections or questions have to be on separate sheets?

    ■ Where must the answers be written?

4   Choose your questions:

    ■ Put a light pencil mark through those questions you can't possibly attempt.

    ■ Put a tick at the side of those you can definitely do.

    ■ Number the ticked questions from easiest to hardest. Do the easy ones first; this will give you confidence and allow more time for the more difficult questions later.

5   Check your questions. Re-read the questions you have ticked, and note the key words.

6   Make notes for each question. Points will flood into your memory in a random way. Switch from one question to another, jotting down the ideas that come to mind.

7   Ration your time:

- If the questions have equal marks give them equal time.

- Jot down a mini-timetable for your chosen questions, e.g.:

Quick notes on chosen questions	9.00-9.30
Q.1	9.30-10.00
Q.4	10.00-10.30
Q.6	10.30-11.00
Q.8	11.00-11.30
Final check	11.30-12.00

If you run short of time, do remember that you can't get more than full marks on a question (and rarely as much as that). So a good pass requires answers to as many questions as the examiners tell you to answer. For example, suppose there are 100 marks and you have to do five questions. If you do three well (say 14 out of 20 for each) you get 42 marks – not enough to pass if the pass mark is 50. But if you can get 4 out of 20 on each of two other questions, you would pass.

So, if you haven't done your full quota of questions and are short of time, use that time to write short notes on the remainder of your quota. In this way you should be able to show the examiner more of your knowledge than by a more elaborate answer to one question.

8   Tackle each question in turn. Write clear, precise answers. Be careful not to over-answer. Each question should take no longer than the time allowed by the examiners, but too often candidates take longer because they exceed the question. So, if a question is taking more than its fair share of time, re-read the question – you may not be answering it.

9   When you have finished the paper:

- Read through all your answers. Check for omissions, poor spelling and illegible phrases. Search your mind for any last minute points. (Better to do it then, than to remember them after the exam is over.)

- Check that your name is on each page.

- Number each page and clip any loose sheets together.

After the exam

Do not waste time in 'post-mortems'. You have done all you can. Go out and relax.

Summary

Key points from this unit:

- Find out exactly what form your assessment will take.

- Use your assessment criteria to mark your own work.

- Prepare a detailed assessment timetable.

- Plan your revision so that you don't leave it all to the last minute.

- Always read questions or instructions very carefully.

- Always plan your answers.

- In exams, make sure you have time to do all the questions.

Draw up your assessment timetable here:

Assessment	Preparation required	Date to start preparing	Date of assessment

EXTRA RESOURCES

Introduction

During your study, you may well need to use a range of resources.

This concluding section looks at some of the key resources:

→ getting support from other people;

→ choosing what to read;

→ using a library;

→ extending your vocabulary;

→ using a dictionary.

Getting support

Gaining the support of other people, and making the most of them, may be the key to your success as a learner. What kinds of support you want from other people – and how much – will depend on your style of learning. For example, some people are very good at sticking to their plans and timetables, while others need regular support if they are to keep going.

1 Look through the list of types of support you might need below. For each one, decide whether you think you will need this kind of help, and if so write an example in the space provided. Then think of someone whom you might be able to ask to give you this support.

Type of support	Examples	Your example	Person(s) to ask
Keeping your morale up	Someone who can cheer you up		
Finding a place to study	Space at home/work		
Help with planning	Discussing timetables		
Testing out ideas	Brainstorming Discussing		

(continued overleaf)

Explaining things to you	*Showing how something works*		
Talking things through	*Planning a piece of work*		
Reading what you write	*Comments on style, spelling*		
Help with daily tasks	*Looking after children*		
Giving feedback	*Comments on clarity*		
Obtaining information	*Suggesting books to read*		
Other:			
Other:			

Different people may be able to help you:

- your tutor, teacher, lecturer or trainer;

- other people like librarians, technicians;

- other learners;

- friends, family and colleagues.

And they may be able to help in different ways:

- your tutor may well be the ideal person to read what you do, give you comments or explain difficult points to you;

- a librarian may be able to help you find information;

- another learner may be helpful for generating ideas, talking things through;

- a friend might be good at keeping your morale up, while your family might be able to give you practical or emotional support.

You should talk with the people you have identified and discuss how they may be able to help. You will need to:

- arrange a time and place to discuss it with them;

- prepare what you will say;

- agree how you will work together;

- monitor how it is going.

2 It is particularly important to prepare what you will say. In the box below, note down the names of the people you have identified and beside each name write down any points you would want to cover when you talk with them.

Person	Points to cover
1	
2	
3	

Points you may want to cover could include:

■ describing briefly what you are learning;

■ explaining your reasons for learning;

■ checking in principle if they would be prepared to help;

■ explaining what kind of support you want from them;

■ discussing practical issues such as how much time might be involved, whether you would need to meet up and how often.

Choosing what you will read

There are a number of ways to find out what to read, including your tutor's recommendations, a course booklist, other learners' recommendations, bibliographies in other books and library catalogues and librarians.

If you are following a set course of study, there will almost certainly be some books which are compulsory reading. In addition to these, there will probably be a list of recommended books. It is very unlikely that you will have time to study more than a small section from the list, so you must choose the books with care.

Buy or borrow?

You will also need to decide whether to buy or borrow publications. It is probably worth buying publications that you will need to refer to often during the course of your learning. These might include compulsory texts, reference books, dictionary and thesaurus and important magazines.

You may prefer to use the library to borrow books you will only need for short periods, e.g. for a particular assignment. Whether you buy or borrow you will need to plan well ahead. Bookshops often do not stock the books you need, and will have to order them for you. Similarly, library books you want to borrow will often be on loan, and to avoid this you will have to book well in advance. You may sometimes have to try two or three libraries for particular texts.

Evaluating a book

To find out quickly whether or not a publication is relevant and likely to be useful, check:

■ Do the title, introduction and contents page relate to the topic you are studying?

■ Is the author a recognised authority on the subject, or is there a section in the book which tells you the author's credentials?

- When was it published? Is it sufficiently up to date?
- Where was it published? Is it relevant to your own country?
- Has your tutor mentioned the publication favourably?
- Is the bibliography comprehensive and up to date?

Your own library

Ideally, you should aim to build up a small collection of books in your subject. This can be a very expensive process, so be on the look out for book sales and second-hand bookshops, and ex-students wishing to sell their books. Although books *are* expensive, bear in mind that your collection will save you many trips to libraries and your books will be available whenever you need to refer to them.

Using a library

Your public library may be one of your main resources, so it pays to make the most of it; in particular, you should become a member if you are not one already. Your library is likely to have both a lending section and a reference section.

The lending section

The lending section is usually the largest part of the library, and any of the books in it may be borrowed by members of the library. The books within this section generally fall into two main categories:

- non-fiction;
- fiction.

Non-fiction

Nearly all public libraries use the Dewey Decimal System to arrange their non-fiction books. Under this system, books are arranged on the shelves in ten main categories:

000	General works	500	Pure science
100	Philosophy	600	Applied science
200	Religion	700	Arts and recreation
300	Social sciences	800	Literature
400	Linguistics	900	History

Each of these categories is then broken down into further sub-sections. To find a book you need to find its Dewey classification, and then look it up on the appropriate shelf.

Fiction

Fiction is usually shelved in alphabetical order, according to the author's surname and initials. So books by Richard Adams come before those by Kingsley Amis, and books by Kingsley Amis come before books by Martin Amis.

The reference section

Any member of the public may use the reference section of a library, whether or not he or she is a member. However, you must use these books in the library, and you cannot borrow them. The reference section is likely to contain dictionaries, directories, atlases and so forth.

Other resources

Your library may also:

- lend records, CDs, cassettes or videotapes;

- keep material on microfilm;

- offer computer services such as Ceefax.

Extending your vocabulary

One of the commonest difficulties when you start to read more academic books is lack of familiarity with the language used by the authors you read. Textbooks often contain words that we do not use in everyday life, and the subject you study may well have its own specialist terms as well.

Extending your vocabulary is quite easy and is nothing like learning the lists of words which teachers used to be so fond of. The lists of difficult words printed in popular magazines do not, as claimed, improve your vocabulary. The mere learning of words and their meanings quickly fades from memory, and as fast as you take in new words you are losing words learnt two to three weeks ago. The keys to extending your vocabulary are these:

Read widely

Almost all the words you know were learnt in context. That is, as a child, you heard others use the words over and over again in many different contexts, and so you learnt the meaning of the word. Any other method of learning would be impossibly complex for a child. Imagine trying to define 'pretty' to a five year old! Yet most five year olds use the word without the slightest difficulty. They do this because they have an intuitive understanding of what 'pretty' means from the various occasions on which it has been used by others.

Similarly, the best way in which adults can broaden their vocabulary is by reading widely so as to meet new words in a variety of contexts. It is, of course, no use just doing a lot of reading in one field. A diet of novels or biology or horror stories will not do. You would not meet enough new words in a sufficient range of contexts to clearly establish them in your own vocabulary.

Use new words

Some new words will find their way into your vocabulary without any conscious effort. But you can also gain something by deliberately using new words as you meet them. It may help to list those words which you feel are of particular importance – e.g. those which you will need for your studies. You can then look at the list and determine to use some of the words in the near future.

Look up words

On the whole, we learn very few words through consulting dictionaries. But occasionally you will meet a word without being able to grasp its meaning from the context. When this happens, look up the word in a dictionary (see the next section) and make a note of its meaning. You can go over such lists from time to time, but don't try to remember the lists themselves. You may also find it useful to have a thesaurus to hand.

Using a dictionary

If you don't have a dictionary, or if you feel your current dictionary is not very helpful, you may need to buy a different one. *Collins New Compact Dictionary* is one that many students use.

A dictionary entry will look something like this:

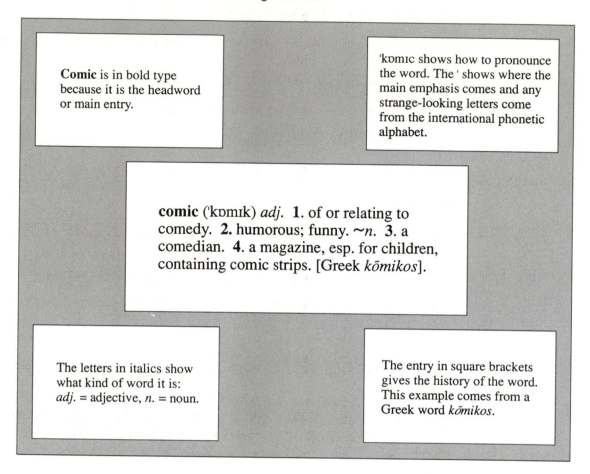

Comic is in bold type because it is the headword or main entry.

'kɒmɪc shows how to pronounce the word. The ' shows where the main emphasis comes and any strange-looking letters come from the international phonetic alphabet.

comic ('kɒmɪk) *adj.* **1.** of or relating to comedy. **2.** humorous; funny. ~*n.* **3.** a comedian. **4.** a magazine, esp. for children, containing comic strips. [Greek *kōmikos*].

The letters in italics show what kind of word it is: *adj.* = adjective, *n.* = noun.

The entry in square brackets gives the history of the word. This example comes from a Greek word *kōmikos*.

Your dictionary will contain a key which explains the system or symbols or abbreviations it uses. They may be a little different from those in the example.

Many words have more than one meaning, and it is always important to check that you have chosen the right definition. For example, in the following sentences, the word 'easy' has two different meanings. Look up 'easy' in your dictionary and see if you can find the two meanings there:

- He is an easy person to persuade.
- She has a very easy manner.

Further reading

If you want to read more on the topics we have covered, these books may be useful to you.

General

Northedge, Andrew *The Good Study Guide,* Open University Press, 1990

Maddox, Harry *How to Study,* Pan Books, 1988

Learning Skills Resource Bank, National Extension College, 1990

Memory

Ansell, G *Make the Most of your Memory*, National Extension College, 1986

Higbee, K L *Your Memory: How It Works and How to Improve It*, Prentice-Hall, 1977

Reading

de Leeuw, M E *Read Better, Read Faster*, Penguin, 1965

Lewis, R and Pugmire, M *How to Use Your Dictionary*, Collins Educational and the National Extension College, 1993

Lloyd, S M (ed) *Roget's Thesaurus*, Longman, 1982

Mares, C *Efficient Reading*, Hodder & Stoughton, 1976

Note-taking

Buzan, Tony *Use Your Head*, BBC Publications, 1974

Writing

Lewis, R *How to Write Essays*, Collins Educational and the National Extension College, 1993

Lewis, R and Inglis, J *Report Writing*, National Extension College, revised edition 1991

Lister, T A *Writing for Everyone*, National Extension College, revised edition 1990

Signing off

We hope you found this book interesting and useful. Remember that to make the most out of it, and out of your studies, you must try and apply its principles at every opportunity. Developing good study habits is a slow job and requires perseverance. If this book has shown you what to do and it encourages you to go on and do it, it has achieved its aim.

Richard Freeman

John Meed

Other books in this series

Clear Thinking

John Inglis and Roger Lewis

An invaluable book for anyone who wants to organise and express their thoughts more effectively, or to analyse the arguments of others. Particularly useful for students preparing for assessment, whether verbally or in writing. Topics covered include: propositions and arguments; assertions; abuses of argument; using source material; applying clear thinking to poetry, prose, and art.

How to Succeed in Exams and Assessments

Penny Henderson

An interactive introduction to the key skills needed for assessment in the 1990s. Includes the latest information on assessment requirements for the new competence-based qualifications, as well as vital hints for tackling A level and GCSE exams. The book also shows how to cope with nerves and stress, and helps students develop their own personal strategy for success.

How to Use Your Dictionary

Roger Lewis and Martin Pugmire

Shows how dictionaries can be used to assist at many stages of study, from clarifying meanings and spellings to finding out about pronunciation and the origins of words. Includes numerous examples from a wide range of dictionaries. Topics include: using a standard dictionary; finding meanings; finding spellings; pronunciation; checking the history of a word.

How to Write Essays

Roger Lewis

An ideal remedy for the blocks many students experience when it comes to essay writing. Covers all the stages of successful essay writing from rough notes to the final presentation, and includes hints on using the comments of friends and tutors. Invaluable for students at all levels, from GCSE to A level and beyond.

1 Fáilte Welcome!

This unit enables learners to: introduce themselves; give praise and make criticism; ask what the Irish word for something is; express gratitude.

Can you pronounce any of the words in the picture?
Can you name any objects in the classroom?

1 Éisteacht *Listening*

How many Irish words do you know? Think about it. They could be people's names, place names, brand names, short expressions, words that passed into English. Discuss your list with other students.

1

Many personal names in Irish have similar sounding English equivalents, such as *Nora* or *Norah* for **Nóra**. In the following recording you will hear six people saying their names. Write the English equivalents of the names.

Pól	Bríd
Pádraig	Art
Síle	Caitlín

Check your answers in *Eochair* at the end of the unit.

2

Listen to the same people introducing themselves. Complete the sentences.

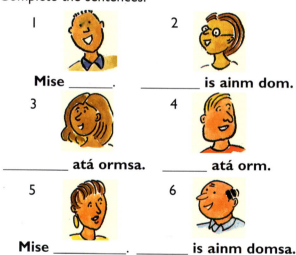

1   Mise _____.

2   _____ is ainm dom.

3   _____ atá ormsa.

4   _____ atá orm.

5   Mise _____.

6   _____ is ainm domsa.

Check *Téipscripteanna* at the end of the unit.

Cumarsáid

2 Communication

1

The following people are meeting for the first time.

Mise Peig.

Mise Bríd.

Donncha atá ormsa.

Éanna atá orm.

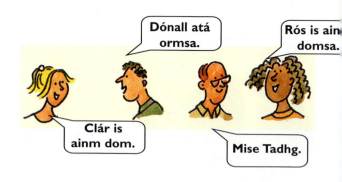

Dónall atá ormsa.

Rós is ainm domsa.

Clár is ainm dom.

Mise Tadhg.

Treasa atá ormsa.

Niall is ainm domsa freisin!

Pádraig is ainm domsa.

Mise Niall.

The exchanges you have just heard illustrate different ways to introduce yourself. Write out three of the ways.

(a) _____

(b) _____

(c) _____

Compare with another student.

> The suffix **sa** implies a contrast with the person you are talking to, and is therefore an indirect way of asking for the other person's name. If other people are first to tell you their names, use the same phrase that they have used, plus the suffix.
>
> **Siobhán atá orm.**
> **Donncha atá ormsa.**
>
> **Diarmuid is ainm dom.**
> **Rós is ainm domsa.**
>
> The suffix is never accented, but rather the word to which it is added.

2

Listen to the recording again while reading the conversations in **2.1**. Practise repeating what each speaker says. Then role-play the different dialogues with another student.

3 **Labhairt** *Speaking*

Introduce yourself to others in the class. If you wish to know the Irish version of your name, ask the teacher.

4 **Éisteacht** *Listening*

1

Deirdre is a new teacher in Scoil Lorcáin. The other teachers are introducing themselves to her. Listen to the recording and write the numbers corresponding to the phrases teachers use to introduce themselves. For example 2 follows Peadar because he says 'Peadar is ainm dom'.

1 **Mise** _____.
2 _____ **is ainm dom.**
3 _____ **atá orm.**

Múinteoirí	
Peadar	**2**
Cáit	
Gormfhlaith	
Dónall	
Treasa	
Seán	

Check your answers in *Téipscripteanna*.

2

In Ireland, friends don't normally shake hands or embrace when they meet. Find out in the group what happens in other countries. Is it different with strangers? Or at formal meetings?

5 **Cultúr** *Culture*

Irish Personal Names

1

In their English forms, a small number of Irish first names such as *Patrick, Eileen, Rory, Maureen,* and *Kathleen* have always been popular, both in Ireland and internationally. In recent years there is a tendency to return to the Irish forms, in these instances **Pádraig**, **Eibhlín**, **Ruaidhrí**, **Máirín**, and **Caitlín**, and also to use a much wider range of names found in Irish history. Popular names for girls to-day include **Áine**, **Aoife**, **Deirdre**, **Gráinne**, **Maedhbh**, **Neasa** and for boys, **Colm**, **Conall**, **Cormac**, **Dara**, **Donncha** and **Oisín**.

Here are 6 famous Irish people from the worlds of politics, acting, writing and music. Can you write their first names?

(a) _____ **Keating**

(b) _____ **McKenna**

(c) _____ **Ní Dhomhnaill**

(d) _____ **de Valera**

(e) _____ **Neeson**

(f) _____ **O'Connor**

2

Common Irish surnames, such as *Kelly, Donovan, Farrell, Rourke,* are often found nowadays as first names, a practice that appears to have originated among Irish emigrants. This is the opposite of the practice long ago in Ireland where first names such as **Dónall, Donncha,** and **Lochlann** eventually became the surnames **Ó Dónaill** *O'Donnell*, **Mac Donncha** *McDonagh* and **Mac Lochlainn** *McLoughlin*. The trend has gone full circle.

Ceist *Question*

Do you recognise the person in the photograph? His name in Irish is Dónall Ó Dónaill.

Bran *Raven* Old Irish   **Marc** *Horse* Old Irish

3

The earliest Irish names were first names, like **Diarmuid** or **Gráinne**. In order to distinguish between people with the same name, **Mac** *son of* or **Ó** *grandson of* were placed in front. So we have the modern **Mac Diarmada** *McDermott* and **Ó Gráinne** *Greaney*. Surnames like this however were unknown in Ireland before the 10th century.

Many personal names appear to have been nicknames or descriptions originally, such as **Dubhghiolla** *dark youth*, or the modern surname *Devilly*. But if **Dubhghiolla** lived long

enough he was eventually old and grey — one good reason that names would tend to be associated in the long run with families rather than individuals. **Dubh** is common in surnames, **Dubhghall** *dark Norman* for example, giving the contemporary *Doyle, Dole, Dowal,* etc.

4

As well as being descriptors of physical characteristics, such as the colour of a person's hair, Irish personal names contained other descriptive elements. For example, people were named after animals, birds, vegetation, places or according to the job or position they held or some personal trait, such as strength or quick temper.

The following are examples of women's and men's first names. Inside the brackets you will find the words on which these names are based. Look up the bracketed words in a dictionary and place them in the appropriate category. Some words may fall into more than one category. The first word has been done for you.

Women's names:
Bláithín (bláth), **Ríona (ríon)**, **Saoirse (saoirse)**, **Gormfhlaith (gorm, flaith)**, **Róisín (rós)**, **Muireann (muir)**, **Órlaith (ór, flaith)**, **Aisling (aisling)**, **Liadán (liath)**, **Bróna (brón)**

Mens' names:
Dallán (dall), **Cúchulainn (cú)**, **Cearnach (cearn)**, **Donncha (donn)**, **Aonghus (aon/gus)**, **Cathal (cath)**, **Fionn (fionn)**, **Ardal (ard)**, **Dara (dair)**, **Rónán (rón)**

animals	
plants	**bláth** *flower*
colours	
status	
physical	
other	

5

Christianity brought the names **Íosa**, **Muire**, **Máire**, **Seosamh**, **Peadar**, **Eoin**, and many others to Ireland, including professional names like **Easpag** *bishop* and **Sagart** *priest* (Latin *episcopus, sacerdos*), and Old Testament names such as **Mícheál** and **Daithí**. They were often prefixed with **Giolla** *servant* or **Maol** *bald,* i.e. *tonsured monk.* They are found today in surnames such as *Gileese* **Giolla Íosa**, *McAleese* **Mac Giolla Íosa**, *Gillespie* **Mac Giolla Easpaig**, *McTaggart* **Mac an tSagairt** and *Mulvihill* **Maol Mhichíl** and in first names like **Maolmhuire** or **Maolmhaodhóg** (also **Malachi**).

Norse names like **Ivor**, **Olaf**, **Ranal** and **Sitric** became popular later, and are found in the modern surnames *McKeever*, *McAuliffe*, *Reynolds* **Mac Ranail** and *McGetterick* **Mac Shitric**. Then followed the Norman names, most obvious today in the *Fitz* (French *fils*, son of) at the beginning of names like *Fitzgerald* **Mac Gearailt** and *Fitzmaurice* **Mac Muiris**. Finally came the English names, now so thoroughly mixed with Irish ones that it is often difficult to tell at a glance which came first.

Strange to say, **Pádraig** became common only in the 13th century, and **Máire** and **Bríd** only in the 17th. In modern Irish **giolla** means a helper or a minder, and in one situation, namely hunting and fishing, the word is found in English in the form *gillie*. (Look it up in an English dictionary.)

Imagine you are choosing an Irish name for a baby. Pick three boys' names and three girls' names. Write them down and ask your teacher how to pronounce them, if necessary. Discuss with other students why you have chosen these names.

6

Tráth na gCeist *Question Time*
Do the quiz with a partner. Try not to look back at what you have read. Questions: Give a first name based on: **1** Colours, **2** Animals, **3** Plants. Give an Irish surname containing: **1** the word **Giolla**, **2** a Norse name, **3** a French name.

Further reading

Mac Lysaght, E. (1982) *More Irish Families,* Dublin: Irish Academic Press.

Ó Droighneáin, M. (1991) *An Sloinnteoir Gaeilge agus an tAinmneoir,* Baile Átha Cliath: Coiscéim.

Ó Corráin, D. and Maguire, F. (1990) *Irish Names.* Dublin: Lilliput Press.

Ó Cuív, B. (1986) Aspects of Irish personal names, *Celtica* 18, 151-184.

Woulfe, P. (1923) *Irish Names and Surnames,* Dublin: McGill & Sons.

 **Gramadach**
Grammar

1

Look up the dictionary to find the meaning of **dom** in the sentence

> **Donncha is ainm dom.**

You will notice that you were referred to the word **do.**

The word **dom** is made up of the preposition **do** *to/for* + the personal pronoun **mé** *me*.

So a literal translation into English would read:

> *Donncha is name to/for me.*

Look up the dictionary again and find the meaning of the word **orm** in the sentence

> **Siobhán atá orm.**

This time you were referred to the word **ar**.

The word **orm** is made up of **ar** *on* and **mé** *me*. A literal translation of **Siobhán atá orm** is *Siobhán is on me.* The combination of prepositions with personal pronouns is rare in non-Celtic languages. Hebrew is an exception.

2

Now look at the following dialogue:

> **Pádraig is ainm domsa.**
> **Treasa atá ormsa.**

The contrastive particle **sa** is added to the prepositional pronoun **dom** to indicate that Pádraig would like to know what Treasa's name is without having to ask her directly.

He could also have said

> **Pádraig atá ormsa.**

This time the contrastive particle is added to the prepositional pronoun **orm.**

3

Mise

Mise is the contrastive form of the first person pronoun **mé** *I*. When the first person pronoun occurs at the beginning of the sentence it becomes **mise**. e.g.

> **Mise Bríd.** *I'm Bríd.*

Mise is made up of **mé** and **se**. **Se** is the slender form of **sa** and is used here because **mé** ends in a slender vowel.

4

Choose a name from the following list:
Cormac Aisling Cian Órla Oisín Nuala.
Pretend this is your name. Go around the classroom introducing yourself to other students. Introduce yourself in as many different ways as you can.

7 Fuaimniú Pronunciation

I

An Aibítir *The Alphabet*

It is usual nowadays to use the letter-names of the English alphabet when spelling Irish words aloud. So **Flann**, spelt aloud would sound like *ef, el, ah, en, en*.

Through most of its history, the Irish alphabet had only eighteen letters, **a, b, c, d, e, f, g, h, i, l, m, n, o, p, r, s, t**, and **u**. But the eight remaining letters of the English alphabet, **j, k, q, v, w, x, y**, and **z**, can all be found in the modern language, often through borrowing, e.g. **jab** *job*, **vóta** *vote*, **x-ghath** *x-ray*.

The lengthening of vowels is indicated with an acute accent, **á, é, í, ó**, and **ú** pronounced **a fada** /a fada/, **e fada** /i: fadə/ etc (**fada** *long*).

Practise spelling the following names aloud: Róisín, Bláithín, Gráinne, Úna. Can you think of men's names containing **fada**?

2

Phonetic Transcriptions

Some Irish language dictionaries supply phonetic transcriptions of words to help pronunciation. Certain symbols may be new to you, particularly if English is your first language, for example /x/ for **ch** (German *lch*) and /ɣ/ for **gh** (Spanish *g* in *agua*).

The use of a tick / ′ / after certain consonants may also be new to you. The consonants of Irish come in two forms, **leathan** *broad* and **caol** *slender**. For example, the **m** in **Máire** is broad, and the **m** in **Mícheál** is slender. In phonetic script, consonants are assumed to be broad unless they have a tick, in which case they are slender. So we have /m′i:xa:l/ with a tick on the **m** for **Mícheál** and /ma:rə/, with no tick on the **m** for **Máire**.

* Broad and slender consonants are dealt with later in the course.

Dán *Poem*

Here is the first verse of a 9th century poem, given here in both Old and Modern Irish with an English translation. A professional scholar compares his own activities to those of his cat, the pursuit of learning with the pursuit of mice.

Messe ocus Pangur bán
cechtar nathar fria saindán:
bith a meanmasan fri seilgg
mu menma céim im saincheirdd.

Mise agus Pangur bán
Ag cleachtadh ár gceirde féin:
Seilg is mian leis sin de ghnáth;
M'aigne féin ar mo shaincheird.

I and white Pangur
Practise each of us his special art:
His mind is set on hunting;
My mind on my special craft.

8 Cumarsáid Communication

I

To ask someone to spell their name you can say:

Litrigh d'ainm le do thoil.
/l′it′ri: danʹəmʹ lə də holʹ/
le do thoil please

Practise saying this sentence. Ask your teacher to check your pronunciation.

2 Obair Bheirte *Pair Work*

Introduce yourself to another student. When you hear the other student's name, ask the spelling. Write down the name. Check the spelling.

9 Éisteacht Listening

I

Write down three situations where you had to spell words aloud or where you observed other people doing so.

2 Plé *Discussion*

Have a short class discussion on this topic. Can you add to the list in 9.1?

3

In this recording a father is helping his daughter Rós with her spelling homework. She has to learn how to spell the names of other pupils in her class. The father calls out different names for her to spell.

Rós has difficulty spelling one of the following names. Which name is it?

Gearóid	❏	**Pádraig**	❏
Siobhán	❏	**Íde**	❏

10 Sa Rang *In Class*

1

The following exercise will help you to recognise phrases your teacher may use to let you know you are correct or to let you know you have made a mistake.

Listen once again to the recording of Rós practising her spelling and read the tapescript as you listen.

Underline the phrases the father uses to let Rós know that she has spelt a name correctly. Write them under 'correct' in the grid below.

Then copy down the phrases the father uses to let her know that she has made a mistake.

Correct	Mistake

2

Compare your lists with others in the group.

3

The following are some of the phrases used by the father in **10**.1 above. Study these phrases carefully. Moving up the scale means you are being more positive in your feedback. Moving down the scale you are being more critical!

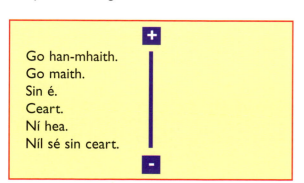

Go han-mhaith.
Go maith.
Sin é.
Ceart.
Ní hea.
Níl sé sin ceart.

4

Listen again to how the phrases in **10**.3 are pronounced. Practise saying them yourself. Think of situations where you could use these phrases. Check your ideas with your teacher or with another student.

5 Rólghlacadh *Role Play*

In this exercise you and your partner will take turns at being teacher and student. The student is trying to recall how to spell four new Irish names. The teacher's role is to ask the student to spell these words and to signal when a spelling is correct or otherwise.

Each partner writes out four to six names in Irish. Do your best to remember the spelling.

Partners work together on the pronunciation of all the names. Ask the teacher or other students to help if necessary.

Exchange lists with your partner. Take it in turns to be student and teacher. Remember to praise your student and to let her or him know when she or he has made a mistake.

Discuss why you chose the particular names you did.

11 Cultúr *Culture*

1

The Ogam Alphabet

The earliest written Irish is found carved around the edges of tall standing stones in a script called Ogam. The name is derived from Ogma, a mythological chief who is reputed to have invented the script.

Ogam, which dates from the 4th century, is a coding of the Roman alphabet. The alphabetic units are represented by notches or short straight lines, in groups of one to five, as you can see in the illustration. The groups of lines were carved in four different orientations to the edge of the stone. Ogam is read from the bottom up on the left, across the top and down the right-hand side. There were twenty characters in the early Ogam alphabet.

Ogam inscriptions are people's names in Old Irish. The writing of the Ogam name or **ainm n-ogaim** in stone was part of the funeral rite,

mainly of people of wealth and status. The Ogam name in the photograph reads **DEGO(S) MAQI MOCOI TOICAKI** (*the stone*) *of Dagis, member of the tribe of Toicacas.*

The notches at the top of the stone in the shape of an **x** stand for the letter **k**. This was an extra character used on the stones. It was used as an alternative representation of the letter **c**. Did you notice the **s** written to the right of **DEGO**? The letter had not been included on the original engraving and was put in later.

Do you know any scripts other than the Roman alphabet? If so, tell the other learners about them and give a demonstration at the board.

Can you figure out the word written on the Ogam stone?

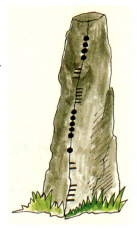

2

Aibítir na gCrann *The Tree Alphabet*

The letters of the Ogam alphabet had names. A number of them are also the names of trees. The letter **a** was called **ailm** /al'm/ *pine* and **b beithe** /b'ehə/ *birch.* So whereas the Latin script is called *The Alphabet*, after the names of the first two letters, the Ogam script was called **In Beithe-Luis** /ənb'ehlis/ since it began with the letters **b** and **l**, the latter called **luis** *rowan tree.* More information on the Tree Alphabet is contained in *Nóta 1* at the end of the unit.

3

Ogam was also written in manuscripts but was written left-to-right with the vowels appearing as vertical strokes bisected by the stemline.

b l f s n h d t c q m g ng k r a o u e i

Try writing your name and another student's name in Ogam. Skip any letters that are not in the Ogam alphabet. Compare results. Now write an Irish word in Ogam. See if other students can figure it out.

Further reading
McManus, D. (1991) *A Guide to Ogam.* Maynooth: An Sagart.

12 Staidéar Pearsanta
Personal Study

1

After class add more first names in Irish to the list you made in exercise **10.5** above.

2

Make a note of where you got these names – in newspapers, telephone directories, from people you know etc.

3

If they have equivalents in other languages (including other Celtic languages), make a note of these.

13 Stór Focal
Vocabulary

1

The words in the following list have to do with the classroom. Do you recognise any of them? Do you know what they mean? If not, can you guess their meaning?

cathaoir	peann	leabhar
foclóir	leabhar nótaí	bord

Discuss the words with another student. Check their meanings in the dictionary. Ask the teacher to help you pronounce the words. Write the words and their meanings in your notebook.

2 Éisteacht *Listening*

In the following recording a teacher points to the six items in **13.1** and asks his students what they are called in Irish. Tick the order in which you hear the items mentioned in the recording. The first one is already ticked off.

	1	2	3	4	5	6
cathaoir						
peann	✓					
leabhar						
foclóir						
leabhar nótaí						
bord						

14 Sa Rang *In Class*

1

If you want to ask what something is in Irish you can say

Cén Ghaeilge atá air seo?
Referring to something nearby

Cén Ghaeilge atá air sin?
Referring to something further away

Cén Ghaeilge atá ar *Patrick*?

You can also say

Cén focal atá air seo?
Asking what the word is for something

2

Read the tapescript of exercise **13.2** and underline any phrases you recognise from the list above. Practise saying these phrases aloud.

3

What do you think the following phrases mean in the tapescript?

Níl a fhios agam.
Tá brón orm ach níl a fhios agam.

Check with your teacher. Practise saying the phrases.

4

Listen to the following dialogues as you read the text:

Gabh mo leithscéal, cén Ghaeilge atá ar *pen?*
PEANN.

Go raibh maith agat.

Cén Ghaeilge atá ar *book?*
LEABHAR.

Cén focal atá air sin?
FUINNEOG.
Go raibh maith agat.

> To get someone's attention, you say
> **Gabh mo leithscéal.**
>
> To thank someone you say
> **Go raibh maith agat!**

Practise saying these phrases. Think of a word and ask the teacher what it is in Irish.

5 Obair Bheirte *Pair Work*

Pick out 3 items in the classroom. One student is A and the other is B. Take turns asking each other what these items are called in Irish. You may ask 3 questions and then change roles or you can change roles after each question.

A

Cén | Ghaeilge focal | atá | air ↗ seo? ↘ sin?
| | | | ar (name of object in English)?

B

Give name in Irish. **Níl a fhios agam.**

Tá brón orm ach níl a fhios agam.

A

Litrigh (name of item in Irish) **le do thoil**.

B

Make an attempt at spelling name.

A

Write down word as spelt by B. **Go raibh maith agat.**

Check the spellings in the dictionary.

15 Gramadach

Grammar

1

Note what happens to the nouns **focal**, **Gaeilge** and **ainm** after **cén**?

> **Cén focal atá air seo?**
> **Cén Ghaeilge atá air seo?**
> **Cén t-ainm atá ort?** *What's your name?*

Problems with the dictionary

In the sentences **Cén Ghaeilge atá air seo?** and **Cén t-ainm atá ort?** the letters **h** and **t-** appear in the words **Gaeilge** and **ainm.** The word **cén** is a combination of **cé** *what* and the article **an** *the* (a is dropped because of the two vowels coming together). Certain words change after **an.** As a result, if you looked up **Ghaeilge** or **t-ainm** in a dictionary you would not find them. You would have to look up the meanings under **Gaeilge** and **ainm.** Other words such as **focal** do not change after **an.** This relates to *gender* which you will be studying later. For the moment, all you need to know is that a **h** following an initial consonant and a **t-** preceding a vowel may have to be removed from a word if you wish to check it in the dictionary.

Look up examples of **an** or **cén** followed by a noun in a piece of text and show them to your teacher.

2

An tAlt *The Article*

There is only one article in Irish – the definite article. To say *That's a chair* in Irish, the indefinite article *a* is not translated. You say **Sin cathaoir** (*lit. That is chair*).

The article in the singular form is **an** e.g. **an leabhar** *the book.* In the plural form it is **na** e.g. **na leabhair** *the books.* The article is covered in more detail in later units.

16 Scileanna Foghlama *Learning Skills*

Finding the Irish word for something

1

Which of the following methods of finding the Irish for a word would you prefer to use:

> asking someone or using a dictionary?

2

Now think about both methods and write down three advantages and three disadvantages of each one.

asking someone		
	advantages	disadvantages
1		
2		
3		

dictionary		
	advantages	disadvantages
1		
2		
3		

Discuss your answers in small groups. One student should act as secretary and write down the different suggestions. The secretary then reports back to the class. Make note of any additional suggestions. See *Nóta 2* at the end of the unit for some more ideas.

Seanfhocal *Proverb*

As in other languages, Irish has many **seanfhocail** /sˈanokilʹ/ *proverbs,* literally *old words.* One that is suitable for our first unit is

> **Tús maith leath na hoibre.**

A good start is half the work.
or: *Well begun is half done.*

Do you know of any similar sayings from other cultures? Tell the group about them.

17 Stór Focal
Vocabulary

1

Work with another student to match the
following pictures to the words in the list:

1 **Éisteacht**

2 **Labhairt**

3 **Léamh**

4 **Scríobh**

5 **Gramadach**

6 **Stór Focal**

7 **Cultúr**

8 **Fuaimniú**

9 **Sa Rang**

Discuss this with other learners.

2

Which do you need most:

to be able to   (a) understand someone saying
                (b) read
                (c) say
                (d) write

the above words?

18 Foclóir Folaithe
Word Sleuth

The following sleuth contains words from the
unit. The words may go from left to right, or from
top to bottom. They may also be diagonal.

Find as many Irish words as you can and write
them in your notebook. The words are in the
Eochair at the end of the unit. You may also find
words not in the *Eochair* or the unit.

G	B	O	R	D	F	G	H	D
A	L	E	A	B	H	A	R	Ó
E	C	É	P	E	A	N	N	N
I	A	U	A	C	P	H	I	A
L	I	N	L	M	E	E	T	L
G	N	É	Í	T	H	A	I	L
E	T	P	Ó	L	Ú	I	R	G
F	O	C	L	Ó	I	R	É	T

   Eibhlín a Rún

Shiúlfainn féin i gcónaí leat, Eibhlín, a rún
Shiúlfainn féin i gcónaí leat, Eibhlín, a rún
Shiúlfainn féin i gcónaí leat,
Síos go Tír Amhlaidh leat,
Mar shúil go mbeinn i gceamhnas leat, Eibhlín, a rún.

Céad míle fáilte romhat, Eibhlín, a rún,
Céad míle fáilte romhat, Eibhlín, a rún,
Céad míle fáilte romhat,
Fáilte agus fiche romhat,
Naoi gcéad míle fáilte romhat, Eibhlín, a rún.

Eileen my Love is a love song from the 13th century.

*The translation, omitting repetitions, is: I would
walk with you always, Down to Tyrawley with you,
Hoping to be married to you, A hundred thousand
welcomes to you, One and twenty welcomes to you,
Nine hundred thousand welcomes to you.*

Achoimre *Summary*

Communication and Vocabulary

Introducing yourself	Mise Peig. Clár is ainm dom. Éanna atá orm. Dónall atá ormsa. Rós is ainm domsa. Niall atá ormsa freisin!
Spelling	Litrigh d'ainm le do thoil. pee, oh fada, el Pól.
In the classroom	Go han-mhaith! Go maith. Sin é. Ceart Ní hea. Níl sé sin ceart. cathaoir peann leabhar foclóir leabhar nótaí bord Gabh mo leithscéal. Cén Ghaeilge atá air seo? Cén focal atá ar *pen*? Níl a fhios agam. Tá brón orm ach níl a fhios agam. Go raibh maith agat.
In the textbook	Éisteacht, Léamh, Scríobh, Labhairt, Gramadach, Stór Focal, Cultúr, Fuaimniú, Sa Rang.

Grammar

- The prepositional pronoun **dom** is made up of **do** and **mé**.
- The prepositional pronoun **orm** is made up of **ar** and **mé**.
- **sa** is added to **dom** and **orm** for contrast.
- **Mise** comprises **mé + se**. **Se** is the slender form of **sa**.
- The only article in Irish is the definite article, **an** sing. **na** pl.
- The article changes the spelling of certain words which follow it e.g.

  Gaeilge, an Ghaeilge
  ainm, an t-ainm

Culture

Irish Personal Names

Recent Trends	• Irish names popular • Surnames used as first names e.g. Kelly.
History	• Only first names originally • **Mac** means *the son of* and **Ó** meant *the grandson of*. • Name often referred to some distinguishing feature e.g. **Dubhghiolla** *dark youth*. • People were also named after animals, birds, vegetation, places, rank or personal quality. • With the coming of Christianity names such as **Eoin**, **Maol Phádraig** and **Giolla Mhuire** were introduced. • Norse names such as **Ranal** were introduced in the ninth, tenth and eleventh centuries. • Examples of Norman names are **(Mac) Gearailt, (Mac) Muiris**.

The Ogam Alphabet

- Ogam is the earliest form of written Irish.
- It dates from the 4th century.
- It is a coding of the Roman alphabet and is carved in groups of straight lines around the edges of tall stones.
- Ogam inscriptions are people's names.
- A number of the letters of the Ogam alphabet are the names of trees e.g. **a = ailm** *pine*.
- The Ogam Alphabet was referred to as **In Beithe-Luis**.

Pronunciation

The most common way to pronounce the Irish alphabet is to use the English letter-names.

Learning Skills

See *Nóta 2* on page 14.

Triail Tú Féin *Test Yourself*

A

Do the following exercises with your teacher.

1

This is your first Irish class. You are getting to know another student.

1 Say your first name in Irish.
2 Ask her or him to spell her or his name.
3 Spell your name.

2

You need to know the Irish word for something.

1 Get the teacher's attention.
2 Ask the Irish for *class*.
3 Point to something at the other side of the room and ask what it is called in Irish (do not use the English name).
4 Point to something near you and ask what it is called in Irish (do not use the English name).
5 Thank the teacher.

3

Another student wants you to check her or his Irish spelling.

1 Ask her or him to spell **cathaoir**.
2 Tell her or him the spelling is incorrect.
3 She or he gets the spelling correct the second time. Praise her or him.

B

Complete the sentences.

(a) **Bríd atá (ar + mé).**
(b) **(mé + se) Aisling.**
(c) **Cén (Gaeilge) atá ar *book*?**
(d) **Cén (focal) atá air sin?**
(e) **Caoimhe atá (ar+mé+sa) freisin!**

C

Unjumble the words.

(a) **TRHAABLI** (b) **SITAHÉETC**
(c) **ÓFICOLR** (d) **IALGGEE**
(e) **ÉMLAH** (f) **EPNAN**

D

True or False?
Mark ✔ for true and ✘ for false in the boxes.

1 **Mac** means *the grandson of.* ❑

2 **Bláithín** is a woman's name and means *little flower.* ❑

3 **Rónán** is named after a tree. ❑

4 **Ranal** is a Norse name. ❑

5 Ogam is the earliest form of written Irish. ❑

6 All the letters of the Ogam alphabet were named after trees. ❑

Téipscripteanna

1.2

Mise Pádraig.
Caitlín is ainm dom.
Bríd atá ormsa.
Art atá orm.
Mise Síle.
Pól is ainm domsa.

4.1 Peadar: Dia duit, a Dheirdre.
Peadar is ainm dom.
Cáit: Mise Cáit.
Gormfhlaith: Fáilte romhat, a Dheirdre.
Gormfhlaith atá orm.
Dónall: Haigh! Dónall is ainm dom.
Treasa: Mise Treasa, an múinteoir matamaitice.
Seán: Mise Seán. Cén chaoi a bhfuil tú?

9.3 agus 10.1
Daid: Anois, a Rós, litrigh 'Gearóid' le do thoil.
Rós: G-E-A-R-Ó-I-D.
Daid: Go maith. Litrigh 'Siobhán'.
Rós: S-I-B-H-Á-N.
Daid: Níl sé sin ceart.
Rós: S-I-B-H-Á-I-N.
Daid: Ní hea. S-I -**O**-B-H-Á-N.
Rós: S-I-O-B-H-Á-N.
Daid: Sin é. Litrigh 'Pádraig'.
Rós: P-Á-D-R-A-I-G.
Daid: Ceart. Agus anois litrigh 'Íde'.
Rós: Í-D-E.
Daid: Go han-mhaith!

13.2

Múinteoir:	Cén Ghaeilge atá air seo? Is ea, a Mháire?
Máire:	Peann.
Múinteoir:	Go maith agus air seo?
Tadhg:	Leabhar nótaí.
Múinteoir:	Agus cén focal atá air sin? A Úna?
Úna:	Sin bord.
Múinteoir:	Ní hea.
Úna:	Ó, sin leabhar.
Múinteoir:	Go maith! Cén focal atá air seo?
Cáit:	Níl a fhios agam.
Múinteoir:	A Phóil?
Pól:	Seo foclóir.
Múinteoir:	Maith an fear! Cén Ghaeilge atá air sin? A Eoghain?
Eoghan:	Tá brón orm ach níl a fhios agam.
Múinteoir:	A Bhrídín?
Brídín:	Cathaoir.
Múinteoir:	Go han-mhaith!

Nóta 1

The following are the letters, their modern Irish names and English translations as found in *An Foclóir Gaeilge-Béarla* by Niall Ó Dónaill, first published in 1977/78. Those followed by a 'D' are found in Dinneen's dictionary (1927). Some letters appear in their Old Irish form only.

b	beith	*birch*
l	luis	*rowan*
f/v	fearn	*alder*
s	sail	*willow/sallow*
n	nion	*ash*
h	uath	*whitethorn*
d	dair	*oak*
t	teithne (D)	*furze (D)*
c	coll	*hazel*
q	(Old Irish = cert)	
m	muin	*vine*
g	gort	*ivy*
ng	(Old Irish = ngetal)	
z	(Old Irish = straif)	
r	ruis	*elder*
p	peith	*dwarf elder*
a	ailm	*pine*
o	oir (D)	*broom (D)*
u	ur (D)	*heath (D)*
e	eabhadh	*aspen*
i	íodha (D)	*ivy (D)*

The idea of the tree alphabet was the subject of great theorising and debate. It was supposed to show the unity of nature and literature in the Celtic mind. The arborealists, as they were called, including the poet Robert Graves, were criticised by the scholars of Old Irish, and the debate is very amusing to read. But in the end the tree-people had a victory of sorts, because the new names did catch on.

Further reading
Graves, R. (1961) *The White Goddess*, London: Faber and Faber.

Nóta 2

Scileanna Foghlama *Learning Skills*

Finding the Irish word for something

asking someone	
advantages	disadvantages
1 immediate feedback, does not interrupt the 'flow' of discourse	1 laziness, makes learner 'passive'
2 can *hear* pronunciation	2 could be confusing if you hear another pronunciation
3 word explained in *context*	3 what if no one is available, over-dependency

dictionary	
advantages	disadvantages
1 more *active*, more effort needed on part of learner, better chance learner will remember word	1 time-consuming
2 can *see* word written down – helps recall	2 pronunciation not always given or, if it is, student must be familiar with IPA symbols
3 learner likely to *write* word down – helps recall	3 more than one meaning given – difficulty knowing the correct meaning in the context
4 learner more independent, can carry dictionary around always	4 does not encourage interaction with others which is important for language learning

1.1 Pól *Paul*, Bríd *Breege/Bridget*, Pádraig *Patrick*,
Art *Art*, Síle *Shelagh/Sheila*, Caitlín *Kathleen*

5.1

(a) Ronan Keating (b) Siobhán McKenna
(c) Nuala Ní Dhomhnaill (d) Éamonn de Valera
(e) Liam Neeson (f) Sinéad O'Connor

5.4

animals	cú *hound* rón *seal*
plants	bláth *flower* rós *rose* dair *oak*
colours	gorm *blue* ór *gold* donn *brown* liath *grey* fionn *fair*
status	ríon *queen/noble lady* flaith *ruler* ard *noble*
physical	ard *tall* dall *blind* gus *vigour*
other	brón *sorrow* saoirse *freedom* aisling *vision* cath *battle* cearn *corner/angle* muir *sea* aon *one*

9.3 Siobhán

10.1

Correct	Mistake
Go maith.	Níl sé sin ceart.
Sin é.	Ní hea.
Ceart.	
Go han-mhaith.	

17.1

A8 B6 C1 D9 E3 F2 G7 H4 I5

18

leabhar, léamh, bord, cultúr, ceart, Dónall, Peig,
Pól, Gaeilge, peann, foclóir

Triail Tú Féin *Test yourself*

B
(a) orm (b) mise (c) Ghaeilge (d) focal
(e) ormsa

C
(a) labhairt (b) éisteacht (c) foclóir
(d) Gaeilge (e) léamh (f) peann

D
1✗ 2✔ 3✗ 4✔ 5✔ 6✗

2 Beannachtaí *Greetings*

This unit enables learners to: greet and say goodbye; describe the weather; ask where certain exercises are in the textbook.

Do you know any greetings in Irish?
Do you know any words in Irish to describe the weather?

1 Éisteacht agus Léamh

I

Listen to the dialogues and match them to the silhouettes.

A   B   C

D   E   F

I
A Chiaráin!
A Aoife!
Cén chaoi a
  bhfuil tú?
Go maith agus
  tú féin?
Go han-mhaith!

2
Dia duit.
Dia is Muire duit.
Mise Gearóid.
Mise Sorcha.

3
Dia daoibh
  ar maidin.
Dia is Muire duit,
  a Áine.
Osclaígí bhur
  leabhair
  leathanach a cúig.

4
Oíche mhaith,
  a stóirín.
Oíche mhaith,
  a Dhaidí.

5
A seacht, a cúig,
  a naoi, a dó, a
  náid, a trí.
A Eibhlín? Daithí
  anseo.
Conas tá tú,
  a Dhaithí?
Tá mé go maith, go
  raibh maith agat.

6
Caithfidh mé
  brostú. Slán
  agaibh!
Slán leat, a Nollaig.
Go n-éirí an bóthar
  leat!

2

If you are greeting one person, would you say:

Dia daoibh
    or
Dia duit?

Which is the most positive reply to the question **Conas tá tú?**

Go han-mhaith
    or
Ceart go leor?

Which phrase would you be likely to use when saying 'goodnight' to someone:

Slán leat
    or
Oíche mhaith?

2 Cumarsáid

I

To greet someone in Irish you can say
    Dia duit.
    /d'iə dit'/
The response is
    Dia is Muire duit.
    /d'iə is mir'ə dit'/
The plural forms are
    Dia daoibh.
    /d'iə di:v'/
    Dia is Muire daoibh.
    /d'iə is mir'ə di:v/
The **d** in **duit** and **daoibh** is often pronounced as if it were followed by a **h**.
    Dia dhuit, dhaoibh.
    /d'iə ɣit',   ɣi:v'/
    Dia is Muire dhuit, dhaoibh.
    /d'iə is mir'ə ɣit',   ɣi:v'/

2

The question that often comes next, *How are you?* has regional forms

    Cad é mar tá tú? Ulster
    Cén chaoi a bhfuil tú? Connaught
    Conas tá tú? Munster

Listen in the recording, and select one for your own use. The teacher will be able to advise you.

The reply to *How are you?* does not depend on the form used. It could be

    Go han-mhaith.
    Go maith.
    Ceart go leor.

You can add **Go raibh maith agat** *thank you* if you wish.

You can also put the phrase **Tá mé** /ta: me:/ *I am* before the replies.

	go han-mhaith.
Tá mé*	go maith.
	ceart go leor.

* Note the position of the personal pronoun **mé**.

Practise saying these phrases. Have a conversation with another student using **tá mé** + one of the three phrases in your reply.

3 📼

Jane and Oisín meet in the street. The conversation is cut short, however, as Jane's bus arrives. Listen to their conversation and read the text at the same time.

Jane:	**Dia duit, a Oisín.**
Oisín:	**Dia is Muire duit, Jane!**
Jane:	**Conas tá tú?**
Oisín:	**Tá mé go han-mhaith agus tú féin?**
Jane:	**Go maith. Ó tá an bus ag teacht. Caithfidh mé imeacht. Slán agat.**
Oisín:	**Slán leat.**

Working with another student, answer the questions:

(i) Oisín tells Jane how he is keeping and he then asks Jane the same question. What phrase does he use to ask this question?

(ii) To say *Goodbye* you can just say **Slán**, or **Slán agat** or **Slán leat**. Jane says **Slán agat** and and Oisín says **Slán leat**. Is there a reason?

Check your answers in the *Eochair*.

3 Labhairt

1

Walk around the class and greet other students. Try to vary the phrases you use.

Student A	Student B
Dia duit.	
	Dia is Muire duit.
Conas tá tú? Cad é mar tá tú? Cén chaoi a bhfuil tú?	
	Go han-mhaith Go maith Ceart go leor → go raibh maith agat.
	Agus tú féin?
Go han-mhaith. Go maith. Ceart go leor.	
Slán leat. To someone who is leaving you. Slán agat. To someone you are leaving behind. Slán.	

2

The teacher in the photograph is about to say something. Write what you think this is in the bubble. Tell another student what you have written.

4 Cultúr

5 Cumarsáid

Beannachtaí

There are many blessings in Irish. The way people greet one another is a good example. **Dia duit** means *God be with you*. The response to **Dia duit**, namely **Dia is Muire duit**, means *God and Mary be with you*. The way people thank is another example. **Go raibh maith agat** means *May you prosper*.

Another common expression in the form of a blessing is **Dia leat,** which can mean *Well done* or *Bravo*. It is often said in encouragement to singers and musicians. It means *Good luck* when said to somebody who is leaving. **Dia linn,** or alternatively, **Dia linn is Muire** is used when somebody sneezes, similar to *Bless you* in English.

Irish contained far more blessings in the past, many of them for special occasions and mishaps. Collections can be found in bookshops.

1 Obair Ghrúpa *Group Work*

Think of blessings in other languages and translate them into English. Describe situations in which they are used.

2 Staidéar Pearsanta

Why not research some popular **beannachtaí** in Irish, for example, what is said when a child is born or when a couple get married. If you are studying in an Irish-speaking area, some of the old people might be able to help you. You could also try **an tIdirlíon** *the Internet*. Start your search with the word **beannachtaí**. Report back to the class on your findings.

Greeting more than one person

1

Note how the speakers greet and say goodbye in the recording.

Caithfidh mé brostú. Slán agaibh.

Slán libh. Bain taitneamh as an turas.

Slán agat, a stór.

Check *Téipscripteanna* for the full conversations.

2

Complete the sentences:

(i) To greet more than one person you say
Dia _____.

(ii) To ask more than one person how they are keeping you say

Conas tá ———
Cén chaoi a bhfuil ———→ _____?
Cad é mar tá ———→

(iii) To say goodbye to more than one person when they are leaving you, you say
Slán _____.

(iv) To say goodbye to more than one person when you are leaving them, you say
Slán _____.

Compare answers with another student. Check the answers in the *Eochair*.

 **Gramadach**

1 Súil Siar *Revision*

Underline the personal pronoun in the following sentence:

Tá mé go maith.

Complete the sentences.

(i) The prepositional pronoun **dom** is made up of the preposition _____ and the personal pronoun _____.

(ii) The prepositional pronoun **orm** is made up of the preposition _____ and the personal pronoun _____.

2

Can you identify the personal pronouns in each of the following sentences?

Conas tá tú?
Cén chaoi a bhfuil sibh?

Check your answers in the *Eochair*.

3

Prepositions	Personal Pronouns	Prepositional Pronouns
do (to)	**tú** *you* sing.	**duit**
do	**sibh** *you* pl.	**daoibh**
le (with)	**tú**	**leat**
le	**sibh**	**libh**
ag (at)	**tú**	**agat**
ag	**sibh**	**agaibh**

4

Write out as many sentences as you can containing one of the following words, for example:

Karen is ainm dom.

7 Staidéar Pearsanta

After class listen out for the different ways people greet each other and say goodbye. Write the different expressions in your notebook.

For example, if you are staying in the Gaeltacht greet people on the road and make a note of their reply. Note how the **Bean an Tí** (female host) or the **Fear an Tí** (male host) greets you and says goodbye or goodnight to you.

If you are staying ouside the Gaeltacht in Ireland, listen to radio and TV presenters. Ask someone to help you write the expressions down.

If you are studying Irish outside Ireland, you may be able to make contact with someone who knows Irish, perhaps using e-mail where you could exchange some friendly greetings in Irish.

Here is a suggestion as to how you could keep a record of your research.

suíomh *situation*	beannacht
Bean an Tí – first thing in the morning	Dia duit ar maidin.

8 Gramadach

1

In the following exercise you will hear four conversations between guests at a wedding. Write down the names of the people who are talking in each conversation. The following is a list of the names. Ask your teacher to help you with the pronunciation of the names before you do the exercise.

Barra, Eibhlín, Criostóir, Deirdre, Fearghal, Gearóid, Máirín, Pádraig, Síle, Tríona

	daoine *people*
1	
2	
3	
4	

Check your answers in *Téipscripteanna*.

2

Read the tapescript again. Do you notice any difference between the way the names are spelt in the conversations and in the list in **8.1**?

Now listen to the recording again. Do you notice any difference between the way the names are pronounced in the recording and the way your teacher pronounced them for you at the beginning of the exercise?

Discuss your observations with another student.

3

An Tuiseal Gairmeach
The Vocative Case

In exercise **8.2** you will probably have noticed that names beginning with a consonant, such as **Barra** or **Deirdre**, become **a Bharra** and **a Dheirdre** when the people in question are being addressed. Adding **h** to the initial consonant is called **séimhiú** /s'e:v'u:/ *lenition* (**séimh** soft, smooth, Latin *lenis*). Lenition is required in this instance because the name is in the **Tuiseal Gairmeach** *Vocative Case*. The Vocative Case is indicated by the use of the vocative particle **a**.

> **A Ghearóid, litrigh 'peann' le do thoil.**
> **Conas tá tú, a Phádraig?**

It also requires that final broad consonants be made slender in the case of male names

> **Seán, a Sheáin**
> **Mícheál, a Mhíchíl**

With names beginning in a vowel, such as **Eibhlín**, the vocative particle **a** cannot usually be heard in normal speech.

This rule does not apply to names that are not in the Irish language e.g.

Conas tá tú Simone?

Write a note to another student asking them how they are. Use the Vocative Case.

When you receive a note from another student, write back saying how you are. Use the Vocative Case.

9 Fuaimniú

1

Séimhiú *Lenition*

Séimhiú or lenition is a distinctive feature of Irish and the other Celtic languages. It occurs not merely in the Vocative Case but also in a lot of other grammatical situations – after certain prepositions and particles, in verbs in the past tense, and so on. As the examples in **8.1** and **2** indicate, the sound of the consonant is changed by lenition:

		Change
A Bharra /ə var ə/		b→v
A Shíle /ə h'i:l'ə/		s'→h'
A Ghearóid /ə ɣaro:d'/		g'→ɣ'

For the moment it is sufficient to be aware of the existence of **séimhiú**. The situations in which it occurs will become clearer as we go on. Look through the full list of changes, given below, and note the basis for the impressionistic idea that the consonants become 'smoother' or 'softer' as a result of **séimhiú**. Note that a séimhiú on **f** deletes it e.g. **A Fhearghail** /ə arɣil'/.

b→v	k→x	d→ɣ
f→( )	g→ɣ	p→f
s→h	t→h	m→v

There is no **séimhiú** on **h, l, n**, and **r**, or on **sc, sm, sp**, and **st**.

2

1 Look at the list of names and ask your teacher to help you to say them.

Bairbre	**Páidín**	**Caitlín**
Daithí	**Fionnuala**	**Nollaig**
Róisín	**Máirtín**	**Tomáisín**
Sorcha	**Gormfhlaith**	**Diarmuid**

2 One student calls out a name, and another addresses the person.

> **Bairbre**
> **A Bhairbre**

3 Obair Bhaile

Séimhiú is always written as the letter **h** added to the first consonant of the word. Look down through a piece of written Irish and note all the words starting **bh, ch, dh**, etc.

10 Cultúr

Mallachtaí *Curses*

Curses, like blessings, were common in Irish long ago. These were prayers or at least wishes that somebody would come to harm. Some curses took the form of actions, such as placing bad eggs or dead animals on somebody's land. Spoken curses like

Mallacht Dé ort! *God's curse on you!*
Mo mhallacht ort! *My curse on you!*
Mo sheacht mallacht ort! *My seven curses on you!*

were very serious matters. They were used to express the most extreme forms of hostility between people. Curses delivered by certain people, such as saints or widows were particularly feared. In the story **Buile Shuibhne** *The Madness of Sweeney* from the 11th century, Sweeney is cursed by Saint Rónán for killing a monk. He goes mad and spends the rest of his life living in trees. Eventually he is murdered in St Mullin's in Co. Carlow.

The curses that survive in today's Irish are less dramatic, mere expressions of annoyance, no stronger than *Damn* or *To Hell with it* in English. Many of them feature **An Diabhal** *The Devil.*

Don diabhal leis! *The Devil take him!*
Bíodh an diabhal acu! *Let the Devil take them!*

Older curses survive in poems and songs. In the song *Bean Pháidín* a woman who is in love with a married man, Páidín, is so in envy of his wife that she wishes her legs were broken!

Obair Ghrúpa *Group Work*

Make a list of curses. If they are in other languages, translate them to English.

Discuss to what extent these curses resemble or differ from one another.

If you know another story with a curse as a theme, like the story of *Buile Shuibhne,* relate it to the group.

Elect a representative to report back to the whole class on what you discussed.

Bean Pháidín

Curfá:
Is é an trua ghéar nach mise, nach mise,
Is é an trua ghéar nach mise bean Pháidín;
Is é an trua ghéar nach mise, nach mise,
Is an bhean atá aige a bheith caillte.

Is do chuaigh mise siar chun an Chlocháin,
Is thart timpeall le Béal Átha na Báighe;
Is do bhreathnaigh mé isteach tríd na fuinneogaí,
Féachaint an bhfeicfinn bean Pháidín.

Is do chuaigh mise siar Tóin an Ruisín,
Is tháinig mé aniar Barr an tSáilín;
Isteach tigh Mhaitiais Uí Chathasaigh,
Féachaint an bhfeicfinn bean Pháidín.

Is do rachainn go Gaillimh, go Gaillimh,
Agus rachainn go Gaillimh, le Páidín;
Ó rachainn go Gaillimh, go Gaillimh,
Agus thiocfainn abhaile sa mbád leis.

Go mbristear do chosa, do chosa,
Go mbristear do chosa, a bhean Pháidín;
Go mbristear do chosa, do chosa,
Go mbristear do chosa is do chnámha.

Páidín's Wife

It's a pity that I am not the wife of Páidín and the wife that he has isn't dead.
I went over to An Clochán, and around by Béal Átha na Báighe,
I looked in through the windows in the hope of seeing Páidín's wife.
I went over to Tóin an Ruisín, and back by Barr an tSáilín, and went into Maitias Ó Cathasaigh's pub, in the hope of seeing Páidín's wife.
I'd go to Galway with Páidín and come home on the boat with him.
May your legs be broken, wife of Páidín, and your bones.

Sa Rang

1

Counting is very important inside and outside the classroom.

(a)

Gaeilge agus Fáilte

In the following recording the teacher is counting a consignment of textbooks which has just arrived. While he is counting, he is interrupted by a visit from the Director. Write down the last number he says before he was interrupted.

Check your answer in the tapescript. Do you know the next number?

(b)

When the Director leaves he starts counting again. How many books are there altogether? Check your answer in *Téipscripteanna*.

(c)

Listen to the recording again. Put an X beside the words which are *not* beside the correct number.

1	a haon
2	a dó
3	a trí
4	a ceathair
5	a cúig
6	a sé
7	a naoi
8	a hocht
9	a seacht
10	a deich
11	a haon déag
12	a dó dhéag

Check your answer in the *Eochair*.

Did you notice the difference in the pronunciation of **a haon déag** and **a dó dhéag**? **A dó dhéag** is an exception because of the *séimhiú*. From 13-19 **déag** is used again.

(d)

Now write out the next numbers in the series.

13	
14	
15	
16	
17	
18	
19	

Check your answer in the *Eochair*.

(e)

Go to page 1 of your textbook **(leathanach a haon)**. Say the page number out loud. Then turn to page 2 and do the same. Continue this way until you reach page 19, saying the numbers out loud.

2 Stór Focal

Aonad /eːnəd/	**Leathanach** /lʼahənəx/
Mír /mʼiːrʼ/	**Uimhir** /ivʼə rʼ/

Find the exercise the teacher is directing you to in the textbook. Part of the information is filled in for you.

Aonad	Mír	Uimhir
	8	

Check answer in *Téipscripteanna*.
Can you say the page number in Irish?

3

(a) Cén Ghaeilge atá ar *What page please?*

To ask politely what page an exercise is on you can say

Cén leathanach, le do thoil?

To ask what unit, section and number

Cén	**t-aonad**	**le do thoil?**
	mhír	
	uimhir	

(b)

Underline the examples of *séimhiú* in the information box above.

(c)

If you need the teacher to repeat what she or he has just said, you can say

Cén	**leathanach**	
	t-aonad	**a dúirt tú?**
	mhír	/ə duːrtʲ tuː/
	uimhir	

Practise saying these phrases. Ask your teacher to check your pronunciation.

4 Obair Bheirte *Pair Work*

Foghlaimeoir *Learner A*
Pick out an exercise in Aonad I but do not tell your partner which one it is.

Foghlaimeoir *Learner B*
Find out which exercise your partner has chosen by asking for the page and section numbers. Pretend you don't understand.

Change roles and continue as before.

Seanfhocal *Proverb*

Ní hé lá na gaoithe lá na scolb.

The windy day is not the day for scollops*.
*scollop = looped stick for securing thatch

What does this proverb mean? When would you use it?
Do you know of similar proverbs in other languages?
Discuss with other students.

12 Stór Focal

An Aimsir *The Weather*

+30°C	an-te
+20°C	te
+15°C	fionnuar
+ 5° C	fuar
+ 0° C	an-fhuar

I

With reference to the scale above, how would you describe the weather where you are today? Complete the sentences using one of the words or phrases from the information box.

Tá sé _____.

You may not agree with the scale. **Te** *hot* for one person may be **fionnuar** *cool* for another, and **fuar** *cold* for one may be **an-fhuar** *very cold* for another. Write your own scale of temperatures and explain it to others.

2 Éisteacht, Léamh agus Fuaimniú

(a)

Listen to the recordings and complete the dialogues using words from the information box above.

(i) Dia duit, a Aisling.
Dia is Muire duit, a Rónáin.
Tá sé _____ inniu.
Tá, cinnte.

(ii) Cén chaoi a bhfuil tú, a Chormaic?
Ceart go leor.
Tá sé _____ amuigh.

(iii) A Áine, conas tá tú?
Go maith agus tú féin?
A thiarcais, tá sé _____ inniu!
Ó, tá sé _____ ar fad!

(iv) Cad é mar tá tú, a Dheirdre?
Go maith. Tá sé _____.
Tá, go bhfóire Dia orainn!

Check answers in *Eochair*.

(b)

Listen to the recordings again, concentrating on the words you just inserted into the dialogues. Repeat these words until you feel you can pronounce them properly.

3 Find these words in your dictionary.

| tirim | fliuch | scamallach | gaofar |

Match the words with the pictures.

(i) _____

(ii) _____

(iii) _____

(iv) _____

4(a)

Listen to the weather forecast. One of the following words has been repeated. Which one?

focail *words*	I	2
gaofar		
tirim		
fliuch		
scamallach		

Check your answers in *Téipscripteanna*.

(b)

Listen to the recordings again. Concentrate on the four words in 4(a). Repeat them until you feel you can pronounce them properly.

5   Scríobh agus léamh

Write a sentence in the speech bubbles describing what each of the women in the photograph might be thinking. Show it to another student.

---

13 Cumarsáid

I

Talking about the weather is a natural part of the greeting process in Irish. To make a comment about the weather you can use the phrase **tá sé** *it is* and add on a weather word or phrase e.g.

Tá sé	**fuar.**
/ta: s'e:/	**te.**
	scamallach.

A suitable reply to such a comment is

Tá or **Cinnte** Definitely or **Tá, cinnte!**

If you wish to make your comment more elaborate you can add words or phrases

Tá sé	**fuar**	**amuigh** *outside*
	te	**inniu** *today*
		nach bhfuil?
		isn't it?

or

| **A thiarcais** | **tá sé** | **fuar!** |
| *My goodness* | | **te!** |

2   Obair Bheirte *Pair Work*

Write the following words on separate pieces of paper (or cards):

fuar, te, an-fhuar, an-te, fionnuar, gaofar, scamallach, fliuch, tirim.

Mix them up and turn them upside down on the table.

Take it in turns to pick up a piece of paper or a card and make a comment on the weather using the phrases in **13.**1. The other student should react appropriately.

3

(a)

Other useful expression are	
Tá an aimsir	**go han-mhaith.**
/ən am's'ər'/	**go maith.**
The weather is	**ceart go leor.**
	go dona *bad.*

Practise saying these sentences. Ask your teacher to check you pronunciation.

(b) Scríobh

The following is a postcard Isolde wrote to her friend Cormac while she was on holiday in Leitir Móir. She has made some spelling mistakes.

Underline the mistakes. Discuss the spellings with your teacher. Re-write the card correctly.

A Cormaic,
Dia is Mura dit. Cén chaoi a bhfuil tu? Tá mise go maith. Tá an aimsir cart go leor.
Slán,
Isolde

Cormac Ó Riada
6 Bóthar na Saile
Baile Mór
Co. Lú

Why do you think **mise** is used instead of **mé**?

 14 Gramadach

1

> ### Bí *Be*
>
> **Bí** is a very useful verb in Irish. You have already used different forms of this verb, for example **tá** and **bhfuil**
>
> **Tá mé go maith**
> **Cén chaoi a bhfuil tú?**
>
> | **Tá mé** | *I am* |
> | **Tá tú** | *you are* (singular) |
> | **Tá sí** /s'i:/ | *she/it is* |
> | **Tá sé** | *he/it is* |
> | **Táimid** /ta:m'i:d'/ | *we are* |
> | **Tá sibh** | *you are* (plural) |
> | **Tá siad** /s'iəd/ | *they are* |

2 Obair Bheirte *Pair Work*

It is a good idea to try to memorise verbs in Irish. Learning by rote may seem old-fashioned but it is a useful learning strategy here. To make the task more exciting, why not work with another student as follows:

Foghlaimeoir A says **tá mé**. *Foghlaimeoir B* says **tá tú**. *Foghlaimeoir A* says **tá sí** and so on. Next time round, *Foghlaimeoir B* starts.

15 Scileanna Foghlama

1 Why learn Irish?

People learn languages for many different reasons, for example, to be able to go on holidays in a country where the language is spoken. But you don't need Irish to holiday in Ireland. So why learn it? Discuss your reasons for learning Irish with other students.

2 Are motives important?

Do you think it is important to know why you are learning a language? Discuss this question with other students.

3 Where can I practise my Irish?

For many Irish people, school provided the only environment in which they could use Irish in a natural way. But there are also many opportunities in everyday life to practise the four language skills of Irish – listening, speaking, reading and writing. Make a list of them, one for each skill, and compare your lists with those produced by other learners.

Scil *Skill*	**Deis** *Opportunity*
Éisteacht	
Labhairt	
Léamh	
Scríobh	

Dán

Séasúir

Bailc shamhraidh sna cnoic –
i dtitim throm thréan na fearthainne
cloisim míle bó bainne á mblí.

I mbáine an gheimhridh sna cnoic
bíonn na bunsoip trom le sioc –
as a gcuid siní sileann tost.

Cathal Ó Searcaigh

Seasons

A heavy summer shower in the hills –
In the teeming downpour,
I hear a thousand cows being milked.

In the winter whiteness of the hills
thatch-eaves are heavy with frost –
from their teats, silence drips.

Translation by Gabriel Fitzmaurice

16 Stór Focal

1

The following is a list of terms which are used frequently throughout the textbook. Match the Irish terms with their equivalents in English.

A	**Súil Siar**	1	Group Work
B	**Foghlaimeoir**	2	Pair Work
C	**Obair Bheirte**	3	Revision
D	**Obair Ghrúpa**	4	Learner/Student

A _____ B _____ C _____ D _____

Look back through the unit to check your answers.

2 Obair Bheirte

Write the Irish terms in **16.1** on separate pieces of paper or cards.

> **Foghlaimeoir A**
> Show the papers/cards one at a time to your partner.

> **Foghlaimeoir B**
> Say the word or phrase in English.

Reverse roles.

17 Dréimire Focal

Word Ladder

Fill in the Irish words on the ladder. The first one is done for you.

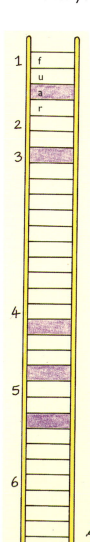

1	Cold
2	Hot
3	Cloudy
4	Dry
5	Wet
6	Very cold

What word can you make from the letters in the coloured spaces on the ladder?

Achoimre *Summary*

Cumarsáid agus Stór Focal

Greeting

Dia duit, daoibh.
Dia is Muire duit, daoibh.
Dia duit, a Phádraig.
Conas tá tú, sibh?
Cén chaoi a bhfuil tú, sibh?
Cad é mar tá tú, sibh?

Go han-mhaith.
(Tá mé) Go maith   go raibh
                 maith agat.
        Ceart go leor.

Agus tú féin?

Leave-taking

Slán (leat, libh, agat, agaibh).
Oíche mhaith.

Commenting
on the
weather

Tá sé   te
           fionnuar   amuigh
           fuar   inniu
           an-te   nach bhfuil?
           an-fhuar
           scamallach
           gaofar
           fliuch
           tirim

Tá an aimsir   go han-mhaith.
                 go maith.
                 ceart go leor.
                 go dona.

A thiarcais, tá sé (fuar)!

Tá/cinnte.

Sa rang

Cén | leathanach
      t-aonad   a dúirt tú?
      mhír
      uimhir

(mír) a haon, a dó...... a naoi déag

Sa téacsleabhar

Súil Siar
Foghlaimeoir
Obair Bheirte
Obair Ghrúpa

Cultúr

Beannachtaí	• The word **beannacht** means blessing.
	• Blessings are used to wish someone well, to greet, thank, praise, encourage, congratulate, show sympathy etc.
Mallachtaí	• The word **mallacht** means a curse.
	• **Mallachtaí** feature strongly in old literature, such as the famous curse put on *Mad Sweeney*.

Fuaimniú

- In **An Tuiseal Gairmeach** the **a** is not usually pronounced before a vowel
  (a) Áine
- A **h** following a consonant is called **séimhiú** *lenition*.
- Consonants become 'smoother' or 'softer' as a result of *séimhiú*.

Scileanna Foghlama

- Why learn Irish?
- Where can I practise Irish?

Gramadach

- do + tú → duit   do + sibh → daoibh
- le + tú → leat   le + sibh → libh
- ag + tú → agat   ag + sibh → agaibh
- A noun is in **An Tuiseal Gairmeach** *The Vocative Case* when it is used to name the person addressed e.g. **Dia duit, a Mháire**
- An Briathar **bí**, *present tense, affirmative*.

Triail Tú Féin *Test Yourself*

A Do the following exercises with your teacher.

1 As you are coming in to class you meet your friend Pádraig.
   1 Greet him by name.
   2 Ask him how he is.
   3 Say goodbye (you leave him talking to his friends).

2 You meet your friend Órla at the bus stop. It is late at night.

   Órla: Dia duit a (d'ainm *your name*).
   Tusa *you*: *Respond.*
   Órla: Conas tá tú?
   Tusa: *Tell her you are very well. Ask her how she is keeping.*
   Órla: Tá sé an-fhuar.
   Tusa: *Agree with her.*
   Órla: Tá an bus ag teacht! Slán agat.
   Tusa: *Say goodnight. Address her by name.*

3 You meet a group of friends in a pub.
   1 Greet them.
   2 Ask them if they would agree that it is very hot.

4 You are not sure about the teacher's instructions.
   1 Ask the teacher what page did she or he call out.
   2 Now ask what section.
   3 Thank the teacher.

B The solutions to the following exercises are in the *Eochair*.

1 Complete the sentences.
   (a) Dia _____. Cén chaoi a bhfuil sibh?
   (b) Conas tá t_____, a Ghearóid?
   (c) Tá _____ scamallach inniu, nach bhfuil?
   (d) Go raibh maith _____, a Bhríd.
   (e) Slán _____ a Chormaic. (Cormac is leaving)

2 Remove the brackets and write correct form.
   (a) Cad é mar tá tú, a (Criostóir)?
   (b) Cén (aonad) a dúirt tú?
   (c) Cén (mír) a dúirt tú?
   (d) Dia (do+tú).

3 Complete the series.

Tá mé, Tá ___, Tá sí, Tá ___, Táimid,
Tá _____, Tá siad.

C Fill in the missing vowels (both long and short).
   (a) f-ghla-meoir   (c) s-il s-ar
   (b) obair ghrúp-   (d) ob-ir bh-irte

D Match the **beannacht** with the occasion.

Beannacht	Ócáid
1 Sláinte!	A When someone has died
2 Dia linn!	B When someone is wearing something new
3 Slán leat.	C When you are having a drink together
4 Beannacht Dé lena anam.	D To say goodbye
5 Go maire is go gcaithe tú é.	E When someone sneezes

1 _____ 2 _____ 3 _____ 4 _____ 5 _____.

1.1 A(6) B(4) C(5) D(2) E(3) F(1)

1.2 Dia duit.
Go han-mhaith.
Oíche mhaith.

2.3 (i) agus tú féin?
(ii) If you are leaving you say **slán agat** to the person who is left.
You say **slán leat** to someone who is leaving you.

5.2 (i) daoibh (ii) sibh (iii) libh
(iv) agaibh

6.1 (i) do, mé (ii) ar, mé

6.2 tú sibh

11.1 (c) 9 = a naoi 7 = a seacht

11.1 (d)

13	a trí déag
14	a ceathair déag
15	a cúig déag
16	a sé déag
17	a seacht déag
18	a hocht déag
19	a naoi déag

12.2(a) (i) te (ii) fionnuar (iii) fuar, an-fhuar
(iv) an-te

12.3 (i) fliuch (ii) scamallach (iii) gaofar (iv) tirim

17 Dréimire Focal

2 Te
3 Scamallach
4 Tirim
5 Fliuch
6 An-fhuar

The word made from the letters in the coloured spaces is **aimsir**.

Triail Tú Féin *Test Yourself*

B

1 (a) duit (b) tú (c) sé (d) agat (e) leat

2 (a) Cad é mar tá tú, a Chriostóir?
(b) Cén t-aonad a dúirt tú?
(c) Cén mhír a dúirt tú?
(d) Dia duit.

3 tú sé sibh

C

(a) o, i (b) a (c) ú, i (d) a, e

D

1C 2E 3D 4A 5B

3 Cárb as tú?
Where are you from?

This unit enables learners to: say where they are from originally and where they are living at present; follow textbook instructions.

Ath-	a ford
Ard-	a height
Balli-	a homestead (from 'baile')
	a ford (from 'béal átha')
Barr-	top
Ben-	a mountain
Bun-	bottom
Caher-	a fortified homestead
Cloghan-	a hamlet
Clon-	a meadow
Derry-	a grove
Drum-	a ridge
Dun-	a homestead, fort
Glen-	a valley
Gort-	a tilled field
Ilaun-	an island
Inish-	an island
Kil-	a church, cell
Knock-	a hill
Liss-	a homestead
Lough-	a lake
Maghera-	a plain
Moy-	a plain
Rath-	a homestead
Rinn-	a point of land
Ross-	a peninsula
Shan-	old
Slieve-	a mountain
Tubber-	a well
Tully-	a hill
-ban	white
-beg	small
-boy	yellow
-derg	red
-duff	black
-een	small
-fad(da)	long
-finn	light-coloured
-more	big
-roe	red
-trasna	across

Do you know any placenames in Ireland which contain the above words?

1 Stór Focal

Names of countries

1 🔊

The group of people in the picture below have just arrived off the ferry to attend an Irish language course on Inis Mór, the largest of the Aran islands. The course director (**An Stiúrthóir**), Póilín is there to meet them.

Léigh an comhrá agus éist leis an téip. Read the dialogue and listen to the recording.

Póilín: Dia daoibh. Mise Póilín, stiúrthóir an chúrsa. Fáilte romhaibh go hInis Mór. Anois, na hainmneacha. Cén t-ainm atá ortsa?

David: Mise David. As Meiriceá mé.

Póilín: Agus cad is ainm duitse?

Ingrid: Ingrid is ainm domsa. As an tSualainn mé.
          (Póilín checks all the names)

Póilín: Ceart go leor. Ar aghaidh linn go dtí an mionbhus.

You probably have guessed that **Meiriceá** means America. Not all Irish words for countries resemble the English forms as in the word *Meiriceá*. **An tSualainn** is a good example of this. At the back of some dictionaries you will find a list of geographical names. Look up the meaning of **an tSualainn** and write it in your notebook. Work in pairs.

2

The following is a list of places. Match the Irish and the English versions.

1	Éire	A	Canada
2	Sasana	B	Spain
3	An Spáinn	C	Scotland
4	An tSeapáin	D	Ireland
5	An Astráil	E	England
6	An Bhriotáin	F	Japan
7	Albain	G	Australia
8	Ceanada	H	Brittany

1 _____ 2 _____ 3 _____ 4 _____

5 _____ 6 _____ 7 _____ 8 _____

Cuir ceist ar an múinteoir conas na focail a rá. Ask the teacher how to say the words.

3 🔊

The following people are introducing themselves to the class:

**Muireann   Anna   Patricia
Yoshiko   Carlos   Morgan**

Can you guess which of the countries already mentioned they come from? Éist leis an téip. Fill in the gaps below.

Ainm: **Anna**   Ainm: _____
Tír: _____   Tír: **An Astráil**

Ainm: _____   Ainm: _____
Tír: _____   Tír: _____

Ainm: _____   Ainm: _____
Tír: _____   Tír: _____

Seiceáil na freagraí sna *Téipscripteanna*.

2 **Cumarsáid**

I

Féach ar an téipscript. Underline the sentences in which the people describe where they are from. Éist leis an téip.

> Someone who is from Australia can say
> **As an Astráil mé.**
>
> If you are also from Australia you can reply
> **As an Astráil mise freisin!**

2 Obair Ghrúpa

Write the Irish names of some countries on separate pieces of paper. You can use the list below, or a list from a dictionary. Check the meanings and pronunciations with your teacher.

> **An Fhrainc An Iodáil**
> **An Spáinn An Rúis An Ghearmáin**
> **An Bheilg An Nua-Shéalainn**
> **An Danmhairg An India**
> **An Phortaingéil An Pholainn**
> **An Ostair An Ungáir An tSín**

Pick a piece of paper and imagine you are from the country named. Introduce yourself to the others, telling them your name and where you are from. If you do not understand what someone is saying, you can use the following phrases:

> **Gabh mo leithscéal.** *Excuse me.*
> **Cén áit?** *Where?*
> **Cén tír?** *What country?*   **a dúirt tú?**
> **Litrigh (é) sin le do thoil.** *Spell that please.*

Fill in where other people are from on the chart.

Foghlaimeoir	Áit *Place*
Leif	An tSualainn

 ### Seanfhocal *Proverb*

Níl aon tinteán mar do thinteán féin.

There is no hearth like your own hearth.
There's no place like home.

Do you agree with this sentiment?
Do you know of any similar proverbs in other languages?
Tell other students about them.

3 **Cultúr**

Obair Bheirte

Look at the three tasks below and read the relevant paragraphs (1-8) in *Recording Irish Placenames* on the next page. Carry out the tasks. When you have finished, read over the whole text together to check that everything is correct.

(i)

Foghlaimeoir A	**Foghlaimeoir B**
Tell your partner about the recording of the oldest placenames in Ireland (*paragraph 1*).	Tell your partner about the *Dinnseanchas* (ask your teacher to pronounce the word for you) (*paragraph 2*).

(ii)

Tell your partner about the developments in Irish placenaming in 1824, in 1905 and in 1946 (*3, 4, 5*).	Tell your partner about the difference between the roles of the Coimisiún Logainmneacha and *The Placenames Branch* (*6*).

(iii)

Give examples of the work being done at the moment by the *Placenames Branch* in Ireland (*7*).	Describe the international dimension of An Coimisiún Logainmneacha (*8*).

Recording Irish Placenames

1 The oldest placenames in Ireland were recorded about 1,900 years ago by Greek geographers and are preserved in the Geography of Ptolemy of Alexandria, who wrote an account of the whole known world. Examples of names recorded by Ptolemy are *Buvinda* (*Bóinn Boyne*) and *Senos* (*Sionainn Shannon*).

2 From the 7th century onwards, the Irish began to record their own placenames. One of the largest collection of placenames is to be found in the *Dinnseanchas* or *History of Places* which is preserved in a 13th century manuscript in the Bodleian Library at Oxford. The *Dinnseanchas* is a collection of legends in prose and verse, explaining the names of famous places, rivers, lakes or hills.

3 The 1824 British Ordnance Survey of Ireland tried to establish appropriate English spellings for Irish placenames.

4 In 1905 *Post-Sheanchas* by Seosamh Laoide, published by the Gaelic League, provided Irish translations for the names of post-offices. Certain local authorities started to change the official English names of their areas to Irish and as a result names such as Dún Laoghaire and Port Laoise came into general use in English although they were not given official recognition until the new independent state was established.

5 In 1946 a Placenames Officer was appointed by the Ordnance Survey and later An Coimisiún Logainmneacha *The Placenames Commission* was set up to research the correct Irish forms of the names of the post offices. Definitive lists were published in 1969.

6 The role of An Coimisiún Logainmneacha is primarily to advise the State on the subject of placenames. The actual work of researching and deciding suitable name-forms in Irish is done by the professional staff of the *Placenames Branch* of the Ordnance Survey.

7 Examples of the work being done by *The Placenames Branch* are: providing the correct Irish form for placenames mentioned in official publications; giving information on the names of the places of origin of ancestors of important foreign people; answering queries about suitable names for new housing estates. The main work of the *Placenames Branch*, however, is to research the names of the administrative units and physical features as part of the mapping programme of the Ordnance Survey.

8 An Coimisiún Logainmneacha is the *National Names Authority* representing Ireland at the United Nations conferences on the standardisation of geographical names. Ireland is also part of the *Celtic Division* which was established within the framework of the United Nations Group of Experts on Geographical Names.

Main information source: Ó Maolfabhail, A. (1992) 'The Background and Present Role of the Placenames Branch of the Ordnance Survey' in Ó Maolfabhail, A. (ed.) *The Placenames of Ireland in the Third Millennium*, An Coimisiún Logainmneacha.

Dán

The Fianna were the legendary warriors of Ireland, led by Fionn Mac Cumhaill. A large collection of stories and poems about them, referred to as **Fiannaíocht**, survived to modern times. The following verses are from a 16th century poem, showing the usual love of nature and attachment to place, and mixed feelings about Christianity. What do you think of the remark, in the last line, about the church bell?

Lon Doire an Chairn

Binn sin, a loin Doire an Chairn!
Ní chuala mé in aird sa bhith
ceol ba bhinne ná do ghuth
agus tú fá bhun do nid.

Doire an Chairn an choill úd thiar
mar a ndéindís an Fhiann fos
ar áille is ar chaoimhe a crann
is ea do cuireadh ann an lon.

An tráth do mhair Fionn is an Fhiann
dob ansa leo sliabh ná cill
ba bhinn leo-san fuighle lon,
gotha na gclog leo níor bhinn.

Prose translation: *That was sweet, Blackbird of Derrycarn! I never heard anywhere on earth music sweeter than your voice, and you perched beneath your nest. Derrycarn is that wood to the west where the Fianna used to rest, on account of the beauty and gentleness of the trees, the blackbird was placed there. When Fionn and the Fianna were alive they preferred mountain to church, the singing of the blackbirds was sweet to them, the ringing of bells to them was not sweet.*

4 Stór Focal

1 Súil Siar *Numbers 1-9*

Éist leis an téip. After each country is named say the matching country dialling code. You will then hear the code repeated correctly for you.

Tír		Cód Tíre *Country Code*
An Bhrasaíl		55
An Danmhairg		45
An Fhrainc		33
An Fhionlainn		358
An Ghearmáin		49
An Ungáir		36
An India		91
Lucsamburg		352
Monacó		377
An Phortaingéil		351

2

Éist agus léigh. Listen and read.

An Rómáin		40

Did you hear the word for zero (0)? Say the country codes in **4.**1 again but this time place the access code 00 before the country code, for example, **a náid, a náid, a cúig, a cúig** for Brazil. If you like, you can work with another student saying every second code.

3 Obair Ghrúpa

One student starts by calling out any country dialling code from the right-hand column (Deir tú). The next student finds the same code in the left-hand column (Cloiseann tú) and then calls the code next to it in the right-hand column. For example, if the first student calls out 505, the correct response from the next student is 240. Continue like this around the group.

Cloiseann tú	Deir tú
670	680
227	505
250	1809
20	670
505	240
1809	507
680	508
508	250
507	227
240	20

4 Staidéar Pearsanta

Find out the Irish names for 5 countries. Check their country dialling codes in the telephone directory. Ask the teacher to help you pronounce the country names. Say the names and the codes in Irish for the group.

5 Cumarsáid

I

Listen to Séamas and Linda as you read the text. They have met for the first time.

Séamas:	Dia duit, mise Séamas.
Linda:	Linda is ainm domsa.
Séamas:	Cárb as tú, a Linda?
Linda:	As Meiriceá mé. Agus cárb as tú féin?
Séamas:	Baile Bhuirne, ach tá mé i mo chónaí i Nua-Eabhrac.
Linda:	Ó tá mise i mo chónaí i Nua-Eabhrac freisin!
	(The drinks arrive).
Séamas:	*(to the barman)* Go raibh maith agat. *(To Linda)* Sláinte!
Linda:	Sláinte!

How did Séamas ask Linda where she was from? How did Linda and Séamas say where they were from? Compare answers with another student. Check with the teacher.

2

To ask where a person is from you can say
Cárb as tú? /ka:rb as tu:/

To answer this question you can just simply say the name of the place
Baile Bhuirne.
or you can say
As Baile Bhuirne mé.
I'm from Ballyvourney.

When someone has asked you where you are from and you want to ask the same question, you can say
Agus cárb as tú féin? /tu: f'e:n'/
And where are you from yourself?

NB. To say you are from Ireland *Éire* you have to change the spelling after the preposition.
As Éirinn mé.

Rólghlacadh

Work with another student. One of you is Séamas and the other is Linda. Practise the sentences in the information box in 2. Role-play the dialogue. Reverse roles.

3

You may not, of course, actually be living in the place you are from originally. Séamas, for example, is not living in Baile Bhuirne at the moment. He is living in Nua-Eabhrac. That is why he says

ach tá mé i mo chónaí i Nua-Eabhrac*
/ax ta: m'e: i mə xo:ni:/

***Eabhrac** (with no *séimhiú* on the c) comes from the Latin for York, **Eboracum**, which is related to **ebor** *yew tree* in Old Irish.

Now practise the whole conversation between Séamas and Linda with another student.

4

If you want to ask where a person is living you can say

Cá bhfuil tú i do chónaí?
/ka: wil' tu: i də xo:ni:/

(a)

Éist leis an gcomhrá. Listen to the dialogue.

Máirín:	Cá bhuil tú i do chónaí anois?
Cathal:	Cill Dara, agus tú féin?
Máirín:	Béal Feirste.

(b) Obair Bheirte

Now talk to your partner about where you are living. Ask your teacher to help you to pronounce the name of the place. Take it in turns to start the conversation.

6 Cultúr

1

Meanings of Irish Placenames

Most placenames in Ireland are to be seen on signposts in both Irish and English. Comparing the two forms can be very useful for learners of Irish. Note that two or three separate Irish words are often run together in the English form, *Glendalough* for **Gleann Dá Loch** *Glen of Two Lakes*, *Kilbeg* for **Cill Bheag** *Small Church*, *Brideswell* for **Tobar Bríde** *Well of Bridget*, and so on. The English forms often contain words that seem to be English but turn out to be Irish. *Donnybrook* does not contain the English word *brook*. It is **Domhnach Broc** *Church of St. Broc*. Sometimes the Irish and English forms are unrelated e.g. **Cill Mhantáin** *Church of Mantán* is the Irish name for *Wicklow*.

The following are examples of words which commonly appear in Irish placenames:

Áth /a:/ *ford*		Áth na Long *Annalong*
Béal /b'e:l/ *mouth*		Béal Feirste *Belfast*
Baile /bal'ə/ *town*		Baile Átha Cliath *Dublin*
Carraig /karəg'/ *rock*		Carraig Airt *Carrickart*
Ceann /k'an/ *head*		Ceann Trá *Ventry*
Cill /k'il'/ *church*		Cill Dara *Kildare*
Cnoc /knok/ *hill*		An Cnoc *Knock*
Cluain /kluən'/ *meadow*		Cluain Meala *Clonmel*
Dún /du:n/ *fort*		An Dún *Down*
Gleann /g'lan/ *glen, valley*		Gleann Dá Loch *Glendalough*
Gort /gort/ *field*		An Gort *Gort*
Inis /in'əs'/ *island*		Inis Oírr *Inisheer*
Lios /l'is/ *ring-fort*		Lios Mór *Lismore*
Loch /lox/ *lake*		Loch Rí *Lough Ree*
Muileann /mil'ən/ *mill*		An Muileann gCearr *Mullingar*
Port /port/ *harbour*		Port an Dúnáin *Portadown*
Ráth /ra:/ *fort*		Ráth Garbh *Rathgar*
Teach /t'ax/ *house*		Teach Munna *Taghmon*

Can you think of other placenames you have come across in Ireland which contain these words? Tell the group about them.

2

Work with another student to complete the signposts with the placenames in the boxes below. The first one is done for you.

Dún Chaoin
Áth Dara
Port an tSalainn
Cill Iníon Léinín
Ráth Eanaigh

Summerhill
Belleek
Ballina
Glencolumbkille
Lisduff

Baile Bhuirne
Ballyvourney

An Lios Dubh

Adare

Gleann Cholm Cille

Raheny

Cnoc an tSamhraidh

Portsalon

Béal an Átha

Dunquin

Béal Leice

Killiney

3 Staidéar Pearsanta

Make a list of Irish placenames (in English) that have some personal interest for you. For example, you might choose the town you are from originally or a place where you spent a nice holiday. You might also choose a place because you like the sound of the name.

Find out the Irish forms, from signposts, by asking people, or with the help of your dictionary. See how many everyday Irish words you can find in them, words such as **baile**, **cill**, **dún**, **cnoc**, **coill**, **mór**, **beag**, **ard** and so on. Two useful and inexpensive books are **Gasaitéar na hÉireann** *Gazetteer of Ireland* and **Eolaí an Phoist** *Post Office Guide*.

Gramadach

I

Read the conversations.

Fiontán:	Cárb as tú, a Chaoimhe?
Caoimhe:	As an nGeata Bán mé. Agus cárb as tú féin?
Fiontán:	As an bPort Rua mé.
Marianne:	As an mBaile Mór mé. Agus tú féin?
Liam:	As an bhFéar Bán mise.
Móna:	Cárb as tú féin, a Risteaird?
Risteard:	As an gClochán mé.

Caoimhe is from **An Geata Bán**. Do you notice the difference between how the placename is spelt here and how it is spelt in the dialogue?

Discuss with another student.

Now write where Fiontán, Marianne, Liam and Risteard are from.

Seiceáil na freagraí san *Eochair*.

2

Urú *Eclipsis*

The small letter inserted before the placename e.g. the **n** in **as an nGeata Bán** *from Whitegate* and the **b** in **as an bPort Rua** *from Portroe*, is another initial mutation in Irish. This is known as **urú** or eclipsis. (*Séimhiú* is the other initial mutation). The *urú* eclipses the initial consonant of the word, so when Marianne says she is **as an mBaile Mór** *from Ballymore*, we no longer hear the initial **B** of **Baile** but only the *urú* **m**, exactly as if the word were **Maile** rather than **Baile**.

Seven initial consonants, **b**, **c**, **d**, **f**, **g**, **p** and **t** can be eclipsed. When eclipsed they become **mb**, **gc**, **nd**, **bhf**, **ng**, **bp** and **dt**. Eclipsis occurs in the case of the placenames above because they followed a preposition plus the article, **as an** *from the*. But there are other situations in which *urú* occurs.

Words that normally have a *séimhiú* lose it when eclipsed e.g. **an Cheathrú Rua** *Carraroe* but **as an gCeathrú Rua** *from Carraroe*.

3 Obair Bheirte

Take it in turns to say you are from the following places:

- An Cnoc
- An Gort
- An Bun Beag
- An Pháirc
- An Fhiacail

Ask the teacher to check your pronunciation.

4 Staidéar Pearsanta

Find a piece of Irish text, a page of a newspaper for example, and mark each *séimhiú* and *urú*. Can you see any patterns, or guess at some situations in which they are found? Which is more common, *séimhiú* or *urú*?

5 Labhairt

Write down where you come from in Irish. Ask the teacher to check your answer.

As _____ mé.

Now have similar conversations to those in **7.**1 with other students.

Cill Liadáin

2

Fágaim le huacht é go n-éiríonn mo chroíse,
Mar ardaíos an ghaoth nó mar scaipeas an ceo,
Tráth a smaoiním ar **Cheara** nó ar **Ghaileang**
    taobh thíos de,
Ar Sceathach an Mhíle is ar Phlánaí Mhaigh Eo.
Cill Liadáin an baile a bhfásann gach ní ann,
Tá sméara is sú craobh ann is meas ar gach sórt,
Is dá mbeinnse i mo sheasamh ann i gceartlár mo
    dhaoine
D'imeodh an aois díom is bheinn arís óg.

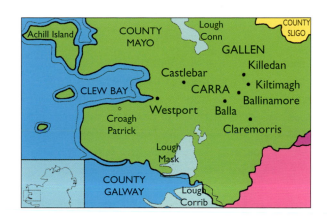

The poet Raftery (Antaine Ó Raiftearaí, 1779-1835) describes his birthplace in County Mayo. He was blind and earned his living writing poetry, singing and playing the fiddle and composing poetry about life in that part of the country.

Only the first two verses of the poem are presented here. Springtime is approaching and Raftery is preparing to take to the roads again. He is planning to visit his native Mayo or Maigh Eo and lists all the places he hopes to visit, the highpoint being Cill Liadáin. The places he will visit are written in bold in the poem.

After you have listened to the recording see if you can trace the route he plans to take on the map.

I

Anois teacht an earraigh beidh an lá dul chun
    síneadh,
Is tar éis na Féile Bríde ardóidh mé mo sheol,
Is ó chuir mé i mo cheann é ní chónoidh mé
    choíche
Go seasfaidh mé thíos i lár Chontae Mhaigh Eo;
I g**Clár Chlainne Mhuiris** a bheas mé an chéad
    oíche,
Is i **mBalla** taobh thíos de is ea thosós mé ag ól
Go **Coillte Mach** rachad go ndéanfad cuairt
    mhíosa ann
I bhfogas dhá mhíle do **Bhéal an Átha Móir.**

8 Gramadach

I

Léigh na comhráite agus éist leis an téip.

Jeaic:	Cá bhfuil tú i do chónaí?
Nóra:	Maigh Eo. Agus tú féin?
Jeaic:	Tá mé i mo chónaí i Sasana.
Liadán:	Cá bhfuil tú i do chónaí, a Chonáin?
Conán:	Baile Átha Cliath. Agus tú féin?
Liadán:	Tá mise i mo chónaí i mBaile Átha Cliath freisin!
Aodán:	Dia duit, a Aisling! Cén chaoi a bhfuil tú?
Aisling:	Go maith. Cá bhfuil tú i do chónaí anois?
Aodán:	In Albain.
Labhrás:	Tá mise i mo chónaí sa Spáinn.
Mícheál:	Tá mise i mo chónaí san Astráil agus san Fhionlainn.
Seosamh:	Tá mé i mo chónaí sa Phortaingéil. Agus tusa?
Patsey:	Ceanada.

Where are the people living? The first one is done for you.

Jeaic	An Spáinn
Nóra	Ceanada
Liadán	An Astráil
Conán	Baile Átha Cliath
Aodán	Maigh Eo
Labhrás	Sasana
Mícheál	An Phortaingéil
Seosamh	Albain
Patsey	An Fhionlainn

2

I *In*

The preposition *in* in English is **i** in Irish. In the conversations you've just heard, when people are saying where they live, you will notice that **i** takes different forms depending on what comes next, e.g.

i Sasana   **in Albain**
sa Phortaingéil   **san Astráil**

Look at the conversations in **8.**1 again. Can you guess at the reason for the four different forms of **i**? Note that two of them take a *séimhiú* and one takes an *urú*.

Rules

1   **i + an = sa** + lenition and
         san before a vowel or f
  an Bheilg, sa Bheilg *in Belgium*
  an Ísiltír, san Ísiltír *in the Netherlands*
  an Fhionlainn, san Fhionlainn *in Finland*

  i + na = sna
  na Cealla Beaga, sna Cealla Beaga
                     in Killybegs
  na Déise, sna Déise *in the Decies*

2   **i** without **an = i** + eclipsis or
             in before a vowel
  Béal Feirste, i mBéal Feirste *in Belfast*
  Corcaigh, i gCorcaigh *in Cork*
  Ard Mhacha, in Ard Mhacha *in Armagh*

Obair Bheirte

Déan abairtí. Make sentences.

Acaill, Airt, Carraig, Na Stáit Aontaithe,
An Fhaiche, An Éigipt, An Bhruiséil

	i
	in
Tá mé i mo chónaí	sa
	san
	sna

3

Complete the grid with more placenames of your choice.

i	in	sa	san	sna

Compare your placenames with another student.

 **9** **Fuaimniú**

I

Urú

Letter	Urú	Fuaimniú Nua *New Sound*
p	bp	b
t	dt	d
c	gc	g
b	mb	m
d	nd	n
g	ng	ng
f	bhf	v

(a)

Éist leis an téip agus léigh an téacs.

Páras	Tá mé i mo chónaí i **bP**áras.
Tamhlacht	Tá mé i mo chónaí i **dT**amhlacht.
Conamara	Tá mé i mo chónaí i **gC**onamara.
Bearna	Tá mé i mo chónaí i **mB**earna.
Doire	Tá mé i mo chónaí i **nD**oire.
Guaire	Tá mé i mo chónaí i **nG**uaire.
Fionntrá	Tá mé i mo chónaí i **bhF**ionntrá.

(b)

Éist leis an téip agus léigh **9**.1(a) arís. Repeat each sentence after you have heard it.

(c) Labhairt

Foghlaimeoir A: Páras
Foghlaimeoir B: Tá mé i mo chónaí i bPáras.

Continue like this until all the places have been said. Reverse roles.

2

Éist leis an téip. Number the placenames in the order you hear them. The first one is done for you.

Fear Manach ____   Casla ____

Gaoth Dobhair ____   Baile na hAbhann 1____

Teamhair_____   Dún Chaoin _____

Port Láirge _____   Fánaid _____

10 Scileanna Foghlama

1

What does 'knowing' a word mean to you? Does it mean being able to

– pronounce the word
– recall the word without having to check in the dictionary or ask someone
– spell or write the word
– know the grammar of the word, for example when you have to use *urú* or *séimhiú*?

Do you have any other ideas?

Productive vs Receptive Vocabulary

If we need to *recognise* a word, for example when someone is talking to us or when we are reading, we say it is a *receptive* item of vocabulary.

If we need to *use* a word for either speaking or writing, we say it is a *productive* item of vocabulary. Learning a word in order to be able to use it is different to learning it to be able to recognise it.

It is important to make this distinction when studying vocabulary.

2

Make two lists of words you plan to learn – one for production and the other for reception.

Productive	Receptive

11 Gramadach

1

Níl *Is not*

Níl, the negative form of **tá** *is*, has already been encountered in **Níl a fhios agam** *I don't know*, or word by word, *is-not its knowledge at-me.* Here are the forms **níl** takes in conjunction with the different personal pronouns.

Níl mé /nʹiːlʹ mʹeː/	*I am not*
Níl tú	*you are not* (singular)
Níl sí	*she, it is not*
Níl sé	*he, it is not*
Nílimid /nʹiːlʹəmidʹ/	*we are not*
Níl sibh	*you are not* (plural)
Níl siad	*they are not*

Foghlaim an briathar. Learn the verb as you did in Unit 2, **14**.2. Ask another student to 'test' you.

You have just asked this man where the bread is – **cá bhfuil an t-arán?** Write his reply in the bubble. Compare with others in the group.

2 Obair Bheirte

Foghlaimeoir A

Think of a positive thing about yourself or the weather today. Tell your partner about it.

Foghlaimeoir B

Think of a negative thing about yourself or the weather today. Tell your partner about it.

Samplaí:

Tá mé go maith inniu.
Níl sé fliuch inniu.

Reverse roles.

12 Stór Focal

I(a)

The following are places you might live in.
Meaitseáil na pictiúir leis na focail.

 A
 B
 C

 D
 E
 F

1 tuath _____
2 sráidbhaile _____
3 árasán _____
4 cathair _____
5 teach _____
6 baile mór _____

Check your answers with other learners, and in the dictionary if necessary.

(b) Obair Ghrúpa

In the following recording a number of people are describing where they live. Divide into groups of three. Each person takes responsibility for listening out for two words from 1(a) (be sure that each person has a different pair of words). As you listen note how many times you hear your words mentioned.

Compare your answers with other groups. Seiceáil na freagraí sna *Téipscripteanna*.

2 Labhairt

Now tell other students where you are living.

Sampla:

Tá mé i mo chónaí in árasán i Nua-Eabhrac.

3 Cultúr

Tuath agus Cúige

Tuath *Countryside*, **Cúige** *Province*

The word **tuath** *countryside* originally meant a group of people, such as **Tuath Dé** *God's People* (the Jews) or **Tuath Dé Danann** *People of the Goddess Danu*. But it came to mean territory also. The **Rí Tuaithe** was the local king (**rí** *king*), and the **tuath** his territory.

The *tuath* was about the size of a modern county. Larger than the *tuath* was the **cúige** *province* ruled by the **Rí Cúige** *Provincial King*. The **Ardrí** *High King* ruled all of Ireland. The *cúigí* eventually became the four modern provinces, **Cúige Uladh** *Ulster*, **Cúige Laighean** *Leinster*, **Cúige Chonnacht** *Connaught* and **Cúige Mumhan** *Munster*. But the word **cúige** actually means one-fifth, from **cúig** *five*, because originally there were five provinces. The lost province is **An Mhí** *Meath*, now part of Leinster.

13 Sa Rang

I Súil Siar

In Aonad 2 you learnt how to count up to 19. In this unit we reviewed numbers 1–9. You were also introduced to the word for zero. Can you remember it? Count out the pages of your textbook up to page 19, a haon, a dó etc.

2(a)

Éist leis an téip. A student is counting the pages of his textbook just like you were. He is continuing on from where you left off. Turn the pages with him and look at the page numbers.

What page does he stop at?

(b) Scríobh

Scríobh an focal ar 20. Write the word for 20.

(c) Fuaimniú

Listen to the recording again. Do you notice any difference between the way **fiche a haon, fiche a dó, fiche a trí** etc are written and the way they are pronounced?

You will probably have noticed that this speaker does not pronounce the **a**. You may find that this makes it easier to say the number.

Now count out loud from **fiche** to **fiche a naoi**.

3(a)

Listen to the recording as the same student continues counting the pages of his textbook. Turn the pages as before. What page does he stop at now?

(b)

Éist leis an téip arís. Say the numbers along with the student.

(c) Scríobh

Scríobh an focal ar 30.

4 Stór Focal

40 – 100
The same pattern is followed when you count from 40 to 100. All you need to know are the Irish words for 40, 50, 60, 70, 80, 90 and 100. Here they are:
daichead /dax'əd/ **caoga** /ki:gə/ **seasca** /s'askə/ **seachtó**/s'axto:/ **ochtó** /oxto:/ **nócha** /no:xə/ **céad** /k'e:d/

5 Obair Bheirte

Take turns opening the textbook at different pages (up to 100). Say the page number out loud.

Biongó

Fill in the numbers of your choice on the bingo card (Cárta Biongó), numbers from 1 to 20 in the first column, numbers from 21 to 40 in the second column, and so on, as shown. The teacher will then call out numbers from 1 to 100 at random, ticking them off from a 10 X 10 number square which you cannot see. As soon as one of your numbers is called out, mark the square on your bingo card. The first person to get five winning numbers in a row, horizontally, vertically or diagonally, calls out **Biongó!**

Cárta Biongó

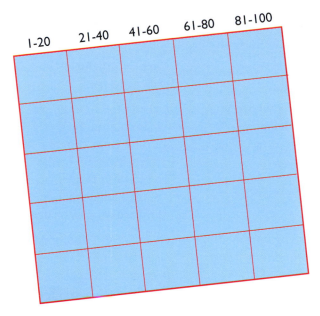

14 Sa Rang

Some of the instructions so far have been given bilingually. In the following units these instructions will be given in Irish only. This exercise will help you to check your understanding of the instructions in Irish you have met so far.

1

Meaitseáil na habairtí. Match the sentences.

Léigh an comhrá.	Ask the teacher.
Éist leis an téip.	Make sentences.
Meaitseáil na habairtí.	Read the conversation.
Seiceáil na freagraí.	Learn the verb.
Cuir ceist ar an múinteoir.	Check the answers.
Féach ar an téipscript.	Write the word.
Déan abairtí.	Look at the tapescript.
Foghlaim an briathar.	Listen to the recording.
Scríobh an focal.	Match the sentences.

2

Write instructions which you would be likely to find in a textbook like this.

Léigh	ar an téipscript
	an téip
Éist	an focal
	leis an téip
Scríobh	ar an bpictiúr
	an comhrá
Féach	leis an gcomhrá

Achoimre *Summary*

Cumarsáid agus Stór Focal

Saying where you are from	As (Éirinn) mé.
Asking where someone is from	Cárb as tú? (Agus) cárb as tú féin?
Saying where you are living	(ach) tá mé i mo chónaí i (Sasana) (anois). Tá mise i mo chónaí i (Nua-Eabhrac) freisin. Tá mé i mo chónaí faoin tuath, i sráidbhaile, i mbaile mór, sa chathair.
Asking where someone is living	Cá bhfuil tú i do chónaí? Agus tú féin? (response to question)
Sa rang	Numbers 0, 20 – 100
Sa téacsleabhar	Léigh an comhrá. Éist leis an téip. Meaitseáil na habairtí. Seiceáil an freagra. Cuir ceist ar an múinteoir. Féach ar an téipscript. Freagair na ceisteanna. Déan abairtí. Foghlaim an briathar. Scríobh an focal.

Gramadach

- **Urú** or eclipsis occurs on seven initial consonants

    b, c, d, f, g, p, t.

- After *urú* they become

    mb, gc, nd, bhf, ng, bp, dt.

- **i** + *urú*, or **in** before a vowel, **i mBaile Átha Cliath, in Albain**

- **i** + **an** = **sa** + *séimhiú*, or **san** before a vowel or f, **sa Phortaingéil, san Astráil, san Fhionlainn**

- **i** + **na** = **sna**, **sna Cealla Beaga**

- **níl mé** *I am not*, **níl tú** *you are not*, etc.

Cultúr

Recording Irish Placenames

- The oldest Irish placenames were recorded by Ptolemy 1,900 years ago.
- From the 7th century on the Irish began to record their own placenames – one of the largest collections is in the *Dinnseanchas*.
- 1824 British Ordnance Survey tried to provide English spellings for Irish placenames.
- 1905 *Post-Sheanchas* was published to provide Irish-language forms of the names of the post-offices.
- 1946 An Coimisiún Logainmneacha *The Placenames Commission* was set up.
- The actual work of researching and deciding name-forms in Irish is done by the *Placenames Branch* of the Ordnance Survey.
- An Coimisiún Logainmneacha is the *National Names Authority* representing Ireland at the United Nations conferences on the standardisation of geographical names.

Meanings of Irish Placenames

- Many placenames consist of two or three words e.g. **Cill Dara** *Church of the Oak*.
- Examples of words which appear frequently in Irish placenames are: **Áth** *ford*, **Béal** *mouth*, **Baile** *town*, **Dún** *fort*, **Gleann** *valley*, **Loch** *lake*, **Port** *harbour*.

Tuath and Cúige

- The **rí tuaithe** ruled over the **tuath**, both people and territory.
- The word **cúige** means a fifth and refers to the five provinces which used to be in Ireland. Nowadays there are only four provinces but the word **cúige** is still used: **Cúige Uladh, Cúige Laighean, Cúige Chonnacht, Cúige Mumhan.**

Fuaimniú

An tUrú

- **bp** has the sound **b** e.g. **i bPáras**
- **dt** has the sound **d** e.g. **i dTamhlacht**
- **gc** has the sound **g** e.g. **i gConamara**
- **mb** has the sound **m** e.g. **i mBearna**
- **nd** has the sound **n** e.g. **i nDoire**
- **ng** has the sound **ng** e.g. **i nGuaire**
- **bhf** has the sound **v** e.g. **i bhFionntrá**

Silent **a** in numbers e.g.

fiche a haon, fiche a dó.

Scileanna Foghlama

Learning Vocabulary

- **Knowing** a word can have many different aspects.
- **Productive** vocabulary is for speaking and writing.
- **Receptive** vocabulary is for listening and reading.

Triail Tú Fein

Déan na cleachtaí seo a leanas leis an múinteoir.
Do the following exercises with the teacher.

1 Get to know your teacher. Scríobh na freagraí.

   Ask her or him where she or he is from originally.
   Ask her or him to spell the name of the place.
   Ask her or him where she or he is living now.

2 You meet Mícheál in a pub. Complete the conversation.

Mícheál:	As an Longfort mé. Cárb as tú féin?
Tusa:	*You are from Longford also but you are living in Cork now.*
Mícheál:	Cén áit?
Tusa:	*In the city.*
Mícheál:	Cá bhfuil tú ag foghlaim na Gaeilge?
Tusa:	*You are studying Irish in Gaoth Dobhair, in Donegal (Dún na nGall).*

3 Your teacher will call out page numbers up to page 100. See how quickly you can find them.

Mark true (✔) or false (✗).

(i)   Féach ar an téipscript. *Listen to the tape.*
(ii) Scríobh an focal. *Write the answer.*
(iii) Freagair na ceisteanna. *Answer the questions.*
(iv) Déan abairtí. *Make sentences.*
(v)   Léigh an comhrá. *Listen to the conversation.*

Remove the brackets. Scríobh na habairtí i gceart *correctly.*

1 (i)   As an (Bóthar Buí) mé.
   (ii) Tá mé i mo chónaí i (Cill Rónáin).
   (iii) As (Iorras) mé.
   (iv) Tá mé ag staidéar i (Árainn).
   (v)   Tá Máire ag obair i (An Pholainn).
   (vi) Tá Gearóid ag obair i (An Abhainn Mhór).

2 Complete the series.
Níl mé, _____ tú, Níl _____, _____ sé, _____,
Níl _____, _____ _____.

D

Correct the mistakes (underlined) on the postcard.

A Chaoimhe, a chara,

Beannachtaí ón Spáin. Níl an aimsir go maith ach tá na daoine go deas! Tá mé ag obair sa chatair ach tá mé i mu chónaí faon tuath.
    Slán go fóill,
    Pádraig

Caoimhe Ní Bheoláin
Bóthar na Trá
Dún Garbhán
Éire

E

Líon na bearnaí sna habairtí. Complete the sentences.

(a)
1 The oldest Irish placenames were recorded by _____ 1,900 years ago.
2 The _____ is a collection of legends in prose and verse, explaining the names of famous rivers, lakes and hills.
3 In 1946 _____ was set up to research the correct Irish forms of the names of _____.
4 The actual work of researching and deciding name-forms today is done by the *Placenames Branch* of the _____.
5 _____ Mhantáin is the Irish for Wicklow.
6 The rí tuaithe ruled over the _____.
7 Nowadays there are only four provinces: Cúige Uladh, Cúige L_____, Cúige Chonnacht, Cúige _____.

(b)
Match the parts to make well-known Irish placenames.

Baile	Dá Loch
Béal	na nGall
Port	Chainnigh
Dún	Feirste
Gleann	Átha Cliath
Cill	Láirge

1.3 & 2.1

Anna:	Anna atá ormsa. As an tSualainn mé.
Patricia:	Dia is Muire daoibh. Mise Patricia. As an Astráil mé.
Yoshiko:	Yoshiko is ainm dom. As an tSeapáin mé.
Muireann:	Dia daoibh. Muireann is ainm dom. As Éirinn mé.
Carlos:	Is mise Carlos. As an Spáinn mé.
Morgan:	Dia daoibh. Morgan atá ormsa. As Sasana mé.

9.2

1 Tá TG4 suite i mBaile na hAbhann.
2 Tá mise i mo chónaí i bhFear Manach.
3 Bhí mé ar saoire i nGaoth Dobhair.
4 Do bhíos-sa lá i bPort Láirge (*amhrán*).
5 Las Naomh Pádraig tine i dTeamhair.
6 Ba mhaith liom a bheith i bhFánaid anois!
7 Tá Raidio na Gaeltachta suite i gCasla.
8 Bhí Peig Sayers ina cónaí i nDún Chaoin.

12.1(b)

Tá mé i mo chónaí in árasán sa chathair.

Tá mise i mo chónaí i sráidbhaile álainn i ndeisceart na Fraince.

Tá mé i mo chónaí sa chathair ach tá teach agam faoin tuath freisin.

Tá cónaí ormsa sa bhaile mór.

Bhí mé i mo chónaí faoin tuath uair amháin ach tá mé i mo chónaí sa chathair anois.

Tá mise i mo chónaí sa Teach Bán!

13.2

(a), (c)
fiche, fiche a haon, fiche a dó, fiche a trí, fiche a ceathair, fiche a cúig, fiche a sé, fiche a seacht, fiche a hocht, fiche a naoi...

13.3(a), (b)

tríocha, tríocha a haon, tríocha a dó, tríocha a trí, tríocha a ceathair, tríocha a cúig, tríocha a sé, tríocha a seacht, tríocha a hocht, tríocha a naoi...

1.2 1D 2E 3B 4F 5G 6H 7C 8A

6.2

An Lios Dubh Lisduff *Áth Dara* Adare
Gleann Cholm Cille Glencolumbkille
Ráth Eanaigh Raheny *Cnoc an tSamhraidh* Summerhill *Port an tSalainn* Portsalon
Béal an Átha Ballina *Dún Chaoin* Dunquin
Béal Leice Belleek *Cill Iníon Léinín* Killiney

Béal and *Baile* can both appear as Ball or Bally in English, *Béal an Átha* Ballina, *Baile Bhuirne* Ballyvourney.

7.1

Fiontán, an Port Rua Marianne, An Baile Mór
Liam, An Féar Bán Risteárd, An Clochán

8.1

Jeaic, Sasana Nóra, Maigh Eo Liadán, Baile Átha Cliath Conán, Baile Átha Cliath Aodán, Albain
Labhrás, An Spáinn Mícheál, An Astráil,
An Fhionlainn Seosamh, An Phortaingéil
Patsey, Ceanada

8.2

in Acaill i gCarraig Airt sa Bhruiséil san Éigipt
san Fhaiche sna Stáit Aontaithe

13.2(b) fiche

13.3(c) tríocha

Triail Tú Féin

B
(i) ✗ (ii) ✗ (iii) ✓ (iv) ✓ (v) ✗

C

1
(i) As an mBóthar Buí mé. (ii) Tá mé i mo chónaí i gCill Rónáin. (iii) As Iorras mé. (iv) Tá mé ag staidéar in Árainn. (v) Tá Máire ag obair sa Pholainn. (vi) Tá Gearóid ag obair san Abhainn Mhór.

2
Níl, sí, níl, nílimid, sibh, níl siad

D
Spáinn chathair mo faoin

E
(a) 1 Ptolemy 2 Dinnseanchas 3 An Coimisiún Logainmneacha *The Placenames Commission*, post-offices 4 Ordnance Survey 5 Cill 6 tuath 7 Laighean, Mumhan

(b) Baile Átha Cliath Béal Feirste Port Láirge Dún na nGall Gleann Dá Loch Cill Chainnigh

Aonad

4 An Teaghlach *The Family*

This unit enables learners to: understand the origin of Irish surnames; introduce members of their families; say they do not understand what someone is saying in Irish; ask for repetition.

Can you guess what these words mean?
uncail, aintín, máthair, athair, mac, iníon

1 Éisteacht agus Léamh

1

Clúdaigh an comhrá agus féach ar an ngrianghraf. Cover the dialogue and look at the photograph. What do you think is happening? Try to guess what the people are saying.

Éist leis an téip agus léigh an comhrá.

Rúnaí:	Dia duit, a Lisa. Conas tá tú?
Lisa:	Go maith, go raibh maith agat.
Rúnaí:	Lisa is ainm duit. Cén sloinne atá ort?
Lisa:	Lapinski.
Rúnaí:	Litrigh é sin dom le do thoil.
Lisa:	Cinnte. L-A-P-I-N-S-K-I.
Rúnaí:	Ceart go leor. Agus cárb as tú?
Lisa:	As Nua-Eabhrac mé.
Rúnaí:	Cén uimhir ghutháin atá agat in Éirinn?
Lisa:	A sé, a haon, a trí, a ceathair, a cúig.

2

Éist leis an gcomhrá arís. Líon isteach an fhoirm. Fill in the form.

Coláiste Samhraidh an Oileáin

Sloinne: _____

Ainm: _____

Tír: _____

Cathair: _____

Fón: _____

---

3 Rólghlacadh

One student is the secretary and another is Lisa. Léigh an comhrá in 1.1 os ard. Léigh arís é. Athraigh na rólanna. Change roles.

2 Cumarsáid

1

Sloinne *Surname*

If you need to know somebody's surname rather than their first name (**céad ainm** *first name* or **ainm baiste** *baptismal name*) you can say

Cén sloinne atá ort?
What's your surname?

Cén t-ainm atá ort? *What's your name?* is not so precise. You could reply, depending on the situation, with your first name, or your surname, or both.

2

Which name is *not* the same as the name in the recording?

(a)

A	B	C

Gearóid Breatnach	Liam Ó Broin	Seán Mac Gearailt

D	E	F

Bríd Ní Chróinín	Máire de Róiste	Nóra Nic Liam

Seiceáil an freagra sna *Téipscripteanna.*

(b) Cluiche

How well can you remember?

Léigh na hainmneacha *the names* in 2(a) arís. Clúdaigh 2(a). Meaitseáil an chéad ainm leis an sloinne.

Máire	Nic Liam
Liam	Mac Gearailt
Seán	Breatnach
Bríd	Ní Chróinín
Gearóid	Ó Broin
Nóra	de Róiste

3

Sloinnte Gaeilge *Irish Surnames*

You will have noticed that it is common for Irish surnames to be preceded by **Ó, Ní, Mac, de,** and other shorter words.

You have already met the words **Mac** and **Ó** (Aonad 1 Mír **5.3**). These words were placed in front of the first name for the sake of distinction. **Mac** meant *son* and **Ó** meant *grandson*. However, with time they began to refer to any male descendant.

The female equivalents of **Ó** and **Mac** are **Ní** and **Nic** respectively.

A number of surnames (male and female) begin with **de** e.g. **de Róiste, de Bhál**

Other surnames (male and female) do not have anything preceding them, e.g. Breatnach, Céitinn.

4   Rólghlacadh

(a)

Abair na hainmneacha in 2(a) os ard. Say the names in 2(a) aloud. Ask your teacher to check your pronunciation. Work with another student. One of you is Gearóid Breatnach and the other is Liam Ó Broin. Have a conversation.

Sampla:

> Gearóid is ainm duit. Cén sloinne atá ort?
> Breatnach. Cén t-ainm atá ortsa?
> Liam Ó Broin

Athraigh na rólanna. Change roles. Do the same for the other names.

(b)

Have similar conversations using your own name.

5

Mná Pósta *Married Women*

Bean *Wife*

Women sometimes use their husbands' names, which may be preceded by **bean** *wife of*

Ó Loinsigh   Máire (Bean) Uí Loinsigh
Mac Liam   Áine (Bean) Mhic Liam

Note how **Ó** changes to **Uí** and **Mac** to **Mhic**. Sometimes the male name is used unchanged, for both married and single women. **Máire Ó Loinsigh** or **Áine Mac Liam**.

How many full names can you make from the following lists?

Aoife	de Buitléir
	Nic Raghnaill
	Ní Riain
Criostóir	Ó Floinn
	Uí Néill
	Mac Aogáin
	Diúc
	Mhic Lochlainn

6

Find out some of the surnames in the group and write them down.

> Cén sloinne atá ort?
> Ó Dónaill.
> Litrigh é sin dom, le do thoil.

A useful list of Irish surnames is *An Sloinnteoir Gaeilge agus an tAinmneoir* (literally *The Irish Surnamer and Namer*) by Muiris Ó Droighneáin (Coiscéim).

3   Staidéar Pearsanta

Find some more surnames in Irish. Have a look in the telephone directory or try other sources. Include some famous people if you like.

de			
Mac			
Ó			
Ní			
Nic			
Uí			
(Bean) Mhic			

Seanfhocal

Briseann an dúchas trí shúile an chait.

Everything takes after its own kind.

Describe some situations where this proverb would be appropriate.

Why is a cat used in the proverb? Is this so for similar proverbs in other languages?

4 **Cultúr**

I

The Evolution of Irish Surnames

Surnames were formed from personal names and were prefixed by *Ó* and *Mac* after the father or the grandfather. Very few women's names were used as surnames.

Gaelic surnames include surnames of Irish, Scottish Gaelic and Manx origin. The Danes and Norse took surnames in the Irish fashion by prefixing *Ó* and *Mac* to the names of their ancestors e.g. **Ó Bruadair** (from *Bruadar*). The Anglo-Normans prefixed *Mac* to surnames in place of the patronymic *Fitz-* e.g. **Mac Gearailt** *from Fitzgerald*. *Costello* was the first Norman name to assume the *Mac* prefix. The Norman *De* was retained in Irish, often in mistake for *Le*, **de Buitléir** or *The*, **de Bláca** for *The Blake* for example.

In the second half of the 16th century Anglo-Irish government officials, who had some knowledge of Irish, set about the anglicisation of Irish surnames. The surnames were written as they were pronounced with no regard to Irish spelling. This meant that different Irish surnames could have the same anglicised form e.g. *Coffey* for **Ó Cobhthaigh, Ó Cathbhadha, Ó Cathbhuaghaigh, Ó Cathmhogha.** In other cases the same Irish surname could have several different realisations in English e.g. **Ó Dubhthaigh** for *Duffy, Dowie, Dooey, Duhig.* Sometimes a surname was substituted for a well-known English name of similar sound and meaning e.g. **Ó Somacháin** for *Summerville* or a name was translated e.g. **Ó Bradáin** for *Salmon*. In certain cases there was no connection between the Irish and the English versions e.g. **Ó Fiannachta** for *Fenton*.

The *Mac* and *Ó* were dropped during the 17th and 18th centuries. These were resumed again under the influence of the Gaelic League, sometimes inaccurately e.g. **Ó Criomhthainn** instead of **Mac Criomhthainn**.

Information source
Woulfe, P. (1923) *Irish Names and Surnames*, Dublin: McGill & Sons.

2(a)

Éist leis an téip. Meaitseáil an leagan Gaeilge agus an leagan Béarla.

Mac Gearailt	*Fisher*
Ó Flaitheartaigh	*Byrne*
de Barra	*Ridge*
Ó Broin	*Flaherty*
Mac an Iomaire	*Barrett*
Mac Muiris	*Fitzmaurice*
Bairéid	*Barry*
Mac an Iascaire	*Fitzgerald*

(b)

Look up the meanings of the words in bold print in the following list and write them in column A.

	A	B
Mac an t**Saoi**	_____	_____
Ó Fiaich (**Fiach**)	_____	_____
Rís	_____	_____
Mac Cuilinn (**Cuileann**)	_____	_____
Mac **Giolla** Íosa	_____	_____
Ó **Rua**	_____	_____

The following are the English forms of these surnames. Match them to the Irish forms writing them in column B above.

Fee, Hunt	*Roe*
Cullen	*Rice*
Mac Aleese, Gilleece	*Mac Entee*

What can you say about these surnames in the light of what you read in **4.1**?

3(a)

In the map on page 53 you will see the distribution of Irish surnames throughout the four provinces. Write the names of the provinces on the map. Ask the teacher for help with pronunciation.

(b) Cluiche Beirte

Pick out 5 surnames from each *Cúige* and write them on separate pieces of paper.
(You can write both Irish and English forms on each paper or you can write the Irish
form only). Write the name of the *Cúige* on the back. Shuffle the papers and deal them
out, giving an equal number to each player.

Foghlaimeoir A places a paper on the table, surname up. *Foghlaimeoir B* tries to name the
Cúige. The paper is turned over. If the answer is correct *Foghlaimeoir B* keeps the paper,
sets it aside and does not play it again. If the answer is not correct *Foghlaimeoir B* places
the paper at the bottom of her or his playing pile. *Foghlaimeoir B* now places a paper on
the table. The game continues until all the papers have been played. The player with the
most papers set aside wins.

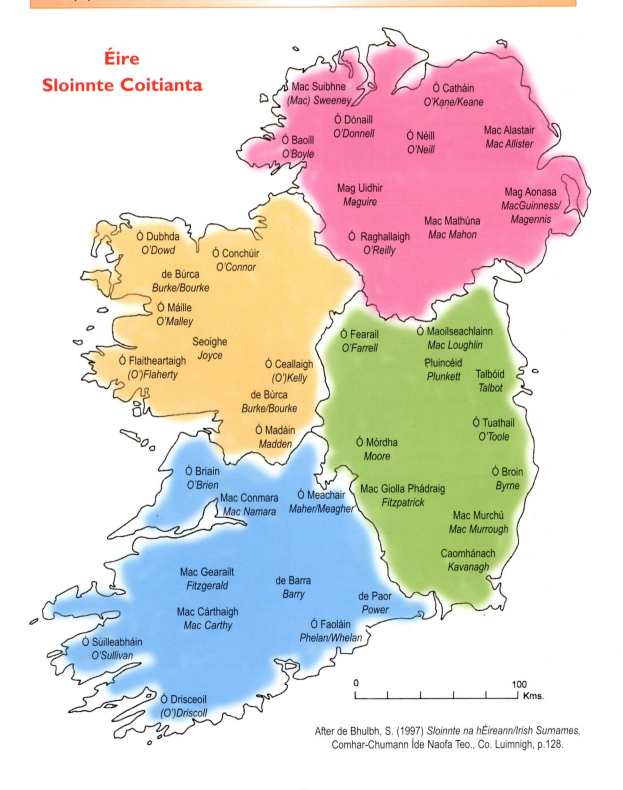

**Éire
Sloinnte Coitianta**

Mac Suibhne
(Mac) Sweeney

Ó Catháin
O'Kane/Keane

Ó Dónaill
O'Donnell

Ó Néill
O'Neill

Mac Alastair
Mac Allister

Ó Baoill
O'Boyle

Mag Uidhir
Maguire

Mag Aonasa
*MacGuinness/
Magennis*

Mac Mathúna
Mac Mahon

Ó Raghallaigh
O'Reilly

Ó Dubhda
O'Dowd

Ó Conchúir
O'Connor

de Búrca
Burke/Bourke

Ó Máille
O'Malley

Ó Fearail
O'Farrell

Ó Maoilseachlainn
Mac Loughlin

Pluincéid
Plunkett

Talbóid
Talbot

Seoighe
Joyce

Ó Flaitheartaigh
(O')Flaherty

Ó Ceallaigh
(O')Kelly

Ó Tuathail
O'Toole

de Búrca
Burke/Bourke

Ó Madáin
Madden

Ó Mórdha
Moore

Ó Broin
Byrne

Ó Briain
O'Brien

Mac Conmara
Mac Namara

Ó Meachair
Maher/Meagher

Mac Giolla Phádraig
Fitzpatrick

Mac Murchú
Mac Murrough

Caomhánach
Kavanagh

Mac Gearailt
Fitzgerald

de Barra
Barry

de Paor
Power

Mac Cárthaigh
Mac Carthy

Ó Faoláin
Phelan/Whelan

Ó Súilleabháin
O'Sullivan

Ó Drisceoil
(O')Driscoll

0   100
Kms.

After de Bhulbh, S. (1997) *Sloinnte na hÉireann/Irish Surnames,*
Comhar-Chumann Íde Naofa Teo., Co. Luimnigh, p.128.

Gramadach

I

Séimhiú and h in surnames

Séimhiú usually follows **Ní, Uí, Mhic, Nic, Nic Giolla, Mac an, Giolla, Maol** e.g. **Áine Ní Cheallaigh, Bríd Uí Bhaoill, Máire Mhic Dhónaill, Eibhlín Nic Dhiarmada, Dónall Mac an Bhaird, Órla Nic Giolla Phádraig, Seán Ó Maolmhuaidh.**

The common surname **Breatnach** *Welsh* or *Walsh(e)*, takes a *séimhiú* for women but not for men, **Nóra Bhreatnach** but **Pól Breatnach**, just like an ordinary adjective, **Máire Bhán** (*blonde, grey*) but **Pól Bán**. This is because originally it just meant *British*, which in Ireland at the time meant Roman Britain, or for practical purposes, Wales. **Déiseach** *Deasey* is another adjectival surname, meaning from the **Déise**, in Co. Wateford.

Note: No *séimhiú* after *Ó* or *Mac*. So **Ó Conaire, Mac Diarmada,** and so on. But **Ó** puts **h** before a vowel, giving most of the Irish surnames that start with *H* in English, such as *Hogan, Horgan, Heffernan, Hurley* from **Ó hÓgáin, Ó hArgáin, Ó hIfearnáin, Ó hUrthaile.**

2

The teacher has just asked the students to write their names on cards so that she can identify them more easily. Some students have difficulty completing their cards. Can you help them? The first one is done for you.

A (Mac Mathúna)
> Gearóidín Nic Mhathúna

B (Mac Donncha)
> Peig Nic

C (Ó Broin)
> Daithí Ó

D (Ó Gealagáin)
> Róisín Ní

E (Déiseach)
> Seán

F (Ó hAogáin)
> Treasa Ní

G (de Brún)
> Pádraig de

H (Mistéil)
> Caitlín

I (Ó Ríordáin)
> Aoife Uí

J (Mac Alastair)
> Íde Mhic

Cultúr

I

People and places

Places often took their names from the ruling family. **Durlas Éile** *Thurles* from the **Éli**, for example, **Ciarraí** *Kerry* from the **Ciarrige** and **Clann Mhuiris** *Clanmaurice* after the Maurice family. **Fear Manach** *Fermanagh* contains a reference to the *Menapii*, a family of Gaullish origin. Other placenames are associated with a particular individual, **Cathair Dónall** *Caherdaniel*, **Tír Eoghain** *Tyrone*, **Cill Bhríde** *Kilbride*, and **Droichead an Bhuitléaraigh** *Butler's Bridge*.

2

Which of the following placenames contain people's names?

1 Clár Chlainne Mhuiris ____
2 An Baile Bán ____
3 Baile Átha Cliath ____
4 Cathair Uí Mhóráin ____
5 Béal Átha Conaill ____
6 Loch Dearg ____
7 Cill Barra ____
8 Gleann Bhriain ____

Do you know any more Irish placenames which contain people's names? If so write them down and compare with other students.

Bríd Óg Ní Mháille

This is a song about a man who is broken-hearted (**mo chroí cráite**) because the beautiful Bríd Óg Ní Mháille is not returning his love. He compares her beauty to that of the moon above the sea (**an ghealach os cionn an tsáile**) and the white flower on the blackthorn tree (**bláth bán na n-airní ag fás ar an draighean**). He says he will not survive (**ní buan i bhfad beo mé**) unless Bríd agrees to marry him.

Is a Bhríd Óg Ní Mháille, is tú d'fhág mo chroí cráite,
Is chuir tú arraingeacha an bháis trí cheartlár mo chroí;
Tá na céadta fear i ngrá le d'éadan ciúin náireach,
Is go dtug tú barr breáthachta ar Thír Oirghialla más fíor.

Níl ní ar bith is áille ná an ghealach os cionn an tsáile,
Ná bláth bán na n-airní ag fás ar an draighean;
Ó siúd mar a bhíonn mo ghrá-sa níos trilsí le breáthacht,
Béilín meala na háilleachta nach ndearna riamh claon.

Is buachaill deas óg mé atá ag triall chun mo phósta,
Is ní buan i bhfad beo mé mura bhfaighidh mé mo mhian;
A chuisle is a stóirín, déan réidh agus bí romhamsa
Ceann deireanach den Domhnach ar Bhóithrín Dhroim Sliabh.

7 Sa Rang

1 Obair Bheirte

You may not have understood the meaning of all the words in *Bríd Óg Ní Mháille*. It was not important that you did as all you needed was to have an idea of what the song was about.

There may, however, be certain words and phrases that you would like to understand.

Pick 3 such words or phrases from the song. You have decided to ask the teacher to explain their meaning. Discuss with your partner how you are going to do this.

2

> **Seeking clarification**
>
> You may well have decided to use the phrases **Cén Béarla atá air seo? Gabh mo leithscéal, cén Béarla atá air seo? Cén Béarla atá air seo, le do thoil?** (Aonad 1)
>
> Another useful phrase to find out the meaning of something is (as you point to the particular item)
>
> **Cad is brí leis seo?** /kad is bri: l'es' s'o/
> *What does this mean?*
>
> If the teacher gives you an explanation that you do not understand you can say
>
> **Ní thuigim é sin.** /n'i: hig'əm e: s'in/
> *I don't understand that.*
>
> And finally, if you would like the teacher to repeat something you can say
>
> **Abair é sin arís le do thoil.**
> /abər' e: s'in ər'i:s'/
> *Repeat that please.*

Éist leis an téip. Abair na habairtí os ard. Say the phrases out loud.

3 Labhairt

You should now be ready to ask the teacher about the words or phrases in the song which you chose earlier. Can you remember how to get the teacher's attention? (Aonad 1).

1 Get the teacher's attention and wait until she or he comes to you.
2 Point to the first word or phrase and ask what it means.
3 If you do not understand say so or ask for repetition.
4 Do the same for the other two words or phrases.

4 Rólghlacadh

You are the teacher and your partner is the student.
Foghlaimeoir: Point to one of the words or phrases your partner has just had explained. Ask her or him what it means. If necessary, say you do not understand the explanation and would like repetition.

Múinteoir: Expain word or phrase. Be as vague as possible!

Athraigh rólanna. Reverse roles.

8 Stór Focal

1

iníon   athair   mac

gariníon   seanmháthair   garmhac

seanmháthair   athair   seanathair   máthair
dearthár   deirfiúr   aintín   uncail   col ceathrair

Obair Bheirte

Cuir na focail sa cholún ceart. Put the words in the correct column.

Mná, cailíní	Fir, buachaillí
máthair	

Seiceáil na focail san fhoclóir.

2

Number the words in the order you hear them. The first one is done for you.

seanmháthair	
seanathair	
máthair	
athair	
iníon	
mac	
gariníon	
garmhac	
aintín	
uncail	I
col ceathrair	

Seiceáil na freagraí san *Eochair*. Abair na focail os ard. Say the words out loud.

 Cumarsáid

I **Teaghlach Aisling**

Aisling

---

35 An Bóthar Mór
Caisleán an Bharraigh
Co. Mhaigh Eo

A Chríostóir, a chara,

Seo mo theaghlach. Tá deartháir amháin agam. Muiris is ainm dó. Máirín is ainm do mo dheirfiúr. Tá mo thuismitheoirí beo* fós. Anna agus Peadar is ainm dóibh. Tá iníon agam freisin. Róisín is ainm di.

This is a letter Aisling wrote to her friend Criostóir describing her family.

Éist leis an téip agus léigh an litir os íseal. Read the letter silently.

Scríobh na hainmneacha faoi na grianghraif *under the photos.*

* *beo* = alive

2

Write out the phrase which Aisling used to introduce her family.

Ag cur do theaghlach in aithne
Introducing your family

In the letter Aisling introduced her family by saying

Seo mo theaghlach.

You can introduce individual members of the family by saying

Seo mo dheartháir Muiris.
/mə g'r'aha:r'/

Mo *my* is followed by a *séimhiú*. It is written **m'** before a vowel or **fh, m'athair** *my father*, **m'fhoclóir** *my dictionary*.

3(a)

Write **mo** in front of the following words:

máthair	mo mháthair
athair	
seanmháthair	
seanathair	
deirfiúr	
deartháir	
iníon	
mac	
aintín	
uncail	
col ceathrair	
gariníon	
garmhac	

Seiceáil na freagraí san *Eochair*.

(b)

Rose is pointing out the members of her family on a photograph. What is her daughter's name? What are her grandchildren's names?

4(a)

Asking who someone is

If you wish to ask who a particular person is you say

Cé hí seo? (in the case of a girl or woman)
/ke: hi:/

Cé hé seo? (in the case of a boy or a man)
/ke: he:/

(b) Obair Bheirte

Draw a picture of your extended family like the one in **9**.2. Don't worry about being artistic, just try to make the gender and age clear.

Have a conversation with your partner like this:

A: Cé hí, hé seo (pointing to a member of your partner's family)?
B: Seo (m'Aintín Deirdre).
A: Agus cé hí, hé sin (pointing to someone further away)?
B: Sin (mo mhac Peadar).

Athraigh rólanna. Change roles.

5 Stór focal

(a)

In the following recording a teacher is checking that all the children are on the mini-bus before they return home after a school outing. Can you tell how many children are present?

Seiceáil do fhreagra sna *Téipscripteanna*.

(b)

Uimhreacha Pearsanta
Personal Numbers

There are special forms of the numbers for counting people. To count people in a group such as the children in 5(a), you say:

1 person	duine or duine amháin	
	/din'ə/	/əwa:n'/
2 people	beirt	/b'er't'/
3	triúr	/t'r'u:r/
4	ceathrar	/k'ahrər/
5	cúigear	/ku:g'ər/
6	seisear	/s'es'ər/
7	seachtar	/s'axtər/
8	ochtar	/oxtər/
9	naonúr	/ni:nu:r/
10	deichniúr	/d'ex'n'u:r/

Abair na huimhreacha os ard. Say the numbers out loud. Count the people in the picture of your extended family.

(c) Léamh agus Scríobh

Tá ... agam *I have*

To say that somebody has something in Irish you say that it is *at them*.

Tá deartháir amháin agam.
I have one brother.

Fill in the speech bubbles with the appropriate sentence from the list below.

B

C

D

1 Tá deartháir amháin agus beirt deirfiúracha agam.
2 Tá ceathrar páistí agam – triúr iníonacha agus mac amháin.
3 Tá cúigear deartháireacha agam.
4 Tá triúr mac agam.

(d)

'not to have'

Níl... agam *I don't have*
If you don't have children you can say

Níl páistí (ar bith) agam.
I don't have (any) children.

6(a)

Naming other people

Look back at Aisling's letter in Mír **9**.1.
To name her brother she says

Muiris is ainm dó.

She uses the prepositional pronoun **dó** *to him*.
Now fill in the blanks in the following sentences:

(a) Róisín is ainm _____.
(b) Anna agus Peadar is ainm _____.

Labhair le foghlaimeoir eile faoi seo. Talk about this with another learner.

(b) Críochnaigh na habairtí. Finish the sentences.

1 Seo mo dheartháir. Uinseann is ainm _____.
2 Tá deirfiúr amháin agam. Caoimhe is ainm

_____.

3 Seo mo thuismitheoirí. Gearóid agus Eibhlín is ainm _____.
4 Tá beirt iníonacha agam. Béibhinn agus Gráinne is ainm _____.
5 Seo mo mháthair. Daire is ainm _____.
6 Seo mise. Jeaic is ainm _____!

10 Fuaimniú

I(a)

Béim *Stress*

Most Irish words are stressed on the first syllable, <u>ath</u>air, <u>máth</u>air, <u>Éir</u>e, <u>Sas</u>ana, <u>Meir</u>iceá, <u>Nór</u>a, <u>Diar</u>muid.

You may notice, however, that people from Munster sometimes place the stress on other syllables e.g. to<u>sach</u>.
Additionally, loan words or some compounds may not be stressed on the first syllable e.g.

    meir<u>eang</u>   *meringue*
    an<u>sin</u>   *there, then*

(b)

Éist leis an téip. Number the syllables.

1 2   1 2 3

Pádraig   Ceanada   amach   gramadach   cultúr
tobac   muileann   gaofar   scamallach   anseo
Breatnach   deirfiúr   seanmháthair   mileoidean

(c)

Éist leis an téip. Underline the stressed syllable. Which word is stressed at the end?

gaofar   tobac   scamallach   cultúr   deirfiúr   Pádraig

2

Other Stress Patterns

The possessive adjective **mo** is never stressed

mo <u>mhá</u>thair

In placenames with more than one word, the stress is on the last one

<u>Baile</u> <u>Átha</u> <u>Cliath</u>
<u>Béal</u> <u>Feirste</u>

Mark the main stress (do not mark the words inside brackets).

1 mo dheirfiúr
2 Dún Dealgan
3 M'Aintín Nóra
4 (Tá mé i) mo chónaí (i) nGaillimh.
5 Mo leabhar nótaí
6 Abair é (sin) arís (le do thoil).

Abair na habairtí.

3

Translate the following words into your own language. Underline the stressed syllable.

Gaeilge	Your language
<u>Cean</u>ada	
fo<u>clóir</u>	
an<u>seo</u>	
cul<u>túr</u>	
<u>gao</u>far	
am<u>ach</u>	

Is there a difference between word stress in your language and word stress in Irish? Labhair le foghlaimeoirí eile faoi seo.

Scileanna Foghlama

1 Strategies for learning vocabulary

How do you prefer to learn vocabulary? Do you prefer to

- See the word written down
- Listen to the word being pronounced and then try to pronounce it yourself
- Learn the word with its translation?

Work with another student to add other strategies to this list. Check *Nóta* on page 66 for more strategies.

2

Grouping words
The following words have been sorted into groups. What has each group got in common? Déan plé le foghlaimeoir eile. Discuss with another learner.

A   leathanach   leabhar   foclóir   mír   fuaimniú

B   a trí   a ceathair   a cúig   a sé   a seacht

C   An Danmhairg   An India   An Phortaingéil   An Fhrainc   An Spáinn

D   Ó Broin   de Barra   Mac Muiris   Mac Gearailt   Ó Rua

3

Sort the words or phrases in the box into groups.

dom   scamallach   go maith   Cáit
orm   gaofar   Eoghan   ceart go leor
fliuch   Bríd   leat   go dona   fuar
agat   Aoife   ní hea
Seán   libh   tirim   Séamas

Compare your groups with those of other students. Does sorting words help you to remember them?

Gramadach

Forainmneacha Réamhfhoclacha

Prepositions combine with personal pronouns to form prepositional pronouns. You will probably recognise some of the prepositional pronouns in the chart below. They are organised in lists, **agam**, **agat**, etc. Read each list aloud several times and then try saying the list without looking. Ask another student to check how well you recall the lists.

preposition	**ag** *at*	**ar** *on*	**do** *to*	**le** *with*
1 Singular	**agam**	**orm**	**dom**	**liom**
2 Singular	**agat**	**ort**	**duit**	**leat**
3 Fem.Sg.	**aici**	**uirthi**	**di**	**léi**
4 Masc.Sg.	**aige**	**air**	**dó**	**leis**
1 Plural	**againn**	**orainn**	**dúinn**	**linn**
2 Plural	**agaibh**	**oraibh**	**daoibh**	**libh**
3 Plural	**acu**	**orthu**	**dóibh**	**leo**

13 **Sa Rang**

I Meaitseáil na habairtí.

1 Líon isteach an fhoirm.	A Repeat.
2 Abair na habairtí.	B Make sentences.
3 Léigh an comhrá os íseal.	C Complete the sentences.
4 Léigh an comhrá os ard.	D Fill in the form.
5 Athraigh na rólanna.	E Talk to another learner about this.
6 Clúdaigh na hainmneacha.	F Say the sentences.
7 Líon na bearnaí sna habairtí.	G Change the roles.
8 Déan athrá.	H Read the conversation silently.
9 Déan abairtí.	I Cover the names.
10 Labhair le foghlaimeoir eile faoi seo.	J Read the conversation out loud.

2 Which sentence matches the picture?

Cluiche

Scríobh na huimhreacha pearsanta 1-9 sna boscaí.

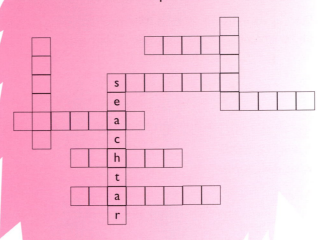

A

1 Scríobh na habairtí.
2 Abair na habairtí.

B

1 Déan athrá.
2 Déan plé le foghlaimeoir eile.

C

1 Léigh an comhrá os ard.
2 Léigh an comhrá os íseal.

D

1 Féach ar an leabhar.
2 Féach ar an múinteoir.

E

1 Clúdaigh an leathanach.
2 Léigh an leathanach.

Achoimre *Summary*

Cumarsáid agus Stór Focal

Stating your name and surname	Bríd Ní Chróinín Cáit Nic Dhiarmada Máire Mhic Dhonncha Nóra Uí Mhurchú Diarmuid Ó Conaire Piaras Mac Gearailt Liam Ó hArgáin
Asking someone what their surname is	Cén t-ainm, sloinne atá ort?
Asking someone to spell their surname	Litrigh do shloinne (é sin) dom, le do thoil.

Introducing your family	Seo mo theaglach.
	Seo mo dheartháir Muiris.
	Seo mo dheirfiúr,
	  mo mhac,
	  mo sheanmháthair,
	  mo sheanathair,
	  mo chol ceathrair,
	  mo ghariníon,
	  mo gharmhac.
	Seo m'aintín, m'iníon
	  m'uncail, m'athair.
	
	(Pól) is ainm dó.
	(Máirín) is ainm di.
	(Róisín agus Donncha)
	  is ainm dóibh.

Enquiring who someone is	Cé hí seo? Cé hé seo?

Counting people	Duine, beirt, triúr,
	  ceathrar, cúigear,
	  seisear, seachtar,
	  ochtar, naonúr, deichniúr.

Sa rang	Cad is brí leis seo?
	(Tá brón orm ach) ní
	  thuigim thú.
	Abair é sin arís le do
	  thoil.

Sa téacsleabhar	Líon isteach an fhoirm.
	Abair na habairtí.
	Léigh an comhrá os ard,
	  os íseal.
	Athraigh na rólanna.
	Clúdaigh na hainmneacha.
	Líon na bearnaí sna
	  habairtí.
	Déan athrá, abairtí.
	Déan plé le
	  foghlaimeoir eile.

Gramadach

- *Séimhiú* after **Ní**, **Nic**, **Mhic** and **Uí** (female)
- No *séimhiú* after **Ó** and **Mac**
- **h** before a vowel after **Ó**: **Ó hÓgáin**
- *Séimhiú* after **mo** *my*: **mo mháthair, mo mhac**
- **m'** for **mo** before vowels or **fh**: **m'athair, m'fhoclóir**
- *Have* in Irish is **tá + ag**: **Tá deartháir amháin agam.** *I have one brother.*
- There are special numbers for counting people: **duine, beirt, triúr** etc.
- The prepositional pronouns **di, dó** (singular), **dóibh** (plural): **Sorcha is ainm di, Mánas is ainm dó, Siobhán agus Úna is ainm dóibh.**

Cultúr

Irish Surnames

- Formed from personal names – prefixed with **Ó** and **Mac**
- Very few women's names used
- Female equivalent of **Ó** is **Ní**, of **Mac** is **Nic**
- The Danes and Norse prefixed **Ó** and **Mac** to their surnames.
- 16th century – anglicisation of Irish surnames
- **Mac** and **Ó** dropped during the 17th and 18th centuries but resumed under Gaelic League
- Today, anglicised forms are dominant.
- Many Irish placenames include a surname.

Fuaimniú

Béim *Stress*

Most words in Irish are stressed on the first syllable.

Scileanna Foghlama

Learning Vocabulary
• The importance of discovering how you prefer to learn vocabulary
• A possible strategy – grouping words according to theme

Triail Tú Féin

A 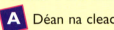 Déan na cleachtaí seo a leanas leis an múinteoir.

I You are working as a receptionist in a hotel called *Óstán an Ghleanna*. A guest arrives who has already booked a room over the telephone. It is late in the evening.

Greet the guest.
> He returns greeting and tells you he booked a room over the phone.

Ask him his name.
> Gives his name.

Ask him to spell his surname.
> Starts to spell name.

(Pretend) you do not understand what he is saying. Apologise. Ask him to repeat it.
> Repeats spelling.

Write it down and say that's fine.
> He introduces his wife.

Greet her. Comment on the weather (today's). You notice a little girl with them. Ask them who she is.
> He tells you she is his daughter, Máire.
> He asks you what the room number is.

Tell him it is **68**. Hand him the key (an eochair).
> The couple thank you.

Wish them a good night.

2 You are enrolling at an Irish Language School for a course in Irish Language and Culture. You talk to the receptionist – **an fáilteoir**.

Cad é mar tá tú?
Freagair. *Respond.*
> Fáilte go Gaoth Dobhair. Cén t-ainm atá ort?

Freagair.
> Litrigh do shloinne le do thoil.

Freagair.
> Cárb as tú?

Freagair.
> Seo uimhir an tseomra ranga – fiche a trí.

Freagair.

B

I Scríobh litir chuig do chara pinn Siobhán. Include the following information:
You are living in the country.
Your mother is still alive.
You have a dog called Conán.

Bóthar na hAbhann
Lios Tuathail
Co. Chiarraí

A _____ a chara,

Conas _____? Tá mise _____. Tá mé _____ faoin tuath. Tá _____ mac agam. Nollaig, Pól agus Diarmuid is ainm _____.

Tá m'athair marbh. Tá mo _____ beo fós.

Sorcha is ainm _____. _____ madra beag _____. Conán _____.

Scríobh chugam go luath.

Do chara,

_____.

2 Complete the names.

(i) Tadhg Ó Cróinín
Bríd_____ (singil *single*)

(ii) Pádraig Mac Piarais
Pádraigín _____ (pósta *married*)

(iii) Antaine de Paor
Caitlín _____ (pósta)

(iv) Aodh Breatnach
Aoife _____ (singil)

(v) Daithí Ó hÓgáin
Áine _____ (pósta)

(vi) Liam Mac Murchú
Síle _____ (singil)

C Déan focail.

dear	air
deir	tín
ain	lach
teagh	fiúr
un	tháir
ath	cail

D Déan abairtí.

Athraigh	athrá
Clúdaigh	abairtí
Líon (isteach)	plé
Abair	an fhoirm
Léigh	na bearnaí
Déan	na rólanna
	na habairtí
	na hainmneacha
	an comhrá os ard
	an comhrá os íseal

Pléigh na freagraí le foghlaimeoir eile agus leis an múinteoir.

E

Underline the stressed syllable.

madra	amach
aréir	pósta
tráthnóna	Atlantach
inniu	singil
amárach	muintir

F

Which of the following statements is *not* true?

1 Surnames were formed from personal or first names.
2 In the 16th century Irish surnames started to be anglicised.
3 *Mac* and *Ó* were dropped as early as the 15th century.
4 Very few women's names were used to form surnames.
5 The Danes and Norse prefixed *Ó* and *Mac* to their surnames.

•••••••••• **Téipscripteanna** ••••••••••

2.2 (a)
A Is mise Gearóid Breathnach. B Liam Ó Broin is ainm dom. C Seán **Puirséil** atá orm.
D Mise Bríd Ní Chróinín. E Máire de Róiste is ainm dom. F Nóra Nic Liam atá orm.

9.3 (b)
Seo mo mháthair, m'athair, mo sheanmháthair agus mo sheanathair.

Cé hí sin?

Sin í mo dheirfiúr Máire.

Agus cé hé seo?

Máirtín, mo dheartháir. Tá sé ag obair san Astráil.

Agus cé hí sin?

Sin Sarah, m'iníon agus seo é mo mhac Máirtín.

D'aithneoinn Sarah asat, ó na súile ach go háirithe.

Agus cé hiad seo?

M'aintín, m'uncail agus mo chol ceathrair Toby. As Meiriceá iad ach tá siad ina gcónaí in Éirinn anois.

Agus na páistí?

Mo gharíníon agus mo gharmhac. Emma agus Jonathan is ainm dóibh.

Féachann siad go hálainn!

9.5 (a)
Bígí ciúin le bhur dtoil.
Duine, beirt, triúr, ceathrar, cúigear, seisear, seachtar, ochtar, naonúr.

Eochair

1.2

Coláiste Samhraidh an Oileáin	
Sloinne: *Lapinski*	Ainm: *Lisa*
Tír: *Na Stáit Aontaithe*	Cathair: *Nua-Eabhrac*
Fón *61345*	

4.2 (a)

Mac Gearailt *Fitzerald* Ó Flaitheartaigh *Flaherty*
de Barra *Barry* Ó Broin *Byrne* Mac an Iomaire
Ridge Mac Muiris *Fitzmaurice* Bairéid *Barrett*
Mac an Iascaire *Fisher*

4.2 (b) Mac an tSaoi *Mac Entee* Ó Fiaich *Fee,*
Hunt Rís *Rice* Mac Cuilinn *Cullen* Mac Giolla
Íosa *Mac Aleese, Gileece* Ó Rua *Roe*

5.2

B Dhonncha C Broin D Ghealagáin E Déiseach
F Aogáin G Brún H Mhistéil I Ríordáin J Alastair

6.2

I, 4, 5, 7, 8.

8.1

Mná/cailíní	Fir/buachaillí
máthair	athair
seanmháthair	seanathair
aintín	uncail
iníon	mac
col ceathrair	col ceathrair
gariníon	garmhac

8.2

I uncail 2 seanmháthair 3 iníon 4 athair
5 máthair 6 aintín 7 mac 8 col ceathrair
9 seanathair 10 gariníon 11 garmhac

9.1 ## Teaghlach Aisling

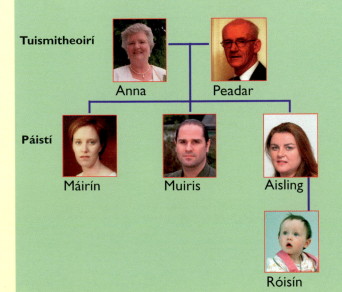

Tuismitheoirí — Anna — Peadar

Páistí — Máirín — Muiris — Aisling

Róisín

9.3(a)

mo mháthair, m'athair, mo sheanmháthair, mo
sheanathair, mo dheirfiúr, mo dhearthair, m'iníon,
mo mhac, m'aintín, m'uncail, mo chol ceathrair,
mo ghariníon, mo gharmhac

9.5(c) IB, 2D, 3A, 4C.

9.6(b)

I dó 2 di 3 dóibh 4 dóibh 5 di 6 dom

10.1(b)

I 2	I 2 3	I 2	I 2 3	I 2
Pádraig	Ceanada	amach	gramadach	cultúr
I 2	I 2	I 2	I 2 3	I 2
tobac	muileann	gaofar	scamallach	anseo
I 2	I 2	I 2 3	I 2 3	
Breatnach	deirfiúr	seanmháthair	mileoidean	

10.1(c)

gaofar tobac scamallach cultúr deirfiúr Pádraig

10.2

I mo dheirfiúr 2 Dún Dealgan 3 M'Aintín Nóra 4 (Tá mé i)
mo chónaí (i) nGaillimh. 5 Mo leabhar nótaí 6 Abair é (sin)
arís (le do thoil).

13.1

ID 2F 3H 4J 5G 6I 7C 8A 9B 10E

13.2

A2 B2 CI DI EI

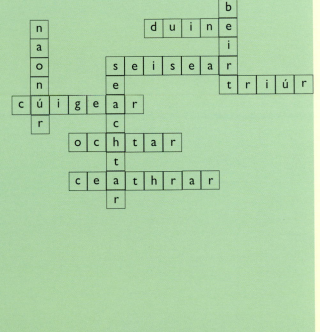

Triail Tú Féin

B

I

Bóthar na hAbhann
Lios Tuathail
Co. Chiarraí

A Shiobhán, a chara,

Conas tá tú? Tá mise go maith (go han-mhaith).

Tá mé i mo chónaí faoin tuath. Tá triúr mac agam.
Nollaig, Pól agus Diarmuid is ainm dóibh.

Tá m'athair marbh. Tá mo mháthair beo fós.
Sorcha is ainm di.

Tá madra beag agam. Conán is ainm dó.

Scríobh chugam go luath,

Do chara,

_____.

2

(i) Bríd Ní Chróinín, Ó Cróinín (ii) Pádraigín
Mhic Phiarais, Mac Piarais, Nic Phiarais (iii) Caitlín
de Paor (iv) Aoife Bhreatnach (v) Áine Uí Ógáin,
Ó hÓgáin, Ní Ógáin (vi) Síle Nic Mhurchú,
Mac Murchú

C

deartháir deirfiúr aintín teaghlach uncail athair

E

m<u>a</u>dra	am<u>ach</u>
ar<u>éir</u>	p<u>ó</u>sta
tráth<u>nó</u>na	At<u>la</u>ntach
inn<u>iu</u>	s<u>i</u>ngil
am<u>á</u>rach	mu<u>i</u>ntir

F

3

Nóta

- Write the word several times.
- Put it with other words of the same topic e.g. **peann** with words to do with the classroom.

Aonad 5

Ceol agus Craic

This unit enables learners to: express their likes and dislikes particularly with regard to music; use Irish to borrow and lend material in the classroom.

is maith liom

Ní maith liom

Can you guess what is **maith liom** and **ní maith liom** mean? Where did the word **craic** come from?

67

1 Cumarsáid

1 Éisteacht agus Léamh

Éist leis an gcomhrá. Two students, Elie and Gearóidín are saying what they like and dislike about the Irish course they are attending. Can you tell from the tone of their voices what they feel about the course?

Elie:	As an Liobáin mé.
Gearóidín:	I ndáiríre? As Gaillimh mise.
Elie:	Is maith liom Gaillimh. Tá na daoine go deas ann.
Gearóidín:	An maith leat an cúrsa Gaeilge?
Elie:	Is maith, ach ní maith liom an ghramadach.
Gearóidín:	Ní maith liomsa an ghramadach ach oiread.

I ndáiríre? *Really?*

Does **ach oiread** mean *also* or *either*?
What does Elie say about Galway?

2 Gramadach

Líon na bearnaí sna habairtí.

To ask someone *if they like* something you say
_____ maith leat (an cúrsa)?
To say you *like* something you say _____ maith liom (an cúrsa).
To say you *do not like* something you say _____ maith liom (an cúrsa).

An Chopail *The Copula*

The verb **Is** in Irish is called the copula. It does not behave like other verbs. For the moment it is sufficient to be able to recognise it.

An is the question form of the copula
An maith leat an cúrsa?

Is is the form used to make an affirmative statement
Is maith liom an cúrsa.

Ní is the form used to make a negative statement
Ní maith liom an cúrsa.

3(a) Stór Focal

Meaitseáil na focail sa bhosca thíos leis na pictiúir.

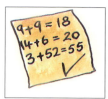

(i)_____ (ii)_____ (iii)_____

(iv)_____ (v)_____ (vi)_____

damháin alla	**luchóga**	**stoirmeacha**
/du:a:n' ˋala/	/luxo:gə/	/stor'm'əxə/
matamaitic	**cait**	**ceol clasaiceach**
/matəmat'ik'/	/kait'/	/k'o:l klasək'əx/

(b) Scríobh

Scríobh abairt faoi gach pictiúr *about each picture*.

Sampla:

Is maith liom cait. Ní maith liom ceol clasaiceach.

Abair na habairtí os ard. Iarr ar an múinteoir éisteacht leat. Ask your teacher to listen to you.

(c) Obair Bheirte

Cleacht an comhrá seo le do pháirtí. Practise this conversation with your partner.

An maith leat cait?
Ní maith. An maith leatsa cait?
Is maith.

Déan plé le do pháirtí faoi na pictiúir in **1**.3(a). Write your partner's opinions in the grid.

	is maith	ní maith
cait		
ceol clasaiceach		
matamaitic		
luchóga		
stoirmeacha		
damháin alla		

(d)

Scríobh

Combining Sentences

1

Líon na bearnaí sna habairtí le **agus**, **ach** nó **ná**.

Samplaí:

Is maith liom cait agus madraí.

Ní maith liom tae ach is maith liom caife.

Ní maith liom an Spáinn ná an Iodáil.

1 Is maith liom Gaeilge _____ ní maith liom an ghramadach.
2 Ní maith le Síle popcheol _____ ceol clasaiceach.
3 Is maith liom an Phortaingéil _____ an Fhrainc.
4 Seo Máire _____ seo Séamas.

2

Scríobh tuairisc ar **1**.3 (c) thuas. Write a report on **1**.3 (c) above.

Sampla 1

Is maith le mo pháirtí luchóga, stoirmeacha agus cait.

Ní maith leis ceol clasaiceach, damháin alla ná matamaitic.

Sampla 2

Is maith le mo pháirtí luchóga, stoirmeacha agus cait ach ní maith leis ceol clasaiceach, damháin alla ná matamaitic.

3

Bord Fáilte *The Irish Tourist Board* wants to know what you like about Ireland, and what you dislike. Scríobh cúpla abairt *a few sentences* as Gaeilge. Be honest!

Seanfhocal

An rud is annamh is iontach.

What's seldom is wonderful.

Is it true? What exactly does it mean?
Do you know similar sayings in other languages?

Fuaimniú

1

Gutaí *Vowels*

In Irish vowels can be either long or short. The long vowels are written **á**, **é**, **í**, **ó**, **ú**.

Phonetically, long vowels are shown by putting /ː/ after the vowel.

It is very important to distinguish between long and short vowels, as replacing one by the other can change the meaning of a word, for example, **lon** /lon/ *blackbird* but **lón** /loːn/ *lunch*.

Vowels without an accent are sometimes pronounced long, e.g. vowels before consonant clusters, such as the first **a** in **Garda**, or vowels in vowel combinations, e.g. **ae** /eː/ as in **Gael**/geːl/.

Irish has one neutral vowel and its phonetic transcription is /ə/, e.g. **solas** /soləs/ *light*.

2

Here is a table of the vowels of Irish. IPA stands for *International Phonetic Alphabet*

I.P.A. Symbol	Irish Examples	Nearest English Equivalent
i	duine, im, sin	sit
i:	buí, naoi, sín	me
e	ceist, te	set
e:	mé, tae	say
a	bean, mac	bat
a:	ard, tá	far
o	obair, seo	son
o:	ceol, mór	more
u	dubh, tiubh	book
u:	siúl, tú	who
ə	mála, míle	the

Breathnaigh ar na focail thíos san fhoclóir agus cuir na focail sa ghreille.

ceol craic fliúit seit seo is dán sí sé rud

a	o	u	i	e	a:	o:	u:	i:	e:
						ceol			

 Éist leis an téip agus abair na focail os ard.

4 Stór Focal

I

What are the different types of music? Tabhair buille faoi thuairim. Have a guess. Write the names.

(i) ceol clasaiceach _____

(ii) snagcheol _____

(iii) ceol tíre _____

(iv) popcheol _____

(v) sean-nós _____

Éist leis an téip agus seiceáil na freagraí.

2 Labhairt

Féach ar na grianghraif *the photographs*. What type of music do you think each person likes? Déan plé le do pháirtí.

Sampla:
Is maith le James ceol clasaiceach.

Róisín

Lao

Ingrid

James

3

Éist leis an téip. You will hear the four people talking about their likes and dislikes. Write down the type of music they like.

Róisín	
Lao	
Ingrid	
James	

4

The following is a list of the cultural activities which are on offer on an Irish Language course.

Scríobh an t-aistriúchán *the translation*. Breathnaigh ar na focail san fhoclóir nó cuir ceist ar an múinteoir. Iarr ar an múinteoir cuidiú leat na focail a rá *to say the words*.

gníomhaíocht	aistriúchán
amhránaíocht	
damhsa	
fíodóireacht	
péintéireacht	
potadóireacht	
sléibhteoireacht	

Talk to another student about activities you like and activities you dislike.

Cultúr

I

An maith leat Ceol Gaelach?

A love of Irish music has often led people to an appreciation and in many cases a desire to study the Irish language. The singer Enya has received thousands of letters from her fans asking for translations of her Irish lyrics simply because they love the sound of the language.

Obair Ghrúpa

Léigh na ceisteanna seo a leanas agus pléigh iad le foghlaimeoirí eile.

(i) Why did you decide to study Irish?
(ii) Did music have anything to do with your decision?
(iii) Has music prompted you to study any other languages? How?

If you know a song in another language apart from your mother-tongue, why not sing it for the group? If you are not happy singing, say the words. Give a short explanation of what the song is about.

2

Irish Music and the Irish Language

There is a strong connection between Irish music and the Irish language.

The most obvious connection is song. This link is particularly evident in **sean-nós** *old style*, which is an unaccompanied form of singing deriving in part from the bardic tradition of professional poetry. The emphasis in sean-nós is on the intensity of the words and the flow of the language. Sean-nós has always been popular in the Gaeltacht but in recent years is becoming more widely appreciated.

Since the 1970's groups like *Planxty, De Danann, The Bothy Band, Stockton's Wing, Clannad, Moving Hearts, The Hothouse Flowers* and more recently *Altan* and artists like Enya have given a new impetus to Irish traditional music and songs in Irish. The way they have combined them with rock, blues, contemporary folk and American and Eastern European folk has produced a uniquely Irish yet contemporary style.

Even in instrumental music the Irish language is echoed. The famous piper Séamas Ennis said that the piper must 'go back to the song' when playing slow airs. Bill Whelan, composer of the music for *Riverdance*, says 'the melodic inflections, particularly of slow airs, obviously spring from the well of the (Irish) language – in the metres and in the rise and fall of the language'.

Obair Ghrúpa

Make a list of songs in Irish you know. Perhaps you might like to sing a verse or two. Give a little explanation of the song if you have an idea what it is about.

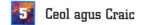

 **Sa Rang**

Sorry, I forgot my...!

I

> Faraor géar, níl mo chárta creidmheasa agam

> An seansgéal céanna..... Tráthúil go leor, tá mo cheannsa agam!

The following people have forgotten something. Meaitseáil na habairtí leis na pictiúir.

(i) (ii)

(iii) (iv)

(v) (vi)

(a) Níl mo scáth fearthainne agam.
(b) Níl m'fhidil agam.
(c) Níl mo pheann agam.
(d) Níl mo théacsleabhar agam.
(e) Níl m'eochracha agam.
(f) Níl m'uaireadóir agam.

2(a)

Cuir an comhrá san ord ceart *in the correct order.*

Go raibh maith agat.
Faraor, níl mo leabhar agam!
Tá fáilte romhat.
Úsáid mo cheannsa.

Tá an comhrá san ord ceart ar an téip.

(b)

> **Offering assistance**
>
> To invite another student to use or share your textbook you can say
>
> **Úsáid mo cheannsa.**
>
> The word **ceann** is very useful in Irish as it can be used to refer to nouns already mentioned or implied without having to repeat these nouns, like the word *one* in English. **Ceannsa** is the contrastive form.
>
> In the dialogue above, **mo cheannsa** refers to **leabhar**.

(c)

Underline the words which **ceann** refer to in the dialogues below.

A dhiabhail, níl mo pheann luaidhe agam!
Tóg mo cheannsa. Tá ceann eile agam.
Go raibh maith agat.
Tá fáilte romhat.

Tá an litriú seo mícheart ach faraor géar níl scriosán agam!
Úsáid mo cheannsa.
Go raibh míle maith agat!
Tá fáilte romhat.

Cheannaigh mé caiséad nua le Enya ach níl mo sheinnteoir caiséad agam inniu.
Úsáid mo cheannsa.
Go raibh maith agat.
Tá fáilte romhat.

Can you figure out what the people have forgotten?

(d)

3 Obair Bheirte

(a) Breathnaigh ar na focail seo san fhoclóir. Iarr ar an múinteoir iad a rá.

scriosán	foclóir	peann luaidhe
leabhar	rialóir	bioróir

(b) Scríobh **mo** roimh gach focal *in front of each word*.

Sampla: mo **bh**ioróir

Iarr ar an múinteoir cuidiú leat na frásaí a rá.

(c) Scríobh na focail (gan 'mo' *without 'mo'*) ar phíosaí páipéir nó ar chártaí. Iompaigh na píosaí páipéir nó na cártaí bun os cionn. Turn the pieces of paper or cards upside down. Take turns picking up a piece of paper or card. You have forgotten to bring the object on the paper or card to class. Have a conversation.

Sampla:
Níl mo bhioróir agam.
Tóg mo cheannsa.
Go raibh míle maith agat.
Tá fáilte romhat.

4(a)

Asking for something

The expression **An bhfuil … agat** can be used to ask if someone has got something. e.g.
An bhfuil bioróir agat?
/ən wil/

A positive reply would be
Tá, seo duit. (Giving the sharpener).

A negative reply would be
Níl. Tá brón orm.

(b) Cluiche do Bheirt

Copy down the chart below. Write 5 words under each of the 4 headings. Do not show the words to your partner.

An Rang	An Teaghlach	Ceol	An Aimsir

Cut the chart into individual word-strips – a single word on each strip. Do not let your partner see the words.

Take turns 'guessing' the words your partner has chosen.

Sampla:
An bhfuil an focal 'deartháir' agat?
Tá. Seo duit.

Partner hands you the word.
An bhfuil an focal 'snagcheol' agat?
Níl. (Tá brón orm).

Now it is your partner's turn. The first person to guess all her or his partner's words correctly wins.

7 Cumarsáid

Describing people

1(a)

Read the following description of Séamus Ó Beaglaoich, accordionist and sean-nós singer.

Tá Séamus Ó Beaglaoich ina chónaí i nGaeltacht Chiarraí. Tá **feirm** 110 acra aige i mBaile na bPoc. Tá triúr mac agus iníon amháin aige. Is amhránaithe ar an sean-nós* iad a dheartháir Breandán agus a dheirfiúracha – Seosaimhín, Máire agus Eibhlín. **Seinn**eann Breandán an bosca ceoil freisin. Is maith le Séamus an **bosca ceoil** E-maol**. Tá sé níos **beoga** dar leis.

* amhránaithe ar an sean-nós *sean-nós singers*
** E-maol *E flat*

(b) Breathnaigh ar na focail i gcló dubh *in bold type* in (a) san fhoclóir.

(c) Obair Bheirte

The following information has been taken from the article about Séamus Ó Beaglaoich. The sentences have been split in two. Meaitseáil na codanna (do not look at the article until you have completed the exercise).

Tá Séamus Ó Beaglaoich ina chonaí	E-maol
Tá feirm 110 acra	aige in mBaile na bPoc
Tá triúr mac agus	an bosca ceoil
Seinneann sé	i nGaeltacht Chiarraí
Is maith leis an bosca ceoil	iníon amháin aige

(d) Scríobh

Imagine you are Séamus Ó Beaglaoich. Write a short description of yourself. Read it out for another student.

Líon na bearnaí.

Séamus Ó Beaglaoich is ainm _____. Tá _____ i _____ chónaí i gCiarraí. Tá triúr mac agus iníon amháin _____. Is maith _____ an bosca ceoil.

2(a) Gramadach

Críochnaigh an ghreille.

feminine	masculine
sí	
	é
aici	
	leis
di	
	air

(b)

The following are descriptions of two well-known people who sing in Irish.

Léigh na téacsanna. Líon na bearnaí leis na focail sna boscaí. **Sé** is already filled in for you.

| air | dó | aige | sé | é | leis |

Tadhg Mac Dhonnagáin is ainm _____.

As Contae Mhaigh Eo _____.

Is maith _____ a bheith ag cumadh ceoil do pháistí óga.

'Feargal Ó Féasóg' an t-ainm eile atá _____.

Tá lipéad speisialta * _____ do cheol do pháistí. *Futa Fata* atá air.

Is maith leis filíocht freisin. Rinne **sé** obair leis an bhfile Gaeilge Michael Davitt.

*Lipéad speisialta *special label*

| léi | í | di | sí | uirthi | aici |

Mairéad Ní Mhaonaigh atá _____.

Tá _____ sa ghrúpa *Altan*.

As Dún na nGall _____.

Tá deartháir amháin _____. Gearóid atá air.

Tá deirfiúr amháin aici. Anna is ainm _____.

Nuair a bhíonn Mairéad saor is maith _____ dul ag siúl cois farraige.

(c)

An Aidiacht Shealbhach 'a'
The Possessive Adjective 'a'

The possessive adjective **a** can mean *her*, *his* or *their*.

The meaning that is intended is indicated by the changes that follow **a**:

a *her*	no *séimhiú*, **h** before a vowel
a *his*	*séimhiú*, no change to a vowel
a *their*	*urú*, **n** before a vowel

So,

> **a páistí** *her children*,
> **a pháistí** *his children*,
> **a bpáistí** *their children*.

And

> **a haintín** *her aunt*,
> **a aintín** *his aunt*,
> **a n-aintín** *their aunt*.

Obair Bheirte

The following are facts about Síle and Pádraig. Some facts are common to both of them **an bheirt acu**. Match the facts to the people. One has already been done for you.

1. Tá Gaeilge ag a hiníon.
2. Níl a athair beo.
3. Tá a deirfiúr ina cónaí i mBéal an Átha.
4. Tá a bpáistí fásta suas.
5. Tá a mhac ina chónaí sna Stáit Aontaithe.
6. Níl a n-eochracha sa seomra.

Síle	Pádraig	An bheirt acu
3		

8 Scríobh agus Caint

Write a short description of yourself – your name, where you are from, where you are living now, your family (number of brothers, sisters, children etc), your likes, dislikes ...

Give this description to your partner.

Read your partner's description of herself or himself. Describe your partner to another student.

Sampla: Yoshiko is ainm di. As Tóiceo í.

An Old Irish Tale

Music features prominently in many of the early Irish stories. One such story is *Oidhe Chloinne Lir* which tells of the fate of the Children of Lear (in Irish 'of Lear' is *Lir*).

The children of Lear – Fiachra, Conn, Aodh and Fionnuala – were turned into swans by their jealous stepmother, Aoife. They spent three hundred years on Loch Dairbhreach, another three hundred years on Sruth na Maoile and a final three hundred years at Iorrus Domhnann and Inis Gluaire. In the end they were turned back into humans but unfortunately they died shortly afterwards.

Painting by Pauline Bewick

The following extract from the story takes place on Loch Dairbhreach. Lear and his followers are standing on the edge of the lake. The four swans are in the lake.

Nuair a chuala Lear agus a mhuintir go raibh a pháistí athraithe ina n-ealaí, lig siad trí gháir chumha, ghoil agus chaointe astu. 'An dteastaíonn uaibh teacht i dtír chugainn...?' a dúirt sé. 'Níl ar ár gcumas taobh a thabhairt le haon duine eile ...' arsa Fionnuala; 'ach tá ár dteanga Ghaeilge féin againn; agus tá ar ár gcumas ceol síreachtach a chanadh, agus is leor an ceol sin chun an cine daonna a shásamh. Mar sin fanaigí linn anocht, agus canfaimid an ceol duit'.

D'fhan Lear agus a mhuintir ag éisteacht le ceol na n-ealaí ar bhruacha Loch Dairbhreach agus chodail siad go sámh an oíche sin.

When Lear and his people heard that his children had been turned into swans, they raised three shouts of grief, crying and lamentation. 'Do you wish', he said, 'to come ashore to us ...?'

'We are unable to associate with any person...' said Fionnuala; 'but we have our own language, Gaeilge; and we are able to chant plaintive music, and that music is sufficient to satisfy the whole human race. So remain with us tonight, and we shall chant music for you.'

Lear and his people remained listening to the music of the swans on the shores of Loch Dairbhreach and they slept peacefully that night.

These extracts are adaptations of *Oidhe Chloinne Lir* published by the Society for the Irish Language (1908), MH Gill and Son.

9 Gramadach

I

feminine (f)	masculine (m)

Feminine or Masculine?

Inscne *Gender*

There are two genders in Irish, feminine and masculine and all nouns fall into one of these categories. Gender in Irish does not just apply to people or animals – objects, ideas, feelings etc can have gender.

feminine	masculine
bean *woman*	**fear** *man*
Gaeilge *Irish*	**ceol** *music*

The easiest way to find out the gender of a word is to check in the dictionary.

You can often find out the gender of a noun by looking at its ending. For example nouns which end with

-óg/-eog, -lann, -(i)úint, -(e)acht

with more than one syllable are generally feminine.

Most names of countries, such as **Éire**, are feminine, whereas occupations tend to be masculine, e.g. **múinteoir** *teacher*, **glantóir** *cleaner*.

(a) Obair Bheirte

Breathnaigh ar na focail san fhoclóir. Déan liosta de na focail faoi *feminine* nó *masculine*.

Have a competition to see who finishes first.

- ainm
- amhrán
- bioróir
- cathair
- cathaoir
- ceist
- cultúr
- fidil
- fliúit
- foclóir
- gramadach

- grúpa
- leabhar
- leathanach
- peann
- obair
- rialóir
- scamall
- sloinne
- téip
- uaireadóir
- uncail

Compare your answers.

An interesting fact …

> You will have noticed that there are almost twice as many masculine nouns as feminine nouns in the exercise you have just completed.
>
> This fact applies to the Irish language in general.

(b)

Can you guess the gender of the following nouns?

1 máthair 2 An tSín 3 bábóg 4 iníon
5 leabharlann 6 uncail 7 canúint
8 fuinneog 9 ceoltóir

Seiceáil na freagraí san fhoclóir.

Write down 6 nouns from the units you have studied. Check their gender.

2

Why know the gender?

It is helpful to know the gender of a noun in Irish when you are a learner of the language, especially if you are not in an environment where Irish is spoken on a regular basis.

Knowing the gender of a noun ensures more accurate spelling and pronunciation.

The following diagram shows how gender can change the spelling of different nouns when **an** *the* is placed before the dictionary headword. (The Irish nouns in brackets are the headwords).

	nouns beginning with consonant	nouns beginning with 's'	nouns beginning with vowel
feminine	*séimhiú* on initial consonant (except l,n,r,t,d,sc,sm,st) An Ghaeilge (Gaeilge)	't' before 's' + vowel or l, n, r an tseilf (seilf) an tsláinte (sláinte) an tsnaidhm (snaidhm) an tsráid (sráid)	no change an aintín (aintín)
masculine	no change an cúrsa (cúrsa)	no change an solas (solas)	't-' before vowel an t-amhrán (amhrán)

Obair Bheirte

Put **an** in front of the headwords in exercise **9.**1 (a) above and make the necessary changes to the spelling of the nouns.

Sampla: ainm, an t-ainm

10 Cultúr

1

Abair Amhrán!

Traditional Song in Irish

The word 'traditional' refers to songs which have been transmitted orally from one generation to the next, or passed from one performer to another.

With the spread of the English language in the early 1800's songs in the Irish language were performed less frequently. However, the cultural renaissance of the 1890's gave a new impetus to songs in Irish. A concerted effort was made to collect and record Irish music and song. Many songs in Irish were written down for the first time.

In 1987 The Traditional Music Archive was set up. The Archive has assembled the largest collection of Irish traditional music in existence. This includes recently-composed music in 'traditional' style.

Traditional songs are growing in popularity, and are performed in both English and Irish.

Logo and trademark of the Irish Traditional Music Archive

The bell of a bronze horn of the Iron Age, the Loughnashade Horn, which is one of the oldest surviving Irish musical instruments. The horn is in the National Museum of Ireland.

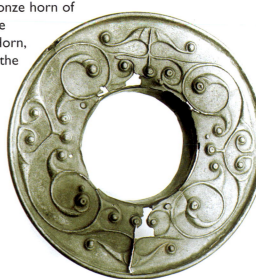

Plé

What value (if any) is there in collecting and recording traditional songs in Irish?

Is it possible to enjoy listening to songs in Irish even if you do not understand the meaning of the words?

2

Many traditional songs we hear today reflect social and cultural changes which have taken place in Ireland throughout the course of Irish history. In the following page there is a description of different types of song in Irish, some of which reflect these changes.

Song Types

Courtly Love Songs: Based on courtly love songs brought to Ireland by the Normans

Praise Songs: 1200–1600 professional poets composed songs to honour their patrons. They were sung by reciters and accompanied by a harp.

Laments: Written after the Flight of the Earls (1607) and the Plantation of Ulster. *Seán Ó Duibhir an Ghleanna* is an example. Laments are probably the oldest form of song to have survived in Ireland. Other forms of Laments were the 'keen' or **caoineadh** in Irish which was sung at wakes (*Caoineadh Airt Uí Laoghaire*) and the 'death song' which recalled tragedies and disasters (*Eanach Dhúin*).

Ballads: Fenian Lays were especially popular in the 16th and 17th centuries. These recorded the deeds of Fionn Mac Cumhaill and the Fianna. They appealed to rural communities with their depiction of outdoor life, athletic and heroic feats. The last singers of Fenian lays were recorded in Ireland in the 1940's.

Love Songs: Mainly written by anonymous poets from the late 17th century onwards. The language was vivid and emotional (*Dónall Óg*).

Aisling Songs: Form of political journalism of the 18th century whereby the poet meets a beautiful woman who claims that Ireland will eventually triumph over her enemies (*Úrchill an Chreagáin*).

Jacobite Songs: Songs which showed a desire for the Stuarts to return and restore the old Gaelic aristocracy (*Mo Ghile Mear*).

Patriotic Songs: Such as *Róisín Dubh* and *Sliabh na mBan*, from the Elizabethan & 1798 Rebellions

Emigration and Famine Songs: Describing the loneliness and nostalgia of the emigrant (*Bánchnoic Éireann Ó*) and the plight of people during the Famine (*Na Fataí Bána*).

Religious Songs: Such as *Caoineadh na dTrí Muire*

Work Songs: e.g. *Dúlamán*, about people selling seaweed

Drinking Songs: Like *Preab san Ól*

Lullabies: e.g. *Seoithín agus Seoithín* with refrains of repeated meaningless words

Sources
Ó hAllmhuráin, G. (1998) *A Pocket History of Irish Traditional Music*, Dublin: The O'Brien Press.
Béaloideas 1995.
Irish Traditional Music Archive – Leaflet 1

3

In the recording you will hear extracts from some of these songs. The words are on page 84. Can you say which category each song belongs to (without looking at the information on the left)?

Amhrán	Catagóir
1	
2	
3	
4	

Déan comparáid le foghlaimeoir eile. Seiceáil na freagraí sa bhosca ar chlé *on the left*.

11 Scileanna Foghlama

Learning Grammar – how important is it?

1

The following are different views on learning grammar:

I think Irish grammar is far too complex at this stage… beginner. It's better to learn to speak the language first and then worry about the grammar.

It's very important to know the basic rules of the language. If you know the rules you have something to build on. It gives you more confidence to use the language.

It's better to introduce grammar only when it is absolutely necessary – when not knowing a particular grammar point would interfere with communication.

Grammar is interesting, especially when you want to compare different languages. How a language is constructed is a fascinating study in itself. You can study a language without having to speak it!

Think about these 4 viewpoints. Write a similar statement about your own attitude to studying grammar.

2 Tuairisc

Prepare a report on the advantages and disadvantages of studying grammar. Elect one person to be secretary for the group. Copy the grid below for your report.

Grammar

Advantages	Disadvantages

Report your findings to the whole class.

Sa Rang

Cuardaigh na habairtí seo a leanas san aonad. Look for the following sentences in the unit. Translate the words in bold print.

Cleacht an comhrá.

Iompaigh na cártaí bunoscionn.

Breathnaigh ar na focail nua.

Cuardaigh na habairtí seo a leanas.

Staidéar Pearsanta

Scríobh cuntas ar dhuine eile faoi na ceannteidil seo a leanas. Write an account of another person under the following headings. If, for example, you had enough information you could write about a famous singer or musician from your own country.

- Ainm
- Sloinne
- Áit dhúchais (where she or he is from)
- Teaghlach
- Na rudaí is maith léi nó leis
- Na rudaí nach maith léi nó leis

Cluiche

Round 1

Class divides into two teams, not more than 6 on each team. Everyone choses a like and a dislike from the first category below – Female Singers. One after the other the members of team A say who they like and dislike. A member of team B reports this information (see example below). One point is awarded for each correct report (a point for each 'like' and a point for each 'dislike').

The members of team B then say which female singers they like and dislike. A member of team A reports this informtaion. Points are awarded as before.

Round 2

Everyone choses a like and a dislike from the second category. The game continues as before until all the categories have been completed.

The team with the highest number of points wins.

Foireann A   **Foireann B**

Is maith liom Enya ach ní maith liom Madonna

Is maith le Pádraig Enya ach ní maith leis Madonna

Na Catagóirí

1 Amhránaithe (mná) *Female Singers*
2 Amhránaithe (fir) *Male singers*
3 Grúpaí ceoil *Music groups*
4 Cineálacha ceoil *Types of music*
5 Gníomhaíochtaí *Activities*
6 Tíortha *Countries*

Achoimre *Summary*

Cumarsáid agus Stór Focal

Stating your likes and dislikes	Is maith liom an cúrsa.
	Ní maith liom an cúrsa.
	Is maith liom cait agus madraí.
	Ní maith liom tae ach is maith liom caife.
	Ní maith liom an Spáinn ná an Iodáil.
Enquiring about likes and dislikes	An maith leat an cúrsa?
Responding	Is maith. Ní maith.
Talking about a third person	Máire is ainm di. Síle atá uirthi.
	Pól is ainm dó. Seán atá air.
	As an Astráil í, é.
	Tá triúr mac aici, aige.
	Tá sí, sé ina c(h)ónaí i bPáras.
	Is maith léi, leis éisteacht le ceol.
	Tá a d(h)eirfiúr ina cónaí in Éirinn.
	Seo a (h)aintín.
Types of music	ceol clasaiceach, popcheol, snagcheol, ceol tíre, sean-nós
Likes and dislikes	cait, matamaitic, luchóga, stoirmeacha, damháin alla
Hobbies and activities	potadóireacht, amhránaíocht, damhsa, fíodóireacht, péintéireacht, sléibhteoireacht
Sa rang	Faraor, níl mo pheann agam!
	Tóg, úsáid mo cheannsa.
	Tá ceann eile agam.
	An bhfuil bioróir agat?
	Tá, seo duit.
	Níl. Tá brón orm.
	Go raibh (míle) maith agat.
	Tá fáilte romhat.
	bioróir, rialóir, scriosán, peann luaidhe, leabhar
Sa téacsleabhar	Cleacht an comhrá.
	Iompaigh na cártaí bun os cionn.
	Breathnaigh ar na focail nua.
	Cuardaigh na habairtí.

Gramadach

- An Chopail
  Positive: **Is** maith liom.
  Negative: **Ní** maith liom.
  Question: **An** maith leat?
- Personal Pronouns 3rd person sing. (subject)
  Tá **sí** ina cónaí sa Bhruiséil (fem).
  Tá **sé** ina chónaí sa Bhruiséil (masc).
- Personal Pronouns 3rd person sing. (object)
  As Gaillimh **í** (fem).
  As Gaillimh **é** (masc).
- Prepositional Pronouns 3rd person sing.
  Tá feirm **aici** (fem). Tá feirm **aige** (masc).
  Máire atá **uirthi** (fem). Seán atá **air** (masc).
  Is maith **léi** luchóga (fem). Is maith **leis** damháin alla (masc).
- Possessive Adjectives 3rd person sing.
  Seo **a m**uintir (fem). Seo **a mh**uintir (masc).
  Seo **a h**aintín (fem). Seo **a a**intín (masc).
- Nouns are either feminine or masculine.
  – The easiest way to know which is which is to look the word up in the dictionary.
  A noun may change after *an* depending on gender: **an bh**ean, **an t-a**mhrán, **an ts**eilf.

Cultúr

- A love of Irish music and song has often led people to study the Irish language.
- Instrumental music can echo the Irish language, slow airs in particular.
- Songs in Irish became less popular in the early 1800's.
- The cultural renaissance of the 1890's gave a new impetus to songs in Irish. Music began to be collected and written down.
- In 1987 The Traditional Music Archive was established, having the largest collection of Irish traditional music in existence.
- Many traditional songs in Irish reflect social, cultural and political changes which have taken place throughout history.
- Different *Song Types*

Fuaimniú

- The symbols used for the short vowels are
  i e a o u
- The symbols used for the long vowels are
  i: e: a: o: u:
- Each sound can have more than one spelling
  /i:/ = buí, naoi, sín

Scileanna Foghlama

- There are many different views on the value of learning grammar at beginner level
  1. no grammar at all
  2. only as need arises
  3. a crucial basis for language learning
  4. something which can be studied in its own right
- Important to be able to weigh up advantages and disadvantages.

Triail Tú Féin

A

Say how you feel about the following classroom activities. Cuir x sa bhosca cuí.

Gníomhaíocht	Is maith	Ní maith
Léamh		
Éisteacht		
Labhairt		
Scríobh		
Gramadach		
Cultúr		

Question two people about the classroom activities they like and dislike. Fill in the replies in the chart below (a sample is given).

	Máire		
Léamh	is maith		
Éisteacht	ní maith		
Labhairt	is maith		
Scríobh	ní maith		
Gramadach	is maith		
Cultúr	is maith		

Which person resembles you most? Tell another student about the likes and dislikes you share and don't share with that person.

Déan an cleachtadh seo leis an múinteoir.

Tusa:	Tell the teacher you have forgotten your pen.
Múinteoir:	Tóg mo cheannsa.
Tusa:	Thank the teacher.

Múinteoir:	An bhfuil bioróir agat?
Tusa:	Say 'yes, here it is'.
Múinteoir:	Go raibh míle maith agat.
Tusa:	Respond.

B Meaitseáil na focail.

potadóireacht   *storms*   snagcheol   damhsa
fiddle   *ruler*   *pencil-parer*   scriosán   *mice*
luchóga   fidil   ceol tíre   stoirmeacha   *jazz*
eraser   rialóir   *pottery*   *country music*
dancing   bioróir

C Líon na bearnaí.

Seo mo chol ceathrair. Mildred is ainm _____. Tá _____ ina cónaí i mBaile na Muc. Tá mac amháin _____. Marc is ainm _____.

Tá a hathair agus a _____ beo fós. Is maith le Mildred ceol tíre. Ní maith _____ luchóga.

Seo mo chara. Tony is ainm _____. As an Astráil _____ ach tá sé ina chónaí in Éirinn anois. Tá deirfiúr amháin _____. Sadie atá _____.

Tá a _____ beo ach tá a mháthair marbh. Is maith le Tony ceol traidisiúnta Éireannach ach ní maith _____ an bodhrán!

D

Are the following nouns feminine or masculine? Cuir x sa bhosca cuí.

Nouns	Feminine	Masculine
an t-amhrán		
an foclóir		
an tsráid		
an chathaoir		
an seomra		
an áit		

E Meaitseáil na focail leis na siombailí.

dó	a:		seo	a
faoi	i:		maith	e
sé	o:		deich	i
tá	u:		sin	o
tú	e:		rud	u

F

Líon na bearnaí sna habairtí.

1   Sean-nós is an unaccompanied form of
    _____.
2   The famous piper Séamas Ennis said that the
    piper must 'go back to the _____'.
3   The Archive has assembled the largest
    collection of _____.
4   Many traditional songs we hear today reflect
    _____.

Meaitseáil an t-amhrán agus an chatagóir.

Amhrán	Catagóir
Dúlamán	Religious
Mo Ghile Mear	Lullaby
Preab San Ól	Jacobite
Úrchill an Chreagáin	Work
Seoithín, Seoithín	Aisling
Caoineadh na dTrí Muire	Drink

Eochair

1.2 an, is, ní

1.3(a)
(i)   matamaitic
(ii) stoirmeacha
(iii) cait
(iv) ceol clasaiceach
(v)   luchóga
(vi) damháin alla

2.1   1 ach   2 ná   3 agus   4 agus

3.2

a	o	u	i	e	a:	o:	u:	i:	e:
craic	seo	rud	is	seit	dán	ceol	fliúit	sí	sé

4.3 Róisín, ceol tíre   Lao, sean-nós
Ingrid, ceol clasaiceach   James, snagcheol

6.1 (i)(c) (ii)(d) (iii)(f)   (iv)(b)   (v)(a)   (vi)(e)
6.2(c) peann luaidhe, scriosán, seinnteoir
          caiséad
6.3(b) mo scriosán, m'fhoclóir, mo pheann
          luaidhe, mo leabhar, mo rialóir

7.1(c)

Tá Séamus Ó Beaglaoich ina chónaí i nGaeltacht
Chiarraí.
Tá feirm 110 acra aige i mBaile na bPoc.
Tá triúr mac agus iníon amháin aige.
Seinneann sé an bosca ceoil.
Is maith leis an bosca ceoil E-maol.

7.1(d)
Séamus Ó Beaglaoich is ainm dom. Tá mé i mo
chónaí i gCiarraí. Tá triúr mac agus iníon amháin
agam. Is maith liom an bosca ceoil.

7.2(a)

fem	sí	í	aici	léi	di	uirthi
masc	sé	é	aige	leis	dó	air

7.2(b)

Tadhg Mac Dhonnagáin is ainm **dó**.
As Contae Mhaigh Eo **é**.
Is maith **leis** a bheith ag cumadh ceoil do
pháistí óga.
'Feargal Ó Féasóg' an t-ainm eile atá **air**.
Tá lipéad speisialta **aige** do cheol do pháistí.
Futa Fata atá air.
Is maith leis filíocht freisin.
Rinne **sé** obair leis an bhfile Gaeilge
Michael Davitt.

Mairéad Ní Mhaonaigh atá **uirthi**.
Tá **sí** sa ghrúpa *Altan*.

As Dún na nGall **í**.
Tá deartháir amháin **aici**. Gearóid atá air.
Tá deirfiúr amháin aici. Anna is ainm **di**.

Nuair a bhíonn Máiréad saor is maith **léi** dul ag siúl cois farraige.

7.2(c)

Síle	Pádraig	An bheirt acu
1	2	4
3	5	6

9.2
An t-ainm, an t-amhrán, an bioróir,
an chathair, an chathaoir, an cheist, an cultúr,
an fhidil, an fhliúit, an foclóir, an ghramadach,
an grúpa, an leabhar, an leathanach, an peann,
an obair, an rialóir, an scamall, an sloinne, an téip, an
t-uaireadóir, an t-uncail

Triail Tú Féin

B

potadóireacht *pottery*, snagcheol *jazz*,
damhsa *dancing*, scriosán *eraser*,
luchóga *mice*, fidil *fiddle*, ceol tíre *country music*,
stoirmeacha *storms*, rialóir *ruler*, bioróir *pencil parer*.

C

Seo mo chol ceathrair. Mildred is ainm **di**. Tá **sí** ina cónaí i mBaile na Muc. Tá mac amháin **aici**. Marc is ainm **dó**. Tá a hathair agus a **máthair** beo fós.

Is maith le Mildred ceol tíre. Ní maith **léi** luchóga.

Seo mo chara. Tony is ainm **dó**.

As an Astráil **é** ach tá sé ina chónaí in Éirinn anois. Tá deirfiúr amháin **aige**. Sadie atá **uirthi**. Tá a athair beo ach tá a mháthair marbh.

Is maith le Tony ceol traidisiúnta Éireannach ach ní maith **leis** an bodhrán!

D

Nouns	Feminine	Masculine
an t-amhrán		x
an foclóir		x
an tsráid	x	
an chathaoir	x	
an seomra		x
an áit	x	

E

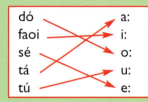

F

1 Sean-nós is an unaccompanied form of **singing**.
2 The famous piper Séamas Ennis said that the piper must 'go back to the **song**'.
3 The Archive has assembled the largest collection of **Irish traditional music in existence**.
4 Many traditional songs we hear today reflect **social and cultural changes**.

Dúlamán, Work

Mo Ghile Mear, Jacobite

Preab san Ól, Drink

Úrchill an Chreagáin, Aisling

Seoithín agus Seoithín, Lullaby

Caoineadh na dTrí Muire, Religious

Amhráin

Bánchnoic Éireann Ó

Beir beannacht ó mo chroí go tír na hÉireann,
Bánchnoic Éireann Ó
Chun a maireann de shíolra Ír agus Éibhir
Ar Bhánchnoic Éireann Ó
An áit úd inarb aoibhinn binn-ghuth
   éan
Mar shámh-chruit chaoin ag caoineadh Gael;
Is é mo chás a bheith míle, míle i gcéin
Ó bhánchnoic Éireann Ó.

The Fair Hills of Ireland Ó

Take a blessing from my heart to the land of Ireland
The fair hills of Ireland Ó
And to those alive of the seed of Éiriú and Heber
The fair hills of Ireland Ó
In that place where delightful were sweet voices
   of birds
Like the tranquil gentle harp lamenting the Irish;
My sorrow to be miles and miles away
From the fair hills of Ireland Ó.

Seoithín agus Seoithín

Agus seoithín agus seoithín agus seoithín agus seó
Agus seoithín agus seoithín agus seoithín agus seó
Agus seoithín agus seoithín agus seoithín agus seó
Ag magadh leat a bhíosa a leanbh bhig ó.

Agus seoithín agus seoithín agus seoithín agus seó
Agus seoithín agus seoithín agus seoithín agus seó
Agus seoithín agus seoithín agus seoithín agus seó
Ag magadh leat a bhíosa a bhuachaill bhig ó.

Seoithín and Seoithín

Seoithín and seoithín and seoithín and seó
Seoithín and seoithín and seoithín and seó
Seoithín and seoithín and seoithín and seó
I was teasing you little child ó.

Seoithín and seoithín and seoithín and seó
Seoithín and seoithín and seoithín and seó
Seoithín and seoithín and seoithín and seó
I was teasing you little boy ó.

Dónall Óg

Is a Dhónaill Óig, má théir thar farraige
Tabhair mé fhéin leat is ná déan dearmad
Beidh agat féirín lá aonaigh is margaidh
Is beidh iníon Rí Sheoirse mar chéile feasta leat.

'Gus gheall tú dhom agus rinne tú bréag liom
Go mbeifeá romham ag cró na gcaorach
Lig mé fead ort is míle béice
Ach ní bhfuair mé romham ann ach na huain
   ag méileach.

Dónall Óg

O Dónall Óg, if you cross the ocean
Take me with you when you are going
At fair or market, you'll be well looked after
And you shall sleep with a great king's daughter.

You said you'd meet me but you were lying
Beside the sheiling when day was dying
I whistled and called you, twelve times repeating
But all I heard was the young lambs bleating.

Translated by *Séamas Ennis*

Mo Ghile Mear

(Ireland speaks as a woman who laments her love, Prince Charles Stuart, who is in exile).

Seal dá rabhas im' mhaighdean shéimh,
Is anois im bhaintreach chaite thréith,
Mo chéile ag treabhadh na dtonn go tréan,
De bharr na gcnoc 's in imigéin.
Curfá:
'Sé mo laoch mo ghile mear,
'Sé mo Chaesar gile mear,
Suan ná séan ní bhfuaireas féin
Ó luadh i gcéin mo ghile mear.

Bímse buan ar buairt gach ló,
Ag caoi go crua is ag tuar na ndeor
Mar scaoileadh uainn an buachaill beo
Is ná ríomhtar tuairisc uaidh mo bhrón.

Gile Mear

Once I was a gentle maiden,
Now I'm a feeble worn widow,
My spouse boldly ploughing the waves,
Over the hills and far away.
Chorus:
He is my hero my Gile Mear,
He is my Caesar my Gile Mear,
Sleep or happiness I have not
Since my Gile Mear has gone away.

I am in grief each day,
Crying lamentable and weeping sore
Because my lively boy was sent away
And sadly no word from him is known.

Nóta

The word **Craic** is not originally an Irish word. It came from an Old English word which meant 'make loud sound'. In Scottish it meant 'brisk talk' or 'news'. Today, (in both Irish and English) it means informal entertainment especially the type found in a pub. The word is spelt *crack* in English.

Aonad

6 Cá bhfuil an . . .?

This unit enables learners to: ask and give directions; describe locations and become familiar with common signs. Learners are also given terms for using a tape-recorder in the classroom.

Write down any words or phrases you know to do with the topic of this unit.

1 Cumarsáid

1 Léamh

Féach ar na comharthaí (signs). Are they familiar? Do you know what they mean? Déan plé le foghlaimeoir eile.

(b)

An Siopa Leabhar	Busáras	Gael-Linn
←	↑	→
ar chlé	**díreach ar aghaidh**	**ar dheis**

Éist leis an téip agus léigh an téipscript arís. Cuir líne faoi na focail **ar chlé, díreach ar aghaidh** agus **ar dheis**. These words indicate the directions in which the people must go to reach their destinations.

(c)

Now see if you can remember where Bord Fáilte, An Siopa Leabhar and TG4 are.

Cá bhfuil	ar chlé	díreach ar aghaidh	ar dheis
Bord Fáilte			
An Siopa Leabhar			
TG4			

Seiceáil na freagraí sna *Téipscripteanna*.

3(a) Obair Bheirte

Clúdaigh an bosca eolais thíos.

(i)   Write down 2 ways of asking for directions.
(ii) What phrase would you use to get someone's attention?

> ### Treoracha *Directions*
>
> The simplest way to ask directions is to name the place you are looking for followed by **le do thoil** *please*.
>
> **Bord Fáilte, le do thoil.**
>
> You can also say
> **Cá bhfuil** + place
> **Cá bhfuil Gael-Linn (le do thoil)?**
>
> To get someone's attention use
> **Gabh mo leithscéal.** *Excuse me.*

2(a) Obair Bheirte

In the following dialogues different people are asking a Garda Síochána for directions. Tick off the places mentioned.

FÁS	
Aer Rianta	
Banc Ceannais na hÉireann	
Gael-Linn	
TG4	
An Siopa Leabhar	
Údarás na Gaeltachta	
Iarnród Éireann	
An Lár	
Busáras	
Bord na Móna	
Bord Fáilte Éireann	
Fir Mná (leithreas)?	

Déan comparáid *comparison* le do pháirtí. Seiceáil na freagraí sna *Téipscripteanna*.

(b)

The picture on the next page shows three buildings. One is **an Siopa Leabhar**, one is **an Siopa Potadóireachta** and the third is **an Siopa Ceoil**. You decide which shop is which but do not tell your partner. Find out where your partner has located her or his shops.

Tá tú anseo

2 Stór Focal

1

Cuardaigh na focail seo san fhoclóir. Check their meanings and their gender.

banc	oifig an phoist
ollmhargadh	aerfort
pictiúrlann	oifig fáilte
linn snámha	scoil

2

Líon na bearnaí sna habairtí leis na focail thuas *the above words*.

(a) Cá bhfuil an _____?

(b) Tá an _____ ar dheis.

(c) Tá _____ ar chlé.

(d) Cá bhfuil an _____ ?

(e) Tá an _____ díreach ar aghaidh.

(f) Seo an _____.

(g) Is maith liom an _____ seo!

(h) Cá bhfuil an _____?

Nóta gramadaí

The definite article **an** *the* is not placed before a name if it already occurs within it. Compare:

> **Tá an Oifig Fáilte ar dheis.**
>
> **Tá Oifig an Phoist ar chlé.**

3

A number of people are being asked where different places are but they do not always give the right directions.

Éist leis an téip agus féach ar an bpictiúr.

Mark the places you think have not been correctly indicated.

Déan comparáid le do pháirtí.
Seiceáil na freagraí sna *Téipscripteanna*.

4 Cluiche do Bheirt

See how well you remember where the different places in 3 above are located.

Sampla:

A *(looking at picture)*: Cá bhfuil an linn snámha?

B *(not looking at picture)*: Ar dheis

A: Go maith.

B *(looking at picture)*: Cá bhfuil an banc?

A *(not looking at picture)*: Ar dheis

B: Ní hea.

After you have finished the game, copy this plan on to a page and change the locations of the different places. Then continue the game as before.

3 Cultúr

1(a)

Bilingual Signs

The first bilingual road-signs appeared in Ireland in 1937. The names on the early road-signs may be inaccurate and inconsistent, since the spelling was often decided locally. Nowadays standard spellings are used, determined by the *Placenames Commission*.

Bus companies like *Bus Éireann* and *Bus Átha Cliath* give destinations on the front of the bus in both English and Irish. But it is common to find bilingual signs in other places too, including supermarkets, book shops and beauty shops.

(b) Obair Bheirte

Discuss the advantages and disadvantages of bilingual signs. Do you think they are a good idea or not? Gives reasons.

Now have a short class discussion on the topic.

2 Obair Bheirte

How well do you remember your numbers?

Foghlaimeoir A: Léigh *Nóta 1* ar leathanach 105.

Foghlaimeoir B: You are making enquiries about which buses go to the following destinations in Dublin. Your partner has this information. Say your destination in Irish (ask your teacher to help you with the pronunciation). Write the bus number in the box on the right.

Cearnóg Mhuirfean **Merrion Square**	
An Lár **City Centre**	
Dún Laoghaire	
Aerfort	

Athraigh na rólanna.
Foghlaimeoir A: Léigh *Nóta 2* ar leathanach 105.

Foghlaimeoir B: Your partner wants to know which buses go to the following destinations in Dublin. When she or he names a destination, say the bus number.

Bóthar Bulfin **Bulfin Road**	19
Sráid an Choláiste **College Street**	83
Páirc Wadelai **Wadelai Park**	11
Faiche Stiabhna	32X

3 Staidéar Pearsanta

If you are studying in Ireland, find out the Irish name of your street or road. Ask your teacher to help you with the pronunciation. Learn how to spell the name also. You will then be able to say or write your name (first name and surname) and your address (e.g. street, town and country) in Irish.

If you are studying outside Ireland write the address of a person or organisation you know in Ireland. Your teacher will help you if you do not know any.

3(a) San Ollmhargadh

Meaitseáil an leagan Gaeilge agus an leagan Béarla.

Bia folláin	*Beverages*
Fíoruisce	*Bread*
Seacláidí	*Health foods*
Crua-earraí	*Spring water*
Arán	*Chocolates*
Deochanna	*Hardware*

(b) Staidéar Pearsanta

Keep an eye out for bilingual signs (if you are outside Ireland, check in magazines, books or on the Internet). Make a note of them and show them to the other students when you return to class.

Seanfhocal *Proverb*

Is fearr a bheith cinnte ná bheith caillte.

It's better to be sure than lost.

4 Stór Focal

I   Líon na bearnaí sna habairtí leis na focail seo a leanas:

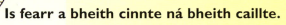

suas	síos	isteach	amach

A   Téigh* _____ an doras.

B   Téigh _____ an staighre.

C   Téigh _____ an fhuinneog!

D   Téigh _____ sa tollán.

E   Téigh _____ an cnoc.

F   _____ leat!

* Téigh /t'e:y'/ = go

2 Scríobh

(a) Críochnaigh na comhráite seo a leanas:

I   *Stop the shop-assistant and ask where the bread is.*
Téigh suas an pasáiste agus tá sé ar dheis, in aice leis na seacláidí.
Thank him.

2   An bhfuil a fhios agat cá bhfuil an phictiúrlann?
Down the street on the left.
Go raibh maith agat.
Say 'You're welcome'.

3   An bhfaca tú m'iníon aon áit?
Tell him she is in the park.
Cá bhfuil an pháirc?
Tell him to go straight ahead and to go in that gate.

4   An bhfuil an leithreas sa treo seo?
Say you are sorry but that you don't know.

5   Cá bhfuil seomra na múinteoirí le do thoil?
Tell him to go out the door and to turn left.
The teachers' room is on the left.
Go raibh maith agat.
Respond.

(b)
Put titles on the above conversations, e.g. I, **San Ollmhargadh.**

(c) Déan abairtí.

Téigh	síos	an	seomra
	isteach	sa	fharraige
	suas	san	doras
	amach		cnoc
			ghairdín
			staighre

Seiceáil na habairtí leis an múinteoir.

Zen – Haiku

Saor faoi dheoidh, d'eitil an chuileog an fhuinneog amach – isteach arís de sciotán léi

Free at last, the fly flew out the window – and then right back in again.

J.W Hackett translated by Gabriel Rosenstock
Drawing by Piet Sluis

Sa Rang

1

Éist leis an gcomhrá. What is happening?

Léigh an téipscript. In the speech bubble write the phrase the student uses to ask the teacher to slow down.

2 Labhairt

Think of a sentence you have learnt in Irish and practise saying it as quickly as you can. Walk around the class. Say your sentence (very quickly) for another student. Repeat the sentence more slowly when you are asked to slow down. Listen to the other student's sentence and ask her or him to slow down if necessary. Write the sentence. Repeat the process with another student. Compare written sentences with others in the class.

Ar dtús *first of all* cleacht an comhrá seo le foghlaimeoir eile.

A: *Say a sentence quickly.*

B: *(If necessary)* Labhair níos moille, le do thoil.

A: *Repeat sentence.*

B: *(If still not understood)* Níos moille fós!

A: *Repeat sentence even more slowly.*

B: *(If you have understood)* Go raibh maith agat.

A: Tá fáilte romhat.

Athraigh rólanna.

6 **Cumarsáid**

1(a) Look at the picture and try and guess the meanings of the prepositions used to show the location of the boats.

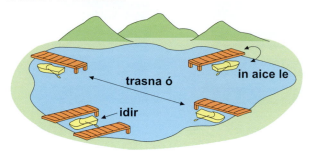

(b)

Éist leis an téip agus léigh an téacs. Can you figure out who the different people are around the table?

You may work with another student if you wish.

Tá Gearóid White ina shuí idir Cáit Ní Bhriain agus Bríd Ní Mháille.

Tá Mary Wilson ina suí in aice le Peadar Ó Dónaill.

Tá Peadar Ó Dónaill trasna ó Cháit Ní Bhriain.

Tá Séamas Mac Giolla Bhuí trasna ó Simone Bouvier.

Tá Simone Bouvier ina suí in aice le Bríd Ní Mháille.

Seiceáil na freagraí san *Eochair.*

(c) Obair Bheirte

Clúdaigh an téacs agus féach ar an bpictiúr in (b) thuas. Déan comhrá le do pháirtí.

Sampla:

> Cá bhfuil Gearóid White ina shuí?*
> Idir Cáit Ní Bhriain agus Bríd Ní Mháille.
> Cá bhfuil Mary Wilson ina suí?**

* **ina shuí** *sitting* masculine
** **ina suí** feminine

2(a) Stór Focal

You are in a language school. Meaitseáil na pictiúir leis na focail.

Leithreas

Leabharlann

Oifig

Seomra na múinteoirí

Ardaitheoir

Seomra Ranga

Seomra an Stiúrthóra

Seiceáil na freagraí san *Eochair*. Seiceáil na focail san fhoclóir freisin.

(b)

Féach ar an bplean agus éist leis an téip.

You will hear 4 statements about where certain rooms are located. Some of the statements are *not* true. Tick these off on the grid below the plan.

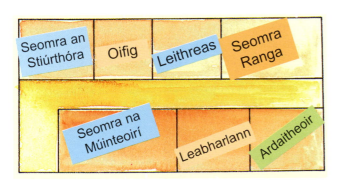

Ráitis *statements*	Ní fíor
1	
2	
3	
4	

Seiceáil na freagraí sna *Téipscripteanna*.

(c) Obair Bheirte

Change around the names on the plan in **(b)**. Do not show these changes to your partner. Ask your partner about the changes on her or his plan. Make a note of them in your plan. Remember to ask for repetition or slower delivery if required.

Sampla:

Cá bhfuil an t-ardaitheoir?
Trasna ón oifig.

Déan comparáid idir na pleananna.

(d)

Design you own language school. Use your dictionary for new words. Present the plan to the class and vote on the best design.

3(a) Gramadach

Clúdaigh an bosca eolais thíos agus léigh na habairtí seo a leanas:

Tá an scoil idir Banc na hÉireann agus
an t-ollmhargadh.
Tá an leabharlann in aice le Banc na hÉireann.
Tá an Oifig Fáilte trasna ó Bhanc na hÉireann.

What can you say about prepositions or prepositional phrases **(idir, in aice le, trasna ó)** and the nouns that come after them, in this case **Banc na hÉireann**?

> ### Preposition + séimhiú
> Some prepositions are followed by *séimhiú*. Others are not.
>
> *séimhiú*: **ar, ó, do, faoi, trí**
> no *séimhiú*: **go, le, idir, ag, as**
>
> Ó chlé go deas *from left to right*, idir Pádraig agus Mícheál *between Pádraig and Mícheál*, do Mháire le grá *to Mary with love*, ar dheis *on the right*, ag baile *at home*, faoi bhun *underneath*, as Doire *from Derry*.

Remove the brackets and add a *séimhiú* if necessary.

1 Suigh idir (Tomás agus Deirdre)
2 In aice le (Gael-Linn)
3 Trasna ó (Siopa Uí Néill)
4 Cas ar (clé).
5 Faoi (Clog Uí Chléirigh)

Nóta: h before a vowel after **go** and **le**, in aice le hOifig an Phoist, go hAlbain.

(b)

Clúdaigh an bosca eolais thíos agus scrúdaigh na habairtí seo:

> Tá an foclóir ar an mbord.
> Tá siopa leabhar ag an gcúinne.
> Tá mo mhála faoin gcathaoir.

Note what happens to the nouns after **ar an**, **ag an** and **faoin**.

Preposition + an

A noun after preposition and the singular article **an** the takes *urú* (Aonad 3, **7**.2). In a few cases, the article changes the form of the preposition:
**faoi+an → faoin, le+an → leis an,
ó+an → ón, trí+an → tríd an.**

Ar an bhfuinneog *on the window,* ag an mbun *at the bottom,* faoin bpictiúr *under the picture,* ón mBéarla *from English,* tríd an ngeata *through the gate.*

Ulster Irish has *séimhiú* instead of an *urú*: ar an bhord, ag an chúinne etc.

Exceptions:
  Don (do+an) mhúinteoir *to the teacher* (*séimhiú*)
  Idir an banc agus an pháirc (no change)
  Ag an doras (no change to nouns beginning with **d** or **t**)

Recall from Aonad 3 that the preposition **i** *in* is different. It takes *urú* on its own, *séimhiú* with **an.**

I mBanc na hÉireann *in the Bank of Ireland,* sa chúinne *in the corner,* san fhoclóir *in the dictionary* (**i+an → sa, san** before a vowel or **fh**).

Remove the brackets and make the necessary changes.

1 In aice le (an linn snámha)
2 Idir (an phictiúrlann) agus an t-ollmhargadh
3 Trasna ó (an leabharlann)
4 Ar (an bord)
5 Faoi (an chathaoir)
6 Trí (an pháirc)

(c) Comparing Towns

Draw a plan of your own town, village or neighbourhood. Do not show it to your partner. Write the names of the buildings or places on a separate piece of paper and give it to your partner. Describe, without pointing, where the different buildings or places are situated in relation to one another. Your partner tries to draw the plan according to your instructions. Compare your plan with your partner's version of it.

---

7 Stór Focal

Orduimhreacha *Ordinal numbers*

1

You will hear three different recordings. What do you think is happening in each one?

An chéad cheann (1st) _____
An dara ceann (2nd) _____
An tríú ceann (3rd) _____

Study how **chéad**, **dara** and **tríú** are used in the tapescripts. Déan plé le foghlaimeoir eile.

2 Meaitseáil na focail leis na huimhreacha.

seacht	1	an t-ochtú
aon	2	an seachtú
deich	3	an dara
naoi	4	an séú
trí	5	an naoú
ocht	6	an cúigiú
sé	7	an tríú
ceathair	8	an deichiú
cúig	9	an chéad
dó	10	an ceathrú

3 Cultúr

Ceann, Cloigeann, Duine

Ceann is the ordinary word for head. Cuir do lámh ar do cheann *Put your hand on your head.* Tá tinneas cinn orm *I have a headache.* But **ceann** is heard far more often as an indefinite pronoun meaning *one*, Cén ceann? *Which one?*, an ceann sin *that one*, an tríú ceann *the third one.*

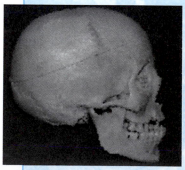

The importance of the head to the Celts is obvious in their art. Apparently Kings passed around the brains of their victims, hardened with lime, to give them wisdom. And perhaps it's no accident that the word **cloigeann** *skull* can be used like **ceann**, when counting people, to mean **duine** *person.* Cé mhéad cloigeann? *How many persons?* Trí chloigne déag. *Thirteen people.*

---

4 Obair Bheirte

Lúnasa	
1	_____
2	_____
3	_____
4	_____
5	_____
6	_____
7	_____
8	_____
9	_____
10	_____

(i)
Which two dates in August are not mentioned in the recording but appear on the calender?

(ii)
Practise saying **an chéad lá, an dara lá** etc.

(iii)
Now repeat (ii) this time leaving out one or two dates. Your partner says which date(s) you have left out.

5

At the hotel reception
The following guests are looking for their rooms. Write the floor numbers.

Aoi Guest	Urlár
Bean Uí Lochlainn	_____
An tUasal Ó hÉalaí	_____
Máire Ní Ghríofa	_____
An tUasal Ó Gráda	_____
Bean Uí Chasaide	_____

Seiceáil na freagraí sna *Téipscripteanna*.

6 Gramadach

Scrúdaigh an tábla.

An chéad	lá	**ch**eann	urlár
An dara	lá	ceann	**h**urlár
An tríú	lá	ceann	**h**urlár
↓	↓	↓	↓
An deichiú	lá	ceann	**h**urlár

Rule: Séimhiú after **chéad** (1st) and *h* before a vowel after **dara**, **tríú**, etc (2nd, 3rd, etc).

Dental Consonants

However, **céad** does not put a *séimhiú* on words beginning with **d, t** and **s**, e.g. **an chéad doras, an chéad teach, an chéad seomra.**

This is another case of a *séimhiú* or *urú* cancelled because the dental consonants (**d, n, t, l, s**) come together. Earlier, in **6.3**(b), they cancelled an *urú*, in **ar an talamh, ag an doras.**

Déan frásaí: an chéad +
                 an dara +
casadh, aonad, seomra, ceann, duine, bóthar, uair, mac

Nóra Bheag

A Nóra Bheag cá raibh tú aréir?
Is é dúirt mo mhamaí liomsa.
I gcúl an tí ag tobar an uisce
Ag foghlaim coiscéim damhsa.

Curfá:
Agus iomba Nóra, Nóra, Nóra
Is iomba is tú mo ghrá geal
Agus iomba Nóra is tú mo stóirín
Tá mise dúnta i ngrá leat.

B'aite le Nóra pis agus pónaire,
B'aite le Nóra bainne,
B'aite le Nóra prátaí rósta,
Is d'íosfadh Nóra an t-im leo.

(1) Little Nora, where were you last night? That's what my mother said to me. Behind the house beside the well, learning to dance a step. (Chorus) And iomba Nóra, Nóra, Nóra and iomba you're my true love, and iomba Nóra you're my darling, I'm madly in love with you. (2) Nora likes peas and beans, Nora likes milk, Nora likes roast potatoes, and Nóra would eat them with butter.

8 Fuaimniú

Défhoghair *Diphthongs*

1

> ### Cad is défhoghar ann?
>
> A diphthong is a vowel sound whose quality changes while it is being pronounced, for example in the word **suas** the vowel starts as an /u:/ and ends as a /ə/ producing the effect of two syllables /uə/.

(a)

Listen carefully and note the difference between /u:/ and /uə/.

	/u:/	/uə/
1	sú	suas
2	tú	tuath
3	úr	uair
4	crú	crua
5	lúth	luath

(b)

Éist leis an téip. There will be a pause for repetition after each pair.

(c)

Clúdaigh 1(a) thuas.

You will hear some of the words again, but not in the same order. Tick the sound that you hear.

	/u:/	/uə/
1		
2		
3		
4		
5		
6		

2

The following are lines from well-known songs. As you listen, pay attention to the /u:/ and /uə/ sounds. When you have listened to all 4 examples, try saying them.

1 An Maidrín Rua, Rua, Rua, Rua, Rua
2 Fill, Fill a Rún Ó, Ó, Ó, Ó
3 'Sé an trua ghéar nach mise, nach mise
   'Sé an trua ghéar nach mise Bean Pháidín
4 Dúlamán na binne buí

9 Cumarsáid

1 Éisteacht agus Léamh

In the following recording a woman wants to buy a jumper. The shop assistant comes to help her.

> Gabh mo leithscéal, cá bhfuil na geansaithe?
> Ar dheis in aice leis na sciortaí.
> Go raibh maith agat.
> Cén dath?
> Dearg.
> Seo ceann deas.
> Ó, ní maith liom an ceann sin. Tá an muineál róleathan! An bhfuil ceann eile agat?
> Fan go bhfeicfidh mé. Seo duit.
> Mmmmm… is fearr liom an chéad cheann, ceapaim!

Freagair na ceisteanna.
A   What colour is the woman looking for?
B   How many jumpers does she look at?
C   Which jumper does she prefer?

Try to answer in Irish. What phrase is used to ask about colour? Abair an frása os ard.

2(a) Stór Focal

Cén dath atá ar an doras? Meaitseáil an dath leis an doras.

(i)   (ii)   (iii)   (iv)   (v)   (vi)   (vii)   (viii)

gorm, bán, donn, glas, liath, dubh, buí, bándearg

(b)

Éist leis an téip. The speaker is saying what colours the doors are but he is deliberately trying to lead you astray. Which statements are true and which are false? **Fíor** *True*, **bréagach** *False*.

Doras	Fíor	Bréagach
1		
2		
3		
4		
5		
6		

(c)

Éist leis an téip. This time the correct colours are given. Abair na dathanna os ard.

3 Obair Bheirte

Spot the differences between the two pictures and tell your partner.

A   B

10 Cultúr

1

Irish Scripts

Irish has been written down in various ways over the centuries, beginning with the Ogam script described in Aonad 1. The Roman alphabet was adopted from the beginning (Ogam was already based on it), but the Roman letters were written in a distinctive Irish style, particularly the letters *a, d, f, g, r, s* and *t.* A punctum or dot on consonants was used to indicate *séimhiú.*

Irish scripts were abandoned in the 1960s and 1970s because of the problems they caused printers and language teachers. The international Roman alphabet was used instead, with *h* for *séimhiú.* All primary schools were using the standard Roman alphabet for Irish by 1964, and all post-primary schools by 1970.

The personal computer has given a new lease of life to Irish scripts, and many fine examples can be copied from the internet (www.sil.org/computing/fonts/lang/Celtic.html). They are often used in letterheads, logos, coats of arms, and the like, and occasionally book-length texts are printed in them.

2 Plé

Do you know of other languages with script problems, past or present? Was anything lost when the international Roman alphabet was adopted for Irish? Is there a case for bringing back the Irish script?

3

Scríobh

Write your name in different Irish scripts. Déan comparáid le foghlaimeoirí eile.

11 Sa Rang

Cas suas í. *Turn it up!*

1

In the following recording you will hear a listening exercise being conducted with a group of students learning Irish. The teacher is operating a tape-recorder (taifeadán). A student wants the volume adjusted.

Which of the following instructions does the teacher get? Cuir ✔ in aice leis an abairt cheart.

Cuir ar siúl (arís) é.	
Cas síos í (an fhuaim).	
Is leor sin.	
Cas suas (beagáinín) í.	
Cuir as é.	

Can you guess the meanings of the sentences above?

2(a) Labhairt

Déan abairtí.

Cuir	as	an fhuaim	(le do thoil)
	suas	an taifeadán	
Cas	ar siúl	é*	
	síos	í**	

* é refers to 'an taifeadán'
** í refers to 'an fhuaim' (the volume)

Ask the teacher to play the tape again. Give instructions using all the sentences you have just made.

Beagáinín

If you only want the volume adjusted *a little* you can use the word **beagáinín** /b'ega:n'i:n'/.

Cas síos an fhuaim beagáinín.
Cas síos beagáinín í.

One student volunteers to operate the tape-recorder. Take it in turns to give her or him instructions.

$\mathcal{A}abc\delta ef\mathcal{G}hijklmnopqrstuvwxyz$

(b) Scríobh

Cuir na focail san ord ceart.

(a) suas fhuaim beagáinín cas an
(b) beagáinín cas í síos
(c) sin leor is
(d) é siúl cuir arís ar
(e) ar arís an taifeadán cuir siúl

12 Gramadach

1 Léamh

> Ag an stáisiún cas ar dheis. Ansin tóg an dara casadh ar chlé. Tá mo theach in aice leis an leabharlann. Tá dath bán air. Tá crann mór in aice leis.
>
> Ag tnúth leat
>
> Áine

Above is part of an e-mail you have just received from Áine giving you instructions to her house. Which word do the pronouns **air** and **leis** refer back to?

2

More about pronouns

In the e-mail above, the prepositional pronouns **air** and **leis** refer back to the noun *teach*. Pronouns are useful in order to avoid repetition.

> **Tá dath bán air** (ar an teach).
> **Tá crann mór in aice leis** (leis an teach).

We have already used pronouns to refer to people e.g.

> **Tá sí sa ghrúpa Altan.**
> **Is maith léi dul ag siúl cois farraige.**

Sí and **léi** refer back to *Mairéad Ní Mhaonaigh* (Aonad 5). The pronouns **sí** and **léi** agree with the noun *Mairéad Ní Mhaonaigh* in gender and number (*feminine, singular*).

3(a) Scríobh

Check the *gender* and *number** of the following nouns. Tá an chéad cheann déanta cheana féin. Féach san fhoclóir.

ainmfhocal	inscne	uimhir
léine peann seacláid planda mairteoil madra bialann	feminine (f)	singular

* *pl* refers to plural in the dictionary.

(b) Líon na bearnaí.

(a) Tá léine nua agam. Tá dath dearg _____.
(b) Níl mo pheann agam. Tá _____ sa bhaile.
(c) Is maith liom an planda seo. Cén t-ainm atá _____?
(d) Ní maith liom an mhairteoil seo. Tá _____ rórighin.
(e) Seo mo mhadra nua. Setanta is ainm _____.
(f) Tá an bhialann ansin. Tá Teach Uí Riain in aice _____.

13 Scileanna Foghlama

1

'Tuning in' to the language

Some people decide to learn a language because they simply like the way it sounds.

Getting used to the rhythms and sounds of a language is very important when you start learning. Listening without trying to understand is known as the 'silent' stage. Have you ever tried listening to a language in this way?

Déan plé le foghlaimeoirí eile.

2 Staidéar Pearsanta

Try to spend half an hour each day listening to *Raidió na Gaeltachta* or *Raidió na Life*. You could also listen to a song in Irish or watch a programme on *TG4*. You do not have to understand every word. At the end of the day, write a short description of your experience, for example:

Dé Luain	Listened to the news on *Raidió na Gaeltachta*. Noticed the difference between the accent of the newsreader and that of the reporter. Preferred the newsreader's accent.

3 Obair Ghrúpa

Listen to a radio programme as a group. Write out your reactions to what you hear. Déan comparáid le foghlaimeoirí eile.

Sa Rang

1 Textbook instructions

Líon na bearnaí sna habairtí leis na focail nó frásaí seo.

Líon   **Déan comparáid**   **Cuir**

leis na focail   **na focail**

Compare with your partner.
(a) .... le do pháirtí.

Underline the words.
(b) .... líne faoi ....

Complete the sentences with the following words.
(c) .... na bearnaí sna habairtí
.... seo a leanas.

Compare the plans.
(d) .... idir na pleananna.

Put the words in the correct order.
(e) .... san ord ceart.

Cuardaigh na habairtí san aonad.

2 Obair Bheirte

Copy out three instructions from any of the units you have studied. Do not let your partner see them.

Write the instructions again, this time changing the order of the words.

Give these sentences to your partner to put back into the correct order. Have a competition to see who can put the sentences into the correct order first.

Am Spóirt

1   Cén dath é?

Class divides into two teams. A member of team A writes a colour on a piece of paper and gives it to the teacher. The student then draws a representation of the colour on the board, for example an apple could represent the colour **dearg**. The other members of team A take it in turn to make a guess at the colour. If the student is unsuccessful at guessing the colour, a member of team B may make a guess. The procedure is repeated with team B.

A point is awarded for each successful guess. The team with the highest number of successful guesses wins.

2   Cad é?

Class divides into two teams. A member of team A writes the name of an object in the room on a piece of paper and gives it to the teacher. The aim of the game is to find out what the object is.

Students from team A take it in turns to ask questions about the object such as: **An bhfuil sé ar dheis? An bhfuil sé in aice leis an mbord? An bhfuil sé dubh (an bhfuil dath dubh air)?** Each student can only ask one question at a time. The answers to these questions can only be **Níl** or **Tá**.

If a student decides to make a guess at naming the object and is successful, a point is awarded to the team. (Remember **Ceart**, **Sin é** to tell people they are right and **Níl sé sin ceart**, **Ní hea** to tell them they are wrong, Aonad 1, **10**.3). If the student is wrong, a member of team B can make a guess. A point is awarded to team B if the guess is correct.

The teacher keeps count of the number of correct guesses *and* the number of questions each team asks. The team that names the most objects correctly using the least amount of questions wins.

Achoimre *Summary*

Cumarsáid agus Stór Focal

Asking where something is located	Bord Fáilte, le do thoil. Gabh mo leithscéal, cá bhfuil Gael-Linn?
Describing where something is located	(Tá sé) díreach ar aghaidh. (Téigh) síos an bóthar. Tá an leabharlann in aice le Banc na hÉireann. An dara doras ar chlé.
Naming colours	(Tá dath) buí (air).
Recognising common signs	Slí amach Deochanna Bóthar an Choláiste Bord Fáilte Éireann
Location words and phrases	ar dheis, ar chlé, díreach ar aghaidh, suas, síos, isteach, amach, in aice le, idir, trasna ó, ar, faoi, trí
Public buildings and locations	linn snámha, Oifig Fáilte, Oifig an Phoist, pictiúrlann, aerfort, scoil, banc, ollmhargadh
Locations in a language school	leabharlann, seomra na múinteoirí, oifig, leithreas, ardaitheoir, seomra ranga, Seomra an Stiúrthóra

Ordinal numbers	an chéad, an dara, an ceathrú, an cúigi an seachtú, an t-och an naoú, an deichiú
Colours	gorm, buí, dearg, bándearg, donn, bán, dubh, liath, glas
Sa rang	(Labhair) níos moille, le do thoil. Níos moille fós. Cas suas, síos an fhuaim, an taifeadán. Cas suas í, é. Cas síos an fhuaim beagáinín. Cas síos beagáinín í. Is leor sin. Cuir an taifeadán ar siúl. Cuir ar siúl é. Cuir as an taifeadán. Cuir as é.
Sa téacsleabhar	Déan comparáid le, idir Cuir líne faoi Cuir ... san ord ceart. Seo a leanas thíos thuas

Gramadach

- **Definite Noun**
  Oifig an Phoist vs An Oifig Fáilte
- **Prepositions + noun**
  ar, do, faoi, ó, trí + séimhiú, e.g. ar dheis
- **Prepositions + an**
  urú on noun (or *séimhiú*) e.g. ar an mbóthar (ar an bhóthar), in aice leis an mbanc (le + an), faoin mbord (faoi + an), tríd an ngeata (trí + an). No *urú* if noun begins with **d** or **t**.
- *Séimhiú* on nouns aften **don (do + an)**, e.g. don mhúinteoir
- **Ordinal numbers + noun**
  an chéad cheann, an dara, tríú etc ceann, an chéad urlár, an dara, tríú etc hurlár, no *séimhiú* on **d, t, s** after **céad**, e.g. an chéad doras
- **Pronouns**
  Must agree with noun in gender and number e.g. Tá **léine** nua agam. Tá dath dearg **uirthi**.

Cultúr

- The first bilingual road-signs appeared in Ireland in 1937.
- The spellings of placenames have become more consistent in recent years.
- Bilingual signs also appear on buses, in supermarkets, bookshops etc.
- The word **ceann** is the equivalent of *one* in English e.g. **An dara ceann** *the second one*.
- The original *Irish* style of writing was based on Latin writing (e.g. Book of Kells).
- As time went by Irish developed its own distinctive script.
- One of the distinctive features of Irish script is the punctum.
- Roman script eventually took over from Irish script and *h* replaced the punctum.

Fuaimniú

A diphthong is a vowel sound whose quality changes while it is being pronounced e.g. **crú**, **crua** (u:➤ u ə)

Scileanna Foghlama

The importance of listening to a language without trying to understand it

Triail Tú Féin

A

1 What would you expect to find in the following places?

(a)	(b)	(c)
Siopa Potadóireachta	An Siopa Leabhar	Fir Mná
_____	_____	_____

(d)	(e)	(f)
An Lár	Bord Fáilte	Leabharlann
_____	_____	_____

2 Which products would you expect to find under the following signs in a supermarket?

(a)	(b)	(c)	(d)
Bia folláin	Seacláidí	Arán	Fíoruisce
_____	_____	_____	_____

B

1 Study the map. Críochnaigh na comhráite ar leathanach 101. Iarr ar an múinteoir iad a cheartú.

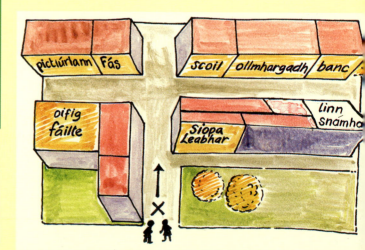

(a)

Fear: Gabh mo leithscéal, cá bhfuil an
phictiúrlann?
Tusa: _____
Fear: Go raibh maith agat.

(b)

Tusa: _____
Bean: An chéad chasadh ar dheis.
Tusa: _____
Bean: Tá fáilte romhat!

(c)

Páiste: An linn snámha le do thoil?
Tusa: _____
Páiste: Trasna ón bpictiúrlann, a dúirt tú?
Tusa: _____
Páiste: Go raibh míle maith agat.

(d)

Tusa: _____
Fear: Tá sí trasna ón bpictiúrlann.
Tusa: _____
Fear: Ná habair é!

2 What does Mike say to Eithne? Líon na bearnaí
sa chomhrá le ceann de na habairtí ón mbosca.

> Abair é sin arís le do thoil.
> Tá sé agam anois!   Níl mé cinnte.
> Tuigim.

Eithne: An bhfuil a fhios agat cá bhfuil mo
theach?
Mike: _____
Eithne: Cas ar chlé ag an linn snámha.
Mike: _____
Eithne: Agus tá sé ansin in aice leis an scoil.
Mike: _____
Eithne: Ceart go leor. Ar chlé ag an linn snámha
agus tá an teach in aice leis an scoil.
Mike: _____

3 Scríobh na focail san ord ceart.

(a) an bhosca Tá sa peann

(b) mbord do an Cuir ar leabhar

(c) mbanc in teach leis an Níl aice an

(d) trasna Nóra bhfuinneog suí Tá ón ina

(e) sos bhfuil agus a dó a haon An idir ann?

(f) staighre Tá faoin cat an

4 Meaitseáil an leagan Gaeilge leis an leagan
Béarla.

Cuir as an taifeadán. *Turn down the volume.*
Cas suas í. *That's enough!*
Cuir ar siúl arís é. *Turn it up.*
Cuir as é. *Play it again.*
Cas síos an fhuaim. *Turn the tape-recorder off.*
Is leor sin! *Turn it off.*

C

1 Scríobh na dathanna in aice leis an mbrat.

1 _____
2 _____
3 _____
4 _____
5 _____
6 _____

2 Críochnaigh an tsraith.

1 _____   2 _____
3 an tríú   4 _____
5 _____   6 _____
7 _____   8 an t-ochtú
9 _____   10 _____

3 Cuir na focail seo sa liosta ceart.

> seomra   isteach   liath   deochanna
> leithreas   leabharlann   síos   bándearg
> seacláidí   amach   aerfort   idir
> glas   tae   donn   crua-earraí

oifig	gorm	suas	arán
_____	_____	_____	_____
_____	_____	_____	_____
_____	_____	_____	_____
_____	_____	_____	_____
_____	_____	_____	_____
_____	_____	_____	_____
_____	_____	_____	_____
_____	_____	_____	_____
_____	_____	_____	_____
_____	_____	_____	_____

Cuir focail eile leis na liostaí.

D

I You have rented the room below while you are attending an Irish course. You are sitting at the desk, facing the window. Write a description of your room from where you are sitting. Imagine this is part of a letter to a friend who knows Irish.

Tá an leaba ar .... Tá an teileafón ....
Tá cófra ar .... Tá fuinneog idir an leaba agus an .... Tá bord faoin .... agus tá planda .... Tá mo chóta sa .... Tá an cat ina shuí in aice leis an .... Toby is ainm .... Tá mise i mo shuí ag an .... ag féachaint amach an ....

2 Remove brackets and write the correct form of the words where applicable.

(a) Tóg an tríú (casadh) ar dheis.
(b) Tá mé ar an gcéad (urlár).
(c) Tá an seomra ar an gceathrú (urlár).
(d) An chéad (teach) ar chlé.
(e) Téigh isteach an chéad (geata).

E Fuaimniú

Which is the odd-one-out?
(a) tú   tríú   urlár   siúcra   fuaimniú
(b) nua   anuas   cuach   casadh   suas

F Fíor nó Bréagach (F nó B)?

(a) The first bilingual road-signs appeared in Ireland in 1947. ❑

(b) The original Irish style of writing was based on Latin writing. ❑

(c) Irish scripts were abandoned in the 1960's and 1970's because they became unfashionable. ❑

Téipscripteanna

I.2(a), (b)
Gabh mo leithscéal, a Gharda, cá bhfuil Busáras le do thoil?
Díreach ar aghaidh.
Go raibh míle maith agat.
Tá fáilte romhat.

Cá bhfuil Gael-Linn?
Cas ar dheis.
Go raibh maith agat.
Slán leat.
Slán.

Gabh mo leithscéal, an bhfuil a fhios agat cá bhfuil an Siopa Leabhar?
Síos an bóthar, ar chlé.
Go raibh maith agat.

Gabh mo leithscéal, Bord Fáilte le do thoil?
An chéad chasadh ar chlé.

Cá bhfuil an leithreas poiblí, le do thoil?
Anseo, ar dheis.
Ó.... go raibh maith agat.
Tá fáilte romhat.

TG4 le do thoil.
Díreach ar aghaidh!
Go raibh maith agat.
Go n-éirí an bóthar leat!

2.3
Gabh mo leithscéal, cá bhfuil Oifig an Phoist?
Ansin, ar dheis.
Go raibh maith agat.

Cá bhfuil an t-ollmhargadh?
Féach, tá sé ansin, ar dheis.
Go raibh maith agat, slán.
Slán.

An bhfuil a fhios agat cá bhfuil an linn snámha?
Fan go bhfeicfidh mé. Suas an bóthar ar chlé, ceapaim.

Gabh mo leithscéal. Cá bhfuil an banc?
Níl a fhios agam. Tá brón orm.

An banc le do thoil?
Tá sé anseo, ar chlé.
Go raibh míle maith agat.
Ná habair é!

An bhfuil an Oifig Fáilte sa treo seo?
Tá. Suas an bóthar ar dheis.

Cá háit a bhfuil an phictiúrlann, le do thoil?
An phictiúrlann? An phictiúrlann.... suas an bóthar ar chlé, ceapaim.
Go raibh maith agat.

An scoil le do thoil.
An scoil náisiúnta?
Is ea.
Suas an bóthar, ar chlé.

An t-aerfort le do thoil?
Díreach ar aghaidh, ar chlé.
Go raibh maith agat.

5.1 Sa rang

Múinteoir:	Inniu beimid ag plé le treoracha. Osclaígí bh...
Foghlaimeoir:	Labhair níos moille le do thoil!
Múinteoir:	Ó gabh mo leithscéal. Inniu beimid ag plé le treoracha.
Foghlaimeoir:	Ceart go leor, ach ní thuigim 'treoracha'!

6.2 (b)

1 Tá an leithreas idir an leabharlann agus an seomra ranga.

2 Tá seomra an stiúrthóra in aice leis an oifig.

3 Tá seomra na múinteoirí trasna ón leabharlann.

4 Tá an leabharlann idir seomra na múinteoirí agus an t-ardaitheoir.

7.1

A dhaoine uaisle, seo torthaí chomórtas amhránaíocht ar an sean-nós. Sa chéad áit tá Bríd Ní Ghallchóir, sa dara háit tá Gearóidín Ní Chléirigh agus sa tríú háit tá Sandra Ní Chuinn. Comhghairdeas leis na buaiteoirí agus mo bhuíochas do na daoine eile a ghlac páirt sa chomórtas.

Fáilteoir:	Ceart go leor, a Uasail Uí Mhóráin. Tá tú i seomra ochtó a sé.
Fear:	Cá bhfuil sé sin?
Fáilteoir:	Ar an gcéad urlár.
Fear:	Go raibh maith agat.
Fáilteoir:	Tá fáilte romhat.
Fear:	Gabh mo leithscéal, an bhfuil a fhios agat cá bhfuil Óstlann na Mara?
Bean:	Fan go bhfeicfidh mé .... Óstlann na Mara .... an dara casadh, ní hea .... an tríú casadh ar chlé trasna ón ngaráiste.
Fear:	Go raibh maith agat.
Bean:	Tá fáilte romhat.

7.4 An chéad lá, an dara lá, an ceathrú lá, an cúigiú lá, an séú lá, an t-ochtú lá, an naoú lá, an deichiú lá.

7.5

Seo d'eochair, a Bhean Uí Lochlainn.
Ó, tá mé ar an tríú hurlár.
Ar mhaith leat cabhair le do mhálaí?
Níor mhaith, go raibh maith agat.

Tá tú i seomra uimhir a cúig chéad seasca, a Uasail Uí Éalaí.
Cá bhfuil sé sin?
Ar an gcúigiú hurlár, in aice leis an staighre.
Go raibh maith agat.

Cá bhfuil mo sheomra le do thoil? Mise Máire Ní Ghríofa.
Ar an séú hurlár, seo an eochair.
Go raibh maith agat.
Ná habair é.

Agus seo duit d'eochair, a Uasail Uí Ghráda. Tá tú ar an dara hurlár i seomra dhá chéad tríocha a cúig.
Go raibh míle maith agat.
Tá fáilte romhat.

Gabh mo leithscéal ach níl a fhios agam cá bhfuil mo sheomra. Nóra Uí Chasaide is ainm dom.
Tá sé ar an seachtú hurlár. Is féidir leat an t-ardaitheoir a thógáil.
Tá go maith. Go raibh maith agat.
Tá fáilte romhat.

8.1(c)
uair tú lúth tuath crú suas

9.2(b)
Tá dath **dearg** ar an gcéad doras.
Tá dath **bán** ar an dara doras.
Tá dath **gorm** ar an tríú doras.
Tá dath **liath** ar an gceathrú doras.
Tá dath **dubh** ar an gcúigiú doras.
Tá dath **donn** ar an séú doras.

9.2(c)
Tá dath **dearg** ar an gcéad doras.
Tá dath **glas** ar an dara doras.
Tá dath **gorm** ar an tríú doras.
Tá dath **buí** ar an gceathrú doras.
Tá dath **bán** ar an gcúigiú doras.
Tá dath **donn** ar an séú doras.

11.1

Múinteoir:	An bhfuil sibh réidh le héisteacht leis an amhrán?
Foghlaimeoirí:	Tá.
Múinteoir:	Ceart go leor. Cuirfidh mé ar siúl é.
Múinteoir:	Conas tá an fhuaim? An bhfuil sí ard go leor?
Foghlaimeoir:	Cas suas beagáinín í. Is leor sin!

Eochair

3.3(a)
Bia folláin, Health foods *Seacláidí*, Chocolates
Crua-earraí, Hardware *Arán*, Bread *Deochanna*,
Beverages

4.1
A amach B síos C isteach D isteach E suas
F amach

6.1(b)
3   Gearóid White
5   Simone Bouvier
6   Mary Wilson
2   Cáit Ní Bhriain
7   Peadar Ó Dónaill
4   Bríd Ní Mháille
1   Séamus Mac Giolla Bhuí

6.2(a)

leithreas

leabharlann

oifig

seomra na múinteoirí

ardaitheoir

seomra ranga

seomra an Stiúrthóra

6.3(a)
1   Suigh idir Tomás agus Deirdre.
2   In aice le Gael-Linn
3   Trasna ó Shiopa Uí Néill
4   Cas ar chlé.
5   Faoi Chlog Uí Chléirigh

6.3(b)
1   In aice leis an linn snámha
2   Idir an phictiúrlann agus
    t-ollmhargadh
3   Trasna ón leabharlann
4   Ar an mbord
5   Faoin gcathaoir
6   Tríd an bpáirc

7.4 an tríú lá, an seachtú lá.

9.1 A dearg *red* B dhá cheann C an chéad
cheann

9.2 (a)
(i) gorm (ii) buí (iii) bándearg (iv) donn
(v) dubh (vi) glas (vii) liath (viii) bán

11.2(b)
(a) Cas suas an fhuaim beagáinín. (b) Cas síos
beagáinín í. (c) Is leor sin. (d) Cuir ar siúl arís é.
(e) Cuir an taifeadán ar siúl arís.

12.3(b)
(a) uirthi (b) sé (c) air (d) sí (e) dó (f) léi

Triail Tú Féin

A

1   (a) pottery (b) books for sale
    (c) toilet (d) city centre (e) tourist office
    (f) books you can borrow
2   (a) health food (b) chocolates (c) bread
    (d) spring water

B
2
Eithne: An bhfuil a fhios agat cá bhfuil mo
          theach?
Mike: Níl mé cinnte.
Eithne: Cas ar chlé ag an linn snámha.
Mike: Tuigim.
Eithne: Agus tá sé ansin in aice leis an scoil.
Mike: Abair é sin arís le do thoil.
Eithne: Ceart go leor. Ar chlé ag an linn snámha
          agus tá an teach in aice leis an scoil.
Mike: Tá sé agam anois!

3
(a) Tá an peann sa bhosca.
(b) Cuir do leabhar ar an mbord.
(c) Níl an teach in aice leis an mbanc.
(d) Tá Nóra ina suí trasna ón bhfuinneog.
(e) An bhfuil sos ann idir a haon agus a dó?
(f) Tá an cat faoin staighre.

4
Cuir as an taifeadán.   Turn down the volume.
Cas suas í.   Turn it off.
Cuir ar siúl arís é.   Turn it up.
Cuir as é.   Play it again.
Cas síos an fhuaim.   Turn the tape-recorder off.

C
1
1 dubh 2 buí 3 glas 4 bán 5 gorm 6 dearg

2 1 an chéad 2 an dara 3 an tríú 4 an ceathrú
5 an cúigiú 6 an séú 7 an seachtú
8 an t-ochtú 9 an naoú 10 an deichiú

3

oifig	gorm	suas	arán
seomra	liath	isteach	deochanna
leithreas	bándearg	síos	seacláidí
leabharlann	glas	amach	crua-earraí
aerfort	donn	idir	tae

D

1 Tá an leaba ar **chlé**. Tá an teileafón **air**. Tá
cófra ar **dheis**. Tá fuinneog idir an leaba agus
an **cófra**. Tá bord faoin **bhfuinneog** agus tá
planda **air**. Tá mo chóta sa **chófra**. Tá an cat
ina shuí in aice leis an **gcathaoir (mbord)**.
Toby is ainm **dó**. Tá mise i mo shuí ag an
mbord ag féachaint amach an **fhuinneog**.

Seiceáil na freagraí leis an múinteoir freisin.

2
(a) Tóg an tríú casadh ar dheis.
(b) Tá mé ar an gcéad urlár.
(c) Tá an seomra ar an gceathrú hurlár.
(d) An chéad teach ar chlé.
(e) Téigh isteach an chéad gheata.

E

(a) urlár (b) casadh

F

(a) bréagach (b) fíor (c) bréagach

Nóta 1

Foghlaimeoir A
Your partner wants to know which buses go to the following destinations in Dublin. When she or he names a destination, say the bus number.

An Lár / City Centre	65B
Dún Laoghaire	46A
Cearnóg Mhuirfean / Merrion Square	13
Aerfort	16A

Nóta 2

Foghlaimeoir A
You want to know the number of the bus for the following destinations. Say the destination in Irish (ask your teacher to help you to pronounce them).

Faiche Stiabhna / Stephen's Green	
Sráid an Choláiste / College Street	
Bóthar Bulfin / Bulfin Road	
Páirc Wadelai / Wadelai Park	

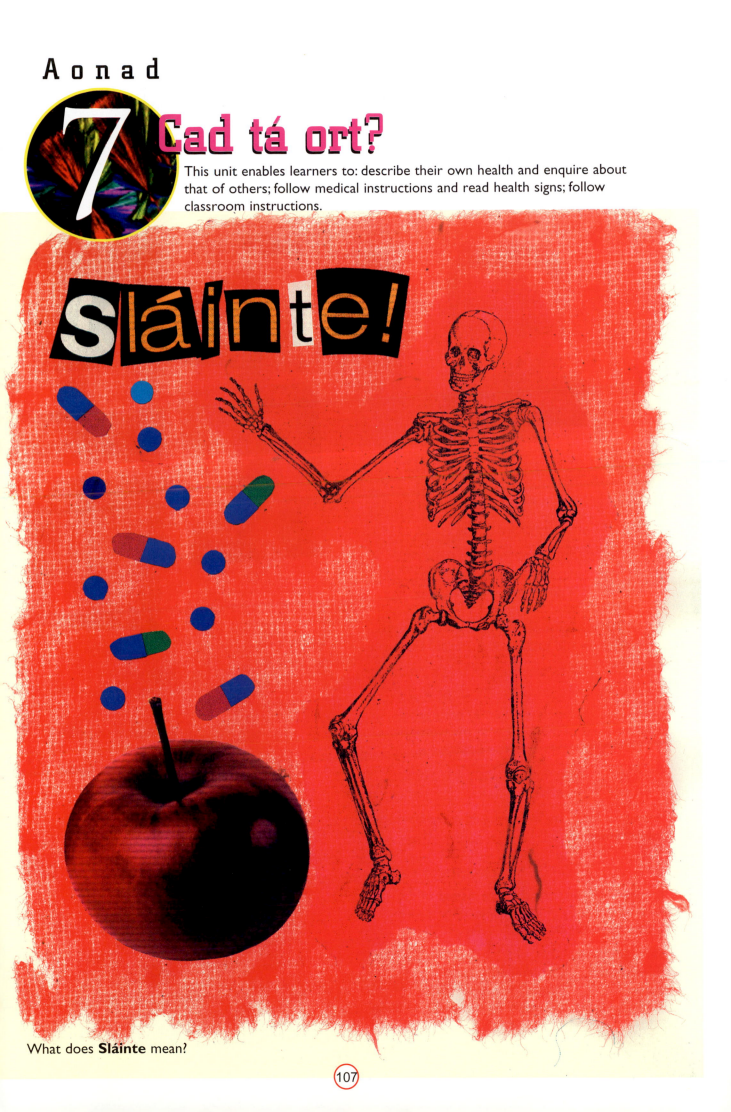

Aonad

7 Cad tá ort?

This unit enables learners to: describe their own health and enquire about that of others; follow medical instructions and read health signs; follow classroom instructions.

Sláinte!

What does **Sláinte** mean?

1 Stór Focal

Na Baill Bheatha *Parts of the Body*

1

Conor has applied to a modelling agency for a job. Caoimhe is looking at his photograph. Imagine what she might be thinking.

Líon na bearnaí sna habairtí le focail ón mbosca.

| súile | cluasa | shrón | bhéal |

(a) Tá a _____ rófhada.

(b) Tá _____ deasa gorma aige.

(c) Is maith liom a _____.

(d) Tá _____ móra air.

2

Éist leis an téip agus seiceáil na focail in 1.1 thuas. Why do, **srón** and **béal** have a *séimhiú*? Labhair le foghlaimeoir eile.

3

Draw a rough sketch of a human body. Label different parts of the body with the words from the list below.

| droim | bolg | cos | lámh |
| fiacail | muineál | rúitín | méar |

Seiceáil na focail san fhoclóir. Add more labels to your drawing.

4 Rólghlacadh

You are teaching your child the names of the parts of the body in Irish. Check if she or he knows them like this:

Sampla:

Tuismitheoir: Cá bhfuil do shrón?
Páiste: *(Pointing to nose)* Anseo.
Tuismitheoir: Go maith! Agus cá bhfuil do bhéal?
Páiste: Tá sé anseo.

Athraigh na rólanna agus cuir ceisteanna faoi na baill bheatha eile.

2 Cumarsáid

1(a)

Meaitseáil na comhráite le trí cinn de na pictiúir seo a leanas:

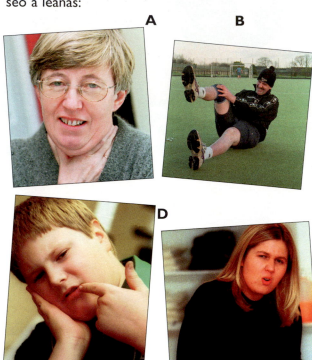

A   B

D

C

Comhrá 1 _____
Comhrá 2 _____
Comhrá 3 _____

(b)

Éist leis an téip arís. Líon na bearnaí na habairtí.

1   Dochtúir: Cad _____ ort?
    Bean: Tá _____ i mo bholg.
    Dochtúir: Luigh _____ ansin le do thoil.

2   Máthair: ___ _____ rud éigin ort, a Mhaidhc?
    Buachaill: Tá _____fiacaile orm.
    Máthair: Maidhc bocht!

3   Fear: _____ ____ _____ar maidin, a Dheirdre?
    Bean: Ní bhraithim go maith. Tá _____ thinn orm.
    Fear: An bhfuil? Agus tá tú ____ freisin.

Seiceáil na freagraí sna *Téipscripteanna*.

2(a)

> ### Cad tá ort? *What's wrong with you?*
>
> To state you have a *pain* somewhere you can say
>
> | **Tá pian i** | **mo lámh.** |
> |---|---|
> | | **mo chluas.** |
> | | **m'fhiacail.** |

Abair na habairtí os ard. Déan abairtí leis na baill bheatha eile.

Sampla: Tá pian i mo chos.

(b)

> ### An bhfuil rud éigin ort?
> *Is there something wrong with you?*
>
> In Irish, many of the states that a person can be in, including health or illness, and also emotional states such as sadness or happiness, are said to be **ar** *on* the person who has them.
>
> **Tá scornach thinn orm.** *I have a sore throat.*
> **Tá biseach orm.** *I am better.*
> **Tá slaghdán orm.** *I have a cold.*
> **Tá cos thinn orm.** *I have a sore foot.*
> **Tá tinneas cinn orm.** *I have a headache.*

Abair na habairtí sa bhosca thuas os ard. Iarr ar an múinteoir cuidiú leat na focail a fhuaimniú.

(c)

Cuardaigh na focail seo a leanas san fhoclóir:

casacht	fiabhras	tuirse	feabhas	fliú

Déan abairtí.
Samplaí: Tá casacht orm.
  Tá fliú orm.

3 Obair Bheirte

Cleacht na comhráite seo.

Samplaí:

Cad tá ort, a Thomáis?

Tá pian i mo ghlúin.

Tomás bocht!

Cad tá ort, a Bhrídín?

Tá súil thinn orm.

Brídín bhocht!

Déan comhráite faoi na pictiúir seo *about these pictures*:

A

B

39°

C

D

 **Fuaimniú**

An Défhoghar /iə/

I(a)

Éist leis an téip. Déan athrá.

	/i:/	/iə/
1	í	ia(d)
2	bí	bia
3	lí	liath
4	díon	dian
5	fíor	fiar

(b)

You will hear 6 different words. Cuir ✔ in aice leis an gcomhartha ceart.

	1	2	3	4	5	6
/i:/						
/iə/						

Seiceáil na freagraí san *Eochair*.

2 Tréanna

The following are examples of **tréanna** or triads. A triad consists of three words or phrases which are succinct expressions of some ancient or folk wisdom.

Éist leis na tréanna. Pay attention to the /i:/ and /iə/ sounds. Abair na tréanna os ard.

1	**An bhruitíneach**	*The measles*
	Trí lá ag teacht	*Three days coming*
	Trí lá ina neart	*Three days at its peak*
	Trí lá ag imeacht	*Three days going*

2	**Na trí rud is géire amuigh**	*The three sharpest things in existence*
	Dealg láibe	*A thorn in mud*
	Fiacail cú	*A hound's tooth*
	Briathar amadáin	*A fool's talk*

3 Cultúr

Do triads or their equivalents exist in other languages or cultures? Give examples if you know them.

Try making a triad in Irish. You could start with single nouns, for example

Na trí bhall den chorp is fusa a ghortú.
The three parts of the body which are most easily injured.

An tsúil	*The eye*
An ghlúin	*The knee*
An uillinn	*The elbow*

Iarr ar an múinteoir cuidiú leat.

 Cultúr

I

Conventional medicine in Ireland

We know very little about Irish medicine before the 14th century. Even though the distinction between qualified and non-qualified doctors was not that apparent, we know that medical schools did exist and that in 860 AD there was a *saoi leighis* or 'master physician' responsible for medicine in the whole country. 'Qualified' doctors belonged to a learned, privileged class. Only the rich could afford such doctors. The majority of people used local healers.

We do, however, have quite a lot of information about Irish medicine from the 14th century onwards. During this time Irish doctors studied in European medical schools and, in some cases, set up their own schools on their return to Ireland. Although the type of medical training these doctors received was based on the Graeco-Arabic tradition, it would appear that there was a cross-over with native medicine whenever the need arose.

Between the 15th and 17th centuries, many of the Latin medical texts were translated into Irish. One of the best known is entitled *Regimen na Sláinte*, from the Latin *Regimen Sanitatis*. The Irish medical manuscripts, most of them in libraries in Ireland, are an important source for the history of medicine in Europe.

Irish doctors originally came from a small number of families, in particular **Ící** (lit. *healer*) *Hickey*, **Ó Casaide** *Cassidy*, **Ó Duinnshléibhe** *Dunleavey*, **Ó Siadhail** *Sheils*, and **Ó Callanáin** *Callanan*.

Further reading
Shaw: F. (1961) 'Irish Medical Men and Philosophers', Ó Cuív, B. (ed.), *Seven Centuries of Irish Learning 1000-1700*, Thomas Davis Lectures, Dublin, cpt VI.

Nic Dhonnchadha, A. (1900) 'Early Modern Irish Medical Writings', *Newsletter of the School of Celtic Studies*, No. 4, Dublin Institute of Advanced Studies.

"...groveling upon couches of straw, their books at their noses, themselves lying flatte prostrate, and so to chaunte out their lessons by peece-meale".

Historie of Ireland Campion
– Medical students in 1571

Plé

Do you know about the history of medicine in other countries? Were healers used? Are healers still used today?

2 Stór Focal

When the Latin medical texts were translated, many terms appeared in Irish for the first time, such as **bruitíneach** for *measles* in *Regimen na Sláinte* just mentioned. Here are some other examples.

Meaitseáil na focail Ghaeilge leis na focail Bhéarla.

muscail	fennel
gaofaireacht	cataract
gúta	soap
cláiréad	flatulence
fionn	muscle
finéal	gout
gallúnach	claret

The word **fionn** means *white*, and **gallúnach** comes from **gall** *foreign* and **uanach** *foamy*.

Seanfhocal

Is fearr an tsláinte ná na táinte.
Health is more important than wealth.

Táinte *herds* refers to wealth measured in cattle or sheep.

Do you agree with this proverb? Do you know of similar proverbs in other languages?

5 Cumarsáid

Ag an dochtúir

1(a)

A woman is phoning the doctor's surgery to make an appointment.

Cuir na habairtí cearta faoi na pictiúir. Put the correct sentences under the pictures.

Beidh an dochtúir saor ar a trí a chlog.
Slán go fóill.
Níl sé róphianmhar.
Tá scornach thinn orm.
Ceart go leor.
Cad tá cearr leat?
An bhfuil sé pianmhar?

Fáilteoir	Othar

_____

_____

_____

_____

_____

_____

(b) Éist leis an téip agus seiceáil an comhrá.

(c) Rólghlacadh

You are a patient in the doctor's waiting room. Talk to other patients about your illnesses.

Foghlaimeoir A		Foghlaimeoir B		
Cad tá	ort? cearr leat?	Tá	pian i mo (chos). (slaghdán) orm.	
An bhfuil	fiabhras ort? sé pianmhar?	Tá Níl	sé	an-phianmhar. róphianmhar.
Is	trua sin! maith			
		Agus cad tá	ortsa? cearr leatsa?	

(d) Scríobh

Scríobh síos na tinnis atá ar na hothair eile.

tinneas	líon daoine
plucamas	2
fliú	4

Scríobh tuairisc mar seo:

Tá plucamas ar bheirt othar.

Tá fliú ar cheathrar othar.

2(a)

Tá an tUasal Ó Riagáin ag caint leis an dochtúir. Éist leis an gcomhrá. An bhfuil nótaí an dochtúra ceart?

Dáta: 7 Deireadh Fómhair
Ainm an othair: Seán Ó Riagáin

Cad tá cearr: Níl fiabhras air. Ag mothú go dona ... trí lá. Scornach thinn air. Ag ithe.

Déan plé le do pháirtí. Seiceáil na freagraí sna *Téipscripteanna*.

(b)

Éist leis an téip. Which of the following instructions does the doctor *not* give the patient?

Ardaigh do lámh.

Cuir amach do lámh.

Coimeád an teirmiméadar faoi d'ascaill.

Dún do bhéal.

Cuir amach do theanga.

Oscail do bhéal.

(c)

What advice does the doctor give?

---

6 Gramadach

1(a)

An Modh Ordaitheach
The Imperative Mood

The Modh Ordaitheach (**ordaigh** *order*) in Irish, apart from its importance in giving instructions and making requests, also gives the base form of the verb, the form that you can look up in the dictionary.

You have encountered it already, particularly in classroom instructions like

Éist leis an téip. *Listen to the tape.*

Oscail an leabhar. *Open the book.*

These are instructions to one person.

If you are addressing more than one person add **–(a)igí** to one syllable verbs and **–(a)ígí** to multi-syllabic verbs.

Éistigí leis an téip. *Listen to the tape.*

Osclaígí na leabhair. *Open the books.*

(b) Obair Bheirte

Cuardaigh samplaí den mhodh ordaitheach sa téacsleabhar. Déan plé le do pháirtí.

(c)

Líon na bearnaí sna habairtí le focail as an mbosca *with words from the box.*

freagair	léigh	téigh	éist	seiceáil
dún	cuardaigh	cuir	oscail	

1 _____ suas an staighre agus _____ an fhuinneog.

2 _____ an téacsleabhar agus _____ an comhrá.

3 _____ as an raidió. Tá mé ag léamh!

4 _____ an focal san fhoclóir.

5 _____ na ceisteanna.

6 _____ leis an gceoltóir sin. Tá sé go han-mhaith ar fad!

Déan comparáid le foghlaimeoirí eile. Seiceáil na freagraí leis an múinteoir.

Cluiche

You have to put one of the pictures into words, e.g.

Cuir lámh amháin ar do cheann.
Cuir lámh eile ar an mbord.

The group has to guess the right picture. Some phrases you will need are **suigh (síos)** *sit (down)*, **luigh (síos)** *lie (down)* and **seas (suas)** *stand (up)*.

You can also try out these positions – *Foghlaimeoir A* whispers instructions to *Foghlaimeoir B. Foghlaimeoir B* tries out the position. The group says which position it is.

2(a)

An Modh Ordaitheach Diúltach
The Negative Imperative

If you want to tell someone *not* to do something you put **ná** before the base form of the verb.

Ná habair é.
Don't mention it.
Ná bac leis.
Don't bother with it.

Note that a **h** follows **ná** if the verb begins with a vowel.

(b)

Déan abairtí faoi na comharthaí *about the signs*. Bain úsáid as na focail sa bhosca. Use each word once. Scríobh an litir in aice leis an abairt.

caith	páirceáil	ól	téigh	tóg

A **B** **C**

D **E**

Ná _____ do mhadra leat.   D

Ná _____ do charr anseo.   ____

Ná _____ an deoch seo.   ____

Ná _____ an treo seo.   ____

Ná _____ tobac.   ____

(c) Léamh agus Scríobh

Here is some advice which Mary wrote in an e-mail to her friend Sharon, who has the 'flu.

Ól deochanna teo. Ná hith aon rud mar tá fiabhras ort. Ná déan an iomarca cainte.

Do you agree with this advice? Write out the advice you would give and then read it out to another student.

Comhairle *Advice*

A piece of advice from the past

Ná bí uaibhreach,	*Don't be proud,*
Ná bí bog,	*Don't be soft,*
Ná bí brónach,	*Don't be sad,*
Ná bí leamh,	*Don't be insipid,*
Ná bí santach,	*Don't be greedy,*
Ná bí cainteach,	*Don't be talkative,*
Ach bí foighneach,	*But be patient*
Agus gheobhaidh tú	*And you will get*
do chuid!	*your share!*

7 Sa Rang

1

Compare the instructions which the teacher gives in the recording to those which are written down. Cad iad na difríochtaí? *What are the differences?*

1 Éist go cúramach leis an téip. Ná scríobh aon rud.
2 Litrigh na focail seo os ard – *rosta, glúin, teanga, droim.*
3 Déan aithris orm. *An bhfuil sé seo pianmhar?*
4 Freagair na ceisteanna seo a leanas.

Déan plé le do pháirtí. Seiceáil na freagraí sna *Téipscripteanna.*

2(a)

Write classroom instructions starting with the following verbs. Remember you can also use **Ná**.

Déan	Abair	Éist	Tóg	Litrigh	Cuir

Seiceáil na habairtí leis an múinteoir.

(b) Obair Bheirte

Now give instructions orally to another student which she or he must carry out immediately. You can use the instructions you wrote out in **7.**2(a), if appropriate, or you can make up new ones.

An Hócaí Pócaí

Now is your chance to sing. If there is anybody in the group who can play a musical instrument, why not arrange to bring it into class to accompany the singers?

Everybody gets in a circle. Each student takes it in turn to call out a part of the body, **lámh**, **cos**, **glúin**, **tóin** etc. Everybody sings, and carries out the instructions.

Cuir do lámh amach
Cuir do lámh isteach
Cuir do lámh amach
Agus croith timpeall í,
Déan an Hócaí Pócaí
Agus iompaigh thart
Sin mar a dhéantar é.

Curfá:
Ó Hócaí, Pócaí, Pócaí
Ó Hócaí, Pócaí, Pócaí
Ó Hócaí, Pócaí, Pócaí
Sin mar a dhéantar é.

You may need to find out the names of parts of the body that you did not learn about in this unit. Iarr ar an múinteoir cuidiú leat nó cuardaigh na focail san fhoclóir.

8 Stór Focal

1 Cá rachaidh mé? *Where will I go?*

Meaitseáil an abairt leis an áit.

(a) Tá tinneas cinn orm. Caithfidh mé piollaí a fháil.
(b) Suigh anseo. Beidh an dochtúir leat gan mhoill.
(c) A thiarcais, tá a chos briste, ceapaim!
(d) Tá pian uafásach agam i m'fhiacail!
(e) Faigh bosca carraigín, le do thoil.
(f) Cá bhfuil an máinlia?

Siopa Bia Folláin

Obrádlann

Ospidéal

Seomra Feithimh

Poitigéir

Fiaclóir

Déan comparáid le foghlaimeoir eile. Seiceáil na focail san fhoclóir.

2 Súil Siar/Obair Bheirte

Take turns asking directions to the places in **8.**1.

 Gramadach

1 Léamh

Léigh na treoracha agus freagair na ceisteanna.

(i) **Tóg trí spúnóg cúig mg ar maidin.**
How many milligrammes are to be taken in a day?

(ii) **Tóg ceann amháin gach oíche ar feadh seacht n-oíche.**
For how many days must the medicine be taken?

2 Numbers with Nouns

(aon) spúnóg amháin
dhá spúnóg
trí spúnóg
ceithre spúnóg
cúig spúnóg
sé spúnog
seacht spúnóg
ocht spúnóg
naoi spúnóg
deich spúnóg
A

(aon) oíche amháin
dhá oíche
trí oíche
ceithre oíche
cúig oíche
sé oíche
seacht n-oíche
ocht n-oíche
naoi n-oíche
deich n-oíche
B

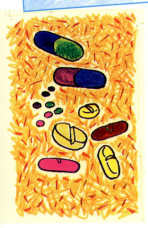

aon phiolla amháin
/piolla amháin
dhá phiolla
trí phiolla
ceithre phiolla
cúig phiolla
sé phiolla
seacht bpiolla
ocht bpiolla
naoi bpiolla
deich bpiolla
C

What 'rules' to do with counting things can be deduced from the examples in A, B and C? Déan plé le foghlaimeoir eile. Críochnaigh na habairtí thíos.

1 The numbers **dó** and **ceathair** change to _____ and _____ respectively.

2 The nouns following the numbers are all _____.

3 **n-** precedes nouns which begin with _____ after _____.

4 Nouns have *séimhiú* after _____.

5 Nouns have an *urú* after _____.

Add any other generalisations you can make.

3 Stór Focal

> **Ith torthaí le haghaidh torthaí sláintiúla.**
> *For healthy results eat fruit.*

(a)
Do you know any Irish names for fruit? Déan plé le foghlaimeoirí eile.

(b)
A child is naming the different fruit in the bowl for her parent.

Éist leis an téip. Scríobh an focal ceart ón liosta thíos ar an lipéad.

| banana | aibreog | péitseog | piorra |
| pluma | líomóid | úll | oráiste |

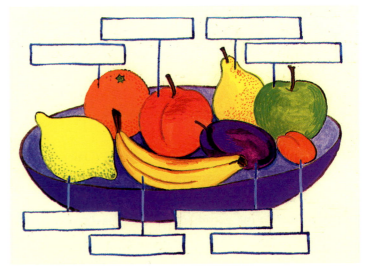

Seiceáil na freagraí san fhoclóir.

4   Rólghlacadh

The instructions for *Foghlaimeoir A* are below and the instructions for *Foghlaimeoir B* are in *Nóta*, page 128.

Foghlaimeoir A
(a)

Your partner is going shopping. Ask her or him to get you the following items:

7 oranges, 8 bananas, 3 apricots, 10 pears.

(b)

You are going shopping. Your partner is going to ask you to buy certain items. Make a shopping list based on what you hear.

5(a)

> **Ceann, Bliain, Uair**
>
> Special plural forms are used for **ceann** *one/head*, **bliain** *year*, **uair** *hour/time* after the numbers 3-10.

trí ...... sé **cinn**
seacht ..... deich **gcinn**

trí ...... sé **bliana**
seacht .... deich **mbliana**

trí ....sé **huaire**
seacht ... deich **n-uaire**

(b)   Scríobh

Líon na bearnaí leis an bhfoirm cheart den ainmfhocal *with the correct form of the noun.*

(a) Cé mhéad oráiste atá uait? Deich _____ le do thoil. (Ceann)

(b) Cén aois é do mhac? Tá sé ceithre _____ d'aois. (Bliain)

(c) Tóg piolla amháin trí _____ sa lá. (Uair)

(d) Seo dhá _____ domsa agus ceithre _____ duitse. (Ceann)

(e) Chuaigh mé go dtí an dochtúir seacht _____. (Uair)

(f) Tá m'iníon ocht _____ d'aois. (Bliain)

> **Cé mhéad uair chodlata a theastaíonn uait?**
> Cúig huaire d'fhear dlí,
> Sé huaire don sclábhaí,
> Dhá uair don ghadaí
> agus naoi n-uaire don leadaí.
>
> ***How many hours of sleep do you need?***
> *Five hours for a lawyer,*
> *Six hours for the labourer,*
> *Two hours for the thief*
> *And nine hours for the good-for-nothing.*

10   Cumarsáid

1   Stór Focal

Scríobh na focail in aice leis na pictiúir. The letters in brackets are used to form the plural. Write the singular form of the words.

deoch leighis

bindealá(i)n

ungadh

piolla(í)

plásta(i)r

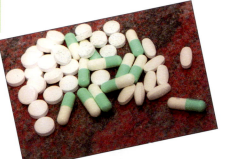

Seiceáil na focail san fhoclóir. Iarr ar an múinteoir cuidiú leat na focail a fhuaimniú.

Cuir focail eile leis an liosta.

2(a) Sa Siopa Poitigéara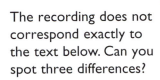

The recording does not correspond exactly to the text below. Can you spot three differences?

Freastalaí:	Dia duit, ar maidin.
Custaiméir:	Dia is Muire duit. Tá sé an-te inniu!
Freastalaí:	Tá, cinnte! An féidir liom cuidiú leat?
Custaiméir:	Tá tinneas cinn ar m'iníon ón oíche aréir. An bhfuil aon rud agat chun an phian a mhaolú?
Freastalaí:	Cén aois í d'iníon?
Custaiméir:	Ocht mbliana.
Freastalaí:	Fan go bhfeicfidh mé. Tá an deoch leighis seo an-mhaith do pháistí den aois sin. Tabhair dhá spúnóg di trí huaire sa lá.
Custaiméir:	Tá go maith. Tógfaidh mé é. Ó, agus tá bindealáin uaim freisin.
Freastalaí:	Cé mhéad atá uait?
Custaiméir:	Trí cinn.
Freastalaí:	Ceart go leor.

Stating what you want

You can use the verb **bí** + *noun* + *prepositional pronoun* **uaim** (**ó** *from* + **mé** *me*) for example

Tá bindealáin uaim. *(lit.- there are bandages from me i.e. I need bandages).*

You could also say

Tá bindealáin ag teastáil uaim. *(lit.-there are bandages needing/wanting from me i.e. I need bandages).*

In an interaction like the one in the pharmacy above you could also just state what you need, for example

Trí bhindealán, le do thoil.
Three bandages, please.

or you could use the imperative

Tabhair trí bhindealán dom, le do thoil.
Give me 3 bandages, please.

Iarr ar an múinteoir cuidiú leat na habairtí thuas a rá.

(b)

Scríobh síos trí rud *three things* atá ag teastáil uait anois.

Sampla:
Tá sos uaim anois! *I need a break!*

Déan comparáid le do pháirtí.

(c)

Asking what someone wants

To enquire about someone's needs or wants, you can say

Cad tá uait? or **Cad tá ag teastáil uait?**

Another way of doing this is to ask if you can help someone

An féidir liom cuidiú leat?
Can I help you?

To ask how many items someone wants, you can say

Cé mhéad bindealán atá uait?
How many bandages do you want?

Note the singular form after **Cé mhéad.**

Iarr ar an múinteoir cuidiú leat na habairtí thuas a rá.

3(a) Stór Focal

Where would you expect to get the items in the box?

ronnach	ticéad	léarscáil
ubh	bileog oibre	rialóir

(i)   seomra ranga
(ii) ollmhargadh
(iii) siopa nuachtán
(iv) pictiúrlann
(v)   Oifig Fáilte
(vi) siopa éisc *fish shop*

Déan plé le foghlaimeoirí eile.

Seiceáil na focail sa bhosca san fhoclóir.

(b)

Scríobh abairtí.

Sampla:
Faigheann tú *you get* ronnach sa siopa éisc.

(c) Singular vs Plural

Listen to the difference between the pronunciation of the singular and plural forms of the words:

Uatha *Singular*	Iolra *Plural*
ticéad	ticéid
léarscáil	léarscáileanna
ubh	uibheacha
bileog	bileoga
rialóir	rialóirí
ronnach	ronnaigh

Note some of the different ways of forming plurals in Irish, adding **–a**, **–í**, **–anna** or **–acha**, or making the final consonant slender, by inserting **i** before it. Irish-English dictionaries often give the plural of nouns.

With some irregular nouns the plural form is completely different e.g.

bean *woman*   **mná** *women*

teach *house*   **tithe** *houses*

4 Comhrá

Imagine you are visiting the different shops or places mentioned in **10.3(a)**. Déan comhráite le do pháirtí agus bain úsáid as na focail in (c) thuas. Remember to change the quantity of what you want each time.

Sampla:

Cad tá (ag teastáil) uait?

Tá ticéid uaim

Tá dhá thicéad uaim.

(Tabhair) dhá thicéad (dom), le do thoil.

Cé mhéad (ticéad) (atá uait)?

Tabhair dhá cheann dom, le do thoil.

(Tá) dhá cheann (uaim).

Ticéad amháin… dhá thicéad. Seo duit.
Go raibh maith agat.

Ná déan dearmad na rólanna a athrú. *Do not forget to change roles.*

11 Cultúr

Folk Medicine

We already know that people often had to resort to local healers because they could not afford conventional doctors. As a result, many folk cures were developed.

Illustration of **Teach Allais** *Sweat House by Philip V Moon*

An illness could have been inherited or contracted from another person but it might have been the result of supernatural agencies or an evil wish.

The first step was to diagnose the illness. One of the ways this was done was to scan the heavens for an indication of what might be wrong.

The second step was the treatment of the illness. Patients were encouraged not to delay in coming for treatment as is evident in the saying: **I dtús an ghalair ná bí mall**. *Do not delay at the start of an illness.* Treatments included blood letting, massage, herbs, hot-air baths in **tithe allais** *sweat houses*, milk-baths, transferring disease to inanimate objects such as the earth.

The recital of **orthaí** *charms* was also common, for example: **Goin an míol, arg an míol, maraigh an míol** *Wound the creature, plunder the creature, kill the creature* – the 'creature' (often a worm) being seen as the source of the illness.

Preventive medicine was also practised – three meals of **neantóga** *nettles* in May would avert headaches for a year. **Bain triail as!**

Information sources
Logan, P. (1972) *Making the Cure,* Dublin: Talbot Press.
Ó Súilleabháin, S. (1942) *A Handbook of Irish Folklore,* Dublin: Educational Company of Ireland.

Plé

(i) Have you ever visited a folk healer? How does this type of treatment compare to more traditional medicine?

(ii) Discuss any similarities or differences between Irish folk cures and folk cures from other cultures.

2

Herbal cures were very popular in Ireland. The following are some of the **luibheanna** *herbs* or plants used in creating such cures. Can you label them?

Seiceáil na focail san fhoclóir.

| Neantóg Caisearbhán Biolar |
| Gairleog Méaracán dearg Nóinín |

(i) _____ (ii) _____ (iii) _____

(iv) _____ (v) _____ (vi) _____

3

The following is a list of the illnesses which the above herbs were said to cure. Can you guess which illness was cured by which herb?

| tinneas san ae   fiabhras croí   gaoth |
| slaghdán   casacht   pianta sna cnámha |

Luibheanna	Tinnis
Nóinín	_____
Neantóg	_____
Caisearbhán	_____
Biolar	_____
Gairleog	_____
Méaracán dearg	_____

4 Plé

(a) Are you aware of any other folk cures for the illnessess in 11.3?

(b) Are you aware of any other illness which can be cured by the herbs in 11.2 and 3?

12 Gramadach

1

Déan aithris ar an téip.

Uaim *from me*

uaim	*from me*
uait	*from you* (singular)
uaithi	*from her*
uaidh	*from him*
uainn	*from us*
uaibh	*from you* (plural)
uathu	*from them*

2 Obair Bheirte

Foghlaimeoir A: Repeat the list in 1 but leave out one word.

Foghlaimeoir B: Listen to your partner. Say which word she or he has left out.

Athraigh na rólanna.
Now try leaving out two words.

3(a)

Léigh na ceisteanna seo a leanas:

A What does Muiris, Hilda's son, want from the shop?

B Why is Órla not totally happy staying with her aunt?

Anois léigh an comhrá ar leathanach 120.

Sa Siopa Áitiúil *In the Local Shop*

Siopadóir:	Dia duit, a Hilda. An féidir liom cuidíu leat?
Hilda:	Dia is Muire duit, a Dhonncha. Tá lítear bainne uaim agus mála siúcra.
Siopadóir:	An bhfuil aon rud eile uait?
Hilda:	Níl.
Siopadóir:	Cad faoi na páistí?
Hilda:	Níl aon rud ag teastáil uathu, ceapaim.
Siopadóir:	Ceart go leor mar sin.
Hilda:	Ó, gabh mo leithscéal! Tá rud éigin ag teastáil ó Mhuiris. Tá dhá bhuidéal oráiste uaidh. Cinn bheaga le do thoil.
Siopadóir:	Agus Órla?
Hilda:	Tá Órla ar saoire lena haintín.
Siopadóir:	Níl aon rud uaithi mar sin.
Hilda:	Níl, ach amháin an teilifís! Níl aon teilifís ag mo dheirfiúr.
Siopadóir:	Órla bhocht!

Freagair ceisteanna A agus B ar leathanach 119.

13 Staidéar Pearsanta

There are many examples of instructions in Irish to be seen in Ireland. Most official notices, such as those for parking, appear in both their Irish and English forms. They may not always appear together on the one sign, for example:

At one end of the street you could find the English version and at the other end the Irish version or you may even find the Irish version in one street and the English version in another street!

Look for bilingual notices and tell other students.

14 Sa Rang

1(a) Sa Téacsleabhar

Líon na bearnaí na habairtí leis na focail nó na frásaí seo a leanas:

as an	san	faoin	faoi na		leis an
	in aice leis an/na		sa	ar an	

(a) *Fill the gaps with the correct form of the noun.*
Líon na bearnaí _____ bhfoirm cheart den ainmfhocal.

(b) *Complete the sentences with words from the box.*
Líon na bearnaí sna habairtí le focail _____ mbosca.

(c) *Put a tick beside the correct sign.*
Cuir tic _____ gcomhartha ceart.

(d) *Put the correct sentences under the pictures.*
Cuir na habairtí cearta _____ pictiúir.

(e) *Write the words beside the pictures.*
Scríobh na focail _____ pictiúir.

(f) *Repeat what is said on the tape.*
Déan aithris _____ téip.

(g) *Check the words in the box in the dictionary.*
Seiceáil na focail _____ bhosca _____ fhoclóir.

Déan comparáid le foghlaimeoir eile. Cuardaigh na habairtí san aonad seo.

(b)

Faoi *Under, About*

Many prepositions have more than one meaning. The preposition **faoi** basically means *under* but it can also mean *about*.

1 **Cuir na habairtí cearta faoi na pictiúir.**
Put the correct sentences under the pictures.

2 **Déan comhráite faoi na pictiúir.**
Make conversations about the pictures.

Cuardaigh abairtí 1 agus 2 san aonad seo.

2 Gramadach

Scríobh na focail san uimhir iolra.
Tá an chéad cheann déanta.

uatha	iolra
ceist	ceisteanna
ainmfhocal	
pictiúr	
freagra	
ról	
abairt	
comhrá	

3

Obair Ghrúpa

Each student writes out 2 instructions on a piece of paper.

Sampla: Seas suas ar dtús. Ansin can amhrán.

All instructions are folded and are put in a bag or box. One student picks a piece of paper and carries out the instructions. Everyone writes down what they think the instructions were. The student who carried out the instructions writes them on the board. Students check what they have written.

Now it's another student's turn.

15 Scileanna Foghlama

Developing your listening skills

In Aonad 6 we talked about the importance of becoming familiar with the sound of the language without trying to understand the meaning of every word. This is a crucial first step in developing listening skills.

We are now going to concentrate on ways of understanding what you hear.

I(a)

(b)

Éist leis an téip. Mark the stressed words.

(a) Cá bhfuil an t-ospidéal?
(b) Tá an deoch leighis seo an-mhaith.
(c) Trí bhindealán le do thoil.
(d) Tá pian uafásach i m'fhiacail.
(e) Tá mé te.
(f) Fan sa seomra feithimh.

Déan comparáid le do pháirtí. Abair na habairtí os ard.

2(a)

Meaitseáil an comhrá leis an bpictiúr ceart.

A

B

Déan comparáid le foghlaimeoir eile. Which words helped you in your decision?
Seiceáil sna *Téipscripteanna*.

(b) Staidéar Pearsanta

Try and listen to some Irish and see if you can guess the key words from the stress.

Líon isteach an ghreille mar seo:

context	word(s)	what I think is being said
weather forecast on TV	amárach fuar	it's going to be cold tomorrow

Am Spóirt

Siosóga *Whispers*

Students form a circle. One students starts by whispering an instruction to the student next to her or him, for example **Cuir an chathaoir ar an mbord**. This student whispers the instruction to the next student who in turn whispers it to the next student and so on. The last student to receive the instruction must carry it out.

How has the instruction changed since it was first given?

Achoimre *Summary*

Cumarsáid agus Stór Focal

Describing your state of health is	Tá pian i mo bholg. Tá scornach thinn orm. Tá feabhas orm. Níl fiabhras air. Tá sé an-phianmhar. Níl sé róphianmhar.
Asking others about their health	Cad tá ort, a Bhrídín? Cad tá cearr leat? An bhfuil rud éigin ort? An bhfuil sé pianmhar? An bhfuil tú ag ithe?
Expressing sympathy	Is maith sin. Is trua sin. Máire bhocht!, Mícheál bocht!
Giving medical instructions	Cuir amach do theanga. Ná hith aon rud. Tóg piolla amháin gach oíche. Fan sa leaba. Luigh (síos), suigh (síos), seas (suas).
Stating what you want	Tá bindealáin uaim. Tá dochtúir ag teastáil uaim. Trí bhindealán, le do thoil. Tabhair trí bhindealán dom.
Asking what someone wants	Cad tá uait? Cad tá ag teastáil uait? An féidir liom cuidiú leat? Cé mhéad atá uait?
Recognising common signs	Siopa Bia Folláin Poitigéir Fiaclóir Dochtúir Seomra Feithimh Ospidéal Obrádlann
Parts of the body	droim, bolg, cos, lámh, scornach, rúitín, méar(a), uilinn(eacha), glúin(e), srón, súil(e), cluas(a), béal, fiacail, teanga, muineál
Ailments and illnesses	slaghdán, fiabhras (croí), pian (sna cnámha), tuirse, feabhas, fliú, tinneas (cinn), casacht, (cos) thinn, galar, gaoth
Medicines and dressings	deoch leighis, ungadh, piolla, plástar, bindealán
Fruit	líomóid, oráiste, úll, piorra, pluma, banana, péitseog, aibreog
Herbs	nóinín, neantóg, caisearbhán, biolar, gairleog, méaracán dearg
Sa rang	
Giving, understanding oral instructions	Déan aithris... Freagair an cheist. Éist leis an téip. Tóg an peann. Litrigh... Cuir.... Ná freagair an cheist.
Sa téacsleabhar	Líon na bearnaí leis an bhfoirm cheart den ainmfhocal, líon na bearnaí sna habairtí le focail as an mbosca, cuir tic in aice leis an gcomhartha ceart, cuir na habairtí cearta faoi na pictiúir, scríobh na focail in aice leis na pictiúir, déan aithris ar an téip, seiceáil na focail sa bhosca san fhoclóir.
Saying the order in which something is to happen	Léigh an comhrá ar dtús. Ansin freagair na ceisteanna.

Gramadach

- **An Modh Ordaitheach** *The Imperative Mood*

  dún an leabhar **ná** déan é sin **ná h**oscail do bhéal

- **Uimhreacha le hAinmfhocail** *Numbers with Nouns*

  (aon) spúnóg amháin, **dhá** spúnóg, trí spúnóg, **ceithre** spúnóg ..... deich spúnóg

  (aon) oíche amháin... sé oíche, seacht... deich **n**-oíche

  aon **ph**iolla amháin/piolla amháin, dhá... sé **ph**iolla... seacht... deich **b**piolla

  trí... sé **cinn**, seacht... deich **gcinn**

  trí... sé **bliana**, seacht... deich **mbliana**

  trí... sé **huaire**, seacht... deich **n-uaire**

- **An Uimhir Iolra** *The Plural*

  ticéad-tic**éid**, bileog-bileo**ga**, rialóir – rialóir**í**, léirscáil-léarscáile**anna**, uillinn-uillinn**eacha**, ronnach-ronn**aigh**, bean – **mná**

  an ticéad – **na** ticéid

- **An Forainm Réamhfhoclach** *The Prepositional Pronoun*

  uaim, uait, uaithi, uaidh, uainn, uaibh, uathu

Fuaimniú

An Défhoghar /iə/ e.g. pian, bia, liath

Scileanna Foghlama

Listening skills – key words

- Do not try to understand every word you hear.
- Listen out for key words.
- Key words are usually the stressed words like nouns, verbs and adjectives.
- You may know a word is important because it is stressed but may not know the meaning of the word. If possible, ask the speaker to explain the meaning of the word for you.

Cultúr

Conventional and Folk medicine in Ireland

- Not much is known about Irish medicine before the 14th century.
- In the year 860 AD we know that there was a **saoi leighis** *master physician* responsible for medicine in the whole country.
- From the 14th century onwards Irish doctors studied in European medical schools and some doctors set up medical schools on their return to Ireland.
- The training doctors received in Europe was based on the Graeco-Arabic tradition but there was a cross-over with traditional Irish medicine.
- The 'new' medicine was translated by scribes from Latin (the language used in European medical schools) to Irish.
- Doctors often belonged to hereditary medical families.
- Many people, however, could not afford medical doctors so they went to local healers.
- Treatments included blood-letting, massage, herbs, hot-air baths in **tithe allais**, milk-baths, transferring disease to inanimate objects.
- The recital of **orthaí** *charms* was common.

7 Cad tá ort?

Triail Tú Féin

A

1

Scríobh abairt amháin faoi gach pictiúr.
Sampla: Tá tinneas cinn orm.

Déan comparáid le foghlaimeoirí eile agus ansin seiceáil leis an múinteoir.

2

Tá dhá chomhrá measctha le chéile *mixed up together* – ceann amháin **Ag an Dochtúir**, ceann eile **Ag an bPoitigéir**. Scríobh na comhráite i gceart.

Tá oideas agam. Seo duit.
An ceann mór nó an ceann beag?
(Five minutes later) Seo do dheoch leighis. Tóg spúnóg amháin trí huaire sa lá.
Tá an t-ungadh seo ag teastáil uaim freisin.
Luigh síos ansin, le do thoil.
Cad tá cearr leat?
Ó a dhiabhail!
An bhfuil sé seo pianmhar?
Ní féidir liom. Tá sé róphianmhar.
Tá pian i mo dhroim.
Ardaigh do chos beagáinín.
An ceann beag.
Tógfaidh sé cúig nóiméad, ceart go leor?
Go raibh maith agat.
An féidir liom cuidiú leat?
Ceart go leor.

3

Críochnaigh na habairtí leis na frásaí sa liosta thíos.

Líon na bearnaí _____.

Cuir tic _____.

Déan aithris _____.

Éist _____.

Léigh na focail ar dtús _____.

agus ansin abair os ard iad

leis an múinteoir

sa bhosca ceart

leis na focail chearta

ar an múinteoir

Seiceáil na freagraí leis an múinteoir.

B

(i)

Cuir na focail i gceithre chatagóir.

bindealán	bolg	oráiste	piolla
teanga	rúitín	casacht	banana
deoch leighis	droim	péitseog	ungadh
slaghdán	úll	fliú	lámh	plástar
aibreog	tuirse	plucamas	

bindealán	**bolg**	**oráiste**	**casacht**
_____	_____	_____	_____
_____	_____	_____	_____
_____	_____	_____	_____
_____	_____	_____	_____

(ii)

Meaitseáil na focail ar chlé leis na focail ar dheis.

ospidéal	cathaoireacha
siopa bia folláin	buidéal leighis
dochtúir	leaba/leapacha
fiaclóir	scian
obrádlann	carraigín
seomra feithimh	teirmiméadar
poitigéir	fiacail lofa

Déan comparáid le foghlaimeoirí eile.

C

1

Give instructions based on the pictures below using the verbs ól, téigh, cas, oscail:

A   B

C   D

2(i)

Scríobh an t-oideas thíos i bhfocail. Léigh an t-oideas os ard. Iarr ar an múinteoir éisteacht leat.

> **Sailéad Torthaí**
> 1 úll
> 2 banana
> 8 aibreog
> 8 pluma
> 2 spúnóg mhóra Grand Marnier
> 4 spúnog mhóra sú oráistí
> 5mg siúcra (más maith leat)

(ii)

Scríobh an fhoirm cheart de na focail idir lúibíní *in brackets*.

(a)   dhá (ceann), ceithre (ceann), naoi (ceann)
(b)   trí (bliain), sé (bliain), seacht (bliain)
(c)   cúig (uair), ocht (uair), dhá (uair)

3

Scríobh an Uimhir Uatha de na focail seo a leanas:

Iolra	Uathu
leabhair	
deochanna	
uillinneacha	
pictiúrlanna	
líomóidí	
scoileanna	
piollaí	

4(i)

Críochnaigh an tsraith.

uaim _____   uaithi _____   uainn _____
uathu

(ii)

Líon na bearnaí.

(a)   'Tá bindealáin _____', arsa mise. (ó, mé)
(b)   Cad tá ag teastáil_____, a Sheáin? (ó, tú)
(c)   Tá cupán tae ó Mháire agus tá briosca _____freisin. (ó, í)
(e)   Cuir ceist ar Sheán cad tá _____. (ó, é)

D

Fuaimniú

Which is the odd-one-out?

(a)   bí ith croí níl trí
(b)   pian siad fuar aniar fiacail

E

Cultúr

Based on what you have read in the cultural sections of this unit, what do you associate with the following:

Saoi Leighis _____

Muintir Ící _____

neantóga _____

teach allais _____

orthaí_____

1.2

Tá a shrón rófhada. Ní maith liom é sin in aon chor! Tá súile deasa gorma aige agus is maith liom a bhéal. Ach faraor! Féach na cluasa móra atá air!

2.1(a) agus (b)

Dochtúir:	Cad tá ort?
Bean:	Tá pian i mo bholg.
Dochtúir:	Luigh síos ansin le do thoil.
Máthair:	An bhfuil rud éigin ort, a Mhaidhc?
Buachaill:	Tá tinneas fiacaile orm.
Máthair:	Maidhc bocht!
Fear:	Conas tá tú ar maidin, a Dheirdre?
Bean:	Ní bhraithim go maith. Tá scornach thinn orm.
Fear:	An bhfuil? Agus tá tú te freisin.

3.1(b)

fiabhras, níl, siad, pian, rí, Liam

5.1(b)

Fáilteoir:	Cad tá cearr leat?
Othar:	Tá scornach thinn orm.
Fáilteoir:	An bhfuil sé pianmhar?
Othar:	Níl sé róphianmhar.
Fáilteoir:	Is maith sin! Beidh an dochtúir saor ar a trí a chlog.
Othar:	Ceart go leor.
Fáilteoir:	Slán go fóill.

5.2(a)

Dochtúir:	Dia duit, a Uasail Uí Riagáin.
Othar:	Dia is Muire duit, a dhochtúir.
Dochtúir:	Suigh síos ansin.
Othar:	Go raibh maith agat.
Dochtúir:	Inniu an deichiú lá. An bhfuil sé sin ceart? Caithfidh mé é a sheiceáil ar an bhféilire. Is ea, bhí an ceart agam. Inniu an deichiú lá de Dheireadh Fómhair. Do chéad ainm?
Othar:	Tadhg.
Dochtúir:	Ceart go leor. Agus cad tá cearr leat, a Thaidhg?
Othar:	Bhuel. Níl mé ag mothú go maith. Tá fiabhras orm le trí lá anuas. Tá scornach thinn orm freisin.
Dochtúir:	An bhfuil tú ag ithe?
Othar:	Níl.

5.2(b)

Dochtúir:	Anois, oscail do bhéal go bhfeicfidh mé do scornach.
Othar:	Á … á … á … á …
Dochtúir:	Cuir amach do theanga le do thoil. Tá do scornach an-dearg ar fad.

	Dún do bhéal arís. Dúirt tú go raibh fiabhras ort le cúpla lá?
Othar:	Le trí lá.
Dochtúir:	Ardaigh do lámh agus coimeád an termiméadar faoi d'ascaill.

5.2(c)

Dochtúir:	Tá teocht ard ort ceart go leor.
Othar:	Cé chomh hard?
Dochtúir:	Tríocha hocht. Téigh caol díreach abhaile agus fan sa leaba.

7.1

1 Éist go cúramach leis an gceist. Scríobh síos na freagraí.

2 Scríobh na focail seo – *rosta, glúin, teanga, droim.*

3 Éist leis an abairt arís: *An bhfuil sé seo pianmhar?*

4 Léigh na ceisteanna seo a leanas.

10.2(a)

Freastalaí:	Dia duit, ar maidin.
Custaiméir:	Dia is Muire duit. Tá sé an-te inniu!
Freastalaí:	Tá, cinnte! An féidir liom cuidiú leat?
Custaiméir:	Tá tinneas fiacaile ar m'iníon ón oíche aréir. An bhfuil aon rud agat chun an phian a mhaolú?
Freastalaí:	Cén aois í d'iníon?
Custaiméir:	Deich mbliana.
Freastalaí:	Fan go bhfeicfidh mé. Tá an deoch leighis seo an-mhaith do pháistí den aois sin. Tabhair trí spúnóg di trí huaire sa lá.
Custaiméir:	Tá go maith. Tógfaidh mé é. Ó, agus tá bindealáin uaim freisin.
Freastalaí:	Cé mhéad atá uait?
Custaiméir:	Trí cinn.
Freastalaí:	Ceart go leor.

15.2(a)

Bean:	Tá sé damanta fuar!
Fear:	Tá cinnte. Ach féach ar na páistí ag déanamh spóirt! Is cuma leo faoin bhfuacht! Is maith is cuimhin liom nuair a bhí mé féin óg….
Bean:	Fainic an liathróid sneachta!
Fear:	A dhiabhail! Ná déan é sin arís!
Bean:	Cad é sin a bhí á rá agat… is ea… is cuimhin leat nuair a bhí tú féin óg…
Fear:	Ná bí ag magadh fúm! Ar mhaith leat cupán tae?
Bean:	Ba mhaith.
Fear:	Rachaimid isteach anseo.

Eochair

2.1(a) 1D, 2C, 3A

3.1(b) 1/iə/ 2/i:/ 3/iə/ 4/iə/ 5/i:/ 6/iə/

4.2

muscail — muscle
gaofaireacht — flatulence
gúta — gout
cláiréad — claret
fionn — fennel
finéal — soap
gallúnach — cataract

6.2(b)
Ná tóg do mhadra leat.   D
Ná páirceáil do charr anseo.   C
Ná hól an deoch seo.   E
Ná téigh an treo seo.   A
Ná caith tobac.   B

9.1 (i) 15mg (ii) 7

9.2
1   The numbers **dó** and **ceathair** change to **dhá** and **ceithre** respectively.
2   The nouns following the numbers are all **singular**.
3   **n-** precedes nouns which begin with a **vowel** after **seacht** …. **deich.**
4   Nouns have *séimhiú* after **aon, dhá** … **sé.**
5   Nouns have an *urú* after **seacht** … **deich.**

9.5(b)
(a) gcinn (b) bliana (c) huaire (d) cheann, cinn
(e) n-uaire (f) mbliana

10.2(a)
tinneas **fiacaile**, **deich** mbliana, **trí** spúnóg

11.2
(i) gairleog (ii) neantóg (iii) méaracán dearg
(iv) caisearbhán (v) nóinín (vi) biolar

11.3
Nóinín – casacht
Neantóg – gaoth
Caisearbhán – tinneas san ae
Biolar – slaghdán
Gairleog – pianta sna cnámha
Méaracán dearg – fiabhras croí

12.3(a)
A two bottles of orange juice
B the aunt does not have a television

14.2

uatha	iolra
ainmfhocal	ainmfhocail
pictiúr	pictiúir
freagra	freagraí
ról	rólanna
abairt	abairtí
comhrá	comhráite

15.1(b)
(a) Cá bhfuil an t-ospidéal?
(b) Tá an deoch leighis seo an-mhaith.
(c) Trí bhindealán le do thoil.
(d) Tá pian uafásach i m'fhiacail.
(e) Tá mé te.
(f) Fan sa seomra feithimh.

15.2(a) B

Triail Tú Féin

A

2

Ag an Dochtúir
Cad tá cearr leat?
Tá pian i mo dhroim.
Luigh síos ansin, le do thoil.
Ceart go leor.
Ardaigh do chos beagáinín.
Ní féidir liom. Tá sé róphianmhar.
An bhfuil sé seo pianmhar?
Ó a dhiabhail!

Ag an bPoitigéir
An féidir liom cuidiú leat?
Tá oideas agam. Seo duit.
Tógfaidh sé cúig nóiméad. Ceart go leor?
Tá an t-ungadh seo ag teastáil uaim freisin.
An ceann mór nó an ceann beag?
An ceann beag.
(five minutes later) Seo do dheoch leighis.
   Tóg spúnóg amháin trí huaire sa lá.
Go raibh maith agat.

B

(i)

bindealán	**bolg**	**oráiste**	**casacht**
piolla	teanga	banana	slaghdán
deoch leighis	rúitín	péitseog	fliú
ungadh	droim	úll	plucamas
plástar	lámh	aibreog	tuirse

(ii) (possible matches)

ospidéal   cathaoireacha
siopa bia folláin   buidéal leighis
dochtúir   leaba/leapacha
fiaclóir   scian
obrádlann   carraigín
seomra feithimh   teirmiméadar
poitigéir   fiacail lofa

C

1   A Téigh suas an staighre, B Oscail do bhéal, C Ná cas ar chlé, D Ná hól an ghloine fíona sin.

2(i)   úll (amháin), dhá bhanana, ocht n-aibreog, ocht bpluma, dhá spúnóg mhóra Grand Marnier, ceithre spúnóg mhóra sú óráistí, cúig mhilleagram siúcra (más maith leat)

2(ii)   (a) dhá cheann, ceithre cinn, naoi gcinn
        (b) trí bliana, sé bliana, seacht mbliana
        (c) cúig huaire, ocht n-uaire, dhá uair

3

Iolra	**Uathu**
leabhair	leabhar
deochanna	deoch
uillinneacha	uillinn
pictiúrlanna	pictiúrlann
líomóidí	líomóid
scoileanna	scoil
piollaí	piolla

4(i)   uait, uaidh, uaibh

4(ii)   (a) 'Tá bindealáin uaim', arsa mise
         (b) Cad tá ag teastáil uait, a Sheáin?
         (c) Tá cupán tae ó Mháire agus tá briosca uaithi freisin.
         (e) Cuir ceist ar Sheán cad tá uaidh.

D

(a) ith   (b) fuar

E

Saoi Leighis	Master Physician
Muintir Ící	hereditary medical family
neantóga	nettles, for preventing headaches
teach allais	Irish-style sauna
orthaí	charms which were recited to rid a patient of an illness

Nóta

Foghlaimeoir B

(a)

You are going shopping. Your partner is going to ask you to buy certain items. Make a shopping list based on what you hear.

(b)

Your partner is going shopping. Ask her or him to buy the following items:

4 apples, 8 peaches, 2 plums, 3 lemons

8 Ó mhaidin go hoíche
Ó Luan go Satharn

This unit enables learners to: enquire about opening and closing times, starting and finishing times; ask about and describe work; select information from notice-boards; understand grammatical terms.

Dé Luain...Dé Máirt...Dé Céadaoin ....Déardaoin Dé hA

Do you recognise the words in the picture? There are some words missing. Can you suggest what they are?

129

1 Cumarsáid

An t-Am *The time*

I

You will hear five conversations about the time. The clocks show the times mentioned in the conversations. Meaitseáil na hamanna (times) leis na comhráite.

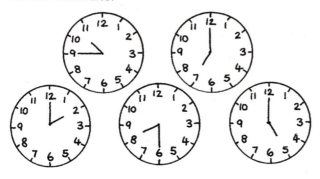

Comhrá	Am
I	5.00
2	
3	
4	
5	

Seiceáil na freagraí sna *Téipscripteanna*. Copy down the phrases used to ask the time. Practise saying them.

2(a)

Críochnaigh na habairtí.

Sampla:
Deich nóiméad **chun** a haon.

1 Leathuair **tar éis** _____.

2 Cúig nóiméad is fiche **tar éis** _____.

3 _____ **a chlog**.

4 Fiche nóiméad **chun** _____.

5 Ceathrú **tar éis** _____.

6 Cúig nóiméad **chun** _____.

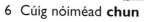

(b)

Draw your own clocks and mark in the following times:

a sé a chlog
cúig nóiméad is fiche tar éis a trí
fiche nóiméad chun a haon
ceathrú tar éis a naoi
deich nóiméad chun a deich
cúig nóiméad chun a hocht
leathuair tar éis a haon déag

Déan comparáid le foghlaimeoirí eile. Iarr ar an múinteoir na freagraí a sheiceáil.

Nóta: you will often hear **i ndiaidh** for **tar éis** *after, past.*

(c)

Éist leis an téip agus líon na bearnaí sna habairtí.

Cén t-am é?

Tá sé fiche nóiméad _____ a cúig.

Tá sé ceathrú _____ a ceathair.

Tá sé a sé _____.

Tá sé _____ nóiméad chun a haon.

Tá sé _____ tar éis a dó.

Tá sé _____ tar éis a haon déag.

(d) Obair Bheirte

Draw more clocks and mark in different times. Ask your partner the time on each clock. Switch roles.

Nóta: In expressions like a **naoi a chlog**/ə ni: ə xlog/ the particle **a** is not emphasised and can scarcely be heard.

3(a) Gramadach

Numbers (11-29) + 'Nóiméad'	
11	aon nóiméad déag
12-19	dhá nóiméad déag ... naoi nóiméad déag
20	fiche nóiméad
21	nóiméad is fiche
22-29	dhá nóiméad is fiche ... naoi nóiméad is fiche

(b)

Scríobh na hamanna i bhfocail.
(i) 2.04 (ii) 4.13 (iii) 5.21 (iv) 6.27

Déan comparáid le foghlaimeoir eile.

(c) Biongó

Pick any five times from column A. Write those five times in any order in the five blank squares in the first column of the bingo card. Pick any five times from column B. Write them in any order in the second column of the bingo card. Do the same for the times in columns C, D and E until your card is completely filled.

A	B	C	D	E
4.01	2.06	3.11	3.16	3.21
5.02	3.07	6.12	3.17	5.22
8.03	11.08	8.13	10.18	11.23
9.04	12.09	10.14	6.19	9.24
10.05	4.10	7.15	1.20	3.25
6.01	12.06	3.11	12.16	11.21
9.02	10.07	5.12	2.17	2.22
2.03	4.08	1.13	3.18	8.23
8.04	6.09	4.14	1.19	2.24
12.05	1.10	9.15	4.20	6.25

Cárta Biongó

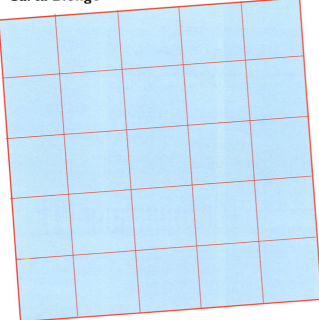

Your teacher will call out the times at random. She or he will also write the times on the board. Mark the times on your card with an X. When you have five x's in a row marked either vertically, horizontally or diagonally, call out Biongó!

(d) Tusa anois!

Now it is your turn to call out the times. Any volunteers?

Dán

Teilifís

(faoi m'iníon Saffron)

Ar a cúig a chlog ar maidin
Theastaigh an teilifís uaithi.
An féidir argóint
  le beainín
Dhá bhliain go leith?
Síos linn le chéile
Níor bhacas fiú le gléasadh
Is bhí an seomra préachta.
Gan solas fós sa spéir
Stánamar le hiontas ar
  scáileán bán.
Anois! Sásta?
Ach chonaic sise sneachta
Is sioráf tríd an sneachta
Is ulchabhán Artach
Ag faoileáil
Os a chionn.

Television

(for my daughter Saffron)

At five o'clock in the morning
She wanted the television.
Who can argue with a little
  woman
Two and a half years old?
Down we went together
I didn't even dress
And the room was freezing.
No light yet in the sky
We stared in wonder at
  the white screen.
Happy now?
But she saw snow
And a giraffe through it
And an artic owl
Wheeling
Above it.

Gabriel Rosenstock
Translated by Gabriel Fitzmaurice

2 Cumarsáid

1(a)

It is Wednesday evening. Kathy and Donncha are trying to decide what television programmes to watch. Kathy is reading the TV guide on page 132.

Before you start listening …

(i) Iarr ar an múinteoir ainmneacha na gclár teilifíse a rá os ard.

(ii) Meaitseáil an Ghaeilge leis an mBéarla.

teilifís	it starts
anocht	interesting
tosaíonn sé	television
clár	tonight
suimiúil	too late
ródhéanach	programme

Now listen to the recording as you read the TV guide. Kathy gives the wrong starting time for one of the programmes. Which one?

Dé Céadaoin

12.00 **RnaG** 83002513 2.30 **Dáil Éireann - Question Time Live** 61361971 4.15 **Traidisiún an Bhia** (TS) 75417890 4.30 **Natural Selection** 95291703 4.58 **Cinnlínte Nuachta** 5.00 **Cúlabúla** 42363074 5.04 **Art Ó Ruairc** (TS) 426371155 5.40 **Thuas san Áiléar** (TS) 44967426

6.00 **Cybernet** (TS) 95116068
Na hiontais is deireanaí ó shaol na gcluichí ríomhaireachta agus deis ar dhuais mhór freisin.

6.30 **Ard San Aer** (TS) 95203548
Clár seachtainiúil do lucht leanta CLG. Buaicphointí.

6.58 **Cinnlínte Nuachta** 380826529

7.00 **Ros na Rún** (GS) 34974703
Sraithdhráma. Tá Caitríona ag dul faoi agallamh. Tagann Vanessa ar chomhaid Andy.

7.30 **EuroNews** 95292432
8.00 **Nuacht** TG4 34983451
8.26 **An Aimsir Láithreach**
8.30 **Nua Gach Bia** (TS) 34979258
Is í an Iodáil foinse ionspioráide an eagráin seo agus is ó shaol na teilifíse na haíonna: Ciara Callaghan (Fair City) agus Síle Nic Chaonaigh (An Gleann Rua).

9.00 **Hollywood Anocht** (TS) 69644529
9.30 **Cead Cainte** 25530364
10.00 **An Aimsir Láithreach**
10.02 **El Che** (OS) 285881838
Cuntas ar shaol Che Guevara, laoch réabhlóidithe na seascaidí.

11.05 **Go Meiriceá Siar** (OS) 64228109
11.30 **Legends of the Isles** 62776258
11.57 **Barabbas** 230129971
11.58 **An Aimsir Láithreach**
Achoimre aimsire.
12.00 **Deireadh Craolta**

Foinse

(b)

Léigh an téipscript. Copy out the sentences which were used to:

ask what time the food programme starts

say what time the food programme starts

ask what time the programme on Che Guevara finishes

Déan comparáid le foghlaimeoir eile. Iarr ar an múinteoir cuidiú leat na habairtí a rá.

Ceist: What happens to the verb after *Cén t-am a …?*

Déan plé le foghlaimeoir eile. Seiceáil an freagra sna *Téipscripteanna* agus leis an múinteoir.

(c) Obair Bheirte

The instructions for *Foghlaimeoir A* are below and the instructions for *Foghlaimeoir B* are in *Nóta 1*, page 143.

Foghlaimeoir A

It is Sunday. You want to record some TV programmes. Your partner has the information you need to complete the card below. Cuir ceist uirthi nó air faoi na hamanna.

Clár	Tosaíonn	Críochnaíonn
Nuacht TG4		7.12
Léargas	7.30	
Ollchlár Ros na Rún		11.20

Seiceáil na freagraí le *Foghlaimeoir B*.

2(a)

Léigh na fógraí seo.

AN SIOPA LEABHAR
The Celtic Bookshop

Amanna Oscailte *Opening hours*
Luan – Aoine *Monday – Friday*
9.30am – 5.30pm

Satharn *Saturday* 10.00am – 4.00pm

(Lón *Lunch* 1.30 – 2.00pm)
6 Sráid Fhearchair

Leabharlann ITÉ

Tráthanna Oscailte
Opening Hours
Máirt – Aoine
Tuesday – Friday
9.30 – 12.30
14.20 – 17.00

31 Plás Mhic Liam
www.ite.ie

It is Wednesday. A man is enquiring over the telephone about the time one of the places above closes. Can you tell which place he is referring to?

(b)

In Aonad 7 you learnt that certain words in Irish are more strongly stressed than others. Before you do the following exercise, look again at Aonad 7 Mír **15.**1(a). Now mark in the stress marks as you listen to the recording. The first one is done for you.

Oscla<u>í</u>onn an <u>Sí</u>opa <u>Lea</u>bhar ar a leathuair tar éis a <u>naoi</u>.

Dúnann sé ar a leathuair tar éis a cúig.

Cén t-am a osclaíonn an banc?

Cén t-am a dhúnann sé?

Abair na habairtí os ard.

(c) Obair Bheirte

The instructions for *Foghlaimeoir A* are below and the instructions for *Foghlaimeoir B* are in *Nóta 2*, page 143.

Foghlaimeoir A

As part of a campaign to promote the use of Irish in your area, you are compiling a list for a new Irish language newsletter of the opening and closing times of different premises. You already have some of this information. Your partner has the rest of the information you need.

Áit	Amanna Oscailte	
Búistéir Uí Fhlaithearta	9.15	–
Ollmhargadh Uí Ghríofa	–	7.00
Potadóireacht Áine	2.30	–
An Cupán Tae	–	6.15

Seiceáil na freagraí le *Foghlaimeoir B*.

3 Cultúr

1 Irish Language Broadcasting

Raidió *Radio*

Two radio stations broadcast entirely in Irish. *Raidió na Gaeltachta*, which has studios in Dublin and in each of the Gaeltacht areas, is broadcast nationally 24 hours a day. *Raidió na Life* broadcasts daily in Dublin. Two thirds of *Raidió na Gaeltachta*'s audience are from outside the Gaeltacht.

While both stations produce news and current affairs, cultural, sports and music programmes, the emphasis in each is different. *Raidió na Gaeltachta* caters to a mixed audience whereas *Raidió na Life* targets a younger, urban audience and this is reflected in the type of music played. *Raidió na Gaeltachta*'s main emphasis is on Irish traditional music but it also broadcasts pop music in Irish and classical music. *Raidió na Life*, on the other hand, focusses on a broad range of music including traditional, jazz, techno, ska, indi, dance etc. Unlike *Raidió na Gaeltachta*, it broadcasts songs in English.

RTÉ (the national broadcasting organisation) and *BBC Radio Ulster*, produce a limited number of Irish language radio programmes every week which include news and current affairs, features and special reports, language learning, programmes for young people and music. Some local radio stations broadcast a weekly Irish language programme.

Learners outside Ireland can access *Raidió na Gaeltachta* either by satellite or through the Internet. The service is carried live to listeners in the UK and throughout Europe on Saturday and Sunday on the ASTRA Satellite system. The service is available daily in North America on the GALAXY Satellite system. *Raidió na Gaeltachta* is also broadcast over the Internet at the following address: http://www.rnag.ie

BBC Radio Ulster broadcasts its Irish language programme *Blas* over the Internet at this address:

http://www.bbc.co.uk/northernireland/blas/realaudio.shtml

Teilifís *Television*

TG4, the national Irish language television service, came on the air in 1996. Its target group is 'that portion of the population which either uses the language on a daily basis or which research indicates has a knowledge of the language'.

RTÉ television broadcasts a small number of Irish language programmes such as daily news bulletins, features, arts and culture programmes. The Irish language unit of *BBC Northern Ireland* has also produced features and series for television. In 1995 *BBC Northern Ireland* and *RTÉ* co-produced a beginners' Irish language course, *Now You're Talking*.

2 Plé

Have you ever listened to an Irish language radio programme or watched an Irish language television programme? What were they? What did you think of them?

In what way(s) could radio and television increase the learner's knowledge of a foreign language? (Think about programmes which are *not* language courses, for example, travel programmes).

How important is the role of TV and radio in the preservation of minority languages? Déan plé le foghlaimeoirí eile.

4 Stór Focal

1(a) Léamh

Laethanta na Seachtaine *The days of the week*

You have just located the Autumn schedule for *Raidió na Life* on the Internet.

Clársceideal an Fhómhair

	Luan	Máirt	Céadaoin	Déardaoin	Aoine	Satharn	Domhnach
12.00						Allagar na Cathrach	Siansa Ceoil
13.00						Rúndrama	Ceol Clasaiceach as an ghnáth
13.30						Gnó 106	
14.00						An Gobán Saor Snagcheol	An Doras Oscailte Ceol Traidisiúnta
15.00						Éist	Saoire Saoire le Bord Fáilte
15.30						An Poc ar Buile Ceol Traidisiúnta	
16.00							An Fhoinse
16.30		An Meangadh Mór				Timpeall Orainn Cúrsaí Timpeallachta	Ar an Imeall
17.00		Seó bóthair, Tráchteolas, Scoth an cheoil agus go leor eile					
17.30						Macalla	Creideamh agus Caint
18.00		Tuairisc Nuacht agus príomhscéalta an lae faoi chaibidil				Clár na Leabhar le hÁis	Gaita Ceol ó Gallicia
18.30	Saoire Saoire le Bord Fáilte	Meascán Mearaí Rogha Ceoil	Timpeall Orainn Cúrsaí Timpeallachta	Clár na Rudaí Beaga	Súil a Sé Ceol Bríomhar	An Port Ard Ceol na gCeilteach	Spórt 106 le Bus Éireann
19.00		Nuacht agus Réamhaisnéis na hAimsire					
19.04	An Gob Fliuch Ceol Traidisiúnta	Beagnach Eicléicteach	Gnó 106 Cúrsaí Gnó	Clár na Rudaí Beaga Comórtais, Cúrsaí na Cathrach*	Súil a Sé Ceol Bríomhar	Ceol Tíre le Oliver Sweeney	Spórt 106 le Bus Éireann
19.30		Scéalta na Gaeltachta le hÚdarás na Gaeltachta	Idir Eatarthu le An Post	Cuaille Éisteachta Ceol Eicléictiúil	An Port Ard Ceol traidisiúnta na hÉireann		Dlúth Yap
20.00		Nuacht agus Réamhaisnéis na hAimsire					
20.04		Fios Feasa Irischlár le cúrsaí ealaíne, cultúir agus ábhar reatha.			Adagio	An Coinín Bán	Stiúidó a 1
20.30					Clár na Leabhar		
21.00		Ceolta na Cruinne Sraith Clár Sainspéise Ceoil					
	Carraigcheol Ceol Éireannach	An Fhuaim Dord is Dráma	Roulette	Jazz 106 Snagcheol	Ar mo Shuaimhneas Cumasc Comhaimseartha	PCP ina Shuí Teicneolaíocht	Electra Ceol Leictreonach
22.30	Neamh Clár ó Phláinéad Eile	Buille Faoi Thuairim Buillí Móra Triphop	Bosca 666 Indí, Úr agus Damhsa	Siosma Ceol Eicléictiúil	Func	Clár Chaoimhe agus Mharia Ailtéarnach*, Electro	Domhancheol

Write down (in your own language) the days of the week the following programmes take place:

Clár	Lá
An Poc ar Buile	
Gaita	
Carraigcheol	
An Fhuaim	
Bosca 666	
Clár na Leabhar	
Jazz 106	

Seiceáil na freagraí san *Eochair*.

(b) Fill in the missing days.

Céadaoin
Déardaoin
Domhnach

2(a)

Ar an Luan *On Mondays*

To state that something happens *on Mondays* you use the phrase **ar an Luan** (lit. on the Monday) e.g.

Osclaíonn an Siopa Leabhar ar a leathuair tar éis a naoi ar an Luan.

Osclaíonn sé ar a deich a chlog ar an Satharn.

Ní osclaíonn an Siopa Leabhar ar an Domhnach.

The Siopa Leabhar does not open on Sundays.

You can also use the word **gach** /gax/ e.g.

Osclaíonn an Siopa Leabhar ar a leathuair tar éis a naoi gach Luan.

The Siopa Leabhar opens at half past nine every Monday.

(b)

Éist leis an téip agus críochnaigh na frásaí sa ghreille.

Luan	ar an Luan
Máirt	ar an
Céadaoin	ar an
Déardaoin	ar an
Aoine	ar an
Satharn	ar an
Domhnach	ar an Domhnach

Seiceáil na freagraí san *Eochair*.

'Dé'

The word **Dé** before the days of the week normally refers to a specific day in the past or in the future, for example

Dé Céadaoin

in the TV programme schedule on page 132 refers to a specific Wednesday. (*Foinse* is a weekly newspaper).

3   Scríobh

Déan abairtí.

Sampla:
Osclaíonn an Siopa Leabhar ar a leathuair tar éis a naoi ar an gCéadaoin.

(i)   Osclaíonn an Siopa Leabhar / 9.30 / Céadaoin.
(ii) Dúnann an Siopa Leabhar / 5.30 / Aoine.
(iii) Dúnann an Siopa Leabhar / 4.00 / Satharn.
(iv) Dúnann Leabharlann ITÉ / 5.00 / Máirt.
(v)   Ní osclaíonn Leabharlann ITÉ / Luan.

Abair na habairtí os ard.

4   Labhairt

Tell others in the class about opening and closing times in your area or country.

5 Gramadach

I

Two verb types

Regular Irish verbs come in two varieties examples of which are

(1) **dún** close, **cuir** put, **éist** listen.

(2) **tosaigh** begin, **éirigh** get up, **oscail** open.

Type 1 verbs, by far the most common, are monosyllabic in base form (the verb as it appears as a headword in the dictionary), and they don't change when verb endings are added to them, e.g. **dúnann**, **cuireann**, **éisteann** in the present tense.

Type 2 verbs have two syllables or more, and the final syllable, which is very often **–igh**, is written as **í** when a verb ending is added in the present tense, e.g. **tosaíonn**, **éiríonn**, **osclaíonn**.

Note what happens with the final syllable of 'oscail' **oscail osclaíonn**

Exception

Polysyllabic verbs ending in **–áil**, such as **seiceáil** check, change to **-ál**, **seiceálann**, and behave as Type 1.

2(a)

Cuir na briathra seo a leanas sa chatagóir cheart:

iompaíonn fágann scríobhann
críochnaíonn cleachtann cuardaíonn
tuigeann litríonn
míníonn déanann

Type 1	Type 2

(b)

Write the base form of each verb.

Samplaí:

iompaíonn **iompaigh**

déanann **déan.**

3(a) Scríobh

Maidin Sheáin *John's Morning*

Scríobh sé abairt.

Éiríonn Seán	tósta.
Ólann sé	an teach ar leathuair tar éis a seacht.
Itheann sé	leis an raidió.
Éisteann sé	ag obair ar a naoi a chlog.
Fágann sé	ar a seacht a chlog gach maidin.
Tosaíonn sé	cupán caife.

Seanfhocal

Ná déan nós agus ná bris nós.
Neither make nor break a custom.

When could you use this proverb? Do you know of similar proverbs in other languages?

(b) Maidin Sylvia

Using sentences like those in 3(a) above, write out six things Sylvia does after she gets up. Déan comparáid le foghlaimeoirí eile.

6 Sa Rang

1 Léamh

Reading Notices

These two notices appeared on the notice board in an Irish language classroom in Dublin.

Léigh na fógraí agus freagair na ceisteanna.

trí·D
CAIFE
DUBLIN'S IRISH LANGUAGE CAFÉ

Ar oscailt 6 lá
Foireann le Gaeilge
Ceapairí, cístí, tae, caife
Ceol, comhrá agus Gaeilge

3 Sráid Dásain, Baile Átha Cliath 2
T: +353-1-474 1050   F: +353-1-474 1055
r-phost: eolas@gael-linn.ie

Club Chonradh na Gaeilge

Bíonn Club an Chonartha ar oscailt gach oíche ó 8 i.n.

6 Sráid Fhearchair, BÁC2
Guthán: (01) 475 1480
eolas@cnag.ie

Ceisteanna:

(i) Someone told you that *Club Chonradh na Gaeilge* was not open on Sunday nights. Is this true?

(ii) What can you do in *Trí·D*?

2 Scríobh

You want to advertise an Irish language conversation circle (ciorcal comhrá) in your area.

Líon na bearnaí san fhógra le focail as an liosta thíos agus le focail eile.

Deochanna, comhrá agus craic

Ar mhaith leat páirt a ghlacadh inár gCiorcal _____?

Buailimid lena chéile gach _____(lá) ar a _____ (am) i (in/sa/san/sna) _____ (áit).

Beidh a___ - _____ agat! T_____ cara leat.
F_____.
R-_____.
            B___ linn!

tóg   r-phost   comhrá   bí
fón   an-chraic

Seiceáil le foghlaimeoirí eile agus leis an múinteoir.

7 Cultúr

1

Laethanta na Seachtaine

A combination of pagan and Christian influences are evident when we examine the etymology of the names of the days of the week in Irish.

Luan *Monday* means *moon* from the Latin *Luna*.
Máirt *Tuesday* is the Irish name for the god *Mars*.
Céadaoin *Wednesday* comes from *Céad Aoine* which means *First Fast*. Christians did not eat meat on Wednesdays or Fridays.
Déardaoin *Thursday* is based on the Old Irish *Dé eter-dí-aín* meaning 'the day between two fasts'. *Dé* meant *day* so in modern Irish this would read: *An lá idir dhá Aoine*.
Aoine *Friday* was originally *aín diden* which meant *end fast*.
Satharn *Saturday* comes from the Roman God *Saturnus*.
Domhnach *Sunday* comes from the Latin *dominicus* meaning *the Lord's day*.

Domhnach also means *church* – as seen in Aonad 3 – and *shrine* or *gospel-case*.

Source *A Dictionary of the Irish Language*, Royal Irish Academy, Dublin: 1988.

2 Obair Ghrúpa

Break up into as many language groups as possible, English, French, German, etc. You can join a group even if you know only a little of the language.

Now write down the names for the days of the week in the language of your group. Do you know where the names originated? Report back to the class.

8 Fuaimniú

Na Défhoghair /au/ agus /ai/

1(a) Déan aithris ar an téip.

feabhas **bodh**rán **Samh**radh **rogh**a **clann**

(b) Which is the odd-one-out?

cabhair aghaidh domhan

2(a) Déan aithris ar an téip.

aghaidh **éi**righ **leigh**eas **veidh**lín **radh**arc

(b) Which is the odd-one-out?

saighdiúir gadhar leabhar

3 Cuir tic sa bhosca ceart.

	/au/	/ai/
Tadhg		
Samhain		
Nua-Eabhrac		
slaghdán		
damhsa		
abhainn		
eidhneán		

4

Éist leis an amhrán *Eibhlín, a Rún*.
Mark /au/ or /ai/ over the words which have these sounds.

Eibhlín a Rún

Shiúlfainn féin i gcónaí leat, 'Eibhlín, a rún.
Shiúlfainn féin i gcónaí leat, 'Eibhlín, a rún.
Shiúlfainn féin i gcónaí, leat,
Síos go Tír Amhlaidh leat,
Mar shúil go mbeinn i gcleamhnas leat,
'Eibhlín, a rún.

Déan comparáid le foghlaimeoirí eile.
Seiceáil na freagraí san *Eochair*.

9 Cumarsáid

Poist

1(a) Stór Focal

Meaitseáil na poist leis na grianghraif.

(i)	(ii)	(iii)

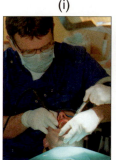  

(iv)	(v)	(vi)

múinteoir	leabharlannaí
freastalaí	cúntóir pearsanta
garraíodóir	fiaclóir

Déan comparáid le foghlaimeoir eile.

(b)

Éist leis na comhráite agus seiceáil na freagraí do **9.**1(a) thuas.
Can you name any other jobs in Irish? Find out the Irish word for your own job.

2(a)

Stating your profession or trade

Éist leis na comhráite arís agus léigh an téipscript.

Pay special attention to the sentences where people say what their jobs are. Then write a similar sentence about your own job.

(b)

Asking about someone's job

Léigh an téipscript uair amháin eile.

Write down 3 different ways of asking someone what their job is. Déan comparáid le foghlaimeoir eile.

(c)

If you are not working

Níl mé ag obair. *I am not working.*
Tá mé dífhostaithe. *I am unemployed.*
/dʹiːostiːhə/

(d) Obair Bheirte

Sampla:

A   Cén obair a dhéanann tú?
B   Is freastalaí mé i mbialann.
    Agus cén post/tslí bheatha atá agat féin?
A   Is múinteoir mé.

Athraigh na rólanna.

Continue until all the jobs in **9.**1(a) have been mentioned. Now talk about your own work.

3(a) Stór Focal 🔊

The same group of people are saying where they work. Éist leis an téip agus meaitseáil an post leis an áit.

Post	Áit
fiaclóir	gairdín
freastalaí	meánscoil
garraíodóir	clinic
leabharlannaí	bialann
múinteoir	oifig
cúntóir pearsanta	leabharlann

(b) Gramadach

Stating where you work – 'tá' or 'bí'?

If you are stating a *general fact* about your working life at the moment, you use *tá*, for example

Tá mé ag obair i meánscoil.
I work in a secondary school.

If you want to describe your work *habits* or *patterns* you use **bí**, for example

Bím* ag obair in óstán trí lá sa tseachtain agus i dteach tábhairne dhá lá sa tseachtain.
I work in a hotel three times a week and in a bar twice a week.

*Bím = bíonn+mé

Cuardaigh na focail seo a leanas san fhoclóir.

seandálaí	banaltra	iriseoir
tiománaí leoraí	ealaíontóir	leictreoir

Meaitseáil na habairtí.

Is seandálaí mé.	Tá mé ag obair i Raidió na Gaeltachta.
Is banaltra mé.	Tá mo chomhlacht leictreachais féin agam.
Is iriseoir mé.	Tá mé ag obair le Dúchas.
Is tiománaí leoraí mé.	Bím ag múineadh sa Choláiste Ealaíne gach maidin.
Is ealaíontóir mé.	Bím ag taisteal san Iodáil agus sa Spáinn go minic.
Is leictreoir mé.	Bím ag obair san ospidéal gach lá.

Déan comparáid le foghlaimeoir eile. If you made different choices, discuss your reasons.

(c)

The following time words and phrases are often used with **bí**:

Gaeilge	Béarla
ar an Luan	on Mondays
ar maidin	in the morning
tráthnóna	in the afternoon/evening
gach lá	every day
gach maidin	every morning
uaireanta	sometimes
go minic	often

Déan aithris ar an téip.

4 Suirbhé

Find out about the work patterns of other students in the class.

Sampla:

Tusa: Cén obair a dhéanann tú?
Foghlaimeoir: Is dochtúir mé. Bím ag obair i mo chlinic féin ar maidin agus san ospidéal tráthnóna.

Foghlaimeoir	Post	Nósanna oibre
David	dochtúir	ag obair ina chlinic féin ar maidin agus san ospidéal tráthnóna

5 Scríobh

Scríobh tuairisc ar 4 thuas.
Sampla:

Is dochtuir é David. Bíonn sé ag obair ina chlinic féin ar maidin agus san ospidéal tráthnóna.

10 Gramadach

1(a)

An Fhoirm Tháite
Synthetic Verb Forms

These are verb forms in which the verb combines with personal pronouns. In the *present* tense, these forms are used in the first persons singular and plural.

fágaim *I leave*
éirímid *we get up*

Type 1 verbs | **Type 2 verbs**

Ith (present tense)
Ithim *I eat*
Itheann tú
Itheann sí/sé
Ithimid
Itheann sibh
Itheann siad

Éirigh (present tense)
Éirím *I get up*
Éiríonn tú
Éiríonn sí/sé
Éirímid
Éiríonn sibh
Éiríonn siad

Dún (present tense)
Dúnaim *I close*
Dúnann tú
Dúnann sí/sé
Dúnaimid
Dúnann sibh
Dúnann siad

Tosaigh (present tense)
Tosaím *I start*
Tosaíonn tú
Tosaíonn sí/sé
Tosaímid
Tosaíonn sibh
Tosaíonn siad

(b)

Clúdaigh an bosca thíos.

Compare the verb endings in the following words. Do you notice any pattern in the spellings?

A Ithim   Dúnaim
      Ithimid   vs   Dúnaimid

B Éirím   Tosaím
      Éirímid   vs   Tosaímid

Déan plé le foghlaimeoir eile. Seiceáil an freagra sa bhosca.

The letter **a** is prefixed to the endings **–im**, **–imid** and **–ím**, **–ímíd** when the preceding vowel is broad **(a, o, u)**.

Scríobh agus Labhairt

Féach arís ar mhír **5.3**(a) 'Maidin Sheáin'. Write similar sentences about your morning.
Sampla: Éirím ar a hocht a chlog …

Read the sentences out for another student.

140

2(a)

Clúdaigh an bosca thíos.
Compare the following verb endings. Do you notice any patterns in the spellings?

A Ólann sé   vs   Itheann sé

B Éiríonn sé   vs   Tosaíonn sé

Déan plé le foghlaimeoir eile.

Caol le caol, leathan le leathan

The verb endings **–ann** and **–íonn** can be attached directly to the stems **ól–** and **éir–** because the vowels match up at either side of the final consonant of the stem. We have broad **a** matching broad **ó** in **ólann** and slender **í** matching slender **i** in **éiríonn**.

We cannot, however, attach **–ann** directly to **ith–** or **–íonn** to **tos–** since the vowels do not match up at either side of the stem. A slender vowel must follow a slender vowel (caol le caol) and a broad vowel must follow a broad vowel (leathan le leathan). In order that the vowels match up an **e** is inserted before **–ann** to give **itheann** and an **a** is inserted before **–íonn** to give **tosaíonn**.

This rule is not just for verb endings. It applies wherever there are vowels at either side of a consonant or a consonant cluster. Go through an Irish text and see for yourself. On either side of internal consonants it is virtually always 'caol le caol agus leathan le leathan'.

(b)

Meaitseáil na siollaí.

fág	e
litr	ic
Aoin	aim
siop	íonn
oscl	a
min	aíonn

11 Scileanna Foghlama

Improving your reading skills

I

Reading Irish

Many people learn Irish to read the language. People who live outside Ireland often consider it more important to be able to read Irish than to speak it. They keep in touch with the language through the written word, for example, through books, magazines, newspapers and the Internet.

How important is it for you to be able to *read* Irish?

very important	❑
important	❑
not important	❑

Déan plé le foghaimeoirí eile.

Some people may need to read Irish in their work. Mícheál Ó Comáin is a Herald of Arms in the Office of the Chief Herald of Ireland. His work involves researching and preparing Grants of Arms for individuals or organisations. Grants of Arms may be given in Irish, in English or in both Irish and English. Reading Irish is, therefore, an important part of Mícheál's work.

A grant of Arms includes the Coat-of-Arms of the individual or organisation and an accompanying text in Irish, English or both.

Eddie Jordan, Formula One racing team owner with his new Grant of Arms.

2

What kinds of text would you like to be able to read in Irish?

Samplaí: postcards, letters from friends, Irish language Web sites, song-words.

Add other examples, if necessary. Déan comparáid le foghlaimeoirí eile.

12 Sa Rang

Grammatical Terms

1(a)

Translate the following grammatical terms:

| abairt | aibítir | siolla | ainmfhocal |
| briathar | forainm | aidiacht | réamhfhocal |

Seiceáil na freagraí san *Eochair.*

(b) Éist leis an téip agus déan aithris ar na focail.

2

Meaitseáil na focail ar chlé leis na samplaí ar dheis.

abairt	teil if ís (teilifís)
aibítir	sí
siolla(í)	idir
ainmfhocal	pianmhar
briathar	A, B, C....
forainm	críochnaíonn
aidiacht	clog
réamhfhocal	Tá mé ag obair i siopa.

3 Use grammatical terms to describe the words in bold print in the sentences below.

Sampla: Osclaíonn *briathar*

Osclaíonn an **leabharlann ar** a leathuair tar éis a naoi.
Cén t-am a dhúnann **sí?**
Tá an **tae** seo an-**te.**
Tá **Máirtín** ag staidéar **i** gColáiste na Tríonóide.

13 Staidéar Pearsanta

1(a)

Look up *an clársceideal* for this week's programmes on *TG4, Raidió na Gaeltachta, Raidió na Life, BBC Radio Ulster.* Make a list of the Irish language programmes you would like to watch or listen to.

You can access many of the above on the Internet (ar an Idirlíon) at the following locations:

Raidió na Gaeltachta
http://www.rnag.ie/gaeilge/sceideal/index.html

Raidió na Life
http://www.iol.ie/~rnl102/sceideal.htm

BBC Radio Ulster
http://www.bbc.co.uk/northernireland/tvr-irish-language-unit.shtml

TG4
http://www.tg4.ie/gaeilge/sceideal/index.htm

Sampla:

Stáisiún	Raidió na Life	
Clár	An Port Ard	
Lá	Satharn	
Am	18.30	

(b) Labhairt

Tell other students about your choices. Use as much Irish as you can to do this. Discuss why you chose different programmes. Iarr ar an múinteoir cuidiú leat.

2

When you have listened to or watched each programme, write a short note about what you thought of it.

Sampla:

An Port Ard
Raidió na Life
Satharn
18.30

Enjoyed the music. Understood many words such as....
Would listen to programme again.

Am Spóirt

1 Slabhra Focal

There are 8 words hidden in the form of a chain (slabhra) in the grid. You will find the words in English in the box. Starting with the highlighted **a** use a pencil to trace the word-chain by moving one square in any direction – up, down, left, right, diagonally.

Tuesday	noun	programme	television	
	lunch	Friday	hospital	verb

p	m	r	á	l	r	ú	p
á	i	s	n	e	c	ó	n
t	r	i	a	l	l	u	b
a	o	m	o	a	f	r	c
i	n	t	a	é	á	m	i
r	n	i	d	ó	t	a	f
m	p	s	c	h	s	í	i
f	o	é	o	r	a	l	ú
h	b	c	a	l	t	e	i

Déan comparáid idir do shlabhra agus slabhraí foghlaimeoirí eile.

2

Write out the words in the order of the word chain, putting **an** *the* in front of each word. Seiceáil na focail san *Eochair*.

3 Obair Ghrúpa

Divide into small groups. Design an exercise similar to 1 above. Choose words which would be useful for learners like yourselves. Give the exercise to another group and see how quickly the chain is traced.

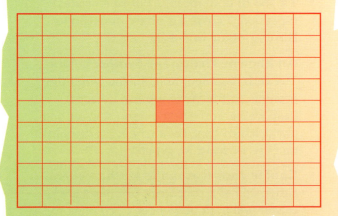

Foghlaimeoir B

It is Sunday. You want to record some TV programmes. Your partner has the information you need to complete the card below. Cuir ceist uirthi nó air faoi na hamanna.

Clár	Tosaíonn	Críochnaíonn
Nuacht TG4	7.00	
Léargas		8.00
Ollchlár Ros na Rún	10.25	

Seiceáil na freagraí le do pháirtí.

Foghlaimeoir B

As part of a campaign to promote the use of Irish in your area, you are compiling a list for a new Irish language newsletter of the opening and closing times of different premises. You already have some of this information. Your partner has the rest of the information you need.

Áit	Amanna Oscailte	
Búistéir Uí Fhlaithearta		– 5.00
Ollmhargadh Uí Ghríofa	9.00	–
Potadóireacht Áine		– 4.30
An Cupán Tae	10.30	–

Seiceáil na freagraí le do pháirtí.

Achoimre

Cumarsáid agus Stór Focal

Asking and saying the time	Cén t-am é? Tá sé deich nóiméad tar éis a haon.
Saying and asking when something starts, finishes, opens, closes	Tosaíonn *Ros na Rún* ar a leathuair tar éis a hocht. Críochnaíonn sé ar a naoi a chlog. Osclaíonn an leabharlann ar a leathuair tar éis a naoi. Dúnann an siopa ar a cúig a chlog. Cén t-am a thosaíonn *Ros na Rún*? Cén t-am a chríochnaíonn sé? Cén t-am a osclaíonn an t-ollmhargadh? Cén t-am a dhúnann sé?
Describing daily routines	Éiríonn Seán, éirím ar a seacht a chlog. Ólann sé, ólaim cupán caife. Itheann sé, ithim tósta.
Stating your profession or trade	Is fiaclóir mé. Níl mé ag obair. Tá mé dífhostaithe.
Asking about someone's profession or trade	Cén post atá agat? Cén tslí bheatha atá agat? Cén obair a dhéanann tú?
Stating where you work	Tá mé ag obair i meánscoil. Bím ag obair in óstán trí lá sa tseachtain.
Time	a haon, a dó…. dó dhéag a chlog, leathuair tar éis a ceathair, ceathrú chun, tar éis a cúig, aon nóiméad déag, dhá nóiméad déag… naoi nóiméad déag chun a haon, fiche nóiméad chun a haon, nóiméad is fiche chun a haon, dhá nóiméad is fiche…. naoi nóiméad is fiche chun a haon

Days of the week	Luan, Máirt, Céadaoin, Déardaoin, Aoine, Satharn, Domhnach
Time phrases	ar an Luan, ar maidin, tráthnóna, gach lá, gach maidin, uaireanta, go minic
Work locations	gairdín, meánscoil, clinic, bialann, oifig, leabharlann
Occupations	fiaclóir, garraíodóir, leabharlannaí, múinteoir, freastalaí, cúntóir pearsanta
Picking out information from notices	Ar oscailt Dé hAoine 13:00-14:00 Ar oscailt gach lá ó 8.00am Guthán, teileafón, fón Facs R-phost, Ríomhphost: ros@ite.ie Tae, caife, craic, comhluadar agus caint Bí linn.
Téarmaí teanga	abairt, aibítir, siolla(í), ainmfhocal, briathar, forainm, aidiacht, réamhfhocal

Gramadach

- **Numbers + 'Nóiméad' (11-19)** Add **déag**, similar to English –*teen*, aon nóiméad **déag**, trí nóiméad **déag. 21-29** add **is fiche** *and twenty*, dhá nóiméad is fiche, trí nóiméad is fiche.

- **Verb types** Verbs in Irish fall into either of two categories, one syllable (in the base form, Imperative Singular, e.g. **scríobh**, **éist**, **léigh**) or more than one, **éirigh**, **iompaigh**, **tosaigh**.

- **Tá** and **bí** both mean *is*. But **bí** indicates repetition. **Tá mé ag obair in óstán** vs **Bím ag obair in óstán**.

- **An Fhoirm Tháite** *The Synthetic Form* The verb is sometimes combined with the pronoun. In the Present tense it happens with *I* and *we*, i.e. in the first person singular and plural, **ithim** *I eat*, **tosaím** *I begin*, **dúnaimid** *we close*, **éirímid** *we get up*.

- **Caol le caol, leathan le leathan** Vowels at either side of a consonant or consonant cluster will both be slender (**i, e**) or both be broad (**a, o, u**).

144

Cultúr

Irish Language Broadcasting

• The radio stations *Raidió na Gaeltachta* and *Raidió na Life* broadcast entirely in Irish. *Raidió na Gaeltachta* broadcasts nationally. *Raidió na Life* broadcasts in Dublin. *Raidió na Gaeltachta* caters to a more mixed audience whereas *Raidió na Life* targets a younger, urban audience. *Raidió na Life* broadcasts songs in English.

• TG4 is the national Irish Language television service in the Republic of Ireland.

• *RTÉ* and *BBC Northern Ireland* produce a number of Irish language programmes for radio and television.

• *Raidió na Gaeltachta* is relayed by satellite to listeners in the UK and Europe on Saturday and Sunday and to listeners in North America on a daily basis.

• *Raidió na Gaeltachta* and *Blas (BBC Radio Ulster)* are also broadcast on the Internet.

Laethanta na Seachtaine
The Days of the Week

The days of the week in Irish derive from pagan and Christian sources e.g. **Máirt** *Mars* (pagan), **Céadaoin** *First fast* (Christian).

Fuaimniú

An Défhoghar /au/ e.g. feabhas, bodhrán

An Défhoghar /ai/ e.g. aghaidh, leigheas

Scileanna Foghlama

Reading skills

• You must decide how important reading Irish is for you. For example, it might be your only contact with the language.

• What kinds of text would you like or need to read?

Triail Tú Féin

1(i) Scríobh an t-am i bhfocail.

5:00	a cúig a chlog
6:15	
4:45	
3:10	
7:30	
7:55	
11:20	

(ii)

You will hear the same clock times being called out. Sometimes the speaker does not call out the correct time. Which times have not been called out correctly?

Seiceáil na freagraí sna *Téipscripteanna*.

2 Obair Bheirte

A: Ask your partner what time she or he gets up in the morning.

B: Answer your partner's question and then ask her or him the same question.

A: Answer your partner's question.

B: Ask your partner what work she or he does.

A: Answer your partner's question and ask her or him the same question.

B: Answer your partner's question.

A: You need to get some foreign currency. Ask what time the bank closes today.

B: Say that the bank closes at 5 on Thursday.

A: Ask what time it is now.

B: Answer your partner's question.

3(i) Rólghlacadh

Foghlaimeoir A
Féach ar **A** thíos.

Foghlaimeoir B
Féach ar **B** in *Nóta 3*, lch 150.

A
You are Leif. Déan cur síos ort féin. Tosaigh mar seo:
Leif Johannesson is ainm dom …

Ainm:	Leif Johannesson
Tír:	An tSualainn
Obair:	Altra
Áit oibre:	Örebro
Uaireanta oibre:	3pm-9:30pm nó 9pm–7.30am
Am saor:	Seinneann sé an bodhrán.

(ii)

Foghlaimeoir A
Féach ar **C** thíos.

Foghlaimeoir B
Féach ar **D** in *Nóta 3*, lch 150.

C
Your partner is Margaret. Listen to what she says and complete the information below. Can you remember what to say if you want a word spelt or repeated?

Ainm:	Margaret _____
Tír:	_____
Obair:	_____ Pearsanta
Áit oibre:	_____ Learphoill
Uaireanta oibre:	_____ am–5pm
Am saor:	Féachann sí ar an _____. Téann sí go dtí _____.

Seiceáil na freagraí le Foghlaimeoir B.

4 Scríobh

Scríobh cur síos ort féin.

B Add more words or phrases to the following lists:

Luan	ar maidin	éiríonn	garraíodóir
Máirt	ar an Luan	itheann	dochtúir
Céadaoin	go minic	éisteann	tiománaí leoraí

C

1 Léamh, scríobh agus éisteacht

(i)
Tá Gormfhlaith Ní Thuairisg ag obair sa seomra nuachta i Raidió na Gaeltachta. The following is a description of how she spends her time both at work and outside work.

Éist leis an téip agus léigh an cur síos. The words in brackets are not in the correct form. The correct form is spoken by Gormfhlaith.

Nuair a bhím ag obair (éiríonn) ar a 5:15 ar maidin. (Tosaíonn) ag obair ar a sé a chlog. (Bíonn) ag coinneáil súile ar scéalta nuachta in Éirinn agus thar lear. (Réitíonn) míreanna nuachta leis an eolas sin. (Cuireann) agallamh ar dhaoine freisin. Is maith liom an obair. Tá mo chomhghleacaithe go deas.

Nuair a bhím saor is maith liom a bheith ag garraíodóireacht. (Téann) ag siopadóireacht go minic. Uaireanta (tugann) cuairt ar chairde.

(ii)
Cuir isteach an fhoirm cheart de na briathra idir lúibíní.

Sampla: (éiríonn) **éirím**

Seiceáil na freagraí sna *Téipscripteanna*.

2(i) Líon na bearnaí sna focail.

(a) seacht-in (b) for-inm (c) daoin- (d) ua-re-nta

(e) buail-m-d (f) d-mhsa (g) si-ll-

(ii) Cuir na litreacha san ord ceart.

Lanu, Mtári, Cnaiodéa, Ddréaaino, Aeino, Shnatar, Dhhmcoan.

D **Fuaimniú**

Which is the odd-one-out?

(i) labhair, Samhain, Londain, Domhnach

(ii) adhmad, éirigh, Maidhc, maidin

E

Read the descriptions and name the radio or TV station.

1 It targets a younger, urban audience.
2 They co-produced a beginners' Irish language course.
3 It came on the air in 1996.
4 Its main emphasis is on Irish traditional music.

Read the definitions and name the day of the week in Irish.

1 It means the Lord's day in Latin.

_____

2 It is named after the God Mars.

_____

3 It means the day between two fasts.

_____

4 It comes from the Latin word for the moon.

_____

Téipscripteanna

1.1
Gabh mo leithscéal. Cén t-am é?
Tá sé a cúig a chlog.
Go raibh maith agat.

Cén t-am é le do thoil?
A seacht a chlog.
Go raibh maith agat.

Cén t-am atá sé?
Leathuair tar éis a hocht.
Ó, caithfidh mé brostú!

Cén t-am é a Rós?
Tá sé ceathrú chun a haon déag.
An bhfuil?

Tá sé ag tarraingt ar a dó a chlog.
Tá mise ag imeacht.
Fan go fóill!

1.2(c)
Tá sé fiche nóiméad tar éis a cúig.
Tá sé ceathrú chun a ceathair.
Tá sé a sé a chlog.
Tá sé cúig nóiméad chun a haon.
Tá sé leathuair tar éis a dó.
Tá sé ceathrú tar éis a haon déag.

2.1(a)

Donncha:	Cad tá ar an teilifís anocht, a stór?
Kathy:	Bhuel, tá *Ros na Rún* ar a seacht a chlog agus tá *Euro News* ar a leathuair tar éis a seacht…. ansin tá *Nuacht* agus *An Aimsir*.
Donncha:	Cén t-am a thosaíonn an clár bia sin… ní cuimhin liom an t-ainm atá air.
Kathy:	*Nua Gach Bia*.
Donncha:	Sin é!
Kathy:	Tosaíonn sé ar a hocht a chlog. Tosaíonn *Hollywood Anocht* ar a naoi a chlog.
Donncha:	Ba mhaith liom é sin a fheiceáil.
Kathy:	Dáiríre?
Donncha:	Is ea, dáiríre!
Kathy:	Tá clár an-suimiúil ar siúl faoi Che Guevara. *El Che* an t-ainm atá air. Tosaíonn sé ar dhá nóiméad tar éis a deich.
Donncha:	Cén t-am a chríochnaíonn sé?
Kathy:	Fan go bhfeicfidh mé. Críochnaíonn sé timpeall a haon déag a chlog.
Donncha:	Tá sin ródhéanach domsa!

2.2(a)

Fear: Ba mhaith liom a fháil amach cén
            t-am a dhúnann sibh inniu.

Bean: Dúnaimid ag* a leathuair tar éis a cúig.

Fear: Go raibh maith agat.

Bean: Tá fáilte romhat.

* *Ag can be used instead of ar.*

9.1(b), **9.**2(a)

(i)   Cén post atá agat?
          Is fiaclóir mé.

(ii)   Cén tslí bheatha atá agat?
          Is freastalaí mé i mbialann.

(iii)   Cén obair a dhéanann tú?
          Is garraíodóir mé.

(iv)   An bhfuil post agat?
          Tá. Is leabharlannaí mé.

(v)   Cén post atá agat?
          Is múinteoir mé.

(vi)   Cén post atá agat?
          Is cúntóir pearsanta mé.

9.3(a)

Cén post atá agat?

Is fiaclóir mé.

Cá mbíonn tú ag obair?

Bím ag obair i mo chlinic féin ar an Luan agus ar
   an Aoine agus san Ollscoil ar an Máirt, ar an
   gCéadaoin agus ar an Déardaoin.

Cén tslí bheatha atá agat?

Is freastalaí i mbialann mé.

An ea? Cá mbíonn tú ag obair?

Bím ag obair in óstán trí lá sa tseachtain agus
   i dteach tábhairne dhá uair sa tseachtain.

Cén obair a dhéanann tú?

Is garraíodóir mé. Bím ag obair i ngairdíní éagsúla
   ar fud na cathrach.

An bhfuil post agat?

Tá. Is leabharlannaí mé. Tá mé ag obair
   i leabharlann Choláiste na Tríonóide.

Cén post atá agat?

Is múinteoir mé.

Cá bhfuil tú ag obair?

Tá mé ag obair i meánscoil.

Cén post atá agat?

Is cúntóir pearsanta mé.

Cá bhfuil tú ag obair?

Tá mé ag obair in Oifig USIT i mBaile Átha Cliath.

Triail Tú Féin

A

I (ii)

Tá sé a cúig a chlog, tá sé fiche nóiméad tar éis a
sé, tá sé ceithre nóiméad déag tar éis a ceathair,
tá sé deich nóiméad tar éis a trí, tá sé leathuair
tar éis a seacht, tá sé cúig nóiméad chun a
seacht, tá sé fiche nóiméad tar éis a haon déag.

C

I (ii)

Nuair a bhím ag obair éirím ar a ceathrú tar éis a
cúig ar maidin. Tosaím ag obair ar a sé a chlog.
Bím ag coinneáil súile ar scéalta nuachta in Éirinn
agus thar lear. Réitím míreanna nuachta leis an
eolas sin. Cuirim agallamh ar dhaoine freisin. Is
maith liom an obair. Tá mo chomhghleacaithe go
deas.

Nuair a bhím saor is maith liom a bheith ag
garraíodóireacht. Téim ag siopadóireacht go
minic. Uaireanta tugaim cuairt ar chairde.

Eochair

1.2(a)
1 a dó dhéag, 2 a ceathair, 3 a ceathair,
4 a haon déag, 5 a trí, 6 a hocht

1.3(b)
(i) ceithre nóiméad tar éis a dó (ii) trí nóiméad déag tar éis a ceathair (iii) nóiméad is fiche tar éis a cúig (iv) seacht nóiméad is fiche tar éis a sé

2.1(a)

teilifís   it starts
anocht   interesting
tosaíonn sé   television
clár   tonight
suimiúil   too late
ródhéanach   programme

2.2(a) An Siopa Leabhar

4.1(a)

Clár	Lá
An Poc ar Buile	Saturday
Gaita	Sunday
Carraigcheol	Monday
An Fhuaim	Tuesday
Bosca 666	Wednesday
Clár na Leabhar	Friday
Jazz 106	Thursday

4.2(b)

Luan	ar an Luan
Máirt	ar an Máirt
Céadaoin	ar an gCéadaoin
Déardaoin	ar an Déardaoin
Aoine	ar an Aoine
Satharn	ar an Satharn
Domhnach	ar an Domhnach

4.3
(ii) Dúnann an Siopa Leabhar ar a leathuair tar éis a cúig ar an Aoine.
(iii) Dúnann an Siopa Leabhar ar a ceathair a chlog ar an Satharn.
(iv) Dúnann Leabharlann ITÉ ar a cúig a chlog ar an Máirt.
(v) Ní osclaíonn Leabharlann ITÉ ar an Luan.

5.2(a)

Type 1	Type 2
fágann	iompaíonn
scríobhann	críochnaíonn
cleachtann	cuardaíonn
tuigeann	litríonn
déanann	míníonn

5.2(b)
fág, fágann scríobh, scríobhann cleacht, cleachtann tuig, tuigeann déan, déanann iompaigh, iompaíonn críochnaigh, críochnaíonn cuardaigh, cuardaíonn litrigh, litríonn mínigh, míníonn

5.3(a)

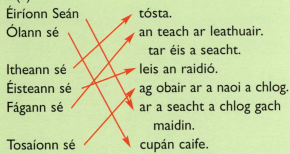

Éiríonn Seán — tósta.
Ólann sé — an teach ar leathuair.
— tar éis a seacht.
Itheann sé — leis an raidió.
Éisteann sé — ag obair ar a naoi a chlog.
Fágann sé — ar a seacht a chlog gach maidin.
Tosaíonn sé — cupán caife.

6.1(i) no (ii) eat, drink, listen to music and talk Irish

8.1(b) aghaidh
8.2(b) leabhar

8.3

	/au/	/ai/
Tadhg		x
Samhain	x	
Nua-Eabhrac	x	
slaghdán		x
damhsa	x	
abhainn	x	
eidhneán		x

8.4

               /ai/
Shiúlfainn féin i gcónaí leat, Eibhlín, a rún
               /ai/
Shiúlfainn féin i gcónaí leat, Eibhlín, a rún
Shiúlfainn féin i gcónaí leat,
           /au/
Síos go Tír Amhlaidh leat,
               /au/   /ai/
Mar shúil go mbeinn i gcleamhnas leat, Eibhlín, a rún.

9.3(a)

Post	Áit
fiaclóir	gairdín
freastalaí	meánscoil
garraíodóir	clinic
leabharlannaí	bialann
múinteoir	oifig
cúntóir pearsanta	leabharlann

9.3(b) Suggested answers:

Is seandálaí mé.	Tá mé ag obair i Raidió na Gaeltachta.
Is banaltra mé.	Tá mo chomhlacht leictreachais féin agam.
Is iriseoir mé.	Tá mé ag obair le Dúchas.
Is tiománaí leoraí mé.	Bím ag múineadh sa Choláiste Ealaíne gach maidin.
Is ealaíontóir mé.	Bím ag taisteal san Iodáil agus sa Spáinn go minic.
Is leictreoir mé.	Bím ag obair san ospidéal gach lá.

10.2(b)

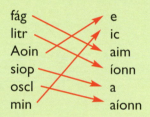

fág	e
litr	ic
Aoin	aim
siop	íonn
oscl	a
min	aíonn

12.1(a)

abairt *sentence*, aibítir *alphabet*, siolla *syllable*, ainmfhocal *noun*, briathar *verb*, forainm *pronoun*, aidiacht *adjective*, réamhfhocal *preposition*

12.2

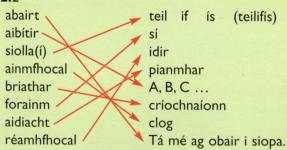

abairt	teil if ís (teilifís)
aibítir	sí
siolla(í)	idir
ainmfhocal	pianmhar
briathar	A, B, C …
forainm	críochnaíonn
aidiacht	clog
réamhfhocal	Tá mé ag obair i siopa.

12.3

leabharlann ainmfhocal, *ar* réamhfhocal,
sí forainm, *tá* briathar, *tae* ainmfhocal,
te aidiacht, *Máirtín* ainmfhocal

Am Spóirt

1 An Aoine 2 an lón 3 an briathar
4 an t-ospidéal 5 an clár 6 An Mháirt
7 an t-ainmfhocal 8 an teilifís

Triail Tú Féin

A

1(i)

5:00	a cúig a chlog
6:15	ceathrú tar éis a sé
4:45	ceathrú chun a cúig
3:10	deich nóiméad tar éis a trí
7:30	leathuair tar éis a seacht
7:55	cúig nóiméad chun a hocht
11:20	fiche nóiméad tar éis a haon déag

C

2(i)
(a) seacht**ain** (b) for**ainm** (c) d**ao**in**e**
(d) u**ai**r**ea**nta (e) bu**ail**imid (f) d**a**mhsa
(g) s**io**lla

2(ii) Luan Máirt Céadaoin Déardaoin Aoine
Satharn Domhnach

D

(i) Londain (ii) maidin

Nóta 3

Foghlaimeoir B
Your partner is Leif. Listen to what he says and complete the information below. Can you remember what to say if you want a word spelt or repeated?

Ainm:	Leif _____
Tír:	_____
Obair:	_____
Áit oibre:	Örebro
Uaireanta oibre:	3pm ___ pm nó __ pm –7.30am
Am saor:	Seinneann sé an _____.

Seiceáil na freagraí le Foghlaimeoir A.

D

You are Margaret. Déan cur síos ort féin. Tosaigh mar seo: *Margaret Farrington is ainm dom …*

Ainm:	Margaret Farrington
Tír:	Sasana
Obair:	Rúnaí Pearsanta
Áit oibre:	Ollscoil Learphoill
Uaireanta oibre:	9.15am–5pm
Am saor:	Féachann sí ar an teilifís. Téann sí go dtí rang Gaeilge.

9 Bia agus deoch

This unit enables learners to: describe their eating habits and food preferences; offer, accept or refuse food or drink; order something to eat or drink; describe a past experience.

BLASTA!

What Irish word is used as a toast? Do you know what is said in other languages?

1 Foclóir

1(a) Obair Bheirte

You may already know some Irish names for foods and drinks, perhaps the names of those in the drawing? Déan liosta.

(b)

Is maith liom spaigití Bologna. Is fuath liom iasc.

Is maith liom cáis chéadair.

Discuss with you partner some foods and drinks that you like or dislike.

2 Léamh

The following is part of the text of a letter sent by Aidan, an Irish chef in the Ritz Carlton Hotel, in Naples, Florida to his sister in Ireland. Aidan describes his routine after he arrives at work in the morning. He also describes what he has to eat for his own breakfast. Can you pick out the words referring to food and drink?

Tosaím ag obair ar a 5:05. Réitím an bricfeasta do na haíonna (idir 10 agus 1,000 duine). Ansin, réitím mo bhricfeasta féin – gránach bran rísíní agus bainne, trí ghloine sú oráistí, dhá ubh bhruite (ceithre nóiméad), dhá chanta aráin doinn, im agus subh, banana, iógart sútha talún, cupán caife. Bíonn an bricfeasta céanna agam gach maidin!

Bia *Food*	Deoch *Drink*

(ii) Cuardaigh na focail nua san fhoclóir nó iarr ar an múinteoir cuidiú leat iad a aistriú.

(iii) What do you usually eat and drink for your breakfast? Cuardaigh na focail san fhoclóir nó cuir ceist ar an múinteoir.

Bricfeasta *Breakfast*	
Ithim	**Ólaim**

3 Obair Bheirte

Tell your partner what you eat and drink for your breakfast. Then tell another student what your partner eats and drinks for breakfast.

4 Cultúr

Béilí *Meals*

In general Irish people eat one main meal a day. This is called **dinnéar**/d'in'e:r/ *dinner*. The time of this meal varies. People who work near home may have dinner around midday whereas people who work far away from home may have dinner in the evening, usually between 6:30 and 7:30. People who have dinner early have a light meal called **tae** /te:/ *tea* around 6:30 while those who have dinner in the evening have a light meal called **lón** /lo:n/ *lunch* around midday.

Bricfeasta /b'r'ik'f'astə/ *breakfast* is eaten after you get up in the morning.

Some people like to eat a light snack before going to bed. This is known as **suipéar**/sup'e:r/ *supper*.

In the Past

In earlier times people who worked in the fields would have a meal before setting out to work in the morning. This was known as **bia na maidine** *morning food*. During the day they would eat when they felt hungry and when they returned home in the evening they would have another meal, known as **bia tráthnóna** *evening food*. Richer people, on the other hand, tended to eat meals at set times in the day – in the morning, at midday and in the evening. By the end of the 19th century the custom of eating meals at set times of the day was the norm everywhere.

Danaher, K (1985) *Irish Country Households*, Dublin: Mercier.

Obair Ghrúpa

Divide into groups of four to discuss the following points:

1   What are the main meals in your country called?

2   At what times are they eaten? Try to answer in Irish e.g. *Bíonn an dinnéar agam/againn ar a seacht a chlog tráthnóna.*

3   What do the meals usually consist of? If you know the Irish words for any of these foods, use them. If you do not understand the meaning of a word another student says, ask (in Irish) for the English equivalent. Can you remember how to do this?

One person from each group reports on 1, 2, 3 to the whole class.

5(a)

Stobhach Gaelach
caoireoil, prátaí, oinniúin, uisce, salann, piobar, peirsil

Sorcha is on a diet. The following is a record of what she had for lunch last week. In the recording she is telling a friend about it. She is trying to impress her friend so she does not always tell the truth about what she ate. Before listening to the recording, can you say which days you think Sorcha is likely to lie about? (Seiceáil na focail nua san fhoclóir).

Déan plé le foghlaimeoir eile.

Dé Luain	sailéad Waldorf
Dé Mairt	stobhach gaelach
Dé Céadaoin	stéig agus sceallóga
Déardaoin	uibheagán
Dé hAoine	sailéad trátaí
Dé Sathairn	torthaí agus iógart
Dé Domhnaigh	bradán

Anois éist leis an téip. Were you correct in your prediction? Seiceáil sna *Téipscripteanna*.

(b)

Féach ar na pictiúir agus meaitseáil na focail leis na huimhreacha.

arán, scónaí, píotsa, cabáiste, toirtín, leitís, sicín, tornapa, quiche, uachtar reoite, mairteoil, brioscaí, iasc, prátaí, piseanna, cáis, císte, uaineoil, bagún, uibheacha.

(c)

Éist leis an téip agus déan aithris ar na focail.

(d) Rólghlacadh

Divide into groups of four. You have rented a house for the duration of an Irish language course. It is Sunday evening and you are planning a dinner-menu for the week ahead. If you don't know the Irish for something, ask the group (in Irish) or the teacher. Or consult your dictionary.

	Dinnéar
Dé Luain	
Dé Máirt	
Dé Céadaoin	
Déardaoin	
Dé hAoine	
Dé Satharn	
Dé Domhnaigh	

Déan comparáid le grúpaí eile.

2 Cumarsáid

1(a)

Peter has just been interviewed by Siobhán about his eating habits. Below are Peter's answers. Work in pairs to see if you can make out the questions he was asked. Bain triail as!

_____?
Bíonn sé agam idir a seacht agus a hocht a chlog.

_____?

Ithim feoil trí huaire sa tseachtain – mairteoil, uaineoil agus sicín de ghnáth. Bíonn béile veigeatórach agam dhá uair sa tseachtain agus iasc dhá uair más féidir.

_____?

Ólaim fíon dearg le mo dhinnéar i gcónaí – gloine nó dhó.

_____?

Ní ólaim ach go fíor-annamh.

_____?

Ní bhíonn riamh. Ach bíonn cupán tae agam uaireanta.

_____?

Go minic. Tá bialann Iodálach in aice liom agus téim féin agus mo bhean ann ar ócáidí speisialta.

(b)

Here are the questions which Siobhán asked Peter but they are not in the correct order. Compare them to your own and put them in order.

An ólann tú fíon geal?
Cad a ólann tú leis an dinnéar?
An dtéann tú amach ag ithe riamh?
Cén t-am a bhíonn an dinnéar agat?
An mbíonn caife agat tar éis an dinnéir?
Cad a itheann tú don dinnéar?

(c)

Éist leis an gcomhrá ar fad agus léigh an téipscript.

(d)

Take turns asking the questions. Give your own answers.

2(a) Gramadach

Scrúdaigh na briathra sna habairtí seo a leanas:

An ólann tú fíon geal?
Ní ólaim ach go fíor-annamh.
An mbíonn caife agat tar éis an dinnéir?
Ní bhíonn riamh.

Now discuss your answers to the following questions.

What effect does the question marker **An** have on
    (a) verbs that begin with a vowel?
    (b) verbs that begin with a consonant?

What effect does the negative marker **Ní** have on
    (c) verbs that begin with a vowel?
    (d) verbs that begin with a consonant?

Scríobh an fhoirm cheart den bhriathar.
A   An (itheann) tú feoil?
     Ní (itheann).
B   An (dúnann) an siopa ar a cúig a chlog inniu?
     Ní (dúnann) sé go dtí a sé a chlog.

Cleacht comhráite A agus B le foghlaimeoir eile.

Make similar conversations using the following verbs:

cuir	éirigh	fág	ól	tosaigh

(b)

Cad, Cén … + a

Questions that begin with words such as **Cad**, **Cén** require an **a** before the verb.

   Cad a ólann tú? _What do you drink?_
   Cén t-am a bhíonn an dinnéar agat?
   What time do you have dinner?

Scrúdaigh na habairtí seo a leanas:

Cén t-am a éiríonn tú ar maidin?

Cén obair a dhéanann tú?

In these two questions decide what effect **a** has on
(a) verbs that begin with a vowel?
(b) verbs that begin with a consonant?

Scríobh an fhoirm cheart den bhriathar.

A Cén t-am a (tosaíonn) tú ag obair?

B Cad a (itheann) tú don bhricfeasta?

(c)

> ### a + tá becomes atá
>
> **a** is joined to **tá** to become **atá**. There is no *séimhiú* on **tá**. **Cén post atá agat?**

3(a) Stór Focal

Léigh freagraí Peter in **2.**1(a) arís. Underline the words that tell *how often* something happens.

Sampla: <u>trí huaire sa tseachtain</u>

Déan comparáid le foghlaimeoir eile.

Note the position of the 'time' words in these sentences:

Ólaim fíon le mo dhinnéar i gcónaí.

Ach bíonn cupán tae agam uaireanta.

An dtéann tú amach ag ithe riamh?

Déan plé le foghlaimeoir eile.

(b) Scríobh iad seo san ord ceart:

go hannamh	i gcónaí	uaireanta
de ghnáth	riamh	go minic

100%

0%

Déan comparáid le foghlaimeoir eile.
Anois abair os ard iad.

(c) Scrúdaigh an ghreille.

Riamh		
?	+	−
An itheann tú iasc **riamh**?	Ithim	ach ní ithim feoil **riamh**.

What have you learnt about the use of **riamh**?
Déan plé le foghlaimeoir eile.

(d)

Make sentences about what you eat and don't eat. Use as many 'time' words as you can.

4(a) Obair Bheirte

Ceistiúchán *Questionnaire*

Find out about your partner's eating habits. Ask questions based on the statements in the grid below. Líon na bearnaí sa ghreille.

Sampla:

Foghlaimeoir A: An itheann tú bricfeasta de ghnáth?

Foghlaimeoir B: Ithim, uaireanta.

Foghlaimeoir A: An dtéann tú ar aiste bia riamh?

Foghlaimeoir B: Ní théim riamh.

Statements	Cathain When?
itheann tú bricfeasta	uaireanta
téann tú ar aiste bia	riamh
ólann tú tae le bainne	
réitíonn tú béile gach tráthnóna	
úsáideann tú im sa chócaireacht	
bíonn fíon agat leis an dinnéar	
níonn tú torthaí	
ceannaíonn tú bia gasta (fast food)	

(b) Scríobh

Scríobh tuairisc ar 4(a) thuas.

Sampla: Itheann Maurice bricfeasta uaireanta. Ní théann sé ar aiste bia riamh …

3 Cultúr

Flaithiúlacht *Hospitality*

Irish people have a reputation for being hospitable or *flaithiúlach* /flahu:lax/. The tradition of keeping 'open house', in other words giving food and sometimes lodgings free of charge to passing travellers, was a feature of Irish life for many centuries. Certain people had a duty to keep open house, for example, clergymen, doctors and poets. A chief and his followers had the right to go from house to house to be fed and entertained. This was known as 'coshering' from the Irish word *cóisir* which means a feast or a party. A more recent version of this is the practice of dropping casually into a neighbour's house for a chat and a cup of tea.

Food played an important role in the hospitality tradition. A host's generosity tended to be measured according to the amount (as distinct from the variety or quality) of the food she or he provided. Many of the old stories tell of great feasts where large amounts of food were served. In the 8th century story *Fled Bricrenn* (modern Irish Fleá Bhricriú *Bricriu's Feast*) Bricriu spent a whole year gathering food for a feast he planned for Conchobar Mac Neasa, the king of Ulster and his warriors. During the feast the warrior of most exceptional skill and valour could claim the

curadhmhír hero's portion – 'a milk-fed hog; an ox that had been fed only on milk, grass and corn; and a hundred wheaten loaves baked in honey'*. A sure way of insulting a guest was to provide a meagre amount of food, as happened to the poet Mac Con Glinne when he was given a drink of whey-water on a visit to a monastery in the 12th century poem *Aislinge Meic Conglinne, or The Vision of Mac Con Glinne*.

The tradition of hospitality was carried on by the Normans, who arrived in Ireland in the 12th century and by many of the Anglo-Irish colonial landlords from the 16th century onwards.

By the 19th century, the 'open house' tradition had begun to die out. Food costs rose and it was also more expensive to hire servants. Many of the Anglo-Irish landlords returned to England. The Great Famine of 1845-47 meant that people had to concentrate on feeding themselves.

Despite these set-backs, the Irish tradition of *flaithiúlacht* still lives on.

Sources
*Dillon, M. (1994) 'Bricriu's Feast', *Early Irish Literature*, Dublin: Four Courts Press.

Mahon, B. (1991) *Land of Milk and Honey*, Dublin: Poolbeg.

Obair Ghrúpa

Pléigh na ceisteanna seo le foghlaimeoirí eile:

(i) Do you think the Irish live up to their reputation for being *flaithiúlach*? Have you had any experience of Irish *flaithiúlacht*? If so, tell other students about it.

(ii) Do you know of any other cultures which have a similar reputation?

(iii) Is your country noted for any particular characteristic?

Seanfhocal

Is maith an t-anlann an t-ocras.
Hunger is a good sauce.

Do you have a similar saying in your language or in another language you know? Say it in the original language for the other students and then give its equivalent in English.

Cumarsáid

1

John is about to go up to the bar to order another drink.

Éist leis an téip agus léigh an comhrá.

John: Ar mhaith leat gloine eile?
Peig: Níor mhaith, go raibh maith agat ach tá ocras orm!
John: Ar mhaith leat ceapaire?
Peig: Ba mhaith.
John: Cén sórt ceapaire a theastaíonn uait?
Peig: Fan go bhfeicfidh mé … ceapaire sicín, ceapaim.

Freagair na ceisteanna.

(i)   Does Peig want any more beer?
(ii) What does she want to eat?
(iii) What do you think *Tá ocras orm* means?

Pléigh na freagraí le foghlaimeoir eile.

2   Léigh an comhrá thuas arís.

Which phrase is used to express
    an offer? _____
    an acceptance? _____
    a refusal? _____

Déan plé le foghlaimeoir eile.

3

Tá … orm

In Aonad 7 you learnt **Tá … orm** to talk about health e.g.

Tá slaghdán orm. *I have a cold.*
Tá tinneas cinn orm. *I have a headache.*

Here are more examples:
Tá tart orm. *I am thirsty.*
Tá ocras orm. *I am hungry.*
Tá áthas orm. *I am happy.*
Tá brón orm. *I am sorry.*
Tá deifir orm. *I am in a hurry.*

4(a) Scríobh agus Labhairt

Líon na bearnaí sna comhráite.

Fear: Tá _____ orm.
Bean: _____ mhaith leat gloine uisce?
Fear: _____ mhaith.
Bean: Seo duit.
Fear: Go raibh maith agat.

Páiste: Tá _____ orm.
Máthair: _____ _____ leat arán agus im?
Páiste: _____ mhaith ach ba mhaith liom píosa císte.
Máthair: Ceart go leor. Seo duit an císte.
Páiste: Go raibh míle maith agat, a mhamaí.

Déan comparáid le foghlaimeoir eile. Seiceáil na freagraí san *Eochair*.

(b)

Cleacht na comhráite thuas le foghlaimeoir eile.

5(a) Stór Focal

Cuir na focail sa chatagóir cheart.

fíon	bainne	leann dubh	líomanáid
	beoir	uisce beatha	tae
	sú oráistí	caife	uisce mianraí

Deochanna *Drinks*	
meisciúla	**neamh-mheisciúla**
fíon	líomanáid

Déan comparáid le foghlaimeoir eile.

(b)

Éist leis an téip agus léigh an téipscript chun na freagraí a sheiceáil.
Cuir focail eile isteach sa dá chatagóir.

6 Obair Bheirte

Déan comhráite mar atá in **4.4**(a) thuas.

Samplaí:

Foghlaimeoir A: Tá tart orm.
Foghlaimeoir B: Ar mhaith leat …
Foghlaimeoir A: Ba mhaith, níor mhaith …
Foghlaimeoir B: Tá ocras orm etc.

5  Gramadach

1 An maith *vs* Ar mhaith?

Roghnaigh an cheist cheart.

(i) Ceist: Ar mhaith leat caife?
              An maith leat caife?
    Freagra: Níor mhaith, go raibh maith agat.

(ii) Ceist: An maith leat uachtar reoite?
              Ar mhaith leat uachtar reoite?
    Freagra: Is maith, cinnte!

(iii) Ceist: Ar mhaith leat bradán?
              An maith leat bradán?
    Freagra: Ba mhaith liom píosa beag.

(iv) Ceist: An maith leat tae?
              Ar mhaith leat cupán tae?
    Freagra: Ní maith.

What have you learnt about the different forms of An Chopail, **an**, **is**, **ní** vs **ar**, **ba**, **níor**?
Déan plé le foghlaimeoir eile.

2 Líon na bearnaí sa ghreille.

+	–	?
is maith		
	níor mhaith	ar mhaith

What happens to **maith** following **ar**, **ba** and **níor**?

Cluiche

Class divides into two teams. Each team makes a list of questions, half the questions beginning with *An maith leat …* and half beginning with *Ar mhaith leat …* Try to use food and drink words. Divide the questions equally between the members of the team. A member of Team A asks a question of a member of Team B. The student answers *Is/ní maith* or *ba/níor mhaith* depending on the question asked. The person who asked the question has to decide whether the answer is grammatically correct e.g. *An maith leat éisc? Ní/is maith* is correct but the reply *níor/ba mhaith* is not. If the answer was correct and the questioner accepts that the answer was correct (the teacher being the final adjudicator), each team gets one point. If the answer was correct and the questioner says it was not correct, Team B gets one point and Team

A gets none. If the answer was not correct and the questioner confirms that it was not correct, Team A gets one point. If the answer was not correct and the questioner said it was correct, neither team scores a point.

A member of Team B then asks a question and so on until all the questions have been asked. The team with the most points wins.

6  Sa Rang

Grammatical Terms

1(a)

Translate the following grammatical terms.

uimhir uatha_____

uimhir iolra _____

guta _____

consan _____

caol _____

leathan _____

baininscneach_____

firinscneach _____

(b)

Éist leis an téip agus déan aithris ar na focail.

2 Scríobh focail ó 1(a) thuas faoi na pictiúir.

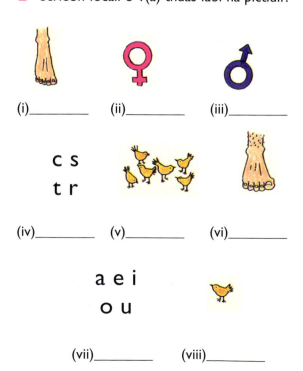

(i)_____   (ii)_____   (iii)_____

c s
t r

(iv)_____   (v)_____   (vi)_____

a e i
o u

(vii)_____   (viii)_____

3 Féach ar an bhfocal seo agus líon na bearnaí sna habairtí.

> veigeatóir

(i) Tá an focal seo san uimhir _____.

(ii) Tá sé _____ inscneach.

(iii) Tá ceithre _____ ann.

(iv) Tá sé (6) _____ ann.

(v) Tá an chéad ghuta _____.

(vi) Tá an ceathrú guta _____.

What does *veigeatóir* mean?
Seiceáil na freagraí san *Eochair*.

Praising a meal

Nua gach bia agus sean gach dí.
Fresh food and mature drink.

Unlike other parts of Europe, the practice of 'hanging' meat for several days to make it tender was not common in Ireland. All food had to be **nua** *new, fresh*. Drink on the other hand was best when it was **sean** *old*. **Dí** is the genitive of **deoch**.

You can use this saying to praise a meal highly, for example, **bhí nua gach bia agus sean gach dí ann** *it was a real feast!* How is a meal praised in other languages? Déan plé le foghlaimeoirí eile.

Bog Braon *Warm a Drop*

This is a lullaby or suantraí (**suan** *sleep*). The baby in the house was often called **an seanduine** *the old one*. The song calls for warm milk for the baby, careful attention, and good food. Listen to the recording and join in the chorus.

Curfá:
Bog braon, bog braon, bog braon don tseanduine,
Bog braon is blais féin, bog braon don tseanduine.

Cuir a chodladh, cuir a chodladh,
Cuir a chodladh an seanduine,
Cuir a chodladh, nigh a chosa,
Bog braon don tseanduine.

Ubh chirce, ubh chirce,
Ubh chirce don tseanduine,
Ubh chirce is blúirín ime
Is é a thabhairt don tseanduine.

Arán úr, arán úr,
Arán úr don tseanduine,
Arán úr is braon sú
Is é a thabhairt don tseanduine.

Prose translation, without repetitions:
*Warm a drop for the old one and taste it yourself
Put him to sleep and wash his feet.
A hen's egg and a little bit of butter, and give it to the old one.
Fresh bread and a drop of soup.*

7 Cultúr

The Irish Diet

For many centuries the Irish ate mostly dairy produce and meat. The importance of the cow is evident in the old, pre-Christian, stories like *Táin Bó Cuailgne/The Cattle Raid of Cooley* (**bó** *cow*, **táin** *herd*), and it comes down to us in modern Irish in words such as **bóthar** *road*, which literally means *cow passage*.

People did, of course, eat other types of food. A vivid description of the different foods available in mediaeval Ireland is given in *Aislinge Meic Conglinne*. Mac Con Glinne sets out in a boat of lard on a lake of new milk to visit the Land of Plenty.

The fort we reached was fair, with earthworks of thick custard, beyond the lake. Its bridge was of butter, its wall of wheat, the palisade was of bacon. Smooth pillars of old cheese, beams of juicy bacon, in due order, fine rafters of thick cream, with laths of curds supported the house. Behind was a spring of wine, rivers of beer and bragget[1], every full pool had a flavour. A flood of smooth malt over a bubbling spring spreads over the floor.[2]

Many other foods are mentioned in *Aislinge Meic Conglinne* such as wheaten bread, salmon, mutton, beef, carrots, kale, whortleberries and hazelnuts.[3]

In the 12th century the Normans introduced cereals, beans and peas. The potato was introduced at the end of the 16th century by Sir Walter Raleigh. By the 17th century English colonial developers were concentrating on the commercial cultivation of grains, fruits and sweet herbs. Fishing also began to be developed as an industry.

After the Famine living standards rose and food prices fell. Foods such as tea, sugar, Indian meal, bread and American bacon were available in shops. These foods were often exchanged for eggs and home-made butter.

The colonists also introduced sugar, tea, coffee, white bread, raisins, currants, and other luxury foods. However, it was mainly the wealthy who ate these foods. A class distinction in eating habits was quite evident by the 18th century. Poorer people still relied on dairy products with supplements of vegetables and grains. The difference in eating habits grew more pronounced and by the 19th century the poor were almost completely dependent on potatoes and milk.

The potato still remains an important part of the Irish diet. Tea is now the national beverage, the national dependency, some might say.

Marbh le tae agus marbh gan é
Dead from tea and dead for want of it!

---

1   Fermented ale and honey mixed together

2   Dillon, M. (1998) *Early Irish Literature*, Dublin: Four Courts Press.

3   Mahon, B. (1991) *Land of Milk and Honey*, Dublin: Poolbeg.

1 Do you know any food stories or poems similar to *Aislinge Meic Conglinne* from other cultures? If so, tell the class.
What are the traditional foods of your country? Déan comparáid le foghlaimeoirí eile.

2 The following foods are still known by their Irish name (although in anglicised form). Match the words to the definitions.

> bacstaí *boxty*   crúibín *crubeen*
> carraigín *carrageen*
> cál ceannann *colcannon*   duileasc *dulse*
> fraochán *fraughan*   poitín *poteen*
> práta *pratie*   praiseach *prashagh*

(a) a dish made of potatoes mashed with butter and milk with kale or (white) cabbage
(a)_____

(b) a whortleberry or bilberry found on the edge of heather
(b)_____

(c) porridge, gruel or stirabout … used figuratively to mean a mess
(c)_____

(d) a burgundy-coloured edible seaweed, dried and chewed raw
(d)_____

(e) home-made (illicit) spirits, distilled from potatoes in a little pot
(e)_____

(f) dish made from raw potatoes grated into a mixture of oatmeal or flour and fried in butter
(f)_____

(g) a delicacy made from boiled pigs' trotters/feet
(g)_____

(h) introduced to Ireland by Sir Walter Raleigh in 1585
(h)_____

(i) type of edible seaweed found on rocks (hence the name) prepared as a blancmange-like dessert
(i)_____

Information source
Dolan T.P. (1988) *A Dictionary of Hiberno-English*, Dublin: Gill & Macmillan.

3 Obair Ghrúpa

Compare Irish diets, past and present, with other diets around the world.

4

For those who are interested in archaeology

Fulacht Fia is the archaeological term used to refer to the remains of a prehistoric outdoor cooking site. It consists of a low grass-covered mound of burnt stone (generally kidney-shaped) and excavations have revealed that cooking took place in a water-filled pit or trough which was heated by adding hot stones from a nearby fire. The surviving mounds are the debris of the shattered stone which was thrown out of the trough after repeated use. They are usually found close to streams or in low-lying marsh areas and for the most part are considered to date from the Bronze Age (c.2000-400 B.C.). The origin of the name Fulacht Fia is not clear. It may derive from *Fiann* for *Fianna* (a legendary band of heroes whose leader was Fionn Mac Cumhaill). The Fianna had a reputation for hunting and would have used the fulacht to cook game. The name could also derive from *fia*, the Irish word for *deer*.

Bullaun Stones The Irish term *ballán* means a bowl or a round hollow in a stone. The anglicised term *Bullaun Stone* has been adopted to refer to artificial basin-like depressions or hollows found on rocks and boulders. The majority of examples are found on or are associated with early ecclesiastical sites (A.D. 500-1100). They appear to have been for grinding foodstuffs and other substances.

If you know of other examples of fulachtaí fia or balláin, tell the group about them.

8 Cumarsáid

I(a) Léamh

Tá tú i *mBialann Ghearóid*. Léigh an Biachlár. Cad ba mhaith leat?

Bialann Ghearóid

Biachlár an Lae

Cúrsaí Tosaigh
Anraith Éisc 'Gearóid'
Bradán Deataithe
agus arán donn
Sailéad Glas
le luibheanna úra

Príomhchúrsaí
Trosc Mornay Scallta
Caoldroim Rósta Mairteola
Uaineoil Ghalstofa agus
Cál Ceannann
Póg Ghlasraí na Feirme

Milseoga
Póg Úll agus Piorraí
Uachtar Reoite Baile
Mousse Seacláide

Tae nó Caife

(b)

Caitríona and Jack are also dining in Bialann Ghearóid. Éist leis an gcomhrá agus líon na bearnaí sa ghreille.

	Caitríona	Jack
Cúrsa tosaigh		
Príomhchúrsa		
Milseog		
Tae/Caife		

Seiceáil na freagraí sna *Téipscripteanna*.

(c)

The following are individual sentences taken from the dialogue you have just heard. Éist leis an téip agus líon na bearnaí sna habairtí.

(a) Beidh an sailéad _____ mar chéad chúrsa.

(b) _____ an uaineoil agam mar sin.

(c) _____ mbeidh cáis nó milseog agaibh?

(d) _____ a bheidh agatsa?

(e) _____ bheidh aon rud eile agam.

Talking about what you are going to eat

To state that you intend to have the salad you can say

Beidh an sailéad agam.

I am going to have the salad.

Beidh is the future tense form of the verb **bí.**
Bí is used because there is no verb *have* in Irish.
To state that you are not going to have something to eat you can say

Ní bheidh aon rud agam.

Ní bheidh rud ar bith agam.

To ask if someone intends to have something to eat you can say

An mbeidh milseog agat?

To ask what someone intends to eat you can say

Cad a bheidh agat?

Abair na habairtí sa bhosca os ard.

(d) Obair Bheirte

Take it in turns to be the waiter and the customer.

Comhrá I
Freastalaí: Cad a bheidh agat?
Custaiméir: Beidh an _____ agam ar dtús.
Freastalaí: Ceart go leor. Agus cad a bheidh agat ansin?
Custaiméir: Beidh an _____ agam.

Comhrá 2
Freastalaí: An mbeidh milseog agat?
Custaiméir: Beidh. Ba mhaith liom an _____.
/Ní bheidh.
Freastalaí: Ar mhaith leat tae nó caife?
Custaiméir: Ba mhaith liom _____/Níor mhaith, go raibh maith agat.

If you cannot pronounce the item on the menu, you can point to it and say: **Beidh an ceann seo agam.**

Sa Phub

If you say **Cad a bheidh agat?** *What will you have?* in a pub, you are offering to pay for the drink!

An mbeidh deoch agat?
Beidh.
Cad a bheidh agat?
Beidh pionta agam.

Ar mhaith leat deoch?
Ba mhaith.
Cad a bheidh agat?
Pionta, le do thoil.

2(a) Stór Focal

Bean: Cad a bheidh agat, a Shéamais?
Fear: Cupán caife.

Bean: Pionta beorach agus cupán caife le
            do thoil.
Freastalaí: Ceart go leor.

What is the woman having to drink?

(b)

Ceangail na focail leis na pictiúir.

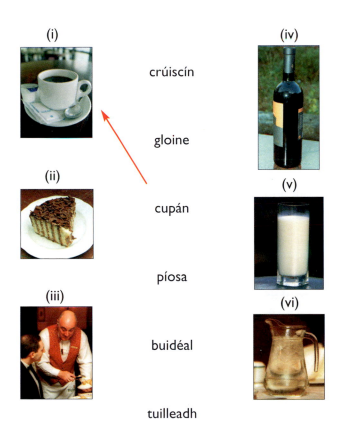

(i)

crúiscín

gloine

(ii)

cupán

píosa

(iii)

buidéal

tuilleadh

(iv)

(v)

(vi)

Seiceáil na focail san *Eochair* agus san fhoclóir.

(c) Líon na bearnaí leis na focail in (b).

buidéal   fíona

_____ prátaí

_____ uisce

_____ císte

_____ bainne

_____ caife

3(a) Gramadach

Tadhg and Máire are having a romantic dinner.
Éist leis an gcomhrá.

Tadhg: An mbeidh rud ar bith eile agat?
Máire: Beidh píosa eile feola agam.
Tadhg: Agus an mbeidh gloine eile fíona agat?
Máire: Ní bheidh. Tá go leor agam anseo.

Notice the change to the words **feoil** *meat* and
fíon *wine* in the expressions **píosa eile feola**
another piece of meat and **gloine eile fíona**
another glass of wine.

An Tuiseal Ginideach
a glass of, a cup of, a slice of ...

There is no Irish word corresponding to the
English *of* in phrases like **gloine fíona** *a glass of
wine*, or **píosa feola** *a piece of meat*. Instead
fíon and **feoil** are put into the **Tuiseal
Ginideach** *Genitive Case* causing their spellings
to change.

For the moment, it is sufficient to be aware of
the change in spelling. In many cases it is quite
minor, **fíon** to **fíona**, **arán** to **aráin**, and so
on. Sometimes there is no change at all, in
nouns ending in a vowel, for example, like **tae**,
caife, **uisce**, **prátaí** and **císte**.

(b)

Now fill in the brackets.

píosa bagúin (bagún)
gloine líomanáide (   )
pionta beorach (   )
gloine uisce (   )
tuilleadh sicín (   )
babhla stobhaigh (   )

Déan plé le foghlaimeoir eile.

4(a)

Tar éis an bhéile *After the meal*

Caitríona and Jack are on their way home from the restaurant. They are talking about the meal. Can you tell what they liked and what they disliked? Listen out for the prefixes **an-** *very* and **ró-** *too*, **an-te** *very hot*, **an-deas** *very nice*, **rómhilis** *too sweet*. The tone of voice is also an important clue, and the negative operators **ní** and **níor** *not*.

Thaitin *Liked*	**Níor thaitin** *Disliked*

Seiceáil na freagraí san *Eochair*.

(b) Stór Focal

Cuardaigh na haidiachtaí seo a leanas san fhoclóir. Write the equivalents in you own language.

Aidiacht	**Aistriúchán**
blasta	
milis	
righin	
úr	
searbh	

Cuir aidiachtaí eile leis an liosta. Déan comparáid le foghlaimeoirí eile.

Réimíreanna *Prefixes*

Prefixes in Irish are followed by a *séimhiú*, **an-mhaith** *very good*, **róshearbh** *too bitter* unless the dental consonants **d, n, t, l, s** come together, **an-searbh** *very bitter*, **an-deas** *very nice*.

A hyphen is used after a prefix if two vowels come together, **ró-úr** *too fresh*, or if the same consonant has to be repeated, **sean-nós** *old-style*.

Two of the most common prefixes, **an-** *very* and **dea-** *well-*, always have a hyphen, **an-mhaith** *very good*, **le dea-mhéin** *with compliments*.

In all other cases, there is no hyphen after prefixes, **rómhilis** *too sweet*, **seanmháthair** *grandmother*.

(c) Gramadach

Cuir líne faoi na briathra. Can you say what tense they are in?

Caitríona: Bhuel, ar thaitin an béile leat?
Jack: Thaitin an uaineoil liom. Bhí sí an-bhlasta. Ar thaitin an béile leatsa?
Caitríona: Níor thaitin an t-iasc liom. Bhí sé rófhuar.

(d) Labhairt

Have similar conversations with other students about a meal you had recently.

(e) Scríobh

Scríobh tuairisc ar cheathrar foghlaimeoirí ó (d) thuas.

Samplaí: Bhí uaineoil ag Jack. Thaitin sí leis. Bhí sí an-bhlasta.
Bhí iasc ag Caitríona. Níor thaitin sé léi mar bhí sé rófhuar.

9 Sa Rang

I

Éist leis an gcomhrá idir Elie agus Maria. They are talking about an Irish lesson they have just had. Can you tell who liked the lesson more?

Déan plé le foghlaimeoir eile agus ansin seiceáil na freagraí sna *Téipscripteanna*. Iarr ar an múinteoir cuidiú leat.

2(a) Stór Focal

The following adjectives can be used to describe a lesson. Can you guess what they mean?

| suimiúil | deacair | maith | éasca |

Déan plé le foghlaimeoir eile. Seiceáil na focail san fhoclóir. Cuir aidiachtaí eile leis an liosta.

(b)

Éist leis an gcomhrá in **9.**1 arís. Pay attention to the words/phrases in the box.

| dada | a lán | ar chor ar bith |
| mórán | go mór |

Críochnaigh gach abairt le ceann de na focail nó na frásaí.

(i) Thaitin sé _____ liom.

(ii) Níor thaitin, _____.

(iii) Ar fhoghlaim tú _____?

(iv) D'fhoghlaim mé _____!

(v) Níor fhoghlaim mé _____!

Déan plé le foghlaimeoir eile agus ansin seiceáil na freagraí sna *Téipscripteanna*

3 Obair Bheirte

Talk to another student about the lesson you have just had. First study the possible answers that *Foghlaimeoir B* could give. They are graded according to how positive or how negative you require the answer to be. Cleacht na habairtí leis an múinteoir.

Sampla:

Foghlaimeoir A:
      Ar thaitin an ceacht leat?

Foghlaimeoir B:
  + Thaitin.   – Níor thaitin.
+++ Thaitin sé go mór liom!   – – – Níor thaitin sé ar chor ar
                                                          bith liom!

  + Bhí sé suimiúil.   – Bhí sé deacair.
 ++ Bhí sé an-suimiúil.   – – Bhí sé an-deacair/
                                                        ródheacair.
+++ Bhí sé an-suimiúil ar fad!   – – – Bhí sé an-deacair/
                                                        ródheacair ar fad!

 ++ D'fhoghlaim mé cuid mhaith.   – – Níor fhoghlaim mé mórán.
+++ D'fhoghlaim mé a lán!   – – – Níor fhoghlaim mé dada!

  Ar thaitin an ceacht leatsa?

Use other adjectives such as *éasca*, *maith* etc.

Athraigh rólanna.
Now have similar conversations about a film (scannán) you have seen or a book you have read.

10 Gramadach

An Aimsir Chaite *The Past Tense*

I

The following are comments by students about an Irish course they are attending. Some comments are about the course in general. Other comments are about a particular class they had yesterday.

(i) Which comments are about the course in general?

(ii) Which comments are about yesterday's lesson?

- D'éist mé go cúramach.

- Imíonn an t-am go tapa.

- Bíonn an rang an-fhada.

- Faighim obair bhaile gach lá.

- Thit mé i mo chodladh!

- Chríochnaigh mé na ceisteanna gramadaí.

- Tá an múinteoir an-deas.

- Titeann na foghlaimeoirí ina gcodladh go minic!

- Fuair mé grád maith sa scrúdú ranga.

Past Tense

To form the past tense of both *Type 1* (**tit**) and *Type 2* (**críochnaigh**) verbs, put

(a) séimhiú on base form

   thit, chríochnaigh

(b) **d'** before vowel or *fh*

   d'éist, d'fhág.

Irregular verbs are covered in Aonad 10.

2(a)

Maria is describing what happened in yesterday's Irish lesson. Líon na bearnaí. Úsáid an Aimsir Chaite de na briathra sa bhosca.

> scríobh   bí   tug   tosaigh
> foghlaim   cuir   éist

_____ an rang ar a leathuair tar éis a naoi. _____ deichniúr foghlaimeoirí i láthair. _____ an múinteoir an téip ar siúl ar dtús. _____ gach duine go cúramach. Ansin _____ an múinteoir ceisteanna dúinn faoin téip. _____ siad an-easca ar fad! _____ mé cárta poist i nGaeilge. _____ mé deich bhfocal nua.

Anois éist le Maria. Seiceáil na freagraí sna *Téipscripteanna*.

(b)

Does the information in the text match that in the photograph? Déan plé le foghlaimeoirí eile. Ansin seiceáil an freagra san *Eochair*.

11 Fuaimniú

I

Na Consain *The Consonants*

Consonants in Irish come in two forms, broad and slender. They are identified by the vowels that are adjacent to them, slender (**i, e**) or broad (**a, o, u**). Compare /l/ and /l'/ in

> **labhair** /laur'/ *speak* and
> **leabhair** /l'aur'/ *books*,

or /r/ and /r'/ in

> **leabhar** /l'aur/ *book* and
> **leabhair** /l'aur'/ *books*.

The tick in the phonetic script indicates a slender consonant. Exactly the same information is carried in ordinary script by the vowels next to the consonant, e.g. **Gaeilge, cúramach**.

2(a)

Hear the Difference?

The broad and slender consonants of Irish are not entirely new sounds. The contrast exists in all languages. English *b* is broad in *boat* and slender in *be*.

In Irish, however, the difference is more pronounced, and the two *b*'s, broad and slender, are distinct phonemes, or different 'letters' in the sound alphabet of Irish. If you switch them, you get a different word, possibly meaningless, but definitely different:

bó /bo:/ *cow*	**beo** /b'o:/ *alive*
buí /bi:/ *yellow*	**bí** /b'i:/ *be*
cad /kad/ *what*	**cead** /k'ad/ *permission*
lón /lo:n/ *lunch*	**leon** /l'o:n/ *lion*
mar /mar/ *because*	**mear** /m'ar/ *quick*
naoi /ni:/ *nine*	**ní** /n'i:/ *not*
tuí /ti:/ *straw*	**ar tí** /t'i:/ *about to*

Listen to the pairs of words in the recording and repeat them.

(b)

You will hear six pairs of words. Meaitseáil an uimhir leis an gconsan ceart.

Péire *Pair*	Consan *Consonant*
I	p
2	s
3	t
4	v
5	f
6	n

3 Obair Bheirte

Write down some Irish phrases that you know. Mark the consonants broad or slender. Discuss the results with your partner. Say the words aloud paying attention to the contrasts between the broad and slender consonants. Iarr ar an múinteoir cuidiú leat.

 **Scileanna Foghlama**

Writing in Irish

1 How do you feel about writing in you own language? The following questions may help you think about this.

(a) Do you like writing? If so, what do you like to write? If you do not like writing, why is this so?

(b) Which do you prefer – using pen and paper or a keyboard? Why?

(c) What things do you admire in other people's writing? What do you not admire?

Déan plé le foghlaimeoirí eile.

2

Do you want to be able to write in Irish? If so, what would you like to write? The following are some suggestions. 'Anois', refers to things you might like to write now, and 'níos déanaí' to what you might hope to achieve at a later stage. Add your own ideas. Think of things you would like to write outside of classroom work.

anois	níos deanaí
Write a greeting e.g. *Nollaig shona*	Write a letter to a penfriend
Write a postcard	Write a poem

3

How can you improve your writing skills in Irish? Here are some methods which other students have suggested. What do you think of them? Have you any more suggestions?

> *… My friend dictates a sentence and I write it down. I then try to add a sentence of my own about the same topic …*

> … I have a piece of text – a note someone wrote – and I make a photocopy of it. I blank out a word here and there, like a pronoun or an adjective, and after a while I try to replace the missing words. I then compare it to the original text.

> *I keep a list of useful expressions, for example, expressions I can use in a postcard* – le grá ó do chara Máire.
>
> – Go raibh maith agat as an gcárta etc

> I started to keep a diary, just a sentence or two about the day. They do not need to be full sentences, for example:
>
> **Thaitin an rang Gaeilge liom. Aimsir go dona.**

Déan plé le foghlaimeoirí eile.

 Staidéar Pearsanta

Dialann

If you have not done so already, start a diary (dialann). Every evening write down one or two things which happened during the day. Read your diary to a friend in class. If you have not written a full sentence you can say a full sentence when you are reading your diary out, for example if you have written 'Aimsir go dona' you can say 'Bhí an aimsir go dona'.

Achoimre

Cumarsáid agus Stór Focal

Asking about, describing eating habits and food preferences	An ólann tú fíon geal? Ní ólaim ach go fíor-annamh. An mbíonn caife agat tar éis do dhinnéir? Ní bhíonn, riamh. Cad a ólann tú de ghnáth? Ólaim fíon dearg. Cén t-am a bhíonn an bricfeasta agat? Ar a hocht a chlog.
Saying you are hungry or thirsty	Tá ocras orm. Tá tart orm.
Offering food or drink	Ar mhaith leat ceapaire? Cad a bheidh agat? (in a pub).
Accepting, refusing an offer of food or drink	Ba mhaith. Níor mhaith, go raibh maith agat. Níor mhaith ach ba mhaith liom píosa císte. Ní bheidh aon rud eile agam.
Ordering a meal or a drink	An mbeidh an uaineoil agat? Ní bheidh. Beidh an sailéad agam. Ar mhaith leat aon rud eile? Ba mhaith liom an t-uachtar reoite.
Commenting on food or drink	Thaitin an bagún liom. Bhí sé an-bhlasta. Ar thaitin an béile leatsa? Níor thaitin an t-iasc liom. Bhí sé rófhuar
Meals	Bricfeasta, Lón, Dinnéar, Suipéar
Foods and drinks	Feoil – mairteoil, bagún Éisc – iasc, trosc, bradán Bia Veigeatórach – uibheacha, cáis Glasraí – cairéid, cabáiste Deochanna – fíon, líomanáid
Frequency words and phrases	i gcónaí, de ghnáth, go minic, uaireanta, go hannamh, riamh
Courses	Biachlár, Cúrsa Tosaigh, Príomhchúrsa, Milseog, Tae nó Caife
Quantity	cupán (caife), gloine (bainne), crúiscín (uisce), píosa (císte), buidéal (fíona), tuilleadh (prátaí).
Adjectives	blasta, milis, righin, úr, searbh, an-bhlasta, róroghin
Commenting on a lesson	Ar thaitin an ceacht leat? Thaitin an ceacht sin liom. Thaitin sé (go mór) liom. Níor thaitin sé (ar chor ar bith) liom. Bhí sé suimiúil, an-suimiúil (ar fad). Bhí sé deacair, ródheacair (ar fad). Bhí sé éasca. D'fhoghlaim mé cuid mhaith, a lán. Níor fhoghlaim mé mórán, dada.
Grammatical terms	uimhir uatha, iolra, guta, consan, caol, leathan, baininscneach, firinscneach, tuiseal ginideach

Gramadach

- **Present Tense: negative statement and interrogative**
  The negative marker **ní** is placed before the verb. If the verb begins with a consonant, it has a *séimhiú* e.g. **Ní bhíonn.**
  The question marker **an** is placed before the verb. If the verb begins with a consonant, an *urú* is placed before it e.g. **An mbíonn ...?**
- **a** after **Cad?** and **Cén?** If the verb begins with a consonant, it has a *séimhiú* e.g. **Cén t-am a bhíonn an lón agat? A** is joined to **tá** to become **atá** e.g. **Cén post atá agat?**
- **An maith leat?** vs **Ar mhaith leat?** Asking about, stating likes: **An maith leat caife? Is, ní maith.** Offering, accepting or refusing an offer: **Ar mhaith leat caife? Ba, níor mhaith.**
- **Genitive Case** In expressions like **gloine fíona** *glass of wine* or **píosa feola** *piece of meat*, there is no Irish word for *of*. Instead, the second noun is in the Genitive Case.

Past Tense
- **Séimhiú**, or **d'** before vowels and *fh*: **dhún, chuir, d'ól, d'fhoghlaim.**

Cultúr

- **Daily Eating Routines**
  Bricfeasta, lón, dinnéar correspond to breakfast, lunch and dinner in English. The time dinner is eaten varies. **Tae** is usually eaten around 6pm. **Suipéar** is a light snack taken before going to bed. Set meal-times were not always common in Ireland.

- **Flaithiúlacht**
  The Irish tradition of showing hospitality goes back a long way. In the past certain people had a duty to keep 'open house' which meant giving free food and lodgings to travellers. A host's generosity was often measured by the amount of food she or he served. It was an insult to a guest not to provide a plentiful amount of food. The Norman and Anglo-Irish colonists continued the tradition of giving hospitality. The tradition of keeping open house began to die out in the 19th century.

- **The Irish Diet over the centuries**
  Meat and dairy produce were the mainstay of the Irish diet for many centuries. Other foods were also consumed from an early date such as fish, wheaten bread, vegetables (including carrots and kale), various berries and nuts, wine, beer and bragget. The Normans introduced cereals, beans and peas in the 12th century. Sir Walter Raleigh introduced the potato in the 16th century. Grains, raisins, currants, tea, sugar, coffee and white bread were introduced by the Anglo-Irish. Potatoes and milk became the main foods for poorer people in the first half of the 19th century. After the Great Famine living standards rose and people bought more imported food in shops.

Fuaimniú

Broad and Slender Consonants
- Irish consonants can be broad or slender.
- Broad consonants have the letters **a**, **o** or **u** beside them.
- Slender consonants have the letters **e** or **i** beside them.

Scileanna Foghlama

Writing in Irish
- Decide what you would like or need to write in Irish.
- Be reasonable in your expectations.
- Think of strategies to help you improve your writing skills in Irish e.g. keeping a list of useful expressions.

Triail Tú Féin

I (i)

Cuir na focail/frásaí san ord ceart.

uaireanta   100%

riamh

go hannamh

go minic

de ghnáth

i gcónaí   0%

(ii)

Scríobh liosta de na rudaí a dhéanann tú de ghnáth. Bain úsáid as na focail/frásaí in I(i).

Sampla: Téim ag snámh uaireanta. Éistim leis an raidió go minic.

(iii)

Now enquire about your partner's habits.

Scríobh amach na ceisteanna ar dtús.

Sampla: An dtéann tú go dtí an phictiúrlann riamh? An dtéann tú go dtí an amharclann?

(iv)

Abair le foghlaimeoir eile cad a dhéanann do pháirtí.

Sampla: Téann Jason go dtí an phictiúrlann go minic. Ní théann sé go dtí an amharclann riamh.

2 Obair Bheirte

Déan comhráite le foghlaimeoir eile.

(i)

Foghlaimeoir A:	Say you are hungry.
Foghlaimeoir B:	Offer your partner something to eat.
Foghlaimeoir A:	Accept or reject your partner's offer.
Foghlaimeoir B:	Say you are thirsty.
Foghlaimeoir A:	Offer your partner something to drink (you are in a pub).
Foghlaimeoir B:	Accept or reject your partner's offer.

(ii) Sa Bhialann

It is lunchtime. *Foghlaimeoir A* is the waiter and *Foghlaimeoir B* is the customer.

Foghlaimeoir A:	Ask the customer if she or he intends to have a starter.
Foghlaimeoir B:	Say you do not plan to have a starter. Say you will have the main course. Say you would like the chicken.
Foghlaimeoir A:	Ask if she or he would like anything else.
Foghlaimeoir B:	Say you would like chips with the chicken.
Foghlaimeoir A:	Ask if she or he intends to have dessert.
Foghlaimeoir B:	Say you do not want anything else as you are on a diet.

Athraigh rólanna agus déan an comhrá le foghlaimeoir eile.

(iii)

Two friends (*Foghlaimeoir A* agus *Foghlaimeoir B*) are having a chat about a meal they have just had and about the Irish class they had earlier.

Foghlaimeoir A:	Ask your friend if she or he enjoyed the meal.
Foghlaimeoir B:	Say you enjoyed the meal but the chicken was a bit tough. Ask your friend if she or he enjoyed the meal.
Foghlaimeoir B:	Say you enjoyed it very much. It was very tasty.
Foghlaimeoir A:	Ask if she or he enjoyed the class this morning.
Foghlaimeoir B:	Say it was very interesting but the grammar was difficult. Ask your friend what she or he thought of the class.
Foghlaimeoir A:	Say it was far too easy and that you did not learn a thing!

B

I   Cuir na focail seo a leanas sa chatagóir cheart:

> scónaí   cáis   cabáiste   mairteoil   sicín
> fíon   píóg   úll   uibheacha   bagún
> leitís   piseanna   brioscaí   toirtín
> pancóg   oinniún   uaineoil   beoir
> píotsa   prátaí   tae   sú oráistí

Feoil	
Císte, arán	
Glasraí	
Deochanna	
Bia veigeatórach (príomhchúrsa)	

2   Obair Ghrúpa

Combining words from the two columns below gives phrases that are acceptable, unacceptable, or doubtful, for example, **gloine uisce beatha** *glass of whiskey*, **píosa caife** *piece of coffee*, and **cupán fíona** *cup of wine*. In groups of four, try to find as many acceptable combinations as possible in 3 minutes. Discuss your answers with other groups.

spúnóg	tae
cupán	fíona
gloine	caife
píosa	aráin
buidéal	prátaí
crúiscín	feola
tuilleadh	uisce beatha
pláta	siúcra
babhla	bagúin
muga	bainne

3

The following words are ways of describing food. Cén focal atá ann?

	Gaeilge	**Translation**
irnihg	righin	tough
labsat	_____	_____
barshe	_____	_____
rú	_____	_____
lisim	_____	_____

4

Líon na bearnaí sna habairtí le ceann de na focail atá idir lúibíní.

Tornapa

(i)   Tá *tornapa* san uimhir _____.
     (uatha, iolra)

(ii)   Tá sé _____.
     (firinscneach, baininscneach)

(iii)   Tá an chéad chonsan _____.
     (caol, leathan)

(iv)   Tá an ceathrú consan _____.
     (caol, leathan)

(v)   Níl aon chonsan _____ san fhocal.
     (caol, leathan)

C

Imagine you are Máirín. You have just received the following e-mail from your friend Luke who is learning Irish. Luke has asked you to correct any mistakes which you may notice.

> A Mháirín, a chara
>
> Conas tá tú? Tá mise go han-mhaith. Éirigh mé ar a cúig a chlog ar maidin mar bhí mo bean chéile ag dul go dtí an t-aerfort. Tá tuirse orm anois. Ná éirím chomh luath sin riamh! Éirím ar a hocht a chlog de gnáth. Cén t-am a éiríonn tusa?
>
> Réitaigh mé dinnéar breá dom féin tráthnóna. Bhí píóg ghlasraí agam ar dtús. Ansin bhí uachtar reoite agus silíní agam. Thaitin na silíní go mór liom. An mhaith leat silíní? Ní maith liom silíní de ghnáth ach bhí na cinn seo an-blasta ar fad! Ól mé leathbhuidéal fíona ach níl mé ar meisce!
>
> Bí mé ag mo rang Gaeilge inniu. D'fhoghlaim mé a lán. Chríochnaigh mé an ceacht gramadaí go luath. Tug an múinteoir ceacht eile dom.
>
> Cheannaigh mé madra nua. *Setanta* atá air. Tá sé an-deas ar fad. Ar maith leat grianghraf de?
>
> Sin an méid atá le rá agam. Scríobh ar ais chugam go luath.
>
> Do chara
>
> Luke.

D

An bhfuil an **t** leathan nó caol sna focail seo a leanas?

bricfeasta	_____
cabáiste	_____
poitín	_____
tae	_____
píotsa	_____
tuinnín	_____

E

I Líon na bearnaí sna habairtí seo a leanas. Scríobh na focail as Gaeilge.

(i) _____ is a light snack eaten before going to bed.

(ii) _____ can be eaten at midday or in the evening.

(iii) _____ is usually eaten when a person gets up in the morning.

(iv) _____ is normally only eaten around midday.

2 The word *flaithiúlach* is sometimes used in Hiberno-English to describe a particular characteristic. Describe this characteristic.

3 Freagair 'fíor' nó 'bréagach'.

(i) Sir Walter Raleigh introduced the potato into Ireland in the 19th century.

(ii) Tea was always drunk in Ireland.

(iii) Sugar was introduced to Ireland by the Anglo-Normans.

Téipscripteanna

1.5(a)

Sorcha:
Dé Luain bhí sailéad Waldorf agam. Dé Máirt... cad a bhí agam Dé Máirt... ó is ea... bhí sailéad eile agam – Sailéad Rúiseach! Dé Céadaoin bhí ceapaire tuinníne agam agus bhí uibheagán agam Déardaoin. Dé hAoine d'ith mé sailéad trátaí. Dé Sathairn ní raibh ach torthaí agus iógart agam agus bhí sól agam Dé Domhnaigh.

Mairéad:
Maith thú, a Shorcha!

2.1(c)

Siobhán:	Cén t-am a bhíonn an dinnéar agat?
Peter:	Bíonn sé agam idir a seacht agus a hocht a chlog.
Siobhán:	Cad a itheann tú don dinnéar?
Peter:	Ithim feoil trí huaire sa tseachtain – mairteoil, uaineoil agus sicín de ghnáth. Bíonn béile veigeatórach agam dhá uair sa tseachtain agus iasc dhá uair más féidir.
Siobhán:	Cad a ólann tú leis an dinnéar?
Peter:	Ólaim fíon dearg le mo dhinnéar i gcónaí – gloine nó dhó.
Siobhán:	An ólann tú fíon geal?
Peter:	Ní ólaim ach go fíor-annamh.
Siobhán:	An mbíonn caife agat tar éis an dinnéir?
Peter:	Ní bhíonn riamh. Ach bíonn cupán tae agam uaireanta.
Siobhán:	An dtéann tú amach ag ithe riamh?
Peter:	Go minic. Tá bialann Iodálach in aice liom agus téim féin agus mo bhean ann ar ócáidí speisialta.

4.5(b)

Deochanna	
meisciúla	**neamh-mheisciúla**
fíon	líomanáid
leann dubh	bainne
beoir	tae
uisce beatha	sú oráistí
	caife
	uisce mianraí

8.1(b)

Freastalaí:	An bhfuil sibh réidh le hordú?
Caitríona:	Tá. Beidh an sailéad agam ar dtús.
Jack:	Beidh an bradán deataithe agamsa.
Freastalaí:	Agus mar phríomhchúrsa?
Caitríona:	Beidh an trosc agamsa.
Jack:	Cad é seo?
Freastalaí:	Cál ceannann, an ea?
Jack:	Is ea.
Freastalaí:	Meascán de phrátaí coipthe agus cabáiste.
Jack:	Tá sé sin spéisiúil! Beidh an uaineoil agus cál ceannann agam, mar sin.
Freastalaí:	Sailéad glas agus Trosc Mornay don bhean uasal. Bradán Deataithe agus Uaineoil Ghalstofa duitse, a dhuine uasail?
Jack:	Go díreach!
Freastalaí:	Ar mhaith libh an liosta fíona a fheiceáil?
Jack:	Ba mhaith.

(Later on in the meal)

Freastalaí: An mbeidh milseog agaibh?

Jack: Beidh.

Freastalaí: Cé acu ceann a bheidh agat?

Jack: Fan go bhfeicfidh mé. Pióg Úll agus Piorraí. Ní maith liom piorraí. Uachtar Reoite. Mousse seacláide. Beidh an t-uachtar reoite agam.

Freastalaí: Agus cad a bheidh agatsa, a bhean uasal?

Caitríona: Tá mise ar aiste bia. Ní bheidh aon rud eile agam.

Freastalaí: Tae nó caife?

Caitríona: Tae, le do thoil.

Jack: Beidh caife dubh agamsa.

8.1(c)

(a) Beidh an sailéad agam mar chéad chúrsa.
(b) Beidh an uaineoil agam mar sin.
(c) An mbeidh cáis nó milseog agaibh?
(d) Cad a bheidh agatsa?
(e) Ní bheidh aon rud eile agam.

8.4(a)

Caitríona: Bhuel, ar thaitin an béile leat?

Jack: Thaitin an uaineoil liom. Bhí sí an-bhlasta. Ar thaitin an béile leatsa?

Caitríona: Ní raibh an t-iasc go deas.

Jack: Cén fáth?

Caitríona: Bhí sé rófhuar ach bhí an sailéad ar fheabhas!

Jack: Níor thaitin an t-uachtar reoite liomsa. Bhí sé beagáinín róbhog.

Caitríona: Is trua sin.

9.1, 9.2(b)

Elie: Ar thaitin* an ceacht leat?

Maria: Thaitin* sé go mór liom! Bhí an ghramadach an-suimiúil. Ar thaitin an ceacht leatsa?

Elie: Níor thaitin ar chor ar bith. Bhí sé ródheacair.

Maria: I ndáiríre? Ar thaitin an rólghlacadh leat?

Elie: Bhí sé ceart go leor. Ar fhoghlaim tú mórán?

Maria: D'fhoghlaim mé a lán! Agus tú féin?

Elie: Níor fhoghlaim mé dada!

Maria: Is trua sin!

* Note two different pronunciations of 'thaitin'

10.2(a)

Thosaigh an rang ar a leathuair tar éis a naoi. Bhí deichniúr foghlaimeoirí i láthair. Chuir an múinteoir an téip ar siúl ar dtús. D'éist gach duine go cúramach. Ansin thug an múinteoir ceisteanna dúinn faoin téip. Bhí siad an-éasca ar fad! Scríobh mé cárta poist i nGaeilge. D'fhoghlaim mé deich bhfocal nua.

11.2(b)

1	sean	san
2	teacht	tacht
3	peaca	paca
4	fonn	fionn
5	Nóra	Neasa
6	bhí mé	vóta

Eochair

2.2(a)

A An itheann tú feoil?
Ní ithim.

B An ndúnann an siopa ar a cúig a chlog inniu?
Ní dhúnann sé go dtí a sé a chlog.

2.2(b)

A Cén t-am a thosaíonn tú ag obair?

B Cad a itheann tú don bhricfeasta?

2.3(a)

trí huaire sa tseachtain, de ghnáth, dhá uair sa tseachtain, dhá uair, i gcónaí, go fíor-annamh, riamh, uaireanta, go minic

2.3(b)

i gcónaí (100%), de ghnáth, go minic, uaireanta, go hannamh, riamh

4.1 (i) no (ii) a chicken sandwich
(iii) I am hungry

4.2 an offer *ar mhaith leat?*, an acceptance *ba mhaith*, a refusal *níor mhaith*

4.4(a)

Fear: Tá tart orm.
Bean: Ar mhaith leat gloine uisce?
Fear: Ba mhaith.
Bean: Seo duit.
Fear: Go raibh maith agat.

Páiste: Tá ocras orm.
Máthair: Ar mhaith leat arán agus im?
Páiste: Níor mhaith ach ba mhaith liom píosa císte.
Máthair: Ceart go leor. Seo duit an císte.
Páiste: Go raibh míle maith agat, a mhamaí.

5.1(i) Ar mhaith leat caife? (ii) An maith leat
uachtar reoite? (iii) Ar mhaith leat bradán?
(iv) An maith leat tae?

5.2

+	–	?
is maith	**ní maith**	**an maith**
ba mhaith	níor mhaith	ar mhaith

6.1(a)
uimhir uatha *singular number*, uimhir iolra
plural number, guta *a vowel*, consan *a consonant*,
caol *slender*, leathan *broad*, baininscneach *feminine
gender*, firinscneach *masculine gender*

6.2(i) caol (ii) baininscneach (iii) firinscneach
(iv) consan (v) uimhir iolra (vi) leathan (vii) guta
(viii) uimhir uatha

6.3(i) Tá an focal seo san uimhir **uatha**.
  (ii) Tá sé **fir**inscneach.
  (iii) Tá ceithre **chonsan** ann.
  (iv) Tá sé **ghuta** ann.
  (v) Tá an chéad ghuta **caol**.
  (vi) Tá an ceathrú guta **leathan**.

veigeatóir *vegetarian*

7.2
(a) cál ceannann (b) fraochán (c) praiseach
(d) duileasc (e) poitín (f) bacstaí (g) crúibín
(h) práta (i) carraigín

8.2(a) a pint of beer

8.2(b) (ii) píosa (iii) tuilleadh (iv) buidéal
(v) gloine (vi) crúiscín

8.2(c)
tuilleadh prátaí, crúiscín uisce, píosa císte, gloine
bainne, cupán caife.

8.3(b)
líomanáid, beoir, uisce, sicín, stobhach

8.4(a)
Thaitin *Liked*: an uaineoil, an sailéad
Níor thaitin *Didn't like*: an t-iasc, an t-uachtar reoite

8.4(c)
ar <u>thaitin</u> … leat *did you like*, <u>thaitin</u> … liom *I liked*,
níor <u>thaitin</u> … liom *I didn't like*, <u>bhí</u> *was*
The verbs are all in the Past Tense.

10.1
(i) Imíonn an t-am go tapa.
  Bíonn an rang an-fhada. Faighim obair bhaile
  gach lá. Tá an múinteoir an-deas. Titeann na
  foghlaimeoirí ina gcodladh go minic.
(ii) D'éist mé go cúramach. Thit mé i mo
  chodladh. Chríochnaigh mé na ceisteanna
  gramadaí. Fuair mé grád maith sa scrúdú
  ranga.

10.2(b)
Tá seisear foghlaimeoirí sa ghrianghraf agus tá
deichniúr foghlaimeoirí sa téacs.

11.2(b) 1s, 2t, 3p, 4f, 5n, 6v

Triail Tú Féin

A
1(i)

i gcónaí 100%
de ghnáth
go minic
uaireanta
riamh 0%

B
1
Feoil: mairteoil, uaineoil, bagún, sicín
Cístí, Arán: píóg úll, scónaí, toirtín, brioscaí
Glasraí: cabáiste, leitís, prátaí, piseanna
Deochanna: fíon, tae, beoir, sú oráistí
Bia Veigeatórach: cáis, uibheacha,
pancóg oinniún, píotsa

3

Gaeilge	Translation
blasta	*tasty*
searbh	*bitter*
úr	*fresh*
milis	*sweet*

4
(i) Tá tornapa san uimhir **uatha**.
(ii) Tá sé **firinscneach**.
(iii) Tá an chéad chonsan **leathan**.
(iv) Tá an ceathrú consan **leathan**.
(v) Níl aon chonsan **caol** san fhocal.

C
d'éirigh mé, mo **bh**ean chéile, **ní** éirím, de **gh**náth,
réi**tigh** mé, an **maith** leat, an-**bh**lasta, **d'**ól mé,
bhí mé, **d'fh**oghlaim mé, **th**ug an múinteoir,
ar **mh**aith leat

D
bricfeasta **leathan**, cabáiste **caol**, poitín **caol**,
tae **leathan**, píotsa **leathan**, tuinnín **leathan**

E
1 (i) suipéar (ii) dinnéar
  (iii) bricfeasta (iv) lón
2 generosity e.g.
  He was very *flaithiúlach* with his money.
3 (i) bréagach (ii) bréagach (iii) fíor

10 Go n-éirí an bóthar leat!

This unit enables learners to: describe places they visited; talk about the future; make travel arrangements; discover the origins of the names of the months and seasons; talk about language ability.

Chuaigh mé trasna an domhain mhóir .....

Have you heard the expression *Go n-éirí an bóthar leat*? If so, what do you think it means?

Cumarsáid

Describing a place you visited

1(a) Stór Focal

Write down a list of countries and cities you have visited. Use the Irish names if you know them. Tell your partner which places you liked and which places you didn't like.

Sampla:

Bhí mé san Astráil agus sna Stáit Aontaithe.
Thaitin an Astráil liom ach níor thaitin na Stáit Aontaithe liom.

(b)

The box below contains a list of adjectives which will help you to describe a place you visited. Which adjectives would you put with which nouns?

cairdiúil	álainn	glan
saor	róthe	ard	eascairdiúil
daor	salach	gránna

Ainmfhocail	Aidiachtaí
daoine	cairdiúil
bia	
taobh tíre	
foirgnimh	
aimsir	
óstán, brú	

Déan comparáid le foghlaimeoir eile.
Seiceáil na focail san fhoclóir. Cuir focail eile leis an liosta. Iarr ar an múinteoir cuidiú leat na focail nua a rá.

(c)

Now you should be ready to describe in more detail what you liked and disliked about a particular place you visited. Ar aghaidh leat! Off you go!

Samplaí:

(a) Thaitin Nua-Eabhrac liom mar bhí na daoine an-chairdiúil.
(b) Bhí an aimsir go hálainn ach bhí an bia ródhaor.

2(a)

Cá bhfuil na háiteanna sna grianghraif thuas? An féidir leat ainm a chur ar na háiteanna seo? Ainm Gaeilge? Déan comparáid le foghlaimeoirí eile.

A   B   C

(b)

Éist leis na trí chomhrá. Meaitseáil na comhráite leis na grianghraif.

3(a) Gramadach

Cuir líne faoi na briathra sa chomhrá thíos.

Fear: Ar thaitin an áit leat?
Bean: Thaitin. Chuir na foirgnimh arda iontas orm.
Fear: An bhfaca tú an *Empire State Building*?
Bean: Chonaic. Chuaigh mé suas go dtí an barr.

What tense are the verbs in? Déan plé le foghlaimeoir eile.

> ### Irregular Verbs
>
> You will have noticed the difference between 'an bhfaca' and 'chonaic'. In the past tense the following verbs are irregular:
>
> Chuaigh (téigh) mé go Gaillimh. *I went to Galway.*
> Tháinig (tar) mé abhaile inné. *I came home yesterday.*
> Chonaic (feic) mé Túr Eiffel. *I saw the Eiffel Tower.*
> Chuala (clois) mé go raibh tú anseo. *I heard you were here.*
> Rug mé ar an liathróid. *I caught the ball.*
> Cad a rinne (déan) tú? *What did you do?*
> Cad a dúirt (abair) tú? *What did you say?*
> Fuair (faigh) mé cárta poist. *I got a postcard.*

(b) Cluiche do Bheirt

Write the verbs in the box above in the base form on slips of paper and place them face down on a table. Turn them over, in turn, and give the past tense.

Sampla:

Foghlaimeoir A: tar
Foghlaimeoir B: tháinig

Foghlaimeoir B: déan
Foghlaimeoir A: rinne

When all verbs have been used, reverse the procedure starting with the past tense.

4(a) Scríobh

Imagine you have just returned from a weekend in Paris. The following is a diary you kept while you were away. Use the diary to write an e-mail to another student describing what you did. Use the past tense of the verbs in the box to make full sentences.

Dé hAoine	béile deas Boulevard Saint Germain tar éis an bhéile ag siúl a chodladh 3 am!
Dé Sathairn	aimsir go dona siopadóireacht
Dé Domhnaigh	Cloig *Notre Dame* *Louvre – Mona Lisa* a lán pictiúr eile ann go dtí 5pm ar ais go Baile Átha Cliath tráthnóna leaba 10pm

bí	téigh	feic	codail	ith
tar	fan	clois	taitin	

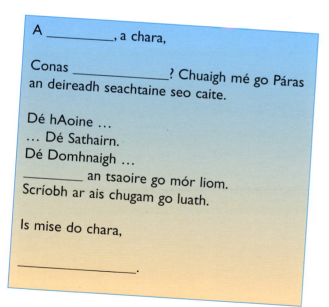

A _____, a chara,

Conas _____? Chuaigh mé go Páras an deireadh seachtaine seo caite.

Dé hAoine …
… Dé Sathairn.
Dé Domhnaigh …
_____ an tsaoire go mór liom.
Scríobh ar ais chugam go luath.

Is mise do chara,

_____.

Déan comparáid le foghlaimeoir eile agus ansin léigh an litir san *Eochair*.

(b)

Now write a letter to another person in the class. Tell them about a holiday you went on. When you have finished, read one another's letters.

2 Gramadach

go, go dtí *to*

1

Léigh na habairtí seo a leanas:

> Chuaigh mé go Páras ag an deireadh seachtaine.
> *I went to Paris at the weekend.*

> Chuaigh mé go hÉirinn ar mo laethanta saoire.
> *I went to Ireland on my holidays.*

An bhfuil an abairt seo a leanas fíor nó bréagach?

> A **h** is placed before a noun after **go**
> if the noun begins with a vowel.

Déan plé le foghlaimeoir eile. Ansin seiceáil an freagra san *Eochair*.

2

Léigh na habairtí seo a leanas:

> Chuaigh Sorcha go dtí an Iodáil anuraidh.

> Chuaigh Seán go dtí an Pholainn an mhí seo caite.

> Chuaigh Muireann go dtí na Stáit Aontaithe.

Líon na bearnaí san abairt seo:

> **Go dtí** is used before _____ or _____.

Déan plé le foghlaimeoir eile. Ansin seiceáil an freagra san *Eochair*.

3

David is back in London after having spent the last year travelling around the world. The places he visited are marked on the map. Which route might he have taken?

Now listen to the recording and follow his actual journey on the map.

How different was your route from David's?
Copy down the places in the order he visited them.

4 Scríobh

The following is a shortened version of David's journey. A number of the places David visited have been left out. Léigh na habairtí agus ansin líon isteach na bearnaí.

Refer to the list you copied down in 3. Don't forget to add *dtí* where appropriate!

Ar dtús chuaigh mé ar eitleán go _____.

Seachtain ina dhiaidh sin chuaigh mé go

_____. Ar aghaidh liom ansin go _____.

Ansin chuaigh mé go _____, go _____

ar dtús agus ansin go Perth. Sé mhí ina dhiaidh sin chuaigh mé go _____ agus as sin go hOileáin Fhidsí. Sa deireadh thaistil mé go _____. Chuaigh mé go _____ ar dtús mar bhí cairde agam ann. Chaith mé dhá mhí ag obair i dteach tábhairne i Nua-Eabhrac sular tháing mé ar ais go _____.

Déan comparáid le foghlaimeoir eile. Seiceáil sna *Téipscripteanna.*

3 Stór Focal

Na míonna *The months of the year*

1(a)

In the following recording you will hear a student reciting the months of the year. After you hear a month named, tick it off on the calendar.

Eanáir							
L	M	C	D	A	S	D
1	2	3	4	5	6	7
8	9	10	11	12	13	14
15	16	17	18	19	20	21
22	23	24	25	26	27	28
29	30	31

Feabhra						
L	M	C	D	A	S	D
				1	2	3	4
5	6	7	8	9	10	11
12	13	14	15	16	17	18
19	20	21	22	23	24	25
26	27	28

| Márta |
| L M C D A S D |
| 1 2 3 4 |
| 5 6 7 8 9 10 11 |
| 12 13 14 15 16 17 18 |
| 19 20 21 22 23 24 25 |
| 26 27 28 29 30 31 |

| Aibreán |
| L M C D A S D |
| 30 1 |
| 2 3 4 5 6 7 8 |
| 9 10 11 12 13 14 15 |
| 16 17 18 19 20 21 22 |
| 23 24 25 26 27 28 29 |

| Bealtaine |
| L M C D A S D |
| 1 2 3 4 5 6 |
| 7 8 9 10 11 12 13 |
| 14 15 16 17 18 19 20 |
| 21 22 23 24 25 26 27 |
| 28 29 30 31 |

| Meitheamh |
| L M C D A S D |
| 1 2 3 |
| 4 5 6 7 8 9 10 |
| 11 12 13 14 15 16 17 |
| 18 19 20 21 22 23 24 |
| 25 26 27 28 29 30 |

| Iúil |
| L M C D A S D |
| 30 31 1 |
| 2 3 4 5 6 7 8 |
| 9 10 11 12 13 14 15 |
| 16 17 18 19 20 21 22 |
| 23 24 25 26 27 28 29 |

| Lúnasa |
| L M C D A S D |
| 1 2 3 4 5 |
| 6 7 8 9 10 11 12 |
| 13 14 15 16 1718 19 20 |
| 21 22 23 24 25 26 27 |
| 28 29 30 31 |

| Meán Fómhair |
| L M C D A S D |
| 1 2 3 |
| 4 5 6 7 8 9 10 |
| 11 12 13 14 15 16 17 |
| 18 19 20 21 22 23 24 |
| 25 26 27 28 29 30 |

| Deireadh Fómhair |
| L M C D A S D |
| 30 31 1 |
| 2 3 4 5 6 7 8 |
| 9 10 11 12 13 14 15 |
| 16 17 18 19 20 21 22 |
| 23 24 25 26 27 28 29 |

| Samhain |
| L M C D A S D |
| 1 2 3 4 5 |
| 6 7 8 9 10 11 12 |
| 13 14 15 16 1718 19 20 |
| 21 22 23 24 25 26 27 |
| 28 29 30 |

| Nollaig |
| L M C D A S D |
| 1 2 3 4 |
| 5 6 7 8 9 10 11 |
| 12 13 14 15 16 17 18 |
| 19 20 21 22 23 24 25 |
| 26 27 28 29 30 31 |

Seachtain · Mí · Lá · Bliain
(Eanáir go Nollaig)

(b)

Éist leis an téip. Abair na míonna *the months* os ard.

(c) Cluiche

Babhta 1 *Round 1*
Divide into groups of 4 – 6 students. *Foghlaimeoir A* names a month. *Foghlaimeoir B* names the following month. *Foghlaimeoir C* names a month. *Foghlaimeoir D* names the following month and so on.

Babhta 2 *Round 2*
In the next round, *Foghlaimeoir A* names a month. *Foghlaimeoir B* names the previous month and so on.

2 📼

Brídín has a successful pottery business in the west of Ireland. Last year she decided to expand her business outside Ireland. During the course of the year she spent a lot of time abroad promoting her product in different countries. The following is an account of her travels.

Éist leis an téip agus freagair na ceisteanna seo: Where did Brídín visit in April, August and December?

Déan comparáid le foghlaimeoir eile. Seiceáil na freagraí sna *Téipscripteanna*.

3(a)

> ## Na Míonna *The Months*
>
> The Irish names for the months are listed again above. In the second column, the Irish word **mí** *month* appears before them, as it must in many situations. One is when you are naming the month in which something happened or will happen.
>
> > **Chuaigh mé go dtí an tSualainn i mí Eanáir.**
> > *I went to Sweden in (the month) of January.*
> > **Beidh mo lá breithe agam i mí Feabhra.**
> > *I will have my birthday in (the month of) February.*
>
> In the second column, the names of the months are in the *Tuiseal Ginideach*.
>
> > **Aibreán, mí Aibreáin** *April, month of April*
>
> similar to
> > **arán, píosa aráin** *bread, piece of bread* (Aonad 9).
>
> The same thing happens to the names for the days of the week when **Dé** appears before them
>
> > **Domhnach, Dé Domhnaigh**
> > *Sunday, on Sunday*

Eanáir	Mí Eanáir
Feabhra	Mí Feabhra
Márta	Mí an Mhárta
Aibreán	Mí Aibreáin
Bealtaine	Mí na Bealtaine
Meitheamh	Mí an Mheithimh
Iúil	Mí Iúil
Lúnasa	Mí Lúnasa
Meán Fómhair	Mí Mheán Fómhair
Deireadh Fómhair	Mí Dheireadh Fómhair
Samhain	Mí na Samhna
Nollaig	Mí na Nollag

(b) Scríobh

Scríobh abairtí faoi na rudaí a rinne tú i rith na bliana agus i rith na seachtaine *during the year and during the week.*

Sampla:

i rith na bliana: Tháinig mé go hÉirinn i mí na Bealtaine.
i rith na seachtaine: Chuaigh mé go dtí an Dánlann Náisiúnta (The National Gallery) Dé Domhnaigh.

Déan comparáid le foghlaimeoirí eile.

4

> ## Other useful phrases for times past
>
> **inné** /ən'e:/ *yesterday*
> > Chonaic mé Leabhar Cheanannais inné.
> > *I saw the Book of Kells yesterday.*
> > Chuaigh mé isteach sa chathair maidin inné.
> > *I went into the city yesterday morning.*
>
> **aréir** /əre:r'/ *last night*
> > Chuaigh mé a chodladh go luath aréir.
> > *I went to bed early last night.*
>
> **seo caite** /s'o kat'ə/ *last*
> > an tseachtain seo caite *last week*
> > an mhí seo caite *last month*
> > an bhliain seo caite *last year*

Now make sentences about yourself.

_____ inné.
_____ maidin inné.
_____ aréir.
_____ an tseachtain seo caite.
_____ an mhí seo caite.
_____ an bhliain seo caite.

Déan comparáid le foghlaimeoirí eile.

4 Cultúr

1(a) How the months and seasons were named

Fadó, fadó... A journey through the old Irish calendar

In older times a special celebration or festival was held to mark the beginning of each of the four seasons of the year.

The new year began with the festival of **Samhain** which introduced **An Geimhreadh** or the Winter season. **An tEarrach** or the Spring season started at the beginning of February with the festival of *Imbolc*. Both these seasons were considered to be in the dark half of the year.

The bright half of the year started at the beginning of May with the festival of *Beltane* **(Bealtaine)**. This also marked the beginning of **An Samhradh** which was the Summer season. The festival of *Lughnasadh* **(Lúnasa)** was held at the beginning of August and marked the beginning of **An Fómhar** which was the Autumn or harvest season.

Matthews, C. (1995) *The Celtic Book of Days*, Dublin: Gill and Macmillan.

Danaher, K. (1972) *The Year in Ireland*, Dublin: Mercier Press.

Scríobh an séasúr faoin bpictiúr ceart.

A   B

C   D

(b)

Scríobh na míonna atá ar iarraidh.

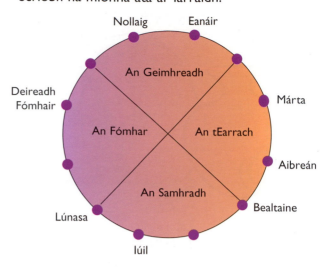

Inniu

For most people in Ireland today the year begins on the first of January. Spring begins on the first day of February and is also known as **Lá Fhéile Bríde** or Saint Brigid's Day, (the Christian Bríd taking the place of an earlier pagan Goddess called Brigit). Some people celebrate the day by making Saint Brigid's crosses out of interwoven rushes. These are often hung over doorways.

The summer season begins on the first of May. The first Monday in May is a public holiday dedicated to the working person. In some parts of Ireland traditional May Day, **(Lá Bealtaine)** rituals are practised.

The beginning of Autumn is marked by another public holiday on the first Monday in August. Traditionally, this was the time of year when marriages were planned. The end of the season is still seen in the farming community as the time for looking for a wife or a husband. Some **Lúnasa** festivals take place at this time.

Winter begins on **Oíche Shamhna** or Hallowe'en night (31 October) when the dead are said to return to speak to their descendants. It is customary for children to dress up and go from house to house collecting sweets and nuts.

2 Plé

(a) When does the New Year begin in your country? Did the New Year ever begin at a different time?

(b) How many seasons do you have? When does each season begin and end? How do the seasons in your country differ from each other (weather, agriculture etc.)?

Déan plé le foghlaimeoirí eile.

3(a)

The Irish names for the months of the year are based on either old Irish words or Latin words. In the following exercise the months are listed on the left and the origins of the words are on the right.

Meaitseáil na míonna ar chlé leis na focail nó na frásaí ar dheis.

Eanáir	*Latin 'Aprilis'*
Feabhra	*Irish meaning 'month in the middle (of Summer)'*
Márta	*Irish meaning 'the end of the harvest'*
Aibreán	*Latin 'Iulius'*
Bealtaine	*Latin 'Natalis'*
Meitheamh	*Lugh, the pagan God of Light*
Iúil	*Latin 'Martius'*
Lúnasa	*Latin 'Januarius'*
Meán Fómhair	*Irish meaning 'end of Summer or bright half of the year'*
Deireadh Fómhair	*Irish meaning 'the fire of Bel'*
Samhain	*Latin 'Februarius'*
Nollaig	*Irish meaning 'the middle of the harvest'*

Déan comparáid le foghlaimeoirí eile.

(b) Plé

Say the months of the year in another language.
Do you know the origin of the words?
Pléigh an cheist le foghlaimeoirí eile.

5 Gramadach

Questions and negatives in the past

1

Maria has just finished her Irish course in the Gaeltacht. The organisers of the course are conducting a survey to find out what students thought about the course, extra-curricular activities, accommodation etc. Pól is asking the questions. Some of the answers Maria gives are positive (dearfach) and some are negative (diúltach). Tick off the answers Maria gives.

Ceist	Freagra Dearfach	Freagra Diúltach
Ar thaitin an cúrsa leat?	thaitin	níor thaitin
Ar fhoghlaim tú mórán?	d'fhoghlaim	níor fhoghlaim
An raibh tú ar chúrsa Gaeilge roimhe seo?	bhí	ní raibh
An ndearna tú potadóireacht?	rinne	ní dhearna
An ndeachaigh tú ag sléibhteoireacht?	chuaigh	ní dheachaigh
Ar fhan tú i dteach lóistín?	d'fhan	níor fhan
An bhfaca tú an scannán aréir?	chonaic	ní fhaca
Ar ith tú duileasc?	d'ith	níor ith

Déan comparáid le foghlaimeoir eile. Seiceáil na freagraí sna *Téipscripteanna*.

2 Féach ar an ngreille thíos.

Ceist	Freagra Dearfach	Freagra Diúltach
Ar thaitin an cúrsa leat?	thaitin	níor thaitin
Ar fhoghlaim tú mórán?	d'fhoghlaim	níor fhoghlaim
An raibh tú ar chúrsa Gaeilge roimhe seo?	bhí	ní raibh
An ndearna tú potadóireacht?	rinne	ní dhearna

Freagair na ceisteanna.
(i) What goes before the verb to ask a question in the past tense?
(ii) What goes before the verb to give a negative answer in the past tense?

Déan plé le foghlaimeoir eile. Seiceáil na freagraí san *Eochair*.

3 Léigh na comhráite seo a leanas.

Comhrá 1
Tadhg: Ar chríochnaigh sibh an ceacht?
Bríd: Chríochnaigh.
Des: Níor chríochnaigh.

Comhrá 2
Cáit: An bhfaca sibh an scannán aréir?
Lelia: Chonaic.
Jerry: Ní fhaca, faraor.

Líon na bearnaí sna habairtí seo:
(i) In the past tense, certain verbs have a special form after **an** and _____.
(ii) A *séimhiú* generally follows **ar**, _____ and **ní**. An *urú* follows _____.

4 Líon na bearnaí sna comhráite.

(i) An bhfaca tú Marie aréir?
Ní _____ ach chonaic mé í an tseachtain seo caite.

(ii) Ar _____ tú i bhfad san Astráil?
D'fhan mé sé seachtaine ann.

(iii) Ar tháinig an post fós?
Níor _____.

(iv) An _____ tú go dtí an Róimh an bhliain seo caite?
Ní dheachaigh ach chuaigh mé ann dhá bhliain ó shin.

(v) An raibh an dráma go maith?
Bhí an scéal suimiúil go leor ach ní _____ an aisteoireacht go maith.

(vi) An _____ tú an císte seo tú féin?
Rinne. An dtaitníonn sé leat?

Déan comparáid le foghlaimeoir eile. Ansin seiceáil na freagraí san *Eochair*.

Cluiche do Thriúir

It is a good idea to learn the question, positive and negative forms of the verb together, for example, *An raibh? Bhí. Ní raibh.* Try the following game:

A chooses a verb from the list below and asks a question, for example *ar ól tú tae aréir?* B answers *D'ól*. C answers *Níor ól*. B picks the next verb and asks a question. C and A answer. Then C picks a verb and asks a question. A and B answer and so on until all the verbs are used.

ól	codail	bí	déan	tar
	téigh	foghlaim	taitin	
feic	clois	oscail	fan	

6 Fuaimniú

d, t

1

Éist leis an téip agus léigh na habairtí nó na frásaí.

Listen to the contrast between the pairs of **d**'s and **t**'s in each sentence.

Dia duit. *Hello.*
D'ól mé deoch leo *I had a drink with them.*
An dara dearmad *The second mistake*
Daoine ag díol rudaí *People selling things*

Taoiseach na tíre seo *The Prime Minister of this country*
Bhí mé tamall ag teagasc. *I was teaching for a while.*
An bhfuil tuilleadh ticéad agat? *Do you have more tickets?*

2

Listen to the pairs of words in the recording. Repeat them. Make sure you mark the contrasts between broad and slender consonants.

/d/	/d'/
dúnta	diúltach
damhsa	deas
fada	maidin
fadó	Brídín
fód	fóid
cad	cuid

/t/	/t'/
talamh	teach
tuiseal	tithe
nóta	caite
atá	ráite
agat	uait
leat	duit

3

You will hear 12 more words. Tick the sounds as you hear them.

	d	d'			t	t'
1	___	___		7	___	___
2	___	___		8	___	___
3	___	___		9	___	___
4	___	___		10	___	___
5	___	___		11	___	___
6	___	___		12	___	___

Seiceáil sna *Téipscripteanna* agus san *Eochair*.

4 Labhairt

Abair na habairtí nó na frásaí ar dtús agus ansin éist leis an téip.

(a) Chuaigh Dónall go Doire inné.
(b) Tháinig Diarmaid ó Londain inné.
(c) Trasna na dtonnta dul siar dul siar
(d) Báidín Fheilimí d'imigh go Toraigh.
(e) Chuaigh siad ag taisteal timpeall na tíre.

Sa Rang

Languages and language ability

1 Críochnaigh na focail ar dheis.

Tír	Teanga
An Fhrainc	Fraincis
An Ghearmáin	Gearmáinis
An Iodáil	Iodáil _____
An tSeapáin	Seapá _____
An Rúis	Rú _____
An Tuirc	T _____

Déan comparáid le foghlaimeoir eile. Seiceáil na freagraí san *Eochair*.

2 Cén Ghaeilge atá ar na teangacha seo? Tá na freagraí sa bhosca thíos.

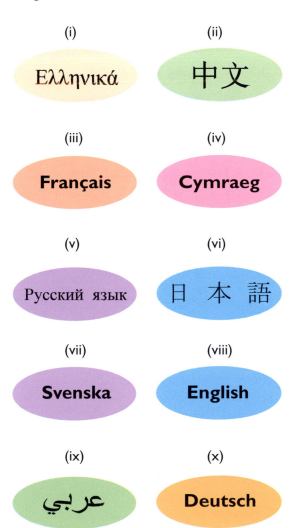

(i) Ελληνικά

(ii) 中文

(iii) **Français**

(iv) **Cymraeg**

(v) Русский язык

(vi) 日 本 語

(vii) **Svenska**

(viii) **English**

(ix) عربي

(x) **Deutsch**

Rúisis   Béarla   Araibis   Sualainnis
Seapáinis   Breatnais   Sínis   Gearmáinis
Fraincis   Gréigis

3
A group of students are talking about the languages they speak. Which language from the list below is *not* mentioned in the recording?

Gearmáinis	Polainnis	Gaeilge na hAlban
Portaingéilis	Tuircis	Béarla
Araibis	Gaeilge	Seapáinis
Briotáinis	Spáinnis	Fraincis

Déan plé le foghlaimeoir eile agus ansin seiceáil an freagra sna *Téipscripteanna*.

4(a)

Déan aithris ar an téip.   100%

Tá Spáinnis líofa agam.
Tá Spáinnis mhaith agam.
Tá Spáinnis réasúnta maith agam.
Tá cúpla focal Spáinnise agam.
Níl Spáinnis ar bith agam.

                                                  0%

(b)

Write about your ability to speak in a language other than English or Irish. Use the sentences above to help you.

(c) Labhairt

Try to find another person in the group who speaks the language you mentioned in (b). Find out about her or his ability in that language. How does it compare to yours?

Samplaí:
An bhfuil Gearmáinis agat?
Tá cúpla focal agam. An bhfuil Gearmáinis agatsa?
Tá Gearmáinis réasúnta maith agam.

An bhfuil Sínis agat?
Níl.
Ná agamsa ach oiread!

Giorraíonn beirt bóthar.

Two shorten the road.

This proverb is used primarily if you are going on a long journey and need company so that the time will pass more quickly.

Do you know any similar proverbs in other languages? Déan plé le foghlaimeoirí eile.

8 Cumarsáid

1

Talking about the Future

You have already seen **beidh** and **ní bheidh** in Aonad 9. Here are some more examples.
   An mbeidh tú saor? *Will you be free?*
   Ní bheidh. *No.*
   Beidh an dráma ag críochnú Dé hAoine.
   The play is ending on Friday.

Other useful words for talking about the future are:
amárach /əma:rəx/ *tomorrow*
   Ní bheidh mé saor amárach.
   I won't be free tomorrow.
   Beidh mé saor maidin Dé Céadaoin.
   I'll be free on Wednesday morning.
seo chugainn /s'o hugin'/*next*
   an tseachtain seo chugainn *next week*
   an mhí seo chugainn *next month*
   an bhliain seo chugainn *next year*

2 Obair Bheirte

The play in the Taibhdhearc is finishing its run this week. Rita is planning to go but would like company. It is Sunday evening. Rita contacts her friend Eibhlín who is willing to go with her. However, they have some difficulty trying to arrange a date. Listen to their telephone conversation. Below are two blank diaries, one for Rita and one for Eibhlín.

Foghlaimeoir A: Fill in Rita's schedule.
Foghlaimeoir B: Fill in Eibhlín's schedule.

	Dialann Rita	Dialann Eibhlín
Dé Luain		
Dé Máirt		
Dé Céadaoin		
Déardaoin		
Dé hAoine		

Féach ar dhialann do pháirtí.

Which night are Rita and Eibhlín going to the theatre?

3(a) Scríobh agus Labhairt

Write your plans for the coming week in note form.

(b)

Cleacht an comhrá seo a leanas le foghlaimeoir eile. Iarr ar an múinteoir cuidiú leat.

Sampla:
An mbeidh tú saor tráthnóna Dé Luain?
Ní bheidh, faraor. Beidh mé ag imirt leadóige.
   Cad faoin Máirt?
Ní bheidh mise saor Dé Máirt. Beidh mé ag
   bualadh le mo chara.
Is trua sin. Cad faoin Aoine?
Beidh mé saor an tráthnóna sin.
Ar fheabhas! Dé hAoine mar sin!
Ceart go leor.

(c)

Now try to arrange to meet another student for a drink or a meal some evening. Check your diary to see when you are free.

4(a)

Éist leis an téip agus léigh an téacs seo thíos.
What are Antaine's plans for (a) tonight? (b) next
year? Write your answers in Irish.

Mise Antaine. Is múinteoir
Matamaitice mé. Tá mé ag
obair i meánscoil i mBaile Átha
Cliath. Bím ag múineadh
Gaeilge do dhaoine fásta
freisin oíche amháin sa
tseachtain. Taitníonn an obair
seo go mór liom. Tá giúmar
maith orm inniu mar beidh an
rang Gaeilge agam anocht.

Is maith liom taisteal nuair a
bhím saor. An bhliain seo caite chuaigh mé go
dtí an Fhrainc in éineacht le m'iníon, Caitríona.
Thaitin Páras liom – na dánlanna ar nós an
Louvre ach go háirithe. Níor thaitin an bia le
Caitríona, áfach. Is veigeatóir í agus taitníonn
feoil leis na Francaigh.

An bhliain seo chugainn beidh mé ag siúl an
Camino de Santiago. Sórt oilithreachta (pilgrimage)
atá ann. Beidh mé ag siúl ó Roncesvalles sa
Fhrainc go dtí Santiago i dtuaisceart na Spáinne.
Tógann sé mí an t-aistear ar fad a dhéanamh.
Caitheann tú sliogán muirín (scallop shell) thart
ar do mhuineál agus bíonn bata mór siúil agat
freisin. Faigheann tú teastas ag deireadh an aistir.
Beidh mo chara, John, ag teacht liom. Fadhb
amháin – ní maith le John siúl. Ceapann sé go
mbeimid ag taisteal i ngluaisteán. Níor lig mé an
cat as an mála fós. John bocht!

Déan comparáid le foghlaimeoirí eile.

(b) Scríobh agus Labhairt

Prepare some notes in Irish about your travel
plans and then tell another student.

9 Stór Focal

Means of Transport

1 Obair Bheirte

The following are places associated with different
forms of travel. Scríobh an modh taistil faoin
bpictiúr.

A

B

long, bád

C

D

E

F

G

H

2

People are looking for directions to different places. Which means of transport are they likely to be using after they reach their destinations?

Sampla:

> Gabh mo leithscéal. Cá bhfuil ionad na dtacsaithe?

Beidh an fear ag taisteal i dtacsaí.

(a)

> Cá bhfuil an calafort le do thoil?

Beidh an bhean ag taisteal ar an _____.

(b)

> Tá mé ag dul go Cabrach. An bhfuil a fhios agat cá bhfuil stad an bhus?

Beidh an cailín ag taisteal ar an _____.

(c)

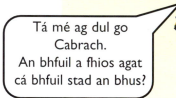

> Cá bhfuil carrchlós Uí Bhroin le do thoil?

Beidh an fear óg ag taisteal ar _____.

(d)

> An stáisiún traenach le do thoil?

Beidh an bhean ag taisteal ar an _____.

(e)

> Gabh mo leithscéal. An bhfuil an t-aerfort sa treo seo?

Beidh an fear ag taisteal ar _____.

(f)

> An bhfuil a fhios agat cá bhfuil Sliabh Mis?

Beidh an buachaill ag _____.

Déan comparáid le foghlaimeoir eile. Seiceáil na freagraí san *Eochair*.

3 Labhairt

Tell another student about how you travelled to class and how you are going home.

Sampla:
Tháinig/thaistil mé anseo i gcarr. Beidh mé ag dul abhaile ar an mbus.

10 Cultúr

I Travel in Irish Literature

The theme of travel was common in Irish literature. Sea-travel had a particular attraction and gave rise to the body of literature known as *Immram (Voyages)*. *Voyages* resembled another group of travel stories known as *Eachtraí (Adventures)* in which people went in search of the Other World, sometimes referred to as *Tír na nÓg* (Land of the Young), where there was neither sickness, old age or death. This land was somewhere in the western sea. While *Adventures* focussed on descriptions of the Other World, *Voyages* dealt mostly with the journey. These stories draw heavily on the experiences of sailors and hermits.

The Voyage of Mael Dúin

The Voyage of Mael Dúin is one of the oldest of these stories. It dates from the 10th century. The story is said to have influenced the writer of the famous mediaeval *Voyage of Saint Brendan*.

Mael Dúin sets off in a boat with his companions in pursuit of his father's murderers. In the course of the journey a great storm breaks out and they lose their way. They decide to let the boat sail in whatever direction it chooses to go. It travels over an endless ocean and brings them to many wonderful islands. Amazing things happen to them on the different islands.

On one island they see a swarm of ants, each as big as a foal. On another the earth is so hot they can hardly stand on it. Wonders happen to them out on the sea. The sea turns into a cloud and they are afraid that it will not be strong enough to support them.

One of the high points of the story is when they reach the *Land of Women*:
'They rowed to an island which, though not large, was fortified by a stronghold; on the stronghold (for all to know) was a firm brass fence. Around the fence was a lovely pool raised high above the sea's waves (no tale can equal this in splendour); before it, was a bridge of glass'.

Seventeen girls are preparing a bath for them. The queen sends one of the girls out to invite them into her fort: 'Her fair cloak, which was shining and beautiful, was surrounded by a hem of red gold. About her feet were silver sandals on which to rest'.

They stay for three months which seems like three years and finally have to leave but not before the queen makes great efforts to stop them. Three times she throws a ball of thread to Mael Dúin and when he catches it she draws the boat back to land. Finally, Mael Dúin asks one of the other men to catch the ball of thread. The ball sticks to his hand but they cut off his arm and sail away.

They visit other islands and on one of these they meet a hermit who tells them to go home. He foretells that they will meet Mael Dúin's father's killer but that, in gratitude for surviving many dangers on the journey, they must not kill him. Mael Dúin and his companions return to Ireland and relate their adventures and the dangers they experienced on sea and land.

Quotations
Murphy, Gerard (1998) *Early Irish Lyrics*, Dublin: Four Courts Press.
Other source
Dillon, M. (1994) *Early Irish Literature*, Dublin: Four Courts Press.

2(a) Obair Bheirte

Below is a shortened version of Mael Dúin's voyage in Irish with some of the words missing. The story has been divided into two sections. *Foghlaimeoir A* is responsible for the first section and *Foghlaimeoir B* the second.

Foghlaimeoir A

This is a description (cur síos) of the journey as far as the *Land of Women* (Tír na mBan). The missing words are in the box below.

Líon na bearnaí sna habairtí leis na focail sa bhosca.

> ansin   chonaic   raibh
> oileán   róthe   bád   bhfarraige

Bhí stoirm mhór ar an _____. D'imigh an _____ le sruth. Thug an bád go hoileáin éagsúla iad. Tharla rudaí iontacha dóibh ar na hoileáin seo. Ar _____ amháin _____ siad seangáin (ants) a bhí chomh mór le searrach. Ní _____ siad ábalta seasamh ar oileán eile mar bhí an talamh _____. _____ shroich siad Tír na mBan.

Foghlaimeoir B

This is a description (cur síos) of the journey after they left the *Land of Women* (Tír na mBan). The missing words are in the box below.

Líon na bearnaí sna habairtí leis na focail sa bhosca.

> isteach   go   freisin   trí
> chuir   oileán   d'fhan

Bhí dún mór ar an _____. Bhí droichead (bridge) gloine ag dul _____ sa dún. _____ an bhanríon fáilte mhór rompu. Bhí folcadh breá acu. Bhí béile blasta acu _____. _____ siad _____ mhí ar an oileán. Thug siad cuairt ar oileáin eile. Ansin tháinig siad ar ais _____ hÉirinn.

Éist leis an téip agus seiceáil na freagraí.

(b)

Anois léigh amach do chuid féin den scéal do do pháirtí.
Tosaigh le *Foghlaimeoir A*.

3 Obair Ghrúpa

Do you know any adventure or voyage stories from other cultures? Do any of these stories resemble *The Voyage of Mael Dúin*? If so, how? Déan plé le foghlaimeoirí eile sa ghrúpa.

11 Sa Rang

Grammatical Terms

1(a)

Which of the following grammatical terms do *not* exist in your language? Translate the terms which *do* exist into your language.

> séimhiú   urú   forainm réamhfhoclach
> aidiacht shealbhach   an chopail
> modh ordaitheach   aimsir láithreach
> aimsir chaite

(b)

Éist leis an téip agus déan aithris ar na focail.

2 Meaitseáil na focail ar chlé leis na samplaí ar dheis.

séimhiú	is
urú	d'ól
forainm réamhfhoclach	téann
aidiacht shealbhach	cuir
an chopail	dom
modh ordaitheach	an fharraige
aimsir láithreach	mo
aimsir chaite	mBan

3

Léigh an téacs thíos. Pick out examples of the grammatical terms listed in 2 above.

Sampla: séimhiú *thaitin*

Téim go dtí an Iodáil go minic ar mo laethanta saoire. Is maith liom an tír mar tá na daoine an-chairdiúil. Uair amháin chuaigh mé go hOileán Ischia ar an mbád. Thaitin an turas go mór liom.

Focal faire, áfach – ná déan dearmad ar do hata gréine!

Déan comparáid le foghlaimeoir eile agus ansin seiceáil na freagraí san *Eochair*.

12 Cumarsáid

1(a) Léamh

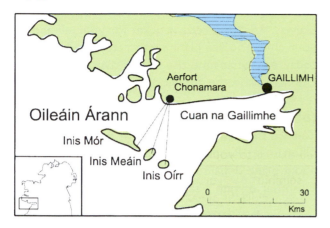

You are thinking of visiting the Aran Islands so you decide to search the Internet for information about different travel packages. You get information about four packages.

The descriptions of the four packages have been separated from their titles. Put the correct title on each description.

Teidil *Titles*

| Traein, eitilt agus lóistín | Bus, eitilt agus lóistín |

| Eitilt agus bád | Eitilt agus lóistín |

Pacáistí *Packages*

A

Faigh an t-eitleán ó Aerfort Chonamara go hInis Mór, lóistín an oíche sin agus ar ais …

B

Bealach amháin ó Aerfort Chonamara agus an bealach eile ar an mbád …

C

Faigh an traein ó áit ar bith sa tír go Gaillimh, an bus ó Ghaillimh go hAerfort Chonamara, an t-eitleán go hInis Meáin, an bus go teach lóistín ar an oileán, lóistín an oíche sin agus ar ais abhaile …

D

Faigh Bus Éireann ó aon áit sa tír go Gaillimh, ansin bus go hAerfort Chonamara, an t-eitleán go hInis Oírr. Lóistín agus ar ais abhaile …

Déan comparáid le foghlaimeoir eile. Seiceáil na freagraí san *Eochair*. Which package would you choose?

(b) Looking out for key words

Did you read *all* the information in the different packages before you made the correct match? If not, why?

Déan plé le foghlaimeoirí eile.

(c)

The following is a list of air fares. Can you guess what the words mean? Déan plé le foghlaimeoir eile.

Táillí	
Ticéad fillte – duine fásta	€45
Ticéad fillte – mac léinn	€37
Ticéad fillte – páiste	€25
Ticéad fillte do PS le pas saor	€15

Freagair na ceisteanna seo:
(a) How much does a student fare cost?
(b) Is it true that Pinsinéirí Seanaoise *Old Age Pensioners* can only buy single tickets?

Déan comparáid le foghlaimeoir eile agus seiceáil na freagraí san *Eochair*.

The woman in the picture is travelling to Inis Mór. Imagine what she is saying. Líon isteach an bolgán.

2 Meaitseáil na habairtí leis na pictiúir.

A
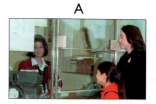

B

_____   _____

C

D

_____   _____

1 Tá mé ag dul go hInis Mór. Ticéad fillte do mhac léinn le do thoil.

2 Ticéad singil do dhuine fásta agus ceann do pháiste.

3 Dhá thicéad do mhic léinn le do thoil.

4 Ticéad singil le do thoil – tá pas saor agam.

Déan comparáid le foghlaimeoir eile.

Anois éist leis an téip chun na freagraí a sheiceáil. Déan aithris ar an téip.

3

> ### Wishing someone a safe journey
>
> If someone is going on a journey by road you can say
>
> **Go n-éirí an bóthar leat!**
> /go nair'i: ən bo:hər l'at/
> _Good luck on the road_
>
> If someone is going on a journey by rail, sea or air it is more appropriate to say
>
> **Go n-éirí do thuras leat!**
> /go nair'i: də hurəs l'at/
> _Good luck on your journey_

Abair na habairtí os ard.

How do you wish someone a safe journey in your own language or in other languages?
Déan plé le foghlaimeoirí eile.

4 Rólghlacadh

The instructions for _Foghlaimeoir A_ are below and the instructions for _Foghlaimeoir B_ are in _Nóta 1_, page 200.

(a) Foghlaimeoir A
You are getting the 09.15 plane from Inis Oírr to Galway. Ask for a return ticket for yourself and your child. You are planning to return to Inis Oírr today. Ask what time the plane leaves Aerfort Chonamara in the afternoon.

(b) Foghlaimeoir A
You are the ticket salesperson in Aerfort Chonamara. Respond to your client's enquiry about plane departure times from Inis Meáin. Wish her or him a safe journey.

Am Imeachta ó na hOileáin	
09.15	10.15
16.15	17.15

13 Scileanna Foghlama

1 Assessing your progress so far

In Aonad 2 you gave your reasons for learning Irish. Do you remember what they were? Which parts of the course have been most successful so far in giving you what you wanted?

Write down three things you liked about the course and three things you did not like. You can write your comments in Irish or in English.

	😊	☹
1		
2		
3		

Déan plé le foghlaimeoirí eile.

2 Planning for the future

Do you plan to continue learning Irish? If so, what aspects of the language would you like to learn more about? The following list may help you. Write a sentence about each aspect you would like to work on.

Sampla:
Léamh – 'I would like to understand the main points of a short newspaper article'.

Labhairt	
Scríobh	
Léamh	
Éisteacht	
Gramadach	
Fuaimniú	
Cultúr	
Eile	

Déan plé le foghlaimeoir eile.

14 Staidéar Pearsanta

1

If you have decided that you would like to continue studying Irish, it is important from time to time that you review what you studied in the course. For example, you could decide to review 6-8 words every day by writing each word on a card and leaving the cards in strategic positions around your home or in your work-place.

The following are some suggestions about how you could practise your Irish after you finish this course. Work with another student to add more suggestions to the list.

Focail ar chártaí – sa teach nó san áit oibre
Teilifís agus raidió
An tIdirlíon

There are some more suggestions in *Nóta 2*, on page 200.

2

Pick 3 suggestions you are going to try out immediately after you finish the course. Go n-éirí an t-ádh leat! *Good luck!*

Báidín Fheilimí *Feilimí's Little Boat*

This is a song about a famous boat, *Feilimí's Little Boat*. Feilimí sailed it to Gola and Tory Islands, off the Donegal coast, and was eventually shipwrecked on Tory. But this is a children's song, and the disaster most likely occured in a bath-tub!

This is one of the best-known of all Irish songs, with a tune that rises and falls like the swell of the sea. Memorise it and sing it together.

Báidín Fheilimí

Báidín Fheilimí d'imigh go Gabhla
Báidín Fheilimí is Feilimí ann.
Báidín Fheilimí d'imigh go Gabhla
Báidín Fheilimí is Feilimí ann.

Curfá:
Báidín bídeach, báidín beosach,
Báidín bóidheach, báidín Fheilimí;
Báidín bídeach, báidín beosach,
Báidín Fheilimí is Feilimí ann.

Báidín Fheilimí d'imigh go Toraigh
Báidín Fheilimí is Feilimí ann.
Báidín Fheilimí d'imigh go Toraigh
Báidín Fheilimí is Feilimí ann.

Báidín Fheilimí briseadh i dToraigh
Báidín Fheilimí is Feilimí ann.
Báidín Fheilimí briseadh i dToraigh
Báidín Fheilimí is Feilimí ann.

Feilimí's little boat went to Gola and Feilimí on it.
A tiny little boat, lively, pretty and Feilimí on it.
Went to Tory and Feilimí on it.
Was shipwrecked on Tory and Feilimí on it.

(i) Do you know any other sea-faring songs in Irish?

(ii) Do you know any sea-faring songs in other languages? Tell the class what they are about. Perhaps you might like to sing them?

Achoimre

Cumarsáid agus Stór Focal

Describing and asking about past experiences	Chuaigh mé go Páras ag an deireadh seachtaine. Bhí béile blasta agam Dé hAoine seo caite. Chonaic mé Túr Eiffel. D'fhan mé i mbrú óige. Thaitin an tsaoire go mór liom. Ar ith tú duileasc? D'ith. Níor ith. An ndeachaigh tú ag sléibhteoireacht? Chuaigh. Ní dheachaigh.
Talking about the future	Beidh mé ag bualadh le Máirín amárach. Beidh an dráma ag críochnú Dé hAoine seo chugainn. Beidh mo chara, John, ag teacht liom.
Arranging to meet	An mbeidh tú saor anocht? Beidh. Ní bheidh. Is trua sin. Ar fheabhas! Cad faoin Aoine? Dé hAoine mar sin? Ceart go leor.
Making travel arrangements	Ticéad fillte do mhac léinn, le do thoil. Ticéad singil do pháiste, le do thoil. Dhá thicéad le do thoil ceann do dhuine fásta agus ceann do pháiste. Tá pas saor agam. Cén t-am a fhágann an eitilt?
Wishing someone well on their journey	Go n-éirí an bóthar leat! Go n-éirí do thuras leat!
Adjectives to describe people and places	cairdiúil, eascairdiúil, álainn, glan, salach saor, daor, ard, róthe, gránna
The months	Eanáir, Feabhra, Márta, Aibreán, Bealtaine, Meitheamh, Iúil, Lúnasa, Meán Fómhair, Deireadh Fómhair, Samhain, Nollaig Mí Eanáir, Mí Feabhra, Mí an Mhárta, Mí Aibreáin, Mí na Bealtaine, Mí an Mheithimh, Mí Iúil, Mí Mheán Fómhair, Mí Dheireadh Fómhair, Mí na Samhna, Mí na Nollag
The seasons	An tEarrach, An Samhradh, An Fómhar, An Geimhreadh
Past time phrases	inné, maidin inné, aréir, an tseachtain seo caite, an mhí seo caite, an bhliain seo caite
Future time phrases	anocht, amárach, maidin amárach, an tseachtain seo chugainn, Dé Luain seo chugainn, an mhí seo chugainn, an bhliain seo chugainn
Means of transport	tacsaí, gluaisteán/carr, traein, long, bád, rothar, gluaisrothar, eitleán, bus ag siúl, ag eitilt
Transport terminals	ionad na dtacsaithe, calafort, stad an bhus, stáisiún traenach, aerfort
Talking about language ability	Teangacha e.g. Fraincis, Spáinnis, Iodáilis, Gaeilge, Béarla. Tá Spáinnis líofa agam. Tá Fraincis mhaith agam. Tá Iodáilis réasúnta maith agam. Tá cúpla focal Seapáinise agam. Níl Iodáilis ar bith agam. An bhfuil Sínis agat(sa)? Níl. Ná agamsa ach oiread.
Grammatical terms	séimhiú, urú, forainm réamhfoclach, aidiacht shealbhach, an chopail, modh ordaitheach, aimsir láithreach, aimsir chaite

Gramadach

- **Go**   Páras, Londain, Conamara
  Go dtí   an Fhrainc, na Stáit Aontaithe

- **Irregular Past Tenses**

Ar chuala?	Chuala	Níor chuala
Ar tháinig?	Tháinig	Níor tháinig
Ar rug?	Rug	Níor rug
An ndeachaigh?	Chuaigh	Ní dheachaigh
An bhfaca?	Chonaic	Ní fhaca
An ndearna?	Rinne	Ní dhearna
An ndúirt?	Dúirt	Ní dúirt
An bhfuair?	Fuair	Ní bhfuair

Fuaimniú

d, t

Leathan **dó** /do:/ **tá** /ta:/

Caol **di** /dʹi/ **tithe** /tʹihə/

Scileanna Foghlama

Assessing your progress
Did the course meet your expectations?
What did you like or dislike about the course?

Planning for the future
Do you plan to continue learning Irish? If so, what would you like to learn more about?

Staidéar Pearsanta

Practising Irish on your own

Words on cards
Fill in the blanks
TV and Radio
Conversation groups
Writing to people – e-mailing
Courses on the Internet
You own ideas

Cultúr

The Celtic Year

The new year began with the festival of **Samhain** – last day of October and first day of November. This was also the beginning of **An Geimhreadh** (Winter). The festival of *Imbolc* was held at the beginning of February. This was the beginning of **An tEarrach** (Spring). **An Samhradh** (Summer) began in May with the festival of Beltane. **An Fómhar** (Autumn) began in August with the festival of *Lughnasadh*.

The Year Today

For most people in Ireland the year begins on the first of January. The seasons still begin at the same time as they did in ancient times. **Lá Fhéile Bríde** (Saint Brigid's Day) has replaced *Imbolc*. *Workers' Day* is celebrated in Ireland on the first Monday of May. The festival of **Samhain** is still celebrated and is known in Irish as **Oíche Shamhna**.

Lúnasa and **Bealtaine** festivals are becoming popular again.

The Voyage Stories

The theme of travel was very common in Irish literature, sea-travel in particular. People often went in search of **Tír na nÓg** (The Land of the Young). These stories, known as *Adventures* or *Voyages*, may have had some factual basis in the experiences of mediaeval sailors and hermits.

Triail Tú Féin

A

1(i)

Write a short letter or e-mail to a friend describing a place you visited recently. Describe the good things and bad things about the place. Use the following headings:

Cén áit? Cathain? Lóistín? Aimsir? Na daoine? Na foirgnimh? An taobh tíre? An bia?

(ii)

Your friend is coming to visit you after returning from a trip to India. Prepare a list of questions to ask her or him about the visit. Use the headings in (i) as a guide.

Sampla: Cá raibh tú ag fanacht?
An raibh an bia go deas?
An bhfaca tú ......?

2(i)

Teastaíonn uait dul ón Daingean go Trá Lí ar an mbus. You are planning to make a telephone call in Irish to Bus Éireann. Plan what you are going to say.

Greet the assistant and ask if she or he can speak Irish.

Ask if there is a bus from Dingle to Tralee.

Ask if there is a bus on Sundays.

Ask what time the bus leaves Dingle on Sunday afternoon.

Ask where the ticket office is.

Thank the assistant.

(ii)

Imagine you are the Bus Éireann assistant who answers the telephone. Reply in Irish to the questions above.

Reply to the greeting and say your Irish is reasonably good.

Say there is a bus from Dingle to Tralee.

Say there are two buses on Sundays.

Say the first bus leaves at 13:30 and the second bus at 16:40.

Say you get your ticket on the bus.

Respond to thanks and say goodbye.

Cleacht an comhrá le foghlaimeoir eile.

(iii)

You are on the bus to Tralee. You are a teacher responsible for a group of children on a school outing. Some teachers and student-teachers are helping you. Your mother has decided to come on the trip. Ask the bus driver for the following tickets:

Three adult tickets

Two student tickets

Seven children's tickets

One single ticket. Your mother has a free pass.

3

Mary is trying to arrange a tennis match with her friend Pádraig. Líon na bearnaí sa chomhrá.

Mary:	An mbeidh tú _____ tráthnóna Dé Céadaoin?
Pádraig:	Ní bheidh faraor. _____ _____ ____ bualadh le cara.
Mary:	_____ _____ Déardaoin?
Pádraig:	Ní bheidh mé saor Déardaoin ach _____. Cad faoin Aoine?
Mary:	_____ _____ _____ saor Dé hAoine. Beidh _____ Seapáinise agam.
Pádraig:	Bhuel, beidh mise saor Dé Sathairn. Cad fútsa?
Mary:	Beidh mise saor Dé Sathairn, _____!
Pádraig:	Ar _____! Dé Sathairn _____ sin?
Mary:	Ceart go leor.

B

1(i)

Cuir na litreacha san ord ceart.

Enaári	_____
Fbehaar	_____
Mtará	_____
Anirábe	_____
Baileneta	_____
Mmatehihe	_____
Ilúi	_____
Lnsúas	_____
Máne Fmóhria	_____
Dhidaree Faóihmr	_____
Snahiam	_____
Nglioal	_____

(ii)

Scríobh an séasúr in aice leis an mí.

Iúil _____

Nollaig _____

Feabhra _____

Lúnasa _____

2

Cuir iad seo san ord ceart:

an mhí seo caite

an tseachtain seo chugainn

tráthnóna amárach

inniu

maidin inné

oíche amárach

an bhliain seo chugainn

an tseachtain seo caite

aréir

future

past

3

Líon na bearnaí sa ghreille.

bád	
	stáisiún traenach
bus	
tacsaí	
	carrchlós
	aerfort

C

1

Criostóir is interviewing Fionnuala about a recent trip she took to the Gaeltacht. Líon na bearnaí. (The little numbers refer to the solutions in the *Eochair*.)

C: Bhí tú sa Ghaeltacht le déanaí. Cén Ghaeltacht?

F: Gaoth Dobhair i gContae Dhún na nGall.

C: _____₁ thaitin an áit leat?

F: Thaitin sí go mór liom. Bhí an taobh tíre go hálainn, na sléibhte ach go háirithe!

C: _____₂ fhan tú in óstán?

F: _____₃ fhan. D'fhan mé i dteach lóistín ag bun na hEaragaile.

C: _____₄ raibh Gaeilge ag na daoine sa teach?

F: Bhí Gaeilge líofa acu. _____₅ siad Gaeilge an t-am ar fad.

C: _____₆ ndeachaigh tú ag snámh san fharraige?

F: Ó _____₇ dheachaigh. Bhí an t-uisce rófhuar! _____₈ mé ag snámh sa linn snámha.

C: Cad a rinne tú sa tráthnóna?

F: Chuaigh mé ag siúl ar an trá dhá uair agus chuaigh mé féin agus bean eile _____₉ an dioscó oíche eile.

C: Cad eile a rinne tú?

F: Chuaigh mé _____₁₀ Toraigh. Bhí Taispeántas Ealaíne ar siúl. Cheannaigh mé pictiúr álainn. Tá sé agam anseo. _____₁₁ dtaitníonn sé leat?

2 Líon na bearnaí sa ghreille.

Aimsir Láithreach	Aimsir Chaite +	Aimsir Chaite -	Aimsir Chaite? ?
Cuireann	Chuir	Níor chuir	Ar chuir
Itheann	D'ith		Ar ith
Foghlaimíonn		Níor fhoghlaim	Ar fhoghlaim
Feiceann	Chonaic		An bhfaca
Cloiseann		Níor chuala	Ar chuala
Codlaíonn			
Tagann	Tháinig	Níor tháinig	
Faigheann	Fuair	Ní bhfuair	
Tá	Bhí		

D

An bhfuil an **d** agus an **t** leathan nó caol sna focail seo a leanas?

seachtain   _____
maidin   _____
d'fhan   _____
teanga   _____
leat   _____
d'imigh   _____

E

1

(i) Críochnaigh na habairtí.
   (a) The Celtic new year began with the festival of _____.
   (b) Today's equivalent of the festival of Imbolc is _____.
   (c) Summer began with the festival of _____.

   (d) Autumn was celebrated with the festival of _____.

(ii) Críochnaigh na habairtí .
   (a) Tosaíonn an Geimhreadh i Mí _____.
   (b) Tosaíonn an tEarrach i Mí _____.
   (c) Tosaíonn an Fómhar i Mí _____.
   (d) Tosaíonn an Samhradh i Mí _____.

2

Freagair na ceisteanna.
(a) In ancient Irish literature, what was the *Other World* often known as?
(b) Which other famous Irish Voyage story is *The Voyage of Mael Dúin* supposed to have influenced?
(c) In which century was *The Voyage of Mael Dúin* originally written?

Téipscripteanna

1.2(b)

Comhrá 1

Fear:	Ar thaitin an áit leat?
Bean:	Thaitin. Chuir na foirgnimh arda iontas orm.
Fear:	Cad faoin mbia?
Bean:	Bhí na bagels an-bhlasta ar fad! Agus na delis! Bhlais mé bia nua gach lá.
Fear:	An ndeachaigh tú ag siopadóireacht?
Bean:	Cinnte. Cheannaigh mé an seaicéad seo. An dtaitníonn sé leat?
Fear:	Is maith liom an dath. Oireann sé duit.
Bean:	Go raibh maith agat!

Comhrá 2

Bean:	Rinneamar malartú tí.
Fear:	Cá raibh an teach suite?
Bean:	Amuigh faoin tuath ach bhí tithe eile in aice leis.
Fear:	Cén sórt tí a bhí ann?
Bean:	Bungaló a bhí ann. Bhí gairdín beag os comhair an tí agus gairdín mór ar chúl an tí.
Fear:	Ar thaitin sé le d'iníon?
Bean:	Thaitin sé go mór léi. Chaith sí go leor ama amuigh sa ghairdín ag léamh agus á grianú féin.
Fear:	Ar thaitin na daoine leat?
Bean:	Bhí siad beagán ciúin, mheas mé, ach bhí siad cairdiúil.

Comhrá 3

Bean 1:	Conas a bhí an aimsir?
Bean 2:	Bhí sé ag stealladh báistí ar dtús ach ansin tháinig an ghrian amach.
Bean 1:	Cad a rinne tú i rith an lae?
Bean 2:	Chuaigh mé ag siúl ar na bóithre agus ar an trá.
Bean 1:	Agus cad a rinne tú nuair a bhí sé ag báisteach?
Bean 2:	D'fhan mé sa teach ag léamh nó chuaigh mé go dtí an pub. Bhí ceol traidisiúnta ar siúl ann cúpla uair.

2.3

Ar dtús chuaigh mé ar eitleán go dtí an Róimh. Seachtain ina dhiaidh sin chuaigh mé go dtí an Aithin. Thaitin an áit sin go mór liom. Bhí na daoine an-chairdiúil. Ar aghaidh liom ansin go hIostanbúl. Bhí cara liom ag pósadh ann. Chaith mé mí in Iostanbúl. Ansin chuaigh mé go dtí an Astráil, go Sydney ar dtús agus ansin go Perth. Fuair mé post i bPerth. Sé mhí ina dhiaidh sin chuaigh mé go dtí an Nua-Shéalainn agus as sin go hOileáin Fhidsi áit a chaith mé saoire seachtaine. Sa deireadh thaistil mé go dtí na Stáit Aontaithe. Chuaigh mé go Los Angeles ar dtús mar bhí cairde agam ann. Thug mé cuairt ar Hollywood ach faraor géar, níor chas mé le réalta ar bith! Chaith mé dhá mhí ag obair i dteach tábhairne i Nua-Eabhrac sular tháinig mé ar ais go Sasana.

3.2

Chuaigh mé go dtí an tSualainn i Mí Eanáir. Bhí cruinniú agam i bPáras i Mí an Mhárta agus i Maidrid i Mí Aibreáin. Ní dheachaigh mé in aon áit i Mí na Bealtaine nó i Mí an Mheithimh. Bhí mé sna Stáit Aontaithe i Mí Lúnasa agus san Astráil i Mí Mheán Fómhair. Chuaigh mé go dtí an tSeapáin i Mí Dheireadh Fómhair, ceapaim, agus go dtí an Ghearmáin ag tús Mhí na Nollag.

5.1

Pól: Gabh mo leithscéal. Ar mhiste leat cúpla ceist a fhreagairt?

Maria: Ceart go leor.

Pól: Ar thaitin an cúrsa leat?

Maria: Thaitin sé go mór liom.

Pól: Ar fhoghlaim tú mórán?

Maria: D'fhoghlaim mé a lán focal nua.

Pól: An raibh tú ar chúrsa Gaeilge roimhe seo?

Maria: Ní raibh.

Pól: Anois cúpla ceist faoi na gníomhaíochtaí a rinne tú. An ndearna tú potadóireacht?

Maria: Ní dhearna, faraor.

Pól: An ndeachaigh tú ag sléibhteoireacht?

Maria: Chuaigh. Bhí mé amuigh ceithre huaire. Bhí an-spórt agam!

Pól: Fiú amháin nuair a bhí sé ag cur báistí?

Maria: Ó is maith liom an bháisteach!

Pól: Ar fhan tú i dteach lóistín?

Maria: Níor fhan. D'fhan mé i mbrú óige.

Pól: Ceist amháin eile. An bhfaca tú an scannán aréir?

Maria: Ní fhaca. Ní raibh a fhios agam go raibh scannán ar siúl.

Pól: Is trua sin. Bhí sé an-ghreannmhar ar fad. *Lip Service* an t-ainm a bhí air. Go raibh maith agat as labhairt liom. Dála an scéil, ar ith tú duileasc riamh?

Maria: Níor ith.

Pól: Seo píosa duit.

Maria: Tá sé an-bhlasta ar fad!

6.3

1 doras, 2 duine, 3 Diarmuid, 4 sráid, 5 staidéar, 6 Pádraig, 7 tá, 8 teanga, 9 áit, 10 romhat, 11 fáilte, 12 Caitlín

7.3

Yannick: Labhraím Fraincis, Briotáinis agus Gaeilge na hAlban.

Chie: Tá Seapáinis agus beagán Béarla agam.

Saïd: Tá Araibis líofa agam – agus beagáinín Gaeilge anois.

Kemal: Is í Tuircis mo theanga dhúchais. Tá beagáinín Spáinnise agam freisin.

Wolfgang: Tá cuid mhaith Polainnise agam agus tá Gearmáinis agam.

Tom: Tá Béarla agus beagáinín Gaeilge agam.

8.2

Rita: A Eibhlín? Rita anseo.

Eibhín: Dia duit, a Rita.

Rita: An bhfuil a fhios agat go mbeidh an dráma atá ar siúl sa *Taibhdhearc* ag críochnú Dé hAoine seo chugainn?

Eibhlín: Ó ní raibh a fhios sin agam.

Rita: Ba mhaith liom dul ann oíche éigin. An dtiocfaidh tú liom?

Eibhlín: Tiocfaidh, cinnte. Cén uair a bhí ar intinn agat dul ann?

Rita: Dé Céadaoin.

Eibhlín: Fan go bhfeicfidh mé … Dé Céadaoin… mmm… Ní bheidh mé saor Dé Céadaoin. Beidh mé ag dul chuig cóisir i dteach Áine. Cad faoin Déardaoin?

Rita: Ní bheidh mise saor Déardaoin. Beidh mo mháthair ag teacht ar cuairt. Dé hAoine, beidh mé ag bualadh le mo chairde sa phub.

Eibhlín: Mise freisin! Fágann sin an Luan agus an Mháirt. Ó, ní féidir liom dul Dé Máirt mar beidh mé ag imirt leadóige ach beidh mé saor Dé Luain. Dé Luain? Sin amárach!

Rita: Beidh mise saor freisin. Oíche amárach mar sin.

Eibhlín: Ceart go leor.

10.2(a)

Bhí stoirm mhór ar an bhfarraige. D'imigh an bád le sruth. Thug an bád go hoileáin éagsúla iad. Tharla rudaí iontacha dóibh ar na hoileáin seo. Ar oileán amháin chonaic siad seangáin a bhí chomh mór le searrach. Ní raibh siad ábalta seasamh ar oileán eile mar bhí an talamh róthe. Ansin shroich siad Tír na mBan.

Bhí dún mór ar an oileán. Bhí droichead gloine ag dul isteach sa dún. Chuir an bhanríon fáilte mhór rompu. Bhí folcadh breá acu. Bhí béile blasta acu freisin. D'fhan siad trí mhí ar an oileán. Thug siad cuairt ar oileáin eile. Ansin tháinig siad ar ais go hÉirinn.

Eochair

1.2(b)
comhrá 1B, comhrá 2C, comhrá 3A

1.3(a) thaitin, chuir, bhfaca, chonaic, chuaigh

1.4(a)

> A Mháire, a chara,
>
> Conas tá tú? Chuaigh mé go Páras an deireadh seachtaine seo caite.
>
> Dé hAoine d'ith mé béile deas i mbialann ar Boulevard Saint Germain. Tar éis an bhéile chuaigh mé ag siúl timpeall na háite. Chuaigh mé a chodladh ar a trí a chlog ar maidin!
>
> Bhí an aimsir go dona Dé Sathairn. Chuaigh mé ag siopadóireacht.
>
> Dé Domhnaigh chuala mé cloig Notre Dame. Chonaic mé an Mona Lisa sa Louvre. Chonaic mé a lán pictiúr eile freisin. D'fhan mé an lá ar fad sa Louvre. Tháinig mé ar ais go Baile Átha Cliath sa tráthnóna. Chuaigh mé a chodladh ar a deich a chlog. Thaitin an tsaoire go mór liom.
>
> Scríobh ar ais chugam go luath.
>
> Is mise do chara,
>
> Bríd

2.1 Fíor *true*

2.2 **Go dtí** is used before **an** or **na**.

4.3(a)

Eanáir	Latin *Aprilis*
Feabhra	Irish meaning 'month in the middle (of Summer)'
Márta	Irish meaning 'the end of the harvest'
Aibreán	Latin 'Iulius'
Bealtaine	Latin 'Natalis'
Meitheamh	Irish, after Lug, the pagan God of Light
Iúil	Latin 'Martius'
Lúnasa	Latin 'Januarius'
Meán Fómhair	Irish meaning 'end of Summer or bright half of the year'
Deireadh Fómhair	Irish meaning 'the fire of Bel'
Samhain	Latin 'Februarius'
Nollaig	Irish meaning 'the middle of the harvest'

5.2
(i) The words **ar** or **an** go before the verb to ask a question in the past tense.
(ii) **Níor** or **ní** go before the verb to give a negative answer in the past tense.

5.3
(i) In the past tense, certain verbs have a special form after **an** and **ní**.
(ii) A *séimhiú* generally follows **ar**, **níor** and **ní**. An *urú* follows **an**.

5.4
(i) ní fhaca (ii) ar fhan (iii) níor tháinig
(iv) an ndeachaigh (v) ní raibh (vi) an ndearna

6.3
1d, 2d, 3d', 4d', 5d', 6d, 7t, 8t', 9t', 10t, 11t', 12t'

7.1

Tír	Teanga
An Iodáil	Iodáilis
An tSeapáin	Seapáinis
An Rúis	Rúisis
An Tuirc	Tuircis

7.2
(i) Gréigis (ii) Sínis (iii) Fraincis
(iv) Breatnais (v) Rúisis (vi) Seapáinis
(vii) Sualainnis (viii) Béarla (ix) Araibis
(x) Gearmáinis

8.4(a)
(a) *Paragraf 1:* … Beidh an rang Gaeilge aige anocht.

(b) *Paragraf 3:* An bhliain seo chugainn beidh sé ag siúl an Camino de Santiago.

Beidh sé ag siúl ó Roncesvalles sa Fhrainc go dtí Santiago i dtuaisceart na Spáinne.

Beidh a chara, John, ag teacht leis.

9.1
A traein C carr (gluaisteán), gluaisrothar D siúl
E eitleán F tacsaí G bus H rothar

9.2
(a) ar an mbád (b) ar an mbus
(c) ar ghluaisrothar (d) ar an traein (e) ar eitleán
(f) ag siúl

11.2

séimhiú · · · · · · · is
urú · · · · · · · d'ól
forainm réamhfhoclach · · · · · téann
aidiacht shealbhach · · · · · cuir
an chopail · · · · · dom
modh ordaitheach · · · · · an fharraige
aimsir láithreach · · · · · mo
aimsir chaite · · · · · mBan

11.3

séimhiú	an-chairdiúil, chuaigh, thaitin
urú	ar an mbád
forainm réamhfhoclach	liom
aidiacht shealbhach	mo, do
an chopail	is maith
modh ordaitheach	ná déan
aimsir láithreach	téim, tá
aimsir chaite	chuaigh, thaitin

12.1(a)
A Eitilt agus lóistín
B Eitilt agus bád
C Traein, eitilt agus lóistín
D Bus, eitilt agus lóistín

12.1(c)

Adult Return Fare	€45
Student Return Fare	€37
Children Return Fare	€25
Free Travel Scheme Return for old age pensioners	€15

Ticéad singil *single ticket*

12.2
A2 B1 C4 D3

Triail Tú Féin

A

2(i)

Dia duit. An bhfuil Gaeilge agat?
An bhfuil bus ón Daingean go Trá Lí?
An mbíonn bus ar an Domhnach?
Cén t-am a fhágann an bus an Daingean
    tráthnóna Dé Domhnaigh?
Cá bhfuil oifig na dticéad?
Go raibh (míle) maith agat.

(ii) Dia is Muire duit. Tá Gaeilge réasúnta
    maith agam.
Tá.
Bíonn dhá bhus ar an Domhnach.
Fágann an chéad bhus ar a leath uair tar éis a
    haon agus fágann an dara bus ar a fiche
    chun a cúig.
Faigheann/ceannaíonn tú an ticéad ar an mbus.
Tá fáilte romhat. Slán.

(iii) Trí thicéad do dhaoine fásta le do thoil.
Dhá thicéad do mhic léinn.
Seacht dticéad do pháistí.
Ticéad singil le do thoil. Tá pas saor ag
mo mháthair.

3 Mary: An mbeidh tú saor tráthnóna
                 Dé Céadaoin?
   Pádraig: Ní bheidh faraor. Beidh mé ag
                 bualadh le cara.
   Mary: Cad faoin Déardaoin?
   Pádraig: Ní bheidh mé saor Déardaoin ach
                 oiread. Cad faoin Aoine?
   Mary: Ní bheidh mé saor Dé hAoine.
                 Beidh rang Seapáinise agam.
   Pádraig: Bhuel, beidh mise saor Dé Sathairn.
                 Cad fútsa?
   Mary: Beidh mise saor Dé Sathairn freisin!
   Pádraig: Ar fheabhas! Dé Sathairn mar sin?
   Mary: Ceart go leor.

B

1(i) Eanáir, Feabhra, Márta, Aibreán, Bealtaine,
Meitheamh, Iúil, Lúnasa, Meán Fómhair, Deireadh
Fómhair, Samhain, Nollaig

(ii) Iúil, An Samhradh Nollaig, An Geimhreadh
Feabhra, An tEarrach Lúnasa, An Fómhar

2

an bhliain seo chugainn, an tseachtain seo chugainn, oíche amárach, tráthnóna amárach, inniu, aréir, maidin inné, an tseachtain seo caite, an mhí seo caite.

3

bád	calafort
traein	stáisiún traenach
bus	stad an bhus
tacsaí	ionad na dtacsaithe
carr/gluaisteán	carrchlós
eitleán	aerfort

C

1   1 ar, 2 ar, 3 níor, 4 an, 5 labhraíonn/labhair, 6 an, 7 ní, 8 chuaigh, 9 go dtí, 10 go, 11 an

2

Cuireann	Chuir	Níor chuir	Ar chuir
Itheann	D'ith	Níor ith	Ar ith
Foghlaimíonn	D'fhoghlaim	Níor fhoghlaim	Ar fhoghlaim
Feiceann	Chonaic	Ní fhaca	An bhfaca
Cloiseann	Chuala	Níor chuala	Ar chuala
Codlaíonn	Chodail	Níor chodail	Ar chodail
Tagann	Tháinig	Níor tháinig	Ar tháinig
Faigheann	Fuair	Ní bhfuair	An bhfuair
Tá	Bhí	Ní raibh	An raibh

D

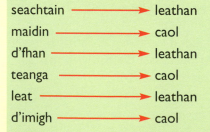

seachtain ⟶ leathan

maidin ⟶ caol

d'fhan ⟶ leathan

teanga ⟶ caol

leat ⟶ leathan

d'imigh ⟶ caol

E

1

(i) (a) Samhain (b) Lá Fhéile Bríde (c) Beltane
(d) Lughnasadh

(ii) (a) Mí na Samhna (b) Mí Feabhra
(c) Mí Lúnasa (d) Mí na Bealtaine

2

(a) Tír na nÓg *Land of the Young*
(b) The Voyage of Saint Brendan
(c) The 10th century AD

Acknowledgements

Author's acknowledgements

Many people have contributed to this project. The author would particularly like to thank

Her colleagues and friends, present and past, in ITÉ for giving so generously of their knowledge and skills and for their support and encouragement throughout the project.

The learners, teachers and others who provided very useful feedback and advice on the material as it was being developed, in particular Mairéad Ní Chraith (University of Liverpool) and Linda Richardson (Authentik).

Aoibheann Nic Dhonnchadha (School of Celtic Studies, Dublin), Damian Mac Manus (Trinity College, Dublin) and Paul Walsh (Dúchas) for their help with some of the Culture sections.

Eoghan Mac Aogáin, ITÉ, and Áine Ó Cuireáin, Gael-Linn, for their editorial work.

The following people for featuring in the textbook: p.141: Mícheál Ó Comáin; p.146: Gormfhlaith Ní Thuairisg; pp.146,150: Margaret Farrington; pp.146,150: Leif Johannesson; p.152: Aidan Byrne; p.185: Antaine Mac Mathúna.

Deirdre d'Auria and Ciara Nic Gabhann for helping to locate the learners who spoke in the recordings.

The City of Dublin Vocational Education Committee for seconding her to ITÉ to write the course.

John, her husband, and Marianne, her daughter, for their insightful comments on the material, their encouragement and good humour.

The author and publishers are grateful to the following copyright holders for permission to reproduce copyright material:

Songs p.11: 'Eibhlín a Rún' by Risteárd Mac Gabhann from *Cúrsa Closamhairc Gaeilge,* Ogmios, 1991; p.23: Cló Iar-Chonnachta for 'Bean Pháidín' by Seán ac Dhonncha from the CD *An Spailpín Fánach*; p.55: Mistletoe Music for 'Bríd Óg Ní Mháille' from the CD *House of the Dolphins* by Melanie O' Reilly (1999); p.78: Gael-Linn for 'Bánchnoic Éireann Ó/The Fair Hills of Ireland by Skara Brae from the CD *Skara Brae*, 1998, 'Dónall Óg' by Seosamh Ó hÉanaí from the CD *Ó mo dhúchas/From my tradition* 1976, 'Mo Ghile Mear' by Deirbhile Ní Bhrolcháin from the CD *Smaointe*, 1990; pp. 78, 93,159: Pádraigín Ní Uallacháin, Garry Ó Briain for 'Seoithín agus Seoithín-Suantraí', 'Nóra Bheag/Little Nora', 'Bog Braon' from the CD *A Stór, 's a Stóirín*, Gael-Linn,1994; p.191: MÓC Music for 'Báidín Fheilimidh' from the CD *Bláth na hÓige*, Cló Iar-Chonnachta, 1997.

Poems, stories and other texts: p.6: Four Courts Press for English translation of 'Mise agus Pangur Bán', *Early Irish Lyrics* by Gerard Murphy, Dublin, 1998; p.28: Cló Iar-Chonnachta for 'Séasúir' (Irish text and recording) by Cathal Ó Searcaigh and translation by Gabriel Fitzmaurice, *Homecoming/An Bealach 'na Bhaile*, 1993; p.36: An Roinn Oideachais agus Eolaíochta for 'Lon Dhoire an Chairn'; p. 70: An Gúm for vowel pronunciation table, *An Foclóir Póca,* Dublin, 1995, pg. xiii; p.89: J.W. Hackett for Haiku 'Free at last the fly', *30 Zen-Haiku,* published by Cló Iar-Chonnachta and An Cumann um Haiku, 1994; Cló Iar-Chonnachta for Irish translation of Haiku 'Saor faoi dheoidh an chuileog' by Gabriel Rosenstock and for the illustration by Pieter Sluis,1994; p.131: Gabriel Rosenstock and An Clóchomhar Teoranta for 'Teilifís' first published in *Óm,* Baile Átha Cliath, 1983; Gabriel Fitzmaurice for translation 'Television' from *An Crann Faoi Bhláth,* Wolfhound Press,1991; p.132: Breandán Delap, Editor "Foinse" for Clársceideal; p.160: Professor John Dillon and Four Courts Press for extracts from 'The Vision of Mac Con Glinne', *Early Irish Literature* by Myles Dillon, Dublin, 1994; p.187: Four Courts Press for extracts from 'The Voyage of Mael Dúin's Currach', *Early Irish Lyrics* by Gerard Murphy, Dublin, 1998.

Art work and photographs: p.75: Pauline Bewick for permission to use painting of swans from *Irish Tales and Sagas* Dragon Granada Publishing, 1985; p.77: National Museum of Ireland for photograph of 'Loughnashade Horn'; p.85: An Post for stamp; p.118: Glaxo Wellcome for illustration of 'Teach Allais/Sweating House' by Philip V Moone from *Making the Cure* by Patrick Logan, Talbot Press, 1972.

Every effort has been made to trace copyright holders, but the publishers will be pleased to make the necessary arrangements if there are any omissions.

The author and publishers wish to thank the following for permission to use or adapt texts:

p.41: Cló Iar-Chonnachta and Mícheál Ó hEidhin, 'Cill Liadáin', from *Cas Amhrán*, Mícheál Ó hEidhin ed.,1990; p.132: Conradh na Gaeilge, notice about opening and closing times of 'An Siopa Leabhar'; p.134: Raidió na Life, 'Clársceideal an Fhómhair'; Raidió na Gaeltachta, BBC Radio Ulster and TG4, for logos; p.137: Trí D Caife, information leaflet; Conradh na Gaeilge, notice 'Club Chonradh na Gaeilge'; p.189: Aer Árann.

The author and publishers are grateful to the following people for contributing photographs:

p.8: Damian McManus (Ogam Stone); p.73: Séamus Ó Beaglaoich and Hummingbird Records; p.74: Tadhg Mac Dhonnagáin and RTÉ; Emi Records (Mairéad Ní Mhaonaigh); p.161: Paul Walsh; John Purvis, p. 68: 'Cat', p.176:'Teach Synge, 'New York', 'An gáirdín sa tSualainn, p.185:'Hillwalkers', p.195:'Sliabh na hEaragaile'.

The author and publishers are also grateful to the following people:

p.41: Ciarán Ó Coigligh for singing 'Cill Liadáin'; pp.41, 53, 189: Paul Walsh for generating maps; p.115: Donncha Ó Cróinín for creating slogan *Ith Torthaí le haghaidh torthaí sláintiúla*.